Option Pricing Models and Volatility Using Excel®-VBA

Founded in 1807, John Wiley & Sons is the oldest independent publishing company in the United States. With offices in North America, Europe, Australia, and Asia, Wiley is globally committed to developing and marketing print and electronic products and services for our customers' professional and personal knowledge and understanding.

The Wiley Finance series contains books written specifically for finance and investment professionals as well as sophisticated individual investors and their financial advisors. Book topics range from portfolio management to e-commerce, risk management, financial engineering, valuation, and financial instrument analysis, as well as much more.

For a list of available titles, visit our Web site at www.WileyFinance.com.

Option Pricing Models and Volatility Using Excel®-VBA

FABRICE DOUGLAS ROUAH
GREGORY VAINBERG

John Wiley & Sons, Inc.

Published by John Wiley & Sons, Inc., Hoboken, New Jersey.
Published simultaneously in Canada.

Wiley Bicentennial Logo: Richard J. Pacifico

For general information on our other products and services or for technical support, please contact our Customer Care Department within the United States at (800) 762-2974, outside the United States at (317) 572-3993 or fax (317) 572-4002.

Wiley also publishes its books in a variety of electronic formats. Some content that appears in print may not be available in electronic books. For more information about Wiley products, visit our Web site at www.wiley.com.

Library of Congress Cataloging-in-Publication Data:

Rouah, Fabrice, 1964-
    Option pricing models and volatility using Excel®-VBA / Fabrice Douglas Rouah, Gregory Vainberg.
        p. cm. –(Wiley finance series)
    Includes bibliographical references and index.
    ISBN: 978-0-471-79464-6 (paper/cd-rom)
    1. Options (Finance)–Prices. 2. Capital investments–Mathematical–Mathematical models.
    3. Options (Finance)–Mathematical models. 4. Microsoft Excel (Computer file) 5. Microsoft Visual Basic for applications. I. Vainberg, Gregory, 1978-II. Title.
      HG6024.A3R678 2007
      332.64'53–dc22
                                                                              2006031250

10 9 8 7 6 5 4 3 2 1

To Jacqueline, Jean, and Gilles
—Fabrice

To Irina, Bryanne, and Stephannie
—Greg

Contents

Preface

This book constitutes a guide for implementing advanced option pricing models and volatility in Excel/VBA. It can be used by MBA students specializing in finance and risk management, by practitioners, and by undergraduate students in their final year. Emphasis has been placed on implementing the models in VBA, rather than on the theoretical developments underlying the models. We have made every effort to explain the models and their coding in VBA as simply as possible. Every model covered in this book includes one or more VBA functions that can be accessed on the CD-ROM. We have focused our attention on equity options, and we have chosen not to include interest rate options. The particularities of interest rate options place them in a separate class of derivatives.

The first part of the book covers mathematical preliminaries that are used throughout the book. In Chapter 1 we explain complex numbers and how to implement them in VBA. We also explain how to write VBA functions for finding roots of functions, the Nelder-Mead algorithm for finding the minimum of a multivariate function, and cubic spline interpolation. All of these methods are used extensively throughout the book. Chapter 2 covers numerical integration. Many of option pricing and volatility models require that an integral be evaluated for which no closed-form solution exists, which requires a numerical approximation to the integral. In Chapter 2 we present various methods that have proven to be extremely accurate and efficient for numerical integration.

The second part of this book covers option pricing formulas. In Chapter 3 we cover lattice methods. These include the well-known binomial and trinomial trees, but also refinements such as the implied binomial and trinomial trees, the flexible binomial tree, the Leisen-Reimer tree, the Edgeworth binomial tree, and the adapted mesh method. Most of these methods approximate the Black-Scholes model in discrete time. One advantage they have over the Black-Scholes model, however, is that they can be used to price American options. In Chapter 4 we cover the Black-Scholes, Gram-Charlier, and Practitioner Black-Scholes models, and introduce implied volatility. The Black-Scholes model is presented as a platform upon which other models are built. The Gram-Charlier model is an extension of the Black-Scholes model that allows for skewness and excess kurtosis in the distribution of the return on the underlying asset. The Practitioner Black-Scholes model uses implied volatility fitted from a deterministic volatility function (DVF) regression, as an input to the Black-Scholes model. It can be thought of as an ad hoc method that adapts the Black-Scholes model to account for the volatility smile in option prices. In Chapter 5 we cover the Heston (1993) model, which is an extension of the Black-Scholes model that allows for stochastic volatility, while in Chapter 6 we cover the Heston and Nandi (2000) GARCH model, which in its simplest form is a discrete-time version of the model in Chapter 5. The call price in each model is available in closed form, up to a complex integral that must be evaluated numerically. In Chapter 6 we also show how to identify the correlation and dependence in asset returns, which the GARCH model attempts to incorporate. We also show how to implement the GARCH(1,1) model in VBA, and how GARCH volatilities can be used for long-run volatility forecasting and for constructing the term structure of volatility. Chapter 7 covers the option sensitivities, or Greeks, from the option pricing models covered in this book. The Greeks for the Black-Scholes and Gram-Charlier models are available in closed form. The Greeks from Heston (1993), and Heston and Nandi (2000) models are available in closed form also, but require a numerical approximation to a complex integral. The Greeks from tree-based methods can be approximated from option and asset prices at the beginning nodes of the tree. In Chapter 7 we also show how to use finite differences to approximate the Greeks, and we show that these approximations are all close to their closed-form values. In Chapter 8 we cover exotic options. Most of the methods we present for valuing exotic options are tree-based. Particular emphasis is placed on single-barrier options, and the various methods that have been proposed to deal with the difficulties that arise when tree-based methods are adapted to barrier options. In Chapter 8 we also cover Asian options, floating-strike lookback options, and digital options. Finally, in Chapter 9 we cover basic estimation methods for parameters that are used as inputs to the option pricing models covered in this book. Particular emphasis is placed on loss function estimation, which estimates parameters by minimizing the difference between market and model prices.

The third part of this book deals with volatility and higher moments. In Chapter 10 we present a thorough treatment of implied volatility and show how the root-finding methods covered in Chapter 1 can be used to obtain implied volatilities from market prices. We explain how the implied volatility curve can shed information on the distribution of the underlying asset return, and we show how option prices generated from the Heston (1993) and Gram-Charlier models lead to implied volatility curves that account for the smile and skew in option prices. Chapter 11 deals with model-free implied volatility. Unlike Black-Scholes implied volatility, model-free implied volatility does not require the restrictive assumption of a particular parametric form for the underlying price dynamics. Moreover, unlike Black-Scholes implied volatilities, which are usually computed using at-the-money or near-the-money options only, model-free volatilities are computed using the whole cross-section of option prices. In Chapter 11 we also present methods that mitigate the discretization and truncation bias brought on by using market prices that do not include a continuum of strike prices, and that are available only over a bounded interval of strike prices. We also show how to construct the Chicago Board Options Exchange® volatility index, the VIX, which is now based on model-free implied volatility. Chapter 12 extends the model-free methods of Chapter 11, and deals with model-free skewness and kurtosis. We show how applying interpolation-extrapolation to these methods leads to much more accurate approximations to the integrals that are used to estimate model-free higher moments. In Chapter 13 we treat volatility returns, which are returns on strategies designed to profit from volatility. We cover simple straddles, which are constructed using a single call and put. Zero-beta straddles are slightly more complex, but have the advantage that they are hedged against market movements. We also introduce a simple model to value straddle options, and introduce delta-hedged gains. Similar to zero-beta straddles, delta-hedged gains are portfolios in which all risks except volatility risk have been hedged away, so that the only remaining risk to the portfolio is volatility risk. Finally, we cover variance swaps, which are an application of model-free volatility for constructing a call option on volatility.

This book also contains a CD-ROM that contains Excel spreadsheets and VBA functions to implement all of the option pricing and volatility models presented in this book. The CD-ROM also includes solutions to all the chapter exercises, and option data for IBM Corporation and Intel Corporation downloaded from Yahoo! (finance.yahoo.com).

ACKNOWLEDGMENTS

We have several people to thank for their valuable help and comments during the course of writing this book. We thank Peter Christoffersen, Susan Christoffersen, and Kris Jacobs. We also thank Steven Figlewski, John Hull, Yue Kuen Kwok, Dai Min, Mark Rubinstein, and our colleagues Vadim Di Pietro, Greg N. Gregoriou, and especially Redouane El-Kamhi. Working with the staff at John Wiley & Sons has been a pleasure. We extend special thanks to Bill Falloon, Emilie Herman, Laura Walsh, and Todd Tedesco. We are indebted to Polina Ialamova at OptionMetrics. We thank our families for their continual support and personal encouragement. Finally, we thank Peter Christoffersen, Steven L. Heston, and Espen Gaarder, for kindly providing the endorsements.

CHAPTER 1

Mathematical Preliminaries

INTRODUCTION

In this chapter we introduce some of the mathematical concepts that will be needed to deal with the option pricing and stochastic volatility models introduced in this book, and to help readers implement these concepts as functions and routines in VBA. First, we introduce complex numbers, which are needed to evaluate characteristic functions of distributions driving option prices. These are required to evaluate the option pricing models of Heston (1993) and Heston and Nandi (2000) covered in Chapters 5 and 6, respectively. Next, we review and implement Newton's method and the bisection method, two popular and simple algorithms for finding zeros of functions. These methods are needed to find volatility implied from option prices, which we introduce in Chapter 4 and deal with in Chapter 10. We show how to implement multiple linear regression with ordinary least squares (OLS) and weighted least squares (WLS) in VBA. These methods are needed to obtain the deterministic volatility functions of Chapter 4. Next, we show how to find maximum likelihood estimators, which are needed to estimate the parameters that are used in option pricing models. We also implement the Nelder-Mead algorithm, which is used to find the minimum values of multivariate functions and which will be used throughout this book. Finally, we implement cubic splines in VBA. Cubic splines will be used to obtain model-free implied volatility in Chapter 11, and model-free skewness and kurtosis in Chapter 12.

COMPLEX NUMBERS

Most of the numbers we are used to dealing with in our everyday lives are real numbers, which are defined as any number lying on the real line $\Re = (-\infty, +\infty)$. As such, real numbers can be positive or negative; rational, meaning that they can be expressed as a fraction; or irrational, meaning that they cannot be expressed as a fraction. Some examples of real numbers are $1/3$, -3, $\sqrt{2}$, and π. Complex numbers, however, are constructed around the imaginary unit i defined as $i = \sqrt{-1}$. While i is not a real number, i^2 is a real number since $i^2 = -1$. A complex number is defined as

$a = x + iy$, where x and y are both real numbers, called the real and imaginary parts of a, respectively. The notation Re[] and Im[] is used to denote these quantities, so that $\text{Re}[a] = x$ and $\text{Im}[a] = y$.

Operations on Complex Numbers

Many of the operations on complex numbers are done by isolating the real and imaginary parts. Other operations require simple tricks, such as rewriting the complex number in a different form or using its complex conjugate. Krantz (1999) is a good reference for this section.

Addition and subtraction of complex numbers is performed by separate operation on the real and imaginary parts. It requires adding and subtracting, respectively, the real and imaginary parts of the two complex numbers:

$$(x + iy) + (u + iv) = (x + u) + i(y + v),$$

$$(x + iy) - (u + iv) = (x - u) + i(y - v).$$

Multiplying two complex numbers is done by applying the distributive axiom to the product, and regrouping the real and imaginary parts:

$$(x + iy)(u + iv) = (xu - yv) + i(xv + yu).$$

The complex conjugate of a complex number is defined as $\bar{a} = x - iy$ and is useful for dividing complex numbers. Since $a\bar{a} = x^2 + y^2$, we can express division of any two complex numbers as the ratio

$$\frac{x + iy}{u + iv} = \frac{(x + iy)(u - iv)}{(u + iv)(u - iv)} = \frac{(xu + yv) + i(yu - xv)}{u^2 + v^2}.$$

Exponentiation of a complex number is done by applying Euler's formula, which produces

$$\exp(x + iy) = \exp(x)\exp(iy) = \exp(x)[\cos(y) + i\sin(y)].$$

Hence, the real part of the resulting complex number is $\exp(x)\cos(y)$, and the imaginary part is $\exp(x)\sin(y)$. Obtaining the logarithm of a complex number requires algebra. Suppose that $w = a + ib$ and that its logarithm is the complex number $z = x + iy$, so that $z = \log(w)$. Since $w = \exp(z)$, we know that $a = e^x\cos(y)$ and $b = e^x\sin(y)$. Squaring these numbers, applying the identity $\cos(y)^2 + \sin(y)^2 = 1$, and solving for x produces $x = \text{Re}[z] = \log(\sqrt{a^2 + b^2})$. Taking their ratio produces

$$b/a = \sin(y)/\cos(y) = \tan(y),$$

and solving for y produces $y = \text{Im}[z] = \arctan(b/a)$.

It is now easy to obtain the square root of the complex number $w = a + ib$, using DeMoivre's Theorem:

$$[\cos(x) + i\sin(x)]^n = \cos(nx) + i\sin(nx). \tag{1.1}$$

By arguments in the previous paragraph, we can write $w = r\cos(y) + ir\sin(y) = re^{iy}$, where $y = \arctan(b/a)$ and $r = \sqrt{a^2 + b^2}$. The square root of w is therefore

$$\sqrt{r}[\cos(y) + i\sin(y)]^{1/2}.$$

Applying DeMoivre's Theorem with $n = 1/2$, this becomes

$$\sqrt{r}[\cos(\tfrac{y}{2}) + i\sin(\tfrac{y}{2})],$$

so that the real and imaginary parts of $\sqrt{w}$ are $\sqrt{r}\cos(\tfrac{y}{2})$ and $\sqrt{r}\sin(\tfrac{y}{2})$, respectively.

Finally, other functions of complex numbers are available, but we have not included VBA code for these functions. For example, the cosine of a complex number $z = x + iy$ produces another complex number, with real and imaginary parts given by $\cos(x)\cosh(y)$ and $-\sin(x)\sinh(y)$ respectively, while the sine of a complex number has real and imaginary parts $\sin(x)\cosh(y)$ and $-\cos(x)\sinh(y)$, respectively. The hyperbolic functions $\cosh(y)$ and $\sinh(y)$ are defined in Exercise 1.1.

Operations Using VBA

In this section we describe how to define complex numbers in VBA and how to construct functions for operations on complex numbers. Note that it is possible to use the built-in complex number functions in Excel directly, without having to construct them in VBA. However, we will see in later chapters that using the built-in functions increases substantially the computation time required for convergence of option prices. Constructing complex numbers in VBA, therefore, makes computation of option prices more efficient. Moreover, it is sometimes preferable to have control over how certain operations on complex numbers are defined. There are other definitions of the square root of a complex number, for example, than that given by applying DeMoivre's Theorem. Finally, learning how to construct complex numbers in VBA is a good learning exercise.

The Excel file Chapter1Complex contains VBA functions to define complex numbers and to perform operations on complex numbers. Each function returns the real part and the imaginary part of the resulting complex number. The first step is to construct a complex number in terms of its two parts. The function Set_cNum() defines a complex number with real and imaginary parts given by set_cNum.rp and set_cNum.ip, respectively.

```
Function Set_cNum(rPart, iPart) As cNum
 Set_cNum.rP = rPart
 Set_cNum.iP = iPart
End Function
```

The function cNumProd() multiplies two complex numbers cNum1 and cNum2, and returns the complex number cNumProd with real and imaginary parts cNumProd.rp and cNumProd.ip, respectively.

```
Function cNumProd(cNum1 As cNum, cNum2 As cNum) As cNum
 cNumProd.rP = (cNum1.rP * cNum2.rP) - (cNum1.iP * cNum2.iP)
 cNumProd.iP = (cNum1.rP * cNum2.iP) + (cNum1.iP * cNum2.rP)
End Function
```

Similarly, the functions cNumDiv(), cNumAdd(), and cNumSub() return the real and imaginary parts of a complex number obtained by, respectively, division, addition, and subtraction of two complex numbers, while the function cNum-Conj() returns the conjugate of a complex number.

The function cNumSqrt() returns the square root of a complex number:

```
Function cNumSqrt(cNum1 As cNum) As cNum
 r = Sqr(cNum1.rP ^ 2 + cNum1.iP ^ 2)
 y = Atn(cNum1.iP / cNum1.rP)
 cNumSqrt.rP = Sqr(r) * Cos(y / 2)
 cNumSqrt.iP = Sqr(r) * Sin(y / 2)
End Function
```

The functions cNumExp() and cNumLn() produce, respectively, the exponential of a complex number and the natural logarithm of a complex number using the VBA function Atn() for the inverse tan function (arctan).

```
Function cNumExp(cNum1 As cNum) As cNum
 cNumExp.rP = Exp(cNum1.rP) * Cos(cNum1.iP)
 cNumExp.iP = Exp(cNum1.rP) * Sin(cNum1.iP)
End Function
```

```
Function cNumLn(cNum1 As cNum) As cNum
 r = (cNum1.rP^2 + cNum1.iP^2)^0.5
 theta = Atn(cNum1.iP / cNum1.rP)
 cNumLn.rP = Application.Ln(r)
 cNumLn.iP = theta
End Function
```

Finally, the functions cNumReal() and cNumIm() return the real and imaginary parts of a complex number, respectively.

The Excel file Chapter1Complex illustrates how these functions work. The VBA function Complexop2() performs operations on two complex numbers:

```
Function Complexop2(rP1, iP1, rP2, iP2, operation)
Dim cNum1 As cNum, cNum2 As cNum, cNum3 As cNum
Dim output(2) As Double
cNum1 = setcnum(rP1, iP1)
cNum2 = setcnum(rP2, iP2)
Select Case operation
 Case 1: cNum3 = cNumAdd(cNum1, cNum2) ' Addition
```

```
Case 2: cNum3 = cNumSub(cNum1, cNum2) ' Subtraction
Case 3: cNum3 = cNumProd(cNum1, cNum2)  ' Multiplication
Case 4: cNum3 = cNumDiv(cNum1, cNum2) ' Division
End Select
 output(1) = cNum3.rP
 output(2) = cNum3.iP
 complexop2 = output
End Function
```

The Complexop2() function requires five inputs, a real and imaginary part for each number, and the parameter corresponding to the operation being performed (1 through 4). Its output is an array of dimension two, containing the real and imaginary parts of the complex number. Figure 1.1 illustrates how this function works. To add the two numbers $11 + 3i$ and $-3 + 4i$, which appear in ranges C4:D4 and C5:D5 respectively, in cell C6 we type

$$= \text{Complexop2(C4,D4,C5,D5,F6)}$$

and copy to cell D6, which produces the complex number $8 + 7i$. Note that the output of the Complexop2() function is an array. The appendix to this book explains in detail how to output arrays from functions. Note also that the last argument of the function Complexop2() is cell F6, which contains the operation number (1) corresponding to addition.

	A	B	C	D	E	F
1						
2		**Operations on Two Complex Numbers**				
3			Real	Imaginary		Operation
4		First Complex Number	11	3		
5		Second Complex Number	-3	4		
6		Addition	8	7		1
7		Subtraction	14	-1		2
8		Multiplication	-45	35		3
9		Division	-0.84	-2.12		4
10						
11						
12		**Operations on a Single Complex Number**				
13			Real	Imaginary		Operation
14		Complex Number	4	5		
15		Conjugate	4	-5		1
16		Square Root	2.2807	1.0962		2
17		Exponentiation	15.4874	-52.3555		3
18		Natural Logarithm	1.8568	0.8961		4

FIGURE 1.1 Operations on Complex Numbers

Similarly, the function Complexop1() performs operations on a single complex number, in this example $4 + 5i$. To obtain the complex conjugate, in cell C15 we type

$$= \text{Complexop2(C14,D14,F15)}$$

and copy to cell D15 This is illustrated in the bottom part of Figure 1.1.

Relevance of Complex Numbers

Complex numbers are abstract entities, but they are extremely useful because they can be used in algebraic calculations to produce solutions that are tangible. In particular, the option pricing models covered in this book require a probability density function for the logarithm of the stock price, $X = \log(S)$. From a theoretical standpoint, however, it is often easier to obtain the characteristic function $\varphi_X(t)$ for $\log(S)$, given by

$$\varphi_X(t) = \int_0^\infty e^{itx} f_X(x)\, dx,$$

where

$$i = \sqrt{-1},$$
$$f_X(x) = \text{probability density function of } X.$$

The probability density function for the logarithm of the stock price can then be obtained by inversion of $\varphi_X(t)$:

$$f_X(x) = \frac{1}{2\pi} \int_{-\infty}^{\infty} e^{-itx} \varphi_X(t)\, dt$$

One corollary of Levy's inversion formula—an alternate inversion formula—is that the cumulative density function $F_X(x) = \Pr(X < x)$ for the logarithm of the stock price can be obtained. The following expression is often used for the risk-neutral probability that a call option lies in-the-money:

$$F_X(k) = \Pr[\log(S) > k] = \frac{1}{2} + \frac{1}{\pi} \int_0^\infty \text{Re}\left[\frac{e^{-itk}\varphi_X(t)}{it}\right] dt,$$

where $k = \log(K)$ is the logarithm of the strike price K. Again, this formula requires evaluating an integral that contains $i = \sqrt{-1}$.

FINDING ROOTS OF FUNCTIONS

In this section we present two algorithms for finding roots of functions, the Newton-Raphson method, and the bisection method. These will become important in later chapters that deal with Black-Scholes implied volatility. Since the Black-Scholes formula cannot be inverted to yield the volatility, finding implied volatility must be done numerically. For a given market price on an option, implied volatility is that volatility which, when plugged into the Black-Scholes formula, produces the same price as the market. Equivalently, implied volatility is that which produces a zero difference between the market price and the Black-Scholes price. Hence, finding implied volatility is essentially a root-finding problem.

The chief advantage of programming root-finding algorithms in VBA, rather than using the Goal Seek and Solver features included in Excel, is that a particular algorithm can be programmed for the problem at hand. For example, we will see in later chapters that the bisection algorithm is particularly well suited for finding implied volatility. There are at least four considerations that must be kept in mind when implementing root-finding algorithms. First, adequate starting values must be carefully chosen. This is particularly important in regions of highly functional variability and when there are multiple roots and local minima. If the function is highly variable, a starting value that is not close enough to the root might stray the algorithm away from a root. If there are multiple roots, the algorithm may yield only one root and not identify the others. If there are local minima, the algorithm may get stuck in a local minimum. In that case, it would yield the minimum as the best approximation to the root, without realizing that the true root lies outside the region of the minimum. Second, the tolerance must be specified. The tolerance is the difference between successive approximations to the root. In regions where the function is flat, a high number for tolerance can be used. In regions where the function is very steep, however, a very small number must be used for tolerance. This is because even small deviations from the true root can produce values for the function that are substantially different from zero. Third, the maximum number of iterations needs to be defined. If the number of iterations is too low, the algorithm may stop before the tolerance level is satisfied. If the number of iterations is too high and the algorithm is not converging to a root because of an inaccurate starting value, the algorithm may continue needlessly and waste computing time.

To summarize, while the built-in modules such as the Excel Solver or Goal Seek allows the user to specify starting values, tolerance, maximum number of iterations, and constraints, writing VBA functions to perform root finding sometimes allows flexibility that built-in modules do not. Furthermore, programming multivariate optimization algorithms in VBA, such as the Nelder-Mead covered later in this chapter, is easier if one is already familiar with programming single-variable algorithms. The root-finding methods outlined in this section can be found in Burden and Faires (2001) or Press et al. (2002).

Newton-Raphson Method

This method is one of the oldest and most popular methods for finding roots of functions. It is based on a first-order Taylor series approximation about the root. To find a root x of a function $f(x)$, defined as that x which produces $f(x) = 0$, select a starting value x_0 as the initial guess to the root, and update the guess using the formula

$$f(x_{i+1}) = x_i - \frac{f(x_i)}{f'(x_i)} \tag{1.2}$$

for $i = 0, 1, 2, \ldots$, and where $f'(x_i)$ denotes the first derivative of $f(x)$ evaluated at x_i. There are two methods to specify a stopping condition for this algorithm, when the difference between two successive approximations is less than the tolerance level ε, or when the slope of the function is sufficiently close to zero. The VBA code in this chapter uses the second condition, but the code can easily be adapted for the first condition.

The Excel file Chapter1Roots contains the VBA functions for implementing the root-finding algorithms presented in this section. The file contains two functions for implementing the Newton-Raphson method. The first function assumes that an analytic form for the derivative $f'(x_i)$ exists, while the second uses an approximation to the derivative. Both are illustrated with the simple function $f(x) = x^2 - 7x + 10$, which has the derivative $f'(x) = 2x - 7$. These are defined as the VBA functions Fun1() and dFun1(), respectively.

```
Function Fun1(x)
  Fun1 = x^2 - 7*x + 10
End Function

Function dFun1(x)
  dFun1 = 2*x - 7
End Function
```

The function NewtRap() assumes that the derivative has an analytic form, so it uses the function Fun1() and its derivative dFun1() to find the root of Fun1. It requires as inputs the function, its derivative, and a starting value x_guess. The maximum number of iterations is set at 500, and the tolerance is set at 0.00001.

```
Function NewtRap(fname As String, dfname As String, x_guess)
Maxiter = 500
Eps = 0.00001
cur_x = x_guess
For i = 1 To Maxiter
  fx = Run(fname, cur_x)
  dx = Run(dfname, cur_x)
    If (Abs(dx) < Eps) Then Exit For
  cur_x = cur_x - (fx / dx)
Next i
  NewtRap = cur_x
End Function
```

The function NewRapNum() does not require the derivative to be specified, only the function Fun1() and a starting value. At each step, it calculates an approximation to the derivative.

```
Function NewtRapNum(fname As String, x_guess)
Maxiter = 500
Eps = 0.000001
delta_x = 0.000000001
cur_x = x_guess
  For i = 1 To Maxiter
    fx = Run(fname, cur_x)
    fx_delta_x = Run(fname, cur_x - delta_x)
    dx = (fx - fx_delta_x) / delta_x
      If (Abs(dx) < Eps) Then Exit For
    cur_x = cur_x - (fx / dx)
  Next i
NewtRapNum = cur_x
End Function
```

The function NewtRapNum() approximates the derivative at any point x by using the line segment joining the function at x and at $x + dx$, where dx is a small number set at 1×10^{-9}. This is the familiar "rise over run" approximation to the slope, based on a first-order Taylor series expansion for $f(x + dx)$ about x:

$$f'(x) \approx \frac{f(x) - f(x + dx)}{dx}.$$

This approximation appears as the statement

```
dx = (fx - fx_delta_x) / delta_x
```

in the function NewtRapNum().

Bisection Method

This method is well suited to problems for which the function is continuous on an interval $[a, b]$ and for which the function is known to take a positive value on one endpoint and a negative value on the other endpoint. By the Intermediate Value Theorem, the interval will necessarily contain a root. A first guess for the root is the midpoint of the interval. The bisection algorithm proceeds by repeatedly dividing the subintervals of $[a, b]$ in two, and at each step locating the half that contains the root. The function BisMet() requires as inputs the function for which a root must be found, and the endpoints a and b. The endpoints must be chosen so that the function assumes opposite signs at each, otherwise the algorithm may not converge.

```
Function BisMet(fname As String, a, b)
Eps = 0.000001
  If (Run(fname, b) < Run(fname, a)) Then
```

```
    tmp = b:  b = a: a = tmp
   End If
Do While (Run(fname, b) - Run(fname, a) > Eps)
  midPt = (b + a) / 2
If Run(fname, midPt) < 0 Then
  a = midPt
Else
  b = midPt
  End If
Loop
  BisMet = (b + a) / 2
End Function
```

We will see in Chapters 4 and 10 that the bisection method is particularly well suited for finding implied volatilities extracted from option prices.

Illustration of the Methods

Figure 1.2 illustrates the Newton-Raphson method with an explicit derivative, the Newton-Raphson method with an approximation to the derivative, and the Bisection method. This spreadsheet appears in the Excel file Chapter1Roots. As before, we use the function $f(x) = x^2 - 7x + 10$, coded by the VBA function Fun1(), with derivative $f'(x) = 2x - 7$, coded by the VBA function dFun1(). It is easy to see by inspection that this function has two roots, at $x = 2$ and at $x = 5$. We illustrate the methods with the first root.

The bisection method requires an interval with endpoints chosen so that the function takes on values opposite in sign at each endpoint. Hence, we choose the

	A	B	C	D	E	F	G	H
1								
2		Function	$f(x) = x^2 - 7x + 10$					
3		Derivative	$f'(x) = 2x - 7$					
4								
5								
6		First Root	Root	Endpoints		Function Values		
7		Bisection:	2	$a =$	1	$f(a) =$	4	
8		Newton-Raphson (derivative)	2	$b =$	3	$f(b) =$	-2	
9		Newton-Raphson (no derivative)	2					
10								
11								
12								
13		Second Root	Root	Endpoints		Function Values		
14		Bisection:	5	$a =$	4	$f(a) =$	-2	
15		Newton-Raphson (derivative)	5	$b =$	7	$f(b) =$	10	
16		Newton-Raphson (no derivative)	5					
17								

FIGURE 1.2 Root-Finding Algorithms

interval $[1, 3]$ for the first root, which appears in cells E7:E8. In cell G7 we type

$$= \text{Fun1}(E7)$$

which yields the value 4 for the function evaluated at the point $x = 1$. Similarly, in cell G8 we obtain the value -2 for the function evaluated at $x = 3$.

Recall that the VBA function BisMet() requires three inputs, a function name enclosed in quotes, and the endpoints of the interval along the x-axis over which the function changes sign. To invoke the bisection method, therefore, in cell C7 we type

$$= \text{BisMet}(\text{"Fun1"}, E7, E8)$$

which produces the root $x = 2$.

To invoke the two Newton-Raphson methods, we choose $x_0 = 1$ as the starting value for the root $x = 2$. The VBA function NewtRap() uses an explicit form for the derivative and requires three inputs, the function name and the derivative name, each enclosed in quotes, and the starting value. Hence, in cell C8 we type

$$= \text{NewtRap}(\text{"Fun1"}, \text{"dFun1"}, 1)$$

and obtain the root $x = 2$.

The VBA function NewRapNum() does not use an explicit form for the derivative, so it requires as inputs only the function name and a starting value. Hence, in cell C9 we type

$$= \text{NewtRapNum}(\text{"Fun1"}, 1)$$

and again obtain the root $x = 2$. The other root $x = 5$ is obtained similarly, using the interval $[4,7]$ for the bisection algorithm and the starting value $x_0 = 4$.

This example illustrates that proper selection of starting values and intervals is crucial, especially when multiple roots are involved. With the bisection method, an interval over which the function changes sign must be found for every root. Sometimes no such interval can be found, as is the case for the function $f(x) = x^2$, which has a root at $x = 0$ but which never takes on negative values. In that case, the bisection method cannot be used.

With Newton's method, it is important to select starting values close enough to every root that must be found. If not, the method might focus on one root only, and multiple roots may never be identified. Unfortunately, there is no method to properly identify appropriate starting values, so these are usually found by trail and error. In the case of a single variable, covered in this chapter, this is relatively straightforward and can be accomplished by dividing the x-axis into a series of starting values, and invoking Newton's method at every starting value. In the multidimensional case, however, more complicated grid-search algorithms must be used.

OLS AND WLS

In this section we present VBA code to perform multiple regression analysis under ordinary least squares (OLS) and weighted least squares (WLS). While functions to perform multiple regression are built into Excel, it is sometimes preferable to write VBA code to run regression, rather than relying on the built-in functions. First, Excel estimates parameters by OLS only, according to which each observation receives equal weight. If the analyst feels more weight should be given to certain observations, and less to others, then estimating parameters by WLS is preferable to OLS. Second, it is straightforward to obtain the entire covariance matrix of parameter estimates with VBA, rather than just its diagonal elements, which are the variance of each parameter estimate. Third, it is easy to obtain the "hat" matrix, whose diagonal elements can help identify the relative influence of each observation on parameter estimates. Finally, changing the contents of one cell automatically updates the results when a function is used to implement regression. This is not the case when OLS is implemented with the built-in regression routine in Excel.

To summarize, writing VBA code to perform regression is more flexible and allows the analyst to have access to more diagnostic tools than relying on the regression functions built into Excel. The OLS and WLS methods are explained in textbooks such as those by Davidson and MacKinnon (1993) and Neter et al. (1996).

Ordinary Least Squares

Suppose we specify that the dependent variable Y is related to $k-1$ independent variables $X_1, X_2, \ldots, X_{k-1}$ and an intercept β_0 in the linear form

$$Y = \beta_0 + \beta_1 X_1 + \beta_2 X_2 + \cdots + \beta_{k-1} X_{k-1} + \varepsilon, \tag{1.3}$$

where

$$
\begin{aligned}
Y &= \text{a vector of dimension } n \text{ containing values of the dependent} \\
  &\quad\text{variable} \\
X_1, X_2, \ldots, X_{k-1} &= \text{vectors of dimension } n \text{ of independent variables} \\
\beta_0, \beta_1, \ldots, \beta_{k-1} &= k \text{ regression parameters} \\
\varepsilon &= \text{a vector of dimension } n \text{ of error terms, containing elements } \varepsilon_i \\
\varepsilon_i &= \text{independently and identically distributed random variables} \\
  &\quad\text{each distributed as normal with mean zero and variance } \sigma^2.
\end{aligned}
$$

The ordinary least-squares estimate of the parameters is given by the well-known formula

$$\hat{\beta}_{OLS} = (X^T X)^{-1} X^T Y \tag{1.4}$$

where

$$\hat{\beta}_{OLS} = \text{a vector of dimension } k \text{ containing estimated parameters}$$
$$X = (\iota X_1 X_2 \cdots X_{k-1}) = \text{a design matrix of dimension } n \times k \text{ containing the independent variables and the vector } \iota$$
$$\iota = \text{a vector of dimension } n \text{ containing ones}$$

Once the OLS parameter estimates are obtained, we can obtain the fitted values as the vector $\hat{Y} = X\hat{\beta}_{OLS}$ of dimension n. If a model with no intercept is desired, then

$$Y = \beta_1 X_1 + \beta_2 X_2 + \cdots + \beta_{k-1} X_{k-1} + \varepsilon,$$

and the design matrix excludes the vector ι containing ones, resulting in a design matrix of dimension $n \times (k-1)$, and the OLS parameters are estimated by (1.4) as before.

Analysis of Variance

It is very convenient to break down the total sum of squares (SSTO), defined as the variability of the dependent variable about its mean, in terms of the error sum of squares (SSE) and the regression sum of squares (SSR). Using algebra, it is straightforward to show that

$$\text{SSTO} = \text{SSE} + \text{SSR}$$

where $\text{SSTO} = \sum_{i=1}^{n} (y_i - \bar{y})^2$

$$\text{SSE} = \sum_{i=1}^{n} (y_i - \hat{y}_i)^2 = (Y - \hat{Y})^T (Y - \hat{Y})$$

$$\text{SSR} = \sum_{i=1}^{n} (\hat{y}_i - \bar{y})^2$$

$y_i = \text{elements of } Y$

$\hat{y}_i = \text{elements of } \hat{Y} (i = 1, 2, \ldots, n)$

$\bar{y} = \dfrac{1}{n} \sum_{i=1}^{n} y_i \text{ is the sample mean of the dependent variable.}$

With these quantities we can obtain several common definitions. An estimate of the variance σ^2 is given by the mean square error (MSE)

$$\hat{\sigma}^2 = \text{MSE} = \frac{\text{SSE}}{n-k}, \tag{1.5}$$

while an estimate of the standard deviation is given by $\hat{\sigma} = \sqrt{MSE}$. The coefficient of multiple determination, R^2, is given by the proportion of SSTO explained by the model

$$R^2 = \frac{SSR}{SSTO}. \tag{1.6}$$

The R^2 coefficient is the proportion of variability in the dependent variable that can be attributed to the linear model. The rest of the variability cannot be attributed to the model and is therefore pure unexplained error. One shortcoming of R^2 is that it always increases, and never decreases, when additional independent variables are included in the model, regardless of whether or not the added variables have any explanatory power. The adjusted R^2 incorporates a penalty for additional variables, and is given by

$$R_a^2 = 1 - \left(\frac{n-1}{n-k}\right)(1 - R^2). \tag{1.7}$$

An estimate of the $(k \times k)$ covariance matrix of the parameter estimates is given by

$$\mathrm{Cov}(\hat{\beta}_{OLS}) = MSE(X^T X)^{-1} \tag{1.8}$$

The t-statistics for each regression coefficient are given by

$$t = \frac{\hat{\beta}_j}{SE(\hat{\beta}_j)} \tag{1.9}$$

where

$\hat{\beta}_j = j$-th element of $\hat{\beta}$
$SE(\hat{\beta}_j) = $ standard error of $\hat{\beta}_j$, obtained as the square root of the jth diagonal element of (1.8).

Each t-statistic is distributed as a t random variable with $n - k$ degrees of freedom, and can be used to perform a two-tailed test that each regression coefficient is zero. The two-tailed p-value is used to assess statistical significance of the regression coefficient. A small p-value corresponds to a coefficient that is significantly different from zero, whereas a large p-value denotes a coefficient that is statistically indistinguishable from zero. Usually $p \leqslant 0.05$ is taken as the cut-off value to determine significance of each coefficient, corresponding to a significance level of 5 percent.

When an intercept term is included in the model, it can be shown by algebra that the condition $0 \leqslant R^2 \leqslant 1$ always holds. When no intercept term is included, however, this condition may or may not hold. It is possible to obtain negative values of R_a^2, especially if SSR is very small relative to SSTO.

Weighted Least Squares

Ordinary least squares attribute equal weight to each observation. In certain instances, however, the analyst may wish to assign more weight to some observations, and less weight to others. In this case, WLS is preferable to OLS. Selecting the weights $w_1, w_2, \ldots, w_n$, however, is arbitrary. One popular choice is to choose the weights as the inverse of each observation. Observations with a large variance receive little weight, while observations with a small variance get large weight.

Obtaining parameter estimates and associated statistics of (1.3) under WLS is straightforward. Define W as a diagonal matrix of dimension n containing the weights, so that $W = \text{diag}[w_1, \ldots, w_n]$. Parameter estimates under WLS are given by

$$\hat{\beta}_{WLS} = (X^T W X)^{-1} X^T W Y \tag{1.10}$$

while SSTO, SSE, and SSR are given by

$$\text{SSTO} = \sum_{i=1}^{n} w_i (y_i - \bar{y})^2$$

$$\text{SSE} = \sum_{i=1}^{n} w_i (y_i - \hat{y}_i)^2 \tag{1.11}$$

$$\text{SSR} = \text{SSTO} - \text{SSE}.$$

The $(k \times k)$ covariance matrix is given by

$$\text{Cov}(\hat{\beta}_{WLS}) = \text{MSE}(X^T W X)^{-1} \tag{1.12}$$

where MSE is given by (1.5), but using the definition of SSE given in (1.11), and the t-statistics are given by (1.9), but using the standard errors obtained as the square root of the diagonal elements of (1.12). The coefficients R^2 and R_a^2 are given by (1.6) and (1.7) respectively, but using the sums of squares given in (1.11).

Under WLS, R^2 does not have the convenient interpretation that it does under OLS. Hence, R^2 and R_a^2 must be used with caution when these are obtained by WLS. Finally, we note that WLS is a special case of generalized least squares (GLS), according to which the matrix W is not a diagonal matrix but rather a matrix of general form. Under GLS, for example, the independence of the error terms can be relaxed to allow for different dependence structures between the errors.

Implementing OLS and WLS with VBA

In this section we present the VBA code for implementing OLS and WLS. We illustrate this with a simple example involving two explanatory variables, a vector of weights, and an intercept. The Excel file Chapter1WLS contains VBA code to implement WLS, and OLS as a special case. The function Diag() creates a diagonal matrix using a vector of weights as inputs:

```
Function Diag(W) As Variant
Dim n, i, j, k As Integer
Dim temp As Variant
n = W.Count
ReDim temp(n, n)
For i = 1 To n
  For j = 1 To n
    If j = i Then temp(i, j) = W(i) Else temp(i, j) = 0
  Next j
Next i
  Diag = temp
End Function
```

The function WLSregress() performs weighted least squares, and requires as inputs a vector y of observations for the dependent variable; a matrix X for the independent variables (which will contain ones in the first column if an intercept is desired); and a vector W of weights. This function produces WLS estimates of the regression parameters, given by (1.10). It is useful when only parameter estimates are required.

```
Function WLSregress(y As Variant, X As Variant, W As Variant) As Variant
Wmat = Diag(W)
n = W.Count
Dim Xtrans, Xw, XwX, XwXinv, Xwy As Variant
Dim m1, m2, m3, m4 As Variant
Dim output() As Variant
Xtrans = Application.Transpose(X)
Xw = Application.MMult(Xtrans, Wmat)
XwX = Application.MMult(Xw, X)
XwXinv = Application.MInverse(XwX)
Xwy = Application.MMult(Xw, y)
b = Application.MMult(XwXinv, Xwy)
k = Application.Count(b)
ReDim output(k) As Variant
  For bcnt = 1 To k
    output(bcnt) = b(bcnt, 1)
  Next bcnt
WLSregress = Application.Transpose(output)
End Function
```

Note that the first part of the function creates a diagonal matrix Wmat of dimension n using the function Diag(), while the second part computes the WLS parameter estimates given by (1.10).

The second VBA function, WLSstats(), provides a more thorough WLS analysis and is useful when both parameter estimates and associated statistics are needed. It computes WLS parameter estimates, the standard error and t-statistic of each parameter estimate, its corresponding p-value, the R^2 and R_a^2 coefficients, and $\sqrt{\text{MSE}}$, the estimate of the error standard deviation σ.

```
Function WLSstats(y As Variant, X As Variant, W As Variant) As Variant
Wmat = diag(W)
n = W.Count
Dim Xtrans, Xw, XwX, XwXinv, Xwy As Variant
Dim btemp As Variant
Dim output() As Variant, r(), se(), t(), pval() As Double
Xtrans = Application.Transpose(X)
Xw = Application.MMult(Xtrans, Wmat)
XwX = Application.MMult(Xw, X)
XwXinv = Application.MInverse(XwX)
Xwy = Application.MMult(Xw, y)
b = Application.MMult(XwXinv, Xwy)
n = Application.Count(y)
k = Application.Count(b)
ReDim output(k, 7) As Variant, r2(n), ss(n), t(k), se(k), pval(k)
              As Double
yhat = Application.MMult(X, b)
For ncnt = 1 To n
 r2(ncnt) = Wmat(ncnt, ncnt) * (y(ncnt) - yhat(ncnt, 1)) ^ 2
 ss(ncnt) = Wmat(ncnt, ncnt) * (y(ncnt) - Application.Average(y)) ^ 2
Next ncnt
sse = Application.Sum(r2): mse = sse / (n - k)
rmse = Sqr(mse): sst = Application.Sum(ss)
rsquared = 1 - sse / sst
adj_rsquared = 1 - (n - 1) / (n - k) * (1 - rsquared)
For kcnt = 1 To k
  se(kcnt) = (XwXinv(kcnt, kcnt) * mse) ^ 0.5
  t(kcnt) = b(kcnt, 1) / se(kcnt)
  pval(kcnt) = Application.TDist(Abs(t(kcnt)), n - k, 2)
  output(kcnt, 1) = b(kcnt, 1)
  output(kcnt, 2) = se(kcnt)
  output(kcnt, 3) = t(kcnt)
  output(kcnt, 4) = pval(kcnt)
Next kcnt
output(1, 5) = rsquared
output(1, 6) = adj_rsquared
output(1, 7) = rmse
For i = 2 To k
  For j = 5 To 7
    output(i, j) = " "
  Next j
Next i
  WLSstats = output
End Function
```

As in the previous VBA function WLSregress(), the function WLSstats() first creates a diagonal matrix Wmat using the vector of weights specified in the input argument W. It then creates estimated regression coefficients under WLS and

	Weight	Dependent Variable (Y)	Intercept	Independent Variables (X)		beta	s.e.(beta)	t-stat	p-value	R²	Adjusted R²	√MSE
4	1	29.04	1	15.75	4.08	23.6639	6.6902	3.5371	0.0036	0.1200	-0.0154	11.0397
5	1	17.84	1	8.45	4.83	-0.0538	0.2487	-0.2164	0.8320			
6	1	6.22	1	9.37	7.21	-1.0134	0.7661	-1.3229	0.2087			
7	1	21.49	1	18.85	0.88							
8	1	10.49	1	17.83	3.30	beta						
9	1	11.93	1	12.68	2.37	23.6639						
10	1	19.92	1	27.83	4.40	-0.0538						
11	1	24.61	1	28.96	0.54	-1.0134						
12	2	3.51	1	34.75	8.79							
13	2	28.28	1	22.26	5.89							
14	2	11.03	1	17.39	9.88							
15	2	12.38	1	5.32	2.01							
16	2	29.00	1	6.52	8.42							
17	2	8.96	1	21.49	6.64							
18	2	17.26	1	18.10	5.31							
19	2	27.91	1	31.67	1.05							

FIGURE 1.3 Weighted Least Squares

the associated statistics. The last loop ensures that cells with no output remain empty.

The WLSregress() and WLSstats() functions are illustrated in Figure 1.3, using $n = 16$ observations. Both functions require as inputs the vectors containing values of the dependent variable, of the independent variables, and of the weights. The first eight observations have been assigned a weight of 1, while the remaining eight observations have been assigned a weight of 2.

The first VBA function, WLSregress(), produces estimated weighted coefficients only. The dependent variable is contained in cells C4:C19, the independent variables (including the intercept) in cells D4:F19, and the weights in cells B4:B19. Hence, in cell G9 we type

$$= WLSregress(C4:C19, D4:F19, B4:B19)$$

and copy down to cells G10:G11, which produces the three regression coefficients estimated by WLS, namely $\hat{\beta}_0 = 23.6639$, $\hat{\beta}_1 = -0.0538$, and $\hat{\beta}_2 = -1.0134$.

The second VBA function, WLSstats(), produces more detailed output. It requires the same inputs as the previous function, so in cell G4 we type

$$= WLSstats(C4:C19, D4:F19, B4:B19),$$

and copy to the range G4:M6, which produces the three estimated regression coefficients, their standard errors, t-statistics and p-values, the R^2 and R^2_a coefficients and $\sqrt{MSE}$.

It is easy to generalize the two WLS functions for more than two independent variables. The Excel file Chapter1WLSbig contains an example of the WLSregress() and WLSstats() functions using five independent variables and an intercept. This is illustrated in Figure 1.4.

	A	B	C	D	E	F	G	H	I	J
1										
2			**Dependent**							
3		**Weight**	**Variable (Y)**	**Intercept**	-----------------	**Independent**	**Variables (X)**	----------------------		
4		1	29.04	1	15.75	4.08	33.23	-30.05	34.03	
5		1	17.84	1	8.45	4.83	25.65	-18.45	16.76	
6		1	6.22	1	9.37	7.21	9.34	-6.23	19.99	
7		1	21.49	1	18.85	0.88	31.01	-22.32	38.76	
8		1	10.49	1	17.83	3.30	13.46	-11.06	35.59	
9		1	11.93	1	12.68	2.37	14.13	-12.75	24.01	
10		1	19.92	1	27.83	4.40	20.00	-21.12	54.90	
11		1	24.61	1	28.96	0.54	22.95	-24.44	60.17	
12		2	3.51	1	34.75	8.79	1.09	-4.55	70.33	
13		2	28.28	1	22.26	5.89	30.47	-30.21	45.87	
14		2	11.03	1	17.39	9.88	11.24	-10.90	34.18	
15		2	12.38	1	5.32	2.01	14.31	-11.34	10.54	
16		2	29.00	1	6.52	8.42	32.09	-28.79	12.44	
17		2	8.96	1	21.49	6.64	10.88	-9.01	42.65	
18		2	17.26	1	18.10	5.31	23.23	-19.40	36.66	
19		2	27.91	1	31.67	1.05	32.65	-28.44	62.05	
20										
21										
22		**beta**		**beta**	**s.e.(beta)**	**t-stat**	**p-value**	**R^2**	**Adjusted R^2**	**√MSE**
23		1.6172		1.6172	1.0936	1.4788	0.1700	0.9937	0.9906	1.0630
24		0.3818		0.3818	0.4295	0.8891	0.3948			
25		-0.0851		-0.0851	0.0878	-0.9702	0.3548			
26		-0.0896		-0.0896	0.1116	-0.8031	0.4406			
27		-1.0632		-1.0632	0.1224	-8.6848	0.0000			
28		-0.2184		-0.2184	0.2147	-1.0172	0.3330			

FIGURE 1.4 Weighted Least Squares with Five Independent Variables

The range of independent variables (including intercept) is now contained in cells D4:I19. Hence, to obtain the WLS regression coefficients in cell B23 we type

$$= \text{WLSregress}(C4:C19,D4:I19,B4:B19)$$

and copy to cells B23:B28. To obtain detailed statistics, in cell D23 we type

$$= \text{WLSstats}(C4:C19,D4:I19,B4:B19),$$

and copy to cells D23:J28.

Suppose that OLS estimates of the regression coefficients are needed, instead of WLS estimates. Then cells B4:B19 are filled with ones, corresponding to equal weighting for all observations and a weighing matrix that is the identity matrix, so that the WLS estimates (1.10) will reduce to the OLS estimates (1.4). This is illustrated in Figure 1.5 with the Excel file Chapter1WLSbig.

Using the built-in regression data analysis module in Excel, it is easy to verify that Figure 1.5 produces the correct regression coefficients and associated statistics.

	A	B	C	D	E	F	G	H	I	J
1										
2			Dependent							
3		Weight	Variable (Y)	Intercept	----------------------		Independent Variables (X)		----------------------	
4		1	29.04	1	15.75	4.08	33.23	-30.05	34.03	
5		1	17.84	1	8.45	4.83	25.65	-18.45	16.76	
6		1	6.22	1	9.37	7.21	9.34	-6.23	19.99	
7		1	21.49	1	18.85	0.88	31.01	-22.32	38.76	
8		1	10.49	1	17.83	3.30	13.46	-11.06	35.59	
9		1	11.93	1	12.68	2.37	14.13	-12.75	24.01	
10		1	19.92	1	27.83	4.40	20.00	-21.12	54.90	
11		1	24.61	1	28.96	0.54	22.95	-24.44	60.17	
12		1	3.51	1	34.75	8.79	1.09	-4.55	70.33	
13		1	28.28	1	22.26	5.89	30.47	-30.21	45.87	
14		1	11.03	1	17.39	9.88	11.24	-10.90	34.18	
15		1	12.38	1	5.32	2.01	14.31	-11.34	10.54	
16		1	29.00	1	6.52	8.42	32.09	-28.79	12.44	
17		1	8.96	1	21.49	6.64	10.88	-9.01	42.65	
18		1	17.26	1	18.10	5.31	23.23	-19.40	36.66	
19		1	27.91	1	31.67	1.05	32.65	-28.44	62.05	
20										
21										
22		beta			beta	s.e.(beta)	t-stat	p-value	R^2	Adjusted R^2	√MSE
23		1.3110			1.3110	1.0675	1.2281	0.2475	0.9935	0.9903	0.8458
24		0.0851			0.0851	0.3873	0.2199	0.8304			
25		-0.0767			-0.0767	0.0861	-0.8906	0.3940			
26		-0.0745			-0.0745	0.0974	-0.7652	0.4618			
27		-1.0501			-1.0501	0.1076	-9.7561	0.0000			
28		-0.0666			-0.0666	0.1929	-0.3451	0.7372			

FIGURE 1.5 Ordinary Least Squares with Five Independent Variables

Finally, suppose that the intercept β_0 is to be excluded from the model (1.3). In that case, the column corresponding to the intercept is excluded from the set of independent variables. This is illustrated in Figure 1.6.

The range of independent variables is contained in cells E4:I19. Hence, in cell D23 we type

$$= \text{WLSstats}(C4{:}C19,E4{:}I19,B4{:}B19)$$

and copy to the range D23:J27, which produces the regression coefficients and associated statistics.

NELDER-MEAD ALGORITHM

The methods to find roots of functions described earlier in this chapter are applicable when the root or minimum value of a single-variable function needs to be found. In many option pricing formulas, however, the minimum or maximum value of a

	A	B	C	D	E	F	G	H	I	J
1										
2			Dependent							
3		Weight	Variable (Y)	Intercept	----------	---------	Independent Variables (X)	----------	---------	
4		1	29.04	1	15.75	4.08	33.23	-30.05	34.03	
5		1	17.84	1	8.45	4.83	25.65	-18.45	16.76	
6		1	6.22	1	9.37	7.21	9.34	-6.23	19.99	
7		1	21.49	1	18.85	0.88	31.01	-22.32	38.76	
8		1	10.49	1	17.83	3.30	13.46	-11.06	35.59	
9		1	11.93	1	12.68	2.37	14.13	-12.75	24.01	
10		1	19.92	1	27.83	4.40	20.00	-21.12	54.90	
11		1	24.61	1	28.96	0.54	22.95	-24.44	60.17	
12		1	3.51	1	34.75	8.79	1.09	-4.55	70.33	
13		1	28.28	1	22.26	5.89	30.47	-30.21	45.87	
14		1	11.03	1	17.39	9.88	11.24	-10.90	34.18	
15		1	12.38	1	5.32	2.01	14.31	-11.34	10.54	
16		1	29.00	1	6.52	8.42	32.09	-28.79	12.44	
17		1	8.96	1	21.49	6.64	10.88	-9.01	42.65	
18		1	17.26	1	18.10	5.31	23.23	-19.40	36.66	
19		1	27.91	1	31.67	1.05	32.65	-28.44	62.05	
20										
21										
22		beta		beta	s.e.(beta)	t-stat	p-value	R^2	Adjusted R^2	$\sqrt{MSE}$
23		0.1197		0.1197	0.3951	0.3031	0.7675	0.9926	0.9899	0.8651
24		-0.0005		-0.0005	0.0611	-0.0080	0.9938			
25		-0.0048		-0.0048	0.0809	-0.0594	0.9537			
26		-0.9936		-0.9936	0.0995	-9.9829	0.0000			
27		-0.0704		-0.0704	0.1973	-0.3566	0.7281			

FIGURE 1.6 Ordinary Least Squares with No Intercept

function of two or more variables must be found. The Nelder-Mead algorithm is a powerful and popular method to find roots of multivariate functions. It is easy to implement, and it converges very quickly regardless of which starting values are used. Many mathematical and engineering packages, such as Matlab™ for example, use the Nelder-Mead algorithm in their optimization routines. We follow the description of the algorithm presented in Lagarias et al. (1999) for finding the minimum value of a multivariate function. Finding the maximum of a function can be done by changing the sign of the function and finding the minimum of the changed function.

For a function $f(x)$ of n variables, the algorithm requires $n + 1$ starting values in x. Arrange these $n + 1$ starting values in increasing value for $f(x)$, so that $x_1, x_2, \ldots, x_{n+1}$ are such that

$$f_1 \leqslant f_2 \leqslant \cdots \leqslant f_n \leqslant f_{n+1} \tag{1.13}$$

where $f_k \equiv f(x_k)$ and $x_i \in \Re^n$ $(i = 1, 2, \ldots, n + 1)$. The best of these vectors is x_1 since it produces the smallest value of $f(x)$, and the worst is x_{n+1} since it produces the largest value. The remaining vectors lie in the middle. At each iteration step, the best values $x_1, \ldots, x_n$ are retained and the worst x_{n+1} is replaced according to the following rules:

1. Reflection rule. Compute the reflection point $x_r = 2\bar{x} - x_{n+1}$ where $\bar{x} = \sum_{i=1}^{n} x_i/n$ is the mean of the best n points and evaluate $f_r = f(x_r)$. If $f_1 \leqslant f_r < f_n$ then x_{n+1} is replaced with x_r, the $n+1$ points $x_1, \ldots, x_n, x_r$ are reordered according to the value of the function as in (1.13), which produces another set of ordered points $x_1, x_2, \ldots, x_{n+1}$. The next iteration is initiated on the new worst point x_{n+1}. Otherwise, proceed to the next rule.
2. Expansion rule. If $f_r < f_1$ compute the expansion point $x_e = 2x_r - \bar{x}$ and the value of the function $f_e = f(x_e)$. If $f_e < f_r$ then replace x_{n+1} with x_e, reorder the points and initiate the next iteration. Otherwise, proceed to the next rule.
3. Outside contraction rule. If $f_n \leqslant f_r < f_{n+1}$ compute the outside contraction point $x_{oc} = \frac{1}{2}x_r + \frac{1}{2}\bar{x}$ and the value $f_{oc} = f(x_{oc})$. If $f_{oc} \leqslant f_r$ then replace x_{n+1} with x_{oc}, reorder the points, and initiate the next iteration. Otherwise, proceed to rule 5 and perform a shrink step.
4. Inside contraction rule. If $f_r \geqslant f_{n+1}$ compute the inside contraction point $x_{ic} = \frac{1}{2}\bar{x} + \frac{1}{2}x_{n+1}$ and the value $f_{ic} = f(x_{ic})$. If $f_{ic} < f_{n+1}$ replace x_{n+1} with x_{ic}, reorder the points and initiate the next iteration. Otherwise, proceed to rule 5.
5. Shrink step. Evaluate $f(x)$ at the points $v_i = x_1 + \frac{1}{2}(x_i - x_1)$ for $i = 2, \ldots, n+1$. The new unordered points are the $n+1$ points $x_1, v_2, v_3, \ldots, v_{n+1}$. Reorder these points and initiate the next iteration.

The Excel file Chapter1NM contains the VBA function NelderMead() for implementing this algorithm. The function uses a bubble sort algorithm to sort the values of the function in accordance with (1.13). This algorithm is implemented with the function BubSortRows().

```
Function BubSortRows(passVec)
Dim tmpVec() As Double, temp() As Double
uVec = passVec
rownum = UBound(uVec, 1)
colnum = UBound(uVec, 2)
ReDim tmpVec(rownum, colnum) As Double
ReDim temp(colnum) As Double
For i = rownum - 1 To 1 Step -1
  For j = 1 To i
  If (uVec(j, 1) > uVec(j + 1, 1)) Then
    For k = 1 To colnum
       temp(k) = uVec(j + 1, k)
       uVec(j + 1, k) = uVec(j, k)
       uVec(j, k) = temp(k)
    Next k
  End If
  Next j
Next i
  BubSortRows = uVec
End Function
```

In this chapter the Nelder-Mead algorithm is illustrated using the bivariate function $f(x_1, x_2) = f(x, y)$ defined as

$$f(x, y) = x^2 - 4x + y^2 - y + xy, \qquad (1.14)$$

and the function of three variables $g(x_1, x_2, x_3) = g(x, y, z)$ defined as

$$g(x, y, z) = (x - 10)^2 + (y + 10)^2 + (z - 2)^2. \qquad (1.15)$$

These are coded as the VBA functions Fun1() and Fun2(), respectively.

```
Function Fun1(params)
 x = params(1)
 y = params(2)
 Fun1 = x ^ 2 - 4 * x + y ^ 2 - y - x * y
End Function

Function Fun2(params)
 x = params(1)
 y = params(2)
 z = params(3)
 Fun2 = (x - 10) ^ 2 + (y + 10) ^ 2 + (z - 2) ^ 2
End Function
```

The function NelderMead() requires as inputs only the name of the VBA function for which a minimum is to be found, and a set of starting values.

```
Function NelderMead(fname As String, startParams)
Dim resMatrix() As Double
Dim x1() As Double, xn() As Double, xw() As Double, xbar()
As Double, xr() As Double, xe() As Double, xc() As Double,
xcc() As Double
Dim funRes() As Double, passParams() As Double
MAXFUN = 1000
TOL = 0.0000000001
rho = 1
Xi = 2
gam = 0.5
sigma = 0.5
paramnum = Application.Count(startParams)
ReDim resmat(paramnum + 1, paramnum + 1) As Double
ReDim x1(paramnum) As Double, xn(paramnum) As Double,
xw(paramnum) As Double, xbar(paramnum) As Double,
xr(paramnum) As Double, xe(paramnum) As Double,
xc(paramnum) As Double, xcc(paramnum) As Double
ReDim funRes(paramnum + 1) As Double, passParams(paramnum)
For i = 1 To paramnum
   resmat(1, i + 1) = startParams(i)
Next i
resmat(1, 1) = Run(fname, startParams)
For j = 1 To paramnum
```

```
  For i = 1 To paramnum
    If (i = j) Then
      If (startParams(i) = 0) Then
        resmat(j + 1, i + 1) = 0.05
      Else
        resmat(j + 1, i + 1) = startParams(i) * 1.05
      End If
    Else
      resmat(j + 1, i + 1) = startParams(i)
    End If
  passParams(i) = resmat(j + 1, i + 1)
  Next i
  resmat(j + 1, 1) = Run(fname, passParams)
Next j
For j = 1 To paramnum
  For i = 1 To paramnum
    If (i = j) Then
      resmat(j + 1, i + 1) = startParams(i) * 1.05
    Else
      resmat(j + 1, i + 1) = startParams(i)
    End If
  passParams(i) = resmat(j + 1, i + 1)
  Next i
  resmat(j + 1, 1) = Run(fname, passParams)
Next j
For lnum = 1 To MAXFUN
  resmat = BubSortRows(resmat)
If (Abs(resmat(1, 1) - resmat(paramnum + 1, 1)) < TOL) Then
  Exit For
End If
  f1 = resmat(1, 1)
  For i = 1 To paramnum
    x1(i) = resmat(1, i + 1)
  Next i
  fn = resmat(paramnum, 1)
  For i = 1 To paramnum
    xn(i) = resmat(paramnum, i + 1)
  Next i
  fw = resmat(paramnum + 1, 1)
  For i = 1 To paramnum
    xw(i) = resmat(paramnum + 1, i + 1)
  Next i
  For i = 1 To paramnum
    xbar(i) = 0
    For j = 1 To paramnum
      xbar(i) = xbar(i) + resmat(j, i + 1)
    Next j
    xbar(i) = xbar(i) / paramnum
  Next i
  For i = 1 To paramnum
    xr(i) = xbar(i) + rho * (xbar(i) - xw(i))
  Next i
  fr = Run(fname, xr)
```

```
      shrink = 0
      If ((fr >= f1) And (fr < fn)) Then
        newpoint = xr
        newf = fr
        ElseIf (fr < f1) Then
          For i = 1 To paramnum
            xe(i) = xbar(i) + Xi * (xr(i) - xbar(i))
          Next i
        fe = Run(fname, xe)
        If (fe < fr) Then
          newpoint = xe
          newf = fe
        Else
          newpoint = xr
          newf = fr
        End If
      ElseIf (fr >= fn) Then
        If ((fr >= fn) And (fr < fw)) Then
          For i = 1 To paramnum
            xc(i) = xbar(i) + gam * (xr(i) - xbar(i))
          Next i
          fc = Run(fname, xc)
          If (fc <= fr) Then
            newpoint = xc
            newf = fc
          Else
            shrink = 1
          End If
        Else
          For i = 1 To paramnum
            xcc(i) = xbar(i) - gam * (xbar(i) - xw(i))
          Next i
          fcc = Run(fname, xcc)
          If (fcc < fw) Then
            newpoint = xcc
            newf = fcc
          Else
            shrink = 1
          End If
        End If
      End If
      If (shrink = 1) Then
        For scnt = 2 To paramnum + 1
          For i = 1 To paramnum
            resmat(scnt, i + 1) = x1(i) + sigma
                          * (resmat(scnt, i + 1) - x1(1))
            passParams(i) = resmat(scnt, i + 1)
          Next i
          resmat(scnt, 1) = Run(fname, passParams)
        Next scnt
      Else
        For i = 1 To paramnum
          resmat(paramnum + 1, i + 1) = newpoint(i)
```

```
      Next i
        resmat(paramnum + 1, 1) = newf
      End If
   Next lnum
   If (lnum = MAXFUN + 1) Then
      MsgBox "Maximum Iteration (" & MAXFUN & ") exceeded"
   End If
   resmat = BubSortRows(resmat)
   For i = 1 To paramnum + 1
      funRes(i) = resmat(1, i)
   Next i
   funRes(1) = funRes(1)
      NelderMead = Application.Transpose(funRes)
   End Function
```

In this function, the maximum number of iterations (MAXFUN) has been set to 1,000, and the tolerance (TOL) between the best value and worst values x_1, and x_{n+1}, respectively, to 10^{-10}. Increasing MAXFUN and decreasing TOL will lead to more accurate results, but will also increase the computing time.

Figure 1.7 illustrates the NelderMead() function on the functions f and g defined in (1.14) and (1.15). It is easy to verify that f takes on its minimum value of -7 at $(x, y) = (3, 2)$ and that g takes on its minimum value of 0 at the point $(x, y, z) = (10, -10, 2)$. We choose large starting values of 10,000 to illustrate the convergence of the Nelder-Mead algorithm.

The starting values for $f(x, y)$ appear in cells F7:F8, and the final values in cells E7:E8. The value of $f(3, 2) = -7$ appears in cell E6. The starting values for $g(x, y, z)$ appear in cells F14:F16, the final values in cells E14:E16 and the value of $g(10, -10, 2) = 0$ in cell E13. Even with starting values that are substantially

	A	B	C	D	E	F
1						
2		**Nelder-Mead Algorithm for the Minimum of a Multivariate Function**				
3						
4		$f(x) = x^2 - 4x + y^2 - y - xy$			Final Values	Starting Values
5						
6		Value of $f(x)$ at Final Values ------------>			-7.00000	
7				x =	3.00000	10,000
8				y =	2.00000	10,000
9						
10						
11		$g(x) = (x - 10)^2 + (y + 10)^2 + (z - 2)^2$			Final Values	Starting Values
12						
13		Value of $g(x)$ at Final Values ------------>			0.00000	
14				x =	10.00000	10,000
15				y =	-10.00000	10,000
16				z =	2.00000	10,000

FIGURE 1.7 Nelder-Mead Algorithm

different than the optimized values, the Nelder-Mead algorithm is able to locate the minimum of each function.

MAXIMUM LIKELIHOOD ESTIMATION

All of the option pricing models presented in this book rely on parameters as input values to the models. Estimates of these parameters must therefore be found. One popular method to estimate parameter values is the method of maximum likelihood. This method is explained in textbooks on mathematical statistics and econometrics, such as that by Davidson and MacKinnon (1993). Maximum likelihood estimation requires a sample of n identically and independently distributed observations $x_1, x_2, \ldots, x_n$, assumed to originate from some parametric family. In that case, the joint probability density function of the sample (the likelihood function) is factored into a product of marginal functions, and the maximum likelihood estimators (MLEs) of the parameters are those values that maximize the likelihood.

In some cases the MLEs are available in closed form. For example, it is well known that if $x_1, x_2, \ldots, x_n$ are from the normal distribution with parameters μ for the mean and σ^2 for the variance, then Davidson and MacKinnon (1993) explain that the Type II maximum likelihood estimators of μ and σ^2 can be found by differentiating the likelihood function. These have the closed form $\hat{\mu} = \bar{x} = \frac{1}{n} \sum x_i$ and $\hat{\sigma}^2 = \frac{1}{n} \sum (x_i - \bar{x})^2$ respectively, where both summations run from $i = 1$ to n.

For most of the option pricing models covered in this book, however, MLEs of parameters are not available in closed form. Hence, we need to apply an optimization routine such as the Nelder-Mead algorithm to find those values of the parameters that maximize the likelihood. If $x_1, x_2, \ldots, x_n$ are independently and identically distributed according to some distribution $f(x_i; \theta)$, where θ denotes a vector of parameters, then the Type I MLE of θ is given by

$$\hat{\theta}_{MLE} = \arg\max_{\theta} \prod_{i=1}^{n} f(x_i; \theta). \tag{1.16}$$

In Chapter 6 we apply the Nelder-Mead algorithm to expressions such as (1.16), to find MLEs of parameters for generalized autoregressive conditional heteroskedastic (GARCH) models of volatility.

CUBIC SPLINE INTERPOLATION

Sometimes functional values $a_i = f(x_i)$ are available only on a discrete set of points x_i $(i = 1, \ldots, n)$, even though values at all points are needed. In Chapter 10, for example, we will see that implied volatilities are usually calculated at strike prices obtained at intervals of \$5, but that it is useful to have implied volatilities at all strike prices. Interpolation refers to a wide class of methods that allow functional values to be joined together in a piecewise fashion, so that a continuous graph can be obtained. Starting with a set of points $\{(x_i, a_i)\}_{i=1}^{n}$, the cubic spline interpolating function is a series of cubic polynomials defined as

$$S_j(x) = a_j + b_j(x - x_j) + c_j(x - x_j)^2 + d_j(x - x_j)^3. \qquad (1.17)$$

Each $S_j(x)$ is defined for values of x in the subinterval $[x_j, x_{j+1}]$, where there are $n-1$ such subintervals. Finding the coefficients b_j, c_j and d_j is done by solving a linear system of equations which can be represented as $\mathbf{Ax} = \mathbf{b}$, where $\mathbf{A}$ is a tridiagonal matrix. Natural cubic splines are produced when the boundary conditions are set as $S''(x_1) = S''(x_n) = 0$, while clamped cubic splines, when $S''(x_1) = f'(x_1)$ and $S''(x_n) = f'(x_n)$. To obtain natural cubic splines, define $h_j = x_{j+1} - x_j$ for $j = 1, \ldots, n-1$, and for $j = 2, \ldots, n-1$ set $\alpha_j = \frac{3}{h_j}(a_{j+1} - a_j) - \frac{3}{h_{j-1}}(a_j - a_{j-1})$. Then initialize $\ell_1 = \ell_n = 1, \mu_1 = \mu_n = 0, z_1 = z_n = 0$, and for $j = 2, \ldots, n-1$ define $\ell_j = 2(x_{j+1} - x_{j-1}) - h_{j-1}\mu_{j-1}, \mu_j = h_j/\ell_j$, and $z_j = (\alpha_j - h_{j-1}z_{j-1})/\ell_j$. Finally, working backward, the coefficients are obtained as

$$c_j = z_j - \mu_j c_{j+1}, b_j = (a_{j+1} - a_j)/h_j - h_j(c_{j+1} + 2c_j)/3,$$
$$d_j = (c_{j+1} - c_j)/(3h_j) \qquad (1.18)$$

for $j = n-1, n-2, \ldots, 1$. The Excel file Chapter1NatSpline contains the VBA function NSpline() for implementing natural cubic splines. The NSpline() function requires as inputs the points $\{x_j\}_{j=1}^{n}$ and the functional values $\{a_j\}_{j=1}^{n}$. It returns $S(x)$ as defined in (1.17) for any value of x.

```
Function NSpline(s, x, a)
n = Application.Count(x)
Dim h() As Double, alpha() As Double
ReDim h(n - 1) As Double, alpha(n - 1) As Double
For i = 1 To n - 1
  h(i) = x(i + 1) - x(i)
Next i
For i = 2 To n - 1
  alpha(i) = 3 / h(i) * (a(i + 1) - a(i)) - 3 / h(i - 1)
             * (a(i) - a(i - 1))
Next i
Dim l() As Double, u() As Double, z() As Double, c() As Double, b() As
            Double, d() As Double
ReDim l(n) As Double, u(n) As Double, z(n) As Double, c(n) As Double, b(n)
            As Double, d(n) As Double
l(1) = 1: u(1) = 0: z(1) = 0
l(n) = 1: z(n) = 0: c(n) = 0
For i = 2 To n - 1
  l(i) = 2 * (x(i + 1) - x(i - 1)) - h(i - 1) * u(i - 1)
  u(i) = h(i) / l(i)
  z(i) = (alpha(i) - h(i - 1) * z(i - 1)) / l(i)
```

```
Next i
For i = n - 1 To 1 Step -1
  c(i) = z(i) - u(i) * c(i + 1)
  b(i) = (a(i + 1) - a(i)) / h(i) - h(i) * (c(i + 1) + 2 * c(i)) / 3
  d(i) = (c(i + 1) - c(i)) / 3 / h(i)
Next i
For i = 1 To n - 1
  If (x(i) <= s) And (s <= x(i + 1)) Then
  NSpline = a(i) + b(i) * (s - x(i))
        + c(i) * (s - x(i)) ^ 2 + d(i) * (s - x(i)) ^ 3
  End If
Next i
End Function
```

Figure 1.8 illustrates this function, with x-values x_j contained in cells B5:B13, and functional values a_j in cells C5:C13.

To obtain the value of (1.17) when $x = 2.6$ in cell E20, for example, in cell F20 we type

$$= \text{NSpline}(\text{E20,B5:B13,C5:C13})$$

which produces $S(2.6) = 0.7357$.

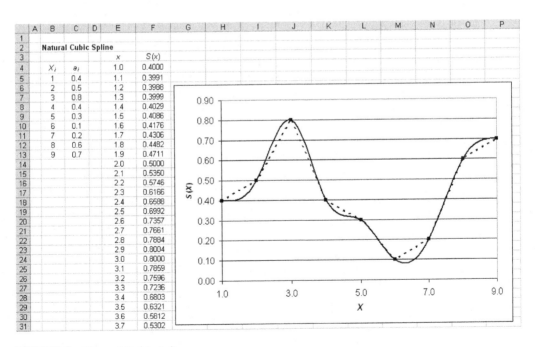

FIGURE 1.8 Natural Cubic Splines

To implement clamped cubic splines, a similar algorithm is used, except that $\alpha_1 = 3(a_2 - a_1)/h_1 - 3f_1'$, $\alpha_n = 3f_n' - 3(a_n - a_{n-1})/h_{n-1}$, where $f_1' = f'(x_1)$ and $f_n' = f'(x_n)$ need to be specified, and the intermediate coefficients are initialized as $\ell_1 = 2h_1$, $\mu_1 = 0.5$, $z_1 = \alpha_1/\ell_1$, $\ell_n = h_{n-1}(2 - \mu_{n-1})$, $z_n = (\alpha_n - h_{n-1}z_{n-1})/\ell_n$, and $c_n = z_n$. The values ℓ_j, μ_j, and z_j for $j = 2, \ldots, n-1$, as well as the coefficients c_j, b_j, and d_j for $j = n-1, n-2, \ldots, 1$ are obtained as before. The Excel file Chapter1ClampSpline contains the VBA function CSpline() for implementing the clamped spline algorithm. It requires as additional inputs values f_1' and f_n' for the derivatives, via the variables fp1 and fpN.

```
Function CSpline(s, x, a, fp1, fpN)
n = Application.Count(x)
Dim h() As Double, alpha() As Double
ReDim h(n - 1) As Double, alpha(n) As Double
For i = 1 To n - 1
   h(i) = x(i + 1) - x(i)
Next i
alpha(1) = 3 * (a(2) - a(1)) / h(1) - 3 * fp1
alpha(n) = 3 * fpN - 3 * (a(n) - a(n - 1)) / h(n - 1)
For i = 2 To n - 1
   alpha(i) = 3 / h(i) * (a(i + 1) - a(i)) - 3 / h(i - 1)
         * (a(i) - a(i - 1))
Next i
Dim l() As Double, u() As Double, z() As Double, c() As Double, b() As
            Double, d() As Double
ReDim l(n) As Double, u(n) As Double, z(n) As Double, c(n) As Double, b(n)
            As Double, d(n) As Double
l(1) = 2 * h(1): u(1) = 0.5: z(1) = alpha(1) / l(1)
For i = 2 To n - 1
   l(i) = 2 * (x(i + 1) - x(i - 1)) - h(i - 1) * u(i - 1)
   u(i) = h(i) / l(i)
   z(i) = (alpha(i) - h(i - 1) * z(i - 1)) / l(i)
Next i
l(n) = h(n - 1) * (2 - u(n - 1))
z(n) = (alpha(n) - h(n - 1) * z(n - 1)) / l(n)
c(n) = z(n)
For i = n - 1 To 1 Step -1
   c(i) = z(i) - u(i) * c(i + 1)
   b(i) = (a(i + 1) - a(i)) / h(i) - h(i) * (c(i + 1) + 2 * c(i)) / 3
   d(i) = (c(i + 1) - c(i)) / 3 / h(i)
Next i
For i = 1 To n - 1
   If (x(i) <= s) And (s <= x(i + 1)) Then
      CSpline = a(i) + b(i) * (s - x(i))
            + c(i) * (s - x(i)) ^ 2 + d(i) * (s - x(i)) ^ 3
   End If
Next i
End Function
```

Clamped Cubic Spline

X_i	a_i	x	$S(x)$	$f'(x_1) =$	0.10
		1.0	0.4000	$f'(x_n) =$	0.10
1	0.4	1.1	0.4083		
2	0.5	1.2	0.4139		
3	0.8	1.3	0.4180		
4	0.4	1.4	0.4216		
5	0.3	1.5	0.4261		
6	0.1	1.6	0.4325		
7	0.2	1.7	0.4419		
8	0.6	1.8	0.4555		
9	0.7	1.9	0.4745		
		2.0	0.5000		
		2.1	0.5326		
		2.2	0.5706		
		2.3	0.6117		
		2.4	0.6538		
		2.5	0.6945		
		2.6	0.7317		
		2.7	0.7631		
		2.8	0.7864		
		2.9	0.7995		
		3.0	0.8000		
		3.1	0.7865		
		3.2	0.7607		
		3.3	0.7249		
		3.4	0.6817		
		3.5	0.6333		
		3.6	0.5823		
		3.7	0.5311		

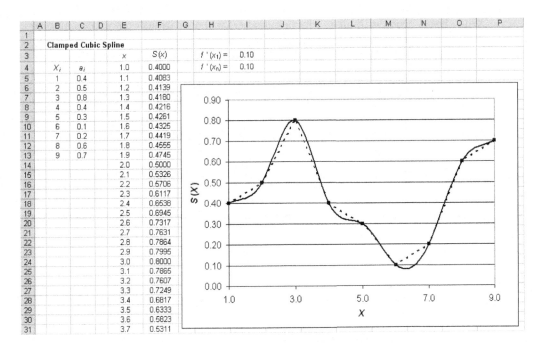

FIGURE 1.9   Clamped Cubic Splines

Figure 1.9 illustrates this function, using the same data in Figure 1.8, and with $f'_1 = f'_n = 0.10$ in cells I3 and I4.

To obtain the value of (1.17) when $x = 2.6$, in cell F20 we type

$$= \text{CSpline}(E20,B5{:}B13,C5{:}C13,I3,I4)$$

which produces $S(2.6) = 0.7317$. Note that clamped cubic splines are slightly more accurate, since they incorporate information about the function, in terms of the first derivatives of the function at the endpoints x_1 and x_n. In this example, however, the values of 0.10 are arbitrary so there is no advantage gained by using clamped cubic splines over natural cubic splines. For a detailed explanation of cubic splines, see Burden and Faires (2001), or Press et al. (2002).

SUMMARY

In this chapter we illustrate how VBA can be used to perform operations on complex numbers, to implement root-finding algorithms and the minimization of multivariate functions, to perform estimation by ordinary least squares and weighted least squares, to find maximum likelihood estimators, and to implement cubic splines.

While Excel provides built-in functions to perform operations on complex numbers, to implement root-finding methods, and to perform regression, there are advantages to programming these in VBA rather than relying on the built-in functions. In the case of root-finding methods, users are not restricted to the methods built into the Goal Seek or Solver Excel modules but can select from a wide variety of root-finding algorithms. Numerical analysis textbooks, such as that by Burden and Faires (2001), present many of the root finding algorithms currently available, and explain cubic splines in detail. Implementing regression with VBA also has its advantages. The most notable is that weighted least squares estimation can be implemented so that users are not restricted to using only ordinary least squares. As well, users can program many additional features, such as diagnostic statistics or the covariance matrix, that are not available in Excel regression module built into Excel. One additional advantage is that regression results are updated automatically every time the user changes the values of a data cell, without having to rerun the regression.

EXERCISES

This section provides exercises to reinforce the mathematical concepts introduced in this chapter. Solutions are contained in the Excel file Chapter1Exercises.

1.1 Write VBA functions to obtain the cosine of a complex number $z = x + iy$, whose real and imaginary parts are given by $\cos(x)\cosh(y)$ and $-\sin(x)\sinh(y)$ respectively, and the sine of a complex number, whose real and imaginary parts are $\sin(x)\cosh(y)$ and $-\cos(x)\sinh(y)$ respectively. The hyperbolic sine and hyperbolic cosine of a real number x are defined as $\sinh(x) = (e^x - e^{-x})/2$ and $\cosh(x) = (e^x + e^{-x})/2$.

1.2 Use DeMoivre's Theorem (1.1) to find an expression for the power of a complex number, and write a VBA function to implement it.

1.3 Find an expression for a complex number raised to the power of another complex number. That is, find an expression for w^z, where w and z are both complex numbers. This requires the angle formulas

$$\sin(\alpha + \beta) = \sin(\alpha)\cos(\beta) + \sin(\beta)\cos(\alpha)$$

$$\cos(\alpha + \beta) = \cos(\alpha)\cos(\beta) - \sin(\alpha)\sin(\beta).$$

1.4 The hat matrix H is very useful for identifying outliers in data. Its diagonal entries, called leverage values, are used to gauge the relative influence of each data point and to construct studentized residuals and deleted residuals. The hat matrix of dimension $(n \times n)$ and is given by

$$H = X(X^T X)X^T,$$

where   I = identity matrix of dimension $n \times n$, and
X = design matrix of dimension $(n \times k)$.

Write VBA code to create the hat matrix. In your code, output the diagonal elements of the hat matrix, h_{ii} $(i = 1, 2, \ldots, n)$ to an array in the spreadsheet. Use the data for two independent variables contained in the spreadsheet Chapter1WLS.

1.5 The global F-test of a regression model under OLS is a test of the null hypothesis that all regression coefficients are zero simultaneously. The F-statistic is defined as

$$F^* = \frac{\text{MSR}}{\text{MSE}} = \frac{\text{SSR}/(k-1)}{\text{SSE}/(n-k)},$$

where SSR is the regression sum of squares, SSE is the error sum of squares, n is the number of observations, and k is the number of parameters (including the intercept). Under the null hypothesis, F^* is distributed as an F random variable with $k - 1$ and $n - k$ degrees of freedom. Write VBA code to append the Excel file Chapter1WLS to include the global F-test. Include in your output a value of the F-statistic, and the p-value of the test. Use the Excel function Fdist() to find this p-value.

SOLUTIONS TO EXERCISES

1.1 Define two new VBA functions cNumCos() and cNumSin() and add these at the bottom of the VBA code in the Excel file Chapter1Complex.

```
Function cNumCos(cNum1 As cNum) As cNum
 cNumCos.rP = Cos(cNum1.rP) * Application.Cosh(cNum1.iP)
 cNumCos.iP = -Sin(cNum1.rP) * Application.Sinh(cNum1.iP)
End Function

Function cNumSin(cNum1 As cNum) As cNum
 cNumSin.rP = Sin(cNum1.rP) * Application.Cosh(cNum1.iP)
 cNumSin.iP = -Cos(cNum1.rP) * Application.Sinh(cNum1.iP)
End Function
```

Modify the VBA function Complexop1() to include two additional cases for the Select Case statement

```
Case 5: cNum3 = cNumCos(cNum)      ' Cosine
Case 6: cNum3 = cNumSin(cNum)      ' Sine
```

The cosine and sine of a complex number can be obtained by invoking the VBA function Complexop1() described in Section 1.1.2. This is illustrated in Figure 1.10.

	A	B	C	D	E	F	G
1	EXERCISE 1.1						
2							
3	Cosine and Sine of a Complex Number						
4							
5			Real	Imaginary		Operation	
6		Complex Number	4	5			
7		Cosine	-48.50685946	56.1571749		5	
8		Sine	-56.16227422	48.5024552		6	
9							

FIGURE 1.10   Solution to Exercise 1.1

	A	B	C	D	E
1	EXERCISE 1.2				
2					
3	Power of a Complex Number				
4					
5			Real	Imaginary	Power
6		Complex Number	4	5	2
7		Raised to Power	-9	40	

FIGURE 1.11   Solution to Exercise 1.2

1.2 Recall that a complex number w can be written $w = r\cos(y) + ir\sin(y)$, where $y = \arctan(b/a)$ and $r = \sqrt{a^2 + b^2}$. Using DeMoivre's Theorem, w raised to the power n can be written as

$$w^n = r^n[\cos(ny) + i\sin(ny)].$$

Hence $\mathrm{Re}[w^n] = r^n\cos(ny)$ and $\mathrm{Im}[w^n] = r^n\sin(ny)$. The functions complexop3() and cNumPower() to obtain w^n are presented below, and their use is illustrated in Figure 1.11.

```
Function complexop3(rP, iP, n)
  Dim cNum1 As cNum, cNum3 As cNum
  Dim output(2) As Double
  cNum1 = setcnum(rP, iP)
cNum3 = cNumPower(cNum1, n.Value)
output(1) = cNum3.rP
  output(2) = cNum3.iP
  complexop3 = output
End Function
Function cNumPower(cNum1 As cNum, n As Double) As cNum
  r = Sqr(cNum1.rP ^ 2 + cNum1.iP ^ 2)
  y = Atn(cNum1.iP / cNum1.rP)
  cNumPower.rP = r ^ n * Cos(y * n)
  cNumPower.iP = r ^ n * Sin(y * n)
End Function
```

For $w = 4 + 5i$ and $n = 2$, the functions produce $w^2 = -9 + 40i$. Note also that when $n = 0.5$ the functions produce the square root of a complex number.

1.3 We seek $w^z = (a + ib)^{c+id}$. Let $r = \sqrt{a^2 + b^2}$ and $\theta = \arctan(b/a)$, then

$$w^z = (re^{i\theta})^{c+id} = r^c e^{-d\theta} e^{ic\theta} r^{id}$$

$$= r^c e^{-d\theta}[\cos(c\theta) + i\cos(c\theta)]r^{id}$$

$$= r^c e^{-d\theta}[\cos(c\theta) + i\cos(c\theta)][\cos(d\ln r) + i\cos(d\ln r)].$$

where $r^{id} = e^{id\ln r}$. Now multiply and group trigonometric terms together

$$w^z = r^c e^{-d\theta} \left\{ \begin{array}{l} [\cos(c\theta)\cos(d\ln r) - \sin(c\theta)\sin(d\ln r)] \\ + i[\sin(c\theta)\cos(d\ln r) + \cos(c\theta)\sin(d\ln r)] \end{array} \right\}.$$

Finally, apply the angle formulas to arrive at

$$w^z = r^c e^{-d\theta}[\cos(c\theta + d\ln r) + i\sin(c\theta + d\ln r)].$$

Hence, the real and imaginary parts of w^z are

$$\mathrm{Re}[w^z] = r^c e^{-d\theta}\cos(c\theta + d\ln r)$$

$$\mathrm{Im}[w^z] = r^c e^{-d\theta}\sin(c\theta + d\ln r).$$

The VBA function cNumPowercNum() implements the exponentiation of a complex number by another complex number.

```
Function cNumPowercNum(cNum1 As cNum, cNum2 As cNum) As cNum
r = Sqr(cNum1.rP ^ 2 + cNum1.iP ^ 2)
y = Atn(cNum1.iP / cNum1.rP)
cNumPowercNum.rP = r ^ cNum2.rP * Exp(-cNum2.iP * y) *
                   Cos(cNum2.rP * y + cNum2.iP * Log(r))
cNumPowercNum.iP = r ^ cNum2.rP * Exp(-cNum2.iP * y) *
                   Sin(cNum2.rP * y + cNum2.iP * Log(r))
End Function

Function complexop4(rP1, iP1, rP2, iP2)
Dim cNum1 As cNum, cNum2 As cNum, cNum3 As cNum
Dim output(2) As Double
  cNum1 = setcnum(rP1, iP1)
  cNum2 = setcnum(rP2, iP2)
  cNum3 = cNumPowercNum(cNum1, cNum2)
output(1) = cNum3.rP
output(2) = cNum3.iP
complexop4 = output
End Function
```

	A	B	C	D
1	EXERCISE 1.3			
2				
3	Power of a Complex Number by Another Complex Number			
4				
5			Real	Imaginary
6	Complex Number (w)		4	5
7	Raised to Complex Number (z)		2	3
8	**Result (w^z)**		1.316	2.458

FIGURE 1.12   Solution to Exercise 1.3

Use of this function is illustrated in Figure 1.12, using $w = 4 + 5i$ and $z = 2 + 3i$. The results indicate that $\text{Re}[w^z] = 1.316$ and $\text{Im}[w^z] = 2.458$.

1.4 The VBA function Hat() creates the hat matrix and outputs its diagonal entries to any cells in the spreadsheet:

```
Option Base 1
Function Hat(X As Variant) As Variant
Dim n, k As Integer
Dim output(), H() As Variant
n = X.Rows.Count
ReDim output(n, n), H(n, n) As Variant
Xt = Application.Transpose(X)
XtX_inv = Application.MInverse(Application.MMult(Xt, X))
XXtX_inv = Application.MMult(X, XtX_inv)
H = Application.MMult(XXtX_inv, Xt)
For k = 1 To n
 output(k, 1) = H(k, k)
Next k
Hat = output
End Function
```

The results of this function appear in Figure 1.13. The function requires as input only the design matrix (including a column for the intercept), which appears in cells B7:D22. Hence, in cell F7 we type

$$= \text{Hat(B7:D22)}$$

and copy the formula as an array to the remaining cells. It can be shown that the trace of H, the sum of its diagonal elements, is equal to k. Hence, in cell F24 we type "=sum(F7:F22)" and obtain $k = 3$. The diagonals of the hat matrix indicate that observation 9, with $h_{9,9} = 0.447412$, has the largest influence, followed by observation 12 with $h_{12,12} = 0.287729$, and so on.

1.5 To implement the global F-test, we must first increase the range for the output, which creates extra room for the F-statistic and its p-value. Hence, we change the

	A	B	C	D	E	F
1	EXERCISE 1.4					
2						
3	Diagonals of the Hat Matrix					
4						
5			Independent			Diagonals of
6			Variables (X)			Hat Matrix
7		1	15.75	4.08		0.073463
8		1	8.45	4.83		0.148321
9		1	9.37	7.21		0.169536
10		1	18.85	0.88		0.177368
11		1	17.83	3.30		0.079438
12		1	12.68	2.37		0.142515
13		1	27.83	4.40		0.133766
14		1	28.96	0.54		0.266010
15		1	34.75	8.79		0.447412
16		1	22.26	5.89		0.086965
17		1	17.39	9.88		0.268214
18		1	5.32	2.01		0.287729
19		1	6.52	8.42		0.266963
20		1	21.49	6.64		0.101181
21		1	18.10	5.31		0.065220
22		1	31.67	1.05		0.285898
23						
24				Trace(H) =		3

FIGURE 1.13 Solution to Exercise 1.4

first part of the ReDim statement from ReDim output(k,5) to ReDim output(k + 2, 5). Then we add the VBA code to create the F-statistic and its p-value using the Fdist() function in Excel, and two statements to output these quantities to the spreadsheet:

```
Dim F As Double
F = (sst - sse) / (k - 1) / mse
Fpval = Application.FDist(F, k - 1, n -  k)
output(4, 5) = F
output(5, 5) = Fpval
For i = 4 To 5
 For j = 1 To 4
  output(i, j) = " "
 Next j
Next i
```

The last output statements ensure that zeros are not needlessly outputted to the spreadsheet. Figure 1.14 illustrates the global F-test using the data for two independent variables contained in the Excel file Chapter1WLS and presented earlier in this chapter (see Figure 1.3). These statements produce $F^* = 0.935329$

	A	B	C	D	E	F	G	H	I	J	K	L	M
1	EXERCISE 1.5												
2													
3	Global F-test for OLS												
4													
5			Dependent		Independent								
6		Weight	Variable (Y)	Intercept	Variables (X)			beta	s.e.(beta)	t-stat	p-value		
7		1	29.04	1	15.75	4.08		22.0222	6.5424	3.3660	0.0051	0.1258	R^2
8		1	17.84	1	8.45	4.83		0.0180	0.2503	0.0718	0.9438	-0.0087	Adjusted R^2
9		1	6.22	1	9.37	7.21		-1.0294	0.7623	-1.3504	0.1999	8.6270	√MSE
10		1	21.49	1	18.85	0.88						0.9353	F-test
11		1	10.49	1	17.83	3.30						0.4173	p-value
12		1	11.93	1	12.68	2.37							
13		1	19.92	1	27.83	4.40							
14		1	24.61	1	28.96	0.54							
15		1	3.51	1	34.75	8.79							
16		1	28.28	1	22.26	5.89							
17		1	11.03	1	17.39	9.88							
18		1	12.38	1	5.32	2.01							
19		1	29.00	1	6.52	8.42							
20		1	8.96	1	21.49	6.64							
21		1	17.26	1	18.10	5.31							
22		1	27.91	1	31.67	1.05							

FIGURE 1.14 Solution to Exercise 1.5

and $p = 0.417336$. Using the built-in regression modules in Excel, or a statistical software package, it is easy to verify that these numbers are correct. The results of the F-test imply that we cannot reject the null hypothesis that the coefficients are all zero, so that the joint values of the coefficients are $\beta_0 = 0, \beta_1 = 0$, and $\beta_2 = 0$.

CHAPTER 2

Numerical Integration

INTRODUCTION

Integration plays a central role in the mathematical models that have been developed to price options. Integration usually involves finding the antiderivative of a function and applying the Fundamental Theorem of Calculus, according to which the antiderivative is evaluated at the endpoints of the integral only. This well-known analytical procedure yields the area under the curve defined by the function, in between the two endpoints.

Unfortunately, while many option pricing models require evaluating the integral of a function to find the area under the curve, it is often impossible to find an antiderivative for the function. One example is the option pricing model of Heston and Nandi (2000) reviewed in Chapter 6, for which they find a semiclosed form solution for an option price, on an underlying asset that has volatility defined by a generalized autoregressive conditional heteroskedasticity (GARCH) process. The solution is in semiclosed form because finding the option price involves a complex integral that must be evaluated by numerical integration. We will need also to apply numerical integration to calculate model-free volatility, skewness, and kurtosis, in later chapters.

This chapter introduces numerical integration, presents algorithms that are used to perform numerical integration, and illustrates the VBA code to implement these algorithms. There are two main families of algorithms that have been developed for numerical integration: Newton-Cotes formulas, also called quadratures, and Gaussian quadratures. The main difference between these algorithms is the way in which the function being integrated is divided into subintervals along the horizontal axis. Newton-Cotes formulas divide the axis into subintervals at each integration point, or abscissa. Lagrange polynomials of varying complexity are used to approximate the areas under the function between successive pairs of abscissas. These areas are then aggregated to produce an approximation to the original integral. The subintervals are usually chosen to be of equal width.

Gaussian quadratures use a much more complex algorithm to approximate the integral. The chief difference is that the abscissas are determined not by the analyst, but by the algorithm itself, as the roots of approximating polynomials.

Gaussian quadratures involve the sum of the product of the function evaluated at the optimal abscissas and a weighting function. The fundamental theorem of Gaussian quadratures defines the abscissas as the roots of the orthogonal polynomial for the same interval and weighting function. Although more complicated than Newton-Coates formulas, Gaussian quadratures are more accurate because they fit polynomials up to degree $2n - 1$ exactly, where n is the number of abscissas. With today's high computer speeds, however, a very large number of points can be chosen, and Newton-Cotes approximations can be computed very quickly. In light of this, for many financial analysts the increased accuracy of the Gaussian quadratures does not justify the extra programming effort required to implement them. It is therefore not surprising that the more straightforward Newton-Cotes formulas are the most widely used of numerical integration algorithms. Consequently, in this chapter we focus mostly on Newton-Cotes formulas. In later chapters, however, the superiority of Gaussian quadratures over Newton-Cotes formulas will become evident.

NEWTON-COATES FORMULAS

In this section, seven popular Newton-Coates numerical integration formulas are introduced: the left-, right-, and midpoint rules, the trapezoidal rule, Simpson's rule and Simpson's three-eighths rule, and Boole's rule. We present the VBA code for implementing each rule, and compare the accuracy of each using a simple example. Finally, we assess how the accuracy of each approximation increases as the number of integration points increases.

The Left-, Right- and Midpoint Rules

Finding the integral of a function is equivalent to finding the area under the curve traced by that function. One way to approximate that area is by dividing the area into rectangles and adding the rectangles together. Suppose we wish to approximate the area under the curve traced by the function $f(x) = x^3 + 10$. This is, of course, a simple function for which an antiderivate exists. It can be integrated exactly, but it is used throughout this chapter to illustrate the methodology of each rule. To approximate the area under the curve within the interval $[a, b]$ on the horizontal axis (x-axis), $n + 1$ equally spaced integration points, or abscissas, are used to divide the interval into a set of n subintervals of equal width:

$$(x_0, x_1), (x_1, x_2), \ldots, (x_{n-1}, x_n),$$

where $x_0 \equiv a$ and $x_n \equiv b$ are the endpoints. A rectangle is constructed in each subinterval and its area is obtained. Aggregating the areas of the rectangles produces the approximation. The left-, right-, and midpoint rules differ only by how the height of the each rectangle is chosen.

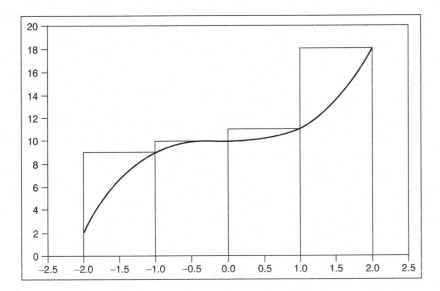

FIGURE 2.1 Right-Point Rule Numerical Integration

According to the right-point rule, the height of each rectangle is defined as the value of the function $f(x)$ at the rightmost endpoint of each subinterval. Figure 2.1 illustrates the right-point rule using our function as an example, with $a = -2$ and $b = 2$. This rule can be expressed mathematically as the approximation

$$\int_a^b f(x)\,dx \approx \Delta x[f(x_1) + f(x_2) + \cdots + f(x_n)] \tag{2.1}$$

where

$$\Delta x = (b-a)/n = \text{the width of each subinterval}$$
$$x_i = \text{the rightmost point of each subinterval}$$
$$a, b = \text{endpoints of the interval over which the integral is evaluated}$$
$$f(x_i) = \text{the value of the function evaluated at } x_i$$
$$n = \text{the number of subintervals.}$$

Note that each abscissas x_i can be expressed in terms of the leftmost endpoint a and the subinterval width Δx as $x_i = a + i\Delta x$, for $i = 0, 1, 2, \ldots, n$. This convenient representation will be exploited later in this chapter, when we implement numerical integration with VBA.

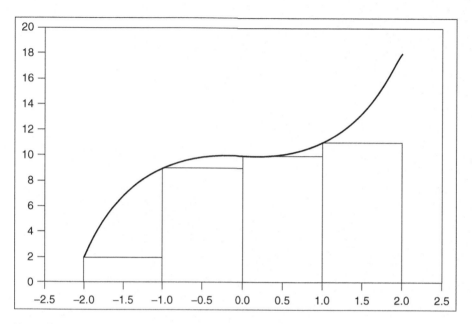

FIGURE 2.2   Left-Point Rule Numerical Integration

The left-point rule sets the height of each rectangle to the leftmost value of $f(x)$ in each subinterval, so that the approximation is

$$\int_a^b f(x)\, dx \approx \Delta x[f(x_0) + f(x_1) + \cdots + f(x_{n-1})]. \tag{2.2}$$

Figure 2.2 illustrates our example using the left-point rule approximation rule. Figures 2.1 and 2.2 demonstrate the shortcomings of the left- and right-point rules. Although these rules each produce a numerical approximation to the integral, a substantial amount of information is lost between the $n + 1$ points defined by the subintervals. It easy to see that when the function is monotone nondecreasing (as in our example), the right-point rule produces an approximation that is too large, while the left-point rule produces one that is too small. The reverse is true for a nonincreasing monotone function.

There are two ways to incorporate information ignored by the left- and right-point rules. The first method requires new function outputs, namely the y-values defined at the midpoint of each subinterval. This is aptly named the midpoint rule. The midpoint rule is identical to the left- and right-point rules, except that it uses the value of $f(x)$ obtained at the midpoint of each subinterval for the height of the rectangles.

Mathematically, the midpoint rule can be expressed as

$$\int_a^b f(x)\, dx \approx \Delta x[f(\overline{x}_1) + f(\overline{x}_2) + \cdots + f(\overline{x}_{n-1}) + f(\overline{x}_n)] \qquad (2.3)$$

where

$\overline{x}_i = \frac{1}{2}(x_i + x_{i-1})$ is the midpoint of each subinterval
$f(\overline{x}_i) = $ value of the function (y-value) evaluated at $\overline{x}_i$.

As illustrated by Figure 2.3, the increase in accuracy brought on by choosing the midpoint rule over either the right-point or left-point rule is substantial. Nevertheless, these three methods are relatively crude compared to the methods that follow.

The Trapezoidal Rule

The trapezoidal rule does not require additional information other than the value of $f(x)$ at each abscissa. Implementing this rule is no more complicated than implementing the left-, right-, or midpoint rules. The interval $[a, b]$ is again divided into a set of n subintervals of equal widthΔx. The goal of this approach, however, is to approximate the rate at which the function $f(x)$ is increasing or decreasing within each subinterval. This is achieved by forming a line segment to join $f(x)$ at

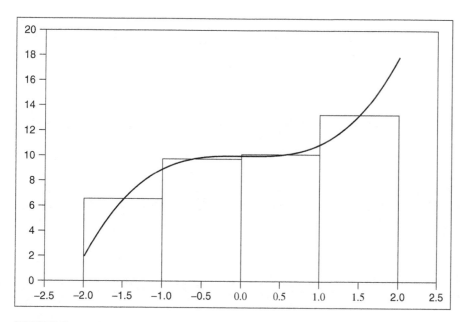

FIGURE 2.3   Midpoint Rule Numerical Integration

the endpoints of each subinterval, which produces a trapezoid instead of a rectangle. The area of the trapezoid defined by the subinterval (x_{i-1}, x_i) is

$$\frac{1}{2}(x_i - x_{i-1})[f(x_i) + f(x_{i-1})] = \frac{\Delta x}{2}[f(x_i) + f(x_{i-1})].$$

Aggregating this quantity for all subintervals produces the trapezoidal rule, which can be expressed mathematically as

$$\int_a^b f(x)\,dx \approx \frac{\Delta x}{2}[f(x_0) + 2f(x_1) + \cdots + 2f(x_{n-1}) + f(x_n)]. \tag{2.4}$$

Because trapezoids are used instead of rectangles, the accuracy of the trapezoidal approximation is much higher than that achieved with the midpoint rule. Figure 2.4 illustrates our example with the trapezoidal rule approximation.

Simpson's Rule

Simpson's rule is a refinement over the trapezoidal rule because it uses parabolas instead of line segments to join points of $f(x)$. Simpson's rule, however, requires that n, the number of subintervals, be an even number. This is needed because the rule jointly approximates each pair of two consecutive areas.

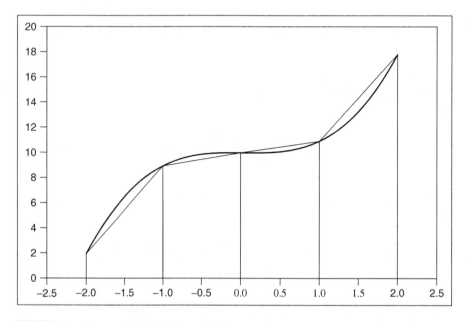

FIGURE 2.4 Trapezoidal Rule Numerical Integration

Simpson's rule is straightforward to derive. For simplicity, assume that we wish to approximate the area under the function $f(x)$ in the interval $[-a, a]$, using $n = 2$ subintervals. We know that a parabola can be fitted to any three points in the xy-plane, so we choose the points $f(-a), f(0)$, and $f(a)$. Suppose that the parabola joining these points is of the form

$$f(x) = Ax^2 + Bx + C.$$

Because the antiderivative of $f(x)$ can be obtained explicitly, the exact area under the parabola in the interval $(-a, a)$ is

$$\int_{-a}^{a} (Ax^2 + Bx + C)\, dx = \left[A\frac{x^3}{3} + B\frac{x^2}{2} + Cx \right]_{x=-a}^{x=a} = \frac{a}{3}(2Aa^2 + 6C).$$

The goal is to express this known area in terms of the three points $f(-a), f(0)$, and $f(-a)$ since these points constitute the only known information for implementing the approximation. Since the parabola passes through the points $(-a, f(-a)), (0, f(0))$, and $(a, f(a))$, we have the following three equations:

$$f(-a) = A(-a)^2 + B(-a) + C = Aa^2 - Ba + C$$
$$f(0) = A(0^2) + B(0) + C = C$$
$$f(a) = A(a^2) + B(a) + C = Aa^2 + Ba + C.$$

Multiplying the second equation by four and adding the three equations, we obtain

$$f(-a) + 4f(0) + f(a) = 2Aa^2 + 6C.$$

Comparing this last equation to the integral derived above, we see that the area under the parabola between $-a$ and a is equal to $\frac{a}{3}[f(-a) + f(0) + f(a)]$. This area will not change if the parabola is shifted along the x-axis, so this relation holds for intervals other than those centered about zero. Considering this fact, we can use this last equation for any three consecutive points on a curve. Hence, we obtain Simpson's rule for numerical integration:

$$\int_{a}^{b} f(x)\, dx \approx \frac{\Delta x}{3}[f(x_0) + 4f(x_1) + f(x_2)],$$

where, as before, $x_0 = a, x_2 = b$, and $\Delta x = (b - a)/2$ is the width of each subinterval.

If the interval $[a, b]$ is very narrow, then Simpson's rule will produce an accurate approximation of the integral. In most applications, however, the interval is wide. The obvious remedy is to break up the interval into a series of small subintervals, and apply Simpson's rule to each subinterval. We can use the rule to approximate the area for any even number of subintervals, by overlapping the three sums for each pair of subintervals. This produces an algorithm sometimes known as the composite Simpson's rule, which can be expressed as the approximation

$$\int_a^b f(x)\,dx \approx \frac{\Delta x}{3}[f(x_0) + 4f(x_1) + 2f(x_2) + 4f(x_3)$$
$$+ 2f(x_4) + \cdots + 4f(x_{n-1}) + f(x_n)],$$

where again $x_0 = a, x_2 = b, \Delta x = (b-a)/n$ is the width of each subinterval, and n is the number of subintervals. In order for this method to work, n must be an even number because each application of the rule requires two subintervals.

Simpson's Three-Eighths Rule and Boole's Rule

Simpson's rule can be refined to yield an approximation method known as Simpson's three-eighths rule. This rule uses a cubic polynomial instead of a parabola to approximate $f(x)$. Hence, to construct the approximation under this rule, four points instead of three are needed in the interval $[a, b]$. The approximation can be derived in a manner similar to that which produces Simpson's rule. Simpson's three-eighths rule can be written as the approximation

$$\int_a^b f(x)\,dx \approx \frac{3\Delta x}{8}[f(x_0) + 3f(x_1) + 3f(x_2) + f(x_3)].$$

As before, we can we can break up the interval $[a, b]$ into a set of n subintervals, where now we require n to be divisible by three, apply Simpson's three-eighths rule in each subinterval, and aggregate the resulting sums. This is known as the composite Simpson's three-eighths rule.

Now that we have Simpson's rule for integrating a function with an even number of integration subintervals, and Simpson's three-eighths rule for a number divisible by three, we can perform a numerical integration for any number of segments by combining the two methods. For example, suppose we have a function that we can evaluate at six evenly spaced points, thus creating five integration subintervals. We could use Simpson's three-eighths rule for the first three segments and Simpson's rule for the remaining two segments. The approximation would therefore be

$$\int_a^b f(x)\,dx \approx \frac{\Delta x}{3}[f(x_0) + 4f(x_1) + f(x_2)]$$
$$+ \frac{3\Delta x}{8}[f(x_2) + 3f(x_3) + 3f(x_4) + f(x_5)].$$

The last Newton-Cotes method we introduce is Boole's rule. This approximation requires four subintervals of integration and can be expressed as

$$\int_a^b f(x)\,dx \approx \frac{\Delta x}{45}[14f(x_0) + 64f(x_1) + 24f(x_2) + 64f(x_3) + 14f(x_4)].$$

As with Simpson's rule and Simpson's three-eighths rule, a composite version of this rule can be applied to a set of n subintervals within $[a, b]$. Since four points are needed for each subinterval, the number of subintervals used in the approximation must be divisible by four.

Finally, the trapezoidal rule, Simpson's rule, Simpson's three-eighths rule, and Boole's rule all use special cases of Lagrange interpolating polynomials. In their most general form, each rule can be written as

$$\int_a^b f(x)\, dx \approx \sum_{i=0}^n a_i f(x_i)$$

where $a_i = \int_a^b L_{n,i}(x)dx$ and $L_{n,i}(x)$ is the Lagrange interpolating polynomial of degree n.

Subintervals of Unequal Width

In the four approximation rules presented so far in this chapter, equally spaced abscissas are specified, or equivalently, subintervals of equal width. While this simplifies the algebraic formulas for the rules, there is no reason to impose equal width in any of these approximations. The VBA functions presented later in this chapter allow the abscissas to be arbitrarily spaced, and not evenly spaced only. This permits subintervals of any width to be used in the approximation. The left-, right-, and midpoint rules, and the trapezoidal rule, allow for intervals of arbitrary width. For example, for arbitrarily spaced points $(x_0, x_1, \ldots, x_n)$ the right-point approximation rule (2.1) becomes

$$\int_a^b f(x)\, dx \approx f(x_1)(x_1 - x_0) + f(x_2)(x_2 - x_1) + \cdots + f(x_n)(x_n - x_{n-1}).$$

As before, the endpoints of the integral are $x_0 = a$ and $x_n = b$.

Adaptive quadrature methods are those that specify small subinterval widths in regions of high functional variation, and larger widths in regions where the function is flatter. It is straightforward to implement adaptive quadrature in the approximation rules. For example, suppose the approximation is over the integration interval $[a, b]$. The interval is broken up into two subintervals $[a, (a + b)/2]$ and $[(a + b)/2, b]$, and two approximations are obtained. One approximation uses the entire interval, and the other uses the sum of the approximations from each subinterval. If the difference between these approximations is larger than some tolerance level, the smaller subintervals are used; otherwise, $[a, b]$ is used.

Improper Integrals and Open Rules

When an integration rule uses all the abscissas $x_0, x_1, \ldots, x_n$ in its formulation, the rule is said to be a closed rule. When the endpoints $x_0 = a$ and $x_n = b$, are excluded, however, the rule is an open rule. Among the rules introduced in this chapter, the midpoint rule is an open rule, while the other rules are all closed. Closed rules can be fully open, so that both endpoints are excluded from the approximation, or semiopen, so that only one endpoint is excluded.

Open rules are needed to approximate improper integrals for which the function cannot be evaluated at the endpoints of the integration interval. For example, the improper integral

$$\int_{-1}^{1} \frac{1}{\sqrt{x+1}} \, dx$$

can be solved analytically, and has the value $2\sqrt{2}$. Using Simpson's rule on this integral, however, would yield an infinite value for the approximation because the function explodes at the left endpoint $a = -1$. Hence, in this example a semiopen rule would be required.

There are at least two simple ways to transform closed rules into semiopen or open rules. The easiest way is to replace the endpoints of the integration integral by values that are shifted by a small amount, ε, so that a and b are replaced by the points $a + \varepsilon$ and $b - \varepsilon$, respectively. Any closed rule can now be applied to this new set of integration points. If ε is too small, however, a large number of abscissas may be required for the approximation to work properly since the function may not be well-behaved at points too close to the endpoints. In the above example, it easy to see that $f(-1 + \varepsilon) = 1/\sqrt{\varepsilon}$ could take on very large values if ε is too small. The only way to mitigate this inflated value in the approximation is to define a very small subinterval width.

Open rules can also be created by choosing $a + \frac{1}{2}\Delta x$ and $b - \frac{1}{2}\Delta x$ as the endpoints. As the number of abscissas increases, these endpoints approach a and b, but the subinterval width becomes smaller. While $f(x)$ becomes evaluated at points progressively closer to a and b, and may take on progressively larger values, $f(x)$ gets multiplied by a subinterval width that becomes progressively smaller. Hence, this approach avoids some of the problems associated with choosing ε too small. Many software packages for numerical integration use this approach to evaluate improper integrals.

Another method to evaluate improper integrals is to write the integrand $f(x)$ as the sum of two functions and create two integrals, at least one of which is not improper so that it can be approximated directly. The other integral may be an improper integral, but it must have an analytical solution so that it can be evaluated without a numerical approximation. In the option pricing models we cover, however, most integrands are too complicated for this method to work.

Finally, integrals with limits $a = -\infty$ or $b = \infty$, or both, are often encountered in financial models. One way to deal with this problem is to transform the integral by change of variable, so that the new integral is finite. In most option pricing models, however, this is not a practical solution. The more popular method is to truncate the limits of integration so that a and b are replaced by very large negative and positive numbers, respectively.

While improper integrals pose a problem with Newton-Cotes rules, this is not always the case for Gaussian quadratures. Later in this chapter we introduce Gaussian quadratures that are designed to work with improper integrals that have limits of integration $(0, \infty)$ and $(-\infty, \infty)$.

IMPLEMENTING NEWTON-COTES FORMULAS IN VBA

There are two different ways of implementing numerical integration in VBA, by passing vector parameters to VBA functions and by using inline functions. We first describe implementing Newton-Cotes methods by passing vector parameters, then by using inline functions. We also compare the accuracy of each rule using a simple functional example for which the exact integral is known.

Passing Vector Parameters

This method of implementing numerical integration refers to how the inputs needed for processing the algorithm are handled. Inputs such as the vector of abscissas or the interval width must be created in a spreadsheet. These inputs are subsequently passed to the function via the function declaration statement.

The Excel file Chapter2Newton contains VBA code to implement the Newton-Cotes rules described in this chapter. The VBA functions RPRnumint(), LPRnumint(), MPRnumint(), and TRAPnumint() construct the right-point, left-point, midpoint, and trapezoidal rules, respectively. Each function requires two vectors as inputs. For all four functions, the vector x being passed contains the abscissas for the interval $[a, b]$, while the vector y contains values of the function to be integrated, evaluated at each element of x for the left- and right-point rules and for the trapezoidal rule, and at the midpoints of the subintervals defined by x for the midpoint rule. These four functions allow the use of subintervals of different width.

The right-point rule uses a summation involving the terms $(x_i - x_{i-1})y_i$, where $y_i \equiv f(x_i)$, as shown in the following code for the RPRnumint() function:

```
Function RPRnumint(x, y) As Double
n = Application.Count(x): RPRnumint = 0
For t = 2 To n
  RPRnumint = RPRnumint + (x(t) - x(t-1))*y(t)
Next t
End Function
```

On the other hand, the function LPRnumint() for the left-point rule uses the terms $(x_i - x_{i-1})y_{i-1}$ in the summation.

```
Function LPRnumint(x, y) As Double
n = Application.Count(x): LPRnumint = 0
For t = 2 To n
  LPRnumint = LPRnumint + (x(t) - x(t-1))*y(t-1)
Next t
End Function
```

In the midpoint rule, which we code as the function MPRnumint() that appears below, the vector x being passed contains the abscissas, just as in the previous two functions for the right- and left-point rules. The vector y, however, must contain the function evaluated at the midpoints of the subintervals defined by x. Hence, the function MPRnumint() requires a different y input than the two previous functions.

```
Function MPRnumint(x, y) As Double
n = Application.Count(x): MPRnumint = 0
For t = 2 To n
  MPRnumint = MPRnumint + (x(t) - x(t-1))*y(t-1)
Next t
End Function
```

The function TRAPnumint() uses the terms $\frac{1}{2}(x_i - x_{i-1})(y_i + y_{i-1})$ in the summation to produce the trapezoidal approximation.

```
Function TRAPnumint(x, y) As Double
n = Application.Count(x): TRAPnumint = 0
For t = 2 To n
  TRAPnumint = TRAPnumint + 0.5*(x(t)-x(t-1))*(y(t-1) + y(t))
Next t
End Function
```

For this first set of four Newton-Cotes methods the VBA functions are simply creating rectangles and trapezoids of different sizes and summing them. Note that each function allows subintervals of different width to be used, so that the integration points passed in the vector x need not be equally spaced. Using more points and subintervals of smaller width in areas where the function is known to be jagged or steep, as done by adaptive quadrature methods, would lead to more precise approximations. However, as mentioned earlier in this chapter, with the computing power available today we may use a high density of abscissas everywhere in the interval $[a, b]$ and arrive at the same accuracy with subintervals of equal width. In the next set of rules we code with VBA, only subintervals of equal width are used.

The functions sSIMPnumint(), SIMPnumint(), sSIMP38numint(), sBOOLEnumint(), and BOOLEnumint() implement Simpson's rule, Simpson's three-eighths rule, and Boole's rule, respectively. We present functions for both versions of each rule, the simple version and the composite version. The simple versions are meant to be applied on individual subintervals, and the composite versions on a set of subintervals. Both versions of each rule require as inputs the vector y of function values and the interval width. The VBA functions for the three simple versions follow.

```
Function sSIMPnumint(deltax, y) As Double
  sSIMPnumint = (1/3)*(y(1) + 4 * y(2) + y(3))*deltax
End Function


Function sSIMP38numint(deltax, y) As Double
  sSIMP38numint = (3/8)*(y(1) + 3*y(2) + 3*y(3) + y(4))*deltax
End Function
```

```
Function sBOOLEnumint(deltax, y) As Double
  sBOOLEnumint = (1/45)*(14*y(1) + 64*y(2) + 24*y(3)
            + 64*y(4) + 14*y(5))*deltax
End Function
```

The next three VBA functions are for the composite versions of these rules.

```
Function SIMPnumint(deltax, y) As Double
n = Application.Count(y): SIMPnumint = 0
For t = 1 To (n-1)/2
 ind = (t*2) - 1
 SIMPnumint = SIMPnumint + (1/3)*(y(ind)
            + 4*y(ind + 1) + y(ind+2))*deltax
Next t
End Function
```

```
Function SIMP38numint(deltax, y) As Double
n = Application.Count(y): SIMP38numint = 0
For t = 1 To (n-1)/3
 ind = (t*3) - 2
 SIMP38numint = SIMP38numint + (3/8)*(y(ind) + 3*y(ind+1)
            + 3*y(ind+2) + y(ind+3))*deltax
Next t
End Function
```

```
Function BOOLEnumint(deltax, y) As Double
n = Application.Count(y): BOOLEnumint = 0
For t = 1 To (n - 1) / 4
   ind = (t * 4) - 3
   BOOLEnumint = (1/45)*(14*y(ind) + 64*y(ind+1) + 24*y(ind+2)
            + 64*y(ind+3) + 14*y(ind+4))*deltax
Next t
End Function
```

It is important to have simple and composite versions of each rule available, since in many cases we do not have a number of subintervals that allows any single rule to be used exclusively. For example, specifying $n = 29$ subintervals would preclude the use of Simpson's three-eighths rule directly, since this number is not divisible by three. We might therefore apply the simple version of Simpson's rule for the first two subintervals, and apply the composite Simpson's three-eighths rule to the remaining $n = 27$ subintervals.

Examples of Passing Vector Parameters

Now that we have all the Newton-Cotes integration rules coded in VBA, we can use Excel to compare their accuracy in approximating the integral of our example function $f(x) = x^3 + 10$. This comparison is in the Newton-cotes worksheet of the Excel file Chapter2Newton, and is illustrated in Figure 2.5. The first step is to create a column of abscissas, which appear in column B of the figure. In the adjacent column (column C), the formula for the function evaluated at each point is entered.

	A	B	C	D	E	F	G	H
1								
2		**Illustration of Newton-Cotes Formulas on a Simple Function**						
3								
4		**delta x =**	1					
5								
6		Abscissas (x)	$f(x)=x^3+10$	Mid Points	$f(x)=x^3+10$	Rule	Integral	
7		-2	2					
8		-1	9	-1.5	6.625	Left-Point	2136	
9		0	10	-0.5	9.875	Right-Point	3144	
10		1	11	0.5	10.125	Mid-Point	2604	
11		2	18	1.5	13.375	Trapezoidal	2640	
12		3	37	2.5	25.625	Simpson's	2616	
13		4	74	3.5	52.875	Simpson's 3/8	2616	
14		5	135	4.5	101.125	Boole's	2616	
15		6	226	5.5	176.375			
16		7	353	6.5	284.625	**Real Integral**	2616	
17		8	522	7.5	431.875	**Value**		
18		9	739	8.5	624.125			
19		10	1010	9.5	867.375			
20								

FIGURE 2.5 Comparison of Newton-Cotes Numerical Integration Methods

To compare across functions, we must ensure that the number of subintervals is divisible by two for Simpson's rule, by three for Simpson's three-eighths rule, and by four for Boole's rule. We will therefore integrate from $a = -3$ to $b = 10$, with a subinterval width $\Delta x = 1$, corresponding to $n = 12$ subintervals. This allows each rule to be implemented. To implement the midpoint rule two additional columns must be created, one containing the midpoints and the other containing the function evaluated at each of the midpoints. These appear in columns D and E of Figure 2.5, respectively.

To implement each approximation rule, its VBA function is invoked using the "=" sign and the function name, and the values needed for the approximation must be specified as inputs. For example, in Figure 2.5, cell G11 contains the trapezoidal approximation, which requires the x and y vectors to be passed to the TRAPnumint() function. The x values appear in the range B7 to B19 while the y values are in the range C7 to C19. Hence, in cell G11 we type

$$= \text{TRAPnumint}(B7{:}B19,C7{:}C19).$$

Alternately, in cell G11 we insert the TRAPnumint() function from the Excel menu, and highlight the required ranges for the x- and y-values in the dialog box that appears. Invoking Simpson's three-eighths rule requires the y-values and the interval width Δx in cell C4 to be passed to the function. Hence, in cell G13 of Figure 2.5 we type

$$= \text{SIMP38numint}(C4,C7{:}C19)$$

or we insert the SIMP38numint() function from the Excel menu and enter the required ranges in the dialog box. The other approximation rules are invoked in a similar manner.

Figure 2.5 presents a comparison of the rules covered so far. The true value of the integral is 2,616. As mentioned earlier, since this is a nondecreasing function the left-point rule produces an underapproximation (2,136), while the right-point rule produces an overapproximation (3,144). The midpoint and trapezoidal approximations are much more accurate, 2,604 and 2,640, respectively, but the two Simpson's rules and Boole's rule each produce approximations that are identical to the true value. The accuracy gained by using the two Simpson's rules and Boole's rule justifies the increased complexity of programming these rules, and the increased computing resources required to implement them. However, as we shall see later in this chapter, increasing the number of subintervals dramatically improves accuracy of the simpler rules.

Inline Functions

The term *inline* means the function to be integrated resides inside the numerical integration procedure. The chief advantage of inline functions is that they are less cumbersome to use because inputs such as the x and y vectors do not have to be created in the spreadsheet—these are created internally by the function. This is an important feature that saves a lot of spreadsheet space when the number of integration points is large. The previous example the function $f(x) = x^3 + 10$ is used to demonstrate how inline functions work. First, a VBA function for $f(x)$ must be defined.

```
Function Examplef(x) As Double
  Examplef = x ^ 3 + 10
End Function
```

The function Examplef() can now be passed to the parent integration function NumericalInt() that appears below. The parent function uses trapezoidal rule, invoked by the TRAPnumint() function.

```
Function NumericalInt(startPoint, endPoint, n, fName As String) As Double
  Dim pass_x() As Double, pass_y() As Double
  ReDim pass_x(n + 1) As Double, pass_y(n + 1) As Double
  delta_x = (endPoint - startPoint) / n
    For cnt = 1 To n+1
      pass_x(cnt) = startPoint + (cnt-1)*delta_x
      pass_y(cnt) = Run(fName, pass_x(cnt))
    Next
  NumericalInt = TRAPnumint(pass_x, pass_y)
End Function
```

Note that in order for this function to work properly, "Option Base 1" must be included at the top of the module in the VBA Editor. This specifies that all arrays begin indexing at one and not at zero.

The function requires the inputs startPoint and endPoint, corresponding to the endpoints a and b, respectively; n, the number of subintervals; and fName, which is a character input for the VBA name of the function to integrate. The variable delta_x creates the subinterval width $\Delta x = (b - a)/n$ while the statement involving pass_x() creates each integration point in terms of the first endpoint of the interval of integration (a, b) and the subinterval width. The statement involving pass_y() fits $f(x) = x^3 + 10$ to the vector of integration points. Hence, pass_x() and pass_y() are the two vectors needed to invoke the trapezoidal approximation that appears in the second-to-last statement of the code. To run this function in Excel for $f(x)$ between $a = -2$ and $b = 10$ with $n = 5$ subintervals, type the following in any cell in the spreadsheet:

$$= \text{NumericalInt}(-2,10,5, \text{"Examplef"}).$$

In this example we implement trapezoidal numerical integration, but any of the approximation rules can be implemented instead. This requires replacing TRAPnumint() in the second-to-last statement of the preceding VBA code with the function corresponding to the rule of choice. With the VBA Select statement, however, it is possible to include each integration rule within the same parent function. In the function declaration statement, the choice of rule appears as an extra parameter that must be specified when invoking the function.

```
Function NumericalInt(startPoint, endPoint, n, fName As String, Method) As
   Double
   Dim pass_x() As Double, pass_y() As Double
   ReDim pass_x(n+1) As Double, pass_y(n+1) As Double
   delta_x = (endPoint-startPoint)/n
     For cnt = 1 To n+1
       pass_x(cnt) = startPoint + (cnt-1) * delta_x
       pass_y(cnt) = Run(fName, pass_x(cnt))
     Next
     Select Case Method
       Case 1: NumericalInt = LPRnumint(pass_x, pass_y)
       Case 2: NumericalInt = RPRnumint(pass_x, pass_y)
       Case 3: NumericalInt = TRAPnumint(pass_x, pass_y)
       Case 4: NumericalInt = SIMPnumint(delta_x, pass_y)
       Case 5: NumericalInt = SIMP38numint(delta_x, pass_y)
       Case 6: NumericalInt = BOOLEnumint(delta_x, pass_y)
     End Select
End Function
```

To implement the integration of our function using Boole's rule, for example, in any cell we type

$$= \text{NumericalInt}(-2,10,5, \text{"Examplef"},6).$$

With this version of the NumericalInt() function we are able to select between the left-point rule, the right-point rule, the trapezoidal rule, Simpson's rule, Simpson's three-eighths rule, and Boole's rule, simply by passing the correct integer to the Method parameter when invoking the function. The NumericalInt() function does not include the midpoint rule function MPRnumint(), since the vector of x values to be passed is different than for the other functions. This function appers in the Excel file Chapter 2 Newton.

Increasing the Accuracy of the Approximation

Up to this point we have ignored the choice of the subinterval width. The choice involves a trade-off between speed and accuracy, since a smaller width yields greater accuracy but requires a higher density of integration points and, consequently, more processing time. This section illustrates the added accuracy in narrowing the width of each subinterval by increasing the number of abscissas.

Figure 2.6 shows that the accuracy of the numerical approximation is improved when n is increased. The disadvantage is that the function needs to be evaluated at more points of integration. If the function is complicated and includes exponents, logarithms, and trigonometric functions, for example, the increase in computing time required to evaluate all the points can be substantial.

This aspect of numerical integration is crucial to understanding the benefits and weaknesses of different integration rules. We compare the accuracy of the different rules in approximating the integral of our example function $f(x) = x^3 + 10$ from $a = -2$ to $b = 10$, brought on by increasing the number of abscissas. This is easily

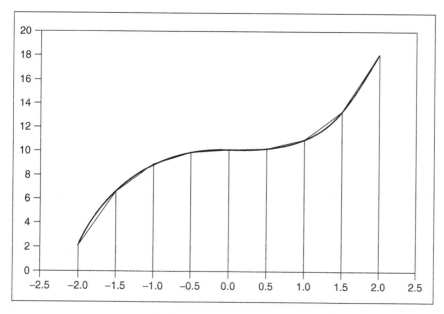

FIGURE 2.6 Increasing the Number of Subintervals for the Trapezoidal Rule

	Rules	\multicolumn{5}{c}{Integral with Increasing Number of Points}	Method Parameter
		$n = 12$	$n = 120$	$n = 1200$	$n = 12000$	$n = 60000$	
	Left-Point	2136.00	2565.84	2610.96	2615.50	2615.90	1
	Right-Point	3144.00	2666.64	2621.04	2616.50	2616.10	2
	Trapezoidal	2640.00	2616.24	2616.00	2616.00	2616.00	3
	Simpson's	2616.00	2616.00	2616.00	2616.00	2616.00	4
	Simpson's 3/8	2616.00	2616.00	2616.00	2616.00	2616.00	5
	Boole's	2616.00	2616.00	2616.00	2616.00	2616.00	6

Increasing Precision of Newton-Cotes Integration Formulas

$a = -2$
$b = 10$

Real Integral Value: 2616

FIGURE 2.7 Increasing Accuracy of Newton-Cotes Numerical Approximations

done using the inline functions, without having to create lengthy columns in the spreadsheet for the x and y values.

Figure 2.7 presents the results of this comparison, which are included in the increasing n worksheet of the Excel file Chapter2Newton. Cells C4 and C5 contain the interval endpoints $a = -2$ and $b = 10$, respectively. For example, to invoke Simpson's three-eighths rule with $n = 1,200$ integration points on our function defined by Examplef(), in cell E13 we type

$$= \text{NumericalInt}(C4, C5, 1200, \text{"Examplef"}, 5)$$

with the Method parameter chosen as 5. Figure 2.7 shows how the six approximation rules that can be invoked by the NumericalInt() function compare when the number of integration points is increased. When 120 abscissas or less are used, Simpson's rule, Simpson's three-eighths rule, and Boole's rule are superior to the left-point, right-point, and trapezoidal rules. With 1,200 abscissas, the trapezoidal rule is very accurate also. Even with 60,000 abscissas, however, the left-point and right-point rules remain inferior to the other rules. Nevertheless, both approximations still converge to the true value of the integral as the number points increases.

From this experiment it is clear that all of the approximation rules converge to the real integral value as we increase the number of abscissas. In practice, as long as enough points are used, any approximation method can be implemented. Thankfully, there is no restriction on the number of abscissas that can be specified. Of the Newton-Cotes methods covered in this chapter, trapezoidal integration is the most commonly used in practice, since its accuracy is quite high and it is easy to implement.

GAUSSIAN QUADRATURES

While Newton-Cotes methods approximate the integral on a set of equally spaced and predetermined abscissas, Gaussian quadratures select the optimal abscissas $x_1, x_2, \ldots, x_n$ at which the function should be evaluated, along with a set of weights $w_1, w_2, \ldots, w_n$. Once these abscissas and weights are obtained, the approximation is straightforward because Gaussian quadratures take the form of a summation involving the weights and the function evaluated at the abscissas.

$$\int_a^b f(x)\, dx \approx \sum_{i=1}^{n} w_i f(x_i).$$

The most difficult part of Gaussian quadratures is finding the abscissas and weights. Hence, it is often simpler to tabulate these into the VBA code, evaluate the function at the abscissas, and take the sum. In this section we present VBA code that uses tabulated values, and VBA code that finds the abscissas and weights for an arbitrary number of points.

Gauss-Legendre quadratures are constructed for integrals over $[-1, 1]$ but can be generalized to other intervals by transformation of variables. The abscissas, which lie in $[-1, 1]$, and weighting coefficients are chosen so that the approximation given by

$$\int_{-1}^{1} f(x)\, dx \approx \sum_{i=1}^{n} w_i f(x_i) \tag{2.5}$$

yields the smallest possible error. Since there are $2n$ parameters involved (abscissas plus weights), choosing the abscissas as the n zeroes of the Legendre polynomial of degree n, along with the correct coefficients, yields exact solutions for polynomials up to degree $2n - 1$. In most applications, 10 points or less are sufficient to yield accurate approximations.

To approximate the integral on a more general interval $[a, b]$, the transformation $y = (2x - a - b)/(b - a)$ is applied, so that the transformed integral has limits $[-1, 1]$ and the Gaussian quadrature is applied to the transformed integrand. Hence, the integral (2.5) becomes

$$\int_a^b f(x)\, dx \approx \sum_{i=1}^{x} w_i f\left(\frac{b+a}{2} + \frac{b-a}{2} x_i\right). \tag{2.6}$$

The same weights are used, but the function is evaluated at the transformed abscissas instead of at the abscissas themselves.

In this section we present three algorithms for Gaussian quadratures. The first algorithm implements Gaussian-Legendre quadrature with 10 abscissas and 10 weights tabulated within the VBA code. The second is Gauss-Legendre quadrature that does not use tabulated abscissas or weights, but rather obtains the abscissas and weights through construction of Legendre polynomials within the VBA function used to code the quadrature. The third is Gauss-Laguerre quadrature, which employs Laguerre polynomials instead of Legendre polynomials, and is designed for integrals over $(0, \infty)$ only. In the appendix to this chapter we provide tabulated values of optimal abscissas and weights for Gauss-Legendre, Gauss-Laguerre, and Gauss-Hermite quadratures. The VBA functions in this section are adapted from Press et al. (2002).

10-Point Gauss-Legendre Quadrature

In this section we use tabulated abscissas and weights to obtain a 10-point Gauss-Legendre quadrature. The Excel file Chapter2Gauss contains the VBA function GLquad10(), which uses our example $f(x) = x^3 + 10$. This function requires as inputs the name of the function to be integrated, and the endpoints of the integration interval.

```
Function examplef(x) As Double
   examplef = x ^ 3 + 10
End Function

Function GLquad10(fname As String, a, b)
Dim x(5) As Double
Dim w(5) As Double
x(1) = 0.1488743389: x(2) = 0.4333953941
x(3) = 0.6794095682: x(4) = 0.8650633666
x(5) = 0.9739065285
w(1) = 0.2955242247: w(2) = 0.2692667193
w(3) = 0.2190863625: w(4) = 0.1494513491
w(5) = 0.0666713443
xm = 0.5 * (b + a): xr = 0.5 * (b - a)
s = 0
For j = 1 To 5
   dx = xr * x(j)
   s = s + w(j)*(Run(fname, xm+dx) + Run(fname, xm-dx))
Next j
GLquad10 = s * xr
End Function
```

This VBA code is simple because it exploits the fact that the abscissas and weights in the algorithm are each symmetric about zero. Only five terms are involved in the summation that produces the approximation. If w_j denotes the weight associated with abscissas x_j and $-x_j$, then the two terms corresponding to these abscissas can be grouped as

$$w_j \left[f \left(\frac{b+a}{2} + \frac{b-a}{2} x_j \right) + f \left(\frac{b+a}{2} - \frac{b-a}{2} x_j \right) \right].$$

This appears as

```
w(j)*(Run(fname, xm+dx) + Run(fname, xm-dx))
```

in the function GLquad10() above.

The Excel file Chapter2Weights contains tabulated abscissas and weights to implement Gauss-Legendre quadratures, using up to 32 points.

Gauss-Legendre Quadrature with Any Number of Points

This algorithm does not use weights and abscissas tabulated within the code, but rather uses Legendre orthogonal polynomials generated by $P_0(x) = 1, P_1(x) = x$, and $P_j(x)$ through the recursive formula

$$jP_j(x) = (2j - 1)xP_{j-1}(x) - (j - 1)P_{j-2}(x).$$

The recursion for Legendre polynomials takes on this simple form because the weighting function is $w(x) = 1$. The function GLquad() is used to implement Gauss-Legendre numerical integration in VBA. This function requires as inputs the name of the function to be integrated, the endpoints, and the number of points to use in the approximation.

```
Function GLquad(fname As String, x1, x2, n)
  Dim x(50) As Double
  Dim w(50) As Double
  m = (n + 1) / 2
  xm = 0.5 * (x2 + x1): xl = 0.5 * (x2 - x1)
  Pi = 3.141592654: EPS = 3E-16
  For i = 1 To m
    z = Cos(Pi*(i - 0.25) / (n + 0.5))
    Do
        p1 = 1: p2 = 0
        For j = 1 To n
          p3 = p2: p2 = p1
          p1 = ((2 * j - 1)*z*p2 - (j - 1)*p3) / j
        Next j
        pp = n * (z * p1 - p2) / (z * z - 1)
        z1 = z: z = z1 - p1 / pp
    Loop Until (Abs(z - z1) < EPS)
    x(i) = xm - xl * z
    x(n + 1 - i) = xm + xl * z
    w(i) = 2 * xl / ((1 - z * z) * pp * pp)
    w(n + 1 - i) = w(i)
  Next i
GLquad = 0
For i = 1 To n
  GLquad = GLquad + w(i) * Run(fname, x(i))
Next i
End Function
```

The GLquad() function uses the roots of Chebychev polynomials, each given by $x_j = \cos[(j - \frac{1}{4})\pi / (n + \frac{1}{2})]$, as initial approximations to the abscissas. It then applies Newton's methods to find more precise abscissas. This requires the first derivative of the Legendre polynomials, given as $P'_0(x) = 0$ and $P'_1(x) = 1$, and found using the recursive relation

$$\frac{x^2 - 1}{j}P'_j(x) = xP_{j-1}(x) - P_{j-2}(x).$$

The GLquad() function stores the abscissas in array x, stores the weights in array w, evaluates the function at the abscissas, and constructs the sum which produces the approximation to the integral.

Gauss-Laguerre Quadrature

The third and last method of Gaussian quadrature presented in this section uses Laguerre polynomials as interpolating polynomials. The function GLAU() in the Excel file Chapter2Gauss contains the VBA code for implementing Gauss-Laguerre quadrature. Since Laguerre polynomials use a weighting function of the form $w(x) = x^{\alpha}e^{-x}$, and since this approximation is designed for integrals over the interval $(0, \infty)$, this function requires as inputs the function to be integrated, a value for α, and the number of points to use in the approximation.

```
Function GLAU(fname As String, n, alpha)
Dim x(100) As Double
Dim w(100) As Double
MAXITER = 10
EPS = 0.0000000000003
For i = 1 To n
  If (i = 1) Then
     z = (1 + alpha) * (3 + 0.92 * alpha)
        / (1 + 2.4 * n + 1.8 * alpha)
  ElseIf (i = 2) Then
     z = z + (15 + 6.25 * alpha) / (1 + 0.9 * alpha + 2.5 * n)
  Else
     ai = i - 2
        z = z + ((1 + 2.55 * ai) / (1.9 * ai) + 1.26 * ai * alpha
           / (1 + 3.5 * ai)) * (z - x(i - 2)) / (1 + 0.3 * alpha)
  End If
For its = 1 To MAXITER
   p1 = 1
   p2 = 0
   For j = 1 To n
      p3 = p2
      p2 = p1
      p1 = ((2 * j - 1 + alpha - z) * p2 - (j - 1 + alpha) * p3) / j
   Next j
   pp = (n * p1 - (n + alpha) * p2) / z
   z1 = z
   z = z1 - p1 / pp
      If (Abs(z - z1) < EPS) Then
         Exit For
      End If
```

```
  Next its
  If (its > MAXITER) Then
    MsgBox "Too many iterations"
  End If
  x(i) = z
  w(i) = -Exp(Application.GammaLn(alpha + n)
      - Application.GammaLn(n)) / (pp * n * p2)
  w(i) = Exp(x(i)) * w(i)
Next i
GLAU = 0
For i = 1 To n
  GLAU = GLAU + w(i) * Run(fname, x(i))
Next i
End Function
```

Similar to the Gauss-Legendre quadrature, the GLAU() function first uses initial guesses for the roots of the Laguerre polynomial, then uses Newton's method to refine the guesses and obtain more precise estimates of the roots. It also uses the Excel function GammaLn() to calculate the log of the Gamma function.

The GLAU() function presented in this section involves finding the roots of the Laguerre polynomials, which are subsequently used as abscissas in the approximation for the integral. Of course, it is possible to simply use tabulated values of the abscissas and weights in the VBA code directly, as in the function GLquad10() described earlier. In that case the algorithm is very simple, since it involves the sum of the product of the weights and the function evaluated at the abscissas. The Excel file Chapter2Weights contains tabulated weights and abscissas to implement Gauss-Legendre and Gauss-Laguerre quadratures, using up to 32 points. The file also includes abscissas and weights to implement Gauss-Hermite quadratures, and is described in more detail in Appendix 2.1.

Comparison of the Methods

In this section we compare the accuracy of the three Gaussian quadrature methods. Figure 2.8 illustrates the Excel spreadsheet Chapter2Gauss. The 10-Point Gauss-Legendre VBA function requires only the endpoints a and b to be specified, along with the function to be integrated. Hence, in cell F10 we type

$$= \text{GLquad10}(\text{"Examplef"},\text{C6},\text{C7})$$

where Examplef() corresponds to the function $f(x) = x^3 + 10$. The Variable-Point Gauss-Legendre function requires the endpoints and the number of points to be specified, so in cell F8 we type

$$= \text{GLquad}(\text{"Examplef"},\text{C6},\text{C7},\text{F6}).$$

Because $f(x)$ is a polynomial of order three, only two points are needed to yield the exact result of 2,616.

	A	B	C	D	E	F
1						
2		**Illustration of Gaussian Quadratures on Simple Functions**				
3						
4		$f(x) = x^3 + 10$				
5						
6		$a =$	-2		**Number of Points (n)**	2
7		$b =$	10			
8					**Variable-Point Gauss-Legendre**	2616
9						
10					**Ten-Point Gauss-Legendre**	2616
11						
12					**Real Integral Value**	2616
13						
14		$f(x) = 1 / (x+1)^3$				
15						
16		$a =$	0		**Number of Points (n)**	12
17		$b =$	∞			
18					**Variable-Point Gauss-Legendre**	0.4996
19						
20					**Real Integral Value**	0.5000
21						

FIGURE 2.8 Comparison of Gaussian Quadratures

We also evaluate the approximation of the integral of $f(x) = 1/(1 + x)^3$ over the interval $(0, \infty)$, which has exact value 0.5. The VBA function Examplef2() contains $f(x)$, so in cell F18 we type

$$= \mathrm{GLAU}(\text{"Examplef2"}, \mathrm{F16}, 0)$$

which invokes the Gauss-Laguerre method and yields an approximation that is very close to the true value even when $n = 12$ points are used.

SUMMARY

This chapter presented some of the more popular algorithms for performing numerical integration, as well as VBA functions to implement them. Newton-Cotes formulas are easy to understand, and writing VBA code for these methods is straightforward. In most applications, either the trapezoidal rule or Simpson's rule will produce sufficiently precise approximations, provided that a large number of abscissas are used. With the speed of today's computers, using a large number of points will not lead to substantial increases in computation or execution time.

We have introduced two Gaussian quadratures, one that can be used over any interval of integration, and one that can be used only on $(0, \infty)$. Gaussian quadratures are much more difficult to understand than Newton-Cotes formulas, but they produce accurate results with much fewer abscissas. Even though their algorithms are more complicated, since the roots of orthogonal polynomials must be found, Gaussian quadratures produce very accurate approximations with little execution time.

Finally, we note that other Gaussian quadratures can be constructed using different weighting functions to generate orthogonal polynomials. Examples of these methods include Gauss-Hermite, Gauss-Chebychev, and Gauss-Jacobi quadratures. Since the focus of this book is not numerical integration, we leave these methods out of this chapter and refer readers to Burden and Faires (2001) or other textbooks on numerical analysis.

EXERCISES

 This section provides reinforcement of the concepts of numerical integration presented in this chapter. Solutions to these problems are in the Excel file Chapter2Exercises provided on the CD-ROM.

2.1 Reproduce Figure 2.5 using the following functions over the interval $(-3, 3)$, using $\Delta x = 0.5$. Recall that Figure 2.5 uses the method of passing parameters.

$$(a)\ f_1(x) = \frac{x \exp(x^2)}{100} + 10$$

$$(b)\ f_2(x) = x^{10} - 7x^8 + x$$

$$(c)\ f_3(x) = \frac{7000x}{x^2 + 1000}.$$

2.2 Repeat Question 1 using in-line functions, using $n = 12, n = 120$, and $n = 1,200$ subintervals in the approximation.

2.3 Write a VBA function for implementing Simpson's rule. If the number of subintervals is odd, use Simpson's three-eighths rule over the first three subintervals, and Simpson's rule over the remaining $n - 3$ subintervals. Apply this to the functions in Question 2.1 above.

2.4 Write VBA code for the sixteen-point Gauss-Legendre quadrature, using the tabulated values for abscissas and weights presented in the appendix to this chapter, which also appears on the CD-ROM. Apply this approximation to the functions in Question 2.1 above.

2.5 Gaussian quadratures produce exact integration for polynomials of degree $2n - 1$ or less, where n is the number of subintervals in the Gaussian quadrature. Use the variable-point Gauss-Legendre quadrature included on the CD-ROM to show that the quadrature yields an exact solution for the function in Question 2.1(b).

SOLUTIONS TO EXERCISES

2.1 The left- and right-point rules produce very poor approximations for the integrals involving functions f_1 and f_3. The other rules produce approximations that are accurate to two decimals. For function f_2, only Boole's rule produces an approximation that is close to the true value. Even that approximation, however, is poor. To save space, Figure 2.9 presents the results only for function f_1.

2.2 This exercise illustrates that dramatically increasing the number of subintervals will in some cases produce approximations that are not adequate. Even with $n = 1,200$ approximations the left- and right-point rules cannot accurately approximate the integrals for f_1 and f_3. Boole's rule produces an accurate approximation for function f_2 even with only $n = 120$ subintervals. This exercise is illustrated in Figure 2.10.

2.3 The VBA function SIMPGENnumint() implements Simpson's rule for an even or odd number of subintervals. This is illustrated in Figure 2.11.

2.4 The VBA function GLquad16() adapts the Ten-Point Gauss-Legendre function GLquad10() described in the section titled "Passing Vector Parameters," to 16 abscissas. This is illustrated in Figure 2.12.

2.5 The degree of the polynomial defined in f_2 is 10, so at least $n = 6$ abscissas are needed provide an exact solution to the integral for f_2. Since $2n - 1 = 2(6) - 1 = 11$, six abscissas provides an exact solution to polynomials up to degree 11 also. Note that $n = 5$ abscissas are not sufficient in this example,

	A	B	C	D	E	F	G
1	EXERCISE 2.1						
2							
3	Function 1.a						
4	Abscissas	f(x) Values	Mid Points	f(x) Values		Rules	Integral
5	-3.00	-233.09					
6	-2.50	-2.95	-2.75	-42.93			
7	-2.00	8.91	-2.25	6.45		Left-Point	-61.55
8	-1.50	9.86	-1.75	9.63		Right-Point	181.55
9	-1.00	9.97	-1.25	9.94		Mid-Point	60.00
10	-0.50	9.99	-0.75	9.99		Trapezoidal	60.00
11	0.00	10.00	-0.25	10.00		Simpson's	60.00
12	0.50	10.01	0.25	10.00		Simpson's 3/8	60.00
13	1.00	10.03	0.75	10.01		Boole's	60.00
14	1.50	10.14	1.25	10.06			
15	2.00	11.09	1.75	10.37		**Real Integral**	**60.00**
16	2.50	22.95	2.25	13.55		**Value**	
17	3.00	253.09	2.75	62.93			

FIGURE 2.9 Solution to Exercise 2.1

	A	B	C	D	E	F	G
1	EXERCISE 2.2						
2		a =	-3				
3		b =	3				
4							
5		Rules		Integral for f₁			
6			n = 12	n = 120	n = 1200		
7		1 Left-Point	-61.55	47.85	58.78		
8		2 Right-Point	181.55	72.15	61.22		
9		3 Trapezoidal	60.00	60.00	60.00		
10		4 Simpson's	60.00	60.00	60.00		
11		5 Simpson's 3/8	60.00	60.00	60.00	**Real**	**60.00**
12		6 Boole's	60.00	60.00	60.00	**Integral**	
13							
14		Rules		Integral for f₂			
15			n = 12	n = 120	n = 1200		
16		1 Left-Point	4519.33	1621.36	1590.84		
17		2 Right-Point	4522.33	1621.66	1590.87		
18		3 Trapezoidal	4520.83	1621.51	1590.86		
19		4 Simpson's	2169.77	1590.61	1590.55		
20		5 Simpson's 3/8	2671.21	1590.70	1590.55	**Real**	**1590.55**
21		6 Boole's	1868.29	1590.55	1590.55	**Integral**	
22							
23		Rules		Integral for f₃			
24			n = 12	n = 120	n = 1200		
25		1 Left-Point	-10.41	-1.04	-0.10		
26		2 Right-Point	10.41	1.04	0.10		
27		3 Trapezoidal	0.00	0.00	0.00		
28		4 Simpson's	0.00	0.00	0.00		
29		5 Simpson's 3/8	0.00	0.00	0.00	**Real**	**0.00**
30		6 Boole's	0.00	0.00	0.00	**Integral**	

FIGURE 2.10   Solution to Exercise 2.2

since that would provide an exact solution for polynomials up to degree $2(5) - 1 = 9$ only. This exercise is illustrated in Figure 2.13.

APPENDIX

Tables for Gaussian Quadratures

This appendix contains abscissas and weights for implementing Gauss-Legendre, Gauss-Laguerre, and Gauss-Hermite quadratures, each tabulated for 8, 16, and 32 abscissas. The weights are available in the Excel file Chapter2Weights. Implementing these rules is straightforward, since they all involve a sum whose terms are the product of the tabulated weights, and the function evaluated at the abscissas (or for Gauss-Legendre quadratures, at a transformation of the abscissas).

	A	B	C	D	E	F	G	H
1	EXERCISE 2.3							
2		*a* =	-3					
3		*b* =	3					
4								
5	Function 1.a				Integral			
6		# subintervals (*n*)	3	4	5	6	7	8
7			60.00	60.00	60.00	47.96	60.00	51.67
8		# subintervals (*n*)	30	31	32	33	34	35
9			59.52	60.00	59.61	60.00	59.68	60.00
10		# subintervals (*n*)	300	301	302	303	304	305
11			60.00	60.00	60.00	60.00	60.00	60.00
12								
13							Real	60.00
14							Integral	
15								
16	Function 1.b				Integral			
17		# subintervals (*n*)	3	4	5	6	7	8
18			26244.00	19656.00	12635.05	9931.12	6692.00	5649.67
19		# subintervals (*n*)	30	31	32	33	34	35
20			1620.65	1607.87	1613.53	1603.97	1608.37	1601.11
21		# subintervals (*n*)	300	301	302	303	304	305
22			1590.55	1590.55	1590.55	1590.55	1590.55	1590.55
23								
24							Real	1590.55
25							Integral	
26								
27	Function 1.c				Integral			
28		# subintervals (*n*)	3	4	5	6	7	8
29			0.00	0.00	0.00	0.00	0.00	0.00
30		# subintervals (*n*)	30	31	32	33	34	35
31			0.00	0.00	0.00	0.00	0.00	0.00
32		# subintervals (*n*)	300	301	302	303	304	305
33			0.00	0.00	0.00	0.00	0.00	0.00
34								
35							Real	0.00
36							Integral	

FIGURE 2.11 Solution to Exercise 2.3

For integrals over the interval $[a, b]$ we use the Gauss-Legendre points and approximate the integral by Equation (2.6). The abscissas and weights are illustrated in Figure 2.14.

For integrals over $(0, \infty)$ we use Gauss-Laguerre points and approximate the integral by

$$\int_0^\infty f(x)\, dx \approx \sum_{i=1}^{x} w_i f(x_i)$$

	A	B	C	D	E	F
1	EXERCISE 2.4					
2						
3	Function 1.a					
4						
5	$a =$	-3		16 Point		60
6	$b =$	3		Gauss Legendre		
7						
8				Real		60.00
9				Integral		
10						
11	Function 1.b					
12						
13	$a =$	-3		16 Point		1590.55
14	$b =$	3		Gauss Legendre		
15						
16				Real		1590.55
17				Integral		
18						
19	Function 1.c					
20						
21	$a =$	-3		16 Point		0
22	$b =$	3		Gauss Legendre		
23						
24				Real		0.00
25				Integral		

FIGURE 2.12 Solution to Exercise 2.4

	A	B	C	D	E	F	G	H
1	EXERCISE 2.5							
2								
3	Function 1.b							
4								
5		$a =$	-3					
6		$b =$	3					
7								
8		# subintervals (n)	1	2	3	4	5	6
9			0.00	-1944.00	-4534.96	-1377.24	1071.18	1590.55
10								
11			7	8	9	10	11	12
12			1590.55	1590.55	1590.55	1590.55	1590.55	1590.55
13								
14						Real		1590.55
15						Integral		

FIGURE 2.13 Solution to Exercise 2.5

	A	B	C	D	E	F	G
1		8 - Abscissas	8 - Weights	16 - Abscissas	16 - Weights	32 - Abscissas	32 - Weights
2	1	-0.960289856498	0.101228536290	-0.989400934992	0.027152459411	-0.997263861849	0.007018145765
3	2	-0.796666477414	0.222381034453	-0.944575023073	0.062253523937	-0.985611511545	0.016277426583
4	3	-0.525532409916	0.313706645878	-0.865631202388	0.095158511684	-0.964762255588	0.025391009833
5	4	-0.183434642496	0.362683783378	-0.755404408355	0.124628971256	-0.934906075938	0.034274547848
6	5	0.183434642496	0.362683783378	-0.617876244403	0.149595988817	-0.896321155766	0.042835989679
7	6	0.525532409916	0.313706645878	-0.458016777657	0.169156519395	-0.849367613733	0.050997873812
8	7	0.796666477414	0.222381034453	-0.281603550779	0.182603415045	-0.794483795968	0.058683939462
9	8	0.960289856498	0.101228536290	-0.095012509838	0.189450610455	-0.732182118740	0.065822060358
10	9			0.095012509838	0.189450610455	-0.663044266930	0.072345609430
11	10			0.281603415045	0.182603415045	-0.587715757241	0.078193695762
12	11			0.458016777657	0.169156519395	-0.506899908932	0.083311711103
13	12			0.617876244403	0.149595988817	-0.421351276131	0.087651868805
14	13			0.755404408355	0.124628971256	-0.331868602282	0.091173645488
15	14			0.865631202388	0.095158511684	-0.239287362252	0.093844159042
16	15			0.944575023073	0.062253523937	-0.144471961583	0.095638475451
17	16			0.989400934992	0.027152459411	-0.048307665688	0.096539841581
18	17					0.048307665688	0.096539841581
19	18					0.144471961583	0.095638475451
20	19					0.239287362252	0.093844159042
21	20					0.331868602282	0.091173645488
22	21					0.421351276131	0.087651868805
23	22					0.506899908932	0.083311711103
24	23					0.587715757241	0.078193695762
25	24					0.663044266930	0.072345609430
26	25					0.732182118740	0.065822060358
27	26					0.794483795968	0.058683939462
28	27					0.849367613733	0.050997873812
29	28					0.896321155766	0.042835989679
30	29					0.934906075938	0.034274547848
31	30					0.964762255588	0.025391009833
32	31					0.985611511545	0.016277426583
33	32					0.997263861849	0.007018145765

FIGURE 2.14 Abscissas and Weights for Gauss-Legendre Quadratures

	A	B	C	D	E	F	G
1		8 - Abscissas	8 - Weights	16 - Abscissas	16 - Weights	32 - Abscissas	32 - Weights
2	1	0.170279632305	0.437723410493	0.087649410479	0.225036314864	0.044489365833	0.114187105768
3	2	0.903701776799	1.033869347670	0.462696328915	0.525836052762	0.234526109520	0.266065216898
4	3	2.251086629280	1.669709765660	1.141057774830	0.831961391687	0.576884629302	0.418793137325
5	4	4.266700170290	2.376924701760	2.129283645100	1.146099240960	1.072448753820	0.572532846497
6	5	7.045905402390	3.208540913350	3.437086633890	1.471751316980	1.722408776440	0.727648788453
7	6	10.758516010200	4.268575510830	5.078018614560	1.813134687360	2.528336706430	0.884536718946
8	7	15.740678641300	5.818083368670	7.070338535010	2.175517519370	3.492213272850	1.043618875970
9	8	22.863131736900	8.906226215290	9.438314336490	2.565762749640	4.616456772230	1.205349205950
10	9			12.214223368600	2.993215083440	5.903958483350	1.370221719690
11	10			15.441527369400	3.471234497090	7.358126808600	1.538775959060
12	11			19.180156855400	4.020044100190	8.982941267320	1.711645945920
13	12			23.515905695900	4.672516611460	10.783012089000	1.889564968300
14	13			28.578729741200	5.487420636160	12.763745476000	2.073188512350
15	14			34.583398703200	6.585361244490	14.930911798100	2.265901444440
16	15			41.940452647400	8.276357975490	17.293266137200	2.469974189880
17	16			51.701160339600	11.824277548900	19.853623649300	2.642967094940
18	17					22.635778962400	2.764644374620
19	18					25.620148202400	3.228905429810
20	19					28.873933686900	2.920193619630
21	20					32.333329401700	4.392847980900
22	21					36.113204224500	4.279086731890
23	22					40.133737705600	5.204803985190
24	23					44.522408536200	5.114362129610
25	24					49.208660566500	4.155614921730
26	25					54.350181332400	6.198510605670
27	26					59.879119284500	5.347957801280
28	27					65.983361704100	6.283392124570
29	28					72.684268322200	6.891983409690
30	29					80.188374790600	7.920910942440
31	30					88.735192639000	9.204405558030
32	31					98.829552318400	11.163743290400
33	32					111.751398227000	15.390241768800

FIGURE 2.15 Abscissas and Weights for Gauss-Laguerre Quadratures

	A	B	C	D	E	F	G
		8 - Abscissas	8 - Weights	16 - Abscissas	16 - Weights	32 - Abscissas	32 - Weights
1							
2	1	-2.930637420260	1.071930144250	-4.688738939310	0.936874492884	-7.125813909830	0.824566523071
3	2	-1.981656756700	0.866752606563	-3.869447904860	0.738245622278	-6.409498149280	0.640950485906
4	3	-1.157193712450	0.792890048386	-3.176999161980	0.655755672876	-5.812225949460	0.561749015435
5	4	-0.381186990207	0.764544128652	-2.546202157850	0.609736958256	-5.275550986640	0.515037283347
6	5	0.381186990207	0.764544128652	-1.951787990920	0.581247275401	-4.777164503340	0.483571441630
7	6	1.157193712450	0.792890048386	-1.380258539200	0.563217829088	-4.305547953470	0.460786455454
8	7	1.981656756700	0.866752606563	-0.822951449145	0.552441957367	-3.853755485420	0.443553185862
9	8	2.930637420260	1.071930144250	-0.273481046138	0.547375205038	-3.417167492820	0.430163710393
10	9			0.273481046138	0.547375205038	-2.992490825010	0.419597752949
11	10			0.822951449145	0.552441957367	-2.577249537730	0.411206128685
12	11			1.380258539200	0.563217829088	-2.169499183610	0.404557061809
13	12			1.951787990920	0.581247275401	-1.767654109460	0.399354844618
14	13			2.546202157850	0.609736958256	-1.370376410950	0.395393939396
15	14			3.176999161980	0.655755672876	-0.976500463590	0.392531864366
16	15			3.869447904860	0.738245622278	-0.584978765436	0.390672744629
17	16			4.688738939310	0.936874492884	-0.194840741569	0.389757342027
18	17					0.194840741569	0.389757342027
19	18					0.584978765436	0.390672744629
20	19					0.976500463590	0.392531864366
21	20					1.370376410950	0.395393939396
22	21					1.767654109460	0.399354844618
23	22					2.169499183610	0.404557061809
24	23					2.577249537730	0.411206128685
25	24					2.992490825010	0.419597752949
26	25					3.417167492820	0.430163710393
27	26					3.853755485420	0.443553185862
28	27					4.305547953470	0.460786455454
29	28					4.777164503340	0.483571441630
30	29					5.275550986640	0.515037283347
31	30					5.812225949460	0.561749015435
32	31					6.409498149280	0.640950485906
33	32					7.125813909830	0.824566523071

FIGURE 2.16 Abscissas and Weights for Gauss-Hermite Quadratures

where, as before, w_i and x_i denote the tabulated values of the weights and abscissas, respectively. These appear in Figure 2.15.

Finally, for integrals over $(-\infty, \infty)$ we use Gauss-Hermite points and approximate the integral by

$$\int_{-\infty}^{\infty} f(x)\, dx \approx \sum_{i=1}^{x} w_i f(x_i).$$

The abscissas and weights for this method appear in Figure 2.16. Note that the Gauss-Legendre quadrature (2.6) is the only one that requires the function to be evaluated at the transformed values of the abscissas. In both other quadratures, the function is evaluated at the abscissas themselves.

CHAPTER 3

Tree-Based Methods

INTRODUCTION

In this chapter we introduce tree-based methods for obtaining option prices, which are especially popular for pricing American options since many closed-form formulas currently available are for European options only. Binomial and trinomial trees can be used to price many options, including plain vanilla options, but also exotic options such as barrier options, digital options, Asian options, and others. Trees make this possible by mapping out price movements of the underlying security. These price movements are represented by a grid of equally spaced time steps, with a series of nodes at each step indicating the price of the security and of the option. At each node, the security moves up or down by a certain amount, according to a prespecified probability. The price of the option is evaluated at each node, and then discounted back to obtain the price at the first node, representing time zero. For many of these trees, the price of a European option converges to the Black-Scholes price. Valuation of American options is done by assessing whether early exercise is profitable at each node in the tree.

The advantage of binomial and trinomial trees is that not only can they can be used to value just about any type of option, but they are very easy to implement. The drawback of binomial trees is that the amount of increase or decrease of the security at each node, as well as the probability of an increase or a decrease, is usually fixed. In these models, jumps in asset prices are not permitted.

In this chapter we introduce several binomial trees, the popular Cox, Ross, and Rubinstein (1979) (CRR) binomial tree, the Leisen and Reimer (1996) binomial tree, the flexible binomial tree of Tian (1999), the Edgeworth binomial tree of Rubinstein (1998), and the trinomial tree of Boyle (1986). In the CRR binomial tree we allow dividends in the form of payments at prespecified periods. We also introduce the implied binomial tree of Derman and Kani (1994); the implied trinomial tree of Derman, Kani, and Chriss (1996); and the adaptive mesh method (AMM) of Figlewski and Gao (1999). In Chapter 7 we show how option sensitivities (the Greeks) can be extracted from these trees, and in Chapter 8 we use trees to obtain prices of exotic options.

CRR BINOMIAL TREE

Suppose an option with maturity T and strike K is to be priced, using a binomial tree with n time increments on a stock with spot price S with volatility σ when the risk free rate is r. In the CRR model the stock moves up in increments of $u = \exp(\sigma\sqrt{dt})$ and down in increments of $d = 1/u$ at each time step of length $dt = T/n$. The probability of an up move is $p = (\exp(r \times dt) - d)/(u - d)$, and the probability of a down move is $1 - p$. European call options are priced at the final time step as

$$\text{Call} = \exp(-rT) \sum_{i=0}^{n} \binom{n}{i} p^i (1-p)^{n-i} \max(Su^i d^{n-i} - K, 0) \qquad (3.1)$$

where

$$\binom{n}{i} = \frac{n!}{i!(n-i)!}$$

is the "n choose i" notation, $n! = n \times (n-1) \cdots 2 \times 1$ is the factorial notation, and where $0!$ is defined as 1. To price a put option, replace $Su^i d^{n-i} - K$ in the last term of Equation (3.1) by $K - Su^i d^{n-i}$. This formula represents the expected value of the option at the final time step, discounted by the risk-free rate. Since it is in closed form, it is very easy to implement. Valuing European and American calls and puts with the CRR tree is explained in the textbook by Hull (2006).

The Excel file Chapter3CompareEuroBS produces the CRR binomial price of a European call or put option with the VBA function EuroBin(). It requires as inputs the spot price (S), the strike price (K), the time period (T), the risk-free rate (rf), the volatility (sigma), the number of time steps (n), and whether a call or put is to be priced (PutCall).

```
Function EuroBin(S, K, T, rf, sigma, n, PutCall As String)
dt = T / n: u = Exp(sigma * (dt ^ 0.5))
d = 1 / u: p = (Exp(rf * dt) - d) / (u - d)
EuroBin = 0
  For i = 0 To n
   Select Case PutCall
    Case "Call":
     EuroBin = EuroBin + Application.Combin(n, i)
       * p ^ i * (1 - p) ^ (n - i)
       * Application.Max(S * u ^ i * d ^ (n - i) - K, 0)
    Case "Put":
     EuroBin = EuroBin + Application.Combin(n, i)
       * p ^ i * (1 - p) ^ (n - i)
       * Application.Max(K - S * u ^ i * d ^ (n - i), 0)
   End Select
  Next i
EuroBin = Exp(-rf * T) * EuroBin
End Function
```

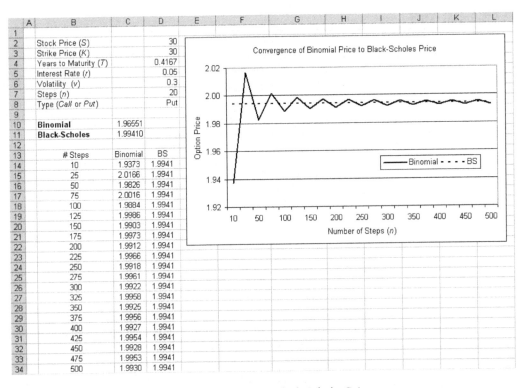

FIGURE 3.1 Convergence of CRR Binomial Price to Black-Scholes Price

The Excel file also shows how the CRR price of an option converges to the Black-Scholes price as the number of time steps n increases. This is illustrated in Figure 3.1. For convenience, the cells for input values have been named using the range name commands in Excel. In cell C10 we type

$$= \text{EuroBin}(S,K,T,RF,V,D7,PutCall)$$

to obtain the binomial price of $1.9655 for a European put option with strike $30 maturing in 5 months on a stock with spot price $30 and annual volatility 30 percent when the risk-free rate is 5 percent annually, using $n = 20$ time steps. In cell C11 we type

$$= \text{BlackScholes}(S,K,RF,T,V,PutCall)$$

to obtain the Black-Scholes price as $1.99410. The Black-Scholes model will be covered in Chapter 4. In Figure 3.1 we increase the number of time steps to illustrate the convergence of the CRR tree to the Black-Scholes price. The figure indicates that the convergence to the Black-Scholes price is slow. Even with 500 time steps, the

	A	B	C	D	E
1	0	$1 \times dt$	$2 \times dt$	$3 \times dt$	$T = 4 \times dt$
2					
3					Su^4
4				Su^3	
5			Su^2		Su^3d
6		Su		Su^2d	
7	S		S		S
8		Sd		Sud^2	
9			Sd^2		Sud^3
10				Sd^3	
11					Sd^4
12					
13					
14	$S(1,1) = S$	$S(1,2) = Su$	$S(1,3) = Su^2$	$S(1,4) = Su^3$	$S(1,5) = Su^4$
15		$S(2,2) = Sd$	$S(2,3) = S$	$S(2,4) = Su^2d$	$S(2,5) = Su^3d$
16			$S(3,3) = Sd^2$	$S(3,4) = Sud^2$	$S(3,5) = S$
17				$S(4,4) = Sd^3$	$S(4,5) = Sud^3$
18					$S(5,5) = Sd^4$

FIGURE 3.2 Stock Price Movements in the Binomial Tree

binomial price is only accurate to two decimal places. In later sections will we see that the convergence of trinomial trees is much faster.

Figure 3.2 illustrates how stock price movements in the binomial tree are treated in this book, using time steps. The top portion presents the binomial tree, while the second portion corresponds to how the prices are placed in a matrix for coding in VBA. To contain all possible price movements under a binomial tree with n steps, we need a square matrix of dimension $n + 1$, equal to 5 in the figure. In the matrix, up movements in the stock price are represented by horizontal moves along any row, while down movements in the stock price by moves downward to the next row. The stock price at node (i, j) is given by $S_{i,j} = Su^{j-i}d^{i-1}$.

Options are priced by obtaining the price at the last time step and working back through the tree, discounting the value of the option by the risk free at each step. The Excel file Chapter3Binomial presents the VBA function Binomial() for pricing an American put or call option. For now, we ignore the code for incorporating dividends and for obtaining the option sensitivities. To conserve space, throughout this chapter we remove the Dim and ReDim statements in the VBA code that we present.

```
Function Binomial(Spot, K, T, r, sigma, n, PutCall As String, EuroAmer As
             String, Dividends)
dt = T / n: u = Exp(sigma * (dt ^ 0.5))
d = 1 / u: p = (Exp(r * dt) - d) / (u - d)
S(1, 1) = Spot
```

```
For i = 1 To n + 1
  For j = i To n + 1
    S(i, j) = S(1, 1) * u ^ (j - i) * d ^ (i - 1)
  Next j
Next i
For i = 1 To n + 1
Select Case PutCall
  Case "Call"
    Op(i, n + 1) = Application.Max(S(i, n + 1) - K, 0)
  Case "Put"
    Op(i, n + 1) = Application.Max(K - S(i, n + 1), 0)
End Select
Next i
For j = n To 1 Step -1
For i = 1 To j
  Select Case EuroAmer
    Case "Amer"
    If PutCall = "Call" Then
      Op(i, j) = Application.Max(S(i, j) - K, Exp(-r * dt)
        * (p * Op(i, j + 1) + (1 - p) * Op(i + 1, j + 1)))
    ElseIf PutCall = "Put" Then
      Op(i, j) = Application.Max(K - S(i, j), Exp(-r * dt)
        * (p * Op(i, j + 1) + (1 - p) * Op(i + 1, j + 1)))
    End If
    Case "Euro"
      Op(i, j) = Exp(-r * dt) * (p * Op(i, j + 1)
                + (1 - p) * Op(i + 1, j + 1))
  End Select
Next i
Next j
Binomial = Op(1, 1)
```

The function requires as inputs the spot price (Spot), the strike price (K), the maturity of the option (T), the annual risk-free rate (r) and volatility (sigma), the number of time steps (n), whether a call or put is to be priced (PutCall), whether the option is American or European (EuroAmer), and dividend payments (Dividends), which we ignore for now.

The value of a call option at the terminal nodes contained in the array $CallOp(i, n+1)$ is given by $\max(S_{i,n+1} - K, 0)$, for $i = 1, 2, \ldots, n+1$. To value an American call option, we work backward through the tree. If we are at node (i, j) and the option is exercised at that time, we earn $S_{i,j} - K$. If the option is not exercised, its value is the expected value from the two previous nodes joining (i, j), namely the up node $(i, j+1)$ and the down node $(i+1, j+1)$, discounted at the risk-free rate for one time period,

$$e^{-r \times dt}[pS_{i,j+1} + (1-p)S_{i+1,j+1}]. \tag{3.2}$$

Hence, the value of an American call option at node (i, j) is given by

$$\max\{S_{i,j} - K, e^{-rdt}[pS_{i,j+1} + (1-p)S_{i+1,j+1}]\}. \tag{3.3}$$

	A	B	C	D	E	F	G
1							
2		**CRR Binomial Tree Price for an American or European Option**					
3		**on a Dividend Paying Stock**					
4					Time (τ)	Dividend	Interest
5		Spot Price (S)	30		0.000	0.00	0.00
6		Strike Price (K)	30		0.000	0.00	0.00
7		Years to Maturity (T)	0.4167		0.000	0.00	0.00
8		Interest Rate (rf)	0.05		0.000	0.00	0.00
9		Volatility (v)	0.3		0.000	0.00	0.00
10		Steps (n)	100		0.000	0.00	0.00
11		Type (Call or Put)	Put		0.000	0.00	0.00
12		Option (Amer or Euro)	Amer		0.000	0.00	0.00
13					0.000	0.00	0.00
14					0.000	0.00	0.00
15		**Option Price**	2.0462				

FIGURE 3.3 CRR Binomial Tree Price of European and American Options

For a European call option, we cannot exercise early, so its value at node (i, j) is Equation (3.2). For European and American options, the value at time zero is contained in Op(1,1), the first element of array Op().

This function is illustrated in Figure 3.3. For now we assume no dividends, so in cells E5:G14 we enter zeros, and we ignore the option sensitivities included in the Excel file Chapter3Binomial.

As in the previous section, cells have been assigned range names for convenience. Using the same values as in Figure 3.1 with $n = 100$ steps, in cell C15 we type

$$= \text{Binomial}(S,K,T,RF,V,N,\text{PutCall},\text{EuroAmer},\text{Dividend})$$

to obtain the value of an American put option as \$2.0462, which, as expected, is higher than the \$1.9884 for a European put option given in cell C18 of Figure 3.1.

LEISEN-REIMER BINOMIAL TREE

The CRR binomial tree is easy to implement but requires many time steps to converge to the true option price. Leisen and Reimer (1996) have proposed an improvement that uses normal approximations to the binomial distribution using inversion formulas. In this chapter we implement the two Peizer-Pratt inversions suggested in their paper. These two methods work for an odd number of steps only.

Leisen and Reimer (1996) use subscripts on the CRR binomial tree parameters to emphasize their dependence on n, the number of time steps. Hence, they denote

$u_n = \exp(\sigma\sqrt{T/n}), d_n = 1/u_n, r_n = \exp(rT/n)$, and the risk-neutral probability of an up move as $p_n = (r_n - d_n)/(u_n - d_n)$. The parameters of their new binomial model are $u = r_n p'/p$ and $d = (r_n - pu)/(1 - p)$, where $p' = h^{-1}(d_1)$ and $p = h^{-1}(d_2)$. The two inversion formulas $h^{-1}(z)$ for the probabilities that we present are the Peizer-Pratt method 1:

$$h^{-1}(z) = \frac{1}{2} + \frac{\text{Sign }(d_1)}{2}\sqrt{1 - \exp\left[\left(\frac{z}{n + \frac{1}{3}}\right)^2\left(n + \frac{1}{6}\right)\right]} \qquad (3.4)$$

and the Peizer-Pratt method 2:

$$h^{-1}(z) = \frac{1}{2} + \frac{\text{Sign }(d_1)}{2}\sqrt{1 - \exp\left[\left(\frac{z}{n + \frac{1}{3} + \frac{0.1}{n+1}}\right)^2\left(n + \frac{1}{6}\right)\right]} \qquad (3.5)$$

where

$$d_1 = \frac{\log(S/K) + (r + \sigma^2/2)T}{\sigma\sqrt{T}} \qquad (3.6)$$

and d_2 is identical to d_1 except that $r + \sigma^2/2$ is replaced by $r - \sigma^2/2$. The tree is constructed exactly as the CRR tree, but using the Leisen Reimer parameters $p, u,$ and d defined above.

　　　The Excel file Chapter3LRBinomial contains the VBA function LRBinomial() for implementing Leisen and Reimer trees. The first part of the function ensures that the time steps are odd. The second part computes the terms d_1 and d_2, the CRR up and down increments u_n and d_n, the terms needed in the Peizer-Pratt inversion, and the Leisen and Reimer up and down increments, u and d. The rest of the LRBinomial() function is similar to the CRR() binomial function presented earlier.

```
Function LRBinomial(Spot, K, T, r, v, n, PutCall As String, EuroAmer As
             String)
If n Mod 2 = 0 Then
  n = n + 1
End If
dt = T / n: exp_rT = Exp(-r * dt)
d1 = (Log(Spot / K) + (r + v ^ 2 / 2) * T) / v / Sqr(T)
d2 = (Log(Spot / K) + (r - v ^ 2 / 2) * T) / v / Sqr(T)
u_n = Exp(v * Sqr(dt)): d_n = Exp(-v * Sqr(dt))
r_n = Exp(r * dt)
Term1 = (d1 / (n + 1 / 3 - (1 - Method) * 0.1
          / (n + 1))) ^ 2 * (n + 1 / 6)
pp = 0.5 + Sgn(d1) * 0.5 * Sqr(1 - Exp(-Term1))
Term1 = (d2 / (n + 1 / 3 - (1 - Method) * 0.1
          / (n + 1))) ^ 2 * (n + 1 / 6)
```

	A	B	C	D
1				
2		**Leisen-Reimer Binomial Tree Price**		
3		**for an American or European Option**		
4				
5		Spot Price (*S*)	30	
6		Strike Price (*K*)	30	
7		Years to Maturity (*T*)	0.4167	
8		Interest Rate (*rf*)	0.05	
9		Volatility (*v*)	0.3	
10		Steps (*n*)	100	
11		Type (*Call* or *Put*)	Put	
12		Option (*Amer* or *Euro*)	Euro	
13		Method (*1* or *2*)	2	
14		*1* = Peizer-Pratt Inversion 1		
15		*2* = Peizer-Pratt Inversion 2		
16				
17		**Option Price**	1.99409	

FIGURE 3.4 Leisen-Reimer Binomial Tree Price of European and American Options

```
p = 0.5 + Sgn(d2) * 0.5 * Sqr(1 - Exp(-Term1))
u = r_n * pp / p: d = (r_n - p * u) / (1 - p)
```

Figure 3.4 illustrates the use of the LRBinomial() function. For comparison, we use the same inputs as those in Figure 3.1. We use the second Peizer-Pratt inversion, so in cell C17 we type

= LRBinomial(S,K,T,RF,V,N,PutCall,EuroAmer,Method)

to obtain the price of $1.99409 for a European call option.

Comparing with Figure 3.1, even with $n = 100$ steps the Leisen-Reimer tree obtains a call price that is closer to the Black-Scholes price of $1.99410 than the CRR binomial tree with $n = 500$ steps.

EDGEWORTH BINOMIAL TREE

The CRR and generalized binomial trees introduced in the previous two sections are a discrete-time approximation of the Black-Scholes formula for European options. Hence, these models assume a normal distribution for returns and do not allow for excess kurtosis or nonzero skewness. The tree we review in this section, created by Rubinstein (1998), introduces skewness and kurtosis into asset prices via an Edgeworth series expansion of the binomial distribution. This model is also explained in Duan et al. (2003).

In this model, terminal asset prices are obtained first, and remaining asset prices are obtained by working backward through the tree. The price at the first node of the tree is the spot price. Terminal prices are based on values of the standardized binomial distribution Y, with $E[Y] = 0$ and $Var[Y] = 1$, whose values are given by $y_j = (2j - n)/\sqrt{n}$ for $j = 0, 1, 2, \ldots, n$, with probability $b_j = (1/2)^n n!/[j!(n-j)!]$. The Edgeworth expansion for b_j is

$$f_j = \left[1 + \tfrac{1}{6}\xi(y_j^3 - 3y_j) + \tfrac{1}{24}(\kappa - 3)(y_j^4 - 6y_j^2 + 3) + \tfrac{1}{72}\xi^2(y_j^5 - 10y_j^3 + 15y_j)\right]b_j \tag{3.7}$$

where ξ and κ are the desired skewness and kurtosis, respectively, for the asset price distribution. The f_j are transformed into probabilities by scaling each by their sum, to yield $P_j = f_j/\sum_{k=0}^{n} f_k$.

Rubinstein (1998) defines the random variable X to have zero mean and unit variance. Its values are given by $x_j = (y_j - M)/\sqrt{V^2}$, where $M = \sum_{k=0}^{n} P_k y_k$ and $V^2 = \sum_{k=0}^{n} P_k(y_k - M)^2$ are the mean and variance of Y under the Edgeworth expansion. The asset prices at the $(n+1)$ terminal nodes are then given by $S_j = S\exp(\mu T + \sigma\sqrt{T}x_j)$ where S is the spot price, σ is the asset volatility, and

$$\mu = r - \frac{1}{T}\ln\left[\sum_{k=0}^{n} P_j \exp(\sigma\sqrt{T}x_j)\right]. \tag{3.8}$$

Once the terminal prices are obtained (namely at the last time step n), we require the terminal probabilities given by $p_j = P_j(n - j)!j!/n!$. With the terminal prices, the rest of the tree can be constructed by working backward at each pair of upper and lower nodes. The upper node j contains the probability p_j and the asset price S_j, while the lower node $j + 1$ contains the probability p_{j+1} and the asset price S_{j+1}. The probability and price at the preceding node joining nodes j and $j + 1$ are given by $p = p_j + p_{j+1}$ and $S = e^{-r\times dt}[p_{j+1}S_{j+1}/p + p_jS_j/p]$, respectively. The algorithm continues until the asset price at time zero is reached. If the algorithm is programmed properly, the time zero price will correspond to the spot price for the asset.

 To implement the Edgeworth binomial tree in Excel, some modifications are required since the method requires sums from 0 to n, but in VBA it is more convenient to work with sums running from 1 to $n + 1$. The Excel file Chapter3EdgeworthBin contains the VBA function EWBin() which illustrates how this is accomplished. Again, for now we ignore option sensitivities, and present only the part of EWBin() relevant for this section.

```
Function EWBin(Spot, K, r, v, T, n, skew, kurt, PutCall As String,
               EuroAmer As String)
dt = T / n
For j = 1 To n + 1
  y(j) = (2 * (n - j + 1) - n) / Sqr(n)
  b(j) = Application.Combin(n, j - 1) * (0.5) ^ n
```

```
     f(j) = (1 + (1 / 6) * skew * (y(j) ^ 3 - 3 * y(j))
       + (1 / 24) * (kurt - 3) * (y(j) ^ 4 - 6 * y(j) ^ 2 + 3)
       + (1 / 72) * skew ^ 2 * (y(j) ^ 5 - 10 * y(j) ^ 3
       + 15 * y(j))) * b(j)
Next j
For j = 1 To n + 1
  P(j) = f(j) / Application.Sum(f)
  SmallP(j, n + 1) = P(j) / Application.Combin(n, j - 1)
  BigP(j, n + 1) = SmallP(j, n + 1)
  Mean(j) = P(j) * y(j)
Next j
M = Application.Sum(Mean)
For j = 1 To n + 1
  PyM(j) = P(j) * (y(j) - M) ^ 2
Next j
V2 = Application.Sum(PyM)
For j = 1 To n + 1
  x(j) = (y(j) - M) / Sqr(V2)
  Pe(j) = P(j) * Exp(v * Sqr(T) * x(j))
Next j
mu = r - (1 / T) * Log(Application.Sum(Pe))
```

The array y() contains values y_j of the random variable Y, array b() contains the raw probabilities b_j, and array f() contains the Edgeworth probabilities f_j. The probabilities P_j for the terminal nodes are contained in array P(), the modified probabilities are contained in SmallP(), and M and V2 contain the Edgeworth mean and variance of Y, respectively. The scalar μ defined in (3.8) is contained in the variable mu. The asset prices at the terminal nodes are contained in the subarray S(1,n+1) to S(n+1,n+1).

```
For j = 1 To n + 1
  S(j, n + 1) = Spot * Exp(mu * T + v * Sqr(T) * x(j))
Next j
For j = n To 1 Step -1
  For i = 1 To j
  BigP(i, j) = BigP(i, j + 1) + BigP(i + 1, j + 1)
  SmallP(i, j) = BigP(i, j + 1) / BigP(i, j)
  S(i, j) = (SmallP(i, j) * S(i, j + 1) + (1 - SmallP(i, j))
        * S(i + 1, j + 1)) * Exp(-r * dt)
  Next i
Next j
```

The asset prices at the remaining nodes are contained in the array S(). With the asset prices obtained, we price European and American options exactly in the same way as before, except that the probabilities of up and down moves are no longer constant but vary from node to node. The terminal prices of calls and puts are obtained exactly as in the previous sections.

```
For i = 1 To n + 1
Select Case PutCall
```

```
Case "Call"
   Op(i, n + 1) = Application.Max(S(i, n + 1) - K, 0)
Case "Put"
   Op(i, n + 1) = Application.Max(K - S(i, n + 1), 0)
End Select
Next i
```

We work our way backward through the tree as in the CRR and LR binomial trees, except at each step we set the probability of an up move to p_j.

```
For j = n To 1 Step -1
For i = 1 To j
Pr = SmallP(i, j)
Select Case EuroAmer
   Case "Amer"
      If PutCall = "Call" Then
         Op(i, j) = Application.Max(S(i, j) - K, Exp(-r * dt)
            * (Pr * Op(i, j + 1) + (1 - Pr) * Op(i + 1, j + 1)))
      ElseIf PutCall = "Put" Then
         Op(i, j) = Application.Max(K - S(i, j), Exp(-r * dt)
            * (Pr * Op(i, j + 1) + (1 - Pr) * Op(i + 1, j + 1)))
      End If
   Case "Euro"
         Op(i, j) = Exp(-r * dt) * (Pr * Op(i, j + 1)
            + (1 - Pr) * Op(i + 1, j + 1))
   End Select
Next i
Next j
```

The value of the option is contained in Op(1,1). Figure 3.5 illustrates the Edgeworth binomial tree. Again, we defer discussion of the option sensitivities to Chapter 7.

We follow the European call example of the previous sections and use the same inputs, and include a skewness of zero and kurtosis of three, corresponding to the normal distribution. In cell C16 we type

$$= \text{EWBin}(S,K,RF,V,T,N,\text{Skew},\text{Kurt},\text{PutCall},\text{EuroAmer})$$

and obtain the price of a European call as $1.9939 with $n = 500$ steps, close to the value of $1.9930 from the CRR binomial tree with the same number of steps in Figure 3.1, and close to the value from the Leisen-Reimer binomial tree in Figure 3.4. Finally, Exhibit 2 of Rubinstein (1998) presents a locus of acceptable values of skewness and kurtosis for which the density (3.7) is guaranteed to be non-negative. With $n = 100$ steps, this locus is roughly elliptical, centered at $(\kappa, \xi) = (4.4, 0)$ approximately, and runs from $\kappa = 3.0$ to $\kappa = 5.4$, and from $\xi = -0.60$ to $\xi = 0.60$ approximately.

	A	B	C	D
1				
2		**Edgeworth Binomial Tree Price**		
3		**for American or European Options**		
4				
5		Spot (*S*)	30	
6		Strike (*K*)	30	
7		Risk Free Rate (*r*)	0.05	
8		Volatility (*v*)	0.30	
9		Time (*T*)	0.4167	
10		Number of Steps (*n*)	500	
11		Skewness (ξ)	0	
12		Kurtosis (κ)	3	
13		Type (*Call* or *Put*)	Put	
14		Option (*Amer* or *Euro*)	Euro	
15				
16		**Option Price**	1.993915	

FIGURE 3.5 Edgeworth Binomial Tree Price of European and American Options

FLEXIBLE BINOMIAL TREE

Tian (1999) proposed a binomial that allows prices in the CRR tree to be tilted upward or downward. In this model the up and down stock price moves are specified by $u = \exp(\sigma\sqrt{dt} + \lambda\sigma^2 dt)$ and $d = \exp(-\sigma\sqrt{dt} + \lambda\sigma^2 dt)$. The tilt parameter λ determines the degree and direction of the tilt. When $\lambda = 0$ the flexible binomial tree reduces to the CRR binomial tree, and the center of the tree forms a horizontal line on which asset prices are the same. When $\lambda > 0$ the tree is titled upward and the center line contains asset prices that increase with the time steps, so that the center of the tree forms a line that slopes upward. When $\lambda < 0$, the opposite is true. See Figure 1 of Tian (1999).

The chief advantage of the flexible binomial tree is that the tilt parameter can be chosen to ensure convergence that is smooth, and not oscillating as is the case for the CRR tree and the Edgeworth tree. Tian (1999) shows that in a tree with n time steps, the value of that ensures smooth convergence is given by

$$\lambda = \frac{\log(K/S) - (2j_0 - n)\sigma\sqrt{dt}}{n\sigma^2 dt}, \tag{3.9}$$

where

$$j_0 = \frac{\log(K/S) - n\log(d_0)}{\log(u_0/d_0)}, \tag{3.10}$$

and where u_0 and d_0 are the CRR values of the up and down moves, namely u and d defined in the previous paragraph but with $\lambda = 0$ in each. With λ specified, the values of u, d, and of the risk neutral up probability $p = (\exp(r \times dt) - d)/(u - d)$ are obtained, and the tree is constructed exactly in the same fashion as the CRR tree.

The Excel file Chapter3FlexibleBin contains the VBA function FlexBin() for implementing the flexible binomial tree. It accepts any value of the tilt parameter, except that 999 is reserved for the value of λ given by (3.9). Again, for now we ignore terms involving the option sensitivities.

```
Function FlexBin(Spot, K, T, r, sigma, n, PutCall As String, EuroAmer As
                String, Lambda)
dt = T / n: u0 = Exp(sigma * Sqr(dt))
d0 = 1 / u0
If Lambda = 999 Then
  j0 = Application.Round((Log(K / Spot) - n * Log(d0)) / Log(u0 / d0), 0)
  L = (Log(K / Spot) - (2 * j0 - n) * sigma * Sqr(dt)) / n
              / sigma ^ 2 / dt
Else
  L = Lambda
End If
u = Exp(sigma * Sqr(dt) + L * sigma ^ 2 * dt)
d = Exp(-sigma * Sqr(dt) + L * sigma ^ 2 * dt)
p = (Exp(r * dt) - d) / (u - d)
```

Figure 3.6 illustrates this function on the European put example used throughout this chapter. Specifying 999 in cell C13 sets λ to the automatic value defined in (3.9). In cell C19 we type

$$= \text{FlexBin}(S,K,T,RF,V,N,PutCall,EuroAmer,Tilt)$$

and obtain the price of a European put as \$1.9908507 with $n = 175$ time steps. When $\lambda = 0$ the function produces a price of \$1.9973022, which is exactly that obtained with the CRR tree in Figure 3.1.

Tian (1999) shows how the approximation of the flexible binomial tree can be significantly improved by extrapolating prices obtained with n and $n/2$ time steps. Denote $f_{FB}(n)$ the price of a European or American call or put obtained with the flexible binomial tree using n steps and tilt parameter λ given by (3.9). The extrapolated price $f_{EFB}(n)$ is given by

$$f_{EFB}(n) = 2f_{FB}(n) - f_{FB}(n/2). \tag{3.11}$$

The Excel file Chapter3ExtrapFlexBin contains the VBA function EFB() to generate option prices under the extrapolated flexible binomial tree, using the same European put example as in the previous sections of this chapter.

```
Function EFB(S, K, T, r, sigma, n, PutCall As String,
EuroAmer As String)
If n Mod 2 = 1 Then
  n = n + 1
```

	A	B	C	D
1				
2		**Flexible Binomial Tree Price**		
3		**for an American or European Option**		
4				
5		Spot Price (S)	30	
6		Strike Price (K)	30	
7		Years to Maturity (T)	0.4167	
8		Interest Rate (rf)	0.05	
9		Volatility (v)	0.3	
10		Steps (n)	175	
11		Type (Call or Put)	Put	
12		Option (Amer or Euro)	Euro	
13		Tilt Parameter (λ)	999	
14		λ = 0 for CRR		
15		λ > 0 for Positive Tilt		
16		λ < 0 for Negative Tilt		
17		λ = 999 for Automatic		
18				
19		**Option Price**	1.9908507	
20		**Delta (Δ)**	-0.4190189	
21		**Gamma (Γ)**	0.1368605	
22		**Theta (Θ)**	-2.4495386	
23		**Vega (V)**	-133.2072541	
24		**Rho (ρ)**	-6.0672512	
25				

FIGURE 3.6 Flexible Binomial Tree Price of European and American Options

```
End If
EFB = 2 * FlexBin(S, K, T, r, sigma, n, PutCall, EuroAmer) —
      FlexBin(S, K, T, r, sigma, n / 2, PutCall, EuroAmer)
End Function
```

The first part of the function ensures that an even number of time steps is being used, while the second uses the VBA function FlexBin() to compute the extrapolated price. The EFB() function is illustrated in Figure 3.7.

Recall that the Black Scholes price for this option is $1.99411. With only $n = 75$ steps, the extrapolated flexible binomial tree produces a price of $1.994079, which is very close to the true price.

TRINOMIAL TREE

The trinomial tree was first introduced by Boyle (1986) and is explained in the textbooks by Hull (2006) and Haug (1998). In a trinomial tree, at any node the

	A	B	C	D
1				
2		**Extrapolated Flexible Binomial Tree Price**		
3		**for an American or European Option**		
4				
5		Spot Price (S)	30	
6		Strike Price (K)	30	
7		Years to Maturity (T)	0.4167	
8		Interest Rate (rf)	0.05	
9		Volatility (v)	0.3	
10		Steps (n)	75	
11		Type (Call or Put)	Put	
12		Option (Amer or Euro)	Euro	
13				
14		**EFB Option Price**	1.994079	

FIGURE 3.7 Extrapolated Flexible Binomial Tree for European and American Options

asset price can move up or down, or stay at the same price. Trinomial trees are more flexible than binomial trees since three movements are possible rather than two. In this section we present the trinomial tree of Boyle, but other versions exist, such as that from Kamrad and Ritchken (1991). Figure 3.8 illustrates the stock price dynamics in trinomial tree, using $n = 4$ time steps.

The top portion presents the trinomial tree, while the second portion corresponds to how the prices are placed in a matrix for coding in VBA. To contain all possible price movements under a trinomial tree with n steps, we need a matrix with $2n + 1$ rows and $n + 1$ columns, corresponding to a matrix of dimension (9×5) in the Figure. Since $d = 1/u$, the stock price at node (i, j) can be written $S_{i,j} = Su^j d^i$.

In the trinomial tree, the up move increment is given by $u = \exp(\sigma \sqrt{2dt})$, the probability of an up movement by

$$p_u = \left(\frac{\exp(\frac{1}{2}rdt) - \exp(-\sigma\sqrt{\frac{1}{2}dt})}{\exp(\sigma\sqrt{\frac{1}{2}dt}) - \exp(-\sigma\sqrt{\frac{1}{2}dt})} \right)^2,$$

the probability of a down movement by

$$p_d = \left(\frac{\exp(\sigma\sqrt{\frac{1}{2}dt}) - \exp(\frac{1}{2}rdt)}{\exp(\sigma\sqrt{\frac{1}{2}dt}) - \exp(-\sigma\sqrt{\frac{1}{2}dt})} \right)^2,$$

and the probability of a lateral move by $p_m = 1 - p_u - p_d$.

To price American and European calls and puts, we proceed by working backward from the terminal prices in a fashion analogous to binomial trees, except

	A	B	C	D	E
1	0	1×dt	2×dt	3×dt	T = 4×dt
2					
3					Su^4
4					
5				Su^3	Su^3
6					
7			Su^2	Su^2	Su^2
8					
9		Su	Su	Su	Su
10					
11	S	S	S	S	S
12					
13		Sd	Sd	Sd	Sd
14					
15			Sd^2	Sd^2	Sd^2
16					
17				Sd^3	Sd^3
18					
19					Sd^4
20					
21					
22	S(1,1) = S	S(1,2) = Su	S(1,3) = Su^2	S(1,4) = Su^3	S(1,5) = Su^4
23		S(2,2) = S	S(2,3) = Su	S(2,4) = Su^2	S(2,5) = Su^3
24		S(3,2) = Sd	S(3,3) = S	S(3,4) = Su	S(3,5) = Su^2
25			S(4,3) = Sd	S(4,4) = S	S(4,5) = Su
26			S(5,3) = Sd^2	S(5,4) = Sd	S(5,5) = S
27				S(6,4) = Sd^2	S(6,5) = Sd
28				S(7,4) = Sd^3	S(7,5) = Sd^2
29					S(8,5) = Sd^3
30					S(9,5) = Sd^4

FIGURE 3.8   Stock Price Movements in the Trinomial Tree

that we work with three probabilities instead of two. For example, at node (i, j), the value of an American call with strike price K is

$$C_{i,j} = \max\{S_{i,j} - K, e^{-r \times dt}[p_u C_{i,j+1} + p_m C_{i+1,j+1} + p_d C_{i+2,j+1}]\} \qquad (3.12)$$

while the value of a European call is

$$C_{i,j} = e^{-r \times dt}[p_u C_{i,j+1} + p_m C_{i+1,j+1} + p_d C_{i+2,j+1}] \qquad (3.13)$$

 The Excel file Chapter3Trinomial contains the VBA function Trinomial() for implementing calls and puts. Again, for now we ignore option sensitivities. The function requires the same inputs as the CRR binomial tree.

```
Function Trinomial(Spot, K, T, r, v, n, PutCall As String, EuroAmer As
        String)
```

```
dt = T / n: u = Exp(v * Sqr(2 * dt)): d = 1 / u
pu = (Exp(r * dt / 2) - Exp(-v * Sqr(dt / 2))) ^ 2
   / (Exp(v * Sqr(dt / 2)) - Exp(-v * Sqr(dt / 2))) ^ 2
pd = (Exp(v * Sqr(dt / 2)) - Exp(r * dt / 2)) ^ 2
   / (Exp(v * Sqr(dt / 2)) - Exp(-v * Sqr(dt / 2))) ^ 2
pm = 1 - pu - pd
S(1, 1) = Spot
For j = 2 To (n + 1)
  For i = 1 To (2 * j - 1)
    S(i, j) = S(1, 1) * u ^ j * d ^ i
  Next i
Next j
```

The terminal values of calls and puts are obtained in the same manner as for the binomial tree.

```
For i = 1 To (2 * n + 1)
Select Case PutCall
  Case "Call"
    Op(i, n + 1) = Application.Max(S(i, n + 1) - K, 0)
  Case "Put"
    Op(i, n + 1) = Application.Max(K - S(i, n + 1), 0)
End Select
Next i
```

Working backward through the tree, the values of American and European calls and puts are coded in the array Op(), of dimension $(2n + 1, n + 1)$.

```
For j = n To 1 Step -1
For i = 1 To (2 * j - 1)
Select Case EuroAmer
Case "Amer":
  If PutCall = "Call" Then
    Op(i, j) = Application.Max(S(i, j) - K, Exp(-r * dt)
            * (pu * Op(i, j + 1) + pm * Op(i + 1, j + 1)
            + pd * Op(i + 2, j + 1)))
  ElseIf PutCall = "Put" Then
    Op(i, j) = Application.Max(K - S(i, j), Exp(-r * dt)
            * (pu * Op(i, j + 1) + pm * Op(i + 1, j + 1)
            + pd * Op(i + 2, j + 1)))
  End If
Case "Euro":
    Op(i, j) = Exp(-r * dt) * (pu * Op(i, j + 1)
        + pm * Op(i + 1, j + 1) + pd * Op(i + 2, j + 1))
End Select
Next i
Next j
```

As before, the option price is contained in Op(1,1). Figure 3.9 illustrates the trinomial tree using the VBA function Trinomial(). We use the same inputs as in the previous examples.

	A	B	C	D
1				
2		**Trinomial Tree Price for an**		
3		**American or European Option**		
4				
5		Spot Price (*S*)	30	
6		Strike Price (*K*)	30	
7		Years to Maturity (*T*)	0.4167	
8		Interest Rate (*r*)	0.05	
9		Volatility (*v*)	0.3	
10		Steps (*n*)	100	
11		Type (*Call* or *Put*)	Put	
12		Option (*Amer* or *Euro*)	Euro	
13				
14		**Option Price**	1.991228	

FIGURE 3.9 Trinomial Tree Price of European and American Options

To obtain the price of a European put, in cell C14 we type

$$= \text{Trinomial}(S, K, T, RF, V, N, PutCall, EuroAmer),$$

which produces a price of \$1.9912 when $n = 100$ steps are used. We will see in the next sections that the trinomial tree requires much fewer steps than the binomial tree to produce accurate prices.

ADAPTIVE MESH METHOD

This method is due to Figlewski and Gao (1999). The method enhances the trinomial tree by grafting a series of finer trees (meshes) at the nodes where the option payoff is linear, namely around the strike price. We will see in Chapter 8 that this method is extremely useful for obtaining prices of exotic barrier options when the barrier is close to the spot price.

The probabilities of up, down, and horizontal moves are

$$p_u = \frac{1}{2}\left(\frac{\sigma^2 k}{h^2} + \frac{\alpha^2 k^2}{h^2} + \frac{\alpha k}{h}\right), \tag{3.14}$$

$$p_d = \frac{1}{2}\left(\frac{\sigma^2 k}{h^2} + \frac{\alpha^2 k^2}{h^2} - \frac{\alpha k}{h}\right), \tag{3.15}$$

and $p_m = 1 - p_u - p_d$, where $\alpha = r - \sigma^2/2, k = T/n$ is the time increment and $h = \sigma\sqrt{3k}$ is the price increment. The coarse mesh is constructed from log prices $A_{ij} = \log S_{ij}$ as in the regular trinomial tree, using the probabilities given above. The fine mesh is constructed from the terminal nodes on the coarse mesh containing

	A	B	C	D	E
1	0	1×dt	2×dt	...	$T = n \times dt$
2					
3					$S(1,n+1) = Su^n$
4					$S(2,n+1) = Su^{n-1}$
5				...	...
6			$S(n-1,3) = Su^2$	...	$S(n-1,n+1) = Su^2$
7		$S(n,2) = Su$	$S(n,3) = Su$	...	$S(n,n+1) = Su$
8	$S(n+1,1) = S$	$S(n+1,2) = S$	$S(n+1,3) = S$	...	$S(n+1,n+1) = S$
9		$S(n+2,2) = Sd$	$S(n+2,3) = Sd$	...	$S(n+2,n+1) = Sd$
10			$S(n+3,3) = Sd^2$	...	$S(n+3,n+1) = Sd^2$
11				...	...
12					$S(2n,n+1) = Sd^{n-1}$
13					$S(2n+1,n+1) = Sd^n$

FIGURE 3.10 Price Movements in the Adaptive Mesh Method

the log of the strike price. Option prices from the fine mesh are then grafted on the coarse mesh at the second to last time step, and the option prices from the coarse mesh are obtained through the usual backward recursion to time zero. This is illustrated in Figure 2 of Figlewski and Gao (1999).

Figure 3.10 illustrates the array we use in VBA to store these movements for the AMM. For n time steps, an array with $2n + 1$ rows and $n + 1$ columns is needed.

The Excel file Chapter3TrinomialAMM contains the VBA function AMM() for implementing the adaptive mesh method. The first part of the function defines the required parameters, the coarse mesh stored in array A() and the cells surrounding the strike price, at the second to last time step.

```
Function AMM(Spot, Strike, T, r, v, n, PutCall As String, EuroAmer As
             String)
alpha = r - v ^ 2 / 2: K = T / n: h = v * Sqr(3 * K)
pu = (v ^ 2 * K / h ^ 2 + alpha ^ 2 * K ^ 2 / h ^ 2 + alpha * K / h) / 2
pd = (v ^ 2 * K / h ^ 2 + alpha ^ 2 * K ^ 2 / h ^ 2 - alpha * K / h) / 2
pm = 1 - pu - pd
logK = Log(Strike): exp_rT = Exp(-r * T / n)
A(n + 1, 1) = Log(Spot)
For j = 2 To n + 1
  For i = n - j + 2 To n + j
    A(i, j) = A(n + 1, 1) + (n - i + 1) * h
  Next i
Next j
' Identify Cells for the Fine Mesh
```

```
For i = 2 To 2 * n
  If (A(i, n) >= logK And logK >= A(i + 1, n)) Then
    Locate = i
  End If
Next i
For i = 1 To 8
  Ind(i, 2) = A(Locate - 4 + i, n + 1)
Next i
For i = 3 To 6
  Ind(i, 1) = Ind(i, 2)
Next i
```

The next part of the function defines the fine mesh, stored in array F() with 15 rows and 5 columns, imputes the log of prices for the fine mesh, and exponentiates all entries to obtain prices.

```
' Compute the Fine Mesh 15 x 5, First Column
For i = 3 To 6
  F(2 * i - 1, 1) = Ind(i, 1)
Next i
' Compute the Fine Mesh 15 x 5, Last Column
For i = 1 To 8
  F(2 * i - 1, 5) = Ind(i, 2)
Next i
' Impute Prices for the Fine Mesh, Last Column
For i = 1 To 7
  F(2 * i, 5) = F(2 * i - 1, 5) - h / 2
Next i
' Impute Prices for the Fine Mesh, Remaining Columns
For j = 4 To 2 Step -1
  For i = 6 - j To 10 + j
    If F(i, j + 1) <> 0 Then F(i, j) = F(i, j + 1)
  Next i
Next j
' Convert to Prices
Dim expF(), S() As Double
ReDim expF(15, 5), S(2 * n + 1, n + 1) As Double
For j = 1 To 5
  For i = 1 To 15
    If F(i, j) <> 0 Then expF(i, j) = Exp(F(i, j))
    End If
  Next i
Next j
For j = 1 To n + 1
  For i = 1 To 2 * n + 1
    If A(i, j) <> 0 Then S(i, j) = Exp(A(i, j))
    End If
  Next i
Next j
```

Next, the option prices along the fine mesh, stored in array FineOp(), and along the coarse mesh for the last two time steps only and stored in array Op(), are obtained. The prices on the first time step of the fine mesh are grafted onto the second to last time step of the coarse mesh, for nodes identified around the strike price with the variable Locate defined above. To conserve space, we include the code for a European call only.

```
' Option Prices for Fine Mesh
For i = 1 To 15
  FineOp(i, 5) = Application.Max(expF(i, 5) - Strike, 0)
Next i
For j = 4 To 1 Step -1
For i = 6 - j To 10 + j
  FineOp(i, j) = exp_rT * (pu * FineOp(i - 1, j + 1)
      + pm * FineOp(i, j + 1) + pd * FineOp(i + 1, j + 1))
Next i
Next j
' Option Prices for Coarse Mesh
' Last two Time Steps
For i = 1 To 2 * n + 1
  Op(i, n + 1) = Application.Max(S(i, n + 1) - Strike, 0)
Next i
For i = 2 To 2 * n
  Op(i, n) = exp_rT * (pu * Op(i - 1, n + 1) + pm *
          Op(i, n + 1) + pd * Op(i + 1, n + 1))
Next i
' Impute Option Prices from Fine Mesh
' At Second to Last Step
Op(Locate - 1, n) = FineOp(5, 1)
Op(Locate, n) = FineOp(7, 1)
Op(Locate + 1, n) = FineOp(9, 1)
Op(Locate + 2, n) = FineOp(11, 1)
' Obtain remaining prices on Coarse mesh
For j = n - 1 To 1 Step -1
For i = n - j + 2 To n + j
  Op(i, j) = exp_rT * (pu * Op(i - 1, j + 1)
          + pm * Op(i, j + 1) + pd * Op(i + 1, j + 1))
Next i
Next j
AMM = Op(n + 1, 1)
```

The option price is stored in Op(n+1,1). The code for the AMM() function also includes a provision to price American options. For these options, the Op() array is constructed using (3.12) instead of (3.13). Figure 3.11 illustrates the adaptive mesh method, using the same inputs as before. The figure represents the Excel file Chapter3TrinomialAMM.

In cell C14 we type

$$= AMM(S,K,T,RF,V,N,PutCall,EuroAmer)$$

to obtain the AMM price of $1.99380 with $n = 500$ time steps. Finally, we note that it is possible to enhance the accuracy of the adaptive mesh method, by progressively

	A	B	C	D	E
1					
2		**Adaptive Mesh Method for an American or European Option**			
3		**Trinomial Tree With One Grafted Level**			
4					
5		Spot Price (*S*)	30		
6		Strike Price (*K*)	30		
7		Years to Maturity (*T*)	0.4167		
8		Interest Rate (*r*)	0.05		
9		Volatility (*v*)	0.3		
10		Steps (*n*)	500		
11		Type (*Call* or *Put*)	Put		
12		Option (*Amer* or *Euro*)	Euro		
13					
14		**Option Price**	1.99380		
15					
16		**Black-Scholes Price**	1.99410		

FIGURE 3.11 Adaptive Mesh Method Price of European and American Options

grafting a series of meshes on the fine mesh. In this book, however, we only use one level of grafting.

COMPARING TREES

In this section we compare the convergence of a European put option, priced using many of the models covered in this chapter, to the Black-Scholes price. We use a spot price of $S = 30$, a strike price $K = 30$, time to maturity $T = 5$ months, an annual risk-free rate of $r = 0.05$, and a stock volatility of $\sigma = 0.30$. The number of steps range from $n = 15$ to $n = 500$. The results are in the Excel file Chapter3CompareBinTri and appear in Figure 3.12.

The Black-Scholes price for this option is $1.99410. The binomial tree and Edgeworth binomial tree with kurtosis equal to three (cell C13) and skewness equal to zero (cell C12) show a similar convergence pattern. The trinomial tree and the AMM also converge together, although the AMM produces better approximations at all time steps. All methods, however, pale in comparison to the Leisen-Reimer tree. Indeed, this method produces approximations that are virtually indistinguishable from the Black-Scholes price beyond $n = 100$ steps.

Also noteworthy is the behavior of the flexible binomial tree. While it does not produce values that converge to the Black-Scholes price faster than those of the CRR tree, clearly its convergence is smooth and not oscillating, unlike the CRR or Edgeworth trees. The extrapolated flexible binomial tree produces approximations that are erratic at first, but that converge very quickly once the number of time steps is increased.

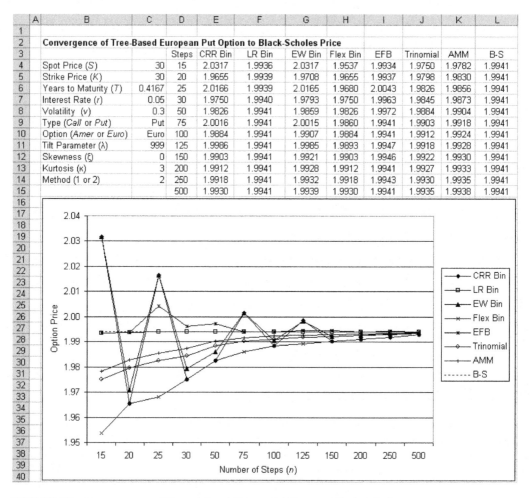

	A	B	C	D	E	F	G	H	I	J	K	L
1												
2		**Convergence of Tree-Based European Put Option to Black-Scholes Price**										
3				Steps	CRR Bin	LR Bin	EW Bin	Flex Bin	EFB	Trinomial	AMM	B-S
4		Spot Price (S)	30	15	2.0317	1.9936	2.0317	1.9537	1.9934	1.9750	1.9782	1.9941
5		Strike Price (K)	30	20	1.9655	1.9939	1.9708	1.9655	1.9937	1.9798	1.9830	1.9941
6		Years to Maturity (T)	0.4167	25	2.0166	1.9939	2.0165	1.9680	2.0043	1.9826	1.9856	1.9941
7		Interest Rate (r)	0.05	30	1.9750	1.9940	1.9793	1.9750	1.9963	1.9845	1.9873	1.9941
8		Volatility (v)	0.3	50	1.9826	1.9941	1.9859	1.9826	1.9972	1.9884	1.9904	1.9941
9		Type (Call or Put)	Put	75	2.0016	1.9941	2.0015	1.9860	1.9941	1.9903	1.9918	1.9941
10		Option (Amer or Euro)	Euro	100	1.9884	1.9941	1.9907	1.9884	1.9941	1.9912	1.9924	1.9941
11		Tilt Parameter (λ)	999	125	1.9986	1.9941	1.9985	1.9893	1.9947	1.9918	1.9928	1.9941
12		Skewness (ξ)	0	150	1.9903	1.9941	1.9921	1.9903	1.9946	1.9922	1.9930	1.9941
13		Kurtosis (κ)	3	200	1.9912	1.9941	1.9928	1.9912	1.9941	1.9927	1.9933	1.9941
14		Method (1 or 2)	2	250	1.9918	1.9941	1.9932	1.9918	1.9943	1.9930	1.9935	1.9941
15				500	1.9930	1.9941	1.9939	1.9930	1.9941	1.9935	1.9938	1.9941

FIGURE 3.12   Convergence of Binomial and Trinomial Trees to Black-Scholes

IMPLIED VOLATILITY TREES

In this section we present the implied binomial tree of Derman and Kani (1994) and the implied trinomial tree of Derman, Kani, and Chriss (1996). The main advantage of these trees is that volatility smiles are accounted for in the option price. Volatility smiles will be discussed thoroughly in Chapter 10. These trees are constructed forward in time from the first step to the last step. At each step the stock prices above and below the current node are implied, based on past stock prices, prices of futures on the stock, prices of Arrow-Debreu securities, and prices of put and call options. The option prices are preferably market prices, but prices from the

Black-Scholes formula or from the binomial or trinomial tree can also be used. In this chapter we use prices from the CRR binomial tree.

Implied Volatility Binomial Tree

The left part of Figure 3.13 shows the notation for stock price movements in the implied binomial tree from step n to step $n + 1$, while the right part shows how these movements are represented in a matrix for coding in VBA. We use the VBA coding in the formulas we present for the implied binomial and trinomial trees. More detailed notation can be found in the textbook by Haug (1998). The tree is explained fully in the textbook by Chriss (1997).

At time zero ($j = 1$) the price of the Arrow-Debreu security is $\lambda_{1,1} = 1$, the spot price is $S_{1,1} = S$, and the forward price is $F_{1,1} = Se^{r \times dt}$, where $dt = T/n$ is the time increment and r is the risk-free rate. At each time step j, stock prices at the central node are obtained first, working from step $j - 1$. For odd time steps j, the price at the central node $S_{(j+1)/2,j}$ is the spot price S. For even time steps, the upper central node is

$$S_{j/2,j} = \frac{S(e^{rdt}C(S,t_{j-1}) + \lambda_{j/2,j}S - \Sigma)}{\lambda_{j/2,j-1}F_{j/2,j-1} - e^{rdt}C(S,t_{j-1}) + \Sigma} \tag{3.16}$$

where $F_{j/2,j-1} = S_{j/2,j-1}e^{rdt}$ is the forward price of $S_{j/2,j-1} = S$, $\lambda_{j/2,j-1}$ is the price of the Arrow-Debreu security, $C(S,t_{j-1})$ is the price of a European call with strike equal to the spot price S and with volatility at node ($\frac{j}{2}, j - 1$) and time to maturity $t_{j-1} = (j - 1) \times dt$, and where

$$\Sigma = \sum_{k=1}^{j/2-1} \lambda_{k,j-1}(F_{k,j-1} - S_{j/2,j-1}). \tag{3.17}$$

	A	B	C	D	E
1	step n	step $n+1$		step $j-1$	step j
2					
3					
4					
5		S_{i+2}		$S(i-1,j-1)$ ⟶	$S(i-1,j)$
6	S_{i+1}				
7					
8		S_{i+1}		$S(i,j-1)$ ⟶	$S(i,j)$
9	S_i				
10		S_i			$S(i+1,j)$
11					

FIGURE 3.13 Stock Price Movements in the Implied Volatility Binomial Tree

In this last expression, the sum runs over all nodes above $S_{j/2,j-1}$. The price at the bottom central node is then given by $S_{j/2+1,j} = S^2/S_{j/2,j}$.

Once the prices of the central node or the two central nodes are obtained, the prices above the central node(s) are obtained using call prices as

$$S_{i,j} = \frac{S_{i+1,j}(e^{rdt}C(S_{i,j-1}, t_{j-1}) - \Sigma) + \lambda_{i,j-1}S_{i,j-1}(F_{i,j-1} - S_{i+1,j})}{e^{rdt}C(S_{i,j-1}, t_{j-1}) - \Sigma - \lambda_{i,j-1}(F_{i,j-1} - S_{i+1,j})} \qquad (3.18)$$

where $C(S_{i,j-1}, t_{j-1})$ is the price of a European call with strike $S_{i,j-1}$, with volatility at node $(i, j-1)$, and with time to maturity $t_{j-1} = (j-1)dt$, and where

$$\Sigma = \sum_{k=1}^{i-1} \lambda_{k,j-1}(F_{k,j-1} - S_{i,j-1}).$$

In this last expression, the sum runs over all nodes above $S_{i,j-1}$. Prices below the central node(s) are obtained using put prices

$$S_{i,j} = \frac{S_{i-1,j}(e^{rdt}P(S_{i-1,j-1}, t_{j-1}) - \Sigma) + \lambda_{i-1,j-1}S_{i-1,j-1}(F_{i-1,j-1} - S_{i-1,j})}{e^{rdt}P(S_{i-1,j-1}, t_{j-1}) + \Sigma - \lambda_{i-1,j-1}(F_{i-1,j-1} - S_{i-1,j})},$$

where $P(S_{i-1,j-1}, t_{j-1})$ is the price of a European put option with strike price $S_{i-1,j-1}$, volatility at node $(i-1, j-1)$, and time to maturity $t_{j-1} = j-1$. The Σ term is now

$$\Sigma = \sum_{k=1}^{j-1} \lambda_{k,j-1}(S_{i-1,j-1} - F_{k,j-1}),$$

where the summation runs over all nodes below $S_{i-1,j-1}$.

Once all prices at time step $n+1$ are obtained, the forward prices, transition probabilities, Arrow-Debreu prices, and volatilities can be updated. The forward prices are given as $F_{i,j} = S_{i,j}e^{rdt}$ and the no-arbitrage condition on prices is imposed so that if the condition $F_{i,j-1} < S_{i,j} < F_{i-1,j-1}$ does not hold, the stock price is changed to $S_{i,j} = S_{i-1,j-1}S_{i+1,j}/S_{i,j-1}$. The transition probabilities from $S_{i,j-1}$ to $S_{i,j}$ are obtained as $p_{i,j-1} = (F_{i,j-1} - S_{i+1,j})/(S_{i,j} - S_{i+1,j})$ for $i = 1, \ldots, j-1$, while the Arrow-Debreu prices as

$$\lambda_{i,j} = \begin{cases} p_{1,j-1}\lambda_{1,j-1}e^{-rdt} & \text{if } i = 1 \\ ((1 - p_{i-1,j-1})\lambda_{i-1,j-1} + p_{i,j-1}\lambda_{i,j-1})e^{-rdt} & \text{if } 1 < i < j \\ (1 - p_{j-1,j-1})\lambda_{j-1,j-1}e^{-rdt} & \text{if } i = j. \end{cases}$$

The volatility is updated to $v_{i,j} = v_{1,1} - \text{Skew}\,(S_{i,j} - S_{1,1})/10$, where Skew is the amount of change in volatility for every 10-point change in the stock price, and $v_{1,1}$

is the initial volatility. Once the entire tree is constructed, the implied volatility at node (i, j) is

$$\text{IV}_{i,j} = \sqrt{\frac{p_{i,j}(1 - p_{i,j})}{dt}} \frac{\ln(S_{i,j+1})}{S_{i+1,j+1}}.$$

The Excel file Chapter3DKBinomial contains the VBA function DKBinomial() for calculating option prices from the Derman-Kani implied binomial tree. The first part of the function initializes the arrays and inputs their values at time zero.

```
Function DKBinomial(Spot, Strike, T, r, sV, n, Skew, PutCall
As String)
dt = T / n: u = Exp(sV * Sqr(dt)): d = 1 / u: m = T + 1
S(1, 1) = Spot: F(1, 1) = S(1, 1) * Exp(r)
v(1, 1) = sV: A(1, 1) = 1
```

The Derman-Kani algorithm is started at the first time step, corresponding to $j = 2$. The algorithm calculates the value of the stock price $S_{i,j}$ at each node. The prices of European call and put options are obtained using the CRR binomial tree with the VBA function Fbinomial(). This function is similar to the VBA function Binomial() described in Section 3.1, except that Fbinomial() is used only to price European options.

Stock prices at the central nodes are obtained first, and prices at the upper and lower nodes are obtained afterward.

```
For j = 2 To m
'Even Steps: Centering Condition on Two Central Nodes
If j Mod 2 = 0 Then
 Ca = fbinomial(Spot, S(j / 2, j - 1), r, v(j / 2, j - 1), dt,
               (j - 1), "C")
 Eu = 0
 For K = 1 To j / 2 - 1
   Eu = Eu + A(K, j - 1) * (F(K, j - 1) - S(j / 2, j - 1))
 Next K
 num_u = Spot * (Exp(r) * Ca + A(j / 2, j - 1) * Spot - Eu)
 den_u = A(j / 2, j - 1) * F(j / 2, j - 1) - Exp(r) * Ca + Eu
 S(j / 2, j) = num_u / den_u
 S(j / 2 + 1, j) = Spot ^ 2 / S(j / 2, j)
End If
'Odd Steps: Center Node is Spot Price
If j Mod 2 = 1 Then
  S((j + 1) / 2, j) = Spot
End If
'Calculate Upper Nodes
For i = (j - 2 + (j Mod 2)) / 2 To 1 Step -1
 Ca = fbinomial(Spot, S(i, j - 1), r, v(i, j - 1), dt, (j - 1), "C")
 Eu = 0
```

```
      For K = 1 To i - 1
        Eu = Eu + A(K, j - 1) * (F(K, j - 1) - S(i, j - 1))
      Next K
      num_u = S(i + 1, j) * (Exp(r) * Ca - Eu) - A(i, j - 1)
             * S(i, j - 1) * (F(i, j - 1) - S(i + 1, j))
      den_u = (Exp(r) * Ca - Eu) - A(i, j - 1)
             * (F(i, j - 1) - S(i + 1, j))
      S(i, j) = num_u / den_u
    Next i
    'Calculate Lower Nodes
    For i = (j + 4 - (j Mod 2)) / 2 To j
      Pu = fbinomial(Spot, S(i - 1, j - 1), r, v(i - 1, j - 1),
           dt, (j - 1), "P")
      Ed = 0
      For K = i To (j - 1)
        Ed = Ed - A(K, j - 1) * (F(K, j - 1) - S(i - 1, j - 1))
      Next K
      num_d = S(i - 1, j) * (Exp(r) * Pu - Ed) + A(i - 1, j - 1)
             * S(i - 1, j - 1) * (F(i - 1, j - 1) - S(i - 1, j))
      den_d = (Exp(r) * Pu - Ed) + A(i - 1, j - 1)
             * (F(i - 1, j - 1) - S(i - 1, j))
      S(i, j) = num_d / den_d
    Next i
```

At each time step, the forward prices $F_{i,j}$ are updated and the no-arbitrage condition is imposed, and the probabilities $p_{i,j}$, the Arrow-Debreu prices $A_{i,j}$, and volatility $v_{i,j}$ are all updated.

```
For i = 1 To j
  F(j - i + 1, j) = S(j - i + 1, j) * Exp(r)
  If j >= 3 And i >= 2 And i <= j - 1 Then
    If ((F(i, j - 1) > S(i, j))
      Or (F(i - 1, j - 1) < S(i, j)))
    Then
      S(i, j) = S(i - 1, j - 1) * S(i + 1, j) / S(i, j - 1)
    End If
  End If
Next i
For i = 1 To j - 1
  P(j - i, j - 1) = (F(j - i, j - 1) - S(j - i + 1, j))
                   / (S(j - i, j) - S(j - i + 1, j))
  If P(j - i, j - 1) > 1 Or P(j - i, j - 1) < 0
  Then P(j - i, j - 1) = (Exp(r * dt) - d) / (u - d)
Next i
A(1, j) = P(1, j - 1) * A(1, j - 1) * Exp(-r * dt)
A(j, j) = (1 - P(j - 1, j - 1)) * A(j - 1, j - 1) * Exp(-r * dt)
For i = 2 To j - 1
  A(i, j) = ((1 - P(i - 1, j - 1)) * A(i - 1, j - 1)
          + P(i, j - 1) * A(i, j - 1)) * Exp(-r * dt)
Next i
For i = 1 To j
  v(i, j) = v(1, 1) - Skew * (S(i, j) - S(1, 1)) / 10
```

```
Next i
Next j      ' End of Derman-Kani Algorithm
```

The implied volatilities are then calculated using the logarithm of the stock prices and the probabilities.

```
For j = 1 To m - 1
 For i = 1 To j
  IV(i, j) = Sqr(P(i, j) * (1 - P(i, j))) * Log(S(i, j + 1)
          / S(i + 1, j + 1)) / Sqr(dt)
 Next i
Next j
```

Finally, the prices of calls and puts are calculated by working backward through the stock prices, and stored in array Op().

```
For i = 1 To m
Select Case PutCall
  Case "Call"
    Op(i, m) = Application.Max(S(i, m) - Strike, 0)
  Case "Put"
    Op(i, m) = Application.Max(Strike - S(i, m), 0)
End Select
Next i
For j = m - 1 To 1 Step -1
For i = 1 To j
  Pr = P(i, j)
  Op(i, j) = Exp(-r * dt) * (Pr * Op(i, j + 1) + (1 - Pr)
            * Op(i + 1, j + 1))
 Next i
Next j
```

As before, the option price is stored in Op(1,1). The DKBinomial() function is illustrated in Figure 3.14 on a European call. We use a spot price of $S = 30$, a strike price of $K = 30$, $T = 5$ years to maturity, $n = 5$ steps, a risk-free rate of $r = 5$ percent, initial stock volatility of $v = 15$ percent, and a skew of $c = 0.05$ that causes volatility to rise (fall) by 5 percent for every 10-point decrease (increase) in the stock price.

In cell C14 we type

$$= \text{DKBinomial}(S,K,T,RF,V,N,\text{Skew},\text{PutCall}),$$

which produces $6.8910 for the call price. The price of a European put is $2.3115. If we set $c = 0$ so that constant volatility is assumed, we obtain the prices of a call and a put as $7.8502 and $1.2142, respectively. By comparison, the Black-Scholes prices of the call and put are $7.8006 and $1.1647.

	A	B	C	D	E	F
1						
2		**Derman-Kani Implied Binomial Tree Price of a European Option**				
3						
4		Spot Price (S)	30			
5		Strike Price (K)	30			
6		Years to Maturity (T)	5			
7		Interest Rate (r)	0.05			
8		Initial Volatility (v)	0.15			
9		Steps (n)	5			
10		Volatility Skew (c)	0.05			
11		Type (Call or Put)	Call			
12						
13						
14		**Option Price**	6.8910			

FIGURE 3.14   Implied Volatility Binomial Tree Price of European Options

Implied Volatility Trinomial Tree

The main disadvantage of the Derman-Kani implied binomial tree is that negative probabilities and probabilities outside of the unit interval can be produced. This is possible even when the no-arbitrage condition is imposed, since this condition does not act on prices at cells at the uppermost and lowermost nodes at each time step. Obtaining negative probabilities can lead to negative stock and option prices and implied volatilities that take on imaginary values.

The implied volatility trinomial tree of Derman, Kani, and Chriss (1996) is much better suited to producing option prices, and it is easier to implement in VBA than the Derman-Kani implied binomial tree. As in the trinomial tree of Boyle (1986), three price movements are possible at each node. The left part of Figure 3.15 presents the notation for stock price movements from step n to step $n+1$, while the right part shows how these movements are represented in a matrix for coding in VBA along with the transition probabilities. At node (i, j) the probability of an up move to $(i, j+1)$ is $p_{i,j}$, the probability of a down move to $(i+2, j+1)$ is $q_{i,j}$, and the probability of a lateral move to $(i+1, j+1)$ is $1 - p_{i,j} - q_{i,j}$.

In the Derman-Kani-Chriss implied trinomial tree, stock prices are obtained using the trinomial tree described earlier in this chapter. At node (i, j) the forward price is obtained as $F_{i,j} = S_{i,j} e^{r \times dt}$ and the volatility as $v_{i,j} = v_{1,1} - \text{Skew}(S_{i,j} - S_{1,1})/10$. We use the trinomial tree to also obtain prices of European calls and puts for the implied trinomial tree. At time zero $(j = 1)$ the Arrow-Debreu price is $\lambda_{1,1} = 1$, the probability of a down move is

$$q_{1,1} = \frac{e^{rdt} P(S_{1,1}, t_1)}{\lambda_{1,1}(S_{2,2} - S_{3,2})},$$

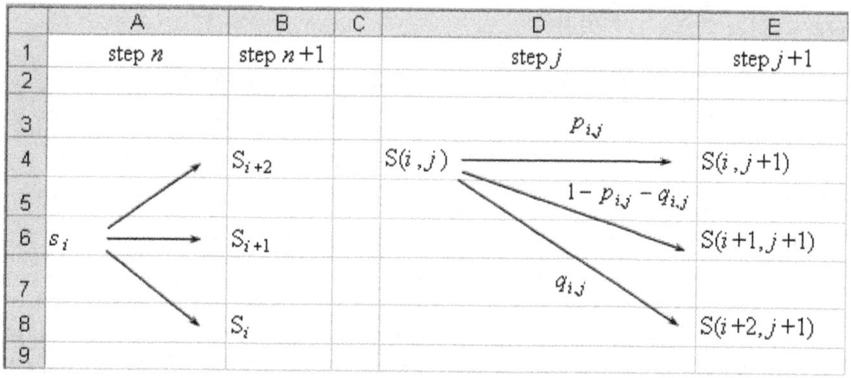

	A	B	C	D	E
1	step n	step $n+1$		step j	step $j+1$
2					
3				$p_{i,j}$	
4		S_{i+2}	$S(i,j)$	$\longrightarrow$	$S(i,j+1)$
5				$1-p_{i,j}-q_{i,j}$	
6	s_i	S_{i+1}			$S(i+1,j+1)$
7				$q_{i,j}$	
8		S_i			$S(i+2,j+1)$
9					

FIGURE 3.15 Stock Price Movements in the Implied Volatility Trinomial Tree

and the probability of an up move is

$$p_{1,1} = \frac{F_{1,1} + q_{1,1}(S_{2,2} - S_{3,2}) - S_{2,2}}{S_{1,2} - S_{2,2}},$$

where $P(S_{1,1}, t_1)$ is the price of a European call with spot price $S_{1,1}$, strike price $S_{1,1}$, maturity $t_1 = dt$ (where $dt = T/n$), risk-free rate r, volatility $v_{1,1}$, obtained with the trinomial tree with $n = 1$ steps. The Arrow-Debreu prices are updated at time 1 ($j = 2$) as $\lambda_{1,2} = p_{1,1}\lambda_{1,1}e^{-rdt}$, $\lambda_{2,2} = (1 - p_{1,1} - q_{1,1})\lambda_{1,1}e^{-rdt}$, and $\lambda_{3,2} = q_{1,1}\lambda_{1,1}e^{-rdt}$.

At time j, probabilities at nodes on the center of the tree and below are given by

$$q_{i,j} = \frac{e^{rdt}P(S_{i,j}, t_j) - \Sigma}{\lambda_{i,j}(S_{i+1,j+1} - S_{i+2,j+1})}$$

and

$$p_{i,j} = \frac{F_{i,j} + q_{i,j}(S_{i+1,j+1} - S_{i+2,j+1}) - S_{i+1,j+1}}{S_{i,j+1} - S_{i+1,j+1}},$$

where $P(S_{i,j}, t_j)$ is the price of a European call with spot price $S_{1,1}$, strike price $S_{i,j}$, maturity $t_j = j \times dt$, and volatility $v_{i,j}$, using $n = j$ time steps. If either probability lies outside the unit interval, the probabilities are changed to

$$p_{i,j} = \frac{1}{2}\left(\frac{F_{i,j} - S_{i+1,j+1}}{S_{i,j+1} - S_{i+1,j+1}} + \frac{F_{i,j} - S_{i+2,j+1}}{S_{i,j+1} - S_{i+2,j+1}}\right)$$

and

$$q_{i,j} = \frac{1}{2}\left(\frac{S_{i,j+1} - F_{i,j}}{S_{i,j+1} - S_{i+2,j+1}}\right)$$

when $S_{i+1,j+1} < F_{i,j} < S_{i,j+1}$, and to

$$p_{i,j} = \frac{1}{2}\left(\frac{S_{i,j+1} - F_{i,j}}{S_{i,j+1} - S_{i+2,j+1}} + \frac{S_{i+1,j+1} - F_{i,j}}{S_{i+1,j+1} - S_{i+2,j+1}}\right)$$

and

$$q_{i,j} = \frac{1}{2}\left(\frac{F_{i,j} - S_{i+2,j+1}}{S_{i,j+1} - S_{i+2,j+1}}\right)$$

when $S_{i+2,j+1} < F_{i,j} < S_{i+1,j+1}$. Arrow-Debreu prices are more complicated to update than in the implied binomial tree. Since each node can be reached from three separate nodes in the previous time step, at each time step we need a separate expression for Arrow-Debreu prices at the top two nodes ($i = 1$ and $i = 2$), the bottom two nodes ($i = 2j$ and $i = 2j + 1$), and all nodes in between ($2 < i < 2j$).

$$\lambda_{i,j+1} = \begin{cases} p_{1,j}\lambda_{1,j}e^{-rdt} & \text{if } i = 1 \\ (p_{2,j}\lambda_{2,j} + (1 - p_{1,j} - q_{1,j})\lambda_{1,j})e^{-rdt} & \text{if } i = 2 \\ (q_{i-2,j}\lambda_{i-2,j} + p_{i,j}\lambda_{i,j} + (1 - p_{i-1,j} - q_{i-1,j})\lambda_{i-1,j})e^{-rdt} & \text{if } 2 < i < 2j \\ (q_{2j-2,j}\lambda_{2j-j,j} + (1 - p_{2j-1,j} - q_{2j-1,j})\lambda_{2j-1,j})e^{-rdt} & \text{if } i = 2j \\ q_{2j-1,j}\lambda_{2j-1,j}e^{-rdt} & \text{if } i = 2j + 1. \end{cases}$$

Once the tree is completed, the implied volatilities are obtained as

$$\text{IV}_{i,j} = \sqrt{\frac{p_{i,j}(S_{i,j+1} - F_0)^2 + (1 - p_{i,j} - q_{i,j})(S_{i+1,j+1} - F_0)^2 + q_{i,j}(S_{i+2,j+1} - F_0)^2}{F_0^2\, dt}},$$

where

$$F_0 = [p_{i,j}S_{i,j+1} + (1 - p_{i,j} - q_{i,j})S_{i+1,j+1} + q_{i,j}S_{i+2,j+1}]e^{rdt}.$$

The Excel file Chapter3DKCTrinomial contains the VBA function DKCTrinomial() for implementing the implied trinomial tree. The first part of the function creates the stock prices $S_{i,j}$, the forward prices $F_{i,j}$, and the volatility structure $v_{i,j}$, which imposes a change in volatility by an amount specified by the variable skew.

```
Function DKCTrinomial(Spot, Strike, T, r, v, n, skew, PutCall As String)
dt = T / n: u = Exp(v * Sqr(2 * dt)): d = 1 / u
pu = (Exp(r * dt / 2) - Exp(-v * Sqr(dt / 2))) ^ 2
    / (Exp(v * Sqr(dt / 2)) - Exp(-v * Sqr(dt / 2))) ^ 2
pd = (Exp(v * Sqr(dt / 2)) - Exp(b * dt / 2)) ^ 2
    / (Exp(v * Sqr(dt / 2)) - Exp(-v * Sqr(dt / 2))) ^ 2
```

```
pm = 1 - pu - pd
S(1, 1) = Spot
For j = 2 To (n + 1)
  For i = 1 To (2 * j - 1)
    S(i, j) = S(1, 1) * u ^ j * d ^ i
  Next i
Next j
F(1, 1) = Spot * Exp(r * dt)
For j = 2 To (n + 1)
  For i = 1 To (2 * j - 1)
    F(i, j) = S(i, j) * Exp(r * dt)
  Next i
Next j
For j = 1 To (n + 1)
  For i = 1 To (2 * j - 1)
    vol(i, j) = v * skew * (S(i, j) - Spot) / 100
  Next i
Next j
```

The Arrow-Debreu securities prices and the probabilities of up and down moves are initialized at time steps zero and one.

```
AD(1, 1) = 1
q(1, 1) = Exp(r * dt) * EuroTri(Spot, S(1, 1), 1 * dt, r,
    vol(1, 1), 1, "Put") / AD(1, 1) / (S(2, 2) - S(3, 2))
p(1, 1) = (F(1, 1) + q(1, 1) * (S(2, 2) - S(3, 2))
        - S(2, 2)) / (S(1, 2) - S(2, 2))
AD(1, 2) = p(1, 1) * AD(1, 1) * Exp(-r * dt)
AD(2, 2) = (1 - p(1, 1) - q(1, 1)) * AD(1, 1) * Exp(-r * dt)
AD(3, 2) = q(1, 1) * AD(1, 1) * Exp(-r * dt)
```

The Arrow-Debreu prices and probabilities are then obtained at the remaining time steps in the "j" loop. The first "i" loop calculates the nodes at the center of the tree and below, while the second loop calculates nodes above the center of the tree. European calls and puts are obtained using the trinomial tree with the VBA function EuroTri() that uses volatility from the array Vol() described above.

```
For j = 2 To n
For i = j To 2 * j - 1
 E = 0
 For K = i + 1 To 2 * j - 1
   E = E + AD(K, j) * (S(i, j) - F(K, j))
 Next K
q(i, j) = (Exp(r * dt) * EuroTri(Spot, S(i, j), j * dt, r,
            vol(i, j), j, "Put") - E) / AD(i, j)
        / (S(i + 1, j + 1) - S(i + 2, j + 1))
p(i, j) = (F(i, j) + q(i, j) * (S(i + 1, j + 1)
        - S(i + 2, j + 1)) - S(i + 1, j + 1))
        / (S(i, j + 1) - S(i + 1, j + 1))
```

```
If q(i, j) <= 0 Or q(i, j) >= 1 Or p(i, j) <= 0
 Or p(i, j) >= 1 Then
  F1 = F(i, j)
  S0 = S(i, j + 1)
  S1 = S(i + 1, j + 1)
  S2 = S(i + 2, j + 1)
  If S1 < F1 And F1 < S0 Then
    p(i, j) = ((F1 - S1) / (S0 - S1) + (F1 - S2) / (S0 - S2)) / 2
    q(i, j) = (S0 - F1) / (S0 - S2) / 2
  ElseIf S2 < F1 And F1 < S1 Then
    p(i, j) = ((S0 - F1) / (S0 - S2) + (S1 - F1) / (S1 - S2)) / 2
    q(i, j) = (F1 - S2) / (S0 - S2) / 2
  End If
End If
Next i
For i = 1 To j - 1
 E = 0
 For K = 1 To i - 1
  E = E - AD(K, j) * (S(i, j) - F(K, j))
 Next K
 p(i, j) = (Exp(r * dt) * EuroTri(Spot, S(i, j), j * dt, r,
          vol(i, j), j, "Call") - E) / AD(i, j)
         / (S(i, j + 1) - S(i + 1, j + 1))
 q(i, j) = (F(i, j) - p(i, j) * (S(i, j + 1)
         - S(i + 1, j + 1)) - S(i + 1, j + 1))
         / (S(i + 2, j + 1) - S(i + 1, j + 1))
 If q(i, j) <= 0 Or q(i, j) >= 1 Or p(i, j) <= 0
  Or p(i, j) >= 1 Then
    F1 = F(i, j): S0 = S(i, j + 1)
    S1 = S(i + 1, j + 1): S2 = S(i + 2, j + 1)
    If S1 < F1 And F1 < S0 Then
     p(i, j) = ((F1 - S1) / (S0 - S1) + (F1 - S2) / (S0 - S2)) / 2
     q(i, j) = (S0 - F1) / (S0 - S2) / 2
    ElseIf S2 < F1 And F1 < S1 Then
     p(i, j) = ((S0 - F1) / (S0 - S2) + (S1 - F1) / (S1 - S2)) / 2
     q(i, j) = (F1 - S2) / (S0 - S2) / 2
    End If
 End If
Next i
```

This loop updates the prices of the Arrow-Debreu securities.

```
For i = 1 To 2 * j + 1
 If i = 1 Then
  AD(i, j + 1) = p(i, j) * AD(i, j) * Exp(-r * dt)
 ElseIf i = 2 Then
  AD(i, j + 1) = (p(i, j) * AD(i, j) + (1 - p(i - 1, j)
          - q(i - 1, j)) * AD(i - 1, j)) * Exp(-r * dt)
 ElseIf i = 2 * j Then
  AD(i, j + 1) = (q(2 * j - 2, j) * AD(2 * j - 2, j)
          + (1 - p(2 * j - 1, j) - q(2 * j - 1, j))
          * AD(2 * j - 1, j)) * Exp(-r * dt)
```

```
ElseIf i = 2 * j + 1 Then
 AD(i, j + 1) = q(2 * j - 1, j) * AD(2 * j - 1, j) * Exp(-r * dt)
Else
 AD(i, j + 1) = (q(i - 2, j) * AD(i - 2, j) + p(i, j)
              * AD(i, j) + (1 - p(i - 1, j) - q(i - 1, j))
              * AD(i - 1, j)) * Exp(-r * dt)
End If
Next i
Next j
```

The next loop calculates the implied volatilities $IV_{i,j}$ from the stock prices and probabilities.

```
IV(1, 1) = v
For j = 2 To n
  For i = 1 To 2 * j - 1
    pu = p(i, j): pd = q(i, j): pm = 1 - pu - pd
    FO = (pu * S(i, j + 1) + pm * S(i + 1, j + 1)
       + pd * S(i + 2, j + 1)) * Exp(r * dt)
    IV(i, j) = Sqr((pu * (S(i, j + 1) - FO) ^ 2
              + pm * (S(i + 1, j + 1) - FO) ^ 2
              + pd * (S(i + 2, j + 1) - FO) ^ 2)
              / (FO ^ 2 * dt))
  Next i
Next j
```

Finally, the prices of European calls and puts are obtained. The probabilities of up and down moves are not constant, so at each time step we set these to $p_{i,j}$ and $q_{i,j}$.

```
For i = 1 To (2 * n + 1)
Select Case PutCall
  Case "Call"
    Op(i, n + 1) = Application.Max(S(i, n + 1) - Strike, 0)
  Case "Put"
    Op(i, n + 1) = Application.Max(Strike - S(i, n + 1), 0)
End Select
Next i
For j = n To 1 Step -1
For i = 1 To 2 * j - 1
  pu = p(i, j): pd = q(i, j): pm = 1 - p(i, j) - q(i, j)
  Op(i, j) = Exp(-r * dt) * (pu * Op(i, j + 1)
         + pm * Op(i + 1, j + 1) + pd * Op(i + 2, j + 1))
Next i
Next j
```

The prices of European calls and puts obtained from the implied trinomial tree are contained in Op(1,1). Note that the end of the function DKCTrinomial() is slightly different since it outputs also the sensitivities calculated from these options. These sensitivities will be examined in Chapter 7.

	A	B	C	D
1				
2		**Derman-Kani-Chriss Implied Trinomial Tree**		
3		**Price for a European Option**		
4				
5		Spot Price (S)	30	
6		Strike Price (K)	30	
7		Years to Maturity (T)	5	
8		Interest Rate (r)	0.05	
9		Volatility (v)	0.15	
10		Steps (n)	25	
11		Volatility Skew (c)	0.05	
12		Type (Call or Put)	Call	
13				
14				
15		**Option Price**	7.779984	

FIGURE 3.16 Implied Volatility Trinomial Tree Price of European Options

Figure 3.16 illustrates how European options are priced using the Derman, Kani, and Chriss (1996) implied trinomial tree coded in the function DKC-Trinomial() described above. We use a spot price of $S = 30$, a strike price of $K = 30, T = 5$ years to maturity, $n = 25$ steps, a risk-free rate of $r = 5$ percent, initial stock volatility of $v = 15$ percent, and a volatility skew of $c = 0.05$.

In cell C15 we type

$$= \text{DKCTrinomial(S,K,T,RF,V,N,Skew,PutCall)}$$

and obtain the price of a European call as $7.7799. The price of a European put is $1.1440. Recall that the Black-Scholes prices of the call and put are $7.8006 and $1.1647, respectively.

ALLOWING FOR DIVIDENDS AND THE COST-OF-CARRY

Modifying the binomial and trinomial trees when dividend payments form a continuous stream of payments at annual rate q is straightforward. It is useful to consider such dividends as a special case of the cost-of-carry rate of the asset, b, and incorporate b into the tree. In that case the trees can be used to value options on a variety of assets. For options on stocks paying a continuous dividend rate q, the cost-of-carry is $b = r - q$; for options on currencies with foreign risk-free rate r_F, the cost-of-carry is $b = r - r_F$; and for options on futures, the cost-of-carry is $b = 0$.

Incorporating the cost-of-carry in binomial and trinomial trees involves modifying some of the tree parameters, usually replacing r with b. In the CRR tree, for example, the up probability becomes $p = (e^{b \times dt} - d)/(u - d)$, while in the trinomial tree the up and down probabilities become

$$p_u = \left(\frac{\exp(\frac{1}{2}b \times dt) - \exp(-\sigma\sqrt{\frac{1}{2}dt})}{\exp(\sigma\sqrt{\frac{1}{2}dt}) - \exp(-\sigma\sqrt{\frac{1}{2}dt})} \right)^2$$

and

$$p_d = \left(\frac{\exp(\sigma\sqrt{\frac{1}{2}dt}) - \exp(\frac{1}{2}b \times dt)}{\exp(\sigma\sqrt{\frac{1}{2}dt}) - \exp(-\sigma\sqrt{\frac{1}{2}dt})} \right)^2$$

respectively. In the Edgeworth binomial tree r is replaced by b in the expression for μ defined in Equation (3.8). In this case, the price at the first node will no longer be the spot price S, but the spot price discounted by $\exp(-(r-b) \times T)$. For example, in the case of an option on a stock paying a dividend yield of q, the price at the first node of the Edgeworth binomial tree will be $Se^{-q \times T}$. Modification of these trees to include a cost-of-carry term is left as an exercise.

When dividends are paid at discretely spaced time intervals during the life of the option, it is not as easy to incorporate dividend payments. One problem is that the dividends decrease the asset prices at certain times and not others, so that the tree will not necessarily recombine at all nodes. As described in Hull (2006) and Chriss (1997), however, it is possible to adjust the asset prices so that the nodes recombine. For the CRR binomial tree this involves obtaining the sum D of N dividend payments, each discounted to time zero by the appropriate interest rate,

$$D = \sum_{z=1}^{N} D_i \exp(-r_z \times \tau_z) \tag{3.19}$$

where D_z is the ith dividend payment, paid out at time τ_z and discounted to time zero using interest rate r_z ($z = 1, \ldots, N$). This sum is subtracted from the spot price

$$S^* = S - D \tag{3.20}$$

and a temporary tree for asset prices based on the adjusted spot price S^* is formed. Next, a tree is constructed that adds the present value of the dividends at each node, but only at nodes before each dividend date. Finally, the option prices are obtained by the usual process of backward recursion on this last tree.

Most of the Excel files for implementing binomial and trinomial trees described in this chapter allow for continuous dividend payments. The VBA function Binomial() contained in the Excel file Chapter3Binomial allows for dividends in the CRR binomial tree to paid at discretely timed intervals.

```
Function Binomial(Spot, K, T, r, sigma, n, PutCall As String, EuroAmer As
                String, Dividends)
dt = T / n: u = Exp(sigma * (dt ^ 0.5)): d = 1 / u
a = Exp(r * dt): p = (a - d) / (u - d)
ndivs = Application.Count(Dividends) / 3
```

The dividend payments are contained in array Div(), the time of the payments in array Tau(), and the interest rate applied to each dividend payment in array Rate(). The sum of the dividend payments discounted at the rates based on (3.19) is stored in the variable divsum.

```
divsum = 0
For i = 1 To ndivs
  Tau(i) = Dividends(i, 1): Div(i) = Dividends(i, 2)
  Rate(i) = Dividends(i, 3)
  divsum = divsum + Div(i) * Exp(-Rate(i) * tau(i))
Next i
```

A temporary tree for the asset prices is created, exactly as in the usual CRR binomial tree, but using the adjusted spot price in (3.20).

```
temp(1, 1) = Spot - divsum
For i = 1 To n + 1
  For j = i To n + 1
    temp(i, j) = temp(1, 1) * u ^ (j - i) * d ^ (i - 1)
  Next j
Next i
```

Next, a tree that adds the sum of discounted dividends at each node is created. Only dividends before or at the time of each node are used. Suppose we are at node (i, j), corresponding to time $(j - 1)dt$, and that the dividend amount D_z is paid at time τ_z. If τ_z occurs prior to time $(j - 1)dt$ then the price of the asset on the new tree is equal to the price at the temporary tree. Otherwise, the price of the asset on the new tree is set to the price at the temporary tree minus the present value of the dividend at time $(j - 1)dt$, namely the dividend discounted at the rate r_z for a time of $\tau_z - (j - 1)dt$.

```
S(1, 1) = temp(1, 1) + divsum
For j = 2 To n + 1
  For i = 1 To j
    If tau(1) < (j - 1) * dt Then S(i, j) = temp(i, j)
    Else S(i, j) = temp(i, j) + Div(1)
            * Exp(-Rate(1) * (tau(1) - (j - 1) * dt))
  Next i
Next j
For z = 2 To ndivs
  For j = 2 To n + 1
    For i = 1 To j
      If tau(z) < (j - 1) * dt Then S(i, j) = S(i, j)
      Else S(i, j) = S(i, j) + Div(z)
```

```
                        * Exp(-Rate(z) * (tau(z) - (j - 1) * dt))
              Next i
          Next j
      Next z
```

Finally, the new tree with nodes $S_{i,j}$ is used to price the option using backward recursion.

Figure 3.17 illustrates the VBA function Binomial() with five dividend payments contained in cells E4:G8, each discounted at the same rate of 0.05. Recall that this

	A	B	C	D	E	F	G
1							
2		**CRR Binomial Tree Price for an American or European Option**					
3		**on a Dividend Paying Stock**					
4					Time (τ)	Dividend	Interest
5		Spot Price (S)	30		0.400	1.06	0.05
6		Strike Price (K)	30		0.350	1.25	0.05
7		Years to Maturity (T)	0.4167		0.300	1.10	0.05
8		Interest Rate (rf)	0.05		0.280	1.15	0.05
9		Volatility (v)	0.3				
10		Steps (n)	50				
11		Type (*Call* or *Put*)	Put				
12		Option (*Amer* or *Euro*)	Amer				
13							
14							
15		**Option Price**	4.5870				

FIGURE 3.17 CRR Binomial Tree Option Price with Five Dividend Payments

	A	B	C	D	E	F	G
1							
2		**CRR Binomial Tree Price for an American or European Option**					
3		**on a Dividend Paying Stock**					
4					Time (τ)	Dividend	Interest
5		Spot Price (S)	30		0.400	1.06	0.05
6		Strike Price (K)	30		0.350	1.25	0.05
7		Years to Maturity (T)	0.4167		0.300	1.10	0.05
8		Interest Rate (rf)	0.05		0.280	1.15	0.05
9		Volatility (v)	0.3		0.240	1.35	0.05
10		Steps (n)	50		0.180	1.03	0.05
11		Type (*Call* or *Put*)	Put		0.150	1.10	0.05
12		Option (*Amer* or *Euro*)	Amer		0.100	1.12	0.05
13					0.075	1.45	0.05
14					0.025	1.23	0.05
15		**Option Price**	11.1216				

FIGURE 3.18 CRR Binomial Tree Option Price, with Ten Dividend Payments

function is contained in the Excel file Chapter3Binomial. In cell C15 we type

$$= \text{Binomial}(S,K,T,RF,V,N,\text{PutCall},\text{EuroAmer},\text{Dividend})$$

and obtain the price of an American put as \$4.5870.

Incorporating more than five dividend payments is straightforward. We simply add more lines in columns E, F, and G, and increase the range corresponding to dividends in the argument for the Binomial() function. Figure 3.18 illustrates this with 10 dividends, contained in cells F4:G13.

In cell C15 of Figure 3.18, we type

$$= \text{Binomial}(S,K,T,RF,V,N,\text{PutCall},\text{EuroAmer},\text{Dividend})$$

to obtain the price of \$11.1216 of the American put option.

SUMMARY

The popularity of the binomial tree of Cox, Ross, and Rubinstein (1979) and the trinomial tree of Boyle (1986) have prompted researchers to develop alternative models that refine these original trees and speed up their convergence. In this chapter we present some of these tree-based methods, describe the VBA functions to implement them, and compare their convergence. The chief advantage of tree-based methods is that they can be used to price American options, and that any number of dividends paid out at discrete time intervals can used. Binomial and trinomial trees are easy to understand and implement, but most of these trees assume constant volatility and lognormal distribution of asset prices. It is possible, however, to incorporate time-varying interest rates in these models (see Chriss, 1997). Implied volatility trees match asset prices to market option prices and account for volatility smiles, but these are more difficult to implement.

EXERCISES

This section presents several exercises that deal with the subject matter discussed in this chapter. Solutions are in the Excel file Chapter3Exercises.

3.1 The expression for the price of European options from the CRR binomial tree in Equation (3.1) can be made simpler by noting that at the lower set of terminal nodes in the tree the call price will be zero when the asset price is less than the strike price, and at the upper set of terminal nodes the put price will be zero when the reverse is true. Moreover, these nodes will not overlap, and there will be exactly as many of them as there are terminal nodes. This implies that we can write the price of a call as

$$\text{Call} = \exp(-rT) \sum_{i=a}^{n} \binom{n}{i} p^i (1-p)^{n-i} (Su^i d^{n-i} - K),$$

and the price of a put as

$$\text{Put} = \exp(-rT) \sum_{i=0}^{a-1} \binom{n}{i} p^i (1-p)^{n-i} (K - Su^i d^{n-i}),$$

where a represents the number of terminal nodes for which the asset price is less than the strike price. Find an expression for a, and code in VBA the price of a call and put using these simplified formulas. This formulation will run faster than Equation (3.1), since fewer terms are used in the summation, and the maximum function is not used.

3.2 Update the CRR binomial tree, the Edgeworth binomial tree, and the Boyle trinomial tree to include a cost-of-carry term, b, as described in this chapter. Compare these prices to the Black-Scholes formula of Chapter 4 that includes a cost-of-carry term.

3.3 Analyze the effect of skewness on European call prices, by comparing the prices using the Edgeworth binomial tree when the skewness is $\xi = -0.2$, and when $\xi = +0.2$, to the Black-Scholes price. Use the values $K = 30, r = 0.05, b = 0.05, \sigma = 0.30, T = 1/12$ years, $\kappa = 3.3$, and $n = 100$ steps. For each value of ξ, plot the difference between the Edgeworth prices and the Black-Scholes prices, when the spot price varies from $S = 20$ to $S = 40$ in increments of 1.

SOLUTIONS TO EXERCISES

3.1 We need the smallest integer value of a such that $Su^a d^{n-a} = K$. Solving this equation yields $a = \text{Ceiling}|\ln(K/Sd^n) \div \ln(u/d)|$, where $||$ denotes the absolute value and where the ceiling function rounds up to the nearest integer. See Cox, Ross, and Rubinstein (1979), Tian (1999), or Leisen and Reimer (1996) for details. Programming the simplified formula requires the use two additional Excel functions, the Ceiling() and Abs() functions. The term a is coded as

```
a = Application.Ceiling(Abs(Log(K/S/d^ n) / Log(u/d)), 1)
```

while the summations for a call and put involve the terms

	A	B	C	D	E	F	G	H	I
1	EXERCISE 3.2								
2									
3		Binomial and Trinomial Tree Price for an American or European Option with Cost of Carry							
4									
5		CRR Binomial Tree			Edgeworth Binomial Tree			Trinomial Tree	
6									
7		Spot Price (S)	30		Spot (S)	30		Spot Price (S)	30
8		Strike Price (K)	30		Strike (K)	30		Strike Price (K)	30
9		Years to Maturity (T)	0.4167		Risk Free Rate (r)	0.05		Years to Maturity (T)	0.4167
10		Interest Rate (r)	0.05		Cost of Carry (b)	0.02		Interest Rate (r)	0.05
11		Cost of Carry (b)	0.02		Volatility (v)	0.30		Cost of Carry (b)	0.02
12		Volatility (σ)	0.3		Time (T)	0.4167		Volatility (v)	0.3
13		Steps (n)	100		Number of Steps (n)	100		Steps (n)	100
14		Type (Call or Put)	Call		Skewness (ξ)	0		Type (Call or Put)	Call
15		Option (Amer or Euro)	Euro		Kurtosis (κ)	3		Option (Amer or Euro)	Euro
16					Type (Call or Put)	Call			
17					Option (Amer or Euro)	Euro			
18									
19		Option Price	2.3951		Option Price	2.4040		Option Price	2.3980
20		Black-Scholes Price	2.4008		Black-Scholes Price	2.4008		Black-Scholes Price	2.4008

FIGURE 3.19 Solution to Exercise 3.2

```
Application.Combin(n, i) * P ^ i * (1 - P) ^ (n - i)
   * (S * u ^ i * d ^ (n - i) - K)
Application.Combin(n, i) * P ^ i * (1 - P) ^ (n - i)
   * (K - S * u ^ i * d ^ (n - i))
```

respectively. The summation for the put involves *a* terms and runs from 0 to *a* − 1, while the summation for the call runs from *a* to *n*. Note that since asset price nodes are constructed at the terminal nodes only, the method cannot be used for American options.

3.2 For each of the trees, we create a new VBA function that includes an additional input for the cost-of-carry, and modify the appropriate section of the function. For the CRR binomial tree, the VBA statement p = (Exp(r * dt) − d)/(u − d) is changed to p = (Exp(b * dt) − d)/(u − d) in the function BinCC(), while for the Edgeworth binomial tree the statement

```
mu = r - (1 / T) * Log(Application.Sum(Pe))
```

is changed to

```
mu = bb - (1 / T) * Log(Application. Sum(Pe))
```

in the function EWBinCC(). We use bb instead of b, since b is a variable already used for the binomial probabilities driving the tree. Finally, in the trinomial tree the statements for the up and down probabilities are modified similarly. The CRR binomial tree, Edgeworth binomial tree, and the trinomial tree, each modified to include the cost-of-carry, are illustrated in Figure 3.19.

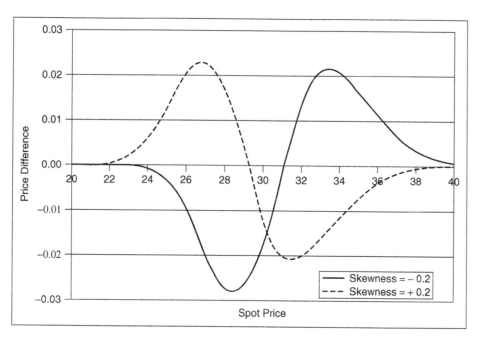

FIGURE 3.20 Solution to Exercise 3.3

3.3 We use the EWBinCC() function included in the exercises, and set the parameter values accordingly. The results are presented in Figure 3.20. The right part of Figure 3.20 corresponds to in-the-money (ITM) calls, and the left part corresponds to out-of-the-money (OTM) calls. When skewness is negative, the difference is negative for OTM calls, which means that the Edgeworth tree produces higher prices for OTM calls than does Black-Scholes. However, the difference is positive for ITM calls, so that Edgeworth prices are lower than Black-Scholes prices. The opposite is true when skewness is positive. This will be explained more clearly in Chapter 5, when we examine the Heston (1993) option pricing model.

CHAPTER 4

The Black-Scholes, Practitioner Black-Scholes, and Gram-Charlier Models

INTRODUCTION

In this chapter we review the Black-Scholes option pricing model and present the VBA code to implement it. We do not derive this model nor spend too much time explaining it since so much has been written about it already, in textbooks such as those by Hull (2006), Haug (1998), and Chriss (1997). We review implied volatility and the moneyness and maturity biases that give rise to volatility smiles. We then review the Practitioner Black-Scholes model, which uses the Deterministic Volatility Function of Dumas, Fleming, and Whaley (1998). Finally, we discuss the model of Backus, Foresi, and Wu (2004), which introduces skewness and excess kurtosis into the Black-Scholes model to account for moneyness and maturity biases.

THE BLACK-SCHOLES MODEL

This model hardly needs introduction. It is the most popular option pricing model, due to its simplicity, closed-form solution, and ease of implementation. The Black and Scholes (1973) price at time t for a European call option with maturity at time $t + T$ with strike price K on a stock paying no dividends is

$$C_{BS} = S_t \Phi(d) - e^{-rT} K \Phi(d - \sigma \sqrt{T}) \tag{4.1}$$

where

S_t = time t price of the stock
σ = annual stock return volatility (assumed constant)
r = annual risk-free interest rate
T = time to maturity in years

$$\Phi(d) = \int_{-\infty}^{d} \phi(u)du = \text{cumulative distribution function of a standard normal variable}$$

$$\phi(x) = \exp(-x^2/2)/\sqrt{2\pi} = \text{density function of a standard normal variable}$$

$$d = \frac{\log(S_t/K) + T(r + \sigma^2/2)}{\sigma\sqrt{T}}.$$

Some authors use the notation $d_1 = d, d_2 = d - \sigma\sqrt{T}, N(x) = \Phi(x)$, and $n(x) = \phi(x)$.

To price a put option, the put-call parity relation can be used, which produces

$$P_{BS} = C_{BS} - S_t + Ke^{-rT}, \tag{4.2}$$

or C_{BS} can be substituted into (4.2) to get

$$P_{BS} = Ke^{-rT}\Phi(\sigma\sqrt{T} - d) - S_t\Phi(-d).$$

The Excel file Chapter4BlackScholes contains VBA code for implementing the Black-Scholes model. The VBA function BS_call() produces the Black-Scholes price of a European call given by Equation (4.1), while function BS_put() uses the put-call parity relationship (4.2) to produce the price of a European put. Both functions require as inputs the spot price of the asset (S), the strike price (K), the risk-free rate of interest (r), the time to maturity (T) and the volatility (σ).

```
Function Gauss(X)
 Gauss = Application.NormSDist(X)
End Function

Function BS_call(S, K, r, T, v)
 d = (Log(S / K) + T * (r + 0.5 * v ^ 2)) / (v * Sqr(T))
 BS_call = S * Gauss(d) - Exp(-r * T) * K * Gauss(d - v * Sqr(T))
End Function

Function BS_put(S, K, r, T, v)
 BS_put = BS_call(S, K, r, T, v) -S + K * Exp(-r * T)
End Function
```

The function Gauss() is used to save space. It replaces the VBA statement Application.NormSDist() with the simpler Gauss() statement whenever cumulative values of the standard normal distribution are needed.

We illustrate these functions in Figure 4.1. Suppose we wish to price a five-month option with strike price $30 on a non-dividend-paying stock with spot price $30 and annual volatility 30 percent, when the risk-free rate is 5 percent. Hence, $S = 30, K = 30, r = 0.05, T = 5/12$, and $\sigma = 0.3$. The cells that contain these inputs have been assigned names for convenience, so in cell E4 we type

$$= BS\_call(S,K,RF,T,V),$$

	A	B	C	D	E	F
1						
2		**Black-Scholes Call and Put Price for Non-Dividend Paying Stock**				
3						
4		Underlying Price (S)	30.00	Black Scholes Call Price	2.612638	
5		Strike Price (K)	30.00			
6		Risk-Free Rate (r)	0.05	Black Scholes Put Price	1.994104	
7		Time to Maturity (T)	0.41667			
8		Volatility of the Underlying (σ)	0.3			
9						

FIGURE 4.1   Black-Scholes Price of Calls and Puts

which produces the Black-Scholes price of the call as $2.612638.

Similarly, the function BS_put() in cell E6 shows that the Black-Scholes price of the put is $1.994104.

Black-Scholes with Dividends

The value of a call option on a dividend-paying stock can be obtained, provided that the current stock price S is assumed to be equal to the sum of all discounted future dividends. For illustration, suppose that a stock pays quarterly dividends, so that in the ith quarter, a dividend in the amount of D_i is paid. Suppose also that this dividend is discounted at the risk-free rate r_i. The current stock price can therefore be expressed as the discounted dividend stream

$$S = D_1 \exp(-r_1 \times \tfrac{1}{4}) + D_2 \exp(-r_2 \times \tfrac{2}{4}) + D_3 \exp(-r_3 \times \tfrac{3}{4}) + \cdots. \qquad (4.3)$$

The closer the ex-dividend dates, the more accurately the value of the dividend payments can be predicted. When a stock is purchased, the buyer hopes that future dividends will increase. The same is true for call options: a bet on future dividends is being made. If the call option expires in seven months, the first two dividends will be paid out and the stock price will drop to S^*. This price can be expressed as the sum of future dividends starting in seven months,

$$S^* = D_3 \exp(-r_3 \times \tfrac{3}{4}) + D_4 \exp(-r_4 \times \tfrac{4}{4}) + \cdots$$
$$= S - D_1 \exp(-r_1 \times \tfrac{1}{4}) - D_2 \exp(-r_2 \times \tfrac{2}{4}). \qquad (4.4)$$

The Black-Scholes formula can be used to price European call options on stocks that pay dividends, simply by using S^* in (4.1) instead of S, and keeping all other parameter values the same. This approximation works best for option with short maturities, since dividends are more predictable in the short term. In the more general case wherein dividends are paid at irregular times τ_i, the discount factors in (4.3) and (4.4) become $\exp(-r_i \times \tau_i)$. The Excel file Chapter4BlackScholesDiv contains the VBA function BS_div_call() to price European call options on a dividend-paying stock.

```
Function BS_div_call(S, K, r, T, v, Div)
Divnum = Application.Count(Div) / 3
PVD = 0
  For i = 1 To Divnum
    PVD = PVD + Div(i, 2) * Exp(-Div(i, 1) * Div(i, 3))
  Next i
Smod = S - PVD
BS_div_call = BS_call(Smod, K, r, T, v)
End Function
```

The stock price S^* is stored in the variable Smod, and the function BS_call() for the Black-Scholes call price defined earlier in this chapter is used, but with the spot price S replaced by S^*. The times to ex-dividend dates, dividends, and risk-free rates are stored in the first, second, and third columns of array Div(), respectively.

This reasoning can be extended to American-style options by employing Black's approximation. Using arbitrage, it can be shown that it is never optimal to exercise prior to maturity an American call option on a stock paying no dividends (Hull, 2006; Chriss, 1997). For a stock paying dividends, it is never optimal to exercise an American call option on the stock anytime other than immediately prior to an ex-dividend date. This implies that we must only verify the value of the call prior to all ex-dividend dates and at maturity, and set the current value of the call to the greatest of these values. This procedure can be implemented by extending the previous algorithm. We have to calculate the value of all the call options expiring at the ex-dividend dates, by modifying the time to maturity and calculating the appropriate adjusted price S^*. The function BS_div_amer_call() implements the procedure.

```
Function BS_div_amer_call(S, K, r, T, v, div)
Dim allCall() As Double
divnum = Application.Count(div) / 3
ReDim allCall(divnum + 1) As Double
  For j = 1 To divnum
    PVD = 0
    For i = 1 To j
      If (i < j) Then
        PVD = PVD + div(i, 2) * Exp(-div(i, 1) * div(i, 3))
      End If
    Next i
    Smod = S - PVD
    allCall(j) = BS_call(Smod, K, r, div(j, 1), v)
  Next j
allCall(divnum + 1) = BS_div_call(S, K, r, T, v, div)
BS_div_amer_call = Application.Max(allCall)
End Function
```

Figure 4.2 illustrates the use of these functions on a stock with spot price $S = \$100$ and volatility $\sigma = 30$ percent, when the strike price is $K = \$100$, the time

	A	B	C	D	E	F	G
1							
2		**Black-Scholes Call and Put Price for a Dividend Paying Stock**					
3		**American and European Options**					
4					Time (τ)	Dividend	Interest
5		Underlying Price (S)	100.00		0.250	2.00	0.05
6		Strike Price (K)	100.00		0.500	2.00	0.05
7		Risk-Free Rate (r)	0.05				
8		Time to Maturity (T)	0.58333				
9		Volatility of the Underlying (σ)	0.3				
10							
11							
12		**Black Scholes Price (European)**	8.295116				
13							
14		**Black Scholes Price (American)**	8.508572				

FIGURE 4.2   Black-Scholes Call Price on a Dividend-Paying Stock

to maturity is $T = 7$ months, and the risk-free rate is $r = 5$ percent. There are two dividends of \$2 each ($D_1 = D_2 = 2$), paid out quarterly ($\tau_1 = 0.25, \tau_2 = 0.50$) and each dividend is discounted at the rate of five percent ($r_1 = r_2 = 0.05$). In cell C12 we type

$$= BS\_div\_call(S,K,RF,T,V,Dividend)$$

and obtain the price of a European call as \$8.2951. Similarly, the price of an America call appears in cell C14 as \$8.508572. In this example, it is optimal to exercise prior to the last dividend date, so the American call price is higher than the European price.

IMPLIED VOLATILITY AND THE DVF

In this section we introduce implied volatilities, which are volatilities extracted from option prices, and the deterministic volatility function (DVF). Implied volatilities differ from realized volatilities, which are volatilities estimated from historical returns. Implied volatilities are often preferred to realized volatilities, since implied volatilities are prospective estimates that reflect future expectations about stock price volatility. Realized volatilities, however, are retrospective estimates that reflect only past stock price volatility. Realized volatilities can be obtained by using simple estimators such as the standard deviation of historical returns, or by applying more sophisticated methods such as an exponential weighted average or the generalized autoregressive conditional heteroskedasticity (GARCH) model. Implied volatilities are obtained by matching a set of market option prices with given strike price and maturity to those produced by an option pricing model using the same strike price and maturity.

Black-Scholes implied volatilities are extracted using the Black-Scholes formula. This must be done numerically because the formula cannot be solved for σ in terms of the other parameters. If σ_{iv} denotes the implied volatility, $C_{obs}(K, T)$ denotes the observed call price with strike price K and time to maturity T, and $C_{BS}(\sigma, K, T)$ denotes the Black-Scholes price of the call with same strike price and maturity, then σ_{iv} is the value of volatility in the Black-Scholes formula such that

$$C_{obs}(K, T) = C_{BS}(\sigma_{iv}, K, T).$$

To find implied volatilities numerically, the objective function $f(\sigma)$ is often defined by the squared loss function

$$f(\sigma) = [C_{obs}(K, T) - C_{BS}(\sigma, K, T)]^2. \tag{4.5}$$

Implied volatility is that value of volatility $\sigma = \sigma_{iv}$ which produces a zero difference between the observed price and the Black-Scholes price

$$f(\sigma_{iv}) = 0. \tag{4.6}$$

Squaring the difference ensures that a minimization algorithm such as the Newton-Raphson method does not produce large negative values for $f(\sigma_{iv})$ instead of a root. It is possible to use objective functions other than that specified by (4.5). This will become evident in Chapter 10. In that chapter, implied volatilities are treated more thoroughly.

One important feature of Black-Scholes implied volatilities is that they resemble a smile or smirk when plotted against moneyness. The smile is more pronounced for options with short maturities. This smile-shaped pattern, which consistently appears in volatilities extracted from a wide variety of options, has provided evidence against the constant volatility assumption inherent in the Black-Scholes model.

Obtaining Implied Volatility with VBA

In this section we present VBA code to obtain Black-Scholes implied volatilities from a cross-section of option prices. The Excel file Chapter4IV contains volatilities implied from call options on IBM stock paying no dividends, with strike price ranging from \$40 to \$115, and maturity of 137 days. The BS_call() function defined earlier in this chapter is used for the Black-Scholes call price, and the NewtRaph() function defined in Chapter 1 is used to find the root of our objective function (4.5). This objective function is defined as the VBA function ImpliedVolatility().

```
Function ImpliedVolatility(S, K, r, q, T, v, CallPrice)
   ImpliedVolatility = (CallPrice - BS_call(S, K, r, q, T, v)) ^ 2
End Function
```

The VBA function NewtRaph() is similar to that defined in Chapter 1, except that it uses the VBA function ImpliedVolatility() as the objective function and uses the Taylor approximation to the derivative.

```
Function NewtRaph(S, K, r, q, T, x_guess, CallPrice)
' More VBA statements
fx = Run("ImpliedVolatility", S, K, r, q, T, cur_x, CallPrice)
cur_x_delta = cur_x - delta_x
fx_delta = Run("ImpliedVolatility", S, K, r, q, T, cur_x_delta, CallPrice)
dx = ((fx - fx_delta) / delta_x)
' More VBA statements
End Function
```

Figure 4.3 illustrates how these functions are used to find implied volatilities from a single call price, from a series of call prices, and to plot an implied volatility smile. In the first case, a spot price of $S = 100$ (in cell E4), a strike price of $K = 100$ (cell E5), a risk-free rate of $r = 0.03$ (cell E6), no dividend yield ($q = 0$ in cell E7), a time to maturity of 137 days ($T = 137/365$ or 0.3753 years in cell E8), and a volatility $v = 0.6$ (cell E9) are used. To obtain the Black-Scholes price in cell E11 we type

$$= BS\_call(S, K, RF, Q, T, V),$$

						Multiple Implied Volatilities			
Call Option on IBM : Black-Scholes Implied Volatilities							Spot Price (S) =	88.43	
			Single Implied Volatility						
			Spot Price (S) =	100		Implied	Strike	Call Price	Call Price
			Strike Price (K) =	100		Volatility	Price (K)	Bid	Ask
			Risk-Free rate (r) =	0.03					
			Div Yield/Foreign rate (q) =	0.00		0.4955	40	48.80	49.00
			Time to Maturity (T) =	0.3753		0.4857	45	43.90	44.10
			Volatility (v) =	0.60		0.4477	50	39.00	39.20
						0.4018	55	34.10	34.30
Initial Guess =	0.4		Black-Scholes Call =	15.0676		0.3529	60	29.20	29.40
			Implied Volatility =	0.6000		0.3027	65	24.30	24.50
						0.2686	70	19.50	19.70
						0.2357	75	14.80	15.00
						0.2119	80	10.40	10.60
						0.1917	85	6.50	6.70
						0.1788	90	3.50	3.70
						0.1725	95	1.65	1.75
						0.1735	100	0.70	0.80
						0.1810	105	0.30	0.40
						0.1854	110	0.10	0.20
						0.1945	115	0.05	0.10

FIGURE 4.3 Black-Scholes Implied Volatilities

which produces a call price of $15.0676. The NewtRaph() function, using a starting value of 0.4 in cell C11, is used to obtain the Black-Scholes implied volatility from the Black-Scholes price. Hence, in cell E12 we type

$$= NewtRaph(S, K, RF, Q, T, Guess, E11),$$

which produces the original volatility of 0.6000, as expected.

To obtain multiple implied volatilities, shown in the right set of columns in Figure 4.3, assume a spot price of $S = 88.43$ (in cell I1), strike prices ranging from 40 to 115 (cells H7:H22), and the same risk-free rate and dividend yield as in the previous example. The market price of each option is defined as the midpoint between the bid price (column I) and the ask price (column J). In the NewtRaph() function we use the same starting value as in the previous example. Hence, in cell G7 we type

$$= NewtRaph(Spot, H7, RF, Q, T, Guess, (I7+J7)/2),$$

which produces the implied volatility of 0.4995 for the option with strike price of $K = 40$. The formula in cell G7 can then be copied to cells G8:G22, which produces the remaining implied volatilities.

Finally, the plotting wizard can be invoked to produce a graph for the Black-Scholes implied volatility smile, using cells H7:H22 for values of the x-axis, and cells G7:G22 for values of the y-axis.

Deterministic Volatility Functions

The parabolic shape of the volatility smile, and its dependence on moneyness and maturity, has motivated researchers to model implied volatility as a quadratic function of moneyness and maturity. Dumas, Fleming, and Whaley (1998) describe this as the deterministic volatility function (DVF) approach to modeling implied volatility. They consider four specifications for the DVF:

$$\sigma_{iv} = a_0 \tag{4.7}$$

$$\sigma_{iv} = a_0 + a_1 K + a_2 K^2 \tag{4.8}$$

$$\sigma_{iv} = a_0 + a_1 K + a_2 K^2 + a_3 T + a_5 KT \tag{4.9}$$

$$\sigma_{iv} = a_0 + a_1 K + a_2 K^2 + a_3 T + a_4 T^2 + a_5 KT \tag{4.10}$$

where

$$\sigma_{iv} = \text{Black-Scholes implied volatility}$$
$$K = \text{strike price}$$
$$T = \text{time to maturity}$$
$$a_0, a_1, a_2, a_3, a_4, a_5 = \text{model parameters.}$$

Each of these specifications stipulates a different form of the volatility function. Equation (4.7) assumes constant volatility with no dependence on the strike price or the time to maturity, and corresponds to the Black-Scholes model. Equation (4.8) stipulates volatility be a quadratic function of strike price, with no dependence on maturity. Equation (4.9) adds a dependence on maturity, with an interaction between moneyness and maturity contained in its last term. Equation (4.10) allows for the relationship between volatility and maturity to be quadratic also. In each of these models, a threshold of 0.01 is introduced to eliminate possible negative values of fitted volatility. For example, the model being fitted in Equation (4.9) is actually

$$\sigma_{iv} = \max(0.01, a_0 + a_1 K + a_2 K^2 + a_3 T + a_5 KT).$$

Finally, a fifth model is defined which switches between models (4.8), (4.9), and (4.10) depending on whether the different expiration dates in the cross-section of option prices is one, two or three, respectively. Estimation of model parameters is done by minimizing error sum of squares between observed and fitted option prices.

DVF modeling is useful because it provides estimates of volatility for a combination of moneyness and maturity that is not available in observed option prices. For any such combination, volatility can be estimated from the fitted function. If a set of observed option prices contained a continuum of strike prices and time to maturity, there would be no need for the function. We would simply extract implied volatility from a cross-section of option prices with the strike price and time to maturity we require.

Dumas, Fleming, and Whaley (1998) show that of the five models under consideration, the Black-Scholes model leads to the largest valuation errors, consistent with the notion that volatility is not constant across moneyness and maturity. Most of the improvement over Black-Scholes, however, is from including K, K^2, T, and KT into the volatility function. There is little improvement to be gained by introducing T^2, squared maturity. This implies that volatility depends on both moneyness and maturity, but that smiles are dependent on moneyness only. The effect of maturity on volatility is linear only. In some cases, only K and K^2 are needed. Hence, simple functions of volatility, such as those specified in Equations (4.8) and (4.9), are often sufficient for modeling volatility.

THE PRACTITIONER BLACK-SCHOLES MODEL

This model is referred to as the Practitioner Black-Scholes (PBS) model by Christoffersen and Jacobs (2004a), and as the ad-hoc model by Dumas, Fleming, and Whaley (1998). It constitutes a simple way to price options, based on implied volatilities and the Black-Scholes pricing formula. The assumption of constant volatility in the Black-Scholes model is circumvented by using volatility that is not constant, but rather depends on moneyness and maturity.

Implementing the Practitioner Black-Scholes Model

Implementing the PBS model is straightforward, since all that is required is a series of Black-Scholes implied volatilities on which to run multiple regression under ordinary least squares (OLS). This model can be summarized in four steps:

1. Use a cross-section of option prices with a variety of strike price and time to maturity to obtain a set of Black-Scholes implied volatilities.
2. Choose a deterministic volatility function and estimate its parameters.
3. For a given strike price and maturity, obtain the volatility as the fitted value of the volatility function in step 2.
4. Obtain the option price using the Black-Scholes formula, using the fitted volatility from step 3 and the same strike price and maturity.

While this model provides a rudimentary method of obtaining option prices, its performance in terms of pricing errors is remarkably effective. Christoffersen and Jacobs (2004a) compare the pricing errors of two option pricing models: the PBS model and the Heston (1993) model. When a different loss function is used for the estimation of model parameters and for the evaluation of the model in terms of pricing errors, the Heston (1993) model prevails. When the same loss function is used for estimation and evaluation, however, the PBS model prevails. Christoffersen and Jacobs (2004a) argue that using the same loss functions for estimation and evaluation is preferable. Furthermore, when evaluating the performance of different models, the same loss function should be used across models, which will avoid making unfair comparisons. According to the results of their paper, the PBS model is preferable to the Heston (1993) model for pricing options. The fact that the PBS model is easy to implement makes it all the more attractive. In-sample and out-of-sample loss function estimation will be presented in Chapter 9.

 The Excel file Chapter4PBS contains the PBS model to obtain fitted implied volatilities through the most general regression given by Equation (4.10). It uses the VBA functions BS_call(), which produces the Black-Scholes price for a call option, PBSparams(), which returns the six coefficients of the regression (4.10) estimated by OLS, and PBSvol(), which uses the estimated coefficients to produce fitted volatility for a given strike price and maturity. The function PBSparams() requires as inputs a vector of implied volatilities, impV, of strike prices, K, and of maturities, T. It returns the six regression coefficients a_0 through a_5 defined in Equation (4.10) and estimated by OLS using the VBA function OLSregress() introduced in Chapter 1.

```
Function PBSparams(impV, K, T)
n = Application.Count(impV)
Dim RHS() As Double
ReDim RHS(n, 6) As Double
For cnt = 1 To n
RHS(cnt, 1) = 1
```

```
RHS(cnt, 2) = K(cnt)
  RHS(cnt, 3) = K(cnt) ^ 2
  RHS(cnt, 4) = T(cnt) / 365
  RHS(cnt, 5) = (T(cnt) / 365) ^ 2
  RHS(cnt, 6) = K(cnt) * T(cnt) / 365
Next cnt
  betas = OLSregress(impV, RHS)
  PBSparams = betas
End Function
```

The function PBSvol() requires as inputs the six regression coefficients, a strike price, and a maturity, and returns a fitted volatility based on (4.10) or a value of 0.01 if the fitted volatility is negative.

```
Function PBSvol(p, K, T)
PBSvol = p(1) + p(2)*K + p(3)*K^2 + p(4)*T/365
       + p(5)*(T/365)^ 2 + p(6)*K*T/365
If PBSvol < 0 Then PBSvol = 0.01
End Function
```

Figure 4.4 illustrates how these functions are used to construct PBS fitted volatilities, using December 15, 2005, call options on IBM non-dividend-paying stock with spot price of $83.53 (in cell I4), strike price ranging from $50 to $120 in increments of $5 (cells A5:A47), and maturity ranging from 37 to 309 days (cells D5:D47). Figure 4.4 is from the Excel file Chapter4PBS, and has been truncated at 32 rows to conserve space.

The first step is to obtain a set of Black-Scholes implied volatilities. These appear in cells E5:E47. Figure 4.4 uses a starting value of 0.7 for implied volatility (cell I7), along with a risk-free rate of 0.03 (cell I5), and the midpoint of the call option bid and ask price (cells B5:B47 and C5:C47, respectively) for the market price. Hence, in cell E5 we type

$$= \text{NewtRaph}(S, A5, RF, Q, D5/365, \text{Guess}, (B5+C5)/2)$$

to produce the Black-Scholes implied volatility of 0.6218. The formula in cell E5 is then copied to cells E6:E47 to produce the remaining implied volatilities.

The second step is to select a deterministic volatility function. The VBA function PBSparams() uses the most general function given in (4.10) and requires as inputs implied volatilities, strike prices, and times to maturity. Hence, in cell I10 we type

$$= \text{PBSparams}(E5:E47, A5:A47, D5:D47),$$

and copy down to cells I11:I15, which produces estimates of the six parameters of (4.10), given by $\hat{a}_0 = 1.23951, \hat{a}_1 = -0.01598, \hat{a}_2 = 0.00006, \hat{a}_3 = -0.78490, \hat{a}_4 = 0.21275$, and $\hat{a}_5 = 0.00552$.

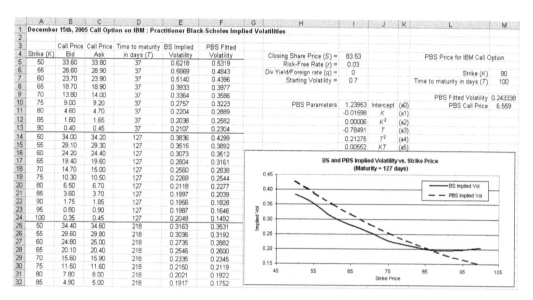

FIGURE 4.4   Practitioner Black-Scholes Model

The third step is to obtain fitted volatilities for each strike price and time to maturity. The VBA function PBSvol() uses the six parameters estimated by PBSparams() to produce a fitted volatility from (4.10) using a given strike price and maturity. Hence, in cell F5 we type

$$= PBSvol(I10:I15, A5, D5)$$

to obtain a fitted volatility of 0.5319 for a strike price of $K = 50$ and a time to maturity of $T = 37$ days. As before, this formula is copied to cells F6:F47 to obtain the remaining fitted volatilities.

The fourth and final step of the PBS model is to price an option using the Black-Scholes pricing formula and the fitted volatility from (4.10) with parameters appearing in cells I10:I15. Figure 4.4 illustrates this for a strike price of $K = 80$ (cell M6) and a maturity of $T = 100$ days (cell M7). To obtain the fitted volatility for combination of strike price and maturity, in cell M9 we type

$$= PBSvol(I10:I15, M6,M7)$$

to produce a fitted volatility of 0.243338. To obtain the PBS price using this fitted volatility and the VBA function BS_call(), in cell M10 we type

$$= BS\_call(S, M6, RF, Q, M7/365, M9)$$

to obtain the call option price of 6.56. It is also instructive to compare the PBS price with the market price. For example, replacing the strike price with $K = 50$ and the maturity with $T = 37$ days in cells M6 and M7, respectively, produces a PBS call price of 33.69, close to the bid and ask prices of 33.60 and 33.80 appearing in cells B5 and B6, respectively.

Finally, Figure 4.4 also includes a volatility smile for the Black-Scholes (BS) and PBS implied volatilities, for a maturity of $T = 127$ days. Hence the x-axis contains cells A14:A24 while the y-axis contains cells E14:E24 for the BS implied volatilities, and cells F14:F24 for the PBS implied volatilities. It is evident that the PBS implied volatilities produce a steeper curve and can therefore better capture the smile than the BS implied volatilities, which produce a curve that is flatter.

THE GRAM-CHARLIER MODEL

This model, which we refer to as the Gram-Charlier model, was developed by Backus, Foresi, and Wu (2004) and provides a simple way to account for both skewness and kurtosis. They use a Gram-Charlier expansion up to the fourth order in the distribution of returns of the underlying asset. This allows for skewness and greater kurtosis than the normal distribution to be introduced into option pricing. This model, however, still assumes that volatility is constant over time.

Define the one-period return on the asset as $R_{t+1} = \log S_{t+1} - \log S_t$, where S_t is the price of the asset at time t. Then the return over T periods is $R_{t+1}^T = \log S_{t+T} - \log S_t$, which can be written $R_{t+1}^T = \sum_{j=1}^{T} R_{t+j}$ as the sum of the previous one-period returns. Suppose that R_{t+1} has cumulant-generating function given by

$$\psi(t) = \sum_{j=1}^{\infty} \kappa_j \frac{t^j}{j!} = \kappa_1 t + \kappa_2 \frac{t^2}{2!} + \kappa_3 \frac{t^3}{3!} + \cdots,$$

where κ_j are the cumulants of R_{t+1}. If returns are identically and independently distributed, then the cumulants of their sum R_{t+1}^T are given as $T\kappa_j$ so that the T-period return has mean and variance given by $\mu_T = T\mu$ and $\sigma_T^2 = T\sigma^2$, respectively. Back, Foresi, and Wu (2004) use the fact that if

$$\gamma_1 = E\left[\left(\frac{R_{t+1} - \mu}{\sigma}\right)^3\right] = \frac{\kappa_3}{\kappa_2^{3/2}}$$

and

$$\gamma_2 = E\left[\left(\frac{R_{t+1} - \mu}{\sigma}\right)^4\right] - 3 = \frac{\kappa_4}{(\kappa_2)^2}$$

denote the one-period skewness and excess kurtosis respectively, then the T-period skewness and excess kurtosis are given by $\gamma_{1T} = \gamma_1/\sqrt{T}$ and $\gamma_{2T} = \gamma_2/T$ respectively.

Backus, Foresi, and Wu (2004) use the first four terms of the Gram-Charlier expansion to arrive at the following probability density for the standardized T-period return $w_T = (R_{t+1}^T - \mu_T)/\sigma_T$:

$$f(w_T) = \phi(w_T)\left[1 - \frac{\gamma_{1T}}{3!}\phi^{(3)}(w_T) + \frac{\gamma_{2T}}{4!}\phi^{(4)}(w_T)\right],$$

where

$\phi(x) = \exp(-x^2/2)/\sqrt{2\pi}$, the density of the standard normal distribution
$\phi^{(k)}(x) =$ the kth derivative of $\phi(x)$.

It is easy to show by straightforward differentiation that $\phi^{(3)}(x) = (3x - x^3)\phi(x)$ and $\phi^{(4)}(x) = (x^4 - 6x^2 + 3)\phi(x)$, so the density $f(w_T)$ is readily available.

The Gram-Charlier Call Price

Backus, Foresi, and Wu (2004) use the density $f(w_T)$ in the integral for the price of a call option with strike price K:

$$C_{GC} = e^{-rT}E[\max(S_{t+T} - K), 0] = e^{-rT}\int_{\log(K/S_t)}^{\infty} (S_t e^x - K)f(x)\, dx,$$

where r is the continuously compounded n-period interest rate and K is the strike price of the option. Substituting the Gram-Charlier density $f(w_T)$ for $f(x)$, the call price becomes

$$C_{GC} = \int_{w^*}^{\infty} (S_t e^{\mu T + \sigma_T w_T} - K)f(w_T)dw_T$$

$$= \int_{w^*}^{\infty} (S_t e^{\mu T + \sigma_T w_T} - K)\left(\phi(w_T)\left[1 - \frac{\gamma_{1T}}{3!}\phi^{(3)}(w_T) + \frac{\gamma_{2T}}{4!}\phi^{(4)}(w_T)\right]\right)dw_T,$$

where $w^* = (\log(K/S_t) - \mu_T)/\sigma_T$. Backus, Foresi, and Wu (2004) break the integral into four parts and evaluate each separately. The first integral produces the usual Black-Scholes pricing formula, while the other integrals adjust the price for skewness and excess kurtosis. The resulting call price is shown to be approximately

$$C_{GC} \approx S_t\Phi(d) - Ke^{-rT}\Phi(d - \sigma_T)$$

$$+ S_t\phi(d)\sigma_T\left[\frac{\gamma_{1T}}{3!}(2\sigma_T - d) - \frac{\gamma_{2T}}{4!}(1 - d^2 + 3d\sigma_T - 3\sigma_T^2)\right]. \qquad (4.11)$$

Note that when skewness and excess kurtosis are both zero, the terms inside the square brackets in (4.11) become zero, and the Gram-Charlier formula for the call price C_{GC} reduces to the Black-Scholes call price.

The form of d is identical to that given in the Black-Scholes formula, and depends on which type of option being priced. For options on a non-dividend-paying stock,

$$d = \frac{\log(S_t/K) + T(r + \sigma^2/2)}{\sigma_T} = \frac{\log(S_t/K) + Tr + \sigma_T^2/2}{\sigma_T},$$

since $\sigma_T^2 = T\sigma^2$. For a stock that pays dividends at rate q per period, in the pricing formula for C_{GC} we replace S_t by its discounted value $S_t e^{-qT}$ and use

$$d = \frac{\log(S_t/K) + T(r - q + \sigma^2/2)}{\sigma_T} = \frac{\log(S_t/K) + T(r - q) + \sigma_T^2/2}{\sigma_T}.$$

For currency options, we use this latter formula for d, except that q denotes the foreign risk-free rate.

The price P_{GC} of a put option with same maturity as the call is given by put-call parity. Hence,

$$P_{GC} = C_{GC} + Ke^{-rT} - S_t e^{-qT}. \tag{4.12}$$

For options on stock paying no dividends, $q = 0$ and the last term is simply S_t. By differentiating (4.11) and (4.12), it is possible to obtain closed-form expressions for the option sensitivities (the Greeks) of Gram-Charlier calls and puts. This will be done in Chapter 7.

The Excel file Chapter4GramCharlier contains the VBA function GC_call() to obtain the Gram-Charlier price (4.11) of a European call, and the VBA function GC_put() for the price of a European put using put-call parity (4.12).

```
Function fz(x)
 fz = Exp(-x ^ 2 / 2) / Sqr(2 * Application.Pi())
End Function

Function GC_call(S, K, r, q, n, v, skew, kurt)
Nskew = skew / Sqr(n): Nkurt = kurt / n
Nvol = Sqr(n) * v
d = (Log(S / K) + n * (r - q) + Nvol ^ 2 / 2) / Nvol
GC_call = S * Exp(-q * n) * Gauss(d) - K * Exp(-r * n)
        * Gauss(d - Nvol) + S * Exp(-q * n) * fz(d)
        * Nvol * ((Nskew / 6) * (2 * Nvol - d)
        - (Nkurt / 24) * (1 - d ^ 2 + 3 * d * Nvol - 3 * Nvol ^ 2))
End Function

Function GC_put(S, K, r, q, n, v, skew, kurt)
 GC_put = GC_call(S, K, r, q, n, v, skew, kurt) + K * Exp(-r*n)
        - S*Exp(-q*n)
End Function
```

The VBA function GC_call() requires the same inputs as the Black-Scholes function BS_call, plus the one-period skewness and kurtosis. The VBA function

	A	B	C
1			
2		**Gram-Charlier Price of Calls and Puts**	
3		**Period = Monthly**	
4			
5		Underlying Price (*S*)	30.00
6		Strike Price (*K*)	30.00
7		Risk Free Rate Per Year (*r×12*)	0.05
8		Risk Free Rate Per Period (*r*)	0.004167
9		Foreign Rate or Dividend Yield Per Year (*q×12*)	0
10		Foreign Rate or Div Yield Per Period (*q*)	0
11		Periods Until Maturity (*T*)	5
12		Volatility Per Year (σ×√12)	0.30
13		One-Period Volatility (σ)	0.086603
14		One-Period Skewness (γ₁)	-2.3
15		One-Period Kurtosis (γ₂)	1.2
16			
17		**Gram-Charlier Call Price**	2.519584
18			
19		**Gram-Charlier Put Price**	1.901049

FIGURE 4.5 Gram-Charlier Prices for a Non-Dividend-Paying Stock

fz() computes the standard normal density, while the VBA function Gauss() computes cumulative probabilities of the standard normal distribution. Both functions are used to conserve space in subsequent functions.

Suppose an option on the non-dividend-paying stock presented in Figure 4.1 is to be priced, and suppose further that the one-month skewness and kurtosis of the stock are -2.3 and 1.2, respectively. Then $S = 30, K = 30, r = 0.05/12$ is the one-month risk-free rate, $T = 5$ months, and $\sigma = 0.3/\sqrt{12}$ is the one-month volatility. Figure 4.5 illustrates the use of the VBA functions for Gram-Charlier prices, contained in the Excel file Chapter4GramCharlier.

In cell C17 we type

$$= GC\_call(S, K, RF, Q, T, V, Skew, Kurt)$$

which produces the call price of $2.519584. Similarly, in cell C19 we type

$$= GC\_put(S, K, RF, Q, T, V, Skew, Kurt)$$

which produces the put price of $1.901049. Note that when kurtosis and skewness are both set to zero in cells C14 and C15, the VBA functions produce the Black-Scholes prices of $2.612638 for the call and $1.994104 for the put, exactly as in the example presented in Figure 4.1.

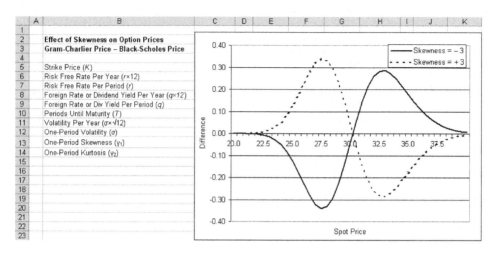

	A	B	C	D	E	F	G	H	I	J	K
1											
2		**Effect of Skewness on Option Prices**									
3		**Gram-Charlier Price – Black-Scholes Price**									
4											
5		Strike Price (*K*)									
6		Risk Free Rate Per Year (*r*×12)									
7		Risk Free Rate Per Period (*r*)									
8		Foreign Rate or Dividend Yield Per Year (*q*×12)									
9		Foreign Rate or Div Yield Per Period (*q*)									
10		Periods Until Maturity (*T*)									
11		Volatility Per Year (σ×√12)									
12		One-Period Volatility (σ)									
13		One-Period Skewness (γ₁)									
14		One-Period Kurtosis (γ₂)									

FIGURE 4.6 Effect of Skewness on Option Prices

We illustrate the effect of skewness on option prices, using the experiment outlined in Exercise 3.3. We obtain the price of a call option with one month to maturity, using the Black-Scholes formula, and using the Gram-Charlier model with one period skewness equal to −3 and +3. We use a strike price of $K = 30$, vary the spot price from $S = 20$ to $S = 40$ in increments of $2.50 and plot the difference between the Gram-Charlier price and the Black-Scholes price. The results of this experiment are presented in the Excel file Chapter4CompareCGBS, and are illustrated in Figure 4.6.

As expected, the Gram-Charlier model accounts for positive skewness (dashed line) by assigning a higher price than Black-Scholes to out-of-the money calls, but a lower price for in-the-money calls. The opposite is true when negative skewness is introduced into the Gram-Charlier price (solid line).

Finally, we evaluate how the Gram-Charlier model compares with the Edgeworth binomial tree of Chapter 3. Since both of these models introduce skewness and kurtosis, prices obtained from both models should be similar. The file Chapter4CompareGCEW evaluates the effect of skewness on both models, using parameter values that have been matched. This is illustrated in Figure 4.7. For each model, a plot of the difference in call price between the model and the Black-Scholes call price is produced in a manner identical to that in Figure 4.6.

The following parameter values are used, $S = 30, K = 30$, yearly volatility $\sigma = 0.30$, time to maturity $T = 0.5$ years or 6 months. The kurtosis and skewness for the Edgeworth tree must be chosen so that they fall within the locus illustrated in Exhibit 2 of Rubinstein (1998). The 6-month skewness is $\xi = -0.4$ in the Edgeworth tree, so in cell C23 the one-month skewness for the Gram-Charlier model must be set to $\gamma_1 = -0.4 \times \sqrt{6}$ or $\gamma_1 \approx -0.98$. Similarly, the

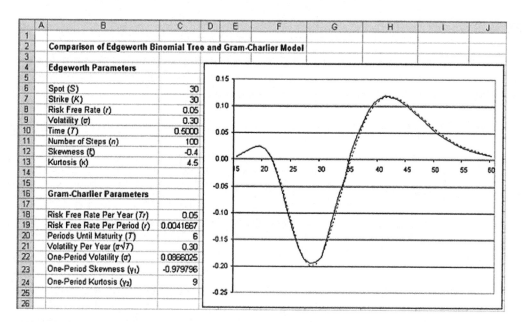

	A	B	C	D	E	F	G	H	I	J
1										
2		**Comparison of Edgeworth Binomial Tree and Gram-Charlier Model**								
3										
4		**Edgeworth Parameters**								
5										
6		Spot (S)	30							
7		Strike (K)	30							
8		Risk Free Rate (r)	0.05							
9		Volatility (σ)	0.30							
10		Time (T)	0.5000							
11		Number of Steps (n)	100							
12		Skewness (ξ)	-0.4							
13		Kurtosis (κ)	4.5							
14										
15										
16		**Gram-Charlier Parameters**								
17										
18		Risk Free Rate Per Year (Tr)	0.05							
19		Risk Free Rate Per Period (r)	0.0041667							
20		Periods Until Maturity (T)	6							
21		Volatility Per Year (σ√T)	0.30							
22		One-Period Volatility (σ)	0.0866025							
23		One-Period Skewness (γ₁)	-0.979796							
24		One-Period Kurtosis (γ₂)	9							
25										
26										

FIGURE 4.7   Comparison of Edgeworth and Gram-Charlier Call Prices

6-month kurtosis is $\kappa = 4.5$ in the Edgeworth tree, so in cell C24 the one-month kurtosis is set to $\gamma_2 = (4.5 - 3) \times 6$ or $\gamma_2 = 9$. Since the Gram-Charlier model uses excess kurtosis, three must be subtracted from the Edgeworth kurtosis before multiplying the result by the number of months. Figure 4.7 is similar to the solid line in Figure 4.6, and indicates that the Edgeworth tree and the Gram-Charlier model both account for skewness. Moreover, the price differences produced by the Edgeworth tree (solid line) and the Gram-Charlier model (dashed line) are fairly close, even when only $n = 100$ steps are used in the Edgeworth tree.

SUMMARY

This chapter deals with the Black-Scholes model, the most popular option pricing model, and extends this model to allow for dividends paid out at discrete time intervals. We also introduce Black-Scholes implied volatilities, which are volatilities extracted from option prices with the Black-Scholes formula. The Practitioner Black-Scholes (PBS) exploits the volatility smile by using implied volatilities as the volatility input to the Black-Scholes option price. Finally, the Gram-Charlier model provides a closed-form solution that allows for skewness and kurtosis in the returns distribution.

EXERCISES

This section presents exercises that involve the Black-Scholes, PBS, and Gram-Charlier models introduced in this chapter. All VBA code for these exercises is contained in the Excel file Chapter 4 Exercises.

4.1 Obtain implied volatilities in the Excel file Chapter4 IV using two additional methods.
   1. By deriving the analytic derivative of the objective function (4.5) and incorporating this derivative into the Newton-Raphson method.
   2. By using the objective function $f(\sigma) = C_{BS}(\sigma, K, T) - C_{obs}(K, T)$ and the Bisection method to find the value σ_{iv} for σ that produces $f(\sigma_{iv}) = 0$.
      Compare the accuracy of both methods using a small number of iterations. Which root-finding algorithm is the best for finding Black-Scholes implied volatilities?

4.2 Using the most general deterministic volatility function in (4.10) may not be the optimal choice if some of the regression coefficients are not statistically significant. Modify the function OLSregress() in the Excel file Chapter4PBS to include p-values for the estimated coefficients. Using the data in that worksheet on options with maturity $T = 37, 127$, and 218 days only, exclude all coefficients that are not significant at the 1 percent level, and use a simpler deterministic volatility function. Obtain new parameter estimates and fitted volatilities using this simpler function.

4.3 By including a cost-of-carry term, the Black-Scholes formula can easily be generalized to price European options for stocks paying dividends, for futures, and for foreign currencies. The Black-Scholes formula becomes

$$C_{BS} = e^{(b-r)T} S_t \Phi(d) - e^{-rT} K \Phi(d - \sigma \sqrt{T})$$

for calls, and

$$P_{BS} = K e^{-rT} \Phi(\sigma \sqrt{T} - d) - S_t e^{(b-r)T} \Phi(-d)$$

for puts, where $d = [\log(S_t/K) + T(b + \sigma^2/2)]/[\sigma \sqrt{T}]$ (Haug, 1998). For stocks paying dividends at a continuous rate q, we set $b = r - q$, for options on futures we set $b = 0$ and replace the stock price S_t by $F_t = S_t e^{rT}$ in the expressions for C_{BS}, P_{BS}, and d, and for options on currencies we set $b = r - r_F$, where r_F is the foreign risk-free rate. Program this general form of the Black-Scholes model in VBA.

SOLUTIONS TO EXERCISES

4.1 We will see in Chapter 10 that the bisection method, along with the objective function $f(\sigma) = C_{BS}(\sigma, K, T) - C_{obs}(K, T)$, is particularly well suited for finding implied volatility. To find a positive value of f we simply choose a very large value of σ, and to find a negative value of f we choose a very small value. Hence, the values $a = 100$ and $b = 0.01$ are used as starting values for the bisection algorithm. Figures 4.8 and 4.9 both show that the implied volatilities obtained by the three methods are virtually indistinguishable from one another.

4.2 We can use the formulas in the Excel file Chapter1WLS to obtain the standard errors, t-statistics, and p-values for each regression coefficient of the deterministic volatility function, modified for OLS. Hence, we modify the VBA function OLSregress() by adding statements that produce these statistics. Running the regression (4.10) on all implied volatilities, excluding those for options with maturity $T = 390$ days, produces the values in Table 4.1 for the coefficients and their associated p-values. The results indicate that the coefficient for Maturity^2 has a p-value of 0.04015, which is not significant at the 1 percent level. Hence, we exclude that term from the regression and opt for model (4.9) instead, which specifies implied volatility as a function of Strike, Strike^2, Maturity, and Maturity $\times$ Strike. We therefore create a new VBA function PBSparams2(), to estimate by OLS the parameters of (4.9).

EXERCISE 4.1

Call Option on IBM : Black-Scholes Implied Volatilities — Spot Price (S) = 88.43

Endpoints: a = 100, b = 0.01

		Implied Vol Exact Value	N.-R. Approx Derivative	N.-R. Exact Derivative	Bisection Method	Strike Price (K)	Call Price Bid	Call Price Ask	f(a)	f(b)
Single Implied Volatility										
Spot Price (S) =	100.0000	0.4955	0.4954	0.4955	0.4955	40	48.80	49.00	39.53	-0.02
Strike Price (K) =	100.0000	0.4857	0.4856	0.4857	0.4857	45	43.90	44.10	44.43	-0.07
Risk-Free rate (r) =	0.0300	0.4477	0.4476	0.4477	0.4477	50	39.00	39.20	49.33	-0.11
Div Yield/Foreign rate (q) =	0.0000	0.4018	0.4018	0.4018	0.4018	55	34.10	34.30	54.23	-0.15
Time to Maturity (T) =	0.3753	0.3529	0.3529	0.3529	0.3529	60	29.20	29.40	59.13	-0.20
Volatility (v) =	0.6000	0.3027	0.3026	0.3027	0.3027	65	24.30	24.50	64.03	-0.24
		0.2686	0.2686	0.2686	0.2686	70	19.50	19.70	68.83	-0.39
Black-Scholes Call =	15.0676	0.2357	0.2357	0.2357	0.2357	75	14.80	15.00	73.53	-0.63
Bisection Implied Volatility =	0.6000	0.2119	0.2118	0.2119	0.2119	80	10.40	10.60	77.93	-1.17
Exact N-R Implied Volatility =	0.6000	0.1917	0.1916	0.1917	0.1917	85	6.50	6.70	81.83	-2.22
Approx N-R Implied Volatility =	0.5999	0.1788	0.1787	0.1788	0.1788	90	3.50	3.70	84.83	-3.56
Endpoint	Objective	0.1725	0.1725	0.1725	0.1725	95	1.65	1.75	86.73	-1.70
0.55	-1.20	0.1735	0.1734	0.1735	0.1735	100	0.70	0.80	87.68	-0.75
0.65	1.19	0.1810	0.1809	0.1810	0.1810	105	0.30	0.40	88.08	-0.35
Initial guess	0.5	0.1854	0.1852	0.1854	0.1854	110	0.10	0.20	88.28	-0.15
		0.1945	0.1945	0.1945	0.1945	115	0.05	0.10	88.36	-0.08

FIGURE 4.8 Solution to Exercise 4.1

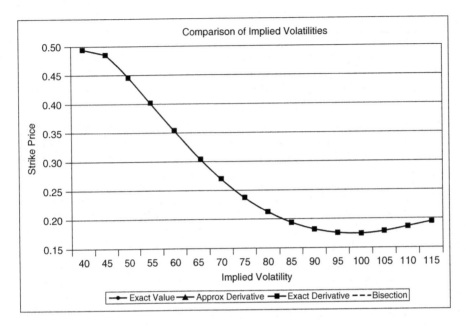

FIGURE 4.9   Solution to Exercise 4.1

TABLE 4.1   Regression Coefficients and p-Values
Based on (4.10)

Coefficient	Estimate	p-Value
Intercept (a_0)	1.69346	<0.00001
Strike (a_1)	−0.02541	<0.00001
Strike^2 (a_2)	0.00010	0.00039
Maturity (a_3)	−1.49915	<0.00001
Maturity^2 (a_4)	0.41584	0.04015
Strike × Maturity (a_5)	0.01322	<0.00001

```
Function PBSparams2(impV, K, T)
n = Application.Count(impV)
Dim RHS() As Double
ReDim RHS(n, 5) As Double
For cnt = 1 To n
  RHS(cnt, 1) = 1: RHS(cnt, 2) = K(cnt)
  RHS(cnt, 3) = K(cnt) ^ 2
  RHS(cnt, 4) = T(cnt) / 365
  RHS(cnt, 5) = K(cnt) * T(cnt) / 365
Next cnt
```

```
    betas = OLSregress(impV, RHS)
    PBSparams2 = betas
End Function
```

Table 4.2 presents the parameter estimates and p-values for regression (4.9) produced by the PBSparams2() function. As expected, all coefficients are significant at the one percent level. We also create a new function, PBSvol2(), to produce fitted volatilities based on (4.9).

```
Function PBSvol2(p, K, T)
PBSvol2 = p(1) + p(2) * K + p(3) * K ^ 2 + p(4) * T / 365
        + p(5) * K * T / 365
If PBSvol2 < 0 Then PBSvol2 = 0.01
End Function
```

The results of this Exercise are presented in Figure 4.10. The coefficients of model (4.10) appear in cells I11:I16, while those of model (4.9) appear in cells M11:M15. To fit the model (4.9), in cell M11 we type

$$= \text{PBSparams2(E5:E36,A5:A36,D5:D36)},$$

and copy to the range M12:M15 to produce the estimated coefficients. To produce the fitted volatilities, in cell G5 we type

$$= \text{PBSvol2(M11:M15,A5,D5)}$$

to produce the PBS fitted volatility based on (4.9) of 0.5891, which is lower than the fitted volatility of 0.5953 based on (4.10) in cell F5. The formula in cell G5 is then copied to cells G6:G36 to produce the remaining fitted volatilities based on (4.9). The PBS price of the IBM call option with strike price of $K = 80$ and maturity of $T = 100$ days is $6.38 (cell N7), 20 cents higher than the

TABLE 4.2 Regression Coefficients and p-Values Based on (4.9)

Coefficient	Estimate	p-value
Intercept (a_0)	1.66256	<.00001
Strike (a_1)	−0.02522	<.00001
Strike^2 (a_2)	0.00010	0.00098
Maturity (a_3)	−1.25650	<.00001
Strike × Maturity (a_4)	0.01397	<.00001

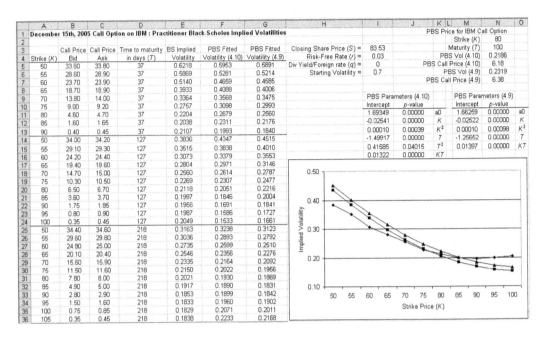

	A	B	C	D	E	F	G
1	December 15th, 2005 Call Option on IBM : Practitioner Black-Scholes Implied Volatilities						
3		Call Price	Call Price	Time to maturity	BS Implied	PBS Fitted	PBS Fitted
4	Strike (K)	Bid	Ask	in days (T)	Volatility	Volatility (4.10)	Volatility (4.9)
5	50	33.60	33.80	37	0.6218	0.5953	0.5891
6	55	28.60	28.90	37	0.5869	0.5281	0.5214
7	60	23.70	23.90	37	0.5140	0.4659	0.4585
8	65	18.70	18.90	37	0.3933	0.4088	0.4006
9	70	13.80	14.00	37	0.3364	0.3568	0.3475
10	75	9.00	9.20	37	0.2757	0.3098	0.2993
11	80	4.60	4.70	37	0.2204	0.2679	0.2560
12	85	1.60	1.65	37	0.2038	0.2311	0.2176
13	90	0.40	0.45	37	0.2107	0.1993	0.1840
14	50	34.00	34.20	127	0.3836	0.4347	0.4515
15	55	29.10	29.30	127	0.3515	0.3838	0.4010
16	60	24.20	24.40	127	0.3073	0.3379	0.3553
17	65	19.40	19.60	127	0.2804	0.2971	0.3146
18	70	14.70	15.00	127	0.2560	0.2614	0.2787
19	75	10.30	10.50	127	0.2269	0.2307	0.2477
20	80	6.50	6.70	127	0.2118	0.2051	0.2216
21	85	3.60	3.70	127	0.1997	0.1846	0.2004
22	90	1.75	1.85	127	0.1956	0.1691	0.1841
23	95	0.80	0.90	127	0.1987	0.1586	0.1727
24	100	0.35	0.45	127	0.2049	0.1533	0.1661
25	50	34.40	34.60	218	0.3163	0.3238	0.3123
26	55	29.60	29.80	218	0.3036	0.2893	0.2792
27	60	24.80	25.00	218	0.2735	0.2599	0.2510
28	65	20.10	20.40	218	0.2546	0.2356	0.2276
29	70	15.60	15.90	218	0.2335	0.2164	0.2092
30	75	11.50	11.60	218	0.2160	0.2022	0.1956
31	80	7.80	8.00	218	0.2021	0.1930	0.1869
32	85	4.90	5.00	218	0.1917	0.1890	0.1831
33	90	2.80	2.90	218	0.1853	0.1899	0.1842
34	95	1.50	1.60	218	0.1833	0.1960	0.1902
35	100	0.75	0.85	218	0.1829	0.2071	0.2011
36	105	0.35	0.45	218	0.1838	0.2233	0.2168

Side panel (columns H–I):

Closing Share Price (S) =	83.53
Risk-Free Rate (r) =	0.03
Div Yield/Foreign rate (q) =	0
Starting Volatility =	0.7

Right panel (columns L–O): PBS Price for IBM Call Option

Strike (K)	80
Maturity (T)	100
PBS Vol (4.10)	0.2186
PBS Call Price (4.10)	6.18
PBS Vol (4.9)	0.2319
PBS Call Price (4.9)	6.38

PBS Parameters (4.10):

Intercept	p-value	
1.69349	0.00000	a0
-0.02541	0.00000	K
0.00010	0.00039	K^2
-1.49917	0.00000	T
0.41585	0.04015	T^2
0.01322	0.00000	KT

PBS Parameters (4.9):

Intercept	p-value	
1.66259	0.00000	a0
-0.02522	0.00000	K
0.00010	0.00098	K^2
-1.25652	0.00000	T
0.01397	0.00000	KT

FIGURE 4.10   Solution to Exercise 4.2

price of $6.18 produced by the fitted implied volatility using (4.10) which appears in cell N5.

4.3 The VBA functions GenBS_Call() and GenBS_Put() produce the price of a call and put from the generalized Black-Scholes model, respectively.

```
Function Gauss(X)
  Gauss = Application.NormSDist(X)
End Function

Function genbs_call(S, K, r, b, T, v)
d = (Log(S / K) + T * (b + 0.5 * v ^ 2)) / (v * Sqr(T))
genbs_call = Exp((b - r) * T) * S * Gauss(d)
             - Exp(-r * T) * K * Gauss(d - v * Sqr(T))
End Function

Function genbs_put(S, K, r, b, T, v)
genbs_put = K * Exp(-r * T) * Gauss(v * Sqr(T) - d)
            - S * Exp((b - r) * T) * Gauss(-d)
End Function
```

	A	B	C	D	E
1	EXERCISE 4.3				
2					
3		**Generalized Black-Scholes Call and Put Price**			
4					
5		Underlying Price (S)	30.00	Black-Scholes Call Price	**2.400839**
6		Strike Price (K)	30.00		
7		Risk-Free Rate (r)	0.05	Black-Scholes Put Price	**2.132818**
8		Cost-of-Carry (b)	0.02		
9		Time to Maturity (T)	0.41667		
10		Volatility of the Underlying (σ)	0.3		

FIGURE 4.11   Solution to Exercise 4.3

These functions are illustrated on Figure 4.11, using the same inputs as in Figure 4.1, but on a stock paying a continuous dividend yield of 2 percent annually. The price of the call is $2.400839 and the price of the put is $2.132818.

CHAPTER 5

The Heston (1993) Stochastic Volatility Model

INTRODUCTION

The Black-Scholes model and Practitioner Black-Scholes model covered in Chapter 4 have the advantages that they express the option price in closed form and they are easy to implement. These models, however, make the strong assumption that the continuously compounded stock returns are normally distributed with constant mean and variance. The Black-Scholes formula does not depend on the mean of the returns, but it does depend on the volatility (the square root of the variance of returns). A number of empirical studies have pointed to time-varying volatility in asset prices and to the fact that this volatility tends to cluster. The assumption of constant volatility is the most restrictive assumption in the Black-Scholes model, so many of the advanced option pricing models encountered in the literature have sought to overcome this assumption by incorporating time-varying volatility. In this chapter we present the Heston (1993) model, a stochastic volatility model that has become popular and is relatively easy to implement in VBA.

Stochastic Volatility

One approach for modeling option prices under time-varying volatility is to assume that the asset price and its volatility each follow a continuous time diffusion process. Hull and White (1987) generalize the Black-Scholes model for time-varying volatility. Their model represents a general framework for stochastic volatility models in which the asset price and asset volatility each follow their own diffusion process. In their model, the option price is the expected value of the Black-Scholes price, obtained by integration over the distribution of mean volatility during the life of the option, and assuming zero correlation between the asset price and the volatility. Obtaining the density of the mean volatility requires solving a differential equation by numerical methods. While their simulations are generalized for nonzero correlation, no closed-form solution for the option price is available. Hence, while the option price expressed as the average Black-Scholes price over the mean volatility of the asset is intuitively appealing, obtaining option prices under the Hull and White (1987) model is computationally intensive.

Recall that in the model of Backus, Foresi, and Wu (2004) presented in Chapter 4, skewness and kurtosis in the distribution of the underlying asset are accounted for through a Gram-Charlier expansion of the distribution. Alternatively, incorporating skewness can be achieved by introducing correlation between the diffusion driving the underlying asset price and the diffusion driving its volatility. Incorporating skewness can be done by introducing jumps into the diffusion driving asset prices. Models with both these features are known as stochastic volatility, stochastic interest rate models with jumps (SVSI-J). Bakshi, Cao, and Chen (1997) analyze the SVSI-J model and compare its performance to the Black-Scholes model, models incorporating stochastic volatility only (SV), and models incorporating stochastic volatility and jumps (SVJ). They conclude that the most important improvement over the Black-Scholes model is achieved by introducing stochastic volatility into option pricing models. Once this is done, introducing jumps and stochastic interest rates leads to only marginal reductions in option pricing errors. Hence, in this book we ignore models that use stochastic interest rates and jumps.

THE HESTON (1993) MODEL

Contrary to the model of Hull and White (1987), the Heston (1993) model does yield a closed-form solution. Moreover, this model is better suited at allowing correlation between the asset price and the asset volatility. The model assumes a diffusion process for the stock price that is identical to that underlying the Black-Scholes model, except that the volatility is allowed to be time varying. Hence, this model is a generalization of the Black-Scholes model for time-varying volatility. The option price is obtained by calculating the probability of a call option expiring in-the-money. Although such a probability cannot be obtained directly, it can be obtained through inversion of the characteristic function of the log price of the underlying asset.

The Heston (1993) model assumes that the stock price S_t follows the diffusion

$$dS_t = \mu S_t \, dt + \sqrt{v_t} S_t dz_{1,t}$$

where μ is a drift parameter, and $z_{1,t}$ is a Weiner process. The volatility $\sqrt{v_t}$ follows the diffusion

$$d\sqrt{v_t} = -\beta \sqrt{v_t} \, dt + \delta dz_{2,t}$$

where $z_{2,t}$ is a Weiner process that has correlation ρ with $z_{1,t}$. To simplify the implementation of the model, Ito's lemma is applied to obtain the variance process v_t, which can be written as a Cox, Ingersoll, and Ross (1985) process:

$$dv_t = \kappa[\theta - v_t] \, dt + \sigma \sqrt{v_t} dz_{2,t} \qquad (5.1)$$

where

θ = the long-run mean of the variance

κ = a mean reversion parameter

σ = the volatility of volatility.

The time t price of a European call option with time to maturity $(T - t)$, denoted Call(S, v, t), is given by

$$\text{Call}(S, v, t) = S_t P_1 - K P(t, T) P_2 \qquad (5.2)$$

where

S_t = the spot price of the asset

K = the strike price of the option

$P(t, T)$ = a discount factor from time t to time T.

For example, assuming a constant rate of interest, r, we can write $P(t, T) = e^{-r \times (T-t)}$. The price of a European put option at time t is obtained through put-call parity and is given by

$$\text{Put}(S, v, t) = \text{Call}(S, v, t) + K P(t, T) - S_t. \qquad (5.3)$$

The quantities P_1 and P_2 are the probabilities that the call option expires in-the-money, conditional on the log of the stock price, $x_t = \ln[S_t] = x$, and on the volatility $v_t = v$, each at time t. In order to price options we need the risk-neutral dynamics, expressed here in terms of the risk-neutral parameters κ and θ.

$$dx_t = \left[r - \frac{1}{2} v_t \right] dt + \sqrt{v_t} dz^*_{1,t}$$
$$dv_t = \kappa [\theta - v_t] dt + \sigma \sqrt{v_t} dz^*_{2,t}. \qquad (5.4)$$

In the appendix to this chapter it is shown how these risk-neutral versions are derived. Using these dynamics, the probabilities can be interpreted as risk-adjusted or risk-neutral probabilities. Hence,

$$P_j = \Pr(x_T \geqslant \ln(K) | x_t = x, v_t = v) \qquad (5.5)$$

for $j = 1, 2$. The probabilities P_j can be obtained by inverting the characteristic functions f_j defined below. Thus,

$$P_j = \frac{1}{2} + \frac{1}{\pi} \int_0^\infty \text{Re} \left[\frac{e^{-i\phi \ln(K)} f_j}{i\phi} \right] d\phi \qquad (5.6)$$

where

$$f_j = \exp(C_j + D_j v + i\phi x) \text{ with } v = v_t$$

$$C_j = r\phi i\tau + \frac{\kappa\theta}{\sigma^2}\left\{(b_j - \rho\sigma\phi i + d_j)\tau - 2\ln\left[\frac{1 - g_j e^{d_j\tau}}{1 - g_j}\right]\right\}$$

$$D_j = \frac{b_j - \rho\sigma\phi i + d_j}{\sigma^2}\left[\frac{1 - e^{d_j\tau}}{1 - g_j e^{d_j\tau}}\right]$$

$$g_j = \frac{b_j - \rho\sigma\phi i + d_j}{b_j - \rho\sigma\phi i - d_j}$$

$$d_j = \sqrt{(\rho\sigma\phi i - b_j)^2 - \sigma^2(2u_j\phi i - \phi^2)}.$$

In these expressions $\tau = T - t$ is the time to maturity, $i = \sqrt{-1}$ is the imaginary unit, $u_1 = 1/2, u_2 = -1/2, b_1 = \kappa + \lambda - \rho\sigma$, and $b_2 = \kappa + \lambda$. The parameter λ represents the price of volatility risk as a function of the asset price, time, volatility, and time. Although (5.2) and (5.3) are considered to be closed-form solutions, each requires evaluating the two complex integrals in (5.6). The operations on complex numbers and numerical integration procedures, defined in Chapters 1 and 2, respectively, are used to approximate these complex integrals and obtain the option prices.

VBA Code for Implementing the Heston Model

The Excel file Chapter5Heston contains the VBA code for implementing the Heston (1993) model. The file contains both the full valuation approach and the analytical closed-form approach. The valuation approach is a Monte Carlo method that requires many possible price paths to be simulated, while the analytical approach is a closed-form solution up to a complex integral that must be evaluated numerically using the methods of Chapter 2. Both of these approaches are described in the sections that follow.

The Full Valuation Approach

This approach is a Monte Carlo simulation. A large number of stock price paths are simulated over the life of the option, using the stochastic process for S_t. For each stock price path, the terminal price and the value of the option at the terminal price are obtained, and the option value is discounted back to time zero at the risk-free rate. This produces the option price for a single path. This process is repeated many times, and the price of the option is taken as the mean of the option prices for each path.

Recall the Heston risk-neutral stochastic equations from (5.4):

$$dx_t = \left[r - \frac{1}{2}v_t\right]dt + \sqrt{v_t}dz_{1,t}^*$$

$$dv_t = \kappa[\theta - v_t]dt + \sigma\sqrt{v_t}dz_{2,t}^*. \tag{5.7}$$

Unfortunately, it is possible to obtain negative variances when Euler discretization is applied directly to this process. There are a number of ways to deal with this problem. The simulated variance can be inspected to check whether it is negative ($v < 0$). In this case, the variance can be set to zero ($v = 0$), or its sign can be inverted so that v becomes $-v$. Alternatively, the variance process can be modified in the same way as the stock process, by defining a process for natural log variances $y_t = \ln[v_t] = y$, which insures a positive variance. This is the approach we use. The second equation in (5.7) can easily solved for the process $y = \ln v$ by applying Ito's Lemma:

$$d\ln v_t = \frac{1}{v_t}\left(\kappa(\theta - v_t) - \frac{1}{2}\sigma^2\right)dt + \sigma\frac{1}{\sqrt{v_t}}dz_{2,t}^*. \tag{5.8}$$

The first equation in (5.7) and Equation (5.8) can both be discretized, which will allow the stock price paths to be simulated:

$$\ln S_{t+\Delta t} = \ln S_t + \left(r - \frac{1}{2}v_t\right)\Delta t + \sqrt{v_t}\sqrt{\Delta t}\varepsilon_{S,t+1}$$

$$\ln v_{t+\Delta t} = \ln v_t + \frac{1}{v_t}\left(\kappa(\theta - v_t) - \frac{1}{2}\sigma^2\right)\Delta t + \sigma\frac{1}{\sqrt{v_t}}\sqrt{\Delta t}\varepsilon_{v,t+1}. \tag{5.9}$$

Shocks to the volatility, $\varepsilon_{v,t+1}$, are correlated with the shocks to the stock price process, $\varepsilon_{S,t+1}$. This correlation is denoted ρ, so that $\rho = \text{Corr}(\varepsilon_{v,t+1}, \varepsilon_{S,t+1})$ and the relationship between the shocks can be written

$$\varepsilon_{v,t+1} = \rho\varepsilon_{S,t+1} + \sqrt{1 - \rho^2}\varepsilon_{t+1}$$

where ε_{t+1} are independently and identically distributed standard normal variables that each have zero correlation with $\varepsilon_{S,t+1}$. Broadie and Özgür (2005) explain that the discretization in (5.9) introduces a bias in the simulation of the stock price and variance, and that a large number of time steps is required to mitigate this bias. They propose a method that simulates the stock price and variance exactly.

Using the discretized equations (5.9) it is possible to generate a stochastic volatility price path. The Excel file Chapter5Simulate contains the following VBA code to generate simulated stock paths. We illustrate this simulation using $S = 100, K = 100, r = 0, \tau = 180/365 = 0.5, v = 0.01, \rho = 0, \kappa = 2, \theta = 0.01, \lambda = 0,$ and $\sigma = 0.1$. These are the same values as those used in Heston (1993).

```
For daycnt = 1 To daynum
  e = Application.NormSInv(Rnd)
  eS = Application.NormSInv(Rnd)
  ev = rho * eS + Sqr(1 - rho ^ 2) * e
  lnSt = lnSt + (r - 0.5 * curv) * deltat + Sqr(curv) * Sqr(deltat) * eS
  curS = Exp(lnSt)
  lnvt = lnvt + (kappa * (theta - curv) - lambda
        * curv - 0.5 * sigmav) * deltat + sigmav
        * (1 / Sqr(curv)) * Sqr(deltat) * ev
  curv = Exp(lnvt)
  allS(daycnt) = curS
Next daycnt
```

This loop generates one potential price path under the Heston stochastic volatility price process, over a time period of daynum days (daynum/365 years). Figure 5.1 shows one such possible stock price path, taken from the Excel file Chapter5Simulate. If this were the only possible price path, the option would be priced by using the terminal value of the stock price, $S_T = 104.26$.

Suppose a call option with strike $K = 100$ is to be priced. Then the price of this call is $S_T - K$ discounted to time zero, namely $(104.26 - 100)e^{-r \times (180/365)}$, which produces a price of \$4.16 when $r = 0.05$. The path in Figure 5.1 is obviously not the only price path that the stock can follow, and what is needed is the distribution

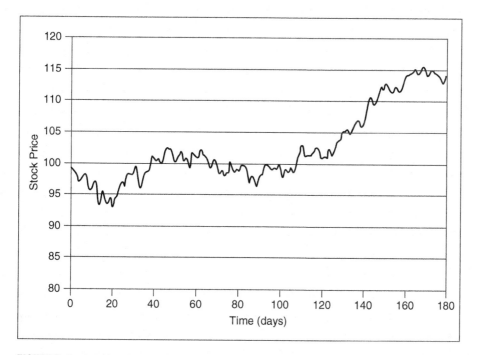

FIGURE 5.1 Simulated Stock Price Path

of the terminal stock price, which is unavailable in closed form. By simulating many stock price paths, however, this distribution can be approximated. The terminal value of the option at each simulated terminal price can be obtained, and discounted back to time zero. The option price can then be defined as the mean of the set of discounted values. The VBA function simPath(), which appears as part of the Excel file Chapter5Simulate, produces a number of simulated paths equal to the value of ITER, and evaluates the price of the call for each path.

```
Function simPath(kappa, theta, lambda, rho, sigmav, daynum, startS, r,
              startv, K)
For itcount = 1 To ITER
  lnSt = Log(startS): lnvt = Log(startv)
  curv = startv: curS = startS
    For daycnt = 1 To daynum
      ' Stock Path Generating VBA Code ...
    Next daycnt
Next itcount
  simPath = Application.Transpose(allS)
End Function
```

This procedure, however, is very computationally expensive. For example, with 1,000 iterations and a call option with $\tau = 180$ days to maturity, a total of 360,000 random standard normal variables must be generated with the NormSInv() function. In Figure 5.1 only one possible stock price path is simulated, so ITER=1.

It is straightforward to extent the code to generate the Heston (1993) call price by Monte Carlo. The Excel file Chapter5HestonMC contains the VBA function HestonMC() to perform this routine. It is the same as the function simPath(), except that the discounted call price is obtained at the end of each daycnt loop, and the function returns the average of these call prices.

```
Function HestonMC(kappa, theta, lambda, rho, sigmav, daynum, startS, r,
              startv, K, ITER)
' More VBA Code
For itcount = 1 To ITER
    For daycnt = 1 To daynum
      ' Stock Path Generating VBA Code ...
    Next daycnt
simPath = simPath + Exp((-daynum / 365) * r) *
        Application.Max(allS(daynum) - K, 0)
Next itcount
  HestonMC = simPath / ITER
End Function
```

Figure 5.2 illustrates this function on a call option with a time to maturity of 30 days. Using 5,000 iterations, the call price obtained by Monte Carlo simulation is $1.1331. The analytical price of this option, using the functions described in the latter parts of this chapter, is $1.1345.

	A	B	C	D
1				
2		**Heston (1993) Call Price**		
3		**by Monte Carlo**		
4				
5		Spot Price (S)	100	
6		Strike Price (K)	100	
7		Risk Free Rate (r)	0	
8		Time to Maturity (T − t)	30	
9		Rho (ρ)	0	
10		Kappa (κ)	2	
11		Theta (θ)	0.01	
12		Lambda (λ)	0	
13		Volatility of Variance (σ)	0.1	
14		Current variance (v)	0.01	
15		Number of Simulations	5,000	
16				
17		**Heston Call Price**	1.1331	
18				

FIGURE 5.2 Heston (1993) Call Price by Monte Carlo

The Closed-Form Approach

The closed-form solution is much faster at producing option prices, since stock price paths do not have to be simulated. This method, however, is more difficult to implement because it requires that the complex integrals in (5.6) be evaluated. The closed-form requires the user to input the spot price S_t of the asset, the strike price K, the time to maturity $\tau = T - t$, and the risk-free rate of interest r (assumed constant). It also requires estimates of the parameters driving the drift processes, namely the long-run variance θ, the current variance v_t, the price of volatility risk λ, the mean reversion parameter κ, the volatility of variance σ, and the correlation between the processes driving the asset price and the volatility, ρ. Note that in earlier chapters we set $t = 0$ so that the time to maturity was simply T.

The Excel file Chapter5Heston contains the VBA function Heston() to implement the closed-form solution of the Heston (1993) model. This function contains four main elements:

1. A complex library introduced in Chapter 1 that defines operations on complex numbers and that will be required at various stages of implementing the model.
2. A function for the integrands in Equation (5.6).
3. Functions that implement numerical integration of each integral in (5.6) so that P_1 and P_2 can be obtained.

4. A function that calculates the Heston (1993) price of a European call option given in Equation (5.2), and put option price through put-call parity given in (5.3).

We now describe the four different sections of the Heston() function. There are two complex integrals to be computed in (5.6), for each of the probabilities in (5.5). The VBA function HestonP1() defines the function $Re[e^{i\phi \ln(K)}f_1/i\phi]$, which is integrated to yield P_1, and the function HestonP2() defines $Re[e^{i\phi \ln(K)}f_2/i\phi]$, which is integrated to yield P_2.

```
Function HestonP1(phi, kappa, theta, lambda, rho, sigma, tau, K, S, r, v)
mu1 = 0.5
b1 = set_cNum(kappa + lambda - rho * sigma, 0)
d1 = cNumSqrt(cNumSub(cNumSq(cNumSub(set_cNum(0, rho *
    sigma * phi), b1)), cNumSub(set_cNum(0, sigma ^ 2 *
    2 * mu1 * phi), set_cNum(sigma ^ 2 * phi ^ 2, 0))))
g1 = cNumDiv(cNumAdd(cNumSub(b1, set_cNum(0, rho
    * sigma * phi)), d1), cNumSub(cNumSub(b1,
    set_cNum(0, rho * sigma * phi)), d1))
DD1_1 = cNumDiv(cNumAdd(cNumSub(b1, set_cNum(0, rho
    * sigma * phi)), d1), set_cNum(sigma ^ 2, 0))
DD1_2 = cNumSub(set_cNum(1, 0), cNumExp(cNumProd(d1,
    set_cNum(tau, 0))))
DD1_3 = cNumSub(set_cNum(1, 0), cNumProd(g1,
    cNumExp(cNumProd(d1, set_cNum(tau, 0)))))
DD1 = cNumProd(DD1_1, cNumDiv(DD1_2, DD1_3))
CC1_1 = set_cNum(0, r * phi * tau)
CC1_2 = set_cNum((kappa * theta) / (sigma ^ 2), 0)
CC1_3 = cNumProd(cNumAdd(cNumSub(b1, set_cNum(0, rho
    * sigma * phi)), d1), set_cNum(tau, 0))
CC1_4 = cNumProd(set_cNum(2, 0), cNumLn(cNumDiv
        (cNumSub(set_cNum(1, 0), cNumProd(g1,
        cNumExp(cNumProd(d1, set_cNum(tau, 0))))),
        cNumSub(set_cNum(1, 0), g1))))
cc1 = cNumAdd(CC1_1, cNumProd(CC1_2,
    cNumSub(CC1_3, CC1_4)))
f1 = cNumExp(cNumAdd(cNumAdd(cc1, cNumProd(DD1,
    set_cNum(v, 0))), set_cNum(0,
    phi * Application.Ln(S))))
HestonP1 = cNumReal(cNumDiv(cNumProd(cNumExp(
        set_cNum(0, -phi * Application.Ln(K))), f1),
        set_cNum(0, phi)))
End Function
```

The function HestonP2() is identical to HestonP1(), except that different values of u_j and b_j are used, in accordance with the definitions that follow (5.6).

Once these functions are implemented the trapezoidal integration rule from Chapter 2 can be used to obtain the integrals P_1 and P_2. As shown in Heston (1993), the integrals converge very quickly so a very large upper limit of integration is not needed. This will become evident later in the next section of this chapter, in which the rate of convergence of the complex integral in (5.6) is examined. In the Heston() function described below, the limits of integration are set to [0,100], and a fine grid with step size of 0.1 is used. Note that the last statements ensure that the probabilities P_1 and P_2 both lie in the interval [0,1].

```
Function Heston(PutCall As String, kappa, theta, lambda, rho, sigma, tau,
          K, S, r, v)
Dim P1_int(1001) As Double, P2_int(1001) As Double, phi_int(1001) As
          Double
Dim p1 As Double, p2 As Double, phi As Double, xg(16) As Double, wg(16) As
          Double
cnt = 1
For phi = 0.0001 To 100.0001 Step 0.1
  phi_int(cnt) = phi
  P1_int(cnt) = HestonP1(phi, kappa, theta, lambda, rho, sigma, tau,
          K, S, r, v)
  P2_int(cnt) = HestonP2(phi, kappa, theta, lambda, rho, sigma, tau,
          K, S, r, v)
  cnt = cnt + 1
Next phi
p1 = 0.5 + (1 / thePI) * TRAPnumint(phi_int, P1_int)
p2 = 0.5 + (1 / thePI) * TRAPnumint(phi_int, P2_int)
If p1 < 0 Then p1 = 0
If p1 > 1 Then p1 = 1
If p2 < 0 Then p2 = 0
If p2 > 1 Then p2 = 1
```

The final step of the closed-form solution is the evaluation of the call and put prices. The call price can be obtained easily by using (5.2) once the risk-neutral probabilities P_1 and P_2 are obtained. With the call price, put-call parity (5.3) can be used to obtain the price of the put.

```
HestonC = S * p1 - K * Exp(-r * tau) * p2
If PutCall = "Call" Then
  Heston = HestonC
ElseIf PutCall = "Put" Then
  Heston = HestonC + K * Exp(-r * tau) - S
End If
End Function
```

Figure 5.3 illustrates the use of the VBA functions to implement the Heston call and put prices contained in the Excel file Chapter5Heston. As in the previous chapters, range names are assigned to the 10 input values in cells C4:C13 required for the Heston() function. To obtain the price of a call, the Heston() function requires "Call" as the first argument. Hence, in cell C16 we type

= Heston("Call", kappa, theta, lambda, rho, sigmav, dtm, K,S, rf,V),

	A	B	C	D
1				
2		**Heston (1993) Price of a Call or Put Option**		
3				
4		Spot Price (S)	100	
5		Strike Price (K)	100	
6		Risk Free Rate (r)	0.05	
7		Time to Maturity ($T - t$)	0.5	
8		Rho (ρ)	0	
9		Kappa (κ)	2	
10		Theta (θ)	0.01	
11		Lambda (λ)	0	
12		Volatility of Variance (σ)	0.225	
13		Current variance (v)	0.01	
14				
15				
16		**Heston Call Price**	4.0852	
17		**Heston Put Price**	1.6162	
18				

FIGURE 5.3   Closed-Form Heston (1993) Option Prices

and the function produces a price of \$4.0852. Similarly, to price a put option the Heston() function requires "Put" as the first argument of the function. Hence, in cell C17 we type

$$= \text{Heston("Put", kappa, theta, lambda, rho, sigmav, dtm, K, S, rf, V)}$$

and the function produces a price of \$1.6162.

The computational weakness of the Heston (1993) comes from the requirement of a numerical integration. The prices are sensitive to the width of the integration slices (abscissas). To increase computation speed, a Gaussian quadrature could be used, or the abscissas could be varied as a function of the ϕ parameter. In the next section we show how combining the functions $\text{Re}[e^{i\phi \ln K} f_j / i\phi]$ leads to a function that is well-behaved and much easier to integrate.

INCREASING INTEGRATION ACCURACY

The Heston (1993) model contains two complex integrals in (5.6), each of which are used to obtain risk-neutral probabilities. Figure 5.4 illustrates the convergence of the two functions used in (5.6). Each graph is a plot of $\text{Re}[e^{i\phi \ln K} f_j / i\phi]$ as a function of ϕ, $j = 1, 2$. Each function converges quickly to zero, and each displays a similar pattern.

Figure 5.4 highlights two important points. First, both functions are zero for values of ϕ beyond, say, 75. This implies that the upper integration limits in the

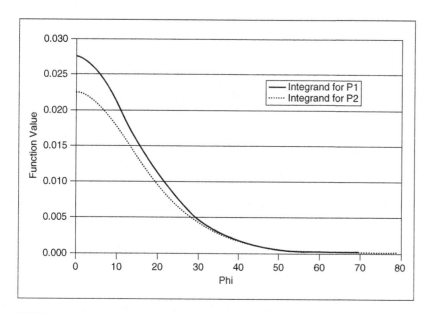

FIGURE 5.4 Convergence of Functions Used in Integration

numerical algorithms to implement (5.6) need not be excessively high, and that the limit of 100 that we select is more than adequate. Second, the similar convergence pattern of each function implies that the integrals in (5.6) could be combined into the same integral. Recall the equation for the Heston (1993) call price (5.2)

$$\text{Call}(S, v, t) = S_t P_1 - e^{-r(T-t)} K P_2 \tag{5.10}$$

and the expression for the risk-neutral probabilities (5.6)

$$P_j = \frac{1}{2} + \frac{1}{\pi} \int_0^\infty \text{Re}\left[\frac{e^{-i\phi \ln(K)} f_j}{i\phi} \right] d\phi. \tag{5.11}$$

These two equations can be combined to arrive at the following formula for the Heston call price:

$$\text{Call}(S, v, t) = \frac{1}{2}(S_t - Ke^{-r(T-t)})$$

$$+ \frac{1}{\pi} \left\{ \int_0^\infty \left(S_t \text{Re}\left[\frac{e^{i\phi \ln K} f_1}{i\phi} \right] - Ke^{-r(T-t)} \text{Re}\left[\frac{e^{i\phi \ln K} f_2}{i\phi} \right] \right) d\phi \right\}. \tag{5.12}$$

Although this formula for the call price is less intuitive than (5.2), it combines the two sinusoidal functions into one well-behaved and fast-converging function. Figure 5.5 plots the function appearing in the integral of (5.12), as a function of ϕ.

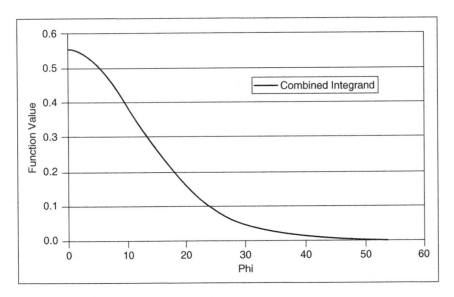

FIGURE 5.5   Convergence of Combined Function

Figure 5.5 illustrates that the shape of the combined integrand in (5.12) is smooth and well behaved. Hence, using (5.12) will not cause any problems with the numerical integration required to obtain the call price. Moreover, since (5.12) requires only one numerical integration to produce the call price, rather than two integrations in (5.10), it will calculate the call price much faster. Moreover, since the integrand in (5.12) is smooth and well behaved, it will be possible to obtain accurate approximations to the integral regardless of which numerical integration algorithm is applied.

The Excel file Chapter5Integral contains the VBA function Heston2() used to generate Figures 5.4 and 5.5. The function uses the VBA functions HestonP1() and HestonP2() defined earlier in this chapter.

```
Function Heston2(kappa, theta, lambda, rho, sigma, tau, K, S, r, v)
Dim P1_int(1001) As Double, P2_int(1001) As Double, phi_int(1001) As
                Double
Dim P1 As Double, P2 As Double, phi As Double, xg(16) As Double, wg(16) As
                Double, HestonC As Double
Dim allP(1001, 4)
cnt = 1
For phi = 0.0001 To 100.0001 Step 0.1
  phi_int(cnt) = phi
  allP(cnt, 1) = phi
  P1_int(cnt) = HestonP1(phi, kappa, theta, lambda, rho, sigma, tau,
                K, S, r, v)
  P2_int(cnt) = HestonP2(phi, kappa, theta, lambda, rho, sigma, tau,
                K, S, r, v)
```

```
   allP(cnt, 4) = S * P1_int(cnt) - K * Exp(-r * tau) * P2_int(cnt)
   cnt = cnt + 1
Next phi
For i = 1 To 1001
   allP(i, 2) = P1_int(i)
   allP(i, 3) = P2_int(i)
Next i
   Heston2 = allP
End Function
```

The output of the function is the array allP(). The values of ϕ are stored in the first column of allP(), while the values of the integrands for P_1 and P_2 are stored in the second and third columns, respectively. Finally, the value of the integrand in (5.12) is stored in the fourth column of allP().

THE FUNDAMENTAL TRANSFORM

Although regrouping both integrals into a single integral leads to greater accuracy and speed, there is another way this can be achieved. Lewis (2000) shows how the call price $C(S, V, \tau)$ for the Heston (1993) model can be written in terms of the fundamental transform $\hat{H}(k, V, \tau)$, where $k = k_r + ik_i$ is a complex number, V is the volatility, and $\tau = T - t$ is the time to maturity. In VBA, this leads to option prices that are faster to obtain and more accurate, since only one integration is required. The general formula for the call price under a general class of stochastic volatility models is

$$C(S, V, \tau) = Se^{-\delta\tau} - Ke^{-r\tau} \frac{1}{2\pi} \int_{ik_i-\infty}^{ik_i+\infty} e^{-ikX} \frac{\hat{H}(k, V, \tau)}{k^2 - ik} \, dk \qquad (5.13)$$

where $X = \ln S/K + (r - \delta)\tau, k_i = 1/2$, and δ is the dividend yield. For Heston model, the fundamental transform takes the form

$$\hat{H}(k, V, \tau) = \exp[f_1(t) + f_2(t)V_t] \qquad (5.14)$$

where

$$f_1(t) = \tilde{\omega}\left[tg - \ln\left(\frac{1 - h\exp(td)}{1 - h}\right)\right], \quad f_2(t) = g\left(\frac{1 - \exp(td)}{1 - h\exp(td)}\right), \quad (5.15)$$

$$d = (\hat{\theta}^2 + 4\tilde{c})^{1/2}, g = \frac{1}{2}(\hat{\theta} + d), \quad h = \frac{\hat{\theta} + d}{\hat{\theta} - d}, \qquad (5.16)$$

$$\hat{\theta} = \frac{2}{\sigma^2}\left[(1 - \gamma - ik)\rho\sigma + \sqrt{\kappa^2 - \gamma(1 - \gamma)\sigma^2}\right] \text{ for } \gamma < 1, \qquad (5.17)$$

and where $t = \sigma^2 \tau / 2$, $\tilde{\omega} = 2\kappa\theta/\sigma^2$, $\tilde{c} = 2c(k)/\sigma^2$, and $c(k) = (k^2 - ik)/2$. When $\gamma = 1$, $\hat{\theta}$ is set to $\hat{\theta} = \kappa$. The parameter γ is the representative agent's risk-aversion parameter (Huang and Litzenberger, 1988), and is restricted to $\gamma \leqslant 1$. It is another way to represent the volatility risk premium. The implementation presented in Heston (1993) and shown at the beginning of this chapter, assumes risk-neutrality and specifies a form for the volatility risk premium specified by λ, where λ is restricted to be proportional to the variance. The derivation of the model presented here specifies the risk-aversion parameter of the representative agent, which implies a volatility risk premium.

The Excel file Chapter5HTrans contains VBA functions for implementing the Heston (1993) call price using the fundamental transform. The function intH() produces the integrand in (5.13). Note that in the first part of the function, the parameters κ, θ, and σ from Heston (1993) are transformed to make them consistent with the parameters ω, ξ, and θ from Lewis (2000). Hence, $\omega = \kappa\theta$ (omega), $\xi = \sigma$ (ksi), and $\theta = \kappa$ (theta).

```
Function intH(K As cNum, X, VO, tau, thet, kappa, SigmaV, rho, gam) As
              Double
Dim b As cNum, im As cNum, thetaadj As cNum, c As cNum
Dim d As cNum, f As cNum, h As cNum, AA As cNum,.BB As cNum
Dim Hval As cNum, t As cNum, a As cNum, re As cNum

omega = kappa * thet: ksi = SigmaV: theta = kappa
t = set_cNum(ksi ^ 2 * tau / 2, 0)
a = set_cNum(2 * omega / ksi ^ 2, 0)
If (gam = 1) Then
  thetaadj = set_cNum(theta, 0)
Else
  thetaadj = set_cNum((1 - gam) * rho * ksi
          + Sqr(theta ^ 2 - gam * (1 - gam) * ksi ^ 2), 0)
End If
im = set_cNum(0, 1)
re = set_cNum(1, 0)
b = cNumProd(set_cNum(2, 0), cNumDiv(cNumAdd(thetaadj,
    cNumProd(im, cNumProd(K, set_cNum(rho * ksi, 0)))),
    set_cNum(ksi ^ 2, 0)))
c = cNumDiv(cNumSub(cNumSq(K), cNumProd(im, K)),
    set_cNum(ksi ^ 2, 0))
d = cNumSqrt(cNumAdd(cNumSq(b),
    cNumProd(set_cNum(4, 0), c)))
f = cNumDiv(cNumAdd(b, d), set_cNum(2, 0))
h = cNumDiv(cNumAdd(b, d), cNumSub(b, d))
AA = cNumSub(cNumProd(cNumProd(f, a), t),
    cNumProd(a, cNumLn(cNumDiv(cNumSub(re,
    cNumProd(h, cNumExp(cNumProd(d, t)))),
    cNumSub(re, h)))))
BB = cNumDiv(cNumProd(f, cNumSub(re, cNumExp(
    cNumProd(d, t)))), cNumSub(re, cNumProd(h,
    cNumExp(cNumProd(d, t)))))
```

```
Hval = cNumExp(cNumAdd(AA, cNumProd(BB, set_cNum(V0, 0))))
intH = cNumReal(cNumProd(cNumDiv(cNumExp(cNumProd(cNumProd(
       set_cNum(-X, 0), im), K)), cNumSub(cNumSq(K),
       cNumProd(im, K))), Hval))
End Function
```

The function HCTrans() uses the trapezoidal rule to approximate the integral in (5.13), and returns the call price. The range of integration is over $(0, k_{max})$, where $k_{max} = \max(1000, 10/\sqrt{\tau V_0})$.

```
Function HCTrans(S, K, r, delta, V0, tau, ki, thet, kappa, SigmaV, rho,
                gam, PutCall As String)
Dim int_x() As Double, int_y() As Double
Dim pass_phi As cNum
omega = kappa * thet: ksi = SigmaV: theta = kappa
kmax = Round(Application.Max(1000, 10 / Sqr(V0 * tau)), 0)
ReDim int_x(kmax * 5) As Double, int_y(kmax * 5) As Double
X = Application.Ln(S / K) + (r - delta) * tau
cnt = 0
For phi = 0.000001 To kmax Step 0.2
  cnt = cnt + 1
  int_x(cnt) = phi
  pass_phi = set_cNum(phi, ki)
  int_y(cnt) = intH(pass_phi, X, V0, tau, thet, kappa, SigmaV, rho, gam)
Next phi
CallPrice = (S * Exp(-delta * tau) - (1 / thePI) * K *
            Exp(-r * tau) * TRAPnumint(int_x, int_y))
If PutCall = "Call" Then
  HCTrans = CallPrice
ElseIf PutCall = "Put" Then
  HCTrans = CallPrice + K * Exp(-r * tau) - S * Exp(-delta * tau)
End If
End Function
```

Figure 5.6 illustrates these functions, using the same parameter values as in Figure 5.3, with $k_i = 0.5$ and $\gamma = 1$. In cell C19 we type

$$= \text{HCTrans(S, K, rf, delta, V0, tau, ki, thet, kappa, SigmaV, rho, gam, "Call")}$$

which produces a price of \$4.0852, exactly that in Figure 5.3.

SENSITIVITY ANALYSIS

As mentioned in the introduction to this chapter, the Heston (1993) model defines a diffusion process for the stock price that is identical to that which underlies the Black-Scholes model, except that the Heston model incorporates time-varying volatility. The volatility is allowed to be stochastic and evolves in accordance with

	A	B	C	D
1				
2		**Heston (1993) Call Price**		
3		**Using Fundamental Transform**		
4				
5		Spot Price (S)	100	
6		Strike Price (K)	100	
7		Risk Free Rate (r)	0.05	
8		Dividend Yield (δ)	0	
9		Time to Maturity (τ = T − t)	0.5	
10		Rho (ρ)	0	
11		Kappa (κ)	2	
12		Theta (θ)	0.01	
13		Volatility of Variance (σ)	0.225	
14		Current variance (v)	0.01	
15		Imaginary Part of k (k_i)	0.5	
16		Gamma (γ)	1	
17				
18				
19		**Heston Call Price**	4.0852	
20		**Heston Put Price**	1.6162	
21				

FIGURE 5.6 Heston (1993) Call Price Using the
Fundamental Transform

a separate diffusion process. In this section we investigate how the incorporation of stochastic volatility affects call prices.

There are two parameters from the Heston (1993) call prices that merit particular attention, the correlation between shocks to the stock price and shocks to the variance, ρ, and the volatility of variance, σ. A negative value of ρ will induce negative skewness in the stock price distribution, so that negative shocks to the stock price will result in positive shocks to variance. This negative relationship between the stock price and variance implies that drops in the stock price are followed by increases in variance, leading to the possibility of even bigger drops in the stock price. The opposite is true when ρ is positive. How does negative or positive skewness affect option prices? When stock prices are negatively skewed, the probability of large losses is higher than predicted by the Black-Scholes model. In other words, when the correlation ρ is negative, the right tail of the stock price distribution is narrowed, and the left tail is thickened. To illustrate how this affects call prices, we replicate the experiment of Heston (1993). For different levels of moneyness, call prices are generated using the Heston model and the Black-Scholes model. For each call price, the difference between the Heston price and the Black-Scholes price is obtained, and this difference is plotted against the spot price of the stock. The same parameter values as Heston (1993) are used, namely

$S = 100, K = 100, r = 0, \tau = 0.5, v = 0.01, \kappa = 2, \theta = 0.01, \lambda = 0$, and $\sigma = 0.225$. The experiment is performed with $\rho = -0.5$ and repeated with $\rho = +0.5$, both with spot price ranging from \$75 to \$125 in increments of \$2.50.

In order for this experiment to work properly, the volatility parameter in the Black-Scholes model must be matched to the square root of the variance parameter in the Heston model, so that the average volatility over the life of the option is the same for both models. This can be done using the characteristic functions f_j defined by the model and that appear under (5.6), since moments can always be derived from the characteristic function. The volatility parameters defined in the last paragraph, however, have already been matched by Heston (1993). When rho is equal to zero ($\rho = 0$) the Black-Scholes volatility parameter is $\sigma_{BS} = 0.99985$, when $\rho = -0.5$ it is $\sigma_{BS} = 0.099561$, and when $\rho = +0.5$ it is $\sigma_{BS} = 0.100409$. The call prices and the differences obtained from the Heston (1993) experiments are presented in the Excel file Chapter5Correlation, and illustrated in Figure 5.7. The Heston prices are obtained using the HCTrans() function described in the previous section.

The Black-Scholes prices use the matched volatilities that appear in cells C20 and C21. The differences between the Heston and Black-Scholes call prices appear

	A	B	C	D	E	F	G	H	I	J	K	L
1												
2							$\rho = -0.5$				$\rho = +0.5$	
3		**Heston (1993) Parameters**			Spot	Heston	B-S	Difference		Heston	B-S	Difference
4					75.0	0.00	0.00	0.00		0.00	0.00	0.00
5		Current variance (v)	0.01		77.5	0.00	0.00	0.00		0.00	0.00	0.00
6		Kappa (κ)	2		80.0	0.00	0.00	0.00		0.01	0.00	0.01
7		Theta (θ)	0.01		82.5	0.00	0.01	0.00		0.03	0.01	0.02
8		Lambda (λ)	0		85.0	0.01	0.02	-0.01		0.06	0.02	0.04
9		Volatility of Variance (σ)	0.1		87.5	0.04	0.07	-0.04		0.14	0.08	0.06
10		Strike Price (K)	100		90.0	0.13	0.20	-0.07		0.29	0.20	0.09
11		Risk Free Rate (r)	0		92.5	0.36	0.46	-0.10		0.57	0.47	0.10
12		Dividend Yield (δ)	0		95.0	0.82	0.93	-0.11		1.03	0.95	0.08
13		Time to Maturity (T − t)	0.5		97.5	1.62	1.70	-0.08		1.75	1.72	0.03
14		Type (Call or Put)	Call		100.0	2.78	2.81	-0.02		2.80	2.83	-0.03
15		Imaginary Part of k (k_i)	0.5		102.5	4.31	4.27	0.04		4.20	4.29	-0.09
16		Gamma (γ)	1		105.0	6.13	6.04	0.09		5.94	6.06	-0.12
17					107.5	8.19	8.08	0.11		7.97	8.09	-0.12
18		**Black-Scholes Matched Volatilities**			110.0	10.41	10.30	0.11		10.21	10.31	-0.10
19					112.5	12.74	12.65	0.09		12.59	12.65	-0.06
20		Volatility for ρ = − 0.5	0.099561		115.0	15.13	15.07	0.07		15.03	15.07	-0.04
21		Volatility for ρ = + 0.5	0.100409		117.5	17.58	17.53	0.05		17.51	17.53	-0.02
22					120.0	20.04	20.01	0.03		20.00	20.01	-0.01
23					122.5	22.52	22.50	0.02		22.50	22.50	0.00
24					125.0	25.01	25.00	0.01		25.00	25.00	0.00
25					127.5	27.51	27.50	0.01		27.50	27.50	0.00
26					130.0	30.00	30.00	0.00		30.00	30.00	0.00
27					132.5	32.50	32.50	0.00		32.50	32.50	0.00
28					135.0	35.00	35.00	0.00		35.00	35.00	0.00

FIGURE 5.7 Impact of Correlation on Call Prices

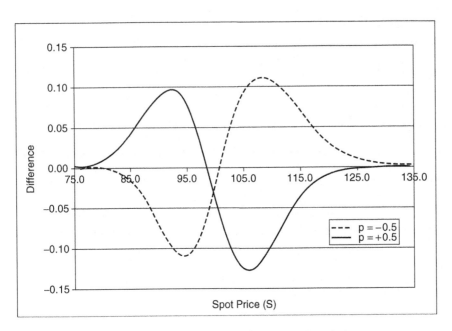

FIGURE 5.8 Plots of Call Price Differences with Varying Correlation

in cells H4:H28 for $\rho = -0.5$ and in cells L4:L28 for $\rho = +0.5$. These differences are plotted as a function of the spot price in Figure 5.8.

The portion of Figure 5.8 to the right of the spot price of $100 corresponds to in-the-money (ITM) call options, while the portion to the left of $100 corresponds to out-of-the-money (OTM) call options. Recall that these plots are for option prices for which the underlying stock price under both models has the same average volatility over the life of the option, so the differences in call prices plotted in the figure are not due to differences in volatility. With negative correlation (dashed line) the difference for OTM options is negative, which means that OTM Heston call options are less expensive than Black-Scholes call options. Since negative correlation induces negative skewness in the stock price distribution and decreases the thickness of the right tail, the price of Heston OTM calls relative to Black-Scholes OTM calls is decreased. This result is intuitive because OTM options are sensitive to the thickness of the right tail of the stock distribution. The Heston model is able to detect this decrease in thickness and decrease the call price accordingly, whereas the Black-Scholes model is unable to detect skewness in the stock price distribution. In-the-money call options, on the other hand, are more sensitive to the left tail of the distribution. With negative correlation the left tail is thickened, so the call prices under the Heston model are higher than under the Black-Scholes model. When the correlation parameter is positive (solid line) the opposite is true. The Heston model reduces the price of ITM calls relative to Black-Scholes, but increases the price of OTM calls.

The second experiment examines the effect on call option prices of varying the volatility of variance parameter, σ. In the simplest case, a volatility of variance of zero ($\sigma = 0$), corresponds to deterministic variance in the process (5.1) driving the volatility dynamics. Volatility of variance controls the kurtosis of the return distribution. Higher volatility of variance increases the kurtosis of the distribution, while lower volatility of variance decreases the kurtosis. This experiment is identical to the previous experiment in that the difference between the call price obtained with the Heston and the call price is plotted against the spot price of the stock. The same parameters as in the previous experiment are used, but with $\rho = 0$. The parameter σ takes on two values, $\sigma = 0.1$ and $\sigma = 0.2$. These differences are presented in Figure 5.9, and their plots as a function of the spot price are presented in Figure 5.10. The results and the plots are in the Excel file Chapter5Variance. Again, the Heston prices are generated using the HCTrans() function described in the previous section.

The plots in Figure 5.10 indicate that the differences between the Heston and Black-Scholes call prices are essentially symmetrical for ITM and OTM options, about the at-the-money (ATM) price of $100. The Heston model gives lower ATM call option prices than the Black-Scholes model, but higher ITM and OTM call option prices. This illustrates the fact that the volatility of variance parameter affects the kurtosis of the distribution, with little or no effect on the skewness. Higher kurtosis induces thicker tails at both ends of the returns distribution. The Heston

	A	B	C	D	E	F	G	H	I	J	K	L
1												
2							$\sigma = 0.1$				$\sigma = 0.2$	
3		**Heston (1993) Parameters**			**Spot**	**Heston**	**B-S**	**Difference**		**Heston**	**B-S**	**Difference**
4					75.0	0.00	0.00	0.00		0.00	0.00	0.00
5		Current Variance (v)	0.01		76.0	0.00	0.00	0.00		0.00	0.00	0.00
6		Rho (ρ)	0		77.0	0.00	0.00	0.00		0.00	0.00	0.00
7		Kappa (κ)	2		78.0	0.00	0.00	0.00		0.00	0.00	0.00
8		Theta (θ)	0.01		79.0	0.00	0.00	0.00		0.01	0.00	0.01
9		Lambda (λ)	0		80.0	0.00	0.00	0.00		0.01	0.00	0.01
10		Strike Price (K)	100		81.0	0.01	0.00	0.00		0.01	0.00	0.01
11		Risk Free Rate (r)	0		82.0	0.01	0.00	0.00		0.02	0.00	0.01
12		Dividend Yield (δ)	0		83.0	0.01	0.01	0.00		0.03	0.01	0.02
13		Time to Maturity (T − t)	0.5		84.0	0.02	0.01	0.01		0.04	0.01	0.02
14		Type (Call or Put)	Call		85.0	0.03	0.02	0.01		0.05	0.02	0.03
15		Imaginary Part of k (k_i)	0.5		86.0	0.05	0.04	0.01		0.07	0.04	0.03
16		Gamma (γ)	1		87.0	0.07	0.06	0.01		0.10	0.06	0.04
17					88.0	0.10	0.09	0.01		0.13	0.09	0.04
18		**Black-Scholes Matched Volatility**			89.0	0.15	0.14	0.01		0.18	0.14	0.04
19					90.0	0.21	0.20	0.01		0.24	0.20	0.04
20		σ_{BS} =	0.099985		91.0	0.29	0.29	0.01		0.32	0.29	0.03
21					92.0	0.40	0.40	0.01		0.42	0.40	0.02
22					93.0	0.54	0.54	0.00		0.55	0.54	0.01
23					94.0	0.72	0.72	0.00		0.71	0.72	-0.01
24					95.0	0.93	0.94	-0.01		0.91	0.94	-0.03
25					96.0	1.20	1.21	-0.02		1.16	1.21	-0.06

FIGURE 5.9 Impact of Volatility of Variance on Call Price Differences

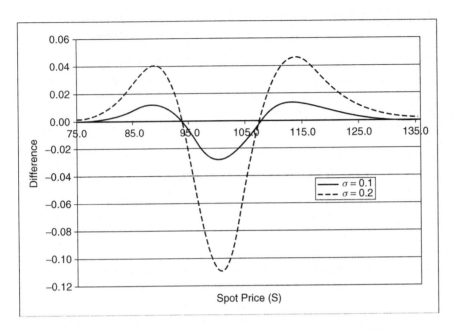

FIGURE 5.10   Plots of Call Price Differences with Varying Volatility of Variance

model is able to detect these thickened tails, and increases the price of ITM and OTM calls relative to the Black-Sholes model, which cannot detect thicker tails. Not surprisingly, since higher volatility of variance induces larger kurtosis, the price difference between the Heston prices and the Black-Scholes prices is higher for $\sigma = 0.2$ than it is for $\sigma = 0.1$.

SUMMARY

In this chapter we present the Heston (1993) option pricing model for plain-vanilla calls and puts. This model extends the Black-Scholes model by incorporating time varying stock price volatility into the option price. One simple way to implement the Heston model is through Monte Carlo simulation of the process driving the stock price. However, this method is computationally expensive. Alternatively, it is possible to obtain closed-form solutions for the option prices, but this requires that a complex integral be evaluated. Empirical experiments demonstrate that the Heston model accounts for skewness and kurtosis in stock price distributions and adjusts call prices accordingly. By combining the two integrals in the expression for the Heston (1993) call price, faster approximations to the integral are possible since only one integral must be evaluated. This is especially true when the Heston call price is obtained using the fundamental transform. The smoothness of the integrand in this combined integral suggests that good approximations to the integral are possible regardless of which numerical integration rule is used.

EXERCISES

This section provides exercises that deal with the Heston option pricing model. Solutions to these exercises are in the Excel file Chapter5Exercises.

5.1 Use the 10-point Gauss-Legendre quadrature VBA function GLquad10() presented in Chapter 2 to implement the Heston (1993) call price, using the parameter values in Figure 5.2. Compare the results with the implementation in this chapter that uses a 1,001-point trapezoidal numerical integration.

5.2 Use the variable-point Gauss-Laguerre quadrature VBA function GLAU() presented in Chapter 2 to implement the Heston (1993) call price, using the parameter values in Figure 5.2 and varying the number of integration points (abscissas) from 1 to 16. Compare with the results implementation in this chapter that uses a 1,001-point trapezoidal numerical integration.

SOLUTIONS TO EXERCISES

5.1 Instead of looping from 0.0001 to 100.0001 in the trapezoidal rule (1,001 points) the 10-point Gauss-Legendre formula requires only that the integrand be evaluated at 10 predetermined points.

```
Function HestonGL10(CorP, kappa, theta, lambda, rho, sigma, tau, K, S,
          r, v)
Dim x(5) As Double, dx As Double
Dim w(5) As Double, xr As Double, xm As Double
x(1) = 0.1488743389: x(2) = 0.4333953941
x(3) = 0.6794095682: x(4) = 0.8650633666
x(5) = 0.9739065285
w(1) = 0.2955242247: w(2) = 0.2692667193
w(3) = 0.2190863625: w(4) = 0.1494513491
w(5) = 0.0666713443
xm = 0.5 * (100): xr = 0.5 * (100)
p1 = 0: p2 = 0
  For j = 1 To 5
     dx = xr * x(j)
     p1 = p1 + w(j) * (HestonP1(xm + dx, kappa, theta,
        lambda, rho, sigma, tau, K, S, r, v)
        + HestonP1(xm - dx, kappa, theta, lambda, rho,
        sigma, tau, K, S, r, v))
```

```
      p2 = p2 + w(j) * (HestonP2(xm + dx, kappa, theta,
          lambda, rho, sigma, tau, K, S, r, v)
        + HestonP2(xm - dx, kappa, theta, lambda, rho,
          sigma, tau, K, S, r, v))
  Next j
p1 = p1 * xr: p2 = p2 * xr
p1 = 0.5 + (1 / thePI) * p1
p2 = 0.5 + (1 / thePI) * p2
If p1 < 0 Then p1 = 0
If p1 > 1 Then p1 = 1
If p2 < 0 Then p2 = 0
If p2 > 1 Then p2 = 1
HestonC = S * p1 - K * Exp(-r * tau) * p2
If PutCall = "Call" Then
    HestonGL10 = HestonC
ElseIf PutCall = "Put" Then
    HestonGL10 = HestonC + K * Exp(-r * tau) - S
End If
End Function
```

The Gauss-Legendre implementation of the Heston (1993) call price is presented in Figure 5.11. The price of a call option and put option implemented with Gauss-Legendre appear in cells C19 and C20, respectively. Even with

	A	B	C	D
1				
2		**Heston (1993) Price of a Call or Put Option**		
3				
4		Spot Price (S)	100	
5		Strike Price (K)	100	
6		Risk Free Rate (r)	0.05	
7		Time to Maturity (T − t)	0.5	
8		Rho (ρ)	0	
9		Kappa (κ)	2	
10		Theta (θ)	0.01	
11		Lambda (λ)	0	
12		Volatility of Variance (σ)	0.225	
13		Current variance (v)	0.01	
14				
15				
16		**Heston 1001-point Trapezoidal Call Price**	4.0852	
17		**Heston 1001-point Trapezoidal Put Price**	1.6162	
18				
19		**Heston GL 10-point Call Price**	4.0852	
20		**Heston GL 10-point Put Price**	1.6162	
21				

FIGURE 5.11 Solution to Exercise 5.1

only 10 abscissas, the Gauss-Legendre method produces option prices that are identical to trapezoidal integration with 1,001 abscissas.

5.2 To implement the Gauss-Laguerre quadrature, the GLAU() function is modified so that the Heston (1993) parameters can be passed to it.

```
Function GLAU(fname As String, n, alpha, kappa, theta, lambda, rho,
            sigma, tau, K, S, r, v)
' More VBA Statements
For i = 1 To n
GLAU = GLAU + w(i) * Run(fname, x(i), kappa, theta,
        lambda, rho, sigma, tau, K, S, r, v)
Next i
End Function
```

The function HestonGLAU() calculates the Heston option price using the GLAU() function above.

```
Function HestonGLAU(CorP, kappa, theta, lambda, rho, sigma, tau, K, S,
            r, v, GLAUpoint)
Dim P1_int(1001) As Double, P2_int(1001) As Double, phi_int(1001) As
            Double
Dim p1 As Double, p2 As Double, phi As Double, xg(16) As Double,
            wg(16) As Double
Dim cnt As Integer, HestonC As Double
cnt = 1
p1 = 0.5 + (1 / thePI) * GLAU("HestonP1", GLAUpoint, 0,
    kappa, theta, lambda, rho, sigma, tau, K, S, r, v)
p2 = 0.5 + (1 / thePI) * GLAU("HestonP2", GLAUpoint, 0,
    kappa, theta, lambda, rho, sigma, tau, K, S, r, v)
If p1 < 0 Then p1 = 0
If p1 > 1 Then p1 = 1
If p2 < 0 Then p2 = 0
If p2 > 1 Then p2 = 1
HestonC = S * p1 - K * Exp(-r * tau) * p2
If PutCall = "Call" Then
    Heston = HestonC
ElseIf PutCall = "Put" Then
    Heston = HestonC + K * Exp(-r * tau) - S
End If
End Function
```

The Heston option price using the Gauss-Laguerre quadrature is presented in Figure 5.12. Not surprisingly, Figure 5.12 indicates that the accuracy of the option prices increases as the number of abscissas increases. With 16 points, the approximations are reasonable, but in general the approximations with Gauss-Legrendre quadratures are more accurate.

	A	B	C	D	E
1					
2		**Heston (1993) Price of a Call or Put Option**			
3					
4		Spot Price (S)	90		
5		Strike Price (K)	100		
6		Risk Free Rate (r)	0.05		
7		Time to Maturity (T − t)	0.5		
8		Rho (ρ)	0		
9		Kappa (κ)	2		
10		Theta (θ)	0.01		
11		Lambda (λ)	0		
12		Volatility of Variance (σ)	0.225		
13		Current variance (v)	0.01		
14					
15					
16		**Heston 1001-point Trapezoidal Call Price**	0.4425		
17		**Heston 1001-point Trapezoidal Put Price**	7.9735		
18					
19				Call	Put
20		**Heston Gauss-Laguerre**	Points (#)	Price	Price
21		**Variable Point Integration**	1	-2.8408	4.6902
22			2	-1.8062	5.7248
23			3	-0.9024	6.6286
24			4	-0.2298	7.3011
25			5	0.2013	7.7323
26			6	0.4369	7.9679
27			7	0.5402	8.0712
28			8	0.5667	8.0977
29			9	0.5555	8.0864
30			10	0.5301	8.0611
31			11	0.5033	8.0343
32			12	0.4807	8.0116
33			13	0.4638	7.9948
34			14	0.4525	7.9835
35			15	0.4457	7.9767
36			16	0.4420	7.9730

FIGURE 5.12 Solution to Exercise 5.2

APPENDIX

In this appendix we derive the Heston (1993) risk-neutral processes for the stock price and variance. Start with the process for the stock price given by

$$dS = \mu S dt + \sqrt{v} S dz_1, \qquad (5.18)$$

where $S = S_t, v = v_t$, and $dz_1 = dz_{1,t}$. By Ito's Lemma the process for $x = \ln S$ is

$$dx = \left(\mu - \tfrac{1}{2}v\right)dt + \sqrt{v}dz_1. \tag{5.19}$$

The process for the square root of the variance $\sqrt{v}$ is

$$d\sqrt{v} = -\beta\sqrt{v}\,dt + \delta dz_2, \tag{5.20}$$

where β and δ are parameters, and where $z_2 = z_{2,t}$. Applying Ito's Lemma, the process for the variance v is the Cox, Ingersoll, and Ross (1985) (CIR) process:

$$dv = \kappa(\theta - v)dt + \sigma\sqrt{v}\,dt \tag{5.21}$$

where $\kappa = 2\beta$, $\theta = \delta^2/(2\beta)$, and $\sigma = 2\delta$. Write (5.19) as the risk-neutral process

$$\begin{aligned} d\ln S &= \left(r - \tfrac{1}{2}v\right)dt + (\mu - r)dt + \sqrt{v}dz_1 \\ &= \left(r - \tfrac{1}{2}v\right)dt + \sqrt{v}dz_1^* \end{aligned} \tag{5.22}$$

where r is the risk-free rate, and where

$$z_1^* = \left(z_1 - \frac{\mu - r}{\sqrt{v}}t\right). \tag{5.23}$$

The risk-neutral version of the process (5.21) for v is

$$dv = \kappa(\theta - v)dt - d\lambda + \sigma dz_2^* \tag{5.24}$$

where $\lambda = \lambda(t, S_t, v_t)$ is the price of volatility risk, and

$$z_2^* = \left(z_2 + \frac{\lambda}{\sigma}t\right). \tag{5.25}$$

Hence, the processes for the stock price and for the variance are

$$d\ln S = \left(r - \tfrac{1}{2}v\right)dt + \sqrt{r}dz_1^* \tag{5.26}$$

and

$$dv = \kappa(\theta - v)dt - \lambda\,dt + \sigma dz_2^* \tag{5.27}$$

respectively, where

$$\begin{pmatrix} z_1^* \\ z_2^* \end{pmatrix} = \begin{pmatrix} z_1 + \dfrac{\mu - r}{v}t \\ z_2 + \dfrac{\lambda}{\sigma}t \end{pmatrix}. \tag{5.28}$$

Under the probability measure P, we have $z_1 \sim N(0, T)$ and $z_2 \sim N(0, T)$. A new measure Q needs to be found so that $z_1^* \sim N(0, T)$ and $z_2^* \sim N(0, T)$ under Q. By the Girsanov Theorem, the measure Q exists provided that $\lambda(t, S_t, v_t)$ and $(\mu - r)t/\sqrt{v}$ satisfy Novikov's condition. As explained in Heston (1993), Breeden's (1979) consumption-based model applied to the CIR process yields a volatility risk premium of the form $\lambda(t, S_t, v_t) = \lambda v$. The process (5.27) for the variance becomes

$$
\begin{aligned}
dv &= \kappa(\theta - v)\, dt - \lambda v dt + \sigma\, dz_2^* \\
&= (\kappa + \lambda)\left(\frac{\kappa\theta}{\kappa + \lambda} - v\right) dt + \sigma\, dz_2^* \\
&= \kappa^*(\theta^* - v)\, dt + \sigma\, dz_2^*
\end{aligned}
\tag{5.29}
$$

where $\kappa^* = \kappa + \lambda$ and $\theta^* = \kappa\theta/(\kappa + \lambda)$ are the risk-neutral parameters. In Chapter 5 we simply drop the asterisk from κ^* and θ^* and write the processes for the stock price and for the variance as

$$
\begin{aligned}
dx_t &= \left[r - \frac{1}{2}v_t\right] dt + \sqrt{v_t}\, dz_{1,t}^* \\
dv_t &= \kappa[\theta - v_t]\, dt + \sigma\sqrt{v_t}\, dz_{2,t}^*.
\end{aligned}
\tag{5.30}
$$

These are equations (5.4).

CHAPTER 6

The Heston and Nandi (2000) GARCH Model

INTRODUCTION

In Chapter 5 it was argued that the constant volatility in the Black-Scholes model is untenable, and presented the time-varying volatility model of Heston (1993) that allows this assumption to be relaxed. Two other assumptions that underlie the Black-Scholes model are that of uncorrelated asset returns, and that these returns are independent. Although returns often show little autocorrelation, they are usually not independent. This chapter begins by examining the effect of dependence in asset returns on asset prices, and by presenting the generalized autoregressive conditional heteroskedasticity (GARCH) model, which is tremendously useful for modeling volatility clustering in asset prices.

Given the popularity of GARCH modeling, it is not surprising that researchers have attempted to incorporate GARCH effects into option pricing, in an attempt to account for the time-varying volatility and volatility clustering of the asset prices that these options are written on. Unfortunately, in most GARCH option pricing models, such as that of Duan (1995) no closed-form analytic solution for the option price is available—the price is available only through Monte Carlo simulation. Heston and Nandi (2000), however, have proposed a closed-form GARCH model for option pricing. The final part of this chapter will develop this model and the VBA functions to implement it, building on the GARCH tools presented beforehand.

PERSISTENT VOLATILITY IN ASSET RETURNS

One of the consequences of dependency in asset returns is that the volatility of these returns tends to exhibit patterns that are not random. Volatility tends to manifest itself in clusters, and these clusters tend to be persistent in time. What effect does this persistency have on option pricing? Suppose options are to be priced using the Black-Scholes formula, and that the volatility of the underlying asset is to be estimated using the unconditional volatility s, the standard deviation of n historical returns $r_1, r_2, \ldots, r_n$:

$$\hat{\sigma} = s = \sqrt{\frac{1}{(n-1)} \sum_{t=1}^{n} (r_t - \bar{r})^2}, \qquad (6.1)$$

where $\bar{r} = \frac{1}{n} \sum_{t=1}^{n} r_t$ is the sample mean of the returns and where the return at time t is the natural logarithmic return defined as $r_t = \ln(S_t/S_{t-1})$. Using volatility estimated through (6.1) can be problematic for pricing options. Suppose that the Black-Scholes formula is used to price an option, and that the historical yearly volatility over the last five years, estimated by using (6.1), is $\hat{\sigma}_s = 0.2$. Suppose further that a GARCH model estimates the current volatility at $\hat{\sigma}_G = 0.3$ instead. The Black-Scholes option using $\hat{\sigma}_s$ is under-priced, since it does not incorporate the true current volatility. However, if a GARCH model estimates the current volatility at $\hat{\sigma}_G = 0.10$, then the option that uses $\hat{\sigma}_s$ is overpriced. An investor could realize a profit by trading these under- and overpriced options.

Uncorrelated and Independent

This section proposes methods that can help verify or refute the assumptions of uncorrelated and independent returns that underlie the Black-Scholes model. This model assumes the following diffusion process for the stock price S_t,

$$dS_t = \mu S_t\, dt + \sigma S_t\, dz \qquad (6.2)$$

where μ is the drift and σ is the volatility. This specification implies that logarithmic returns are distributed according to a lognormal distribution with constant variance, and are independent of each other and uncorrelated. One simple way to verify the latter assumption is by examining the sample autocorrelation function of the returns for different values of the lag k. The kth sample autocorrelation is defined as

$$r_k = \frac{\sum_{t=1}^{n-k} (x_t - \bar{x})(x_{t+k} - \bar{x})}{\sum_{t=1}^{n-1} (x_t - \bar{x})^2} = \frac{\hat{\gamma}_k}{\hat{\gamma}_0}, \qquad (6.3)$$

which is the ratio of the kth sample autocovariance $\hat{\gamma}_k$ to the sample variance $\hat{\gamma}_0$. It is convenient to plot the autocorrelations r_k as a function of k to see what pattern, if any, emerges. Such a plot is often called a correlogram. In Excel, it is easy to generate autocorrelations, by using the CORREL() function.

 If asset returns are independently distributed, there should be no correlation between returns and lagged returns, and the correlogram should be devoid of any pattern or large spikes. Figure 6.1 presents a correlogram of daily closing returns

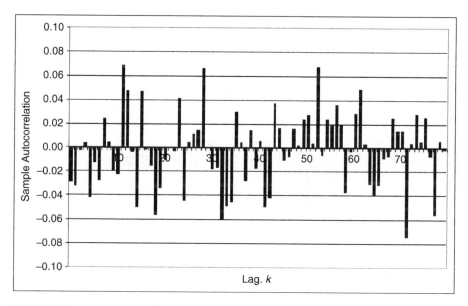

FIGURE 6.1 Correlogram for Daily Returns on the S&P 500 Index

on the Standard and Poor's (S&P) 500 index, for the period running from January 1, 2000, to December 31, 2005, and using up to 80 lags. The data for this figure are contained in the Excel file Chapter6GARCH.

The correlogram in Figure 6.1 clearly indicates the absence of any relationship between the returns on the S&P 500 index and its lags. All of the autocorrelations are very close to zero, and none is greater than 0.08 in absolute value. Moreover, these appear to be random, and do not follow any discernable pattern. These results, though encouraging since they indicate that the returns are not correlated, do not imply that the returns are independently distributed. This becomes apparent when the daily logarithmic returns r_t from the Chapter6GARCH Excel file are plotted against time. This plot appears in Figure 6.2.

Figure 6.2 indicates discernable patterns in the volatility of the returns. In the middle section of the graph the volatility of the index is much larger than in the later part of the graph. Volatility tends to cluster, and periods of high and low volatility can be identified. The figure clearly indicates that the assumption of constant variance is not consistent with the data. This time-varying persistent volatility can be visualized through a correlogram of the return variance. Since the expected daily return is zero, $\bar{r} \approx 0$ and an estimate of the unconditional variance can be expressed as

$$\hat{\sigma}^2 = s^2 = \frac{1}{n-1} \sum_{t=1}^{n} r_t^2. \tag{6.4}$$

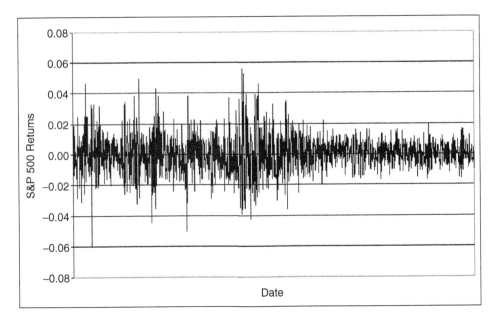

FIGURE 6.2   Daily Log Returns of S&P 500 Index

 Any persistence in volatility can therefore be identified by plotting the autocorrelations of squared logarithmic returns in a correlogram. This appears in Figure 6.3, using again the data contained in the Excel file Chapter6GARCH.

Now the pattern of autocorrelation is much stronger. The autocorrelations are larger and seem to persist for large values of k. This suggests that while the autocorrelations for logarithmic returns presented in Figure 6.1 are uncorrelated, the variances show strong autocorrelation, and this autocorrelation persists for a long time.

GARCH VARIANCE MODELING

The development of autoregressive conditional heteroskedasticity (ARCH) and GARCH models has been nothing short of revolutionary for modeling financial time series, to the extent that Robert Engle, who first introduced the ARCH model, shared the 2003 Nobel Prize in Economics for his discovery. The original GARCH models have spurned a number of extensions, including multivariate versions and applications to option pricing. Bollerslev, Chou, and Kroner (1992) present a literature review of some of the important academic studies on ARCH and GARCH modeling in finance.

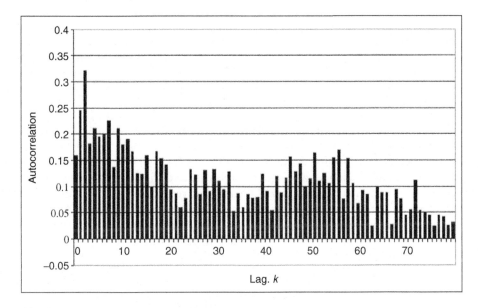

FIGURE 6.3 Correlogram of Squared Daily Returns on the S&P 500 Index

The GARCH(p, q) forecast of volatility for time $t + 1$, based on values observed at time t, is given by

$$\sigma_{t+1}^2 = \omega + \sum_{i=1}^{p} \alpha_i r_{t+1-i}^2 + \sum_{j=1}^{q} \beta_j \sigma_{t+1-j}^2 \qquad (6.5)$$

where σ_{t+1-j}^2 are past estimates of the variance, r_{t+1-j}^2 are past squared returns, and ω, α_i, and β_j are parameters that are all greater than zero $(i = 1, \ldots, p$ and $j = 1, \ldots, q)$. The simplest GARCH model and the most widely used is that which results when $p = 1$ and $q = 1$, aptly named GARCH(1,1),

$$\sigma_{t+1}^2 = \omega + \alpha r_t^2 + \beta \sigma_t^2. \qquad (6.6)$$

In this model, $\alpha + \beta$ measures the volatility persistence, and $\alpha + \beta < 1$ is required for the variance to be mean-reverting. The closer the value of $\alpha + \beta$ to one, the more volatility will persist, and the closer $\alpha + \beta$ is to zero, the faster volatility will revert to the long-run variance. In the model (6.6) the forecast variance for time $t + 1$, σ_{t+1}^2, is a weighted average of the squared return at time t, r_t^2, and the time-t estimate of the variance, σ_t^2. The difference between the GARCH(1,1) estimator (6.6) and the unconditional estimator (6.4) is worth emphasizing. Although both use squared returns to estimate the variance, the GARCH(1,1) model puts more weight on the most recent squared return. This is illustrated in the following example.

Suppose 1,000 days of returns are available to estimate the variance. With the unconditional variance (6.4), all squared returns are assigned the same weight 1/999, regardless of whether the return is recent or ancient. Suppose the GARCH(1,1) model is fitted to the 1,000 returns, using the parameter values $\omega = 0.000002$, $\alpha = 0.1$, and $\beta = 0.85$. This means that the most recent return is assigned a weight of 0.1, which is considerably more weight than the 1/999 assigned by unconditional variance.

The parameter values can be used to define a GARCH(1, 1) model, to illustrate the effectiveness of the model in capturing volatility clusters. With parameter values plugged into (6.6), the variance σ^2_{t+1} can be estimated for each day in the time series, using past estimated variances and squared returns, and the starting value $\sigma^2_0 = s^2$ obtained from (6.1). Finally, the squared logarithmic returns can be standardized by dividing each by the square root of its estimated variance from the GARCH model. This produces a time series of standardized returns defined as $z_t = r_t/\sigma_t$, where σ_t is obtained from (6.6). A correlogram of squared standardized returns z^2_t can then help ascertain whether the GARCH variance model is able to capture the volatility clustering. This correlogram is contained in the Excel file Chapter6GARCH and appears in Figure 6.4.

Figure 6.4 indicates that even with these arbitrary values for the parameters ω, α, and β, the GARCH model is able to capture time varying volatility in the

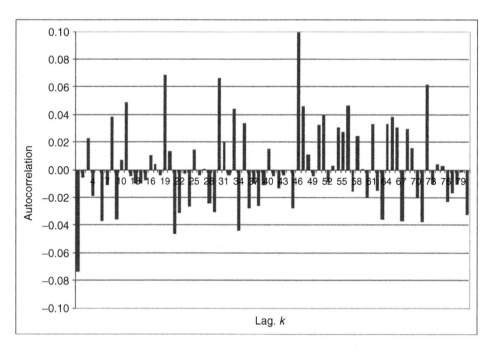

FIGURE 6.4   Correlogram of Squared Daily Standardized Returns on the S&P 500 Index

returns. This is reflected in the correlogram for the standardized logarithmic returns z_t^2. The correlogram displays a series of autocorrelations that are weak for all lags, and that show no discernable or persistent pattern. Hence, accounting for time-varying volatility in returns through a GARCH process effectively eliminates autocorrelations in squared returns.

Implementing the GARCH(1,1) Model

The parameter values for ω, α, and β in the previous example were chosen arbitrarily. In practice, the parameters in the GARCH(1,1) model would need to be estimated from the data. One popular technique for parameter estimation is maximum likelihood estimation introduced in Chapter 1. On a given day $t - 1$, returns for the next day t are assumed to be conditionally distributed as a normal random variable with mean zero and variance σ_t^2. This implies that $E_{t-1}[r_t] = 0$ and $E_{t-1}[r_t^2] = \sigma_t^2$, where $E_{t-1}[]$ denotes expectations taken at $t - 1$, and that the conditional probability density function for r_t is

$$f(r_t) = \frac{1}{\sqrt{2\pi\sigma_t^2}} \exp\left(\frac{-r_t^2}{2\sigma_t^2}\right) \tag{6.7}$$

Assuming that the returns r_t are independent, the joint density of $r_1, \ldots, r_n$ can be factored as the product of marginal densities (6.7). Hence the joint density can be expressed as the likelihood function L given by

$$L(r_1, \ldots, r_n) = \prod_{t=1}^{n} f(r_t) = \prod_{t=1}^{n} \frac{1}{\sqrt{2\pi\sigma_t^2}} \exp\left(\frac{-r_t^2}{2\sigma_t^2}\right) \tag{6.8}$$

Values of the parameters ω, α, and β that produce the maximum value of (6.8) are the maximum likelihood estimates (MLEs) of the parameters. To simplify the equation and make it easier to work with, it is customary to use the natural logarithm of the likelihood function and ignore the constant terms

$$\ell(r_1, \ldots, r_n) \propto \sum_{t=1}^{n} \left(-\ln\sigma_t^2 - \frac{r_t^2}{\sigma_t^2}\right). \tag{6.9}$$

The symbol $\propto$ is read "proportional to." When obtaining MLEs we can ignore constants and work with the kernel of the distribution $f(r_t) \propto \exp(-0.5r_t^2/\sigma_t^2)/\sigma_t$, rather than the probability density function itself $f(r_t) = (-0.5r_t^2/\sigma_t^2)/\sqrt{2\pi\sigma_t^2}$.

The Excel file Chapter6GARCH includes two functions to find the MLEs of the GARCH(1, 1) parameters ω, α, and β based on the function (6.9). The function GARCHMLE() is used to construct (6.9), and the function GARCHparams() uses the Nelder-Mead algorithm introduced in Chapter 1 to find values of the parameters that produce the maximum value of (6.9).

```
Function GARCHMLE(rets, startParams)
Dim VARt() As Double
n = Application.Count(rets)
ReDim VARt(n) As Double
omega = startParams(1)
alpha = startParams(2)
beta = startParams(3)
If ((omega < 0) Or (alpha < 0) Or (beta < 0)) Then
  GARCHMLE = -9999
Else
  VARt(n) = Application.VAR(rets)
  GARCHMLE = -Log(VARt(n)) - (rets(n) ^ 2 / VARt(n))
  For cnt = n - 1 To 1 Step -1
    VARt(cnt) = omega + alpha * rets(cnt + 1) ^ 2 + beta * VARt(cnt + 1)
    GARCHMLE = GARCHMLE - Log(VARt(cnt)) - (rets(cnt) ^ 2 / VARt(cnt))
  Next cnt
End If
  GARCHMLE = -GARCHMLE
End Function

Function GARCHparams(rets, startParams)
  GARCHparams = NelderMead("GARCHMLE", rets, startParams)
End Function
```

Three features of these functions merit special attention. First, since the Nelder-Mead algorithm finds the minimum of a function, the objective function in GARCHMLE() needs to be redefined, as the negative of (6.9). Second, since all estimated parameters must be positive, GARCHMLE() includes a penalty provision, so that a large value of the objective function (equal to 9999) is produced when negative estimates are encountered. Third, the GARCHparams() function requires a slight modification to the NelderMead() function of Chapter 1. This is because to construct the GARCH(1,1) likelihood and calculate MLEs, a vector of returns must be passed to the NelderMead() function. Whenever the statement

```
Run(fname, params)
```

is encountered in the NelderMead() function, it must be replaced with the statement

```
Run(fname, rets, params)
```

since the GARCHMLE() function requires the array rets() of returns. The exact implementation of this code is in the Excel file Chapter6GARCH, which also contains the MLEs produced by the functions GARCHMLE() and GARCHparams(). This spreadsheet appears in Figure 6.5.

The date t and the level of the S&P 500 index, S_t, appear in columns A and B, respectively. The logarithmic returns $r_t = \ln(S_t/S_{t-1})$ and the squared returns r_t^2 are

Date	S&P500	Log Return	(Log Return)²	GARCH for σ_t^2	Log Likelihood	(Std Return)²	Lag, k	r_k for R_t	r_k for R_t^2	r_k for R_t^2/σ_t^2	Arbitrary Parameters	
t	S_t	$R_t = Log(S_t/S_{t-1})$	R_t^2	$\sigma_t^2 = GARCH(1,1)$	$-log(\sigma_t^2) - \eta_t^2/\sigma_t^2$	R_t^2/σ_t^2					$\omega =$	0.0000020
30-Dec-05	1248.29	-4.90E-03	2.40E-05	2.63E-05	9.63E+00	9.13E-01	0	-0.029	0.159	-0.073	$\alpha =$	0.10
29-Dec-05	1254.42	-2.98E-03	8.91E-06	2.75E-05	1.02E+01	3.24E-01	1	-0.032	0.246	-0.006	$\beta =$	0.85
28-Dec-05	1258.17	1.30E-03	1.68E-06	2.98E-05	1.04E+01	5.63E-02	2	-0.002	0.321	0.022	Log Likelihood =	12,155.52
27-Dec-05	1256.54	-9.60E-03	9.21E-05	2.19E-05	6.52E+00	4.20E+00	3	0.003	0.181	-0.019	GARCH LL =	-12,155.52
23-Dec-05	1268.66	4.26E-04	1.81E-07	2.34E-05	1.07E+01	7.74E-03	4	-0.042	0.211	0.000		
22-Dec-05	1268.12	4.21E-03	1.77E-05	2.31E-05	9.91E+00	7.68E-01	5	-0.013	0.195	-0.036		
21-Dec-05	1262.79	2.51E-03	6.32E-06	2.41E-05	1.04E+01	2.62E-01	6	-0.028	0.199	-0.010		
20-Dec-05	1259.62	-2.38E-04	5.67E-08	2.60E-05	1.06E+01	2.18E-03	7	0.025	0.226	0.039		
19-Dec-05	1259.92	-5.86E-03	3.43E-05	2.42E-05	9.21E+00	1.42E+00	8	0.005	0.137	-0.036		
16-Dec-05	1267.32	-2.85E-03	8.14E-06	2.51E-05	1.03E+01	3.24E-01	9	-0.020	0.211	0.007	Estimated Parameters	
15-Dec-05	1270.94	-1.42E-03	2.00E-06	2.70E-05	1.04E+01	7.43E-02	10	-0.022	0.180	0.049	GARCH LL =	-12,241.26
14-Dec-05	1272.74	4.18E-03	1.75E-05	2.73E-05	9.87E+00	6.40E-01	11	0.068	0.191	-0.004	$\omega =$	0.0000007
13-Dec-05	1267.43	5.54E-03	3.07E-05	2.62E-05	9.38E+00	1.17E+00	12	0.047	0.167	-0.010	$\alpha =$	0.075
12-Dec-05	1260.43	8.41E-04	7.08E-07	2.83E-05	1.04E+01	2.50E-02	13	-0.003	0.126	-0.010	$\beta =$	0.921
9-Dec-05	1259.37	2.81E-03	7.86E-06	3.01E-05	1.02E+01	2.62E-01	14	-0.050	0.124	-0.007		
8-Dec-05	1255.84	-1.22E-03	1.48E-06	3.28E-05	1.03E+01	4.51E-02	15	0.047	0.159	0.010		
7-Dec-05	1257.37	-5.02E-03	2.52E-05	3.33E-05	9.55E+00	7.57E-01	16	-0.002	0.099	0.004		
6-Dec-05	1263.7	1.27E-03	1.63E-06	3.67E-05	1.02E+01	4.43E-02	17	-0.015	0.167	-0.004		
5-Dec-05	1262.09	-2.37E-03	5.60E-06	4.01E-05	9.98E+00	1.40E-01	18	-0.056	0.153	0.068		
2-Dec-05	1265.08	3.24E-04	1.05E-07	4.48E-05	1.00E+01	2.34E-03	19	-0.034	0.141	0.013		
1-Dec-05	1264.67	1.21E-02	1.46E-04	3.32E-05	5.92E+00	4.40E+00	20	-0.010	0.094	-0.046		

FIGURE 6.5 Maximum Likelihood Estimates of GARCH Model

in columns C and D, respectively. The arbitrary values of $\omega = 0.000002$, $\alpha = 0.10$, and $\beta = 0.85$ appear in cells M2, M3, and M4, respectively, and these are used to construct the GARCH(1, 1) variances

$$\sigma_{t+1}^2 = 0.000002 + 0.10 \times r_t^2 + 0.85 \times \sigma_t^2 \qquad (6.10)$$

which appear in column E. These are used to construct the squared standardized returns z_t^2 in column G. The autocorrelations for r_t, r_t^2, and z_t^2, which appear in Figures 6.1, 6.3, and 6.4, respectively, are in columns I, J, and K.

The individual terms from (6.9) are constructed by using returns in column D and GARCH variances from column E, and appear in column F. These individual terms are summed to produce a value of 12,155.52 for (6.9), which appears in cell M5. Applying the GARCHMLE() function to the arbitrary parameter values produces exactly the same value for (6.9) and appears in cell M6, except that the sign is reversed.

Finally, Figure 6.5 includes also the GARCH(1, 1) parameters estimated by maximum likelihood, using the arbitrary parameter values in cells M2:M4 as starting values for the Nelder-Mead algorithm. Recall that in the output of the NelderMead() function of Chapter 1 the value of the objective function is listed first and the values of the optimized parameters are listed underneath. The logarithmic returns are contained in C3:C1509 and the starting values in cells M2:M4, so in cell M13 we type

$$= GARCHparams(C3{:}C1509, M2{:}M4)$$

and copy to cells M14:M16, as usual. This produces the MLEs $\hat{\omega} = 0.000007$, $\hat{\alpha} = 0.075$, and $\hat{\beta} = 0.921$, and a value of the function (6.9) of 12,241.26, which, as expected, is higher than for arbitrary parameter values.

Long-Run Volatility Forecasting and Term Structure

The long-run variance in the GARCH(1,1) model (6.6) is given by

$$\sigma^2 = \frac{\omega}{1 - \alpha - \beta},\tag{6.11}$$

so that (6.6) can be written as

$$\sigma_t^2 = \sigma^2(1 - \alpha - \beta) + \alpha r_{t-1}^2 + \beta \sigma_{t-1}^2.\tag{6.12}$$

For n days ahead, the GARCH variance is therefore

$$\sigma_{t+n}^2 = \sigma^2(1 - \alpha - \beta) + \alpha r_{t+n-1}^2 + \beta \sigma_{t+n-1}^2\tag{6.13}$$

so that

$$\sigma_{t+n}^2 - \sigma^2 = \alpha(r_{t+n-1}^2 - \sigma^2) + \beta(\sigma_{t+n-1}^2 - \sigma^2).\tag{6.14}$$

At day t, the expected value of r_{t+n-1}^2 is $E_t[r_{t+n-1}^2] = \sigma_{t+n-1}^2$, so taking expectations of (6.14) and repeating substitutions produces

$$E_t[\sigma_{t+n}^2 - \sigma^2] = (\alpha + \beta)E_t[\sigma_{t+n-1}^2 - \sigma^2]$$
$$= (\alpha + \beta)^n(\sigma_t^2 - \sigma^2)\tag{6.15}$$

since $E_t[\sigma_t^2] = \sigma_t^2$.

The procedure described in Chapter 19 of Hull (2006) can be used to obtain the volatility term structure from the GARCH(1,1) model. Defining $V(n) = E_t[\sigma_{t+n}^2]$ and $a = -\ln(\alpha + \beta)$, the function $V(n)$ can be written

$$V(n) = \sigma^2 + e^{-an}[V(0) - \sigma^2].\tag{6.16}$$

The average variance over $(0, T)$ is

$$\frac{1}{T}\int_{u=0}^{T} V(u)\,du = \frac{1}{T}\left(u\sigma^2 - \frac{e^{-au}}{a}[V(0) - \sigma^2]\right)\Bigg|_{u=0}^{u=T}$$
$$= \sigma^2 + \frac{1 - e^{-aT}}{aT}[V(0) - \sigma^2]\tag{6.17}$$

where $V(0) = \sigma_t^2$ is the current GARCH variance from (6.12). Since equation (6.17) represents the average daily variance, it must be multiplied by 252 to produce an average annual variance, $\sigma(T)^2$. Hence,

$$\sigma(T)^2 = 252 \times \left(\sigma^2 + \frac{1 - e^{-aT}}{aT} [V(0) - \sigma^2] \right), \tag{6.18}$$

and the yearly average volatility, $\sigma(T)$ is the square root of (6.18). The term structure of volatility predicted through the GARCH(1,1) model can be obtained by plotting $\sigma(T)$ against T. When the current GARCH variance σ_{t+1}^2 is less than the long term variance σ^2, the slope will be positive (increasing in T). This is because when the long-term variance (6.11) is not infinite, namely when $\alpha + \beta < 1$, the current GARCH variance is mean-reverting to the long-term variance. Hence, the current variance will want to increase toward the long-term variance. The opposite is true when $\sigma_{t+1}^2 > \sigma^2$, so that the current variance will want to decrease towards toward the long term variance, and a plot of the term structure will have negative slope.

The Excel file Chapter6LongRun contains the very simple VBA function Year-Vol() for computing $\sigma(T)$.

```
Function YearVol(T, alpha, beta, omega, V0)
  Var = omega / (1 - alpha - beta)
  a = -Log(alpha + beta)
  YearVol = Sqr(252 * (Var + (1 - Exp(-a * T)) / a / T * (V0 - Var)))
End Function
```

This function and the term structure of volatility are illustrated in Figure 6.6.

The current GARCH(1,1) variance is $\sigma_{t+1}^2 = 2.63 \times 10^{-5}$ in cell P3, based on the maximum likelihood estimates that appear in column M of the sheet and presented in Figure 6.5. Recall from that figure that the estimates of ω, α and β are in cells M14, M15, and M16, respectively. Hence to obtain the long-run variance, in cell P4 we type "=M14/(1-M15-M16)", which produces $\sigma^2 = 1.63 \times 10^{-4}$. The values of $\sigma(T)$ for various maturities appear in cells P9:P16. To obtain $\sigma(25)$, for example, in cell P11 we type

$$= \text{YearVol(O11, M15,M16,M14,P3)}$$

which produces $\sigma(25) = 0.09201$. The other values of $\sigma(T)$ are obtained similarly, and these appear as the solid line in the figure. As expected, since $\sigma_{t+1}^2 < \sigma^2$, the volatility term structure is increasing. To illustrate how the volatility term structure decreases when $\sigma_{t+1}^2 > \sigma^2$, in cell S3 we assign the arbitrary value $\sigma_{t+1}^2 = 0.30^2/252 \approx 3.57 \times 10^{-4}$, produce the values of $\sigma(T)$ in cells S9:S16, and portray these values as the dashed line in the plot. Clearly, this term structure has a negative slope. Finally, since the annualized long-term volatility is $\sigma_A^2 = \sqrt{252} \times \sigma^2 \approx 0.20254$, we would expect each set of values to converge to 0.20254. Using very large values for T indicates that this is indeed the case.

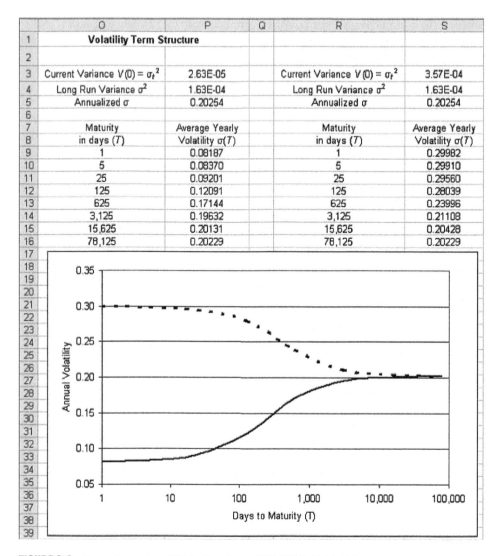

	O	P	Q	R	S
1	**Volatility Term Structure**				
2					
3	Current Variance $V(0) = \sigma_t^2$	2.63E-05		Current Variance $V(0) = \sigma_t^2$	3.57E-04
4	Long Run Variance σ^2	1.63E-04		Long Run Variance σ^2	1.63E-04
5	Annualized σ	0.20254		Annualized σ	0.20254
6					
7	Maturity	Average Yearly		Maturity	Average Yearly
8	in days (T)	Volatility $\sigma(T)$		in days (T)	Volatility $\sigma(T)$
9	1	0.08187		1	0.29982
10	5	0.08370		5	0.29910
11	25	0.09201		25	0.29560
12	125	0.12091		125	0.28039
13	625	0.17144		625	0.23996
14	3,125	0.19632		3,125	0.21108
15	15,625	0.20131		15,625	0.20428
16	78,125	0.20229		78,125	0.20229

FIGURE 6.6   Term Structure of Volatility from GARCH(1,1) Model

THE HESTON AND NANDI (2000) MODEL

In the remainder of this chapter we present the Heston and Nandi (2000) closed-form solution for the option price. In this model the variance follows a GARCH(p, q) process. Although the solution is in closed form, coefficients for the generating function must be derived recursively, working backward from the time to maturity of the option. Once the generating function is derived, by using inversion in a manner similar to the Heston (1993) stochastic volatility model covered in Chapter 5, it is straightforward to obtain probabilities required for the call price. This requires numerical integration, however, since the integral representing the probabilities cannot be derived analytically.

In this chapter only the case $p = q = 1$ is analyzed, corresponding to a GARCH(1,1) process for the return variance in the Heston and Nandi (2000) model. Although the GARCH(p, q) representation is more general, in most applications the single-lag version is sufficiently powerful and reduces the computational burden. Moreover, in Appendix B of Heston and Nandi (2000) it is shown that the single-lag version converges to the Heston (1993) model when the time increment between successive observations shrinks. Finally, we note that there are many GARCH option pricing models available. See Christoffersen and Jacobs (2004b) for a review of these models. The model of Heston and Nandi (2000) is particularly attractive because the call price can be obtained in closed form, up to a complex integral that must be approximated numerically. In other GARCH models, the call price is obtained by Monte Carlo simulation.

In the Heston and Nandi (2000) model the logarithmic return $r_{t+1} = \ln(S_{t+1}/S_t)$ is assumed to follow the GARCH(1,1) process driven by the pair of equations

$$r_{t+1} = r + \lambda\sigma_{t+1}^2 + \sigma_{t+1}z_{t+1} \tag{6.19}$$

$$\sigma_{t+1}^2 = \omega + \beta\sigma_t^2 + \alpha(z_t - \gamma\sigma_t)^2 \tag{6.20}$$

where

$$
\begin{aligned}
r &= \text{risk-free interest rate} \\
\sigma_t^2 &= \text{conditional variance} \\
z_t &= \text{error term distributed as a standard normal variable, } z_t \sim N(0,1) \\
\lambda, \omega, \beta, \alpha, \gamma &= \text{model parameters.}
\end{aligned}
$$

The equation (6.20) is a variant of the classical GARCH(1,1) model in (6.6). Instead of the process containing squared returns r_t^2 in the term involving α, the process contains the term $(z_t - \gamma\sigma_t)^2$. Heston and Nandi (2000) establish several properties of this version of the GARCH(1,1) model. Since the variance persistence is $\beta + \alpha\gamma^2$, the process will be mean-reverting if $\beta + \alpha\gamma^2 < 1$. By rearranging the equation driving σ_t^2 they show that in this model, α determines kurtosis while γ determines skewness.

The risk-neutral version of this model can be written as

$$
\begin{aligned}
r_{t+1} &= r - \frac{1}{2}\sigma_{t+1}^2 + \sigma_{t+1}z_{t+1}^* \\
\sigma_{t+1}^2 &= \omega + \beta\sigma_t^2 + \alpha(z_t^* - \gamma^*\sigma_t)^2.
\end{aligned}
\tag{6.21}
$$

Proposition 1 of Heston and Nandi (2000) ensures that the risk-neutral process has the same form as the real process, with λ replaced by $-1/2$, and γ replaced by $\gamma^* = \gamma + \lambda + \frac{1}{2}$.

The price at time t of a European call option with maturity at time $t + T$ and with strike price K is given by

$$\text{Call} = e^{-rT} E_t^*[(S_{t+T} - K, 0)] = S_t P_1 - K e^{-rT} P_2 \qquad (6.22)$$

where

$$
\begin{aligned}
T &= \text{time to maturity} \\
E_t^*[] &= \text{expectation at time } t \text{ under the risk-neutral distribution} \\
S_t &= \text{price of the underlying asset at time } t \\
P_1, P_2 &= \text{risk-neutral probabilities.}
\end{aligned}
$$

Under this model, P_1 is the delta of the call option and P_2 represents the probability that the price of the underlying asset at maturity is greater than the strike price, so that $P_2 = \Pr[S_{t+T} > K]$.

Generating Function of the Asset Price

To obtain the call price, the values of P_1 and P_2 that appear in the pricing formula (6.22) for the call must be calculated. Since $E_t[S_{t+T}^\phi] = E_t[\phi \log S_{t+T}]$, the generating function of the price of the underlying asset, $f(\phi) = E_t[S_{t+T}^\phi]$, is also the moment generating function of the log price of the asset. The generating function denoted $f^*(\phi)$ is that taken under the risk neutral distribution, so $f^*(\phi) = E_t^*[S_{t+T}^\phi]$. Heston and Nandi (2000) show that the generating function takes the following log-linear form for the GARCH(1,1) model

$$f(\phi) = S_t^\phi \exp(A_t + B_t \sigma_{t+1}^2) \qquad (6.23)$$

where

$$A_t = A_{t+1} + \phi r + B_{t+1}\,\omega - \frac{1}{2}\log(1 - 2\alpha B_{t+1})$$

$$B_t = \phi(\lambda + \gamma) - \frac{1}{2}\gamma^2 + \beta B_{t+1} + \frac{\frac{1}{2}(\phi - \gamma)^2}{1 - 2\alpha B_{t+1}}.$$

Note that A_t and B_t are defined recursively, by working backward from the time of maturity $t + T$ of the option. Note also that A_t and B_t are functions of $t, t + T$, and ϕ, so that $A_t \equiv A(t; t + T, \phi)$ and $B_t \equiv B(t; t + T, \phi)$, but in this chapter the simpler notation is adopted for convenience. Both of these terms can be solved recursively from time $t + T$, working back through time and using the terminal conditions

$$A_{t+T} = B_{t+T} = 0. \qquad (6.24)$$

For example, the next terms in the backward recursion would be $A_{t+T-1} = \phi r$ and

$$B_{t+T-1} = \phi(\lambda + \gamma) - \frac{1}{2}[\gamma^2 + (\phi - \gamma)^2].$$

As mentioned earlier, for pricing options the risk-neutral distribution must be used. To obtain the risk-neutral generating function $f^*(\phi)$, in all terms A_t and B_t we replace λ with $-1/2$, and γ with γ^*.

Integrals for the Call Price

Recall that the value of the call at time t is given in (6.22) as $C = S_t P_1 - Ke^{-rT}P_2$, which requires the probabilities P_1 and P_2 to be evaluated. This is done by inverting the risk-neutral generating function $f^*(\phi)$. Heston and Nandi (2000) show that probabilities have the form

$$P_1 = \frac{1}{2} + \frac{e^{-rT}}{\pi S_t} \int_0^\infty \mathrm{Re}\left[\frac{K^{-i\phi} f^*(i\phi + 1)}{i\phi} \right] d\phi \qquad (6.25)$$

and

$$P_2 = \frac{1}{2} + \frac{1}{\pi} \int_0^\infty \mathrm{Re}\left[\frac{K^{-i\phi} f^*(i\phi)}{i\phi} \right] d\phi. \qquad (6.26)$$

With these probabilities, the call price can be obtained using (6.22), and the put price can be obtained by put-call parity.

Implementation in VBA

In this section we show how to implement the Heston and Nandi (2000) call price using VBA. The Excel file Chapter6HN contains the VBA code to find the characteristic function, the probabilities P_1 and P_2 through numerical integration, and the call price. The VBA function NHC_f() obtains the characteristic function by backward recursion and extracts the real part of the functions defined in (6.25) and (6.26).

```
Function HNC_f(phi As cNum, alpha, beta, gamma, omega, lambda, S, k, r, v,
          dtm)
Dim a() As cNum, b() As cNum
Dim A1 As cNum, B1 As cNum
Dim tHNC_f1 As cNum
Dim curA As cNum, curB As cNum
ReDim a(dtm + 1) As cNum, b(dtm + 1) As cNum
a(1) = set_cNum(0, 0)
b(1) = set_cNum(0, 0)
  For i = 2 To dtm + 1
    a(i) = cNumAdd(cNumAdd(a(i - 1), cNumProd(phi,
          set_cNum(r, 0))), cNumProd(set_cNum(omega, 0), b(i - 1)))
    a(i) = cNumSub(a(i), cNumProd(set_cNum(0.5, 0),
          cNumLn(cNumSub(set_cNum(1, 0),
          cNumProd(set_cNum(2 * alpha, 0), b(i - 1))))))
    b(i) = cNumProd(phi, set_cNum(lambda + gamma, 0))
    b(i) = cNumSub(b(i), set_cNum(0.5 * gamma ^ 2, 0))
```

```
      b(i) = cNumAdd(b(i), cNumProd(set_cNum(beta, 0), b(i - 1)))
      b(i) = cNumAdd(b(i), cNumDiv(cNumProd(set_cNum(0.5, 0),
             cNumPowercNum(cNumSub(phi, set_cNum(gamma, 0)),
             set_cNum(2, 0))), cNumSub(set_cNum(1, 0),
             cNumProd(set_cNum(2 * alpha, 0), b(i - 1)))))
   Next i
A1 = a(dtm + 1): B1 = b(dtm + 1)
tHNC_f1 = cNumPowercNum(set_cNum(k, 0), set_cNum(0, -phi.iP))
tHNC_f1 = cNumProd(tHNC_f1, cNumPowercNum(set_cNum(S, 0), phi))
tHNC_f1 = cNumProd(tHNC_f1, cNumExp(cNumAdd(A1, cNumProd(B1,
          set_cNum(v, 0)))))
tHNC_f1 = cNumDiv(tHNC_f1, set_cNum(0, phi.iP))
HNC_f   = cNumReal(tHNC_f1)
End Function
```

The last step is the numerical evaluation of the integrals, which produces the risk-neutral probabilities, and the computation of the call price. This is achieved with the VBA function HNC(), which employs the trapezoidal rule for the integration. Note that the probabilities are each restricted to lie in the interval [0,1].

```
Function HNC(alpha, beta, gamma, omega, lambda, S, K, r, v, dtm)
Dim phi As cNum
Dim int_x(401) As Double, int_y1(401) As Double, int_y2(401) As Double
Dim int1 As Double, int2 As Double
cnt = 0
For phicnt = 0.000001 To 100.000001 Step 0.25
   cnt = cnt + 1
   phi = set_cNum(1, phicnt)
   int_x(cnt) = phicnt
   int_y1(cnt) = HNC_f(phi, alpha, beta, gamma, omega, lambda,
             S, K, r, v, dtm)
   phi = set_cNum(0, phicnt)
   int_y2(cnt) = HNC_f(phi, alpha, beta, gamma, omega, lambda,
             S, K, r, v, dtm)
Next phicnt
int1 = TRAPnumint(int_x, int_y1)
int2 = TRAPnumint(int_x, int_y2)
P1 = (1 / 2) + (1 / S / thePI) * Exp(-r * dtm) * int1
P2 = (1 / 2) + (1 / thePI) * int2
If P1 < 0 Then P1 = 0
If P1 > 1 Then P1 = 1
If P2 < 0 Then P2 = 0
If P2 > 1 Then P2 = 1
   HNC = S * P1 - K * Exp(-r * dtm) * P2
End Function
```

The Excel file Chapter6HN for obtaining the Heston and Nandi (2000) call price is presented in Figure 6.7. We illustrate this model on a call option with $T = 100$ days to maturity and strike price $K = 100$ written on a stock with spot price $S = 100$, using the risk-free rate $r = 0$, and GARCH parameter values $\alpha = 0.00000132$, $\beta = 0.589$, $\gamma = 421.39$, $\omega = 0.00000502$, and $\lambda^* = -0.5$. The current GARCH

	A	B	C	D
1				
2		**Heston and Nandi (2000) Call Price**		
3				
4		Spot Price (S)	100	
5		Strike Price (K)	100	
6		Risk Free Rate (r)	0	
7		Time to Maturity (days)	100	
8		Alpha (α)	0.00000132	
9		Beta (β)	0.589	
10		Gamma (γ*)	421.39	
11		Omega (ω)	0.00000502	
12		Lambda (λ*)	-0.5	
13		Current GARCH Variance (σ^2_{t+1})	8.92857E-05	
14				
15		**Heston-Nandi Call Price**	2.476704	
16				

FIGURE 6.7   Heston and Nandi (2000) Call Price

variance is set at $\sigma^2_{t+1} = 0.15^2/252$, or 0.0000893 approximately. In cell C15 we type

$$= \text{HNC(alpha, beta, gamma, omega, lambda, S, K, RF, V, T)},$$

and obtain the Heston and Nandi (2000) price of \$2.4767 for this call option. With a yearly interest rate of 5 percent, the call price becomes \$3.4735. This requires a daily rate as input, so "= 0.05/252" must be entered in cell C6, which specifies 252 trading days per year and corresponds to a daily rate of 0.0198 percent.

Note that the choice of the GARCH parameter σ^2_{t+1} is arbitrary, and that we have chosen a daily variance based on an annual volatility of 15 percent and 252 trading days. While the Heston and Nandi (2000) option price uses GARCH parameters from the second equation of (6.21), at first glance it seems odd that an arbitrary choice for σ^2_{t+1} should be used. In this chapter, we simply use this value for σ^2_{t+1}, and arbitrary values for the other parameters also. In Chapter 9 we will encounter methods to estimate parameters, for all the option pricing models covered in this book.

Improving Performance

In Chapter 5 it was pointed out that the computational speed of the VBA functions used to implement the Heston (1993) model can be increased by combining the two integrals that make up the call price into a single integral. In this section

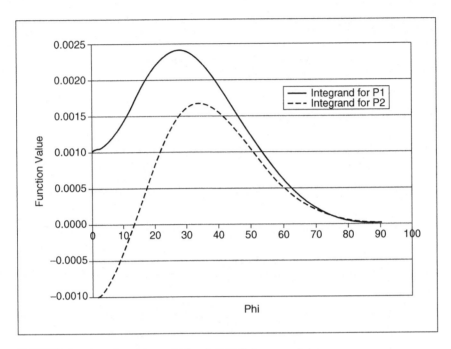

FIGURE 6.8 Plot of Heston and Nandi (2000) Integrands

it is demonstrated that a similar improvement can be achieved with the Heston and Nandi (2000) model.

The Excel file Chapter6Integral contains values of the functions that appear in the integrals (6.25) and (6.26). These functions are plotted against ϕ in Figure 6.8 and also appear in the Excel file Chapter6Integrals.

The solid line in Figure 6.8 is a plot of $e^{-rT}Re[K^{-i\phi}f^*(i\phi + 1)/(i\phi)]/S_t$ versus ϕ and the dashed line is a plot of $Re[K^{-i\phi}f^*(i\phi)/(i\phi)]$ versus ϕ. Both functions clearly display an oscillating pattern similar to the functions of the Heston (1993) model. Moreover, the function for the second integral (dashed line) takes on negative values, which complicates further the numerical integration of the function.

The efficiency of the VBA functions can be improved, by combining the two integrands into a single integrand. Recall the price of a call option under the Heston and Nandi (2000) model given in (6.22):

$$\text{Call} = S_t P_1 - Ke^{-rT}P_2 \tag{6.27}$$

where the risk-neutral probabilities are

$$P_1 = \frac{1}{2} + \frac{e^{-rT}}{\pi S_t} \int_0^\infty \text{Re}\left[\frac{K^{-i\phi}f^*(i\phi + 1)}{i\phi}\right] d\phi \tag{6.28}$$

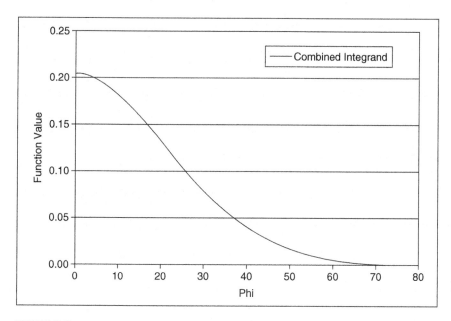

FIGURE 6.9 Plot of Combined Integrand

and

$$P_2 = \frac{1}{2} + \frac{1}{\pi} \int_0^\infty \mathrm{Re}\left[\frac{K^{-i\phi}f^*(i\phi)}{i\phi}\right] d\phi. \tag{6.29}$$

Equation (6.27) can be written

$$\mathrm{Call} = \frac{1}{2}(S_t - Ke^{-rT}) + P_{12} \tag{6.30}$$

where P_{12} is an integral that combines (6.28) and (6.29):

$$P_{12} = \frac{e^{-rT}}{\pi} \int_0^\infty \left\{\mathrm{Re}\left[\frac{K^{-i\phi}f^*(i\phi + 1)}{i\phi}\right] - K\mathrm{Re}\left[\frac{K^{-i\phi}f^*(i\phi)}{i\phi}\right]\right\} d\phi. \tag{6.31}$$

Figure 6.9 presents a plot of the integrand in (6.31) as a function of ϕ. The combined integrand is smoother than the individual integrands in Figure 6.8, and does not take on negative values. The data used to generate the figure are contained in the Excel file Chapter6Integral.

The Excel file Chapter6Integral also contains the VBA function HNCint(), which

is used to produce the graphs in Figures 6.8 and 6.9.

```
Function HNCint(alpha, beta, gamma, omega, lambda, S, K, r, v, dtm)
Dim phi As cNum
Dim int_values(4, 401) As Double, int_ycom(401) As Double
```

```
Dim int1 As Double, int2 As Double
cnt = 0
  For phicnt = 0.000001 To 100.000001 Step 0.25
    cnt = cnt + 1
    phi = set_cNum(1, phicnt)
    int_values(1, cnt) = phicnt
    int_y1 = HNC_f(phi, alpha, beta, gamma, omega, lambda,
                S, K, r, v, dtm)
    int_values(2, cnt) = (1 / S) * Exp(-r * (dtm / 252)) * int_y1
    phi = set_cNum(0, phicnt)
    int_y2 = HNC_f(phi, alpha, beta, gamma, omega, lambda,
                S, K, r, v, dtm)
    int_values(3, cnt) = int_y2
    int_ycom(cnt) = int_y1 - K * int_y2
    int_values(4, cnt) = int_ycom(cnt)
  Next phicnt
HNCint = Application.Transpose(int_values)
End Function
```

Plotting these three functions in Excel using VBA functions is straightforward. The output to this function is contained in the array int_values(). The values of ϕ are contained in the first column of this array, and the functions for P_1, P_2, and P_{12} are in the second, third, and fourth columns, respectively.

SUMMARY

In this chapter we show that correlograms can be used to illustrate that asset returns are generally uncorrelated. Correlograms, however, show also that returns are not independent, and that volatility in asset returns tends to cluster and show some degree of persistence. This provides strong evidence against one of the assumptions underlying the Black-Scholes model, namely that of constant volatility. We implement the simple GARCH model with maximum likelihood estimation, and show that this model can adequately capture volatility clusters in the S&P 500 index over the 2000 to 2005 period. We also show how the term structure of volatility can be obtained from GARCH variances. Finally, we cover the GARCH option pricing model of Heston and Nandi (2000) and show how combining integrals that make up the call price can simplify the required calculations.

EXERCISES

This section presents exercises that deal with some of the concepts introduced in this chapter. Solutions are in the Excel file Chapter6Exercises.

6.1 Use the put-call parity relationship to obtain the Heston and Nandi (2000) price of a put option.

6.2 Write a VBA function to find the standard errors of the MLEs of the parameters from the GARCH(1, 1) model. These can be obtained through the second derivative of the log-likelihood function. If $\hat{\theta}_{MLE}$ denotes the vector of MLEs, then $\hat{\theta}_{MLE} \sim N_3(\theta, \mathbf{I}^{-1})$ where $\mathbf{I}$ is the Fisher information matrix and where $N_3(,)$ denotes the multivariate normal distribution of dimension 3. The standard errors of the MLEs are the square roots of the diagonal entries of $\mathbf{I}^{-1}$. The information matrix is defined as the symmetric matrix of expected second derivatives

$$\mathbf{I} = -E\left[\sum_{t=1}^{n} \frac{\partial^2 \ell_t}{\partial \theta^T \partial \theta}\right] = -\sum_{t=1}^{n} E\begin{pmatrix} \dfrac{\partial^2 \ell_t}{\partial \omega^2} & \dfrac{\partial^2 \ell_t}{\partial \omega \partial \alpha} & \dfrac{\partial^2 \ell_t}{\partial \omega \partial \beta} \\[2mm] \dfrac{\partial^2 \ell_t}{\partial \alpha \partial \omega} & \dfrac{\partial^2 \ell_t}{\partial \alpha^2} & \dfrac{\partial^2 \ell_t}{\partial \alpha \partial \beta} \\[2mm] \dfrac{\partial^2 \ell_t}{\partial \beta \partial \omega} & \dfrac{\partial^2 \ell_t}{\partial \beta \partial \alpha} & \dfrac{\partial^2 \ell_t}{\partial \beta^2} \end{pmatrix},$$

where $\ell_t \propto -(\ln \sigma_t^2 + r_t^2/\sigma_t^2)$ and $\sigma_t^2 = \omega + \alpha r_{t-1}^2 + \beta \sigma_{t-1}^2$. The inverse of a matrix A is defined as $A^{-1} = \mathrm{adj}(A)/\det(A)$, where $\det(A)$ is its determinant, and $\mathrm{adj}(A)$ is its adjoint, defined as

$$\mathrm{adj}(A) = \begin{pmatrix} m_{11} & -m_{21} & m_{31} \\ -m_{12} & m_{22} & -m_{32} \\ m_{13} & -m_{23} & m_{33} \end{pmatrix}.$$

In this expression m_{ij} is the (i, j) minor of A, defined as the determinant of the 2×2 matrix obtained by deleting row i and column j from A. Hence, finding A^{-1} requires finding ten determinants, one for A itself, and nine that define each minor. Note that the determinant of a 2×2 matrix with elements a_{11}, a_{12}, a_{21} and a_{22} is given by $a_{11}a_{22} - a_{12}a_{21}$, and that the determinant of a 3×3 matrix

$$A = \begin{pmatrix} a_{11} & a_{12} & a_{13} \\ a_{21} & a_{22} & a_{23} \\ a_{31} & a_{32} & a_{33} \end{pmatrix}$$

is given by decomposing the matrix into its minors along any row or column. For example, decomposition on the first row produces

$$\det(A) = a_{11}\det\begin{pmatrix} a_{22} & a_{23} \\ a_{32} & a_{33} \end{pmatrix} - a_{12}\det\begin{pmatrix} a_{21} & a_{23} \\ a_{31} & a_{33} \end{pmatrix} + a_{13}\det\begin{pmatrix} a_{21} & a_{22} \\ a_{31} & a_{32} \end{pmatrix}$$

$$= a_{11}m_{11} - a_{12}m_{12} + a_{13}m_{31}.$$

6.3 Use the standard errors obtained in Exercise 6.2 to construct 95 percent confidence intervals for ω, α, and β.

SOLUTIONS TO EXERCISES

6.1 Recall the put price can be obtained from the put-call parity relationship as

$$\text{Put} = \text{Call} + Ke^{-rT} - S_t.$$

As seen in Chapter 5, implementing this in VBA is straightforward. We use the VBA function HNP(), which uses the function HNC() for the Heston and Nandi (2000) call price.

```
Function HNP(alpha,beta,gamma,omega,lambda,S,K,r,v,dtm)
  HNP = HNC(alpha, beta, gamma, omega, lambda, S,
           K, r, v, dtm) + K * Exp(-r * dtm) - S
End Function
```

6.2 Write $h_t = \sigma_t^2$ for notational simplicity. Applying the chain rule, the quotient rule, and the product rule for derivatives, the elements of the information matrix are

$$\frac{\partial^2 \ell_t}{\partial \omega^2} = \frac{w_t}{h_t^2}, \quad \frac{\partial^2 \ell_t}{\partial \alpha^2} = \frac{r_{t-1}^4 \, w_t}{h_t^2}, \quad \frac{\partial^2 \ell_t}{\partial \beta^2} = \frac{h_{t-2}}{h_t} \left(\frac{r_t^2}{h_t} - 1 \right) + \frac{h_{t-1}^2 \, w_t}{h_t^2},$$

$$\frac{\partial^2 \ell_t}{\partial \omega \partial \alpha} = \frac{r_{t-1}^2 \, w_t}{h_t^2}, \quad \frac{\partial^2 \ell_t}{\partial \omega \partial \beta} = \frac{h_{t-1} \, w_t}{h_t^2}, \quad \frac{\partial^2 \ell_t}{\partial \alpha \partial \beta} = \frac{h_{t-1} r_{t-1}^2 \, w_t}{h_t^2},$$

where $w_t = (1 - 2r_t^2/h_t)$. The VBA function GARCHSE() computes the information matrix, and the covariance matrix by using the VBA function Minv(). The function Minv() obtains the inverse $B = A^{-1}$ of a 3×3 matrix A with elements a_{11} through a_{33} by constructing the minors of A and calculating its determinant.

```
Function MInv(a11, a12, a13, a21, a22, a23, a31, a32, a33)
Dim B() As Double
ReDim B(3, 3) As Double
m11 = a22 * a33 - a23 * a32: m12 = a21 * a33 - a31 * a23
m13 = a21 * a32 - a22 * a31: m21 = a12 * a33 - a32 * a13
m22 = a11 * a33 - a13 * a31: m23 = a11 * a32 - a31 * a12
m31 = a12 * a23 - a13 * a22: m32 = a11 * a23 - a21 * a13
m33 = a11 * a22 - a12 * a21
detA = a11 * m11 - a12 * m12 + a13 * m13
B(1, 1) = m11 / detA: B(1, 2) = -m21 / detA
B(1, 3) = m31 / detA: B(2, 1) = -m12 / detA
B(2, 2) = m22 / detA: B(2, 3) = -m32 / detA
B(3, 1) = m13 / detA: B(3, 2) = -m23 / detA
B(3, 3) = m33 / detA
MInv = B
End Function
```

The function GARCHSE() obtains the covariance matrix of the MLEs and stores these in the array Cov(). Taking the square root of the diagonal elements of Cov() produces the standard errors.

```
Function GARCHSE(r, startParams)
theta = NelderMead("GARCHMLE", r, startParams)
omega = theta(2, 1)
alpha = theta(3, 1)
beta = theta(4, 1)
n = Application.Count(r)
Dim h() As Double
ReDim h(n) As Double
h(n) = Application.Var(r)
  For t = n - 1 To 1 Step -1
    h(t) = omega + alpha * r(t + 1) ^ 2 + beta * h(t + 1)
  Next t
Dim w() As Double, Dww() As Double, Daa() As Double, Dbb() As Double,
            Dwa() As Double, Dwb() As Double, Dab() As Double
ReDim w(n - 2) As Double, Dww(n - 2) As Double, Daa(n - 2) As Double,
            Dbb(n - 2) As Double, Dwa(n - 2) As Double, Dwb(n - 2)
            As Double, Dab(n - 2) As Double
  For t = n - 2 To 1 Step -1
    w(t) = (1 - 2 * r(t) ^ 2 / h(t))
    Dww(t) = w(t) / h(t) ^ 2
    Daa(t) = r(t + 1) ^ 4 * w(t) / h(t) ^ 2
    Dbb(t) = (h(t + 2) / h(t)) * ((r(t) ^ 2 / h(t)) - 1) +
            h(t + 1) ^ 2 * w(t) / h(t) ^ 2
    Dwa(t) = r(t + 1) ^ 2 * w(t) / h(t) ^ 2
    Dwb(t) = h(t + 1) * w(t) / h(t) ^ 2
    Dab(t) = h(t + 1) * r(t + 1) ^ 2 * w(t) / h(t) ^ 2
  Next t
WW = -Application.Sum(Dww): AA = -Application.Sum(Daa)
BB = -Application.Sum(Dbb): WA = -Application.Sum(Dwa)
WB = -Application.Sum(Dwb): AB = -Application.Sum(Dab)
Dim Cov() As Double
ReDim Cov(3, 3) As Double
Cov = MInv(WW, WA, WB, WA, AA, AB, WB, AB, BB)
Dim SE(3) As Double
SE(1) = Sqr(Cov(1, 1))
SE(2) = Sqr(Cov(2, 2))
SE(3) = Sqr(Cov(3, 3))
GARCHSE = Application.Transpose(SE)
End Function
```

Figure 6.10 illustrates the use of these functions, on the S&P 500 index data contained in the Excel file Chapter6GARCH. Note that the parameter estimates are the same as in Figure 6.5. The standard errors of the MLEs appear in cells F9:F11. For example, the standard error of $\hat{\beta}$ is 0.053372 and appears in cell F11.

6.3 A $(1 - \alpha)100\%$ confidence interval for a maximum likelihood estimator $\hat{\theta}$ is given by $(\hat{\theta} - Z_{1-\alpha/2} \, SE(\hat{\theta}), \hat{\theta} + Z_{1-\alpha/2} \, SE(\hat{\theta}))$, where $SE(\hat{\theta})$ is its standard error

	A	B	C	D	E	F	G	H
1	Date	S&P500	Log Return	Starting Values				
2	t	S_t	$R_t = Log(S_t/S_{t-1})$	$\omega =$	0.0000020			
3	30-Dec-05	1248.29	-0.0048987	$\alpha =$	0.10			
4	29-Dec-05	1254.42	-0.00298497	$\beta =$	0.85		Confidence Level	
5	28-Dec-05	1258.17	0.001296372				$\alpha =$ 0.05	
6	27-Dec-05	1256.54	-0.009599313					
7	23-Dec-05	1268.66	0.000425737	Estimated Parameters		Standard Errors	Confidence Interval	
8	22-Dec-05	1268.12	0.00421193	GARCH LL =	-12,241.26		Lower Limit	Upper Limit
9	21-Dec-05	1262.79	0.002513471	$\omega =$	0.0000007	3.41641E-06	-5.9755E-06	7.4166E-06
10	20-Dec-05	1259.62	-0.000238139	$\alpha =$	0.075	0.027154352	0.0213	0.1278
11	19-Dec-05	1259.92	-0.005856208	$\beta =$	0.921	0.053371919	0.8164	1.0256

FIGURE 6.10 Solution to Exercise 6.2 and 6.3

and $Z_{1-\alpha/2}$ is the $(1-\alpha/2)$ point of the standard normal distribution. A value of $\alpha = 0.05$ produces a 95 percent confidence interval. The VBA function CI() implements the confidence intervals for any value of α using the standard errors obtained from the GARCHSE() function.

```
Function CI(mle, se, alpha)
Dim output() As Double
ReDim output(2) As Double
 output(1) = mle - Application.NormSInv(1 - alpha / 2) * se
 output(2) = mle + Application.NormSInv(1 - alpha / 2) * se
CI = output
End Function
```

The confidence intervals produced by this function appear in Figure 6.10. For example, cells G11 and H11 contain the 95 percent confidence interval for $\hat{\beta}$, given as $(0.8164, 1.0256)$.

CHAPTER 7

The Greeks

INTRODUCTION

In this chapter we present the so-called "Greeks," which are the sensitivities of the option prices to the variables used as inputs to the prices. The Greeks are important for portfolio construction and dynamic hedging because the magnitude and sign of these sensitivities indicate how much the option price will change when the variables change. Suppose that f denotes the price of the call or put option. There are five Greeks that are commonly encountered in option pricing and that we present in this book:

1. Delta is the sensitivity of the option to the price of the underlying asset, $\Delta = \frac{\partial f}{\partial S}$.
2. Gamma is the sensitivity of delta to the price of the underlying asset, $\Gamma = \frac{\partial \Delta}{\partial S} = \frac{\partial^2 f}{\partial S^2}$.
3. Vega is the sensitivity of the option to volatility, $V = \frac{\partial f}{\partial \sigma}$.
4. Rho is the sensitivity of the option to the risk-free rate, $\rho = \frac{\partial f}{\partial r}$.
5. Theta is the sensitivity of the option to the time to maturity, $\Theta = -\frac{\partial f}{\partial T}$, expressed as a negative derivative to represent the sensitivity of the price with decreasing maturity.

This chapter will explain how to obtain the Greeks for the option pricing models encountered in this book. For the Black-Scholes model and the Gram-Charlier model of Chapter 4, the Greeks are available in closed form. For the binomial and trinomial trees of Chapter 3, some of the Greeks can be approximated by considering the price of the option at different nodes of the tree. Others must be approximated by finite differences—inducing a small perturbation in the value of an input variable and calculating the change in option price relative to the perturbation. For the Heston (1993) model of Chapter 5 and the Heston and Nandi (2000) model of Chapter 6, the Greeks are also available in closed form, except that a complex integral must often be evaluated through numerical integration.

BLACK-SCHOLES GREEKS

Recall from Chapter 4 that the Black-Scholes price at time t of a European call and put on a non-dividend-paying stock with spot price S_t, strike price K, time to maturity T years, when the annual volatility of the stock is σ and the risk-free rate is r, are given by

$$C_{BS} = S_t \Phi(d) - Ke^{-rT}\Phi(d - \sigma\sqrt{T}) \tag{7.1}$$

and

$$P_{BS} = Ke^{-rT}\Phi(\sigma\sqrt{T} - d) - S_t\Phi(-d) \tag{7.2}$$

respectively, where

$\phi(x) = \exp(-x^2/2)/\sqrt{2\pi}$ is the pdf of a standard normal variable,

$\Phi(x) = \int_x^\infty \phi(u)du$ is its cdf, and

$d = \dfrac{\ln(S/K) + (r + \sigma^2/2)T}{\sigma\sqrt{T}}.$

By taking partial derivatives of the expressions for C_{BS} and P_{BS}, the Greeks from the Black-Scholes model have the forms shown in Table 7.1. Details can be found in textbooks such as those by Hull (2006) or Haug (1998). Notice that gamma and vega are the same for calls and puts. To make the notation slightly less cumbersome, we have set $S_t = S$.

TABLE 7.1   Greeks from the Black-Scholes Model

Greek	Call	Put
Delta (Δ)	$\dfrac{\partial C}{\partial S} = \Phi(d)$	$\dfrac{\partial P}{\partial S} = [\Phi(d) - 1]$
Gamma (Γ)	$\dfrac{\partial^2 C}{\partial S^2} = \dfrac{\phi(d)}{S\sigma\sqrt{T}}$	$\dfrac{\partial^2 P}{\partial S^2} = \dfrac{\phi(d)}{S\sigma\sqrt{T}}$
Vega (V)	$\dfrac{\partial C}{\partial \sigma} = S\phi(d)\sqrt{T}$	$\dfrac{\partial P}{\partial \sigma} = S\phi(d)\sqrt{T}$
Rho (ρ)	$\dfrac{\partial C}{\partial r} = TKe^{-rT}\Phi(d - \sigma\sqrt{T})$	$\dfrac{\partial P}{\partial r} = -TKe^{-rT}\Phi(\sigma\sqrt{T} - d)$
Theta (Θ)	$-\dfrac{\partial C}{\partial T} = -\dfrac{S\phi(d)\sigma}{2\sqrt{T}}$ $- rKe^{-rT}\Phi(d - \sigma\sqrt{T})$	$-\dfrac{\partial P}{\partial T} = -\dfrac{S\phi(d)\sigma}{2\sqrt{T}}$ $+ rKe^{-rT}\Phi(\sigma\sqrt{T} - d)$

The Excel file Chapter7BSGreeks contains VBA code for implementing all
of the Black-Scholes Greeks. These are coded in the VBA function BSDelta(),
BSGamma(), BSVega(), BSRho(), and BSTheta(). As in Chapter 4, the functions
Fz() and Gauss() are used to save space.

```vba
Function Fz(x)
 Fz = Exp(-x ^ 2 / 2) / Sqr(2 * Application.Pi())
End Function

Function Gauss(x)
 Gauss = Application.NormSDist(x)
End Function

Function BSDelta(S, K, T, r, v, PutCall As String)
d = (Log(S / K) + T * (r + 0.5 * v ^ 2)) / (v * Sqr(T))
Select Case PutCall
 Case "Call": BSDelta = Gauss(d)
 Case "Put": BSDelta = Gauss(d) - 1
End Select
End Function

Function BSGamma(S, K, T, r, v)
 d = (Log(S / K) + T * (r + 0.5 * v ^ 2)) / (v * Sqr(T))
 BSGamma = Fz(d) / S / v / Sqr(T)
End Function

Function BSVega(S, K, T, r, v)
 d = (Log(S / K) + T * (r + 0.5 * v ^ 2)) / (v * Sqr(T))
 BSVega = S * Fz(d) * Sqr(T)
End Function

Function BSRho(S, K, T, r, v, PutCall As String)
 d = (Log(S / K) + T * (r + 0.5 * v ^ 2)) / (v * Sqr(T))
 Select Case PutCall
 Case "Call": BSRho = T * K * Exp(-r * T) * Gauss(d - v * Sqr(T))
 Case "Put": BSRho = -T * K * Exp(-r * T) * Gauss(v * Sqr(T) - d)
 End Select
End Function

Function BSTheta(S, K, T, r, v, PutCall As String)
 d = (Log(S / K) + T * (r + 0.5 * v ^ 2)) / (v * Sqr(T))
 Select Case PutCall
  Case "Call": BSTheta = -S * Fz(d) * v / 2 / Sqr(T)
    - r * K * Exp(-r * T) * Gauss(d - v * Sqr(T))
  Case "Put": BSTheta = -S * Fz(d) * v / 2 / Sqr(T)
    + r * K * Exp(-r * T) * Gauss(v * Sqr(T) - d)
 End Select
End Function
```

	A	B	C	D	E	F	G
1							
2		**Black-Scholes Greeks for a European Call or Put**					
3							
4		Spot Price (S)	30		B-S Call Price	2.6126	
5		Strike Price (K)	30		B-S Put Price	1.9941	
6		Years to Maturity (T)	0.4167				
7		Interest Rate (r)	0.05				
8		Volatility (v)	0.3				
9		Type (Call or Put)	Call				
10							
11		**Delta (Δ)**	0.5810				
12		**Gamma (Γ)**	0.0673				
13		**Vega (V)**	7.5658		**Vega Per %**	0.0757	
14		**Rho (ρ)**	6.1737		**Rho Per %**	0.0617	
15		**Theta (Θ)**	-3.4645		**Theta Per Day**	-0.0095	
16							

FIGURE 7.1 Black-Scholes Greeks

Figure 7.1 illustrates the Black-Scholes Greeks for a European call with strike price $30 and maturity 5 months, on a stock with spot price $30 and annual volatility 30 percent, when the annual risk-free rate is 5 percent. To obtain the delta of the call, for example, in cell C9 we type "Call" and in cell C11 we type

$$= \text{BSDelta(C4,C5,C6,C7,C8,C9)}.$$

Figure 7.2 presents a simulation in Excel that demonstrates how the price of a European call option with a maturity of six months and strike price of $100 on a non-dividend-paying stock with a volatility of 10 percent changes with respect to the underlying stock price when the risk-free rate is 2 percent. This figure is contained in the Excel file Chapter7Figures.

Figure 7.2 illustrates that the relationship between the underlying asset price and option value is not linear. For the call, the slope is always positive, which illustrates that $\Delta > 0$, while for the put, the opposite is true and $\Delta < 0$. This implies that the delta of the option changes depending of the direction of the price movements of the underlying asset. A portfolio that includes both the asset and options on the asset, remains hedged against movements in the underlying price only for a short period of time, and must be rebalanced continuously to make the portfolio delta neutral. Delta-neutral and gamma-neutral portfolios are explained in the textbooks by Hull (2006) and Taleb (1997).

It is straightforward to demonstrate that there exists an intimate relationship between the Greeks from an option (or any other derivative) whose value f is derived from the price S of a non-dividend-paying stock, and the Black-Scholes-Merton (BSM) differential equation. The BSM differential equation can be derived

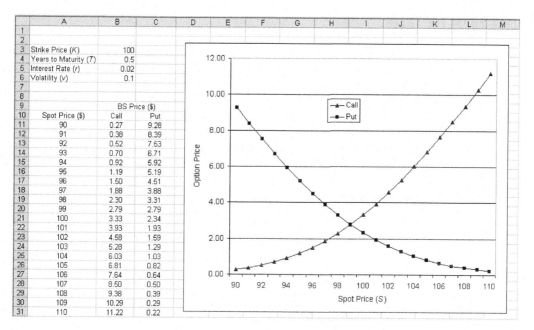

The spreadsheet shows the following values:

	A	B	C
3	Strike Price (K)	100	
4	Years to Maturity (T)	0.5	
5	Interest Rate (r)	0.02	
6	Volatility (v)	0.1	
9		BS Price ($)	
10	Spot Price ($)	Call	Put
11	90	0.27	9.28
12	91	0.38	8.39
13	92	0.52	7.53
14	93	0.70	6.71
15	94	0.92	5.92
16	95	1.19	5.19
17	96	1.50	4.51
18	97	1.88	3.88
19	98	2.30	3.31
20	99	2.79	2.79
21	100	3.33	2.34
22	101	3.93	1.93
23	102	4.58	1.59
24	103	5.28	1.29
25	104	6.03	1.03
26	105	6.81	0.82
27	106	7.64	0.64
28	107	8.50	0.50
29	108	9.38	0.39
30	109	10.29	0.29
31	110	11.22	0.22

FIGURE 7.2 Sensitivity of Black-Scholes Price to Changes in Stock Price

by forming a portfolio that is short one option on a stock, and long an amount of the stock equal to $\partial f/\partial S$, where S is assumed to evolve as geometric Brownian motion $dS_t = \mu S_t dt + \sigma S_t dz_t$. When Itô's Lemma is applied to the process df, the random component dz is eliminated, implying that the portfolio must earn the risk-free rate. Hence, the BSM differential equation is

$$\frac{\partial f}{\partial t} + rS\frac{\partial f}{\partial S} + \frac{1}{2}\sigma^2 S^2 \frac{\partial^2 f}{\partial S^2} = rf, \tag{7.3}$$

where r is the risk-free rate. Note that the partial derivatives in this equation are the Black-Scholes Greeks. The price f of a single derivative satisfies the BSM differential equation, and so does the price Π of a portfolio of derivatives. Hence, the equation can be expressed in terms of the Greeks as

$$\Theta + rS\Delta + \frac{1}{2}\sigma^2 S^2 \Gamma = r\Pi. \tag{7.4}$$

When the portfolio is delta-neutral, then $\Delta = 0$ and the last equation can be written as

$$\Theta + \frac{1}{2}\sigma^2 S^2 \Gamma = r\Pi. \tag{7.5}$$

For details, see Chapters 13 and 15 of Hull (2006).

GREEKS FROM THE TREES

In this section we illustrate how the Greeks can be obtained from the binomial and trinomial trees. For the binomial and trinomial trees, and for the adaptive mesh method, delta, gamma, and theta can be obtained by evaluating the change in the option price at the beginning nodes of the tree. Pelsser and Vorst (1994) explain that this produces better approximation to the Greeks than finite differences. Moreover, it requires less computation time, since only one option price need be calculated. Since volatility and interest rates are assumed constant in these trees, however, rho and vega must be obtained by finite differences.

Greeks from the Binomial Trees

For the CRR binomial tree, the Edgeworth binomial tree, the Leisen and Reimer binomial tree, and the Derman and Kani implied binomial tree, we follow the approach explained in Pelsser and Vorst (1994), and in textbooks such as those by Chriss (1997) or Hull (2006), and examine the change in the option price at the beginning nodes. Figure 7.3 illustrates the stock price movements at the first time steps in these trees. Since delta measures the sensitivity of the option price to the asset price, a natural approximation to delta is the change in the option price to the change in the asset price, both obtained at the first time step, namely at time $1 \times dt$. If $f_{i,j}$ and $S_{i,j}$ are the price of the option and the asset, respectively, at node (i, j), then an approximation to delta is

$$\Delta \approx \frac{f_{1,2} - f_{2,2}}{S_{1,2} - S_{2,2}}. \tag{7.6}$$

Since gamma measures the sensitivity of delta to the asset price, the prices of the option and asset at the second time step $2 \times dt$ can be used to approximate two values of delta, one using nodes $(1, 3)$ and $(2, 3)$, and the other using nodes $(2, 3)$ and $(3, 3)$. Gamma is the change in these two deltas from node $(1, 2)$ to $(2, 2)$ with respect

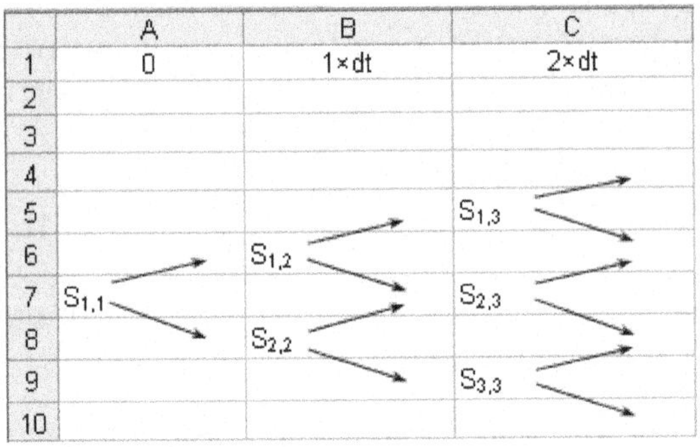

FIGURE 7.3 Stock Price Movements in First Nodes of the Binomial Trees

to changes in the asset price at that time. The first delta is can be approximated as $(f_{1,3} - f_{2,3})/(S_{1,3} - S_{2,3})$ and the second as $(f_{2,3} - f_{3,3})/(S_{2,3} - S_{3,3})$. The change in delta is obtained as the asset price moves from node $(1, 2)$ to $(2, 2)$. This change in price is $(S_{1,2} - S_{2,2})$, so that an approximation to gamma is

$$\Gamma \approx \frac{(f_{1,3} - f_{2,3})/(S_{1,3} - S_{2,3}) - (f_{2,3} - f_{3,3})/(S_{2,3} - S_{3,3})}{(S_{1,2} - S_{2,2})}. \quad (7.7)$$

Theta is the sensitivity of the option to time, so a natural approximation to theta is the change in the option price across time steps, divided by the length of time in between. Since the asset price must be kept constant, we must use option prices at nodes $(1, 1)$ and $(2, 3)$, corresponding to a time step of $2 \times dt$

$$\Theta \approx \frac{f_{2,3} - f_{1,1}}{2dt}. \quad (7.8)$$

Finally, to approximate vega with finite differences, first obtain the price of the option $f(\sigma)$ using the desired volatility σ, then induce a small perturbation $d\sigma$ in the volatility and obtain the new price $f(\sigma + d\sigma)$. An approximation to vega is then

$$V \approx \frac{f(\sigma + d\sigma) - f(\sigma)}{d\sigma}. \quad (7.9)$$

Rho is obtained in an analogous manner, as $\rho \approx [f(r + dr) - f(r)]/dr$. Finite differences will be treated more thoroughly later in this chapter.

The Excel files Chapter3Binomial, Chapter3Edgeworth, Chapter3LRBinomial and Chapter3DKBinomial all contain VBA code for approximating the Greeks. Because the VBA code for the Greeks is exactly the same in each file, we illustrate with Chapter3Binomial on calls only. The price of the asset is stored in the array S(), the option prices in array CallOp(), and delta, gamma, and theta in variables Delta, Gamma, and Theta.

```
Delta = (Op(1, 2) - Op(2, 2)) / (S(1, 2) - S(2, 2))
Gamma = ((Op(1, 3) - Op(2, 3)) / (S(1, 3) - S(2, 3)) -
    (Op(2, 3) - Op(3, 3)) / (S(2, 3) - S(3, 3))) /
    (S(1, 2) - S(2, 2))
Theta = (Op(2, 3) - Op(1, 1)) / dt / 2
```

Figure 7.4 illustrates this on a European call option with strike price $K = 30$ on a stock paying no dividends with spot price $S = 30$, time to maturity $T = 5$ months, risk-free rate 5 percent, and annual volatility 30 percent, using the CRR binomial tree with $n = 250$ time steps.

The price of the option is \$2.6103, and the Greeks are approximated as $\Delta = 0.5809$, $\Gamma = 0.0675$, and $\Theta = -3.4731$. Using the VBA functions included the Excel file Chapter7BSGreeks, we see that these values are close to the Black-Scholes values of $\Delta = 0.5810$, $\Gamma = 0.0673$, and $\Theta = -3.4645$.

	A	B	C	D	E	F	G
1							
2		**CRR Binomial Tree Price for an American or European Option**					
3		**on a Dividend Paying Stock**					
4					Time (r)	Dividend	Interest
5		Spot Price (S)	30		0.000	0.00	0.05
6		Strike Price (K)	30		0.000	0.00	0.05
7		Years to Maturity (T)	0.4167		0.000	0.00	0.05
8		Interest Rate (rf)	0.05		0.000	0.00	0.05
9		Volatility (v)	0.3		0.000	0.00	0.05
10		Steps (n)	250		0.000	0.00	0.05
11		Type (Call or Put)	Call		0.000	0.00	0.05
12		Option (Amer or Euro)	Euro		0.000	0.00	0.05
13					0.000	0.00	0.05
14					0.000	0.00	0.05
15		**Option Price**	2.6103				
16		**Delta (Δ)**	0.5809				
17		**Gamma (Γ)**	0.0675				
18		**Theta (Θ)**	-3.4731				
19		**Vega (V)**	7.5582				
20		**Rho (ρ)**	6.1736				

FIGURE 7.4   Greeks from the CRR Binomial Tree

The VBA function Vega() calculates the price of the option using σ as input, then using σ + Change, where Change is a small number, takes their difference and divides by Change, in accordance with (7.9).

```
Function Vega(Spot, K, T, rf, sigma, n, PutCall As String, EuroAmer As
            String, Dividends)
Change = 0.000001
 f = Binomial(Spot, K, T, rf, sigma, n, PutCall, EuroAmer, Dividends)
 fs = Binomial(Spot, K, T, rf, sigma + Change, n, PutCall, EuroAmer,
            Dividends)
Vega = (fs(1, 1) - f(1, 1)) / Change
End Function
```

The function Rho() works exactly the same way, except that a change to r is induced.

```
Function Rho(Spot, K, T, rf, sigma, n, PutCall As String, EuroAmer As
            String, Dividends)
Change = 0.000001
 f = Binomial(Spot, K, T, rf, sigma, n, PutCall, EuroAmer, Dividends)
 fs = Binomial(Spot, K, T, rf + Change, sigma, n, PutCall, EuroAmer,
            Dividends)
Rho = (fs(1, 1) - f(1, 1)) / Change
End Function
```

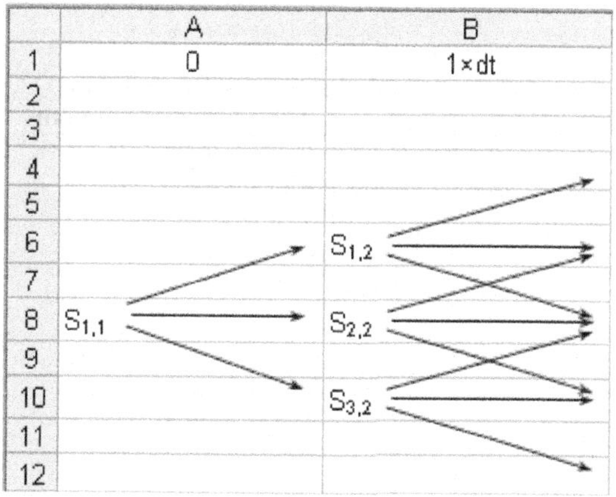

FIGURE 7.5 Stock Price Movements in First Nodes of the Trinomial Tree

Figure 7.4 shows that these Greeks are $V = 7.5582$ and $\rho = 6.1736$, which are close to their Black-Scholes values of $V = 7.5658$ and $\rho = 6.1737$.

Greeks from the Trinomial Tree

Obtaining the Greeks in the trinomial tree of Boyle (1986), the adaptive mesh method of Figlewski and Gao (1999), and the implied trinomial tree of Derman, Kani, and Chriss (1996), is done in a manner analogous to that done with binomial trees, except that different nodes are used because the structure of the trinomial tree is not the same. This is illustrated in Figure 7.5.

Using the same arguments as in the previous section, delta can be approximated at the first time step as

$$\Delta \approx \frac{f_{1,2} - f_{3,2}}{S_{1,2} - S_{3,2}}. \tag{7.10}$$

To approximate gamma, as in the binomial tree we obtain two deltas, one using nodes $(1, 2)$ and $(2, 2)$, the other nodes $(2, 2)$ and $(3, 2)$. However, in the denominator for gamma we must use the change in stock price obtained halfway between these nodes. This change is $\frac{1}{2}(S_{1,2} + S_{2,2}) - \frac{1}{2}(S_{2,2} + S_{3,2})$, or $(S_{1,2} - S_{3,2})/2$. Hence, gamma can be approximated by

$$\Gamma \approx \frac{(f_{1,2} - f_{2,2})/(S_{1,2} - S_{2,2}) - (f_{2,2} - f_{3,2})/(S_{2,2} - S_{3,2})}{(S_{1,2} - S_{3,2})/2}. \tag{7.11}$$

An approximation to theta (per year) is given by

$$\Theta \approx \frac{f_{2,2} - f_{1,1}}{dt}. \tag{7.12}$$

	A	B	C	D
1				
2		**Trinomial Tree Price for an**		
3		**American or European Option**		
4				
5		Spot Price (S)	30	
6		Strike Price (K)	30	
7		Years to Maturity (T)	0.4167	
8		Interest Rate (r)	0.05	
9		Volatility (v)	0.3	
10		Steps (n)	250	
11		Type (Call or Put)	Call	
12		Option (Amer or Euro)	Euro	
13				
14		**Option Price**	2.6115	
15		**Delta (Δ)**	0.5809	
16		**Gamma (Γ)**	0.0674	
17		**Theta (Θ)**	-3.4688	
18		**Vega (V)**	7.5620	
19		**Rho (ρ)**	6.1737	

FIGURE 7.6   Greeks from the Trinomial Tree

To approximate vega and rho, we proceed exactly as in the binomial trees, by inducing a small perturbation in the volatility and risk-free rate, respectively, and calculating the ratio of the change in the option price to the perturbation.

The Excel file Chapter3Trinomial contains VBA code for implementing the Greeks in the trinomial tree. This file is illustrated in Figure 7.6, using the same inputs as those in Figure 7.4. The price of the call is $2.6115, while the Greeks are $\Delta = 0.5809$, $\Gamma = 0.0674$, $\Theta = -3.4688$, $V = 7.5620$, and $\rho = 6.1737$. Not surprisingly, these are closer to the Black-Scholes values than the Greeks derived from the CRR binomial tree with the same number of steps.

We close this section by comparing the Greeks from the different tree models covered in Chapter 3, using a European call option with strike price $K = 105$ and maturity $T = 2$ years, on a non-dividend-paying stock with spot price $S = 100$ and annual volatility $\sigma = 0.30$, when the risk-free rate is $r = 0.05$, and using $n = 250$ steps. The additional parameters are $\kappa = 3$ and $\xi = 0$ for the Edgeworth tree of Rubinstein (1998), Method = 1 for the Leisen and Reimer (1996) binomial tree, $\lambda = 999$ for the flexible binomial tree of Tian (1999) and number of steps for the implied binomial tree of Derman and Kani (1994) and the implied trinomial tree of Derman, Kani, and Chriss (1996). This comparison appears in the Excel file Chapter7GreeksComp, and is illustrated in Figure 7.7.

	A	B	C	D	E	F
1						
2		**Comparison of Greeks from Tree-Based Models**				
3					**Additional Parameters**	
4		Spot Price (S)	100		Kurtosis	3
5		Strike Price (K)	105		Skewness	0
6		Years to Maturity (T)	2.0		Lambda	999
7		Interest Rate (r)	0.05		Method	1
8		Volatility (v)	0.3		Volatility Skew	0
9		Number of Steps (n)	250		Number of Steps	2
10		Type (Call or Put)	Call		Number of Steps	20
11		Option (Euro or Amer)	Euro			
12						**Leisen-Reimer**
13			**Black-Scholes**	**CRR Binomial**	**Trinomial**	**Binomial**
14		Option Price	18.9937	18.9867	18.9980	18.9937
15		Delta (Δ)	0.6304	0.6301	0.6303	0.6303
16		Gamma (Γ)	0.0089	0.0089	0.0089	0.0089
17		Theta (Θ)	-6.2056	-6.2170	-6.2090	-6.2056
18		Vega (V)	53.3789	53.6799	53.2788	53.3790
19		Rho (ρ)	88.0867	88.0547	88.0601	88.0868
20						
21			**Edgeworth**	**Flexible**	**Derman-Kani**	**Derman-Kani-Chriss**
22			**Binomial**	**Binomial**	**Implied Binomial**	**Implied Trinomial**
23		Option Price	19.0021	18.9760	18.1532	19.0704
24		Delta (Δ)	0.6302	0.6301	0.6147	0.6291
25		Gamma (Γ)	0.0089	0.0181	0.0148	0.0090
26		Theta (Θ)	-5.8974	-6.3736	-9.0766	-6.2418
27		Vega (V)	52.8939	53.3240	47.6851	53.4059
28		Rho (ρ)	90.2183	88.0708	86.6363	87.7316

FIGURE 7.7 Comparison of the Greeks from the Tree-Based Models

The figure indicates that with $n = 250$ time steps, most of the trees approximate the Black-Scholes Greeks reasonably well. This is especially true for the Greeks derived from the Leisen and Reimer (1996) binomial tree.

GREEKS FROM THE GRAM-CHARLIER MODEL

This section deals with the Greeks from the Gram-Charlier model of Chapter 4. We present the formulas for the Greeks, the VBA code to implement them, and an illustration of the spreadsheet that contains the code. The derivation of the Gram-Charlier Greeks appears in the appendix to this chapter.

Recall from Chapter 4 that the Gram-Charlier price of a European call is

$$C_{GC} = S\Phi(d) - Ke^{-rT}\Phi(d - \sigma_T)$$
$$+ S\phi(d)\sigma_T \left[\frac{\gamma_{1T}}{3!}(2\sigma_T - d) - \frac{\gamma_{2T}}{4!}(1 - d^2 + 3d\sigma_T - 3\sigma_T^2) \right]$$

where

$$d = \frac{\ln(S/K) + rT + \sigma_T^2/2}{\sigma_T}$$

$\sigma_T = \sigma\sqrt{T}$ = volatility for T periods

$\gamma_{1T} = \gamma_1/\sqrt{T}$ = skewness for T periods

$\gamma_{2T} = \gamma_2/T$ = kurtosis for T periods

and where $S = S_t$. As shown in the appendix to this chapter, the Greeks for the Gram-Charlier calls can be obtained from the partial derivatives of C_{GC}. Hence, we have the following expressions for the Gram-Charlier call delta, gamma, vega, rho, and theta, respectively:

$$\Delta_{Call} = \Phi(d) - \frac{\gamma_{1T}}{3!}\phi(d)(1 - d^2 + 3d\sigma_T - 2\sigma_T^2)$$

$$+ \frac{\gamma_{2T}}{4!}\phi(d)[3d(1 - 2\sigma_T^2) + 4d^2\sigma_T - d^3 - 4\sigma_T + 3\sigma_T^2],$$

$$\Gamma_{Call} = \frac{\phi(d)}{S\sigma_T} - \frac{\gamma_{1T}}{3!}\frac{\phi(d)}{S\sigma_T}[d^3 + d(2\sigma_T^2 - 3) + 3\sigma_T(1 - d^2)]$$

$$+ \frac{\gamma_{2T}}{4!}\frac{\phi(d)}{S\sigma_T}[d^4 + 3(1 - d^2)(1 - 2\sigma_T^2) + 4d\sigma_T(3 - d^2) - 3d(\sigma_T^2 + d)],$$

$$V_{Call} = S\phi(d)\sqrt{T} + \frac{\gamma_{1T}}{3!}S\phi(d)\sqrt{T}[3\sigma\sqrt{T}(1 + d^2) - d(d^2 + 2\sigma^2 T)]$$

$$+ \frac{\gamma_{2T}}{4!}S\phi(d)\sqrt{T}[(1 - d^2 + 3d\sigma\sqrt{T} - 3\sigma^2 T)(\sigma\,dd' - 1) + 2dd'\sigma + 3\sigma^2 T],$$

where

$$d' = \sqrt{T} - d/\sigma,$$

$$\rho_{Call} = KTe^{-rT}\Phi(d - \sigma_T) - \frac{\gamma_{1T}}{3!}ST\phi(d)[-d^2 + 2d\sigma_T + 1]$$

$$+ \frac{\gamma_{2T}}{4!}ST\phi(d)[-d^3 + 3(d\sigma_T + 1)(d - \sigma_T)],$$

$$\Theta_{Call} = -rKe^{-rT}\Phi(d - \sigma\sqrt{T}) - S\phi(d)\frac{\sigma}{2\sqrt{T}}$$

$$- \frac{\gamma_1}{3!}S\sigma\phi(d)\left[(d - 2\sigma\sqrt{T})\,dd' + \left(\frac{\sigma}{\sqrt{T}} - d'\right)\right]$$

$$- \frac{\gamma_2}{4!}S\sigma\phi(d)\left[\left(\frac{1}{\sqrt{T}}(3 - d^2) + 3d\sigma - 3\sigma^2\sqrt{T}\right)dd'\right.$$

$$\left. + \frac{1}{2T^{3/2}}(1 - d^2) - 3\sigma d' + \frac{3\sigma^2}{2\sqrt{T}}\right],$$

where $d' = \frac{r + \sigma^2/2}{\sigma\sqrt{T}} - \frac{d}{2T}$.

The Greeks for the Gram-Charlier puts are obtained by using put-call parity and taking the partial derivatives of $P_{GC} = C_{GC} + Ke^{-rT} - S$. Hence the Gram-Charlier put delta, gamma, vega, rho, and theta are $\Delta_{Put} = \Delta_{Call} - 1, \Gamma_{Put} = \Gamma_{Call}, V_{Put} = V_{Call} = V, \rho_{Put} = \rho_{Call} - KTe^{-rT}$, and $\Theta_{Put} = \Theta_{Call} + Kre^{-rT}$, respectively.

Note that vega, rho, and theta are the Gram-Charlier Greeks for a single period. To make these Greeks comparable to the Black-Scholes Greeks, theta must be scaled by M, vega must be scaled by $1/\sqrt{M}$, and rho must be scaled by $1/M$, where M is the number of periods in the year. For example, suppose that we are using monthly periods in the Gram-Charlier prices of calls, and we wish to obtain yearly Greeks. Then $M = 12$, $V^{Year} = V/\sqrt{12}$, $\rho_{Call}^{Year} = \rho_{Call}/12$, and $\Theta_{Call}^{Year} = \Theta_{Call} \times 12$. In the case of vega, for example,

$$V^{Year} = \frac{\partial C}{\partial \sigma_T} = \frac{\partial C}{\partial (\sigma \sqrt{T})} = \frac{1}{\sqrt{T}} \frac{\partial C}{\partial \sigma} = \frac{1}{\sqrt{T}} V, \qquad (7.13)$$

where $T = 12$. The same scaling argument applies to rho and theta from puts. Scaling the Greeks from the Gram-Charlier model is illustrated later in this section with an example.

The Excel file Chapter7GCGreeks contains VBA code for implementing the Greeks for the Gram-Charlier model. As before, the VBA functions Gauss() and fz() are used to conserve space.

```
Function Gauss(x)
 Gauss = Application.NormSDist(x)
End Function


Function fz(x)
 fz = Exp(-x ^ 2 / 2) / Sqr(2 * Application.Pi())
End Function


Function GCDelta(Spot, K, r, T, v, skew, kurt, PutCall As String)
nskew = skew / Sqr(T)
nkurt = kurt / T
S = Sqr(T) * v
d = (Log(Spot / K) + T * r + S ^ 2 / 2) / S
Delta = Gauss(d) - (nskew / 6) * fz(d)
   * (1 - d ^ 2 + 3 * d * S - 2 * S ^ 2) + (nkurt / 24)
   * fz(d) * (3 * d * (1 - 2 * S ^ 2) + 4 * d ^ 2
   * S - d ^ 3 - 4 * S + 3 * S ^ 3)
Select Case PutCall
 Case "Call"
  GCDelta = Delta
 Case "Put"
  GCDelta = Delta - 1
End Select
End Function


Function GCGamma(Spot, K, r, T, v, skew, kurt)
nskew = skew / Sqr(T): nkurt = kurt / T
```

```
S = Sqr(T) * v
d = (Log(Spot / K) + T * r + S ^ 2 / 2) / S
GCGamma = fz(d) / Spot / S - (nskew / 6) * fz(d) / Spot / S
  * (d ^ 3 + d * (2 * S ^ 2 - 3) + 3 * S * (1 - d ^ 2))
  + (nkurt / 24) * fz(d) / Spot / S * (d ^ 4 + 3
  * (1 - d ^ 2) * (1 - 2 * S ^ 2)
  + 4 * S * d * (3 - d ^ 2) - 3 * d * (d + S ^ 2))
End Function

Function GCVega(Spot, K, r, T, v, skew, kurt)
nskew = skew / Sqr(T): nkurt = kurt / T
d = (Log(Spot / K) + (r + v ^ 2 / 2) * T) / v / Sqr(T)
dp = Sqr(T) - d / v
GCVega = Spot * fz(d) * Sqr(T) + Spot * fz(d)
  * (nskew / 6) * Sqr(T) * (3 * v * Sqr(T) * (1 + d ^ 2)
  - d * (d ^ 2 + 2 * v ^ 2 * T)) + Spot * fz(d)
  * (nkurt / 24) * Sqr(T) * ((1 - d ^ 2 + 3 * d * v
  * Sqr(T) - 3 * v ^ 2 * T) * (d * dp * v - 1)
  + (2 * d * dp + 3 * v * T) * v)
End Function

Function GCRho(Spot, K, r, T, v, skew, kurt, PutCall As String)
nskew = skew / Sqr(T)
nkurt = kurt / T
S = Sqr(T) * v
d = (Log(Spot / K) + T * r + S ^ 2 / 2) / S
Rho = K * T * Exp(-r * T) * Gauss(d - S) - (nskew / 6)
  * fz(d) * Spot * T * (2 * S * d - d ^ 2 + 1)
  + (nkurt / 24) * fz(d) * Spot * T * (-d ^ 3 + 3
  * (S * d + 1) * (d - S))
Select Case PutCall
 Case "Call"
  GCRho = Rho
 Case "Put"
  GCRho = Rho - K * T * Exp(-r * T)
End Select
End Function

Function GCTheta(Spot, K, r, T, v, skew, kurt, PutCall As String)
d = (Log(Spot / K) + (r + v ^ 2 / 2) * T) / v / Sqr(T)
dp = (r + v ^ 2 / 2) / v / Sqr(T) - d / 2 / T
T1 = K * r * Exp(-r * T)
  * Gauss(d - v * Sqr(T)) + Spot * fz(d) * v / 2 / Sqr(T)
T2 = Spot * v * fz(d) * (skew / 6)
  * ((d - 2 * v * Sqr(T)) * d * dp + (v / Sqr(T) - dp))
T3 = Spot * v * fz(d) * (kurt / 24) * (((3 - d ^ 2)
  / Sqr(T) + (3 * d * v) - 3 * v ^ 2 * Sqr(T)) * d * dp
  + T ^ (-1.5) * (1 - d ^ 2) / 2 - 3 * v * dp
  + 3 * v ^ 2 / 2 / Sqr(T))
Theta = -T1 - T2 - T3
Select Case PutCall
 Case "Call"
```

```
    GCTheta = Theta
  Case "Put"
    GCTheta = Theta + K * r * Exp(-r * T)
End Select
End Function
```

Figure 7.8 illustrates the use of the VBA functions for the Gram-Charlier Greeks on a stock with a spot price of $100, a risk-free rate of 5 percent annually (0.4167 percent monthly), yearly volatility of 30 percent ($30/\sqrt{12} = 8.66$ percent monthly), monthly skewness and kurtosis of -0.5 and 0.5, respectively, on a call option with five months maturity and a strike price of $100. The Gram-Charlier price of the call is $8.6268. To obtain the delta of the call, in cell C18 we type

$$= \text{GCDelta(S, K, RF, T, V, Skew, Kurt, PutCall)}$$

and obtain $\Delta_{Call} = 0.5953$. The other Greeks are obtained similarly.

	A	B	C	D
1				
2		**Gram-Charlier Greeks**		
3		**Period = Monthly**		
4				
5		Underlying Price (*S*)	100.00	
6		Strike Price (*K*)	100.00	
7		Risk Free Rate Per Year (*Tr*)	0.05	
8		Risk Free Rate Per Period (*r*)	0.004167	
9		Periods Until Maturity (*T*)	5	
10		Volatility Per Year ($\sigma\sqrt{T}$)	0.30	
11		One-Period Volatility (σ)	0.08660254	
12		One-Period Skewness (γ_1)	-0.5	
13		One-Period Kurtosis (γ_2)	0.5	
14		Type (*Call* or *Put*)	Call	
15				
16		**Gram-Charlier Option Price**	8.6268	
17				
18		**Delta (Δ)**	0.5953	
19		**Gamma (Γ)**	0.0204	
20		**Vega (V)**	85.1567	
21		**Rho (ρ)**	254.5199	
22		**Theta (θ)**	-0.9608	
23				
24		**Vega Per Year ($V/\sqrt{M}$)**	24.5826	
25		**Rho Per Year (ρ/M)**	21.2100	
26		**Theta Per Year (θM)**	-11.5298	
27				

FIGURE 7.8 Greeks from the Gram-Charlier Model

	A	B	C	D
1				
2		**Gram-Charlier Greeks**		
3		**Period = Monthly**		
4				
5		Underlying Price (*S*)	30.00	
6		Strike Price (*K*)	30.00	
7		Risk Free Rate Per Year (*Tr*)	0.05	
8		Risk Free Rate Per Period (*r*)	0.004167	
9		Periods Until Maturity (*T*)	5	
10		Volatility Per Year ($\sigma\sqrt{T}$)	0.30	
11		One-Period Volatility (σ)	0.08660254	
12		One-Period Skewness (γ_1)	0	
13		One-Period Kurtosis (γ_2)	0	
14		Type (*Call* or *Put*)	Call	
15				
16		**Gram-Charlier Option Price**	2.6126	
17				
18		**Delta (Δ)**	0.5810	
19		**Gamma (Γ)**	0.0673	
20		**Vega (V)**	26.2086	
21		**Rho (ρ)**	74.0842	
22		**Theta (Θ)**	-0.2887	
23				
24		**Vega Per Year (V/$\sqrt{M}$)**	7.5658	
25		**Rho Per Year (ρ/M)**	6.1737	
26		**Theta Per Year (ΘM)**	-3.4645	
27				

FIGURE 7.9   Black-Scholes Greeks as a Special Case of Gram-Charlier Greeks

As mentioned earlier, vega, rho, and theta are Greeks for one period, monthly in this case. To make vega, rho, and theta comparable to the yearly Black-Scholes Greeks, vega, rho, and theta must be scaled by the appropriate time factor. Since we are dealing with monthly periods, $M = 12$. To obtain the yearly vega for calls, in cell C24 we type "= C20/SQRT(12)", which produces $V_{Call}^{Year} = 24.5826$. Similarly, to obtain the yearly rho for calls, in cell C25 we type "= C21/12", which produces $\rho_{Call}^{Year} = 21.2100$.

Since the Gram-Charlier option prices reduce to the Black-Scholes prices when skewness and excess kurtosis are each zero, the same should happen for the Greeks. Figure 7.9 illustrates this on a European call with a strike price of $30 and maturity of five months, on a stock with a spot price of $30 and annual volatility of 30 percent, when the annual risk-free rate is 5 percent.

Comparing Figure 7.9 with Figure 7.1, which used the same input variables, we see that the option price, and the call delta, gamma, and the yearly vega, yearly rho, and yearly theta are exactly the same.

GREEKS FROM THE HESTON (1993) MODEL

In this section the Greeks from the Heston (1993) model are derived, and implemented using VBA. The Greeks from a general stochastic model with jumps, that includes the Heston (1993) as a special case, are derived in Bakshi, Cao, and Chen (1997). Recall from Chapter 5 that the Heston (1993) call price has the following form:

$$\text{Call} = S_t P_1 - Ke^{-r(T-t)} P_2 \qquad (7.14)$$

where $e^{-r(T-t)}$ is used for the discount factor $P(t, T)$. The Heston (1993) put price, by put-call parity, is

$$\text{Put} = \text{Call} + Ke^{-r(T-t)} - S_t \qquad (7.15)$$

where

$$P_j = \frac{1}{2} + \frac{1}{\pi} \int_0^\infty \text{Re}\left[\frac{e^{-i\phi \ln K} f_j}{i\phi} \right] d\phi \qquad (7.16)$$

are the risk-neutral probabilities. These are derived from the characteristic functions

$$f_j = \exp(C_j + D_j v + i\phi x) \qquad (7.17)$$

where $x = \ln S$. From (7.14) the delta of the Heston (1993) call is

$$\Delta_{Call} = \frac{\partial \text{Call}}{\partial S(t)} = P_1. \qquad (7.18)$$

This has been employed by several authors, including Bakshi, Cao, and Chen (1997) and Bakshi and Madan (2000). By put-call parity (7.15) the delta of the put is

$$\Delta_{Call} = \frac{\partial \text{Put}}{\partial S(t)} = P_1 - 1. \qquad (7.19)$$

Gamma is given by differentiating again

$$\Gamma = \frac{\partial \Delta}{\partial S} = \frac{\partial P_1}{\partial S} = \frac{1}{\pi} \frac{\partial}{\partial S} \int_0^\infty \text{Re}\left[\frac{e^{-i\phi \ln K} f_1}{i\phi} \right] d\phi$$

$$= \frac{1}{\pi} \int_0^\infty \text{Re}\left[\frac{e^{-i\phi \ln K} \partial f_1 / \partial S}{i\phi} \right] d\phi = \frac{1}{\pi S} \int_0^\infty \text{Re}[e^{-i\phi \ln K} f_1] \, d\phi \qquad (7.20)$$

since

$$\frac{\partial f_1}{\partial S} = \exp(C_1 + D_1 v + i\phi x)i\phi \frac{\partial x}{\partial S} = \frac{1}{S}f_1 i\phi. \tag{7.21}$$

Rho for the call is obtained from (7.14) as

$$\rho_{Call} = \frac{\partial Call}{\partial r} = Ke^{-r(T-t)}(T-t)P_2. \tag{7.22}$$

Rho from the put is obtained from the put-call parity relationship (7.15)

$$\begin{aligned} \rho_{Put} &= \rho_{Call} + Ke^{-r(T-t)}(T-t) \\ &= Ke^{-r(T-t)}(T-t)(P_2 - 1). \end{aligned} \tag{7.23}$$

To obtain vega, we must choose which variance is used to differentiate the call and put price. Choosing the current (spot) variance leads to the following expression for vega:

$$V = \frac{\partial Call}{\partial v} = S_t \frac{\partial P_1}{\partial v} - Ke^{-r(T-t)}\frac{\partial P_2}{\partial v} \tag{7.24}$$

where

$$\frac{\partial P_j}{\partial v} = \frac{1}{\pi}\int_0^\infty \mathrm{Re}\left[\frac{e^{-i\phi \ln K}f_j D_j}{i\phi}\right]d\phi. \tag{7.25}$$

Expression (7.25) results from the fact that

$$\frac{\partial f_j}{\partial v} = \frac{\partial}{\partial v}\exp(C_j + D_j v + i\phi x) = f_j D_j. \tag{7.26}$$

It is easy to see that (7.24) is also the vega for a put.

Obtaining theta is more complicated, since the time to maturity, $\tau = T - t$, also appears in the functions C_j and D_j that make up f_j in (7.17). For the call, theta is

$$\Theta_{Call} = -\frac{\partial Call}{\partial \tau} = -S\frac{\partial P_1}{\partial \tau} + Ke^{-r\tau}\left(\frac{\partial P_2}{\partial \tau} - rP_2\right). \tag{7.27}$$

To obtain theta we need to evaluate

$$\frac{\partial P_j}{\partial \tau} = \frac{1}{\pi}\int_0^\infty \mathrm{Re}\left[\frac{e^{-i\phi \ln K}\partial f_j/\partial \tau}{i\phi}\right]d\phi, \tag{7.28}$$

which requires the partial derivative

$$\frac{\partial f_j}{\partial \tau} = \exp(C_j + D_j v + i\phi x)\left(\frac{\partial C_j}{\partial \tau} + \frac{\partial D_j}{\partial \tau}v + i\phi x\right). \qquad (7.29)$$

Equation (7.29) further requires

$$\frac{\partial C_j}{\partial \tau} = r\phi i + \frac{\kappa\theta}{\sigma^2}\left[(b_j - \rho\sigma\phi i + d_j) + 2\left(\frac{g_j d_j e^{d_j\tau}}{1 - g_j e^{d_j\tau}}\right)\right] \qquad (7.30)$$

and

$$\frac{\partial D_j}{\partial \tau} = \left(\frac{b_j - \rho\sigma\phi i + d_j}{\sigma^2}\right)\left[\frac{d_j e^{d_j\tau}(g_j e^{d_j\tau} - 1) + (1 - e^{d_j\tau})g_j d_j e^{d_j\tau}}{(1 - g_j e^{d_j\tau})^2}\right]. \qquad (7.31)$$

Substituting (7.28) through (7.31) into (7.27), produces the call theta. The put theta is obtained through put-call parity.

$$\Theta_{Put} = -\frac{\partial \text{Put}}{\partial \tau} = \Theta_{Call} + Kre^{-r\tau} \qquad (7.32)$$

The Excel file Chapter7HestonGreeks contains the VBA functions HDelta(), HGamma(), HRho(), HVega(), and HTheta() to implement the Heston (1993) Greeks, based on the equations derived above.

The function HDelta() uses the function HestonP1() to calculate the probability P_1, which is restricted to lie in the interval $[0, 1]$.

```
Function HDelta(PutCall As String, kappa, theta, lambda, rho, sigma, tau,
          K, S, r, v)
Dim P1_int(1001) As Double, P2_int(1001) As Double, phi_int(1001) As
          Double
Dim p1 As Double, p2 As Double, phi As Double, xg(16) As Double, wg(16) As
          Double
Dim cnt As Integer, HestonC As Double
cnt = 1
For phi = 0.0001 To 100.0001 Step 0.1
 phi_int(cnt) = phi
 P1_int(cnt) = HestonP1(phi, kappa, theta, lambda, rho, sigma, tau,
          K, S, r, v)
 cnt = cnt + 1
Next phi
p1 = 0.5 + (1 / thePI) * TRAPnumint(phi_int, P1_int)
If p1 < 0 Then p1 = 0
If p1 > 1 Then p1 = 1
If PutCall = "Call" Then
 HDelta = p1
```

```
ElseIf PutCall = "Put" Then
 HDelta = p1 - 1
End If
End Function
```

Gamma requires the partial derivative (7.20), obtained by modifying the integral for P_1 so that the function $\text{Re}[e^{-i\phi \ln K} f_1]$ is integrated. This is done by creating the function dP1_dS(), which is identical to the VBA function HestonP1() defined in Chapter 5, but with the last statement modified to be $\text{Re}[e^{-i\phi \ln K} f_1]$ rather than $\text{Re}[e^{-i\phi \ln K} f_1/i\phi]$.

```
Function dP1_dS(phi, kappa, theta, lambda, rho, sigma, tau, K, S, r, v)
' More VBA Statements
dP1_dS = cNumReal(cNumProd(cNumExp(set_cNum(0, -phi *
    Application.Ln(K))), f1))
End Function
```

The VBA function HGamma() produces gamma by integrating the dP1_dS() function, in the same way that the Heston() function in Chapter 5 integrates the function HestonP1().

```
Function HGamma(PutCall As String, kappa, theta, lambda, rho, sigma, tau,
            K, S, r, v)
Dim P1_int(1001) As Double, P2_int(1001) As Double, phi_int(1001) As
            Double
Dim p1 As Double, p2 As Double, phi As Double, xg(16) As Double, wg(16) As
            Double
Dim cnt As Integer, HestonC As Double
cnt = 1
 For phi = 0.0001 To 100.0001 Step 0.1
  phi_int(cnt) = phi
  P1_int(cnt) = dP1_dS(phi, kappa, theta, lambda, rho, sigma, tau,
            K, S, r, v)
  cnt = cnt + 1
 Next phi
HGamma = (1 / thePI / S) * TRAPnumint(phi_int, P1_int)
End Function
```

Vega requires the partial derivatives (7.25). These are obtained with the VBA functions dP1_dV() and dP2_dV(), which are identical to the HestonP1() and HestonP2() functions, with a modification to the final statement so that the functions $\text{Re}[e^{-i\phi \ln K} f_j D_j/i\phi], j = 1, 2$, are produced.

```
Function dP1_dV(phi, kappa, theta, lambda, rho, sigma, tau, K, S, r, v)
' More VBA Statements
dP1_dV = cNumReal(cNumDiv(cNumProd(cNumProd(cNumExp
    set_cNum(0, -phi * Application.Ln(K))), f1), DD1), set_cNum(0, phi)))
End Function
```

The VBA function dP2_dV() is similar to dP1_dV() and is not presented here. The function HVega() produces the integrals in (7.25), then calculates and vega in accordance with (7.24).

```
Function HVega(PutCall As String, kappa, theta, lambda, rho, sigma, tau,
               K, S, r, v)
Dim P1_int(1001) As Double, P2_int(1001) As Double, phi_int(1001) As
               Double
Dim p1 As Double, p2 As Double, phi As Double, xg(16) As Double, wg(16) As
               Double
Dim cnt As Integer, HestonC As Double
cnt = 1
 For phi = 0.0001 To 100.0001 Step 0.1
  phi_int(cnt) = phi
  P1_int(cnt) = dP1_dV(phi, kappa, theta, lambda, rho,
       sigma, tau, K, S, r, v)
  P2_int(cnt) = dP2_dV(phi, kappa, theta, lambda, rho,
       sigma, tau, K, S, r, v)
 cnt = cnt + 1
Next phi
dp1 = 0.5 + (1 / thePI) * TRAPnumint(phi_int, P1_int)
dp2 = 0.5 + (1 / thePI) * TRAPnumint(phi_int, P2_int)
 HVega = S * dp1 - K * Exp(-r * tau) * dp2
End Function
```

The function HRho() obtains the probability P_2, restricts this probability to lie in the interval $[0, 1]$, and returns the value of rho.

```
Function HRho(PutCall As String, kappa, theta, lambda, rho, sigma, tau, K,
               S, r, v)
Dim P1_int(1001) As Double, P2_int(1001) As Double, phi_int(1001) As
               Double
Dim p1 As Double, p2 As Double, phi As Double, xg(16) As Double, wg(16) As
               Double
Dim cnt As Integer, HestonC As Double
cnt = 1
For phi = 0.0001 To 100.0001 Step 0.1
 phi_int(cnt) = phi
 P2_int(cnt) = HestonP2(phi, kappa, theta, lambda, rho,
       sigma, tau, K, S, r, v)
 cnt = cnt + 1
Next phi
p2 = 0.5 + (1 / thePI) * TRAPnumint(phi_int, P2_int)
If p2 < 0 Then p2 = 0
If p2 > 1 Then p2 = 1
If PutCall = "Call" Then
 HRho = K * Exp(-r * tau) * tau * p2
ElseIf PutCall = "Put" Then
 HRho = K * Exp(-r * tau) * tau * (p2 - 1)
End If
End Function
```

Finally, the VBA function HTheta() obtains theta.

```
Function HTheta(PutCall As String, kappa, theta, lambda, rho, sigma, tau,
          K, S, r, v)
Dim P1p_int(1001) As Double, P2p_int(1001) As Double, P2_int(1001) As
          Double, phi_int(1001) As Double
Dim p1p As Double, p2p As Double, p2 As Double, phi As Double, xg(16) As
          Double, wg(16) As Double
Dim cnt As Integer, HestonC As Double
cnt = 1
For phi = 0.0001 To 100.0001 Step 0.1
 phi_int(cnt) = phi
 P1p_int(cnt) = dP1_dT(phi, kappa, theta, lambda, rho,
        sigma, tau, K, S, r, v)
 P2p_int(cnt) = dP2_dT(phi, kappa, theta, lambda, rho,
        sigma, tau, K, S, r, v)
 P2_int(cnt) = HestonP2(phi, kappa, theta, lambda, rho,
        sigma, tau, K, S, r, v)
 cnt = cnt + 1
Next phi
p1p = (1 / thePI) * TRAPnumint(phi_int, P1p_int)
p2p = (1 / thePI) * TRAPnumint(phi_int, P2p_int)
p2 = 0.5 + (1 / thePI) * TRAPnumint(phi_int, P2_int)
If p2 < 0 Then p2 = 0
If p2 > 1 Then p2 = 1
Th = -S * p1p + K * Exp(-r * tau) * (p2p - r * p2)
Select Case PutCall
 Case "Call": HTheta = Th
 Case "Put": HTheta = Th + K * r * Exp(-r * tau)
End Select
End Function
```

The HTheta() function integrates the VBA function HestonP2() defined in Chapter 5 for the integral (7.16), and two additional functions, dP1_dT() and dP2_dT(), for the partial derivatives in (7.28). Unfortunately, these functions are both lengthy.

```
Function dP1_dT(phi, kappa, theta, lambda, rho, sigma, tau, K, S, r, v)
mu1 = 0.5
b1 = set_cNum(kappa - lambda - rho * sigma, 0)
d1 = cNumSqrt(cNumSub(cNumSq(cNumSub(set_cNum(0,
   rho * sigma * phi), b1)), cNumSub(set_cNum(0, sigma ^ 2
   * 2 * mu1 * phi), set_cNum(sigma ^ 2 * phi ^ 2, 0))))
g1 = cNumDiv(cNumAdd(cNumSub(b1, set_cNum(0,
   rho * sigma * phi)), d1), cNumSub(cNumSub(b1,
   set_cNum(0, rho * sigma * phi)), d1))
DD1_1 = cNumDiv(cNumAdd(cNumSub(b1, set_cNum(0,
    rho * sigma * phi)), d1), set_cNum(sigma ^ 2, 0))
DD1_2 = cNumSub(set_cNum(1, 0), cNumExp(cNumProd(d1,
    set_cNum(tau, 0))))
DD1_3 = cNumSub(set_cNum(1, 0), cNumProd(g1,
    cNumExp(cNumProd(d1, set_cNum(tau, 0)))))
```

```
DD1 = cNumProd(DD1_1, cNumDiv(DD1_2, DD1_3))
CC1_1 = set_cNum(0, r * phi * tau)
CC1_2 = set_cNum((kappa * theta) / (sigma ^ 2), 0)
CC1_3 = cNumProd(cNumAdd(cNumSub(b1, set_cNum(0,
    rho * sigma * phi)), d1), set_cNum(tau, 0))
CC1_4 = cNumProd(set_cNum(2, 0),
    cNumLn(cNumDiv(cNumSub(set_cNum(1, 0),
    cNumProd(g1, cNumExp(cNumProd(d1,
    set_cNum(tau, 0))))), cNumSub(set_cNum(1, 0), g1))))
CC1 = cNumAdd(CC1_1, cNumProd(CC1_2, cNumSub(CC1_3, CC1_4)))
CC1p_1 = cNumAdd(cNumSub(b1, set_cNum(0,
    rho * sigma * phi)), d1)
CC1p_2 = cNumProd(set_cNum(2, 0), cNumProd(cNumProd(g1, d1),
    cNumExp(cNumProd(d1, set_cNum(tau, 0)))))
CC1p_3 = cNumSub(set_cNum(1, 0), cNumProd(g1,
    cNumExp(cNumProd(d1, set_cNum(tau, 0)))))
CC1p = cNumAdd(set_cNum(0, r * phi),
    cNumProd(set_cNum(kappa * theta / sigma ^ 2, 0),
    cNumAdd(CC1p_1, cNumDiv(CC1p_2, CC1p_3))))
expdtau = cNumExp(cNumProd(d1, set_cNum(tau, 0)))
DD1p_1 = cNumDiv(cNumAdd(cNumSub(b1, set_cNum(0,
    rho * sigma * phi)), d1), set_cNum(sigma ^ 2, 0))
DD1p_2 = cNumProd(d1, cNumProd(expdtau,
    cNumSub(cNumProd(g1, expdtau), set_cNum(1, 0))))
DD1p_3 = cNumProd(cNumSub(set_cNum(1, 0), expdtau),
    cNumProd(g1, cNumProd(d1, expdtau)))
DD1p_4 = cNumSq(cNumSub(set_cNum(1, 0),
    cNumProd(g1, expdtau)))
DD1p = cNumProd(DD1p_1, cNumDiv(
    cNumAdd(DD1p_2, DD1p_3), DD1p_4))
f1 = cNumExp(cNumAdd(cNumAdd(CC1, cNumProd(DD1,
    set_cNum(v, 0))), set_cNum(0, phi * Log(S))))
f1 = cNumProd(f1, cNumAdd(CC1p, cNumProd(DD1p,
    set_cNum(v, 0))))
dP1_dT = cNumReal(cNumDiv(cNumProd(cNumExp(set_cNum(0,
    -phi * Log(K))), f1), set_cNum(0, phi)))
End Function
```

The dP2_dT() function is similar to the dP1_dT() function, and will not be presented here. It is possible to shorten these functions somewhat by combining terms, but this would make some the VBA statements even more difficult to decipher.

Figure 7.10 is taken from the Excel file Chapter7HestonGreeks, and illustrates the Greeks from the Heston (1993) model, using the same parameter values as in the examples in Chapter 5.

With the given parameter values, the call price is $4.0852. To obtain the Heston (1993) delta, for example, in cell C17 we type

= HDelta(putcall, kappa, theta, lambda, rho, sigmav, dtm, K, S, rf, V),

	A	B	C	D
1				
2		**Greeks from the Heston (1993) Model**		
3				
4		Spot Price (S)	100	
5		Strike Price (K)	100	
6		Risk Free Rate (r)	0.05	
7		Time to Maturity (T − t)	0.5	
8		Rho (ρ)	0	
9		Kappa (κ)	2	
10		Theta (θ)	0.01	
11		Lambda (λ)	0	
12		Volatility of Variance (σ)	0.225	
13		Current variance (v)	0.01	
14		Option Type (Call or Put)	Call	
15				
16		**Option Price**	4.0852	
17		**Delta (Δ)**	0.6711	
18		**Gamma (Γ)**	0.0580	
19		**Vega (V)**	82.0548	
20		**Rho (ρ)**	31.5114	
21		**Theta (Θ)**	-5.5476	
22				

FIGURE 7.10 Greeks from the Heston (1993) Model

which produces $\Delta = 0.6711$. The rest of the Greeks are $\Gamma = 0.0580$, $V = 82.0548$, $\rho = 31.5114$, and $\Theta = -5.5476$.

GREEKS FROM THE HESTON AND NANDI (2000) MODEL

Recall from Chapter 6 that the Heston and Nandi (2000) price of a European call option is given by

$$\text{Call} = SP_1 - Ke^{-rT}P_2, \tag{7.33}$$

where T is the time to maturity and $S = S_t$. The price of a put is given by put-call parity

$$\text{Put} = \text{Call} + Ke^{-rT} - S, \tag{7.34}$$

where the cumulative probabilities are

$$P_1 = \frac{1}{2} + \frac{e^{-rT}}{\pi S} \int_0^\infty \text{Re}\left[\frac{K^{-i\phi}f^*(i\phi + 1)}{i\phi}\right]d\phi, \tag{7.35}$$

$$P_2 = \frac{1}{2} + \frac{1}{\pi} \int_0^\infty \text{Re}\left[\frac{K^{-i\phi}f^*(i\phi)}{i\phi}\right]d\phi, \tag{7.36}$$

and where the generating function f^* is

$$f^*(\phi) = S_t^\phi \exp(A_t(\phi) + B_t(\phi)\sigma_{t+1}^2). \tag{7.37}$$

Heston and Nandi (2000) argue that the delta of the call is

$$\Delta_{Call} = P_1. \tag{7.38}$$

By put-call parity (7.34) the delta of the put is

$$\Delta_{Put} = P_1 - 1. \tag{7.39}$$

To obtain gamma, write P_1 as

$$P_1 = \frac{1}{2} + \frac{e^{-rT}}{\pi} \int_0^\infty \text{Re}\left[\frac{K^{-i\phi} S^{i\phi} \exp(g(i\phi + 1))}{i\phi}\right] d\phi \tag{7.40}$$

where $g(\phi) = A_t(\phi) + B_t(\phi)\sigma_{t+1}^2$. Taking the derivative of (7.40) gamma is seen to be

$$\begin{aligned}\Gamma = \frac{\partial P_1}{\partial S} &= \frac{e^{-rT}}{\pi} \int_0^\infty \text{Re}\left[\frac{K^{-i\phi} i\phi S^{i\phi-1} \exp(g(i\phi + 1))}{i\phi}\right] d\phi \\ &= \frac{e^{-rT}}{\pi} \int_0^\infty \text{Re}\left[\frac{K^{-i\phi} f^*(i\phi + 1)}{S^2}\right] d\phi.\end{aligned} \tag{7.41}$$

Obtaining rho is more complicated since r appears not only in the expression for the call and put price, but also in $A_t, A_{t+1}, \ldots, A_{t+T-1}$. Rho for the call is

$$\begin{aligned}\rho_{Call} = \frac{\partial \text{Call}}{\partial r} &= S\frac{\partial P_1}{\partial r} - K\left[-Te^{-rT}P_2 + e^{-rT}\frac{\partial P_2}{\partial r}\right] \\ &= S\frac{\partial P_1}{\partial r} + Ke^{-rT}\left[TP_2 - \frac{\partial P_2}{\partial r}\right].\end{aligned} \tag{7.42}$$

The partial derivative of $f^*(\phi)$ with respect to r is

$$\frac{\partial f^*(\phi)}{\partial r} = S^\phi \exp(A_t + B_t\sigma_{t+1}^2)\frac{\partial A_t}{\partial r} = f^*\frac{\partial A_t}{\partial r} = f^*T\phi, \tag{7.43}$$

since

$$\frac{\partial A_t}{\partial r} = \phi + \frac{\partial A_{t+1}}{\partial r} = 2\phi + \frac{\partial A_{t+2}}{\partial r} = \cdots = T\phi + \frac{\partial A_{t+T}}{\partial r} = T\phi. \tag{7.44}$$

Hence, the partial derivative of $f^*(i\phi + 1)$ with respect to r is $f^*(i\phi + 1)T(i\phi + 1)$. Applying the product rule, the first partial derivative in (7.42) is

$$
\begin{aligned}
\frac{\partial P_1}{\partial r} &= \frac{1}{\pi S}\left\{-Te^{-rT}\int_0^\infty \text{Re}\left[\frac{K^{-i\phi}f^*(i\phi + 1)}{i\phi}\right]d\phi\right\} \\
&\quad + \frac{1}{\pi S}\left\{e^{-rT}\int_0^\infty \text{Re}\left[\frac{K^{-i\phi}f^*(i\phi + 1)T(i\phi + 1)}{i\phi}\right]d\phi\right\} \\
&= T\left(\frac{1}{2} - P_1\right) + \frac{Te^{-rT}}{\pi S}\int_0^\infty \text{Re}\left[\frac{K^{-i\phi}f^*(i\phi + 1)(i\phi + 1)}{i\phi}\right]d\phi.
\end{aligned}
\tag{7.45}
$$

Note that the integrand in (7.45) is very similar to the one for P_1, except that the numerator includes the extra term $i\phi + 1$. Since $\partial f^*(i\phi)/\partial r = f^*(i\phi)Ti\phi$, the other partial derivative needed to evaluate (7.42) is

$$
\frac{\partial P_2}{\partial r} = \frac{T}{\pi}\int_0^\infty \text{Re}[K^{-i\phi}f^*(i\phi)]\,d\phi.
\tag{7.46}
$$

Again, this integral is very similar to the one for P_2. Substituting (7.45) and (7.46) into (7.42) yields ρ_{Call}. Using put-call parity (7.34), rho for the put can be written

$$
\rho_{Put} = \rho_{Call} - TKe^{-rT}.
\tag{7.47}
$$

Vega is derived from the current volatility σ_{t+1}

$$
V = \frac{\partial \text{Call}}{\partial \sigma_{t+1}} = S\frac{\partial P_1}{\partial \sigma_{t+1}} - Ke^{-rT}\frac{\partial P_2}{\partial \sigma_{t+1}}.
\tag{7.48}
$$

Again, two partial derivatives are needed. The first is

$$
\begin{aligned}
\frac{\partial P_1}{\partial \sigma_{t+1}} &= \frac{e^{-rT}}{\pi S}\int_0^\infty \text{Re}\left[\frac{K^{-i\phi}}{i\phi}\frac{\partial f^*(\xi)}{\partial \sigma_{t+1}}\bigg|_{\xi=i\phi+1}\right]d\phi \\
&= \frac{2\sigma_{t+1}e^{-rT}}{\pi S}\int_0^\infty \text{Re}\left[\frac{K^{-i\phi}f^*(i\phi + 1)B_t}{i\phi}\right]d\phi,
\end{aligned}
\tag{7.49}
$$

since $\partial f^*/\partial \sigma_{t+1} = S\exp(A_t + B_t\sigma_{t+1}^2)2B_{t+1}\sigma_{t+1} = 2B_t\sigma_{t+1}f^*$. The second is

$$
\frac{\partial P_2}{\partial \sigma_{t+1}} = \frac{2\sigma_{t+1}}{\pi}\int_0^\infty \text{Re}\left[\frac{K^{-i\phi}f^*(i\phi)B_t}{i\phi}\right]d\phi.
\tag{7.50}
$$

Note that the integrands in (7.49) and (7.50) are similar to those for P_1 and P_2, except that the numerator includes the extra term B_t. Substituting (7.49) and (7.50) into (7.48) produces vega.

Finally, note that obtaining theta is very complicated, since the loop which produces the terms $\{A_i\}_{i=t}^T$ and $\{B_i\}_{i=t}^T$ depends itself on the time to maturity, $T - t$. Hence, in this section we do not derive theta for the Heston and Nandi (2000) model, but estimate theta with finite differences in the next section.

Implementing the Heston and Nandi (2000) Greeks requires that new VBA functions be created, for the integrands of the complex integrals. These functions, however, are straightforward modifications of the VBA functions for the option price defined in Chapter 6. For example, the function HNDelta() uses the VBA function HNC_f() to compute the probability P_1, and returns the Heston (1993) delta.

```
Function HNDelta(alpha, beta, gamma, omega, lambda, S, K, r, v, dtm,
              PutCall As String)
Dim phi As cNum
Dim int_x(401) As Double, int_y1(401) As Double, int_y2(401) As Double
Dim int1 As Double, int2 As Double
cnt = 0
For phicnt = 0.000001 To 100.000001 Step 0.25
 cnt = cnt + 1
 phi = set_cNum(1, phicnt)
 int_x(cnt) = phicnt
 int_y1(cnt) = (1 / S) * Exp(-r * dtm) * HNC_f(phi, alpha,
        beta, gamma, omega, lambda, S, K, r, v, dtm)
Next phicnt
int1 = TRAPnumint(int_x, int_y1)
P1 = 0.5 + (1 / thePI) * int1
If P1 < 0 Then P1 = 0
If P1 > 1 Then P1 = 1
Select Case PutCall
 Case "Call": HNDelta = P1
 Case "Put": HNDelta = P1 - 1
End Select
End Function
```

The TRAPnumint() statement invokes the trapezoidal rule to perform the numerical integration. The VBA function HNC_f_Gamma() produces the integrand in (7.41). It is also identical to HNC_f(), except that the third to last line is modified to accommodate the term S^2 instead of $i\phi$.

```
Function HNC_f_Gamma(phi As cNum, alpha, beta, gamma, omega, lambda, S, K,
              r, v, dtm)
' More VBA Statements
 tHNC_f1 = cNumDiv(tHNC_f1, set_cNum(S ^ 2, 0))
 HNC_f_Gamma = cNumReal(tHNC_f1)
End Function
```

The VBA function HNC_f_Vega() is also identical to HNC_f(), except with the modification to accommodate the addition term B_t in the numerator, in accordance with (7.49) and (7.50).

```
Function HNC_f_Vega(phi As cNum, alpha, beta, gamma, omega, lambda, S, K,
            r, v, dtm)
' More VBA Statements
tHNC_f1 = cNumPowercNum(set_cNum(K, 0), set_cNum(0, -phi.iP))
tHNC_f1 = cNumProd(tHNC_f1, cNumPowercNum(set_cNum(S, 0), phi))
tHNC_f1 = cNumProd(tHNC_f1, cNumExp(cNumAdd(A1, cNumProd(B1,
            set_cNum(v, 0)))))
tHNC_f1 = cNumProd(tHNC_f1, B1)
tHNC_f1 = cNumDiv(tHNC_f1, set_cNum(0, phi.iP))
HNC_f_Vega = cNumReal(tHNC_f1)
End Function
```

Finally, rho also requires several functions to implement. The VBA function HN_P2() computes the probability P_2 for (7.42).

```
Function HN_P2(alpha, beta, gamma, omega, lambda, S, K, r, v, dtm)
Dim phi As cNum
Dim int_x(401) As Double, int_y1(401) As Double, int_y2(401) As Double
Dim int1 As Double, int2 As Double
cnt = 0
For phicnt = 0.000001 To 100.000001 Step 0.25
 cnt = cnt + 1
 phi = set_cNum(0, phicnt)
 int_x(cnt) = phicnt
 int_y1(cnt) = HNC_f(phi, alpha, beta, gamma, omega,
         lambda, S, K, r, v, dtm)
Next phicnt
int1 = TRAPnumint(int_x, int_y1)
HN_P2 = 0.5 + (1 / thePI) * int1
If HN_P2 < 0 Then HN_P2 = 0
If HN_P2 > 1 Then HN_P2 = 1
End Function
```

The function dP_dr_f() produces the integrands needed for the partial derivatives in (7.42), (7.45), and (7.46).

```
Function dP_dr_f(phi As cNum, alpha, beta, gamma, omega, lambda, S, K, r,
            v, dtm)
Dim a() As cNum, b() As cNum
Dim A1 As cNum, B1 As cNum
Dim tHNC_f1 As cNum
Dim curA As cNum, curB As cNum
ReDim a(dtm + 1) As cNum, b(dtm + 1) As cNum
a(1) = set_cNum(0, 0): b(1) = set_cNum(0, 0)
For i = 2 To dtm + 1
 a(i) = cNumAdd(cNumAdd(a(i - 1), cNumProd(phi,
     set_cNum(r, 0))), cNumProd(set_cNum(omega, 0), b(i - 1)))
 a(i) = cNumSub(a(i), cNumProd(set_cNum(0.5, 0),
     cNumLn(cNumSub(set_cNum(1, 0), cNumProd(
     set_cNum(2 * alpha, 0), b(i - 1)))))))
```

```
   b(i) = cNumProd(phi, set_cNum(lambda + gamma, 0))
   b(i) = cNumSub(b(i), set_cNum(0.5 * gamma ^ 2, 0))
   b(i) = cNumAdd(b(i), cNumProd(set_cNum(beta, 0), b(i - 1)))
   b(i) = cNumAdd(b(i), cNumDiv(cNumProd(set_cNum(0.5, 0),
      cNumPowercNum(cNumSub(phi, set_cNum(gamma, 0)),
      set_cNum(2, 0))), cNumSub(set_cNum(1, 0),
      cNumProd(set_cNum(2 * alpha, 0), b(i - 1))))))
Next i
A1 = a(dtm + 1): B1 = b(dtm + 1)
tHNC_f1 = cNumPowercNum(set_cNum(K, 0),
      set_cNum(0, -phi.iP))
tHNC_f1 = cNumProd(tHNC_f1, cNumPowercNum(set_cNum(S, 0), phi))
tHNC_f1 = cNumProd(tHNC_f1, cNumExp(cNumAdd(A1,
      cNumProd(B1, set_cNum(v, 0)))))
tHNC_f1 = cNumProd(phi, cNumDiv(tHNC_f1, set_cNum(0, phi.iP)))
dP_dr_f = cNumReal(tHNC_f1)
End Function
```

Next, the functions dP1_dr() and dP2_dr() return the partial derivatives $\partial P_1 / \partial r$ and $\partial P_2 / \partial r$, respectively.

```
Function dP1_dr(alpha, beta, gamma, omega, lambda, S, K, r, v, dtm)
cnt = 0
For phicnt = 0.000001 To 100.000001 Step 0.25
cnt = cnt + 1
 phi = set_cNum(1, phicnt)
 int_x(cnt) = phicnt
 int_y1(cnt) = (dtm / S / thePI) * Exp(-r * dtm) *
      dP_dr_f(phi, alpha, beta, gamma, omega, lambda,
      S, K, r, v, dtm)
Next phicnt
int1 = TRAPnumint(int_x, int_y1)
Prob1 = HN_P1(alpha, beta, gamma, omega, lambda, S, K, r, v, dtm)
dP1_dr = dtm * (0.5 - Prob1) + int1
End Function


Function dP2_dr(alpha, beta, gamma, omega, lambda, S, K, r, v, dtm)
cnt = 0
For phicnt = 0.000001 To 100.000001 Step 0.25
 cnt = cnt + 1
 phi = set_cNum(0, phicnt)
 int_x(cnt) = phicnt
 int_y1(cnt) = (dtm / thePI) * dP_dr_f(phi, alpha, beta,
         gamma, omega, lambda, S, K, r, v, dtm)
Next phicnt
int1 = TRAPnumint(int_x, int_y1)
dP2_dr = int1
End Function
```

Finally, the function HNRho() computes rho from (7.42) for a call, or from (7.47) for a put.

```
Function HNRho(alpha, beta, gamma, omega, lambda, S, K, r, v, dtm, PutCall
          As String)
DP1 = dP1_dr(alpha, beta, gamma, omega, lambda, S, K, r, v, dtm)
DP2 = dP2_dr(alpha, beta, gamma, omega, lambda, S, K, r, v, dtm)
Prob2 = HN_P2(alpha, beta, gamma, omega, lambda, S, K, r, v, dtm)
Rho = S * DP1 + K * Exp(-r * dtm) * (dtm * Prob2 - DP2)
Select Case PutCall
 Case "Call": HNRho = Rho / 252
 Case "Put": HNRho = (Rho - dtm * K * Exp(-r * dtm)) / 252
End Select
End Function
```

The Excel file Chapter7HNGreeks contains the VBA functions for implementing the Heston and Nandi (2000) Greeks. This file is illustrated in Figure 7.11 using the same parameter values as in Chapter 6, except with an annual risk-free rate of 5 percent. Since this rate must be a daily rate, in cell C6 we type "= 0.05/252".

With the given parameter values, the Heston and Nandi (2000) call price is $3.5941 in cell C16. To obtain delta, in cell C17 we type

= HNDelta(alpha, beta, gamma, omega, lambda, S, K, rf,v,T,Type)

	A	B	C	D
1				
2		**Greeks from the Heston and Nandi (2000) Model**		
3				
4		Spot Price (*S*)	100	
5		Strike Price (*K*)	100	
6		Risk Free Rate (*r*)	0.000198413	
7		Time to Maturity (days)	100	
8		Alpha (α)	0.00000132	
9		Beta (β)	0.589	
10		Gamma (γ*)	421.39	
11		Omega (ω)	0.00000502	
12		Lambda (λ*)	-0.5	
13		Current GARCH Variance (σ^2_{t+1})	8.92857E-05	
14		Type (*Call* or *Put*)	Call	
15				
16		**Heston-Nandi Option Price**	3.5941	
17		**Delta (Δ)**	0.6532	
18		**Gamma (Γ)**	0.0578	
19		**Vega (V)**	31.8295	
20		**Daily Rho (ρ)**	24.4960	
21		**Theta (Θ)**	N / A	
22				

FIGURE 7.11 Greeks from the Heston and Nandi (2000) Model

which produces $\Delta = 0.6532$. The other Greeks are obtained similarly, except for theta, for which we do not derive a closed form.

GREEKS BY FINITE DIFFERENCES

Rather than obtaining Greeks in closed form, it is often simpler to introduce a perturbation in the parameter value, calculate a new option price, and approximate the option sensitivity as the change in the option price relative to the perturbation. This method is required to obtain rho and vega in the tree-based methods. For vega, this approximation is given in Equation (7.9). In this section we show that the numerical approximations to the Greeks derived in this chapter are close to their closed-form values. Since the finite difference method uses option prices evaluated at slightly different points, no new VBA functions are required.

Suppose that the option price is f. Then delta, rho, and vega can be approximated by

$$\text{Greek} = \frac{\partial f}{\partial \alpha} \approx \frac{f(\alpha + d\alpha) - f(\alpha)}{d\alpha} \tag{7.51}$$

where α is either the spot price S (for delta), the interest rate r (for rho), or the volatility σ (for vega), and $d\alpha$ is a small perturbation in α. Theta is approximated in the same way, but by reversing the sign of (7.51) since theta is defined as the negative of the partial derivative of the option price with respect to maturity. To obtain gamma, two values of delta must be obtained

$$\Delta_1 \approx \frac{f(S + dS) - f(S)}{dS}, \tag{7.52}$$

and

$$\Delta_2 \approx \frac{f(S + 2dS) - f(S + dS)}{dS}. \tag{7.53}$$

Gamma is defined as the change in delta relative to the perturbation,

$$\Gamma \approx \frac{\Delta_2 - \Delta_1}{dS} = \frac{f(S + 2dS) - 2f(S + dS) + f(S)}{(dS)^2}. \tag{7.54}$$

The Excel file Chapter7BSGreekSim contains these functions and is illustrated in Figure 7.12, using the same parameter values on the call option used in Figure 7.1. It uses the VBA function BlackScholes() to calculate option prices.

	A	B	C	D	E
1					
2		**Approximated Black-Scholes Greeks**			
3					
4		Spot Price (S)	30		
5		Strike Price (K)	30		
6		Years to Maturity (T)	0.4167		
7		Interest Rate (r)	0.05		
8		Volatility (v)	0.3		**Perturbation**
9		Type (Call or Put)	Call		0.00001
10					
11		**Option Price**	2.6126		**Option Price**
12					**With Perturbation**
13		**Approximated Greeks**			
14		**Delta (Δ)**	0.5810		2.612644
15		**Gamma (Γ)**	0.0672		2.612650
16		**Vega (V)**	7.5658		2.612714
17		**Rho (ρ)**	6.1736		2.612700
18		**Theta (Θ)**	-3.4645		2.612673

FIGURE 7.12   Black-Scholes Greeks by Finite Differences

The option price of \$2.6126 is in cell C11, the perturbation is in cell E9, and the perturbed option prices in cells E14:E18. For simplicity, cells C4:C9 have been named S, K, T, rf, v, and putcall, respectively. To obtain delta, for example, in cell E14 we type

$$= BlackScholes(S+E9,K,T,rf,v,putcall)$$

which produces $f(S + dS) = 2.612644$. The finite difference approximation for delta appears in cell C14 as

$$= (E14-C11)/E9,$$

which produces a delta of 0.5810, identical to that in Figure 7.1. To obtain gamma, in cell E15 we type

$$= BlackScholes(S+2*E9,K,T,rf,v,putcall)$$

which produces $f(S + 2dS) = 2.612650$. Equation (7.54) appears in cell C15

$$= (E15-2*E14+C11)/E9\char`^2$$

which produces a gamma of 0.0672, which is close to the value of 0.0673 in Figure 7.1. The other Greeks are seen to take on values that are close also to those in Figure 7.1.

	A	B	C	D	E
1					
2		**Approximated Gram-Charlier Greeks**			
3		**Period = Monthly**			
4					
5		Underlying Price (*S*)	100.00		
6		Strike Price (*K*)	100.00		
7		Risk Free Rate Per Year (*Tr*)	0.05		
8		Risk Free Rate Per Period (*r*)	0.004167		
9		Periods Until Maturity (*T*)	5		
10		Volatility Per Year ($\sigma\sqrt{T}$)	0.30		
11		One-Period Volatility (σ)	0.08660254		
12		One-Period Skewness (γ_1)	-0.5		
13		One-Period Kurtosis (γ_2)	0.5		**Perturbation**
14		Option Type (*Put* or *Call*)	Call		0.0001
15					
16		**Option Price**	8.6268		**Option Price**
17					**With Perturbation**
18		**Approximated Greeks**			
19		**Delta (Δ)**	0.5953		8.626882
20		**Gamma (Γ)**	0.0204		8.626942
21		**Vega (V)**	85.1563		8.635338
22		**Rho (ρ)**	254.7046		8.652293
23		**Theta (Θ)**	-0.9608		8.626919
24					
25		**Vega Per Year (V/$\sqrt{M}$)**	24.5825		
26		**Rho Per Year (ρ/*M*)**	21.2254		
27		**Theta Per Year (ΘM)**	-11.5297		

FIGURE 7.13 Gram-Charlier Greeks by Finite Differences

Implementing numerical approximations to the Gram-Charlier Greeks using finite differences is straightforward also. The Excel file Chapter7GCGreekSim contains these functions. This file is illustrated in Figure 7.13, using the same parameter values as Figure 7.8. Figure 7.13 illustrates that the approximated Greeks are close to their true values that appear in Figure 7.8.

The Excel file Chapter7HestonGreekSim contains the approximated Greeks for the Heston (1993) model. This file is illustrated in Figure 7.14, using the same parameter values as in Figure 7.10. Again, the approximated Greeks are close to their true values that appear in Figure 7.10.

Finally, in this section we approximate the Greeks for the Heston and Nandi (2000) model. Because the time to maturity, the risk-free rate, and the variance are daily quantities, however, this is slightly more complicated since different perturbation values must be introduced for these parameters. To obtain theta, for example, *T* must be perturbed by an integer value, while the current variance

	A	B	C	D	E
1					
2		**Approximated Greeks from the Heston (1993) Model**			
3					
4		Spot Price (S)	100		
5		Strike Price (K)	100		
6		Risk Free Rate (r)	0.05		
7		Time to Maturity (T − t)	0.5		
8		Rho (ρ)	0		
9		Kappa (κ)	2		
10		Theta (θ)	0.01		
11		Lambda (λ)	0		
12		Volatility of Variance (σ)	0.225		
13		Current Variance (v)	0.01		**Perturbation**
14		Option Type (Call or Put)	Call		0.0001
15					
16		**Option Price**	4.08518738		**Option Price**
17					**With Perturbation**
18		**Approximated Greeks**			
19		**Delta (Δ)**	0.6712		4.085254493
20		**Gamma (Γ)**	0.0579		4.085321611
21		**Vega (V)**	81.9563		4.093383011
22		**Rho (ρ)**	31.5222		4.088339599
23		**Theta (Θ)**	-5.5475		4.085742126

FIGURE 7.14 Heston (1993) Greeks by Finite Differences

σ_{t+1}^2 must be perturbed by a daily volatility value, and then squared. The Excel file Chapter7HNGreeksSim contains the Greeks for the Heston and Nandi (2000) model, obtained by finite differences. This file is illustrated in Figure 7.15, using the same values as in Figure 7.11.

The perturbation for delta, gamma, and rho is 0.00001 and appears in cell E5. The unperturbed option price is \$3.5941 in cell C17. To obtain delta, in cell E20 we type

$$= \text{HNC(alpha, beta, gamma, omega, lambda, S+E5, K, rf, v, T, Type)}$$

to obtain the perturbed option price (with $S + dS$) as \$3.59411. In cell C20 we type "=(E20-C17)/E5" which produces $\Delta = 0.6532$, identical to the true value in Figure 7.11. To obtain gamma, which requires the perturbation $S + 2dS$ in accordance with (7.54), in cell E21 we type

$$= \text{HNC(alpha, beta, gamma, omega, lambda, S+2*E5, K, rf, v, T, Type)}$$

and in cell C21 we type

$$= (E21\text{-}2*E20+C17)/E5\char`^2$$

	A	B	C	D	E
1					
2		**Heston and Nandi (2000) Greeks**			**Perturbations**
3		**Approximated by Finite Differences**			
4					
5		Spot Price (*S*)	100		0.00001
6		Strike Price (*K*)	100		
7		Risk Free Rate (*r*)	0.000198413		
8		Time to Maturity (days)	100		1
9		Alpha (α)	0.00000132		
10		Beta (β)	0.589		
11		Gamma (γ*)	421.39		
12		Omega (ω)	0.00000502		
13		Lambda (λ*)	-0.5		
14		Current GARCH Variance (σ^2_{t+1})	8.92857E-05		1.89082E-07
15		Type (*Call* or *Put*)	Call		
16					
17		**Heston-Nandi Option Price**	3.594106864		
18					**Option Price**
19		**Approximated Greeks**			**With Perturbattion**
20		**Delta (Δ)**	0.6532		3.59411340
21		**Gamma (Γ)**	0.0573		3.59411993
22		**Vega (V)**	31.8444		3.59442531
23		**Daily Rho (ρ)**	24.5982		3.65609430
24		**Theta (Θ)**	-5.7708		3.61700676

FIGURE 7.15 Heston and Nandi (2000) Greeks by Finite Differences

This produces $\Gamma = 0.0573$, close to the analytical value of 0.0578 in Figure 7.11. Theta is similarly obtained, but requires an integer perturbation in cell E8 since the time to maturity is defined in days. Finally, the value of the current variance is $\sigma^2_{t+1} = (0.15/\sqrt{252})^2$ in cell C14, while the perturbed value of this is $\sigma^2_{t+1} = (0.15/\sqrt{252} + 0.00001)^2$. The perturbation in cell E14 is simply the difference between the two. Vega obtained by the finite difference method is 31.8444 in cell C22, again very close to the true value in Figure 7.11.

SUMMARY

In this chapter we have obtained five Greeks for the option pricing models covered in this book. For the Black-Scholes model and the Gram-Charlier model, the Greeks are available in closed form. For tree-based methods, good approximations to delta, gamma, and theta can be obtained from the prices at the beginning nodes of the trees. Vega and rho, however, must be approximated by finite differencing—inducing small perturbations to volatility and interest rates, and calculating the relative change in the option price. For the Heston (1993) model and the model of Heston and Nandi (2000), most of the Greeks are available in closed form, but still require that a complex integral be evaluated numerically. The finite difference approximations to the Greeks from the Black-Scholes, Gram-Charlier, Heston, and Heston and Nandi models are all very close to their analytical values.

EXERCISES

This section provides exercises that deal with the option price sensitivities introduced in this chapter. Solutions to these exercises are in the Excel file Chapter7Exercises.

7.1 Refer to Exercise 4.3. Derive the Greeks for the Black-Scholes calls and puts when there is a cost-of-carry term, and code the Greeks in VBA. Illustrate the Greeks using the same parameter values as in Figure 7.1, with $b = 0.02$.

7.2 Use the BSM differential equation (7.4) to find an alternate expression for the theta of an option. In the CRR binomial trees of Chapter 3, compare this value of theta with that given by (7.8). Use $S = 30, K = 30, T = 5/12$ years, $r = 0.05, \sigma = 0.30$, and $n = 150$ steps, on a European put option.

7.3 The delta of the Heston (1993) call option is given by (7.18) as $\Delta_{Call} = P_1$. Using (7.14) find the derivative of the call price with respect to S, and write a VBA function to show that the last two terms of the derivative sum to zero approximately. Illustrate this using the parameter values that appear in Figure 7.10.

SOLUTIONS TO EXERCISES

7.1 We use the expression for the Black-Scholes price with cost-of-carry presented in Exercise 4.3. It is straightforward to derive the Greeks, which appear in Table 7.2. For details, see Haug (1998). Note that when $b = r$, the Greeks reduce to the Black-Scholes Greeks for a non-dividend-paying stock presented in Table 4.1. Most of the Greeks are identical to the Black-Scholes Greeks with no cost-of-carry presented in Table 7.1, but multiplied by the factor $e^{(b-r)T}$. It is therefore straightforward to modify the Greeks to include the cost-of-carry term. For example, the VBA function GBSdelta computes the delta of a call or put option.

```
Function GBSdelta(S, K, T, r, b, v, PutCall As String)
Dim d As Double
d = (Log(S / K) + T * (b + 0.5 * v ^ 2)) / (v * Sqr(T))
expCC = Exp((b - r) * T)
Select Case PutCall
  Case "Call": GBSdelta = expCC * Gauss(d)
```

```
    Case "Put": GBSdelta = expCC * (Gauss(d) - 1)
End Select
End Function
```

The functions developed for this exercise are illustrated in Figure 7.16. Note that when $b = 0.05$ in cell C9, the Greeks all correspond to the Greeks in Figure 7.1.

TABLE 7.2 Greeks from the Black-Scholes Model with Cost of Carry

Greek	Call	Put
Δ	$e^{(b-r)T}\Phi(d)$	$e^{(b-r)T}[\Phi(d) - 1]$
Γ	$\dfrac{e^{(b-r)T}\phi(d)}{S\sigma\sqrt{T}}$	$\dfrac{e^{(b-r)T}\phi(d)}{S\sigma\sqrt{T}}$
V	$e^{(b-r)T}S\phi(d)\sqrt{T}$	$e^{(b-r)T}S\phi(d)\sqrt{T}$
ρ	$TKe^{-rT}\Phi(d - \sigma\sqrt{T})$	$-TKe^{-rT}\Phi(\sigma\sqrt{T} - d)$
Θ	$-\dfrac{e^{(b-r)T}S\phi(d)\sigma}{2\sqrt{T}}$	$-\dfrac{e^{(b-r)T}S\phi(d)\sigma}{2\sqrt{T}}$
	$-(b - r)Se^{(b-r)T}\Phi(d)$	$+(b - r)Se^{(b-r)T}\Phi(-d)$
	$-rKe^{-rT}\Phi(d - \sigma\sqrt{T})$	$+rKe^{-rT}\Phi(\sigma\sqrt{T} - d)$

	A	B	C	D	E	F
1	EXERCISE 7.1					
2						
3	**Black-Scholes Greeks for a European Call or Put with Cost-of-Carry**					
4						
5		Spot Price (*S*)	30		**B-S Call Price**	2.4008
6		Strike Price (*K*)	30		**B-S Put Price**	2.1550
7		Years to Maturity (*T*)	0.4167			
8		Interest Rate (*r*)	0.05			
9		Cost-of-Carry (*b*)	0.02			
10		Volatility (*v*)	0.3			
11		Type (*Call* or *Put*)	Call			
12						
13		**Delta (Δ)**	0.5487			
14		**Gamma (Γ)**	0.0681			
15		**Vega (V)**	7.5553			
16		**Rho (ρ)**	5.8585			
17		**Theta (Θ)**	-2.9291			

FIGURE 7.16 Solution to Exercise 7.1

	A	B	C	D	E
1	EXERCISE 7.2				
2					
3		CRR Binomial Tree Price for an American or European Option			
4		Comparison of Theta Obtained With Two Methods			
5					
6		Spot Price (S)	30		
7		Strike Price (K)	30		
8		Years to Maturity (T)	0.4167		
9		Interest Rate (r)	0.05		
10		Volatility (σ)	0.3		
11		Steps (n)	150		
12		Type (Call or Put)	Put		
13		Option (Amer or Euro)	Euro		
14					Black Scholes
15			Tree values		Values
16		**Option Price**	1.99027		1.99410
17		**Delta**	-0.41915		-0.41902
18		**Gamma**	0.06761		0.06725
19		**Theta (Tree Value)**	-2.00954		-1.99544
20		**Theta (BSM Equation)**	-2.00980		

FIGURE 7.17   Solution to Exercise 7.2

7.2 Since the BSM equation holds for a portfolio of derivatives, it holds for a single call or put option. Hence, we can write the equation as

$$\Theta + rS\Delta + \frac{1}{2}\sigma^2 S^2 \Gamma = rf$$

where f is the price of the option. Rearranging this expression for theta, we obtain

$$\Theta = rf - rS\Delta - \frac{1}{2}\sigma^2 S^2 \Gamma \tag{7.55}$$

If we know the delta and the gamma of the option, we can use this expression to obtain the theta of the option. This is illustrated in Figure 7.17. The values in cells C16:C20 are produced with the VBA function BinThetas(). Delta, gamma, and theta1 and produced using values of the function at different nodes of the tree, as explained in this chapter. Theta2, however, is produced using the relation (7.55).

```
Function BinThetas(Spot, K, t, r, sigma, n, PutCall As String,
          EuroAmer As String)
' More VBA Statements
Delta = (Op(1, 2) - Op(2, 2)) / (S(1, 2) - S(2, 2))
Gamma = ((Op(1, 3) - Op(2, 3)) / (S(1, 3) - S(2, 3)) -
    (Op(2, 3) - Op(3, 3)) / (S(2, 3) - S(3, 3))) /
    (S(1, 2) - S(2, 2))
```

```
Theta1 = (Op(2, 3) - Op(1, 1)) / dt / 2
Theta2 = r * Op(1, 1) - r * Spot * Delta
    - sigma ^ 2 * Spot ^ 2 * Gamma / 2
output(1, 1) = Op(1, 1): output(2, 1) = Delta
output(3, 1) = Gamma: output(4, 1) = Theta1
output(5, 1) = Theta2
 BinThetas = output
End Function
```

The analytical values in cells E16:E19 are produced using the BSGreeks() VBA function and are valid for European options only. Figure 7.17 indicates that theta1, with a value of −2.00954, and theta2, with a value of −2.00980, are very close to each other and close to the analytical value of −1.99544 in cell E19. In this example, theta obtained from the tree is slightly more accurate than theta obtained from the BSM equation. In other cases, theta obtained from the BSM equation will be more accurate.

7.3 Applying the product rule, the derivative of the call price with respect to S is

$$\frac{\partial \text{Call}}{\partial S} = P_1 + S\frac{\partial P_1}{\partial S} - Ke^{-r(T-t)}\frac{\partial P_2}{\partial S}, \tag{7.56}$$

so we expect $S(\partial P_1/\partial S) - Ke^{-r(T-t)}(\partial P_2/\partial S) = 0$. The VBA function dP2_dS() is similar to the function dP1_dS() presented in this chapter, and calculates the second partial derivative in (7.56). Finally, the VBA function DeltaDiff() calculates the required sum. The results appear in Figure 7.18.

	A	B	C	D
1	EXERCISE 7.3			
2				
3		**Difference Between Delta and P_1**		
4				
5		Spot Price (S)	100	
6		Strike Price (K)	100	
7		Risk Free Rate (r)	0.05	
8		Time to Maturity (T − t)	0.5	
9		Rho (ρ)	0	
10		Kappa (κ)	2	
11		Theta (θ)	0.01	
12		Lambda (λ)	0	
13		Volatility of Variance (σ)	0.225	
14		Current variance (v)	0.01	
15				
16		$S(dP_1/dS) - K\exp(-rT)(dP_2/dS)$	0.00008844	

FIGURE 7.18 Solution to Exercise 7.3

```
Function DeltaDiff(kappa, theta, lambda, rho, sigma, tau, K, S, r, v)
 dp1 = dP1_dS(kappa, theta, lambda, rho, sigma, tau, K, S, r, v)
 dp2 = dP2_dS(kappa, theta, lambda, rho, sigma, tau, K, S, r, v)
DeltaDiff = S * dp1 - K * Exp(-r * tau) * dp2
End Function
```

In cell C16 we type

$$= \text{DeltaDiff(kappa, theta, lambda, rho, sigmav,dtm, K, S, rf, V)}$$

which produces a difference of 8.844×10^{-5}. Increasing the time to maturity to one year in cell C8 produces a difference of -3.97×10^{-6}.

APPENDIX

In this appendix the Greeks for the Gram-Charlier model of Chapter 4 are derived. We define $S = S_t$ to make the notation less cumbersome. The Gram-Charlier price of a European call is

$$C_{GC} = S\Phi(d) - Ke^{-rT}\Phi(d - \sigma_T)$$
$$+ S\phi(d)\sigma_T \left[\frac{\gamma_{1T}}{3!}(2\sigma_T - d) - \frac{\gamma_{2T}}{4!}(1 - d^2 + 3d\sigma_T - 3\sigma_T^2) \right]$$

where $d = [\ln(S/K) + rT + \sigma_T^2/2]/\sigma_T$. In deriving the Greeks we use the fact that $\partial\Phi(d)/\partial d = \phi(d)d', \phi(d - \sigma_T) = \phi(d)Se^{rT}/K$, and $\phi'(d) = \partial\phi(d)/\partial d = -\phi(d)dd'$.

Call delta: First note that $d' = \partial d/\partial S = 1/(S\sigma_T)$. Taking the partial derivative of C_{GC} with respect to S:

$$\Delta_{Call} = \frac{\partial C_{GC}}{\partial S} = \Phi(d) + S\phi(d)d' - Ke^{-rT}\phi(d - \sigma_T)d'$$
$$+ \phi(d)\sigma_T \left[\frac{\gamma_{1T}}{3!}(2\sigma_T - d) - \frac{\gamma_{2T}}{4!}(1 - d^2 + 3d\sigma_T - 3\sigma_T^2) \right]$$
$$+ S\phi'(d)\sigma_T \left[\frac{\gamma_{1T}}{3!}(2\sigma_T - d) - \frac{\gamma_{2T}}{4!}(1 - d^2 + 3d\sigma_T - 3\sigma_T^2) \right]$$
$$+ S\phi(d)\sigma_T \left[\frac{\gamma_{1T}}{3!}(-d') - \frac{\gamma_{2T}}{4!}(-2dd' + 3d'\sigma_T) \right].$$

Substituting for $S\sigma_T d' = 1$ and for $\phi(d - \sigma_T)$, we obtain

$$\Delta_{Call} = \Phi(d) + \phi(d) \left[\frac{\gamma_{1T}}{3!}(2\sigma_T^2 - d\sigma_T) - \frac{\gamma_{2T}}{4!}(\sigma_T - \sigma_T d^2 + 3d\sigma_T^2 - 3\sigma_T^3) \right]$$
$$- \phi(d) \left[\frac{\gamma_{1T}}{3!}(2d\sigma_T - d^2) - \frac{\gamma_{2T}}{4!}(d - d^3 + 3d^2\sigma_T - 3\sigma_T^2 d) \right]$$
$$+ \phi(d) \left[-\frac{\gamma_{1T}}{3!} - \frac{\gamma_{2T}}{4!}(3\sigma_T - 2d) \right].$$

Regrouping terms for $\gamma_{1T}/3!$ and $\gamma_{2T}/4!$ produces

$$\Delta_{Call} = \Phi(d) - \frac{\gamma_{1T}}{3!}\phi(d)(1 - d^2 + 3d\sigma_T - 2\sigma_T^2)$$
$$+ \frac{\gamma_{2T}}{4!}\phi(d)[3d(1 - 2\sigma_T^2) + 4d^2\sigma_T - d^3 - 4\sigma_T + 3\sigma_T^2].$$

Note that this expression reduces to the Black-Scholes delta $\Phi(d)$ when skewness and kurtosis are both zero.

Call gamma:

$$\Gamma_{Call} = \frac{\partial^2 C_{GC}}{\partial S^2} = \phi(d)d' - \frac{\gamma_{1T}}{3!}[\phi'(d)(1 - d^2 + 3d\sigma_T - 2\sigma_T^2) + \phi(d)(-2dd' + 3\sigma_T d')]$$
$$+ \frac{\gamma_{2T}}{4!}\left\{ \begin{array}{l} \phi'(d)[3d(1 - 2\sigma_T^2) + 4d^2\sigma_T - d^3 - 4\sigma_T + 3\sigma_T^2] \\ + \phi(d)[3d'(1 - 2\sigma_T^2) + 8dd'\sigma_T - 3d^2 d'] \end{array} \right\}.$$

Substituting for $d' = 1/(S\sigma_T)$ and for $\phi'(d) = -\phi(d)dd'$, we obtain

$$\Gamma_{Call} = \frac{\phi(d)}{S\sigma_T} - \frac{\gamma_{1T}}{3!}\frac{\phi(d)}{S\sigma_T}[d^3 + d(2\sigma_T^2 - 3) + 3\sigma_T(1 - d^2)]$$
$$+ \frac{\gamma_{2T}}{4!}\frac{\phi(d)}{S\sigma_T}[d^4 + 3(1 - d^2)(1 - 2\sigma_T^2) + 4d\sigma_T(3 - d^2) - 3d(\sigma_T^2 + d)].$$

This reduces to the Black-Scholes gamma $\phi(d)/(S\sigma_T) = \phi(d)/(S\sigma\sqrt{T})$ when skewness and kurtosis are both zero.

Call vega: We differentiate with respect to the one-period volatility $\sigma = \sigma_T/\sqrt{T}$. First note that $d' = \partial d/\partial \sigma = \sqrt{T} - d/\sigma$. As before, we use the fact that $\phi'(d) = -\phi(d)dd'$ and that $\phi(d - \sqrt{T}\sigma) = \phi(d)Se^{rT}/K$. Hence,

$$V_{Call} = \frac{\partial C_{GC}}{\partial \sigma} = S\phi(d)d' - Ke^{-rT}\phi(d - \sigma\sqrt{T})(d' - \sqrt{T})$$
$$+ S\phi(d)\sqrt{T}\left[\frac{\gamma_{1T}}{3!}(2\sigma\sqrt{T} - d) - \frac{\gamma_{2T}}{4!}(1 - d^2 + 3d\sigma\sqrt{T} - 3\sigma^2 T)\right]$$
$$+ S\phi'(d)\sigma\sqrt{T}\left[\frac{\gamma_{1T}}{3!}(2\sigma\sqrt{T} - d) - \frac{\gamma_{2T}}{4!}(1 - d^2 + 3d\sigma\sqrt{T} - 3\sigma^2 T)\right]$$
$$+ S\phi(d)\sigma\sqrt{T}\left[\frac{\gamma_{1T}}{3!}(2\sqrt{T} - d') - \frac{\gamma_{2T}}{4!}(-2dd' + 3\sqrt{T}(d'\sigma + d) - 6\sigma T)\right].$$

Substituting for $\phi'(d)$ and d', and grouping together terms for skewness and kurtosis produces the expression

$$V_{Call} = S\phi(d)\sqrt{T} + \frac{\gamma_{1T}}{3!}S\phi(d)\sqrt{T}[3\sigma\sqrt{T}(1 + d^2) - d(d^2 + 2\sigma^2 T)]$$
$$+ \frac{\gamma_{2T}}{4!}S\phi(d)\sqrt{T}[(1 - d^2 + 3d\sigma\sqrt{T} - 3\sigma^2 T)(\sigma\,dd' - 1) + 2dd'\sigma + 3\sigma^2 T],$$

where $d' = \sqrt{T} - d/\sigma$. This reduces to the Black-Scholes vega, $S\phi(d)\sqrt{T}$, when skewness and kurtosis are both zero.

Call rho: In this case $d' = T/\sigma_T$ and the partial derivative is

$$\rho_{Call} = \frac{\partial C_{GC}}{\partial r} = S\phi(d)d' - Ke^{-rT}\phi(d - \sigma_T)d' + KTe^{-rT}\Phi(d - \sigma_T)$$
$$+ S\sigma_T\phi'(d)\left[\frac{\gamma_{1T}}{3!}(2\sigma_T - d) - \frac{\gamma_{2T}}{4!}(1 - d^2 + 3d\sigma_T - 3\sigma_T^2)\right]$$
$$+ S\sigma_T\phi(d)\left[\frac{\gamma_{1T}}{3!}(-d') - \frac{\gamma_{2T}}{4!}(-2dd' + 3\sigma_T)\right].$$

Substituting for $\sigma_T d' = T$, for $\phi(d - \sigma_T) = \phi(d)Se^{rT}/K$, and for $\phi'(d) = -\phi(d)dd'$ yields

$$\rho_{Call} = KTe^{-rT}\Phi(d - \sigma_T) - \frac{\gamma_{1T}}{3!}ST\phi(d)[-d^2 + 2d\sigma_T + 1]$$
$$+ \frac{\gamma_{2T}}{4!}ST\phi(d)[-d^3 + 3(d\sigma_T + 1)(d - \sigma_T)].$$

Again, this reduces to the Black-Scholes rho, $KTe^{-rT}\Phi(d - \sigma_T)$ when both skewness and kurtosis are zero.

Call theta: Note that $\sigma_T = \sigma\sqrt{T}, \gamma_{1T} = \gamma_1/\sqrt{T}$ and $\gamma_{2T} = \gamma_2/T$, so the Gram-Charlier call price must be rewritten taking into account the dependence of σ_T, γ_{1T}, and γ_{2T} on T.

$$C_{GC} = S\Phi(d) - Ke^{-rT}\Phi(d - \sigma\sqrt{T})$$
$$+ S\phi(d)\sigma\sqrt{T}\left[\frac{\gamma_1}{\sqrt{T}3!}(2\sigma\sqrt{T} - d) - \frac{\gamma_2}{T4!}(1 - d^2 + 3d\sigma\sqrt{T} - 3\sigma^2 T)\right].$$

which simplifies to

$$C_{GC} = S\Phi(d) - Ke^{-rT}\Phi(d - \sigma\sqrt{T})$$
$$+ S\phi(d)\sigma\left[\frac{\gamma_1}{3!}(2\sigma\sqrt{T} - d) - \frac{\gamma_2}{4!}\left(\frac{1}{\sqrt{T}}(1 - d^2) + 3d\sigma - 3\sigma^2\sqrt{T}\right)\right].$$

The negative partial derivative with respect to T is theta for the call.

$$\Theta_{Call} = -\frac{\partial C_{GC}}{\partial T} = -S\phi(d)d' - rKe^{-rT}\Phi(d - \sigma\sqrt{T}) + S\phi(d)\left[d' - \frac{\sigma}{2\sqrt{T}}\right]$$
$$- S\sigma\phi'(d)\left[\frac{\gamma_1}{3!}(2\sigma\sqrt{T} - d) - \frac{\gamma_2}{4!}\left(\frac{1}{\sqrt{T}}(1 - d^2) + 3d\sigma - 3\sigma^2\sqrt{T}\right)\right]$$
$$- S\sigma\phi(d)\left[\frac{\gamma_1}{3!}\left(\frac{\sigma}{\sqrt{T}} - d'\right) - \frac{\gamma_2}{4!}\left(-\frac{1}{2T^{3/2}}(1 - d^2) + \frac{-2dd'}{\sqrt{T}} + 3\sigma d' - \frac{3\sigma^2}{2\sqrt{T}}\right)\right].$$

Substituting for $\phi'(d)$ and regrouping terms produces

$$\Theta_{Call} = -rKe^{-rT}\Phi(d - \sigma\sqrt{T}) - S\phi(d)\frac{\sigma}{2\sqrt{T}}$$

$$- \frac{\gamma_1}{3!}S\sigma\phi(d)\left[(d - 2\sigma\sqrt{T})\,dd' + \left(\frac{\sigma}{\sqrt{T}} - d'\right)\right]$$

$$- \frac{\gamma_2}{4!}S\sigma\phi(d)\left[\left(\frac{1}{\sqrt{T}}(3 - d^2) + 3d\sigma - 3\sigma^2\sqrt{T}\right)dd'\right.$$

$$\left. + \frac{1}{2T^{3/2}}(1 - d^2) - 3\sigma d' + \frac{3\sigma^2}{2\sqrt{T}}\right],$$

where $d' = (r + \sigma^2/2)/(\sigma\sqrt{T}) - d/(2T)$. Again, this reduces to the Black-Scholes theta, $-rKe^{-rT}\Phi(d - \sigma\sqrt{T}) - S\phi(d)\sigma/(2\sqrt{T})$, when both the skewness and kurtosis are zero. Note that Θ_{Call} involves the one period moments σ, γ_1, and γ_2 rather than the T-period moments σ_T, γ_{1T}, and γ_{2T}.

Recall that the Gram-Charlier price of a European put can be obtained from put-call parity as $P_{GC} = C_{GC} + Ke^{-rT} - S$. Hence the Greeks for European puts can be derived from taking the partial derivatives of this expression for P_{GC}, and using the Greeks for European calls. As expected, gamma and vega are equivalent for calls and puts.

Put delta : $\Delta_{Put} = \dfrac{\partial P_{GC}}{\partial S_t} = \Delta_{Call} - 1.$

Put gamma : $\Gamma_{Put} = \dfrac{\partial^2 P_{GC}}{\partial S_t^2} = \Gamma_{Call}.$

Put vega : $V_{Put} = \dfrac{\partial P_{GC}}{\partial\sigma} = V_{Call}.$

Put rho : $\rho_{Put} = \dfrac{\partial P_{GC}}{\partial r} = \rho_{Call} - KTe^{-rT}.$

Put theta : $\Theta_{Put} = -\dfrac{\partial P_{GC}}{\partial T} = \Theta_{Call} + Kre^{-rT}.$

CHAPTER 8

Exotic Options

INTRODUCTION

In this chapter we introduce methods to price some of the more popular exotic options, including single-barrier options, Asian options, lookback options, and cash-or-nothing and asset-or-nothing options. We emphasize barrier options since these options have become very popular and can be difficult to price, especially when the barrier is close to the spot price of the asset. This is especially true when using tree-based methods, because the barrier rarely corresponds to any of the price nodes on the tree. All the methods covered in this chapter present novel ways to deal with this difficulty. We show that all the methods produce good approximations to the analytic barrier price. Many European barrier options are available in closed form. See Haug (1998) for a thorough treatment of these options.

SINGLE-BARRIER OPTIONS

Single-barrier options are classified as either knock-in or knock-out options. Knock-in options become activated only if the asset price reaches a barrier, while knock-out options become worthless once the barrier is reached. Down-and-in (DI) options become active if the stock price drops below a lower boundary, and up-and-in (UI) options becomes active of the stock price rises above an upper boundary. Down-and-out (DO) options and up-and-out (UO) options work the same way, except that they become worthless once the barrier is reached. For European options, a simple barrier parity relationship exists, according to which the price of a knock-in option plus the price of a knock-out option equals the price of a plain-vanilla option. Hence, for European single barrier calls and puts,

$$DI + DO = \text{Plain Vanilla}$$
$$UI + UO = \text{Plain Vanilla}.$$

$$(8.1)$$

These parity relationships are intuitive, by considering, for example, a portfolio comprised of a single DI option and a single DO option with similar strike and maturity. If the asset price does not reach the barrier, the DO option stays active and the DI option stays worthless. Conversely, if the asset price reaches the barrier, the DO option becomes worthless and the DI option comes into existence. In either case, the portfolio retains the right to exercise the option at the strike price, exactly as if a plain-vanilla option were being held. A similar argument holds for a portfolio comprised of a single UI and a single UO option. We obtain the price of European up-and-in and down-and-in options by first obtaining the prices of their up-and-out and down-and-out counterparts, and then applying this relation. Unfortunately, (8.1) does not hold for American barrier options.

To price American options, we use the reflection principle described by Haug (2001), according to which the price of a down-and-in American call can be expressed as

$$C_t^{DI}(S, K, H, T, r, \sigma) = \left(\frac{S}{H}\right)^{1 - \frac{2r}{\sigma^2}} C_t^{PV}\left(\frac{H^2}{S}, K, H, T, r, \sigma\right), \qquad (8.2)$$

where S is the spot price, K is the strike price, H is the barrier $(H < S)$, T is the time to maturity, r is the risk-free rate, and σ is the volatility of the underlying, and C_t^{PV} is the price of an American plain-vanilla call option, obtained by using methods described in Chapter 3, for example. Similarly, the price of an up-and-in American put is

$$P_t^{UI}(S, K, H, T, r, \sigma) = \left(\frac{S}{H}\right)^{1 - \frac{2r}{\sigma^2}} P_t^{PV}\left(\frac{H^2}{S}, K, H, T, r, \sigma\right). \qquad (8.3)$$

Kwok and Dai (2004) show that (8.2) holds when $H \leqslant K$ only, and that (8.3) holds when $H \geqslant K$ only. In this chapter we present VBA functions for implementing their method, which holds for American down-and-in calls and up-and-in puts under more general conditions.

Pricing barrier options with tree-based methods may seem easy, since at first glance all that is needed is a slight modification that sets the option price to zero when the barrier is reached. However, it is well known that tree-based methods have trouble converging because the generated asset prices rarely lie on the barrier. The models we present all propose novel methods to deal with this difficulty.

Barrier Monitoring

The price of a barrier option depends on how often the barrier is monitored. Many barrier option pricing formulas assume continuous monitoring, however, which implies that the asset price must be constantly monitored to verify whether it has crossed the barrier. Since continuous monitoring is not feasible, monitoring is done at discrete time intervals. For example, a knock-out option monitored daily will be knocked out only if the closing price of the asset reaches the barrier, even though the asset may have reached the barrier during the trading day. Broadie, Glasserman, and Kou (1997, 1999) have proposed an approximation to correct for discrete barrier monitoring. If $f(H)$ denotes the price of a continuous knock-in or knock-out down call or up put with barrier H, then the price $f_m(H)$ of the corresponding discretely monitored option is

$$f_m(H) = f(He^{\pm\beta\sigma\sqrt{T/m}}), \qquad (8.4)$$

where "+" in the exponent is used for up options (when $H > S$), and "−" is used for down options (when $H < S$), and where $\beta \approx 0.5826$. There are two ways to specify monitoring. The first is to specify m, the number of times the barrier will be monitored during the life of the option, T. For example, if the option has a time to maturity of three months (0.25 years) and the barrier is to be monitored five times over the life of the option, then $\sqrt{T/m} = \sqrt{0.25/5}$ appears in the exponent to (8.4). The second is to specify the frequency of monitoring, usually hourly, daily, weekly, or monthly. For example, with monthly monitoring $\sqrt{T/m} = \sqrt{1/12}$ appears in the exponent. Hence, adjusting for discrete monitoring in a barrier option pricing formula is straightforward with the approximation (8.4), because H is simply replaced by $He^{\pm\beta\sigma\sqrt{T/m}}$ everywhere H is encountered in the formula.

The VBA function NewBarrier() is used to adjust the barrier for discrete monitoring. It creates a new barrier based on (8.4) under either monitoring method. If the parameter M1 is set to zero, the second method is used with frequency specified by the parameter M2. Otherwise, the first method is used, with number of monitoring times specified by the value of M1. This barrier adjustment is constructed with 365 days per year.

```
Function NewBarrier(Spot, Bar, T, v, M1, M2 As String)
If Bar > Spot Then
  Sign = 1
Else
  Sign = -1
End If
Select Case M1
 Case Is <> 0
   Bar = Bar * Exp(Sign * 0.5826 * v * Sqr(T / M1))
 Case Is = 0
   Select Case M2
    Case "H": Bar = Bar * Exp(Sign * 0.5826 * v * Sqr(1 / 24 / 365))
    Case "D": Bar = Bar * Exp(Sign * 0.5826 * v * Sqr(1 / 365))
    Case "W": Bar = Bar * Exp(Sign * 0.5826 * v * Sqr(1 / 52))
    Case "M": Bar = Bar * Exp(Sign * 0.5826 * v * Sqr(1 / 12))
   End Select
End Select
NewBarrier = Bar
End Function
```

Two-Stage Flexible Binomial Tree

The flexible tree of Tian (1999) covered in Chapter 3 can easily be modified to price barrier options. In this section we explain how to construct the flexible binomial tree for European single-barrier options when there is continuous monitoring. This requires that a two-stage tree be constructed. The first part of the tree is a flexible binomial tree, tilted so that one of its nodes lies exactly on the barrier. The remaining part of the tree is a CRR binomial tree, corresponding to a flexible tree with a tilt parameter of zero. Since the CRR recombines, in the second part of the flexible tree the barrier will always lie on the tree nodes.

Recall that the parameters of the flexible binomial tree are given by

$$u = e^{\sigma\sqrt{dt}+\lambda\sigma^2\,dt}, \quad d = e^{-\sigma\sqrt{dt}+\lambda\sigma^2\,dt}, \quad p = \left(\frac{e^{r\times dt} - d}{u - d}\right), \tag{8.5}$$

and that the CRR binomial tree parameters u_0, d_0, and p_0 are obtained by setting $\lambda = 0$ in u, d, and p, respectively, in (8.5). Using techniques similar to those outlined in Chapter 3 for the flexible tree of Tian (1999), the tilt parameter can be derived as

$$\lambda = \frac{\ln(H/S_0) + N_0\sigma\sqrt{dt}}{N_0\sigma^2\,dt}, \tag{8.6}$$

where

$$N_0 = \mathrm{int}\left[\frac{\ln(H/S_0)}{\ln d_0}\right], \tag{8.7}$$

where H is the barrier, and where int[] denotes rounding to the nearest integer. As shown by Tian (1999), the first stage of the tree has asset prices given as $S(i,j) = S_0 u^j d^{i-j}$ ($i \leqslant N_0$), while the second stage of the tree, as $S(i,j) = S_0 d^{N_0} u_0 d_0^{i-N_0-j}$ ($i > N_0$). The two-stage flexible binomial tree constructed in this fashion has recombining nodes throughout, and the barrier is reached after exactly N_0 steps.

 To implement the two-stage flexible binomial tree for European single barrier options, we obtain the prices of down-and-out and up-and-out calls and puts directly. To obtain the prices of down-and-in and up-and-in options, we use the parity relation (8.1), along with plain-vanilla prices obtained using the CRR binomial tree. The Excel file Chapter8FBBarrierC contains the VBA function FBBarrierC() to implement the Tian (1999) two-stage flexible binomial tree for single barrier European options. Note that this requires a slight modification of the notation, to reflect the different indexing for pairs (i, j). In Tian (1999) the first index represents time and the second index represents the nodes, but this is reversed in the VBA coding. For example, in the function FBBarrierC() the first stage has asset prices given by $S(i, j) = S_0 u^{j-i} d^{i-1}$ ($j \leqslant N_0 + 1$), while the second stage has asset prices given by $S(i, j) = S_0 d^{N_0} u_0^{j-i} d_0^{i-1-N_0}$ ($j > N_0 + 1$). This is achieved in the first part of the FBBarrierC() function.

```
Function FBBarrierC(Spot, K, H, T, r, sigma, n, OpType As String, PutCall
            As String)
dt = T / n: u0 = Exp(sigma * Sqr(dt)): d0 = 1 / u0
p0 = (Exp(r * dt) - d0) / (u0 - d0)
N0 = Round(Log(H / Spot) / Log(d0))
L = (Log(H / Spot) + N0 * sigma * Sqr(dt)) / N0 / sigma ^ 2 / dt
u = Exp(sigma * Sqr(dt) + L * sigma ^ 2 * dt)
d = Exp(-sigma * Sqr(dt) + L * sigma ^ 2 * dt)
p = (Exp(r * dt) - d) / (u - d)
Dim S() As Double, Op() As Double
ReDim S(n + 1, n + 1) As Double, Op(n + 1, n + 1) As Double
S(1, 1) = Spot
For j = 1 To n + 1
  For i = 1 To j
    If j <= N0 + 1 Then
      S(i, j) = S(1, 1) * u ^ (j - i) * d ^ (i - 1)
    Else
      S(i, j) = S(1, 1) * d ^ (N0) * u0 ^ (j - i) * d0 ^ (i - N0 - 1)
    End If
    S(i, j) = Round(S(i, j) * 10000, 5) / 10000
  Next i
Next j
```

The second part of the function calculates terminal option prices and verifies whether the asset prices lie above or below the barrier.

```
For i = 1 To n + 1
If (S(i, n + 1) <= H And (OpType = "DI" Or OpType = "DO")) Or (S(i, n + 1)
            >= H And (OpType = "UI" Or OpType = "UO")) Then
  Op(i, n + 1) = 0
Else
Select Case PutCall
  Case "Call"
    Op(i, n + 1) = Application.Max(S(i, n + 1) - K, 0)
  Case "Put"
    Op(i, n + 1) = Application.Max(K - S(i, n + 1), 0)
End Select
End If
Next i
```

The next part of the function computes the option price by backward induction, again verifying where the asset prices lie relative to the barrier. Note that the second stage uses the CRR probability p_0, while the first stage uses the probability p from (8.5).

```
For j = n To 1 Step -1
For i = 1 To j
  If (S(i, j) <= H And (OpType = "DI" Or OpType = "DO")) Or
     (S(i, j) >= H And (OpType = "UI" Or OpType = "UO"))
```

```
Then
  Op(i, j) = 0
Else
  If j <= NO Then
    Prob = p
  Else
    Prob = p0
  End If
Op(i, j) = Exp(-r * dt) * (Prob * Op(i, j + 1)
          + (1 - Prob) * Op(i + 1, j + 1))
  End If
Next i
Next j
```

Finally, the last part of the function calculates the option prices and applies the parity relation (8.1) if needed.

```
If OpType = "DO" Or OpType = "UO" Then
  FBBarrierC = Op(1, 1)
Else
  FBBarrierC = Binomial(Spot, K, T, r, sigma, n, PutCall) - Op(1, 1)
End If
End Function
```

This function is illustrated in Figure 8.1, using the same parameter values that were used to generate Table IV of Tian (1999).

	A	B	C	D	E
1					
2		**Flexible Binomial Tree for a European Barrier Option**			
3		**With Continuous Monitoring**			
4					
5		Spot Price (S)	100		
6		Strike Price (K)	100		
7		Barrier (H)	95		
8		Years to Maturity (T)	0.5000		
9		Interest Rate (r)	0.1		
10		Volatility (σ)	0.2		
11		Steps (n)	1,000		
12		Type (Call or Put)	Call		
13		Option (DI or DO)	DO		
14					
15					
16		**Option Price**	5.7168		

FIGURE 8.1 Two-Stage Flexible Binomial Tree

The cells in column C have been named for convenience. To obtain the price of the barrier option with the given parameters, in cell C16 we type

$$= \text{FBBarrierC}(S, K, H, T, RF, V, N, \text{Type}, \text{PutCall})$$

which produces a price of 5.7168. Using the same parameter values, the price of a down-and-in call is 2.5596, close to the analytical value of 2.5615 (see Haug, 1998).

Boyle and Lau (1994) Method

If the CRR binomial tree is used to price barrier options, by setting the option price to zero whenever the barrier is reached, convergence to the true price will be very slow and follow a sawtooth pattern. The error will be small for those values of n that generate asset prices that fall close to the barrier, but will be large when asset prices lie far from the barrier. Hence, using a large number of steps does not necessarily ensure fast converge. Recognizing this, Boyle and Lau (1994) propose to restrict the number of steps in the tree to those values that generate asset prices close to the barrier. They suggest using a value of n that is the largest integer that is smaller than $F(m)$, where

$$F(m) = \frac{m^2 \sigma^2 T}{\log(S/H)^2} \qquad (8.8)$$

for $m = 1, 2, 3 \cdots$.

The Excel file Chapter8BarrierBin contains the VBA function BarrierBin() for implementing the Boyle and Lau (1994) method. The function calculates the prices of knock-out options directly, and calculates the other types of options using the barrier parity relationship (8.1), or the reflection principles (8.2) and (8.3), in accordance with Table 8.1. It is not possible to obtain the prices of American up-and-in calls or American down-and-in puts with this tree.

The first part of the BarrierBin() function updates the barrier according to which type of monitoring is used, which ensures that the barrier lies below (above) the spot price for down-and-out and down-and-in (up-and-out and up-and-in) options.

TABLE 8.1   Pricing Barrier Options with Binomial Tree

	Down-and-In	Down-and-Out	Up-and-In	Up-and-Out
		Call Options		
European	Parity (8.1)	Direct	Parity (8.1)	Direct
American	Reflection (8.2)	Direct	Not Available	Direct
		Put Options		
European	Parity (8.1)	Direct	Parity (8.1)	Direct
American	Not Available	Direct	Reflection (8.3)	Direct

The closest optimal number of steps above the number specified as an input, *n*, is chosen using the function *F*(*m*). If *n* is not large enough, an error message appears that requests a larger value be used.

```
Function BarrierBin(Spot, Strike, Bar, T, r, v, old_n, PutCall As String,
            EuroAmer As String, BarType As String, M1, M2 As String)
Bar = NewBarrier(Spot, Bar, T, v, M1, M2)
If (BarType = "DO" Or BarType = "DI") And Bar > Spot Then
    MsgBox "Error: Barrier Must be Below Spot Price for a
    Down-and-Out or Down-and-In Option"
ElseIf (BarType = "UO" Or BarType = "UI") And Bar < Spot Then MsgBox
            "Error: Barrier Must be Above Spot Price for a
            Up-and-Out or Up-and-In Option"
Else
For m = 1 To 100
  F(m) = m ^ 2 * v ^ 2 * T / (Log(Spot / Bar)) ^ 2
Next m
If old_n < F(1) Then
 MsgBox ("Increase Number Steps to at Least " &
        Application.Floor(F(1) + 1, 1))
Else
For i = 1 To 99
  If (F(i) < old_n) And (old_n < F(i + 1)) Then
    n = Application.Floor(F(i + 1), 1)
  Exit For
  End If
Next i
End If
```

The second part of the function defines the CRR parameters, and constructs the option prices in exactly the same way as in Chapter 3, except that the option price is set to zero when the option crosses the barrier. To conserve space, only the part of the function that calculates European calls is presented.

```
dt = T / n: u = Exp(v * Sqr(dt))
d = 1 / u: p = (Exp(r * dt) - d) / (u - d)
exp_rT = Exp(-r * dt)
For i = 1 To n + 1
AssetPrice = Spot * u ^ (n + 1 - i) * d ^ (i - 1)
  If ((BarType = "DO" Or BarType = "DI")
        And AssetPrice <= Bar) Or
     ((BarType = "UO" Or BarType = "UI")
        And AssetPrice >= Bar) Then
    Op(i, n + 1) = 0
  ElseIf PutCall = "Call" Then
    Op(i, n + 1) = Application.Max(AssetPrice - Strike, 0)
  End If
Next i
For j = n To 1 Step -1
For i = 1 To j
AssetPrice = Spot * u ^ (j - i) * d ^ (i - 1)
  If ((BarType = "DO" Or BarType = "DI")
```

```
      And AssetPrice <= Bar) Or _
   ((BarType = "UO" Or BarType = "UI")
      And AssetPrice >= Bar) Then
   Op(i, j) = 0
 Else
   Op(i, j) = exp_rT * (p * Op(i, j + 1)
           + (1 - p) * Op(i + 1, j + 1))
 End If
Next i
Next j
```

In accordance with Table 8.1, the prices of down-and-out and up-and-out options are outputted directly. The prices of a European down-and-in or down-and-out call or put are obtained from the barrier parity relationship, where the plain-vanilla value is obtained from the CRR binomial through the VBA function fbinomial(). The prices of an American down-and-in call and up-and-in put are obtained using the reflection principle. Finally, since American down-and-in puts and up-and-in calls cannot be obtained with the algorithm, a message box appears if the user attempts to price these options.

```
If BarType = "DO" Or BarType = "UO" Then
    output(1, 1) = Op(1, 1)
Else
Select Case EuroAmer
Case "Euro"
  If PutCall = "Call" Then
    output(1, 1) = fbinomial(Spot, Strike, r, v, T, n,
                   "Call", "Euro") - Op(1, 1)
  ElseIf PutCall = "Put" Then
    output(1, 1) = fbinomial(Spot, Strike, r, v, T, n,
                   "Put", "Euro") - Op(1, 1)
  End If
Case "Amer"
  If PutCall = "Call" And BarType = "DI" Then
    output(1, 1) = (Spot / Bar) ^ (1 - 2 * r / v ^ 2) *
    fbinomial(Bar ^ 2 / Spot, Strike, r, v, T, n,
    "Call", "Amer")
  ElseIf PutCall = "Put" And BarType = "UI" Then
    output(1, 1) = (Spot / Bar) ^ (1 - 2 * r / v ^ 2) *
    fbinomial(Bar ^ 2 / Spot, Strike, r, v, T, n,
    "Put","Amer")
  ElseIf (PutCall = "Put" And BarType = "DI") Then
    MsgBox "You Cannot Price an American Down-and-In Put
          Using This Algorithm"
  ElseIf (PutCall = "Call" And BarType = "UI") Then
    MsgBox "You Cannot Price an American Up-and-In Call
          Using This Algorithm"
  End If
End Select
End If
output(2, 1) = n
```

```
      BarrierBin = output
End Function
```

Figure 8.2 illustrates the BarrierBin() function on a down-and-in American call with strike price $K = 140$, barrier $H = 95$ and time to maturity $T = 1$ year, when the risk-free rate and volatility are $r = 0.10$ and $\sigma = 0.25$, respectively, and with $n = 250$ time steps. The barrier is $H = 95$ and monitored daily, so in cell C17 we put "D" and cell F8 we type

$$= \text{NewBarrier(S, H, T, V, Mon1, Mon2)}$$

which produces an adjusted barrier value of 94.2785. To obtain the option price and the actual number of optimal steps produced by the Boyle and Lau (1994) method, in cell F6 we type

$$= \text{BarrierBin(S, K, H, T, RF, V, N, PutCall, EuroAmer, BarType, Mon1, Mon2)}$$

and copy to cell F7. The price of the option is $0.8156 and appears in cell F6, while the optimal number of time steps is $n = 288$ in cell F7. The price of a European down-and-in call is 0.8154. For comparison, the analytic value of the European down-and-in call is 0.8180 (see Haug, 1998).

	A	B	C	D	E	F
1						
2		**Binomial Tree for European Single Barrier Options**				
3		**With Optimal Number of Steps from Boyle and Lau (1994)**				
4		**Parity Relation and Reflection Principle**				
5						
6		Spot Price (*S*)	100		**Option Price**	0.8156
7		Strike Price (*K*)	140		**Number of Steps**	288
8		Barrier (*H*)	95		**Adjusted Barrier**	94.2785
9		Years to Maturity (*T*)	1			
10		Interest Rate (*r*)	0.1			
11		Volatility (*σ*)	0.25			
12		Steps (*n*)	250			
13		Type (*Call* or *Put*)	Call			
14		Option (*Euro* or *Amer*)	Amer			
15		Barrier Option Type (*DO, DI, UO, UI*)	DI			
16		Barrier Monitoring (*# Observations*)	0			
17		Barrier Monitoring (*C, H, D, W, M*)	D			
18		*C* = Continuous				
19		*H* = Hourly				
20		*D* = Daily				
21		*W* = Weekly				
22		*M* = Monthly				

FIGURE 8.2 Boyle and Lau (1994) Binomial Pricing for Barrier Options

Interpolation Method

Derman et al. (1995) propose an alternate method to price single barrier options. They note that while the specified barrier rarely lies on tree nodes, it always lies above and below the modified barrier and effective barrier, respectively (see their Figure 7). For UO and UI options, the effective barrier consists of asset prices immediately above the barrier, while the modified barrier consists of asset prices immediately below the barrier. Their approach is to interpolate option prices obtained at the modified and effective barriers, using a first order Taylor series expansion.

The Excel file Chapter8BarrierUp contains the VBA function BarrierUp() for pricing European up-and-in and up-and-out options, and for pricing American up-and-in puts using the reflection principle (8.3). The first part of the BarrierUp() function constructs the CRR binomial tree and stores the asset prices in the array S(). The second part creates "naïve" up-and-out option prices, namely, those obtained by using only the effective barrier, and stores them in the array Op(). These are obtained simply by setting the CRR asset prices to zero when they lie above the barrier.

```
Function BarrierUp(Spot, Strike, H, T, r, v, n, PutCall As String,
             EuroAmer As String, UpType As String, M1, M2 As String)
For i = 1 To n + 1
  If S(i, n + 1) >= H Then
    Op(i, n + 1) = 0
  Else
    Select Case PutCall
    Case "Put": Op(i, n + 1) = Application.Max(Strike
                - S(i, n + 1), 0)
    Case "Call": Op(i, n + 1) = Application.Max(S(i, n + 1)
                - Strike, 0)
    End Select
  End If
Next i
For j = n To 1 Step -1
For i = 1 To j
  If S(i, j) >= H Then
      Op(i, j) = 0
  Else
    Select Case EuroAmer
    Case "Euro":
      Op(i, j) = exp_rT * (p * Op(i, j + 1)
              + (1 - p) * Op(i + 1, j + 1))
    Case "Amer":
      If PutCall = "Call" Then
        Op(i, j) = Application.Max(S(i, j) - Strike,
              exp_rT * (p * Op(i, j + 1) + (1 - p)
              * Op(i + 1, j + 1)))
      If PutCall = "Put" Then
        Op(i, j) = Application.Max(Strike - S(i, j),
              exp_rT * (p * Op(i, j + 1) + (1 - p)
              * Op(i + 1, j + 1)))
```

```
      End Select
   End If
Next i
Next j
```

The next part constructs the modified (lower) barrier and interpolates option prices. The array L() identifies which components of the tree contain the modified barrier.

```
' Modified (Lower) Barrier
Dim L() As Double
ReDim L(n + 1, n + 1) As Double
For j = 1 To n
  If (S(1, j) <= H And H <= S(1, j + 1))
  Or (H <= S(1, j + 1)) Then
    L(1, j) = 1
  End If
Next j
L(1, n + 1) = 1
For i = 2 To n + 1
  For j = 2 To n + 1
    If S(i - 1, j - 1) <= H And H <= S(i - 1, j) Then
      For K = j To n + 1
        L(i, K) = 1
      Next K
    End If
  Next j
Next i
' Interpolate Option Prices at the Lower Barrier
For i = 2 To n
  For j = i To n
    If L(i, j) = 1 Then
      d = S(i, j)
      u = S(i - 1, j)
      Op(i, j) = (H - d) / (u - d) * Op(i, j)
    End If
  Next j
Next i
```

The next step is to identify option prices that must be updated along the last column and along the rows of the array L(), and then apply backward recursion to the identified option prices.

```
For j = n To 1 Step -1
For i = 1 To j
  If L(i, j) = 0 Then
  Select Case EuroAmer
  Case "Euro":
    Op(i, j) = exp_rT * (p * Op(i, j + 1) + (1 - p)
            * Op(i + 1, j + 1))
  Case "Amer":
  If PutCall = "Call" Then
    Op(i, j) = Application.Max(S(i, j) - Strike,
```

```
                  exp_rT * (p * Op(i, j + 1) + (1 - p)
                * Op(i + 1, j + 1)))
    If PutCall = "Put" Then
      Op(i, j) = Application.Max(Strike - S(i, j),
                  exp_rT * (p * Op(i, j + 1) + (1 - p)
                * Op(i + 1, j + 1)))
    End Select
    End If
  Next i
  Next j
```

Finally, up-and-out options are stored in Op(1,1) and are outputted directly. The prices of up-and-in puts and calls are obtained by the parity relationship (8.1), and the price of American up-and-in puts are obtained using the reflection principle (8.3). The prices of plain-vanilla options are obtained using the CRR binomial tree and the VBA function Binomial(), stored in separate module within the Excel file Chapter8BarrierUp.

```
If UpType = "UO" Then
  Price = Op(1, 1)
Else
Select Case EuroAmer
Case "Euro"
  If PutCall = "Call" Then
    Price = Binomial(Spot, Strike, T, r, v, n, "Call", "Euro") - Op(1, 1)
  ElseIf PutCall = "Put" Then
    Price = Binomial(Spot, Strike, T, r, v, n, "Put", "Euro") - Op(1, 1)
  End If
Case "Amer"
  If PutCall = "Put" And UpType = "UI" Then
    Price = (Spot / H) ^ (1 - 2 * r / v ^ 2) * Binomial(
        H ^ 2 / Spot, Strike, T, r, v, n, "Put", "Amer")
  End If
End Select
End If
  BarrierUp = Price
End Function
```

Figure 8.3 illustrates the BarrierUp() function for a European up-and-in put, using $n = 500$ steps. In cell F6 we type

= BarrierUp(S, K, H, T, RF, V, N, PutCall, EuroAmer, BarType, Mon1, Mon2)

which produces a price of $7.8160. The exact price of this option is $7.8154 (see Haug, 1998). The price of an American up-and-in put with the same parameter values is $8.0702.

The method of Derman et al. (1995) can also be used for "down" options. Exactly the same methodology is applied, except that the interpolation scheme

	A	B	C	D	E	F
1						
2		**Binomial Tree for European or American Single Barrier "Up" Options**				
3		**With Derman** *et al.* **(1995) Interpolation**				
4		**Parity Relation and Reflection Principle**				
5						
6		Spot Price (*S*)	100		**Option Price**	7.81602
7		Strike Price (*K*)	110			
8		Barrier (*H*)	105		**Adjusted Barrier**	105.0000
9		Years to Maturity (*T*)	0.5			
10		Interest Rate (*r*)	0.05			
11		Volatility (*σ*)	0.3			
12		Steps (*n*)	500			
13		Type (*Call* or *Put*)	Put			
14		Option (*Amer* or *Euro*)	Euro			
15		Barrier Option Type (*UO* or *UI*)	UI			
16		Barrier Monitoring (# *Observations*)	0			
17		Barrier Monitoring (*C*, *H*, *D*, *W*, *M*)	C			
18		*C* = Continuous				
19		*H* = Hourly				
20		*D* = Daily				
21		*W* = Weekly				
22		*M* = Monthly				

FIGURE 8.3 Interpolated Price for a European Up-and-In Put

reflects the fact that the effective barrier now lies below the specified barrier, while the modified barrier lies above.

The Excel file Chapter8BarrierDown contains the VBA function BarrierDown() for implementing European down-and-out options, and American down-and-in calls. The function is similar to the BarrierUp() function described above, so only selected parts of the BarrierDown() function are presented. The "naïve" down-and-out prices are obtained in a similar fashion, except the option prices are set to zero when CRR asset prices lie at or below the barrier.

```
Function BarrierDown(Spot, Strike, H, T, r, v, n, PutCall As String,
            EuroAmer As String, UpType As String, M1, M2 As String)
For i = 1 To n + 1
  If S(i, n + 1) <= H Then
    Op(i, n + 1) = 0
  Else
    Select Case PutCall
    Case "Call": Op(i, n + 1) = Application.Max(S(i, n + 1)
                        - Strike, 0)
    Case "Put": Op(i, n + 1) = Application.Max(Strike
                        - S(i, n + 1), 0)
    End Select
  End If
Next i
```

The other option prices are obtained by the usual method of backward recursion, but the option prices are set to zero when the asset prices fall below the barrier. The next part creates the modified barrier and interpolates option prices between the effective and modified barriers.

```
' Modified Barrier
For j = 1 To n
  For i = 1 To j
    If S(i + 1, j) <= H And H <= S(i, j)
      And S(i + 1, j) <> 0 Then
        L(i, j) = 1
        L(i + 1, j) = 1
    End If
  Next i
Next j
' Interpolate Option Values
For j = 1 To n
  For i = 1 To j
    If L(i, j) = 1 And L(i + 1, j) = 1 Then
      Up = S(i, j)
      Down = S(i + 1, j)
      Op(i, j) = (H - Up) / (Down - Up) * Op(i, j)
    End If
  Next i
Next j
' Identify Which Option Prices to Update
' Last Column
For i = 1 To n + 1
  L(i, n + 1) = 1
Next i
' Impute First Barrier Value and Values Below the Barrier
For j = 2 To n
  For i = 1 To j
    If L(i, j) = 1 And L(i + 1, j) = 1 Then
      L(i, j - 1) = 1
        For k = 1 To n - i + 1
          L(i + k, j) = 1
        Next k
    End If
  Next i
Next j
```

Down-and-out option prices are obtained directly from Op(1,1), European down-and-in options from the parity relationship (8.1), and American down-and-in calls from the reflection principle (8.2).

```
' Final Pass of Backward Induction on Option Prices
For j = n To 1 Step -1
  For i = 1 To j
  If L(i, j) = 0 Then
  Select Case EuroAmer
    Case "Euro":
```

```
        Op(i, j) = exp_rT * (p * Op(i, j + 1) + (1 - p)
                    * Op(i + 1, j + 1))
      Case "Amer":
        If PutCall = "Call" Then
          Op(i, j) = Application.Max(S(i, j) - Strike,
                       exp_rT * (p * Op(i, j + 1) + (1 - p)
                     * Op(i + 1, j + 1)))
        If PutCall = "Put" Then
          Op(i, j) = Application.Max(Strike - S(i, j),
                       exp_rT * (p * Op(i, j + 1) + (1 - p)
                     * Op(i + 1, j + 1)))
      End Select
    End If
    Next i
  Next j
  If UpType = "DO" Then
    Price = Op(1, 1)
  Else
  Select Case EuroAmer
  Case "Euro"
    If PutCall = "Call" Then
      Price = Binomial(Spot, Strike, T, r, v, n, "Call", "Euro") - Op(1, 1)
    ElseIf PutCall = "Put" Then
      Price = Binomial(Spot, Strike, T, r, v, n, "Put", "Euro") - Op(1, 1)
    End If
  Case "Amer"
    If PutCall = "Call" And UpType = "DI" Then
      Price = (Spot / H) ^ (1 - 2 * r / v ^ 2) * Binomial(
        H ^ 2 / Spot, Strike, T, r, v, n, "Call", "Amer")
    End If
  End Select
  End If
    BarrierDown = Price
End Function
```

Figure 8.4 illustrates this function on a European down-and-in call, using values similar to those in Figure 8.3. In cell F6 we type

= BarrierDown(S, K, H, T, RF, V, N, PutCall, EuroAmer, BarType, Mon1, Mon2)

which produces a price of $5.7578. The exact price is $5.7636 (Haug, 1998). The price of an American down-and-in call with the same parameter values is $5.7667.

Kwok and Dai (2004) Method

Kwok and Dai (2004) show that the reflection principle (8.2) for pricing American down-and-in calls, and (8.3) for pricing up-and-in puts can be inaccurate, depending on whether the barrier lies above or below the strike price. Their method is more general because it allows for the barrier to lie anywhere relative to the strike price.

	A	B	C	D	E	F
1						
2		**Binomial Tree for European or American Single Barrier "Down" Options**				
3		**With Derman *et al*. (1995) Interpolation**				
4		**Parity Relation and Reflection Principle**				
5						
6		Spot Price (*S*)	100		**Option Price**	5.7578
7		Strike Price (*K*)	110			
8		Barrier (*H*)	95		**Adjusted Barrier**	95.0000
9		Years to Maturity (*T*)	1			
10		Interest Rate (*r*)	0.05			
11		Volatility (*σ*)	0.3			
12		Steps (*n*)	500			
13		Type (*Call* or *Put*)	Call			
14		Option (*Amer* or *Euro*)	Euro			
15		Barrier Option Type (*DO* or *DI*)	DI			
16		Barrier Monitoring (# *Observations*)	0			
17		Barrier Monitoring (*C, H, D, W, M*)	C			
18		C = Continuous				
19		H = Hourly				
20		D = Daily				
21		W = Weekly				
22		M = Monthly				

FIGURE 8.4   Interpolated Price for a European Down-and-In Call

The free boundary $S^*(T)$ is the stock price at which it is optimal to exercise an American option with maturity T, so that $S^*(0) = \max(rK/q, K)$ and

$$S^*(\infty) = \frac{\mu_+}{\mu_+ - 1} K, \tag{8.9}$$

where r is the risk-free rate, q is the dividend yield, K is the strike price, and

$$\mu_+ = \frac{-(r - q - \sigma^2/2) + \sqrt{(r - q - \sigma^2/2)^2 + 2\sigma^2 r}}{\sigma^2}, \tag{8.10}$$

where σ is the volatility.

When $H \leqslant S^*(\infty)$, Kwok and Dai (2004) show that the price of an American down-and-in call is given by

$$C_{DI}(S, T; K, H) = \left(\frac{S}{H}\right)^{1-2(r-q)/\sigma^2} \left[C\left(\frac{H^2}{S}, T; K\right) - c\left(\frac{H^2}{S}, T; K\right) \right] \\ + c_{di}(S, T; K, H) \tag{8.11}$$

where T is the time to maturity, $C(H^2/S, T; K)$ is the price of a plain-vanilla American call with spot price H^2/S, time to maturity T and strike price K, $c(H^2/S, T; K)$ is the European counterpart, and $c_{di}(S, T; K, H)$ is the price of a European down-and-in call with spot price S, time to maturity T, strike K and barrier H. We use the CRR binomial tree to obtain the price of a down-and-out European call with the same parameters, and use the parity relationship (8.1) to obtain $c_{di}(S, T; K, H)$ in (8.11).

When $H > S^*(\infty)$, Kwok and Dai (2004) show that the price is

$$C_{DI}(S, T; H, K) = (H - K)\left[\left(\frac{S}{H}\right)^{\alpha - \mu}\Phi(e_1) + \left(\frac{S}{H}\right)^{\alpha + \mu}\Phi(e_2)\right] \quad (8.12)$$

where $\Phi()$ is the standard normal cumulative distribution function, and

$$\mu = \frac{\sqrt{(r - q - \sigma^2/2)^2 + 2r\sigma^2}}{\sigma^2}, \alpha = \frac{1}{2} - \frac{r - q}{\sigma^2}, e_1 = \frac{\ln(H/S) + \mu\sigma^2 T}{\sigma\sqrt{T}}. \quad (8.13)$$

In these expressions e_2 is identical to e_1 except that a minus sign replaces the plus sign in the numerator.

For American up-and-in puts, Kwok and Dai (2004) show that the analogous counterpart to (8.11) is

$$P_{UI}(S, T; K, H) = \left(\frac{S}{H}\right)^{1 - 2(r - q)/\sigma^2}\left[P\left(\frac{H^2}{S}, T; K\right) - p\left(\frac{H^2}{S}, T; K\right)\right]$$
$$+ p_{di}(S, T; K, H) \quad (8.14)$$

where $P(H^2/S, T; K)$ is the price of a plain-vanilla American put with spot price H^2/S, and $p(H^2/S, T; K)$ is the price of a plain-vanilla European put.

The Excel file Chapter8AmerDICall contains the VBA function KDAmerCall() for implementing this method on American down-and-in calls. It uses the CRR binomial tree to obtain the value of a plain-vanilla call option and incorporates the optimal number of steps given by Boyle and Lau (1994). The first part of the function adjusts the barrier for barrier monitoring, chooses the optimal number of steps, and defines the CRR tree parameters. The second part of the function calculates the price of a European down-and-out call, which will be used to obtain the price of a European down-and-in call required in (8.11). The down-and-in call price is stored in Op(1,1).

```
Function KDAmerCall(Spot, Strike, Bar, T, r, q, v, old_n, M1, M2 As
            String)
For i = 1 To n + 1
  AssetPrice = Spot * u ^ (n + 1 - i) * d ^ (i - 1)
  If AssetPrice <= Bar Then
    Op(i, n + 1) = 0
  Else
    Op(i, n + 1) = Application.Max(AssetPrice - Strike, 0)
  End If
Next i
For j = n To 1 Step -1
  For i = 1 To j
```

```
AssetPrice = Spot * u ^ (j - i) * d ^ (i - 1)
  If AssetPrice <= Bar Then
    Op(i, j) = 0
  Else
    Op(i, j) = exp_rT * (p * Op(i, j + 1) + (1 - p) * Op(i + 1, j + 1))
  End If
 Next i
Next j
```

The next part of the function defines the free boundary $S^*(\infty)$. Since $S^*(\infty) = \infty$ when $q = 0$, or equivalently, when $\mu_+ = 1, S^*(\infty)$ is set to a large number when $q = 0$ so that Equation (8.12) is used for the call price.

```
If q <> 0 Then
  mu_plus = -(r - q - 0.5 * v ^ 2) / v ^ 2
    + Sqr((r - q - 0.5 * v ^ 2) ^ 2 + 2 * v ^ 2 * r) / v ^ 2
  S_inf = mu_plus * Strike / (mu_plus - 1)
ElseIf q = 0 Then
  S_inf = 999999999
End If
```

Finally, the barrier is compared to $S^*(\infty)$, so that when $H \leqslant S^*(\infty)$ Equation (8.11) is used, but when $H > S^*(\infty)$ Equation (8.12) is used. The option price and optimal number of steps are stored in array Output().

```
Select Case Bar
Case Is <= S_inf
  DIEurocall =
  fbinomial(Spot, Strike, r, q, v, T, n, "Euro") - Op(1, 1)
  output(1, 1) = (Spot / Bar) ^ (1 - 2 * (r - q) / v ^ 2) *
  (fbinomial(Bar ^ 2 / Spot, Strike, r, q, v, T, n, "Amer")
    - fbinomial(Bar ^ 2 / Spot, Strike, r, q, v, T, n,
      "Euro")) + DIEurocall
Case Is >= S_inf
  mu = Sqr((r - q - v ^ 2 / 2) ^ 2 + 2 * r * v ^ 2) / v ^ 2
  alpha = 0.5 - (r - q) / v ^ 2
  e1 = (Log(Bar / Spot) + mu * v ^ 2 * T) / v / Sqr(T)
  e2 = (Log(Bar / Spot) - mu * v ^ 2 * T) / v / Sqr(T)
  output(1, 1) = (Bar - Strike) * (Gauss(e1)
                  * (Spot / Bar) ^ (alpha - mu)
                  + Gauss(e2) * (Spot / Bar) ^ (alpha + mu))
End Select
output(2, 1) = n
  KDAmerCall = output
End Function
```

Figure 8.5 illustrates the KDAmerCall() function, on a down-and-in American call option with strike price $K = 100$, barrier $H = 110$ and time to maturity $\tau = 1$ year, when the spot price is $S = 120.5$, the risk free rate, dividend yield and volatility are $r = 0.10, q = 0.09$, and $\sigma = 0.30$, respectively, and using $n = 1,000$

	A	B	C	D	E	F
1						
2		**Binomial Tree for American Down-and-In Call, Method of Kwok and Dai (2004)**				
3		**With Optimal Number of Steps from Boyle and Lau (1994)**				
4						
5		Spot Price (*S*)	120.5		**Option Price**	12.539202
6		Strike Price (*K*)	100		**Number of Steps**	1082
7		Barrier (*H*)	110		**Adjusted Barrier**	110.0000
8		Years to Maturity (*T*)	1			
9		Risk-Free Rate (*r*)	0.1			
10		Dividend Yield (*q*)	0.09			
11		Volatility (σ)	0.3			
12		Steps (*n*)	1,000			
13		Barrier Monitoring (# *Observations*)	0			
14		Barrier Monitoring (*C*, *H*, *D*, *W*, *M*)	C			
15		*C* = Continuous				
16		*H* = Hourly				
17		*D* = Daily				
18		*W* = Weekly				
19		*M* = Monthly				

FIGURE 8.5 Down-and-In American Call

steps. These are the same values as those used in Table 1 of Kwok and Dai (2004), except that they used $n = 10,000$ steps to obtain the "exact" values in the last column of their table. In cell F5 we type

$$= \text{KDAmerCall}(S, K, H, T, RF, Q, V, N, \text{Mon1}, \text{Mon2})$$

and copy down to cell F6, which produces a price of \$12.5392 in cell F5 with an optimal number of steps $n = 1,082$ in cell F6. The price is close to the value of \$12.5409 obtained by Kwok and Dai (2004) in row 4 of their Table 1. In this example $S^*(\infty) = 207.6$ and $H = 110$, so Equation (8.11) is used for the price. Specifying $S = 180.5$ and $H = 170$ produces a price of \$59.6083 with $n = 1,227$ optimal time steps, reasonably close to the "exact" value of \$59.3874 obtained in the last row, last column of Table 1 in Kwok and Dai (2004).

The Excel file Chapter8AmerUIPut contains the VBA function KDAmerPut() to implement the Kwok and Dai (2004) price of an American up-and-in put. The function is very similar to the KDAmerCall() function, except for the last part, which specifies that (8.14) use prices of puts instead of calls.

```
Select Case Bar
Case Is <= S_inf
  DIEuroPut =
  fbinomial(Spot, Strike, r, q, v, T, n, "Euro") - Op(1, 1)
  output(1, 1) = (Spot / Bar) ^ (1 - 2 * (r - q) / v ^ 2) *
    (fbinomial(Bar ^ 2 / Spot, Strike, r, q, v, T, n, "Amer")
  - fbinomial(Bar ^ 2 / Spot, Strike, r, q, v, T, n,
    "Euro")) + DIEuroPut
```

```
Case Is >= S_inf
  mu = Sqr((r - q - v ^ 2 / 2) ^ 2 + 2 * r * v ^ 2) / v ^ 2
  alpha = 0.5 - (r - q) / v ^ 2
  e1 = (Log(Bar / Spot) + mu * v ^ 2 * T) / v / Sqr(T)
  e2 = (Log(Bar / Spot) - mu * v ^ 2 * T) / v / Sqr(T)
  output(1, 1) = (Bar - Strike) * (Gauss(e1)
              * (Spot / Bar) ^ (alpha - mu)
              + Gauss(e2) * (Spot / Bar) ^ (alpha + mu))
End Select
End If
output(2, 1) = n
  KDAmerPut = output
End Function
```

Figure 8.6 illustrates the KDAmerPut() function on an American up-and-in put with strike price $K = 100$, barrier $H = 110$, and time to maturity $T = 1$ year, when the risk-free rate, dividend yield, and volatility are $r = 0.05, q = 0.05$, and $\sigma = 0.30$, and when $n = 250$ steps are used. In cell F5 we type

$$= \text{KDAmerPut}(S, K, H, T, RF, Q, V, N, Mon1, Mon2)$$

and copy down to cell F5, which produces a price of \$4.5354, with an optimal number of steps $n = 356$.

Adaptive Mesh Method

This method is due to Figlewski and Gao (1999) and was presented in Chapter 3 for pricing plain-vanilla options. It is very useful for pricing barrier options when the

	A	B	C	D	E	F
1						
2		**Binomial Tree for American Up-and-In Put, Method of Kwok and Dai (2004)**				
3		**With Optimal Number of Steps from Boyle and Lau (1994)**				
4						
5		Spot Price (S)	100		**Option Price**	4.5354
6		Strike Price (K)	100		**Number of Steps**	356
7		Barrier (H)	110		**Adjusted Barrier**	110.0000
8		Years to Maturity (T)	1			
9		Risk-Free Rate (r)	0.05			
10		Dividend Yield (q)	0.05			
11		Volatility (σ)	0.3			
12		Steps (n)	250			
13		Barrier Monitoring (# Observations)	0			
14		Barrier Monitoring (C, H, D, W, M)	C			
15		C = Continuous				
16		H = Hourly				
17		D = Daily				
18		W = Weekly				
19		M = Monthly				

FIGURE 8.6 Up-and-In American Put

barrier is close to the spot price. It uses price increments h given

$$h = 2|\log(S) - \log(H)| \qquad (8.15)$$

for building the coarse mesh in terms of log prices, where S is the spot price and H is the barrier, and time increments k given

$$k = \frac{T}{[T\lambda v/h^2]}, \qquad (8.16)$$

where $[x]$ denotes the floor function (the largest integer smaller than x), v is the volatility, and λ is an arbitrary free parameter. Figlewski and Gao (1999) recommend using $\lambda = 3$. The number of steps in the coarse mesh is given by rounding $n = T/k$ to the nearest integer. The tree is constructed using a coarse mesh with $2n + 1$ rows and $n + 1$ columns (the "A" points in Figure 6 of their paper), and a fine mesh with 3 rows and $4n + 1$ columns (the "B" points). Finally, the probability for up moves is given by the function

$$p_u(v, h, k) = \frac{1}{2}\left(\frac{v^2 k}{h^2} + \frac{\alpha^2 k^2}{h^2} + \frac{\alpha k}{h} \right), \qquad (8.17)$$

the probability for a down move by the function

$$p_u(v, h, k) = \frac{1}{2}\left(\frac{v^2 k}{h^2} + \frac{\alpha^2 k^2}{h^2} - \frac{\alpha k}{h} \right), \qquad (8.18)$$

and the probability of a lateral move by

$$p_m(v, h, k) = 1 - p_u(v, h, k) - p_d(v, h, k), \qquad (8.19)$$

where $\alpha = r - v^2/2$ and r is the risk-free rate.

Finally, we note that since the time to maturity T and the volatility v are both fixed, and since h is fixed by (8.15), the only way to increase the number of time steps n in this model is to reduce k in (8.16) by increasing λ. Note also, however, that by virtue of (8.15) and (8.16), the closer the barrier to the spot price, the larger the number of time steps. In this chapter a single fine mesh is grafted on the coarse mesh, but as shown by Figlewski and Gao (1999) and as mentioned in Chapter 3, it is possible to graft a series of meshes, each one progressively finer, which increases the accuracy of the approximation to the option price even further.

 The Excel file Chapter8BarrierAMM contains the VBA function Barrier-AMM() for obtaining European and American single-barrier options with the AMM method. The function uses the VBA functions ProbUp() and ProbDown() for the up and down probabilities given in (8.17) and (8.18), respectively.

```
Function ProbUp(Alpha, v, h, k)
  ProbUp = (v ^ 2 * k / h ^ 2 + Alpha ^ 2 * k ^ 2 / h ^ 2
```

```
            + Alpha * k / h) / 2
End Function

Function ProbDown(Alpha, v, h, k)
  ProbDown = (v ^ 2 * k / h ^ 2 + Alpha ^ 2 * k ^ 2 / h ^ 2
           - Alpha * k / h) / 2
End Function
```

The coarse mesh in terms of log prices (the "A" points) are constructed from a distance of $h/2$ about the log spot price, and stored in the array A(). The asset prices are constructed by exponentiating the "A" points. These are stored in the array S().

```
If BarType = "DO" Or BarType = "DI" Then
  A(n + 1, 1) = Log(Spot) + h / 2
ElseIf BarType = "UO" Or BarType = "UI" Then
  A(n + 1, 1) = Log(Spot) - h / 2
End If
For j = 1 To (n + 1)
For i = (n - j + 2) To (n + j)
  A(i, j) = A(n + 1, 1) + (n - i + 1) * h
    If A(i, j) = 0 Then
      S(i, j) = 0
    Else
      S(i, j) = Exp(A(i, j))
    End If
Next i
Next j
```

Finally, the option prices along the coarse mesh are obtained by the usual method of backward recursion, by using the probabilities given in (8.17) through (8.19) and $\exp(-rk)$ as the discount factor, verifying whether the current asset price lies above or below the barrier at each step, and checking for early exercise in the case of American options.

```
exp_rt = Exp(-r * k): pu = ProbUp(Alpha, v, h, k)
pd = ProbDown(Alpha, v, h, k): pm = 1 - pu - pd
For i = 1 To 2 * n + 1
  Select Case PutCall
  Case "Call":
    Op(i, n + 1) = Application.Max(S(i, n + 1) - Strike, 0)
  Case "Put":
    Op(i, n + 1) = Application.Max(Strike - S(i, n + 1), 0)
  End Select
  If ((BarType = "DO" Or BarType = "DI")
      And A(i, n + 1) <= logH)
  Or ((BarType = "UO" Or BarType = "UI")
      And A(i, n + 1) >= logH) Then
  Op(i, n + 1) = 0
End If
Next i
For j = n To 1 Step -1
For i = (n - j + 2) To (n + j)
```

```
    If ((BarType = "DO" Or BarType = "DI")
        And A(i, j) <= logH) _
  Or ((BarType = "UO" Or BarType = "UI")
        And A(i, j) >= logH) Then
  Op(i, j) = 0
  Else
  Select Case EuroAmer
  Case "Amer"
    If PutCall = "Call" Then
      Op(i, j) = Application.Max(S(i, j) - Strike,
      exp_rt * (pu * Op(i - 1, j + 1) + pm * Op(i, j + 1)
      + pd * Op(i + 1, j + 1)))
    ElseIf PutCall = "Put" Then
      Op(i, j) = Application.Max(Strike - S(i, j),
      exp_rt * (pu * Op(i - 1, j + 1) + pm * Op(i, j + 1)
      + pd * Op(i + 1, j + 1)))
    End If
  Case "Euro"
      Op(i, j) = exp_rt * (pu * Op(i - 1, j + 1)
      + pm * Op(i, j + 1) + pd * Op(i + 1, j + 1))
  End Select
  End If
Next i
Next j
```

The fine mesh (the "B" points) is constructed using time increments of $k/4$, so the discount factor becomes $\exp(-rk/4)$. The upper row retains the price increment h, so the probabilities (8.17) through (8.19) use v, h, and $k/4$. The array temp() contains temporary values which are transferred to the array B() of dimension $3 \times (4n + 1)$in subsequent steps.

```
exp_rt = Exp(-r * k / 4): pu = ProbUp(Alpha, v, h, k / 4)
pd = ProbDown(Alpha, v, h, k / 4): pm = 1 - pu - pd
For j = n + 1 To 2 Step -1
If EuroAmer = "Euro" Then
  temp(j - 1) = exp_rt * (pu * Op(n, j) + pm *
                Op(n + 1, j) + pd * Op(n + 2, j))
ElseIf EuroAmer = "Amer" And PutCall = "Call" Then
  temp(j - 1) = Application.Max(S(n + 1, 1) - Strike,
                exp_rt * (pu * Op(n, j) + pm * Op(n + 1, j)
              + pd * Op(n + 2, j)))
ElseIf EuroAmer = "Amer" And PutCall = "Put" Then
  temp(j - 1) = Application.Max(Strike - S(n + 1, 1),
                exp_rt * (pu * Op(n, j) + pm * Op(n + 1, j)
              + pd * Op(n + 2, j)))
End If
Next j
Dim B() As Double
ReDim B(3, 4 * n + 1) As Double
If BarType = "DO" Or BarType = "DI" Then
 B(1, 4 * n + 1) = Op(n + 1, n + 1)
ElseIf BarType = "UO" Or BarType = "UI" Then
```

```
 B(3, 4 * n + 1) = Op(n + 1, n + 1)
End If
For i = 3 To 4 * n + 1
  If i Mod 4 = 0 Then
    If BarType = "DO" Or BarType = "DI" Then
      B(1, 1) = 0
      B(1, i) = temp(i / 4)
      B(1, i - 1) = B(1, i)
      B(1, i - 2) = B(1, i)
      B(1, i - 3) = B(1, i)
    ElseIf BarType = "UO" Or BarType = "UI" Then
      B(3, 1) = 0
      B(3, i) = temp(i / 4)
      B(3, i - 1) = B(3, i)
      B(3, i - 2) = B(3, i)
      B(3, i - 3) = B(3, i)
    End If
  End If
Next i
```

The middle row uses price increments of $h/2$, so the probabilities (8.17) through (8.19) use $v, h/2$, and $k/4$.

```
pu = ProbUp(Alpha, v, h / 2, k / 4)
pd = ProbDown(Alpha, v, h / 2, k / 4)
pm = 1 - pu - pd
For j = 4 * n To 1 Step -1
If BarType = "DO" Or BarType = "DI" Then
  Asset = Exp(A(n + 1, 1) - h / 2)
ElseIf BarType = "UO" Or BarType = "UI" Then
  Asset = Exp(A(n + 1, 1) + h / 2)
End If
Select Case EuroAmer
  Case "Euro"
    B(2, j) = exp_rt * (pu * B(1, j + 1) + pm * B(2, j + 1)
            + pd * B(3, j + 1))
  Case "Amer"
    Select Case PutCall
      Case "Call"
        B(2, j) = Application.Max(Asset - Strike,
                exp_rt * (pu * B(1, j + 1) + pm *
                B(2, j + 1) + pd * B(3, j + 1)))
      Case "Put"
        B(2, j) = Application.Max(Strike - Asset,
                exp_rt * (pu * B(1, j + 1) + pm *
                B(2, j + 1) + pd * B(3, j + 1)))
    End Select
  End Select
Next j
```

Finally, option prices are obtained in accordance with Table 8.1, using the trinomial tree of Chapter 3 for plain-vanilla options. The function outputs the option price and the number of steps, n, used to construct the meshes.

```
If BarType = "DO" Or BarType = "UO" Then
  output(1, 1) = B(2, 1)
Else
Select Case EuroAmer
Case "Euro"
  If PutCall = "Call" Then
    output(1, 1) = Trinomial(Spot, Strike, T, r, v, n,
                   "Call", "Euro") - B(2, 1)
  ElseIf PutCall = "Put" Then
    output(1, 1) = Trinomial(Spot, Strike, T, r, v, n,
                   "Put", "Euro") - B(2, 1)
  End If
Case "Amer"
  If PutCall = "Call" And BarType = "DI" Then
    output(1, 1) = (Spot / Bar) ^ (1 - 2 * r / v ^ 2) *
                    Trinomial(Bar ^ 2 / Spot, Strike, T, r,
                    v, n, "Call", "Amer")
  ElseIf PutCall = "Put" And BarType = "UI" Then
    output(1, 1) = (Spot / Bar) ^ (1 - 2 * r / v ^ 2) *
                    Trinomial(Bar ^ 2 / Spot, Strike, T, r,
                    v, n, "Put", "Amer")
  ElseIf (PutCall = "Put" And BarType = "DI") Then
    MsgBox "You Cannot Price an American Down-and-In Put
           Using This Algorithm"
  ElseIf (PutCall = "Call" And BarType = "UI") Then
    MsgBox "You Cannot Price an American Up-and-In Call
           Using This Algorithm"
  End If
End Select
End If
output(2, 1) = n
  BarrierAMM = output
End Function
```

Figure 8.7 presents an example of the BarrierAMM() function, on an up-and-in European single-barrier put option monitored continuously, with spot price $S = 100$, strike price $K = 100$, barrier $H = 100.5$, and time to maturity $T = 0.5$ years, when the interest rate is $r = 0.05$, the yearly volatility is $v = 0.30$ (30 percent), and using $\lambda = 3$. In cell F8 we type

$$= \text{NewBarrier(S,H,T,V,Mon1, Mon2)},$$

which produces the same value of 100.5 for the barrier, since "C" appears in cell C17, indicating continuous monitoring. In cell F6 we type

$$= \text{BarrierAMM(S, K, H, T, RF, V, Lambda, PutCall,}$$

$$\text{EuroAmer, BarType, Mon1, Mon2)}$$

and copy the function to cell F7. This produces an option price of $6.7655 in cell F6, and indicates that $n = 1,356$ was used to construct the adaptive mesh in cell

	A	B	C	D	E	F
1						
2		**Adaptive Mesh Method for European or American Single-Barrier Option**				
3		**Using Parity Relation for European Options**				
4		**Reflection Principle for American Options**				
5						
6		Spot Price (S)	100		**Option Price**	6.7655427715
7		Strike Price (K)	100		**Number of Time Steps**	1356
8		Barrier (H)	100.5		**Adjusted Barrier**	100.5000
9		Years to Maturity (T)	0.5			
10		Interest Rate (r)	0.05			
11		Volatility (v)	0.3			
12		Lambda (λ)	3			
13		Type (Call or Put)	Put			
14		Option (Amer or Euro)	Euro			
15		Type (UO, UI, DO or DI)	UI			
16		Barrier Monitoring (# Observations)	0			
17		Barrier Monitoring (C, H, D, W, M)	C			
18		C = Continuous				
19		H = Hourly				
20		D = Daily				
21		W = Weekly				
22		M = Monthly				

FIGURE 8.7 Adaptive Mesh Method for Single Barrier Options

F7. The analytic price of this option is $6.7663 (see Haug, 1998). The price of the American option with identical parameters is $6.9770.

In the last part of this section, prices of down-and-out American single-barrier call options are obtained using different methods and are compared, using the same inputs as in Figure 8.5. This comparison is in the Excel file Chapter8BarrierComp, and appears in Figure 8.8.

With $n = 300$ steps, the Boyle and Lau (1994) method selects $n = 389$ as the optimal number of steps, and produces a price of 15.2295, comparable to that produced by the interpolation method of Derman et al. (1995) and the adaptive mesh method of Figlewski and Gao (1999). The method of Kwok and Dai (2004) produces a price that is slightly lower.

DIGITAL OPTIONS

Digital options are options with discontinuous payoffs. In this section two types of digital options are examined. Cash-or-nothing calls pay a fixed amount, Q, if the asset price is above the strike price, and pay nothing otherwise. Cash-or-nothing puts pay Q if the asset price is below the strike price, and nothing otherwise. Hence

	A	B	C	D	E	F
1						
2		**Comparison of Barrier Option Prices**				
3						
4		Spot Price (S)	120.5			
5		Strike Price (K)	100			
6		Barrier (H)	110			
7		Years to Maturity (T)	1			
8		Interest Rate (r)	0.1			
9		Dividend Yield (q)	0			
10		Volatility (σ)	0.3			
11		Number of Steps (n)	300			
12		Lambda (λ)	20			
13		Type (Call or Put)	Call			
14		Option (Amer or Euro)	Amer			
15		Type (UO, UI, DO or DI)	DI			
16		Barrier Monitoring (# Observations)	0			
17		Barrier Monitoring (C, H, D, W, M)	C			
18						
19			**Boyle and**	**Derman et al.**	**Kwok and**	**Adaptive Mesh**
20			**Lau**	**Interpolation**	**Dai**	**Method**
21						
22		**Option Price**	15.2295	15.2227	15.1839	15.2119
23		**Number of Steps**	389		389	
24		**Adjusted Barrier**	110			

FIGURE 8.8 Comparison of Prices for Barrier Options

the payoff from a cash-or-nothing option is either zero or Q. Asset-or-nothing calls and puts are identical, except that the payoff is the terminal asset price rather than Q.

Pricing European cash-or-nothing and asset-or-nothing options under risk neutrality and assuming stock price dynamics identical to those giving rise to the Black-Scholes formula, is straightforward and is explained in Hull (2006) and Haug (1998). The prices of these options under these conditions are presented Table 8.2. In this table, S_T is the asset price at maturity, $\Phi()$ is the standard normal cumulative distribution function, S is the spot price, K the strike price, T the time to maturity, r and q are the risk-free rate and the dividend yield or foreign risk-free rate, respectively, σ is the volatility, and d_1 and d_2 are the usual quantities

$$d_1 = \frac{\ln(S/K) + (r - q + \sigma^2/2)T}{\sigma\sqrt{T}}, d_2 = \frac{\ln(S/K) + (r - q - \sigma^2/2)T}{\sigma\sqrt{T}}. \qquad (8.20)$$

For American digital calls, the strike price must be above the spot price, and for American digital puts, the strike price must be below the spot price. If this condition is not met and the option price is less than the payoff Q, then an arbitrage opportunity is possible by buying the option and exercising it immediately.

TABLE 8.2 European Digital Options

Digital Option	Payoff $(S_T > K)$	Payoff $(S_T < K)$	European Option Price
Cash-or-Nothing Call	Q	0	$Qe^{-rT}\Phi(d_2)$
Cash-or-Nothing Put	0	Q	$Qe^{-rT}\Phi(-d_2)$
Asset-or-Nothing Call	S_T	0	$Se^{-qT}\Phi(d_1)$
Asset-or-Nothing Put	0	S_T	$Se^{-qT}\Phi(-d_1)$

Cash-or-Nothing Options

The Excel file Chapter8CashorNothing uses the Leisen-Reimer binomial tree to produce the price of European or American cash-or-nothing options, through the VBA function LRCash(). The first part of the function defines the parameters and constructs the tree, stored in array S(). It is identical to the LRBinomial() function of Chapter 3 and will not be presented here. The second part compares the terminal prices to the strike price, and sets the option price to zero or to the payoff, depending on which condition is met. American options are priced by using the usual method of backward recursion. To allow for the dividend yield q, in the Leisen-Reimer tree we define d_1 and d_2 as in (8.20), and we define $r_n = \exp[(r - q)T/n]$ rather than $r_n = \exp[rT/n]$.

```
Function LRCash(Spot, K, PayOff, T, r, q, v, n, PutCall As String,
              EuroAmer As String, Method)
For i = 1 To n + 1
  Select Case PutCall
  Case "Call":
    If S(i, n + 1) >= K Then
      Op(i, n + 1) = PayOff
    Else
      Op(i, n + 1) = 0
    End If
  Case "Put":
    If S(i, n + 1) >= K Then
      Op(i, n + 1) = 0
    Else
      Op(i, n + 1) = PayOff
    End If
  End Select
Next i
```

The next part of the function discounts the expected terminal option prices to time zero (for European options) and compares the option prices to the payoff (for American options), in the usual manner.

```
For j = n To 1 Step -1
For i = 1 To j
  Select Case EuroAmer
```

```
  Case "Euro":
    Op(i, j) = Exp(-r * dt) * (p * Op(i, j + 1)
              + (1 - p) * Op(i + 1, j + 1))
  Case "Amer":
    If S(i, j) >= K Then
      Select Case PutCall
      Case "Call":
        Op(i, j) = Application.Max(PayOff, Exp(-r * dt)
          * (p * Op(i, j + 1) + (1 - p) * Op(i + 1, j + 1)))
      Case "Put":
        Op(i, j) = Application.Max(0, Exp(-r * dt)
          * (p * Op(i, j + 1) + (1 - p) * Op(i + 1, j + 1)))
      End Select
    Else
      Select Case PutCall
      Case "Call":
        Op(i, j) = Application.Max(0, Exp(-r * dt)
          * (p * Op(i, j + 1) + (1 - p) * Op(i + 1, j + 1)))
      Case "Put":
        Op(i, j) = Application.Max(PayOff, Exp(-r * dt)
          * (p * Op(i, j + 1) + (1 - p) * Op(i + 1, j + 1)))
      End Select
    End If
  End Select
Next i
Next j
```

Finally, the option price is contained in Op(1,1), and for European options the analytical price from Table 8.2 is obtained also.

```
If EuroAmer = "Euro" Then
  Select Case PutCall
    Case "Call": Analytic = PayOff * Exp(-r * T)
                * Application.NormSDist(d2)
    Case "Put": Analytic = PayOff * Exp(-r * T)
                * Application.NormSDist(-d2)
  End Select
End If
output(1, 1) = Op(1, 1)
If EuroAmer = "Euro" Then output(2, 1) = Analytic
If EuroAmer = "Amer" Then output(2, 1) = "Euro Only"
  LRCash = output
End Function
```

Figure 8.9 illustrates a cash-or-nothing option with payoff of $10, maturity 6 months and strike price $K = 40$, when the spot price is $S = 30$, the yearly risk-free rate and dividend yield are $r = 0.05$ and $q = 0.01$, respectively, the yearly volatility is $\sigma = 0.30$, and with $n = 250$ steps.

To obtain the price of the cash-or-nothing option with these values, in cell C19 we type

= LRCash(S, K, PayOff, T, RF, Q, V, N, PutCall, EuroAmer, Method)

	A	B	C
1			
2		**Leisen-Reimer Binomial Tree Price for an**	
3		**American or European Cash-or-Nothing Option**	
4			
5		Spot Price (*S*)	30
6		Strike Price (*K*)	40
7		Payoff (*Q*)	10
8		Years to Maturity (*T*)	0.5000
9		Risk-Free Rate (*r*)	0.05
10		Dividend Yield (*q*)	0.01
11		Volatility (σ)	0.3
12		Steps (*n*)	250
13		Type (*Call* or *Put*)	Call
14		Option (*Amer* or *Euro*)	Euro
15		Method (*1* or *2*)	2
16		*1* = Peizer-Pratt Inversion 1	
17		*2* = Peizer-Pratt Inversion 2	
18			
19		**Option Price**	0.8355169
20		**Analytical Price**	0.8355171

FIGURE 8.9 European Cash-or-Nothing Call

which produces a price of $0.8355, identical within six decimal places to the analytical price in cell C20. The price of an American option with the same parameter values is $1.5998.

Asset-or-Nothing Options

As mentioned above, asset-or-nothing options are similar to cash-or-nothing options, except that the payoff is the terminal asset price rather than Q. To price these options, we use the same Leisen-Reimer binomial tree as we used for the cash-or-nothing options, except that whenever the payoff Q is encountered in the function, it is replaced by the current asset price $S(i,j)$. The Excel file Chapter8AssetorNothing produces the prices of European and American asset-or-nothing options, through the VBA function LRAsset(). Figure 8.10 illustrates the function on a European asset-or-nothing call with the same parameters as the cash-or-nothing call presented in Figure 8.9 above.

To obtain the price of the option with these parameter values, in cell C18 we type

= LRAsset(S, K, T, RF, Q, V, N, PutCall, EuroAmer, Method)

and copy down to cell C19, which produces a price of 3.6979. As can be seen from the figure, the option price in cell C18 obtained from the Leisen-Reimer tree is very

	A	B	C
1			
2		**Leisen-Reimer Binomial Tree Price for an**	
3		**American or European Asset-or-Nothing Option**	
4			
5		Spot Price (*S*)	30
6		Strike Price (*K*)	40
7		Years to Maturity (*T*)	0.5000
8		Risk-Free Rate (*r*)	0.05
9		Dividend Yield (*q*)	0.01
10		Volatility (σ)	0.3
11		Steps (*n*)	250
12		Type (*Call* or *Put*)	Call
13		Option (*Amer* or *Euro*)	Euro
14		Method (*1* or *2*)	2
15		1 = Peizer-Pratt Inversion 1	
16		2 = Peizer-Pratt Inversion 2	
17			
18		**Option Price**	3.6979152
19		**Analytical Price**	3.6979142

FIGURE 8.10 European Asset-or-Nothing Call

close to the analytical price in cell C19. The price of an American asset-or-nothing call is $6.4400 when the same parameter values are used.

ASIAN OPTIONS

Asian options are options for which the payoff depends on the average price of the asset during the life of the option. The average asset price can be the arithmetic average $\bar{S} = \sum_{i=1}^{n} S_i / n$ or the geometric average $\tilde{S} = (\prod_{i=1}^{n} S_i)^{1/n}$. In this section we use the method of Hull and White (1993) for path-dependent derivatives to obtain the price of Asian options where the payoff depends on the arithmetic average $\bar{S}$. The payoffs we consider are those of the form $\max(\bar{S} - K, 0)$ for an Asian call, and $\max(K - \bar{S}, 0)$ for an Asian put.

Hull and White (1993) describe a general procedure for valuing path-dependent derivatives, namely derivatives whose payoffs depend not only on the current or final asset price, but also on the price path of the asset during the life of the option. Asian options and lookback options are examples of such derivatives. To price these derivatives using a tree-based method, at each node all possible price paths must be must be evaluated along with the path function, $F(t)$, which can be cumbersome and computationally extensive. The procedure proposed by Hull and White (1993) requires that only representative values of $F(t)$ need be evaluated at each node, such as the minimum and maximum values of $F(t)$, $F_{min}(t)$ and $F_{max}(t)$. The price of the derivative is evaluated at the representative values, and the prices for other values of $F(t)$ are obtained by interpolation. Increasing the time steps and the number of interpolation points increases the accuracy of the approximation. For this method to work, the function payoff must depend on a single path function, and it must be possible to obtain the value of $F(t+dt)$ using only $F(t)$ and the asset price at time t. For further explanation of this procedure, and a thorough example that includes a detailed diagram, see Hull (2006).

The Excel file Chapter8Asian contains the VBA function Asian() for implementing this procedure. This function relies heavily on three-dimensional arrays in VBA. The first part of the function defines the CRR binomial tree parameters and constructs the CRR tree, the values of which are stored in the array S(). The second part of the function defines $F_{min}(t)$ and $F_{max}(t)$, which are the minimum and maximum average stock price values, and are stored in the arrays $F(i,j,1)$ and $F(i,j,\text{NumAvg})$, respectively. NumAvg is a parameter specified by the user for the number of interpolated points between $F_{min}(t)$ and $F_{max}(t)$. Interpolated values of the path function are stored in the arrays $F(i,j,k)$, where $1 < k < \text{NumAvg}$. The value of the path function at time zero, $F(0)$, is set to the spot price.

```
Function Asian(Spot, Strike, T, r, v, n, NumAvg, PutCall As String,
               EuroAmer As String)
Dim F() As Double
ReDim F(n + 1, n + 1, NumAvg) As Double
For j = 2 To n + 1
  For i = 1 To j
    M1 = 0: M2 = 0
    M3 = 0: M4 = 0
    For k = 1 To j - i + 1
      M1 = M1 + S(i, j - k + 1)
    Next k
    For k = 1 To i - 1
      M2 = M2 + S(i - k, i - k)
    Next k
    F(i, j, 1) = (M1 + M2) / j
    For k = 1 To i
      M3 = M3 + S(i - k + 1, j - k + 1)
    Next k
    For k = 1 To j - i
      M4 = M4 + S(1, j - i - k + 1)
    Next k
    F(i, j, NumAvg) = (M3 + M4) / j
    For k = 2 To NumAvg - 1
      F(i, j, k) = F(i, j, 1) + (k - 1) *
          (F(i, j, NumAvg) - F(i, j, 1)) / (NumAvg - 1)
    Next k
  Next i
Next j
For k = 1 To NumAvg
```

```
      F(1, 1, k) = S(1, 1)
Next k
```

The next part of the function works backward through each path function sub-array and creates new values of the path function when the asset price moves up and down, and stores these in the arrays NewFU() and NewFD(), respectively. The values in NewFU(), NewFD(), and F() are then rounded off to the nearest thousandths.

```
For k = 1 To NumAvg
  For j = n To 1 Step -1
    For i = 1 To j
      NewFU(i, j, k) = (j * F(i, j, k) + S(i, j + 1)) / (j + 1)
      NewFU(i, j, k) = Application.Round(NewFU(i, j, k), 4)
      NewFD(i, j, k) = (j * F(i, j, k) + S(i + 1, j + 1)) / (j + 1)
      NewFD(i, j, k) = Application.Round(NewFD(i, j, k), 4)
    Next i
  Next j
Next k
For j = 1 To n + 1
  For i = 1 To j
    For k = 1 To NumAvg
      F(i, j, k) = Application.Round(F(i, j, k), 4)
    Next k
  Next i
Next j
```

Next, the terminal prices of the options are obtained and stored in the array Op().

```
Dim Op() As Variant
ReDim Op(n + 1, n + 1, NumAvg) As Variant
For k = 1 To NumAvg
  For i = 1 To n + 1
    Select Case PutCall
    Case "Call": Op(i, n + 1, k) = Application.Max(0,
              F(i, n + 1, k) - Strike)
    Case "Put": Op(i, n + 1, k) = Application.Max(0,
              Strike - F(i, n + 1, k))
    End Select
  Next i
Next k
```

Finally, the option prices are interpolated using the arrays F(), NewFU(), and NewFD(). Following interpolation, prices for European and American options are obtained by the usual method of backward recursion, and the final price is stored in Op(1,1).

```
For j = n To 1 Step -1
For i = 1 To j
  For k = 1 To NumAvg
    For m = 1 To NumAvg - 1
```

```
            If (F(i, j + 1, m) <= NewFU(i, j, k))
            And (NewFU(i, j, k) <= F(i, j + 1, m + 1)) Then
               X0 = F(i, j + 1, m)
               Y0 = Op(i, j + 1, m)
               X1 = F(i, j + 1, m + 1)
               Y1 = Op(i, j + 1, m + 1)
               X = NewFU(i, j, k)
               UU = Op(i, j + 1, m)
               If X1 <> X0 Then
                  UU = ((X - X0) * Y1 + (X1 - X) * Y0) / (X1 - X0)
               End If
            End If
          Next m
          For m = 1 To NumAvg - 1
            If (F(i + 1, j + 1, m) <= NewFD(i, j, k))
            And (NewFD(i, j, k) <= F(i + 1, j + 1, m + 1)) Then
               X0 = F(i + 1, j + 1, m)
               Y0 = Op(i + 1, j + 1, m)
               X1 = F(i + 1, j + 1, m + 1)
               Y1 = Op(i + 1, j + 1, m + 1)
               X = NewFD(i, j, k)
               DD = Op(i + 1, j + 1, m)
               If X1 <> X0 Then
                  DD = ((X - X0) * Y1 + (X1 - X) * Y0) / (X1 - X0)
               End If
            End If
          Next m
        If k = 1 Then UU = Op(i, j + 1, 1)
        If k = NumAvg Then DD = Op(i + 1, j + 1, NumAvg)
        Select Case EuroAmer
        Case "Euro":
          Op(i, j, k) = exp_rT * (p * UU + (1 - p) * DD)
        Case "Amer":
        If PutCall = "Call" Then
          Op(i, j, k) = Application.Max(F(i, j, k) - Strike,
                        exp_rT * (p * UU + (1 - p) * DD))
        End If
        If PutCall = "Put" Then
          Op(i, j, k) = Application.Max(Strike - F(i, j, k),
                        exp_rT * (p * UU + (1 - p) * DD))
        End If
        End Select
       Next k
     Next i
   Next j
     Asian = Op(1, 1, 1)
   End Function
```

Figure 8.11 illustrates the VBA function Asian(), on an Asian call option of the American type with time to maturity $T = 1$ year and strike price $K = 50$, on a non-dividend-paying stock with spot price $S = 50$, when the risk free rate is $r = 0.10$, the volatility is $\sigma = 0.40$, with $n = 20$ and NumAvg $= 4$ interpolations between $F_{\min}(t)$

	A	B	C	D
1				
2		**Binomial Tree for Average Price Asian Options**		
3		**of the European and American Type**		
4				
5		Spot Price (S)	50	
6		Strike Price (K)	50	
7		Years to Maturity (T)	1	
8		Interest Rate (r)	0.1	
9		Volatility (σ)	0.4	
10		Steps (n)	20	
11		Number of Averages (NumAvg)	4	
12		Type (Call or Put)	Call	
13		Option (Amer or Euro)	Amer	
14				
15		**Option Price**	7.76925	

FIGURE 8.11 Asian Call Option of the American Type

and $F_{max}(t)$. This is the same example that is described in Chapters 22 and 24 of Hull (2006). In cell C15 we type

$$= Asian(S, K, T, RF, V, N, NumAvg, PutCall, EuroAmer)$$

which produces a price of \$7.77. Increasing the steps to $n = 60$ and the number of averages to NumAvg = 100 produces a price of \$6.17. The price of a European option with these latter values is \$5.58.

FLOATING-STRIKE LOOKBACK OPTIONS

Lookback options are another type of path-dependent option. The payoff of these options depends on the maximum stock price, S_{max} or minimum stock price, S_{min} of the asset during the life of the option. The payoffs from a floating strike lookback call and put are given by $\max(S_T - S_{min}, 0)$ and $\max(S_{max} - S_T, 0)$, respectively, where S_T is the terminal asset price. Cheuk and Vorst (1997) describe a simple method to price floating-strike lookback options. At any time, the call price can be expressed as the product of the asset price and a function V, and the put price as the product of the asset price and a function X. Binomial trees are constructed for V (their Figure 2) and for X (their Figure 3), and the option price in terms of X and V is obtained by backward recursion through the trees.

For floating-strike lookback calls, the tree has elements $V(i,j) = 1 - d^{j-i}$ and for puts the tree has elements $X(i,j) = u^{j-i} - 1$. For a tree with n steps the terminal option prices are set as $V(i, n+1)$ and $X(i, n+1)$. When $i \neq j$ the price at the $(i,j)^{th}$

node of an American call f_{ij} is given by

$$f_{ij} = \max\{V(i,j), \exp(-r \times dt)(pf_{i,j+1}u + (1 - p)f_{i+2,j+1}\,d)\}. \qquad (8.21)$$

If f_{ij} denotes the price of a European call, then the maximum comparison with $V(i,j)$ is not made, and the price is

$$f_{ij} = (pf_{i,j+1}u + (1 - p)f_{i+2,j+1}\,d). \qquad (8.22)$$

If f_{ij} denotes the price of an American put, then

$$f_{ij} = \max\{X(i,j), \exp(-r \times dt)((1 - p)f_{i,j+1}\,d + pf_{i+2,j+1}u)\}. \qquad (8.23)$$

When $i = j$ these expressions become

$$f_{ij} = \max\{V(i,j), \exp(-r \times dt)(pf_{i,j+1}u + (1 - p)f_{i+1,j+1}\,d)\}, \qquad (8.24)$$

and

$$f_{ij} = \max\{X(i,j), \exp(-r \times dt)((1 - p)f_{i,j+1}\,d + pf_{i+1,j+1}u)\} \qquad (8.25)$$

for American calls and puts, respectively. The European counterparts are obtained analogously to (8.22), by ignoring the maximum comparison with $V(i,j)$ and $X(i,j)$. For European and American calls and puts the option price is obtained by multiplying $f_{1,1}$ by the spot price. A description of this method is also available as Technical Note 13 on John Hull's Web site. This procedure is very similar to the one proposed by Babbs (2000).

The Excel file Chapter8LookbackFloat contains the VBA function LBFloat() for implementing this method. The first part of the function defines the CRR tree parameters, constructs the trees for V and X and creates the terminal option prices.

```
Function LBFloat(Spot, T, r, q, sigma, n, CallPut As String, EuroAmer As
            String)
dt = T / n: u = Exp(sigma * Sqr(dt))
d = 1 / u: p = (Exp((r - q) * dt) - d) / (u - d)
exp_rT = Exp(-r * dt)
Dim X(), V(), Op() As Double
ReDim V(n + 1, n + 1), X(n + 1, n + 1), Op(n + 1, n + 1) As Double
For i = 1 To n + 1
  For j = i To n + 1
    X(i, j) = u ^ (j - i) - 1
    V(i, j) = 1 - d ^ (j - i)
  If j = n + 1 Then
    Select Case CallPut
      Case "Call": Op(i, j) = V(i, j)
      Case "Put": Op(i, j) = X(i, j)
    End Select
  End If
```

```
    Next j
Next i
```

The next part computes the option prices through backward recursion, using equations (8.21) through (8.25).

```
For j = n To 1 Step -1
For i = 1 To j
If i <> j Then
  Select Case EuroAmer
  Case "Euro":
    If CallPut = "Put" Then
      Op(i, j) = exp_rT * ((1 - p) * Op(i, j + 1) * d
                 + p * Op(i + 2, j + 1) * u)
    ElseIf CallPut = "Call" Then
      Op(i, j) = exp_rT * (p * Op(i, j + 1) * u + (1 - p) *
                 Op(i + 2, j + 1) * d)
    End If
  Case "Amer":
    If CallPut = "Put" Then
      Op(i, j) = Application.Max(X(i, j), exp_rT * ((1 - p)
            * Op(i, j + 1) * d + p * Op(i + 2, j + 1) * u))
    ElseIf CallPut = "Call" Then
      Op(i, j) = Application.Max(V(i, j), exp_rT
            * (p * Op(i, j + 1) * u + (1 - p)
            * Op(i + 2, j + 1) * d))
    End If
  End Select
Else
  Select Case EuroAmer
  Case "Euro":
    If CallPut = "Put" Then
      Op(i, j) = exp_rT * ((1 - p) * Op(i, j + 1) * d
                 + p * Op(i + 1, j + 1) * u)
    ElseIf CallPut = "Call" Then
      Op(i, j) = exp_rT * (p * Op(i, j + 1) * u
                 + (1 - p) * Op(i + 1, j + 1) * d)
    End If
  Case "Amer":
    If CallPut = "Put" Then
      Op(i, j) = Application.Max(X(i, j), exp_rT * ((1 - p)
            * Op(i, j + 1) * d + p * Op(i + 1, j + 1) * u))
    ElseIf CallPut = "Call" Then
      Op(i, j) = Application.Max(V(i, j), exp_rT
                 * (p * Op(i, j + 1) * u + (1 - p)
                 * Op(i + 1, j + 1) * d))
    End If
  End Select
End If
Next i
Next j
  LBFloat = Spot * Op(1, 1)
End Function
```

	A	B	C	D
1				
2		**Binomial Tree for European or American**		
3		**Floating Strike Lookback Option**		
4				
5		Spot Price (S)	100	
6		Years to Maturity (T)	0.5	
7		Risk-Free Rate (r)	0.04	
8		Foreign Risk-Free Rate (q)	0.07	
9		Volatility (σ)	0.2	
10		Steps (n)	50	
11		Type (Call or Put)	Call	
12		Option (Amer or Euro)	Euro	
13				
14		**Option Price**	8.96930	

FIGURE 8.12   Floating-Strike Lookback Call

Figure 8.12 illustrates this function on a floating strike lookback call with maturity $T = 0.5$ years, when the spot price is $n = 1,000$, the risk free rate is $r = 0.04$ and the dividend yield is $q = 0.07$, using $n = 50$ steps. In cell C14 we type

$$= \text{LBFloat}(S, T, RF, Q, V, N, \text{PutCall}, \text{EuroAmer})$$

which produces a price of \$8.97. With $n = 100, n = 500$, and $n = 1,000$ the prices are \$9.20, \$9.52, and \$9.60, respectively. These are the same prices that appear in Table 1 of Cheuk and Vorst (1997).

SUMMARY

Barrier options are very popular among investors, but using tree-based methods to price these types of exotic options can be problematic because the barrier almost never lies on any of the price nodes. Boyle and Lau (1994) provide a very simple solution to this problem, by selecting the number of steps in a binomial tree so that asset prices lie as close as possible to the barrier. In the method due to Tian (1999) the first stage of the tree is tilted to ensure that the asset price nodes lie on the barrier in the second stage. The interpolation method of Derman et al. (1995) and the adaptive mesh method of Figlewski and Gao (1999) are more complicated but also produce good results. Obtaining the price of down-and-out and up-and-out options with tree-based methods is relatively simple. Down-and-in and up-and-in European barrier options can then be priced using the parity relationship (8.1). American barrier options can be priced using the reflection principle and the method of Kwok and Dai (2004). Adjustments to the barrier for discrete monitoring can be done using the method of Broadie, Glasserman, and Kou (1997, 1999).

In this chapter, it is shown also that digital cash-or-nothing and asset-or-nothing options can be priced very effectively using Leisen and Reimer (1996) binomial trees. Asian options can be priced using the method of Hull and White (1993), but unfortunately this method requires many interpolations and can be quite computer intensive. Finally, prices of floating-strike lookback options are obtained using a procedure described by Cheuk and Vorst (1997).

EXERCISES

This section provides exercises that deal with exotic options. Solutions are contained in the Excel file Chapter8Exercises.

8.1 Capped options are similar to plain-vanilla options, except that the payoff is subject to a limit. Boyle and Lau (1994) show that binomial trees can be used to price capped options effectively when the optimal number of steps is chosen by (8.8), where now H represents the payoff limit. For $H > K$, the payoff of a capped call is $H - K$ when $S_T > H$, it is $S_T - K$ when $K < S_T < H$, and it is zero when $S_T < K$, where K is the strike price and S_T is the terminal price of the asset. Write a VBA program for the price of European and American capped calls, using the optimal number of steps suggested by Boyle and Lau (1994).

8.2 A fixed-strike lookback call has payoff given by $\max(0, S_{\max} - K)$, and a fixed-strike lookback put a payoff $\max(0, K - S_{\min})$. By redefining $X(i,j) = u^{j-i}$ and $V(i,j) = d^{j-i}$, using X for calls and V for puts, modify the LRFloat() function to price the European versions of these options.

8.3 A shout floor is a shout option for which the holder of the option can "shout" to the issuer to impose a lower limit on the return. The limit is taken to be the asset price at the time the time of shouting. Dai, Kwok, and Wu (2004) present a model in which the price of a shout floor is

$$R(S, T) = SP(T) \tag{8.26}$$

when $r \leqslant q$, and

$$R(S, T) = \begin{cases} SP(T) & \text{for } T \in (0, T^*] \text{ and } S > 0 \\ e^{-q(T-T^*)}SP(T^*) & \text{for } T \in (0, T^*] \text{ and } S > 0 \end{cases} \tag{8.27}$$

when $r > q$, where T^* is the unique positive root of the derivative $d[e^{-qT}P(T)]/dT$ and where r and q are the risk free rate and the dividend yield, respectively. The price function $P(T)$ is given by

$$P(T) = e^{-rT}\Phi(-d_2) - e^{-qT}\Phi(-d_1), \tag{8.28}$$

where $\Phi(x)$ is the cumulative distribution function of the standard normal variable, where

$$d_1 = \frac{r - q + \sigma^2/2}{\sigma/\sqrt{T}}, \qquad (8.29)$$

and $d_2 = d_1 - \sigma\sqrt{T}$. Write a VBA function to implement this model.

SOLUTIONS TO EXERCISES

8.1 The VBA function CappedCall() to implement the price of a capped call resembles the code for a barrier option, except with additional conditions on the payoff. The first part of the function is identical to the BarrierBin() function described in this chapter. The second part specifies the terminal option prices.

```
Function CallCap(Spot, K, H, T, r, v, old_n, EuroAmer As String)
For i = 1 To n + 1
  AssetPrice = Spot * u ^ (n + 1 - i) * d ^ (i - 1)
    If AssetPrice >= H Then
      Op(i, n + 1) = H - K
    ElseIf (K <= AssetPrice And AssetPrice < H) Then
      Op(i, n + 1) = AssetPrice - K
    Else
      Op(i, n + 1) = 0
    End If
Next i
```

	A	B	C	D	E
1	EXERCISE 8.1				
2		Binomial Tree for European and American Capped Call Options			
3		With Optimal Number of Steps from Boyle and Lau (1994)			
4					
5		Spot Price (S)	25		
6		Strike Price (K)	25		
7		Cap Limit (H)	40		
8		Years to Maturity (T)	4		
9		Interest Rate (r)	0.076961		
10		Volatility (σ)	0.4		
11		Steps (n)	60		
12		Exercise Type (Euro or Amer)	Amer		
13					
14					
15		Option Price	7.6150		
16		Number of Steps	72		

FIGURE 8.13 Solution to Exercise 8.1

The remaining part of the function calculates the price of European capped calls by backward recursion through the tree, and with the additional comparisons on the payoff conditions for American calls. Figure 8.13 illustrates the function on an American capped call with time to maturity 4 years, spot price $S = 25$, strike $K = 25$, limit $H = 40$ and risk free rate $r = \log(1.08)$ when the volatility is $\sigma = 0.40$. These are the same values as those used in Exhibit 4 of Boyle and Lau (1994). The price of the capped call option is \$7.6150, using $n = 72$ steps. When $S = 30$ and with $n = 69$ time steps, the price increases to \$10.1125. These are the same values that appear in Boyle and Lau (1994).

8.2 The VBA function LBFixed() is identical to LBFloat() function described in this chapter, except that the tree for calls is built for X and the tree for puts is built for V.

```
Function LBFixed(S, K, T, r, q, sigma, n, CallPut As String)
For i = 1 To n + 1
  For j = i To n + 1
    X(i, j) = u ^ (j - i)
    V(i, j) = d ^ (j - i)
    If j = n + 1 Then
    Select Case CallPut
      Case "Put": Op(i, j) = V(i, j)
      Case "Call": Op(i, j) = X(i, j)
    End Select
    End If
  Next j
Next i
```

The last part of the function creates the payoff, which uses the strike price discounted to time zero.

	A	B	C	D
1	EXERCISE 8.2			
2		Binomial Tree for European Fixed-Strike Lookback Options		
3		From Cheuk and Vorst (1997)		
4				
5		Spot Price (S)	100	
6		Strike Price (K)	100	
7		Years to Maturity (T)	0.5	
8		Risk-Free Rate (r)	0.04	
9		Foreign Risk-Free Rate (q)	0.07	
10		Volatility (σ)	0.2	
11		Steps (n)	50	
12		Type (Call or Put)	Call	
13				
14		Option Price	9.7404	

FIGURE 8.14 Solution to Exercise 8.2

```
Select Case CallPut
 Case "Call"
 LBFixed = Application.Max(0, S * Op(1, 1) - K * Exp(-r * T))
 Case "Put"
 LBFixed = Application.Max(0, K * Exp(-r * T) - S * Op(1, 1))
 End Select
End Function
```

Figure 8.14 illustrates this function on a European fixed-strike lookback call with strike $K = 100$ and $n = 100$ steps. The function produces a price of \$10.0273 in cell C14. With $n = 500$ steps, the price is \$10.4268. These prices are identical to those in Exhibit 5 of Choi and Jameson (2003).

8.3 When $r \leqslant q$ it is straightforward to obtain the price function $P(T)$, which we store as BigP in the ShoutFloor() VBA function.

```
Function BigP(r, q, T, v)
   d1 = (r - q + 0.5 * v ^ 2) * Sqr(T) / v
   d2 = d1 - v * Sqr(T)
   BigP = Exp(-r * T) * Gauss(-d2) - Exp(-q * T) * Gauss(-d1)
End Function

Function ShoutFloor(S, r, q, T, v, a, b) As Variant
Dim Tstar As Variant
If r <= q Then
   Price = S * BigP(r, q, T, v)
   Tstar = "N / A"
Else
   Tstar = BisMet(a, b, r, q, v)
   If (0 < T) And (T <= Tstar) Then
     Price = S * BigP(r, q, T, v)
   ElseIf T >= Tstar Then
     Price = Exp(-q * (T - Tstar)) * S * BigP(r, q, Tstar, v)
   End If
End If
Dim output() As Variant
ReDim output(2, 1) As Variant
 output(1, 1) = Price
 output(2, 1) = Tstar
 ShoutFloor = output
End Function
```

To find the root T^* we need a root-finding method, such as the bisection method. We modify this method to accept the parameters of the pricing function. Note that the derivative of the pricing function is

$$\frac{dP(T)}{dT} = -e^{-rT}[r\Phi(-d_2) + \phi(-d_2)d_2']$$
$$+ e^{-qT}[q\Phi(-d_1) - \phi(-d_1)d_1'] \tag{8.30}$$

where $d_1' = d_1/(2T)$ and $d_2' = d_1' - \sigma/(2\sqrt{T})$.

```
Function BisMet(a, b, r, q, v)
EPS = 0.000001
MaxIter = 500
  cnt = 0
  If (Theta(r, q, a, v) * Theta(r, q, b, v) > 0) Then
    MsgBox "Choose Other Bisection Parameters"
  Else
    Do While ((Abs(Theta(r, q, a, v) - Theta(r, q, b, v)) >
    EPS) And (cnt < MaxIter))
      midPt = (b + a) / 2
      If Theta(r, q, midPt, v) < 0 Then
        b = midPt
      Else
        a = midPt
      End If
    cnt = cnt + 1
    Loop
  BisMet = (b + a) / 2
End If
End Function

Function Theta(r, q, T, v)
  d1 = (r - q + 0.5 * v ^ 2) * Sqr(T) / v
  d2 = d1 - v * Sqr(T)
  dp1 = d1 / 2 / T
  dp2 = dp1 - v / 2 / Sqr(T)
  BigP2 = Exp(-r * T) * Gauss(-d2) - Exp(-q * T) * Gauss(-d1)
  dBigP = Exp(-r * T) * (-r * Gauss(-d2) - f(-d2) * dp2)
        + Exp(-q * T) * (q * Gauss(-d1) + f(-d1) * dp1)
  Theta = Exp(q * T) * (q * BigP2 + dBigP)
End Function
```

	A	B	C
1	EXERCISE 8.3		
2		**Shout Floor Option (Dai, Kwok, Wu, 2004)**	
3			
4		Spot Price (*S*)	100
5		Strike Price (*K*)	100
6		Risk Free Rate (*r*)	0.06
7		Dividend Yield (*q*)	0.12
8		Years to Maturity (*T*)	5.00
9		Volatility (σ)	0.2
10			
11		**Shout Floor Option**	23.4209
12		**Critical Time (*T**)**	N / A
13		**ATM Put (Black-Scholes)**	23.4209
14			
15		**Bisection Parameters**	
16		*a* =	0.0001
17		*b* =	999.0000

FIGURE 8.15 Solution to Exercise 8.3

When $r \leqslant q$ the ShoutFloor() function calculates the price as the product of the pricing function (8.28) and the spot price. When $r > q$ then function finds the root of the derivative (8.30) using the bisection method via the VBA function BisMet().

```
Function ShoutFloor(S, r, q, T, v, a, b) As Variant
Dim Tstar As Variant
If r <= q Then
  Price = S * BigP(r, q, T, v)
  Tstar = "N / A"
Else
  Tstar = BisMet(a, b, r, q, v)
  If (0 < T) And (T <= Tstar) Then
    Price = S * BigP(r, q, T, v)
  ElseIf T >= Tstar Then
    Price = Exp(-q * (T - Tstar)) * S * BigP(r, q, Tstar, v)
  End If
End If
Dim output() As Variant
ReDim output(2, 1) As Variant
 output(1, 1) = Price
 output(2, 1) = Tstar
ShoutFloor = output
End Function
```

Figure 8.15 illustrates these functions when $S = 100$, $K = 100$, $T = 5$ years, $\sigma = 0.20$, $r = 0.06$, and $q = 0.12$. The price appears in cell C11 as \$23.4209. When $q = 0.03$ the bisection method uses the starting values in cells C16 and C17 to find the root $T^* = 8.91$, which appears in cell C12. This produces a price of \$8.9487. Note that when $T < T^*$ the price of the shout floor is equal to the price of an at-the-money put option. The Black-Scholes put price appears in cell C13. These numbers are all identical to those in Table 5.1 of Dai, Kwok, and Wu (2004).

CHAPTER 9

Parameter Estimation

INTRODUCTION

Up to this point, option prices have been calculated using parameter values that are given. In this chapter, methods that deal with the estimation of model parameters are introduced. For some models, such as the Black-Scholes or the Gram-Charlier model, parameter estimates can be obtained directly from a time series of historical returns, by taking sample moment estimates. This is also true for the Heston and Nandi (2000) model, for which parameter estimates can be obtained by maximum likelihood. Sample moment estimators and maximum likelihood estimators can be thought of as being consistent with returns, since both methods provide parameter estimates that match historical returns as closely as possible. For the Heston (1993) model, we obtain parameter estimates by minimizing the error between model prices and market prices. Three forms of error loss functions are used. This method is consistent with option prices, since it provides parameter estimates that, when used as inputs to option pricing models, provide model prices that match market prices as closely as possible. In this chapter we briefly discuss methods that are consistent with both returns and option prices, but we do not implement any of the models, since these are too complicated to implement in VBA.

Recall that option prices are obtained under the risk-neutral distribution. In the Black-Scholes model the parameters of both the risk neutral and physical distribution can be estimated from the stock return distribution. For stochastic volatility models such as those by Heston (1993) and Heston and Nandi (2000), however, it is not possible to estimate risk-neutral parameters using only the stock price distribution. As explained by Chernov and Ghysels (2000), one way to circumvent this problem is to use option prices instead of stock prices in the estimation. The loss function approach to parameter estimation presented in this chapter is one approach that uses option prices.

UNCONDITIONAL MOMENTS

The simplest models are those that use estimators of moments based on a time-series of historical returns. This produces estimates that are consistent with returns, but not necessarily with market option prices. This approach was already encountered in Chapter 6, where it was noted that a simple estimator of the volatility of the underlying asset is the unconditional volatility s, the unbiased sample standard deviation of n historical returns $r_1, r_2, \ldots, r_n$

$$s = \sqrt{\frac{1}{(n-1)} \sum_{t=1}^{n} (r_t - \bar{r})^2},$$ (9.1)

where $\bar{r} = \frac{1}{n} \sum_{t=1}^{n} r_t$ is the sample mean of the observed returns and where the return at time t is the logarithmic return defined as $r_t = \ln(S_t/S_{t-1})$. This approach is well-suited for the Black-Scholes model, since under the physical and risk-neutral probability measures, the variance parameter is the same.

In this section estimators of the unconditional moments of the random variable $R_t = \ln(S_t/S_{t-1})$ are produced. We focus on the first four moments of R_t, namely the variance, skewness and kurtosis. Working with central moments instead of raw moments simplifies the expressions for the variance, skewness, and kurtosis. The jth central moment ($j \geq 2$) is defined as $\mu_j = E[(R_t - \mu)^j]$, where $\mu = E[R_t]$ is the mean of R_t. Hence, the variance of R_t is simply the second central moment, so that $\sigma^2 = \text{Var}[R_t] = \mu_2$. The skewness of R_t is the third standardized central moment $\gamma_1 = E[(\frac{R_t-\mu}{\sigma})^3]$, which can be written $\gamma_1 = \mu_3/\mu_2^{3/2}$, and the kurtosis is the fourth standardized moment $\beta = E[(\frac{R_t-\mu}{\sigma})^4]$, or $\beta = \mu_4/\mu_2^2$. The excess kurtosis is defined as the kurtosis in excess of that for the normal distribution. Since the normal distribution has a kurtosis of 3, the excess kurtosis of R_t, denoted γ_2, is defined as $\gamma_2 = \mu_4/\mu_2^2 - 3$.

To obtain estimators of variance, skewness, and kurtosis based on a sample of returns $r_1, r_2, \ldots, r_T$, it is very convenient to obtain the k-statistics of the sample and express the estimators in terms of the k-statistics. The k-statistics can be expressed in terms of power sums. The qth power sum is defined as $S_q = \sum_{t=1}^{T} r_t^q$, where q is an integer such that $q \geq 1$. To estimate the variance, skewness, and kurtosis, the first four k-statistics are needed. These are defined in terms of power sums as

$$k_1 = \frac{S_1}{n}, k_2 = \frac{nS_2 - S_1^2}{n(n-1)}, k_3 = \frac{n^2S_3 - 3\,nS_2S_1 + 2S_1^3}{n(n-1)(n-2)},$$
$$k_4 = \frac{(n^3 + n^2)S_4 - 4(n^2 + n)S_3S_1 - 3(n^2 - n)S_2^2 + 12\,nS_2S_1^2 - 6S_1^4}{n(n-1)(n-2)(n-3)}.$$ (9.2)

With these four k-statistics, sample estimators for the mean, variance, skewness and kurtosis can be readily computed. The sample estimators for the mean and variance are given as $\hat{\mu} = k_1$ and $\hat{\sigma}^2 = k_2$, respectively, and for the skewness and excess kurtosis as, respectively,

$$\hat{\gamma}_1 = \frac{k_3}{k_2^{3/2}}, \quad \hat{\gamma}_2 = \frac{k_4}{k_2^2}.$$ (9.3)

For a thorough treatment of cumulants, *k*-statistics, and moments, see Kendall and Stuart (1977).

The Excel file Chapter9Moments contains the VBA functions Skewness() and Kurtosis() to implement these moments with the *k*-statistics. These produce exactly the same values as the built-in Excel functions Skew and Kurt. The Skewness() function, for example, is

```
Function Skewness(data)
n = Application.Count(data)
S1 = 0: S2 = 0: S3 = 0
For i = 1 To n
  S1 = S1 + data(i)
  S2 = S2 + data(i) ^ 2
  S3 = S3 + data(i) ^ 3
Next i
K1 = S1 / n
K2 = (n * S2 - S1 ^ 2) / n / (n - 1)
K3 = (2 * S1 ^ 3 - 3 * n * S1 * S2 + n ^ 2 * S3) / n
    / (n - 1) / (n - 2)
Skewness = K3 / K2 ^ (3 / 2)
End Function
```

To illustrate how these functions might be implemented in practice, consider the Gram-Charlier model of Chapter 4. The Excel file Chapter9GramCharlier contains closing daily prices on IBM stock (ticker IBM), from November 1, 2005, to December 30, 2005, obtained from Yahoo! (finance.yahoo.com). This file is illustrated in Figure 9.1, on an option with time to maturity of 30 days and strike price of $K = 100$, when the annual risk-free rate is 5 percent and the spot price is $S = 82.20$.

Daily returns are being used, contained in cells G5:G45, so the period is daily. To obtain the one-period volatility, skewness, and kurtosis, in cells C12, C13 and C14 we type "=stdev(G5:G45)", "=skewness(G5:G45)", and "=kurtosis(G5:G45)", respectively. In cell C8 we type "=C7/252" to obtain a daily risk-free rate of 0.01984 percent. To obtain the Gram-Charlier call price, in cell C19 we type

$$= \text{GC\_Call(C5,C6,C8,C10,C11,C12,C13,C14)}$$

which produces a price of $3.2254. To compare this price with the Black-Scholes price, the time to maturity and volatility must each be annualized. A time to maturity of 30 days is used in cell C11, so in cell C16 we type "=C11/252" which corresponds to 0.119 years. In cell C17 we type "=C12*SQRT(252)" which produces an annual volatility of 13.86 percent. Finally, to obtain the Black-Scholes price, in cell C20 we type

$$= \text{BS\_Call(C5,C6,C7,C16,C17)}$$

which produces a price of $3.2328, slightly higher than the Gram-Charlier price. This is not surprising in light of the results presented in Chapter 4. Recall from

	A	B	C	D	E	F	G
1							
2		**Estimated Skewness and Kurtosis for Gram-Charlier Model**			**IBM Stock Price**		
3		**Period = Daily**			Date	Close	Return
4					30-Dec-05	82.20	
5		Underlying Price (S)	82.20		29-Dec-05	82.40	0.0024
6		Strike Price (K)	80.00		28-Dec-05	83.04	0.0078
7		Risk Free Rate Per Year (r)	0.05		27-Dec-05	82.99	-0.0006
8		Risk Free Rate Per Period (r)	0.0001984		23-Dec-05	83.48	0.0059
9		Foreign Rate or Dividend Yield Per Year (q)	0		22-Dec-05	83.22	-0.0031
10		Foreign Rate or Div Yield Per Period (q)	0		21-Dec-05	83.12	-0.0012
11		Periods Until Maturity (n)	30		20-Dec-05	82.48	-0.0077
12		One-Period Volatility (σ)	0.008716		19-Dec-05	82.76	0.0034
13		One-Period Skewness (γ₁)	0.257722		16-Dec-05	83.37	0.0074
14		One-Period Kurtosis (γ₂)	1.546643		15-Dec-05	83.53	0.0019
15					14-Dec-05	83.13	-0.0048
16		Maturity for Black-Scholes (in years)	0.119048		13-Dec-05	83.71	0.0070
17		Volatility for Black-Scholes (annual volatility)	0.138362		12-Dec-05	85.96	0.0269
18					9-Dec-05	86.97	0.0117
19		Gram-Charlier Call Price	3.225377		8-Dec-05	87.50	0.0061
20		Black-Scholes Call Price	3.232791		7-Dec-05	88.72	0.0139
21					6-Dec-05	89.14	0.0047
22		Gram-Charlier Put Price	0.550601		5-Dec-05	88.43	-0.0080
23		Black-Scholes Put Price	0.558015		2-Dec-05	88.65	0.0025

FIGURE 9.1 Estimated Moments for Gram-Charlier Model
Source: www.finance.yahoo.com

the Excel file Chapter4CompareGCEW that when skewness is positive, the Black-Scholes model produces a higher price for in-the-money calls than the Gram-Charlier model. This is also true when kurtosis is positive, for calls that are near at-the-money. If the strike price is changed to $K = 85$ the option is out-of-the money, and the Black-Scholes price is lower than the Gram-Charlier price, as expected.

Finally, we note that in practice it is difficult to estimate skewness and kurtosis in this manner. The estimators are sensitive to the sample size and to the sample frequency of the data. To estimate parameters accurately, a long time-series of returns is needed. Using a long time-series of returns, however, makes the assumption that the distributional parameters are constant over that time period.

MAXIMUM LIKELIHOOD FOR GARCH MODELS

Estimation of parameters for the generalized autoregressive conditional heteroskedastic (GARCH) model can be done by maximum likelihood. This was illustrated in Chapter 6 for the GARCH(1,1) model, on a time-series of returns from the Standard and Poor's (S&P) 500 index. In this section we find the maximum likelihood estimators of the parameters from the Heston and Nandi (2000) GARCH option pricing model.

Recall that in the Heston and Nandi (2000) model the logarithmic return $r_{t+1} = \ln(S_{t+1}/S_t)$ follows the GARCH(1,1) process driven by the pair of equations, written here in terms of the physical parameters

$$r_{t+1} = r - \lambda \sigma_{t+1}^2 + \sigma_{t+1} z_{t+1} \tag{9.4}$$

$$\sigma_{t+1}^2 = \omega + \beta \sigma_t^2 + \alpha(z_t - \gamma \sigma_t)^2, \tag{9.5}$$

where $z_t \sim N(0,1)$. The parameters ω, α, β, γ, and λ must be found by maximum likelihood, which requires that a likelihood function be specified. This is accomplished by proceeding in the same way as described in Chapter 6. Recall that the log-likelihood function is proportional to

$$\ell(r_1, \ldots, r_n) \propto \sum_{t=1}^{n} \left(-\ln \sigma_t^2 - \frac{r_t^2}{\sigma_t^2} \right). \tag{9.6}$$

To implement the maximum likelihood estimation of the parameters, we modify the GARCHMLE() function of Chapter 6 for the process described in (9.4) and (9.5). At each step, z_{t+1} is obtained from (9.4) as

$$z_{t+1} = \frac{r_{t+1} - r - \lambda \sigma_{t+1}^2}{\sigma_{t+1}}, \tag{9.7}$$

where σ_{t+1} is obtained from (9.5), using the previous value z_t. The process is initialized by setting the first variance σ_1^2 as the unconditional variance of the returns.

The Excel file Chapter9HNGarch contains the VBA code for calculating the maximum likelihood estimators of the Heston and Nandi (2000) model. The VBA function HNGARCHMLE() is similar to the GARCHMLE() function of Chapter 6 except that it calculates the log-likelihood for the process specified in (9.4) and (9.5). It requires as inputs the returns (rets), starting values of the parameters (startParams), and the daily risk-free rate (rf). Note that the function returns the negative of the log-likelihood. Since the Nelder-Mead algorithm finds a minimum, the parameter values that produce a minimum value of the negative of the log-likelihood are the maximum likelihood estimates.

```
Function HNGARCHMLE(rets, startParams, rf)
Dim VARt() As Double, Z() As Double
n = Application.Count(rets)
ReDim VARt(n) As Double, Z(n) As Double
omega = startParams(1)
alpha = startParams(2)
beta = startParams(3)
gamma = startParams(4)
lambda = startParams(5)
If ((omega < 0) Or (alpha < 0) Or (beta < 0) Or (gamma < 0)
```

```
Or (lambda < 0)) Then
  HNGARCHMLE = -9999999
Else
  VARt(n) = Application.VAR(rets)
  Z(n) = (rets(n) - rf - lambda * VARt(n)) / Sqr(VARt(n))
  HNGARCHMLE = -Log(VARt(n)) - (rets(n) ^ 2 / VARt(n))
For t = n - 1 To 1 Step -1
  VARt(t) = omega + beta * VARt(t + 1) + alpha
            * (Z(t + 1) - gamma * VARt(t + 1)) ^ 2
  Z(t) = (rets(t) - rf - lambda * VARt(t)) / Sqr(VARt(t))
  HNGARCHMLE = HNGARCHMLE - Log(VARt(t)) - (rets(t) ^ 2 / VARt(t))
Next t
End If
  HNGARCHMLE = -HNGARCHMLE
End Function
```

The variance (9.5) is stored in VARt() and the shock term (9.7) is stored in Z().

The GARCHparams() function invokes the Nelder-Mead algorithm with the HNGARCHMLE() function. Since the risk-free rate is a parameter, but not one that needs to be estimated, it needs to be passed to the function separately from the others.

```
Function GARCHparams(rets, startParams, rf)
  GARCHparams = NelderMead("HNGARCHMLE", rets, startParams, rf)
End Function
```

The NelderMead() function of Chapter 1 requires a few modifications to accommodate the GARCHparams() function. First, the function declaration reflects the fact that the risk-free rate is passed separately. Next, every Run() statement in the NelderMean() function must pass the risk-free rate parameter separately also.

```
Function NelderMead(fname As String, rets, startParams, rf)
' More VBA Code
  Run(fname, rets, passParam, rf)
  Run(fname, rets, xcc, rf)
  Run(fname, rets, xr, rf)
  Run(fname, rets, startParams, rf)
' More VBA Code
For i = 1 To paramnum + 1
  funRes(i) = resmat(1, i)
Next i
NelderMead = Application.Transpose(funRes)
End Function
```

These functions are included in the Excel file Chapter9HNGarch, and are illustrated in Figure 9.2 using returns on the S&P 500 index over the period January 3, 2005, to December 30, 2005, a total of 252 observations. The figure presents the leftmost part of the file.

	A	B	C	D	E	F	G	H	I
1	Date	S&P500	Log Return	(Log Return)²	GARCH for σ_t^2	Error Term	Log Likelihood	Starting Values	
2	t	S_t	$R_t = Log(S_t/S_{t-1})$	R_t^2	$\sigma_t^2 = GARCH(1,1)$	Z_t	$-\log(\sigma_t^2) - r_t^2/\sigma_t^2$	$\omega =$	0.00000502
3	30-Dec-05	1248.29	-4.90E-03	2.40E-05	3.19E-05	-9.05E-01	9.60E+00	$\alpha =$	0.00000132
4	29-Dec-05	1254.42	-2.98E-03	8.91E-06	3.29E-05	-5.58E-01	1.01E+01	$\beta =$	0.589
5	28-Dec-05	1258.17	1.30E-03	1.68E-06	3.46E-05	1.84E-01	1.02E+01	$\gamma =$	420.685
6	27-Dec-05	1256.54	-9.60E-03	9.21E-05	2.75E-05	-1.87E+00	7.15E+00	$\lambda =$	0.205
7	23-Dec-05	1268.66	4.26E-04	1.81E-07	2.88E-05	3.97E-02	1.05E+01	$r =$	0.000198413
8	22-Dec-05	1268.12	4.21E-03	1.77E-05	2.87E-05	7.47E-01	9.84E+00	$\gamma^* =$	421.39
9	21-Dec-05	1262.79	2.51E-03	6.32E-06	2.96E-05	4.23E-01	1.02E+01	Log-L =	-2,188.60
10	20-Dec-05	1259.62	-2.38E-04	5.67E-08	3.11E-05	-8.11E-02	1.04E+01		
11	19-Dec-05	1259.92	-5.86E-03	3.43E-05	2.95E-05	-1.12E+00	9.27E+00	Estimated Parameters	
12	16-Dec-05	1267.32	-2.85E-03	8.14E-06	3.02E-05	-5.58E-01	1.01E+01	Log-L =	-2,287.46
13	15-Dec-05	1270.94	-1.42E-03	2.00E-06	3.15E-05	-2.90E-01	1.03E+01	$\omega =$	1.5831E-06
14	14-Dec-05	1272.74	4.18E-03	1.75E-05	3.19E-05	7.02E-01	9.80E+00	$\alpha =$	2.361E-06
15	13-Dec-05	1267.43	5.54E-03	3.07E-05	3.13E-05	9.52E-01	9.39E+00	$\beta =$	0.9010
16	12-Dec-05	1260.43	8.41E-04	7.08E-07	3.29E-05	1.09E-01	1.03E+01	$\gamma =$	4.83
17	9-Dec-05	1259.37	2.81E-03	7.88E-06	3.43E-05	4.43E-01	1.01E+01	$\lambda =$	2.742E-10
18	8-Dec-05	1255.84	-1.22E-03	1.48E-06	3.61E-05	-2.39E-01	1.02E+01	$\gamma^* =$	5.33
19	7-Dec-05	1257.37	-5.02E-03	2.52E-05	3.64E-05	-8.68E-01	9.53E+00		
20	6-Dec-05	1263.7	1.27E-03	1.63E-06	3.86E-05	1.70E-01	1.01E+01	Estimated Current Variance	
21	5-Dec-05	1262.09	-2.37E-03	5.60E-06	4.06E-05	-4.06E-01	9.97E+00	$\sigma_{t+1}^2 =$	3.192E-05

FIGURE 9.2 Estimated Heston and Nandi (2000) Parameters

The returns are in cells C3:C253, and the starting values corresponding roughly to the estimates in Table 1 of Heston and Nandi (2000) in cells I2:I6, and the daily risk-free rate $r = 0.05/252$ is in cell I7. Hence, in cell I9 we type

$$= HNGARCHMLE(C3:C254,I2:I6,I7)$$

which produces a log-likelihood proportional to $\ell = -2,188.60$. To obtain the maximum likelihood estimates, in cell I12 we type

$$= GARCHParams(C3:C254,I2:I6,I7)$$

and copy down to cells I13:I17. This produces the MLEs $\hat{\omega} = 1.583 \times 10^{-6}, \hat{\alpha} = 2.361 \times 10^{-6}, \hat{\beta} = 0.901, \hat{\gamma} = 4.83$, and $\hat{\lambda} = 2.742 \times 10^{-10}$. The risk-neutral parameter is $\hat{\gamma}^* = \hat{\gamma} + \hat{\lambda} + 1/2 = 5.33$ in cell I18. Using these parameter values, the estimated current GARCH variance at December 30, 2005, is $\hat{\sigma}_{t+1}^2 = 3.192 \times 10^{-5}$, or 0.003192 percent.

Recall that in Figure 6.7, the VBA function HNC() from the Excel file Chapter6HN was used to generate a Heston and Nandi (2000) call price of $2.4767. The rightmost part of the Excel file Chapter9HNGarch contains the Heston and Nandi (2000) call price using parameters estimated by Heston and Nandi (2000), and estimated by maximum likelihood. This appears as Figure 9.3.

The Heston and Nandi (2000) price using the parameter starting values is $2.4767 in cell L16. Using the estimated parameters, the call price becomes $2.4838 in cell M16. In this model, the persistence is $\beta + \alpha\gamma^2$. The persistence of the model with the original parameters is 0.823, but with the estimated parameters it is higher, at 0.901.

J	K	L	M
1	**Heston and Nandi Call Price**		
2		**Starting**	**Estimated**
3		**Parameters**	**Parameters**
4	Spot Price (S)	100	100
5	Strike Price (K)	100	100
6	Risk Free Rate (r)	0	0
7	Time to Maturity (days)	100	100
8	Alpha (α)	1.3200E-06	2.3611E-06
9	Beta (β)	0.589	0.9010
10	Gamma (γ*)	421.39	5.33
11	Omega (ω)	5.0200E-06	1.5831E-06
12	Lambda (λ*)	-0.5	-0.5
13	Current GARCH Variance (σ^2_{t+1})	8.92857E-05	3.192E-05
14	Persistence ($\beta + \alpha\gamma^2$)	0.8226	0.9010
15			
16	**Call Price**	2.476704	2.483763

FIGURE 9.3 Heston and Nandi (2000) Call Prices

The HNGARCHMLE() function described above includes VBA statements that impose a penalty whenever negative parameter values are encountered. Specifying a penalty function is one way to ensure that the NelderMean() function always returns positive parameter values. A penalty function can be defined in two ways. The simplest method, that used in the HNGARCHMLE() function, is to return a very large value of the negative log-likelihood when a parameter lies outside the range of acceptable values. Recall that the NelderMead() function seeks to minimize the negative of the log-likelihood, which is equivalent to maximizing the log-likelihood. Hence, the NHGARCHMLE() function returns the value 9999999 whenever ω, α, β, γ or λ are less than zero. The NelderMead() function will therefore avoid negative parameter values and restrict itself to positive values only. The second way to define a penalty function, which will be illustrated in Exercise 9.1, is by using a variable transformation. Instead of returning a large value of the negative log-likelihood when negative parameter values are encountered, the parameters are restricted to lie within an acceptable range of values. This restriction is done by transformation. The logistic and probit functions are well-suited for this task. The logistic function, for example, transforms the parameter θ to $\theta' = L(\theta)$ by the following transformation

$$L(\theta) = \frac{a}{1 + ce^{-\theta}} + b. \qquad (9.8)$$

In this function, the parameters a and b are such that b and $a + b$ become the left and right endpoints of the interval that represents acceptable values for θ, and c shifts the curve along the x-axis. For example, setting $a = 10$ and $b = -2$ maps the range of values $(-\infty, \infty)$ for θ to the range $(-2, 8)$ for θ'. The minimization is the performed on θ' instead of θ. Once the optimal value of the transformed parameter, $\hat{\theta}'$, is obtained, the optimal value of the original parameter, $\hat{\theta}$, is retrieved by the inverse of $L(\theta)$. Hence,

$$\hat{\theta} = L^{-1}(\hat{\theta}') = -\ln\left[\frac{1}{\hat{\theta}' - b} - \frac{1}{a}\right], \tag{9.9}$$

provided that $\hat{\theta}' \neq b$.

ESTIMATION BY LOSS FUNCTIONS

The next way to obtain parameter values is to select the parameters in such a way that the model prices match market prices as closely as possible. In other words, the parameters must be chosen so that the error between the market and model prices is a small as possible, measured by a loss function. Suppose there are N market option prices C_i $(i = 1, 2, \ldots, N)$ and that the model prices $C_i(\Theta)$ depend on a set of parameters Θ. We employ three loss functions, the root mean squared error loss function, \$RMSE; the relative root mean squared error loss function, %RMSE; and the implied volatility root mean squared error loss function, IVRMSE.

The root mean squared error loss function is the square root of the sample mean of the squared estimation errors

$$\$RMSE(\Theta) = \sqrt{\frac{1}{N}\sum_{i=1}^{N} e_i(\Theta)^2}, \tag{9.10}$$

where $e_i(\Theta) = C_i - C_i(\Theta)$ are the estimation errors $(i = 1, \ldots, N)$. The \$RMSE parameters are those which minimize the \$RMSE loss function (9.10). Heston and Nandi (2000) and Baskshi, Cao, and Chen (1997) both use this approach to estimate model parameters.

The relative root mean squared error loss function is defined as

$$\%RMSE(\Theta) = \sqrt{\frac{1}{N}\sum_{i=1}^{N} (e_i(\Theta)/C_i)^2}. \tag{9.11}$$

Unlike the \$RMSE loss function, which minimizes the raw difference between market prices and model prices, the %RMSE loss function (9.11) minimizes the percentage (or relative) difference between these prices.

Both the \$RMSE and %RMSE loss functions select parameters that minimize the distance between market prices and model prices. Alternatively, it is possible to select parameters that minimize the distance between implied volatilities obtained from market prices and implied volatilities obtained from model prices. This is achieved by the implied volatility root mean squared error loss function, defined as

$$IVRMSE(\Theta) = \sqrt{\frac{1}{N}\sum_{i=1}^{N} (\sigma_i - \sigma_i(\Theta))^2}. \tag{9.12}$$

In this expression, σ_i is the Black-Scholes implied volatility obtained by inverting the Black-Scholes formula equated to market prices, and $\sigma_i(\Theta)$ is the Black-Scholes implied volatility obtained by inverting the Black-Scholes formula equated to model prices. Parameter estimates obtained under the IVRMSE loss function can help to fit distributional properties of the returns of the underlying asset, since the shape of the implied volatility curve reflects the distribution of underlying returns. A volatility smirk indicates skewness in the returns distribution, while a volatility smile indicates kurtosis. In Figure 10.2, for example, it will be shown that the implied volatility curve for Google, Inc., is negatively sloped and concave, indicating that Google's stock return distribution is negatively skewed and leptokurtic.

Each of these loss functions assigns weights to options differently. The dollar root mean squared error loss function $RMSE assigns more weight to in-the-money options. This is because in-the-money options are more expensive. Any large potential estimation error—the difference between fitted prices and market prices—will naturally originate from these options, so the $RMSE loss function will tend to produce parameter values that lead to a small pricing errors for in-the-money options. The relative root mean squared error loss function %RMSE, on the other hand, assigns more weight to deep out-of-the-money options, because these options have little value. Since the %RMSE estimation error includes the market price C_i in the denominator (see (9.11)), a given price difference will tend to become amplified when the market price is small—that is, when options are out-of-the-money. Finally, the implied volatility root mean squared error loss function, IVRMSE, assigns approximately equal weight to all options. This is because the IVRMSE loss function seeks to minimize the error between implied volatilities obtained from market prices, and implied volatilities obtained from prices generated from the parametric model. These two sets of volatilities are of similar magnitude across moneyness levels.

VBA functions for loss function estimation using $RMSE, %RMSE, and IVRMSE are included in the Excel files that accompany this chapter. Each method requires two functions. The first function constructs a loss function according to (9.10), (9.11), or (9.12), and the second finds the minimum of the loss function using the Nelder-Mead algorithm. The functions must be modified to incorporate the required model that generates the model prices $C_i(\Theta)$. In this section, as in Christoffersen and Jacobs (2004a), the functions are constructed to obtain parameter estimates for the Practitioner Black-Scholes (PBS) model of Chapter 4, using the most general form for the deterministic volatility function (DVF) given by

$$\sigma_{iv} = a_0 + a_1 K + a_2 K^2 + a_3 T + a_4 T^2 + a_5 KT. \qquad (9.13)$$

Recall from Chapter 4 that the PBS model consists of two stages. In the first stage, a set of option prices is used to estimate the parameters a_0 through a_5 in (9.13), which produces a fitted implied volatility for any combination (K, T). In the second stage, the fitted implied volatility is used as an input to the Black-Scholes formula, along with the same values of K and T. In Chapter 4 the parameters were estimated

	A	B	C	D	E	F	G	H	I	J	K
1											
2		**Google, Inc. Market and Fitted PBS Call and Put Prices**								**PBS Parameter Starting Values**	
3											
4		Current Date	3-Apr-06	Yearly Risk-Free Rate (*r*)		0.0504			Intercept	1.0225
5				Spot Price (*S*)		389.7			*K*	-0.0025
6										*K*²	0.0000
7		Option	Strike	Days to	Moneyness	Closing	B-S Implied	$RMSE		*T*	-0.3810
8		Type	Price	Maturity	(K/S)	Price	Volatility	Prices		*T*²	0.2391
9		Put	330	47	0.85	4.25	0.4520	3.66		*KT*	0.0003
10		Put	340	47	0.87	5.75	0.4418	5.17			
11		Put	350	47	0.90	7.75	0.4340	7.15			
12		Put	360	47	0.92	10.15	0.4241	9.66			
13		Put	370	47	0.95	13.30	0.4184	12.78		**PBS $RMSE Parameter Estimates**	
14		Put	380	47	0.98	17.05	0.4121	16.57			
15		Call	390	47	1.00	23.50	0.4025	23.28		Loss Function	0.3534
16		Call	400	47	1.03	18.80	0.3988	18.54		Intercept	0.8567
17		Call	410	47	1.05	14.80	0.3954	14.52		*K*	-0.0017
18		Call	420	47	1.08	11.40	0.3910	11.17		*K*²	0.0000
19		Call	430	47	1.10	8.65	0.3876	8.45		*T*	-0.2971
20		Call	440	47	1.13	6.55	0.3869	6.27		*T*²	0.1980
21		Call	450	47	1.15	4.95	0.3878	4.58		*KT*	0.0002

FIGURE 9.4 Dollar RMSE Estimates for the PBS Model
Source: www.optionmetrics.com

using OLS through the VBA function PBSparams(). In this section we estimate the parameters using the $RMSE, %RMSE, and IVRMSE loss functions, using the OLS parameter estimates as starting values.

The Excel file Chapter9PBS_RMSE contains the $RMSE estimates of the PBS model, using option prices on Google, Inc., on April 3, 2006, obtained from OptionMetrics (www.optionmetrics.com). Four sets of calls and puts are used, with maturities 47, 75, 166, and 292 days, and moneyness (defined as K/S) ranging from 0.85 to 1.15. The top portion of this file appears in Figure 9.4.

The closing price of Google on April 3, 2006, was $389.70. The Black-Scholes implied volatilities are in column G. For example, in cell G9 we type

$$= \text{BisecBSV}(B9, S, C9, RF, D9/365, 0.00001, 4, F9)$$

which produces an implied volatility of $\sigma_{iv} = 0.4520$, or 45.20 percent, when $K = 330$ and $T = 47$ days. To obtain the OLS estimates of the DVF (9.13), in cell K4 we type

$$= \text{PBSparams}(G9:G60, C9:C60, D9:D60)$$

and copy down to cells K5:K9, which produces the starting values for the $RMSE loss function.

The first step in obtaining the PBS parameters estimated under the $RMSE loss function (9.10) is to construct the loss function itself. This is achieved with the VBA function RMSE():

```
Function RMSE(startParams, PC, S, K, r, T, realPrice)
n = Application.Count(K)
RMSE = 0
For i = 1 To n
  If (PC(i) = "Call") Then
    RMSE = RMSE + (realPrice(i) -  PBSprice(startParams, S,
          K(i), r, T(i), "Call")) ^ 2
  Else
    RMSE = RMSE + (realPrice(i) - PBSprice(startParams, S,
          K(i), r, T(i), "Put")) ^ 2
  End If
Next i
RMSE = Sqr(RMSE / n)
End Function
```

The VBA function RMSEparams() invokes the Nelder-Mead algorithm to find the minimum value of the RMSE() function, and returns the values of the estimated PBS parameters:

```
Function RMSEparams(startParams, PC, S, K, r, T, realPrice)
  RMSEparams = NelderMead("RMSE", startParams, PC, S, K, r, T, realPrice)
End Function
```

To obtain the $RMSE parameter estimates, in cell K15 we type

$$= \text{RMSEparams(K4:K9,B9:B60,G5,C9:C60,G4, D9:D60,F9:F60)}$$

and copy to cells K16:K21, which produces the estimates $\hat{a}_0 = 0.8567, \hat{a}_1 = -0.0017, \hat{a}_2 = 1.64 \times 10^{-6}, \hat{a}_3 = -0.2971, \hat{a}_4 = 0.1980$, and $\hat{a}_5 = 0.0002$. The dollar root mean error is 0.3534, corresponding to an error of roughly 35 cents, on average, between the market prices and the prices produced by the PBS model. Finally, to obtain the PBS prices, we use the PBSprice() function of Chapter 4. For example, in cell H9 we type

$$= \text{PBSprice(K16:K21, S, C9, RF, D9, B9)}$$

which produces a price of \$3.66 for the put option with $K = 330$ and $T = 47$ days.

The %RMSE estimates are obtained in the same fashion, using the same set of options on Google, Inc. These estimates are contained in the Excel file Chapter9PBS_PERRMSE and illustrated in Figure 9.5. As expected, the implied volatilities and starting values are exactly the same as in Figure 9.4.

The VBA function perRMSE() constructs the relative root mean squared error loss function %RMSE from (9.11):

```
Function perRMSE(startParams, PC, S, K, r, T, realPrice)
n = Application.Count(K)
perRMSE = 0
For i = 1 To n
  If (PC(i) = "Call") Then
```

	A	B	C	D	E	F	G	H	I	J	K
1											
2		Google, Inc. Market and Fitted PBS Call and Put Prices								PBS Parameter Starting Values	
3											
4		Current Date	3-Apr-06	Yearly Risk-Free Rate (r)		0.0504				Intercept	1.0225
5				Spot Price (S)		389.7				K	-0.0025
6										K^2	0.0000
7		Option	Strike	Days to	Moneyness	Closing	B-S Implied	%RMSE		T	-0.3810
8		Type	Price	Maturity	(K/S)	Price	Volatility	Prices		T^2	0.2391
9		Put	330	47	0.85	4.25	0.4520	3.94		KT	0.0003
10		Put	340	47	0.87	5.75	0.4418	5.46			
11		Put	350	47	0.90	7.75	0.4340	7.44			
12		Put	360	47	0.92	10.15	0.4241	9.95			
13		Put	370	47	0.95	13.30	0.4184	13.05		PBS %RMSE Parameter Estimates	
14		Put	380	47	0.98	17.05	0.4121	16.82			
15		Call	390	47	1.00	23.50	0.4025	23.51		Loss Function	0.0277
16		Call	400	47	1.03	18.80	0.3988	18.76		Intercept	1.0255
17		Call	410	47	1.05	14.80	0.3954	14.72		K	-0.0025
18		Call	420	47	1.08	11.40	0.3910	11.36		K^2	0.0000
19		Call	430	47	1.10	8.65	0.3876	8.62		T	-0.4125
20		Call	440	47	1.13	6.55	0.3869	6.45		T^2	0.2599
21		Call	450	47	1.15	4.95	0.3878	4.75		KT	0.0003

FIGURE 9.5 Percent RMSE Parameter Estimates for the PBS Model
Source: www.optionmetrics.com

```
         perRMSE = perRMSE + ((realPrice(i) −
                   PBSprice(startParams, S, K(i), r, T(i),
                   "Call")) / realPrice(i)) ^ 2
      Else
         perRMSE = perRMSE + ((realPrice(i) −
                   PBSprice(startParams, S, K(i), r, T(i),
                   "Put")) / realPrice(i)) ^ 2
      End If
   Next i
   perRMSE = Sqr(perRMSE / n)
   End Function
```

The VBA function perRMSEparams() invokes the Nelder-Mead algorithm to find the minimum value of the perRMSE() function, and returns the PBS parameters estimated with the %RMSE loss function. It is similar to the RMSEparams() function and is not presented here. To obtain the %RMSE parameter estimates, in cell K15 we type

= perRMSEparams(K4:K9,B9:B60,G5,C9:C60,G4, D9:D60,F9:F60)

which produces the estimates $\hat{a}_0 = 1.0255, \hat{a}_1 = -0.0025, \hat{a}_2 = 2.518 \times 10^{-6}, \hat{a}_3 = -0.4125, \hat{a}_4 = 0.2599$, and $\hat{a}_5 = 0.0003$. The percent root mean error is 0.0277, which implies an average error of roughly 2.77 percent between market prices and prices produced by the PBS model.

Finally, the IVRMSE estimates of the PBS model are contained in the Excel file Chapter9PBS_IVRMSE, and illustrated in Figure 9.6.

	A	B	C	D	E	F	G	H	I	J	K
1											
2		Google, Inc. Market and Fitted PBS Call and Put Prices								PBS Parameter Starting Values	
3											
4		Current Date	3-Apr-06	Yearly Risk-Free Rate (r)		0.0504				Intercept	1.0225
5				Spot Price (S)		389.7				K	-0.0025
6										K^2	0.0000
7		Option	Strike	Days to	Moneyness	Closing	B-S Implied	IVRMSE		T	-0.3810
8		Type	Price	Maturity	(K/S)	Price	Volatility	Prices		T^2	0.2391
9		Put	330	47	0.85	4.25	0.4520	3.90		KT	0.0003
10		Put	340	47	0.87	5.75	0.4418	5.42			
11		Put	350	47	0.90	7.75	0.4340	7.39			
12		Put	360	47	0.92	10.15	0.4241	9.88			
13		Put	370	47	0.95	13.30	0.4184	12.98		PBS IVRMSE Parameter Estimates	
14		Put	380	47	0.98	17.05	0.4121	16.74			
15		Call	390	47	1.00	23.50	0.4025	23.43		Loss Function	0.0058
16		Call	400	47	1.03	18.80	0.3988	18.68		Intercept	1.0225
17		Call	410	47	1.05	14.80	0.3954	14.64		K	-0.0025
18		Call	420	47	1.08	11.40	0.3910	11.29		K^2	0.0000
19		Call	430	47	1.10	8.65	0.3876	8.56		T	-0.3810
20		Call	440	47	1.13	6.55	0.3869	6.39		T^2	0.2391
21		Call	450	47	1.15	4.95	0.3878	4.70		KT	0.0003

FIGURE 9.6 Implied Volatility RMSE Parameter Estimates for the PBS Model
Source: www.optionmetrics.com

The ivRMSE() function constructs the implied volatility RMSE loss function (9.12):

```
Function ivRMSE(startParams, PC, S, K, r, T, realPrice)
n = Application.Count(K)
ivRMSE = 0
  For i = 1 To n
    ivRMSE = ivRMSE + (realPrice(i) - PBSvol(startParams,
            K(i), T(i) / 365)) ^ 2
  Next i
ivRMSE = Sqr(ivRMSE / n)
End Function
```

The ivRMSEparams() function nests the ivRMSE() function, invokes the Nelder-Mead algorithm, and returns the PBS parameters estimated under the IVRMSE loss function. It is similar to the perRMSEparams() function and is not presented here. To obtain the IVRMSE estimates, in cell K15 we type

$$= \text{ivRMSEparams(K4:K9,B9:B60,G5,C9:C60,G4, D9:D60,G9:G60)}$$

which produces $\hat{a}_0 = 1.0225$, $\hat{a}_1 = 0 - 0.0025$, $\hat{a}_2 = 2.529 \times 10^{-6}$, $\hat{a}_3 = -0.3810$, $\hat{a}_4 = 0.2391$, and $\hat{a}_5 = 0.0003$. Note that these are exactly the same estimates as those produced by the PBSParams() function, which appear in cells K4:K9 and which are used as starting values. This is because the objective function in OLS is the same as the IVRMSE objective function. The dependent variable in the PBS model is a set of implied volatilities, so the estimates produced by the PBS model are exactly the same as the IVRMSE estimates. The implied volatility root mean

	Option Type	Strike Price	Days to Maturity	Moneyness (K/S)	Closing Price	B-S Implied Volatility	$RMSE PBS Prices	B-S Implied Volatility	%RMSE PBS Prices	B-S Implied Volatility	IVRMSE PBS Prices	B-S Implied Volatility
	Put	330	47	0.85	4.25	0.4520	3.66	0.4311	3.94	0.4411	3.90	0.4398
	Put	340	47	0.87	5.75	0.4418	5.17	0.4248	5.46	0.4334	5.42	0.4321
	Put	350	47	0.90	7.75	0.4340	7.15	0.4189	7.44	0.4263	7.39	0.4249
	Put	360	47	0.92	10.15	0.4241	9.66	0.4133	9.95	0.4196	9.88	0.4183
	Put	370	47	0.95	13.30	0.4184	12.78	0.4080	13.05	0.4135	12.98	0.4121
	Put	380	47	0.98	17.05	0.4121	16.57	0.4031	16.82	0.4078	16.74	0.4064
	Call	390	47	1.00	23.50	0.4025	23.28	0.3985	23.51	0.4027	23.43	0.4013
	Call	400	47	1.03	18.80	0.3988	18.54	0.3942	18.76	0.3980	18.68	0.3966
	Call	410	47	1.05	14.80	0.3954	14.52	0.3902	14.72	0.3939	14.64	0.3924
	Call	420	47	1.08	11.40	0.3910	11.17	0.3866	11.36	0.3902	11.29	0.3888
	Call	430	47	1.10	8.65	0.3876	8.45	0.3833	8.62	0.3871	8.56	0.3856
	Call	440	47	1.13	6.55	0.3869	6.27	0.3803	6.45	0.3845	6.39	0.3830
	Call	450	47	1.15	4.95	0.3878	4.58	0.3776	4.75	0.3823	4.70	0.3809

Google, Inc. Market and Fitted Practitioner Black-Scholes Call and Put Prices — Current Date 3-Apr-06, Yearly Risk-Free Rate (r) 0.0504, Spot Price (S) 389.7

FIGURE 9.7 PBS Implied Volatilities
Source: www.optionmetrics.com

squared error is 0.0058, which corresponds to an average raw difference of 0.58 percent between the implied volatilities obtained from market prices and the implied volatilities obtained from the PBS prices. The ivRMSEparams() function is similar to the RMSEparams() and is not presented here.

The Excel file Chapter9PBS_InSample presents the implied volatilities obtained with the three sets of PBS prices. This is illustrated in Figure 9.7. The $RMSE, %RMSE, and IVRMSE estimates are copied from the previous Excel files into columns P, Q, and R, respectively. Each set of prices and implied volatilities are obtained using these parameter estimates. For example, to obtain the implied volatility for a strike price of $K = 330$ and time to maturity $T = 47$ days with the IVRMSE estimates, in cell M10 we type

$$= \text{PBSvol}(R6{:}R11, C10, D10/365)$$

which produces $\sigma_{iv} = 0.4398$. Continuing for each set of estimates produces the desired implied volatilities. These are grouped into maturities, and plotted in Figure 9.8, which is also included in the Excel file Chapter9PRS_InSample.

Model Assessment

Implementing an option pricing model consists of two general stages, estimation and error evaluation. Model parameters are estimated in the first stage, and in the second stage, the fit of the model is assessed by examining the pricing errors between out-of-sample market prices and model prices. Model parameters are estimated with in-sample data in the first stage, and these parameters are used to generate out-of-sample model prices in the second stage, which are then compared with out-of-sample market prices. Both stages can be implemented using loss functions.

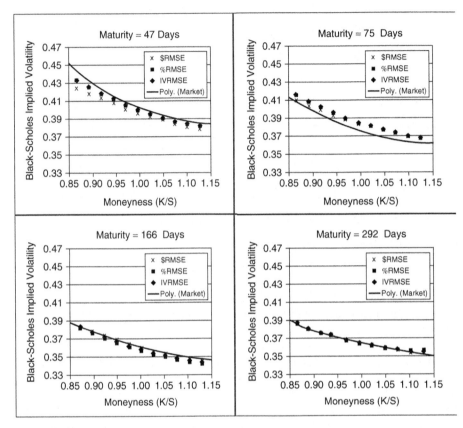

FIGURE 9.8 PBS Implied Volatilities by Maturity
Source: www.optionmetrics.com

A loss function is used to estimate parameters, and another loss function evaluates the distance between out-of-sample model and market prices. Christoffersen and Jacobs (2004a) argue that the same loss function should be used to implement both stages. In particular, to compare the pricing errors of competing models, the same loss function should be used as that which has been used to estimate parameters, to minimize the chance of unfair comparisons.

The Excel file Chapter9PBS_OutSample contains an assessment of the fit of the Practitioner Black-Scholes model, using the Google, Inc., option prices described above. In-sample estimates in the first stage are obtained using prices on April 3, 2006. The out-of-sample pricing errors in the second stage are obtained using prices one week later, on April 10, 2006. The out-of-sample options have the same strike prices as the in-sample options, but with maturities that are seven days shorter. The right-most portion of the In-Sample worksheet of the Excel file Chapter9PBS_OutSample contains in-sample comparisons of the loss functions. This portion of the file is presented in Figure 9.9.

	H	I	J	K	L
1					
2		**PBS Estimated Parameters**			
3					
4			$RMSE	%RMSE	IVRMSE
5		Intercept	0.8567	1.0255	1.0225
6		K	-0.0017	-0.0025	-0.0025
7		K^2	0.0000	0.0000	0.0000
8		T	-0.2971	-0.4125	-0.3810
9		T^2	0.1980	0.2599	0.2391
10		KT	0.0002	0.0003	0.0003
11					
12		**Loss Function Comparison, In-Sample**			
13					
14				Raw Loss	
15			$RMSE	%RMSE	IVRMSE
16		$RMSE Estimates	0.3534	0.0340	0.0065
17		%RSME Estimates	0.4500	0.0277	0.0059
18		IVRMSE Estimates	0.4049	0.0282	0.0058
19					
20				Relative Loss	
21			$RMSE	%RMSE	IVRMSE
22		$RMSE Estimates	1.0000	1.2261	1.1244
23		%RSME Estimates	1.2732	1.0000	1.0183
24		IVRMSE Estimates	1.1456	1.0170	1.0000

FIGURE 9.9 In-Sample Loss Function Comparisons
Source: www.optionmetrics.com

The $RMSE, %RMSE, and IVRMSE parameter estimates for the PBS model are copied directly from the previous Excel files. Values of the three loss functions are compared with the three different sets of parameter estimates. For example, to obtain the value of the $RMSE loss function with the $RMSE estimates, in cell J16 we type

$$= \text{RMSE(J5:J10,B10:B61,G5,C10:C61,G4, D10:D61,F10:F61)}$$

which produces a value of 0.3534. This implies that the $RMSE parameters lead to an average difference of roughly 35 cents between the in-sample market and PBS model prices. To obtain the value of the $RMSE loss function with the %RMSE estimates, in cell J17 we type

$$= \text{RMSE(K5:K10,B10:B61,G5,C10:C61,G4, D10:D61,F10:F61)}$$

which produces a value of 0.4500. This implies that the %RMSE parameters lead to an average difference of 45 cents between the in-sample market and model prices. As a final example, to obtain the value of the %RMSE loss function with the IVRMSE estimates, in cell K18 we type

$$= \text{perRMSE(L5:L10,B10:B61,G5,C10:C61,G4, D10:D61,F10:F61)}$$

	H	I	J	K	L
1					
2		**PBS Estimated Parameters**			
3					
4			$RMSE	%RMSE	IVRMSE
5		Intercept	0.8567	1.0255	1.0225
6		K	-0.0017	-0.0025	-0.0025
7		K^2	0.0000	0.0000	0.0000
8		T	-0.2971	-0.4125	-0.3810
9		T^2	0.1980	0.2599	0.2391
10		KT	0.0002	0.0003	0.0003
11					
12		**Loss Function Comparison One Week Out-of-Sample**			
13					
14				Raw Loss	
15			$RMSE	%RMSE	IVRMSE
16		$RMSE Estimates	1.2526	0.0969	0.0171
17		%RSME Estimates	1.3388	0.0829	0.0160
18		IVRMSE Estimates	1.3091	0.0840	0.0159
19					
20				Relative Loss	
21			$RMSE	%RMSE	IVRMSE
22		$RMSE Estimates	1.0000	1.1685	1.0720
23		%RSME Estimates	1.0688	1.0000	1.0007
24		IVRMSE Estimates	1.0451	1.0136	1.0000

FIGURE 9.10   Out-of-Sample Loss Function Comparisons
Source: www.optionmetrics.com

which produces a value of 0.0282. This means that the IVRMSE estimates lead
to an average difference of roughly 2.82 percent between the in-sample and model
estimates. The relative losses appear immediately below the raw losses, and indicate
that regardless of which loss function is considered, the smallest errors are produced
when the corresponding parameter estimates are used in the loss function.

The Out-of-Sample worksheet of the Excel file ChapterPBS_OutSample contains
the same analysis, but using loss functions on the out-of-sample data, with parameter
estimates obtained with the in-sample data. The right-most part of this worksheet is
illustrated in Figure 9.10.

Again, the three sets of PBS in-sample parameter estimates are copied directly
from the previous Excel files. To obtain the values of the loss function using out-
of-sample data and in-sample parameter estimates, we proceed exactly as in the
previous figure. For example, to obtain the value of the out-of-sample %RMSE loss
function with in-sample $RMSE parameter estimates, in cell K16 we type

$$= \text{perRMSE(J5:J10,B10:B61,G5,C10:C61,G4, D10:D61,F10:F61)}$$

which produces a value of 0.0969. This means that the in-sample $RMSE estimates
lead to a pricing error of roughly 9.69 percent between the out-of-sample market and
model prices. As in the previous figure, the relative losses appear immediately below

the raw losses. Consistent with the findings of Christoffersen and Jacobs (2004a) we find that when the same form of the loss functions for used in-sample estimation and out-of-sample assessment, the objective loss function is minimized.

OTHER ESTIMATION METHODS

In this chapter, parameter estimation methods that are consistent with returns and with option prices are presented. A number of researchers have applied advanced statistical methods that are consistent with both returns and option prices. These include, for example, Markov-chain Monte Carlo methods proposed by Eraker (2001), Eraker, Joannes, and Polson (2003), and Jacquier, Polson, and Rossi (2004), maximum likelihood methods such as that proposed by Aït-Sahalia (2002) and Aït-Sahalia and Kimmel (2007), the generalized method of moments (GMM), efficient method of moments (EMM) and simulated method of moments (SMM). See Chenov and Ghysels (2000) for a review of GMM, EMM, and SMM applied to stochastic volatility option pricing models. Carr and Wu (2006a) apply the Kalman filter before obtaining maximum likelihood estimates, while Christoffersen, Jacobs, Minoui (2006) and Johannes, Polson, and Stroud (2006) use the auxiliary particle filter.

While the methods described above can produce estimators that are consistent with both returns and option prices, they are too complicated and too computationally expensive to implement in VBA. Hence, these methods are not reviewed in this book.

SUMMARY

In this chapter we introduce two methodologies for estimating parameters, consistent with returns and consistent with option prices. Estimates of unconditional moments are easily obtained from stock price returns. Unfortunately, these estimates are for the physical distribution, and not the risk-neutral distribution, so they can be used in the simplest models only, such as the Black-Scholes model for which a simple relationship exists between the two sets of parameters. Many option pricing models include parameters that cannot be estimated with stock price returns alone. Loss function estimates are better suited at estimating parameters from these models. Since they are constructed from option prices, they produce estimates from the risk-neutral distribution. In this chapter, loss function estimation is illustrated for three loss functions. It is also shown how loss functions can be used to assess the fit of models, using both in-sample and out-of-sample data.

EXERCISES

This section provides exercises that deal with parameter estimation. Solutions are contained in the Excel files Chapter9Exercise1, Chapter9Exercise2, Chapter9-Exercise3, Chapter9Exercise4, and Chapter9Exercise5.

9.1 The leverage GARCH model is specified by the two equations

$$\ln(S_t/S_{t-1}) = r + \lambda\sigma_t - \tfrac{1}{2}\sigma_t^2 + \sigma_t z_t$$

$$\sigma_t^2 = \beta_0 + \beta_1\sigma_{t-1}^2 + \beta_2(z_{t-1} - \theta)^2 \qquad (9.14)$$

for $\lambda > 0, \beta_0 > 0, \beta_1 > 0$, and $\beta_2 > 0$ where $\ln(S_t/S_{t-1}) = R_t$ is the return, $z_t \sim N(0,1)$, and where θ is the leverage parameter. Find an expression for the log-likelihood function. Using returns from the S&P 500 index over January 3, 2005, to December 30, 2005, contained in the Excel file ChapterHNGARCH, find estimates of the physical parameters λ, $\beta_0, \beta_1, \beta_2$ and θ, using the NelderMead() VBA function of Chapter 1. Use the logistic transformation (9.8) on β_0, β_1, and β_2, to restrict their range to the interval (0,100). Use as starting values the values estimated by Christoffersen and Jacobs (2004b), $\lambda = 0.0434, \beta_0 = 1.83 \times 10^{-6}, \beta_1 = 0.8847, \beta_2 = 0.0718$, and $\theta = 0.6131$. See Hentschel (1995) for a general framework of asymmetric GARCH models and Christoffersen and Jacobs (2004b) for their application to option pricing.

9.2 Modify the RMSE() and RMSEparameter() functions for estimating parameters of the Heston (1993) model using the $RMSE loss function (9.10), using option prices for Google, Inc., on July 6, 2006. These prices are for options expiring on July 21, 2006, and are contained in the Excel file Chapter9Google. Use the starting values $\rho = -0.3, \kappa = 3, \theta = 0.5, \sigma = 0.9, V_0 = 0.1, k_i = 0.5$, and $\gamma = 0.1$. Use the HCTrans() function introduced in Chapter 5 to generate Heston (1993) option prices, and compare these prices to the market prices of Google, Inc. options.

9.3 Modify the perRMSE() and perRMSEparameter() functions for estimating parameters of the Heston (1993) model using the %RMSE loss function (9.11), using option prices for Google, Inc., on July 6, 2006. These prices are for options expiring on July 21, 2006, and are contained in the Excel file Chapter9Google. Use the starting values $\rho = -0.3, \kappa = 3, \theta = 0.5, \sigma = 0.9, V_0 = 0.1, k_i = 0.5$, and $\gamma = 0.1$. Use the HCTrans() function introduced in Chapter 5 to generate Heston (1993) option prices, and compare these prices to the market prices of Google options. Repeat this exercise, but exclude all options with value less than $0.50. For starting values use the parameter estimates obtained by including all options. Show that the value of the loss function is much lower when these deep out-of-the money options are excluded, and explain why.

9.4 Modify the ivRMSE() and ivRMSEparameter() functions for estimating parameters of the Heston (1993) model using the IVRMSE loss function (9.12), using option prices for Google, Inc., on July 6, 2006. These prices are for options expiring on July 21, 2006, and are contained in the Excel file Chapter9Google.

Use the parameter estimates produced by the \$RMSE loss function in Exercise 9.2 as starting values. For reference, these are $\rho = -0.3274$, $\kappa = 1.8946$, $\theta = 0.5243$, $\sigma = 2.0743$, $V_0 = 0.1453$, $k_i = 0.5051$, and $\gamma = 0.0642$. Use the HCTrans() function introduced in Chapter 5 to generate Heston (1993) option prices, and compare these prices to the market prices on Google options.

9.5 Use the Heston (1993) option prices produced in Exercises 9.2 through 9.4 to generate implied volatilities for each set of prices. Compare these implied volatilities by plotting them as a function of moneyness.

SOLUTIONS TO EXERCISES

9.1 Conditional on σ_{t-1}^2 being known, we can obtain σ_t^2 from the second equation of (9.14), then solve for z_t in the first equation, which is used in turn to update the second equation and obtain σ_{t+1}^2, and so on. For a sample of T returns this produces the set of random variables $\{z_t\}_{t=2}^T$. Since $z_t \sim N(0, 1)$, the probability density function for z_t is

$$f(z_t) = \frac{1}{\sqrt{2\pi}\sigma_t} \exp\left[-\frac{1}{2}\left(\frac{R_t - r - \lambda\sigma_t + \frac{1}{2}\sigma_t^2}{\sigma_t}\right)^2\right]. \tag{9.15}$$

Hence the log-likelihood is proportional to

$$\log L \propto -\sum_{t=2}^T \ln \sigma_t - \sum_{t=2}^T \left(\frac{R_t - r - \lambda\sigma_t + \frac{1}{2}\sigma_t^2}{\sigma_t}\right)^2. \tag{9.16}$$

Note that since the $t = 1$ variance σ_1^2 is used to initialize the equations, the summations in (9.16) begin at $t = 2$. The VBA function LGARCHMLE() produces the log-likelihood (9.16) that can be passed to the NelderMead() function via the LGARCHparams() function. The Run() statements in the NelderMead() function are modified to include the appropriate parameters. These functions are included in the Excel file Chapter9Exercise1.

```
Function LGARCHMLE(rets, startParams, rf, Optional ErrorCheckOff = 0)
Dim h() As Double, z() As Double
n = Application.Count(rets)
ReDim h(n) As Double, z(n) As Double
lambda = startParams(1)
b0 = startParams(2)
b1 = startParams(3)
b2 = startParams(4)
theta = startParams(5)
If (ErrorCheckOff = 0) Then
  b0 = 100 / (1 + 100 * Exp(-b0))
  b1 = 100 / (1 + 100 * Exp(-b1))
  b2 = 100 / (1 + 100 * Exp(-b2))
```

```
End If
h(n) = Application.Var(rets)
z(n) = (rets(n) - rf - lambda * Sqr(h(n)) + 0.5 * h(n)) / Sqr(h(n))
LGARCHMLE = -Log(h(n)) - z(n) ^ 2
For t = n - 1 To 1 Step -1
  h(t) = b0 + b1 * h(t + 1) + b2 * h(t + 1)
      * (z(t + 1) - theta) ^ 2
  z(t) = (rets(t) - rf - lambda * Sqr(h(t)) + 0.5 * h(t)) / Sqr(h(t))
  LGARCHMLE = LGARCHMLE - Log(h(t)) - z(t) ^ 2
Next t
  LGARCHMLE = -LGARCHMLE
End Function
```

Setting $a = 100$ and $b = 0$ in (9.8) restricts the range of the transformed parameters to (0,100). The LGARCHparams() function invokes the Nelder-Mead() function for minimizing the negative log-likelihood, and transforms the parameters back in accordance with (9.9).

```
Function LGARCHparams(rets, startParams, rf)
Dim passParams(5) As Double
For i = 1 To 5
  passParams(i) = startParams(i)
Next i
passParams(2) = -Log(((100 / passParams(2)) - 1) / 100)
passParams(3) = -Log(((100 / passParams(3)) - 1) / 100)
passParams(4) = -Log(((100 / passParams(4)) - 1) / 100)
endParams = NelderMead("LGARCHMLE", rets, passParams, rf)
endParams(3, 1) = 100 / (1 + 100 * Exp(-endParams(3, 1)))
endParams(4, 1) = 100 / (1 + 100 * Exp(-endParams(4, 1)))
endParams(5, 1) = 100 / (1 + 100 * Exp(-endParams(5, 1)))
LGARCHparams = endParams
End Function
```

These functions are illustrated in Figure 9.11. To obtain the estimated parameters using the starting values in cells H4:H8, the risk-free rate in cell H9, and the returns in cells C5:C255, in cell H12 we type

$$= \text{LGARCHparams(C5:C255,H4:H8,H9)}$$

and copy to cells H13:H17, which produces the maximum likelihood estimates $\hat{\lambda} = -0.01267$, $\hat{\beta}_0 = 0.00000126$, $\hat{\beta}_1 = 0.09487$, $\hat{\beta}_2 = 0.00561$, and $\hat{\theta} = 12.4768$. The estimated daily variance on December 30, 2005, is 0.00003552, or 0.0035 percent, which corresponds to a yearly variance of 0.0946, or 9.49 percent. Recall from Figure 9.2 that the estimated GARCH(1,1) variance for that day is 0.003192 percent, corresponding to a yearly variance of 8.97 percent.

9.2 The Excel file Chapter9Exercise2contains the function RMSE() for obtaining the $RMSE loss function (9.10) when Heston (1993) prices are used. The function

	A	B	C	D	E	F	G	H
1	EXERCISE 9.1							
2								
3	Date	S&P500	Log Return	GARCH for σ_t^2	Z_t	Log Likelihood	Starting Values	
4	t	S_t	$R_t = Log(S_t/S_{t-1})$	σ_t^2 = GARCH(1,1)	$(R_t - r - \lambda\sigma_t + \frac{1}{8}\sigma_t^2)/\sigma_t$	$-\log(\sigma_t^2) - z_t^2$	λ =	0.04340000
5	30-Dec-05	1248.29	-0.004899	3.551523E-05	-0.829336	3.761787	β_0 =	0.00000183
6	29-Dec-05	1254.42	-0.002985	3.278537E-05	-0.529702	4.203736	β_1 =	0.88470000
7	28-Dec-05	1258.17	0.001296	3.357100E-05	0.215670	4.427522	β_2 =	0.07180000
8	27-Dec-05	1256.54	-0.009599	2.571952E-05	-1.904619	0.962163	θ =	0.61310000
9	23-Dec-05	1268.66	0.000426	2.550821E-05	0.072371	4.588083	r =	0.00013699
10	22-Dec-05	1268.12	0.004212	2.811035E-05	0.783904	3.936629		
11	21-Dec-05	1262.79	0.002513	2.960986E-05	0.452128	4.324144	Estimated Parameters	
12	20-Dec-05	1259.62	-0.000238	2.902812E-05	-0.054258	4.534237	Log Likelihood	-2,301.40
13	19-Dec-05	1259.92	-0.005856	2.423936E-05	-1.202165	3.170278	λ =	-0.01267371
14	16-Dec-05	1267.32	-0.002852	2.169878E-05	-0.626734	4.270769	β_0 =	0.00000126
15	15-Dec-05	1270.94	-0.001415	2.011699E-05	-0.331169	4.586764	β_1 =	0.09487649
16	14-Dec-05	1272.74	0.004181	2.216395E-05	0.873983	3.890506	β_2 =	0.00561592
17	13-Dec-05	1267.43	0.005538	2.539068E-05	1.087112	3.413513	θ =	12.47682422
18	12-Dec-05	1260.43	0.000841	2.546917E-05	0.154764	4.570034		
19	9-Dec-05	1259.37	0.002807	2.700591E-05	0.529046	4.288652	Persistence	
20	8-Dec-05	1255.84	-0.001218	2.562477E-05	-0.252383	4.527643	$\beta_2(1+\theta^2) + \beta_1$ =	0.97473
21	7-Dec-05	1257.37	-0.005022	2.157596E-05	-1.095592	3.465708		
22	6-Dec-05	1263.7	0.001275	2.177297E-05	0.258861	4.595073		
23	5-Dec-05	1262.09	-0.002366	1.957584E-05	-0.550894	4.404795	Current Variance	0.00003552
24	2-Dec-05	1265.08	0.000324	1.906128E-05	0.057724	4.716516	Annualized	0.0946
25	1-Dec-05	1264.67	0.012084	2.648210E-05	2.336776	-0.883476		
26	30-Nov-05	1249.48	-0.006382	2.146862E-05	-1.392078	2.730355	From Figure 9.2	
27	29-Nov-05	1257.48	0.000016	2.081870E-05	-0.011582	4.681412	Current Variance	0.00003192
28	28-Nov-05	1257.46	-0.008544	1.493428E-05	-2.231789	-0.155068	Annualized	0.0897
29	25-Nov-05	1268.25	0.002084	1.522024E-05	0.513634	4.553759		

FIGURE 9.11   Solution to Exercise 9.1

requires three starting values (startParams), a cross-section of option prices (realPrice) and strikes (K), the spot price (S), time to maturity (T), the risk-free rate (r), the dividend yield (q), and the time to maturity (T). The function includes a penalty for parameter values that are not permissible, which ensures that $V_0 \geqslant 0, \kappa \geqslant 0, \theta \geqslant 0, -1 \leqslant \rho \leqslant 1, \gamma \leqslant 1$, and that $\gamma(1-\gamma)\sigma^2 \leqslant \theta^2$.

```
Function RMSE(startParams, PC, S, K, r, q, t, realPrice)
rho = startParams(1)
kappa = startParams(2)
thet = startParams(3)
SigmaV = startParams(4)
V0 = startParams(5)
ki = startParams(6)
gam = startParams(7)
n = Application.Count(K)
If (V0 > 0) Or (kappa > 0) Or (thet > 0) Or (Abs(rho) > 1)
  Or (gam > 1) Or ((gam * (1 - gam) * SigmaV ^ 2 - thet ^ 2) > 0) Then
  RMSE = 9999999
Else
  RMSE = 0
For i = 1 To n
  If (PC(i) = "Call") Then
RMSE = RMSE + ((realPrice(i) - HCTrans(S, K(i), r, q,
    V0, t, ki, thet, kappa, SigmaV, rho, gam, "Call"))) ^ 2
```

```
Else
  RMSE = RMSE + ((realPrice(i) - HCTrans(S, K(i), r, q,
  VO, t, ki, thet, kappa, SigmaV, rho, gam, "Put"))) ^ 2
  End If
Next i
End If
  RMSE = Sqr(RMSE / n)
End Function
```

The RMSEparams() function invokes the NelderMead() function to find the parameter values that produce the minimum value of RMSE().

```
Function RMSEparams(startParams, PC, S, K, r, q, t, realPrice)
  RMSEparams = NelderMead("RMSE", startParams, PC, S, K, r,
            q, t, realPrice)
End Function
```

These functions are illustrated in Figure 9.12, using the prices contained in the Excel file Chapter9Google. The strike prices of the options expiring on July 21, 2006, appear in cells C10:C31, and their closing prices in cells E10:E31. These

	Option Type	Strike Price	Moneyne (K/S)	Closing Price	B-S Implied Volatility	$RMSE Prices			
1	EXERCISE 9.2								
2	Google, Inc. Market and Fitted Heston (1993) Call and Put Prices						Heston (1993) Parameter Starting Values		
3									
4	Current Date	6-Jul-06	Yearly Risk-Free Rate (r)		0.05185		Dividend Yield (δ)		0
5	Expiry Date	21-Jul-06	Spot Price (S)		423.19		Rho (ρ)		-0.3
6	Time to Maturity (T)	0.0411					Kappa (κ)		3
7							Theta (θ)		0.5
8	Option	Strike	Moneyne	Closing	B-S Implied	$RMSE	Volatility of Variance (σ)		0.9
9	Type	Price	(K/S)	Price	Volatility	Prices	Current variance (V₀)		0.1
10	Put	300	0.709	0.10	0.6842	0.01	Imaginary Part of k (kᵢ)		0.5
11	Put	310	0.733	0.15	0.6566	0.03	Gamma (γ)		0.1
12	Put	320	0.756	0.20	0.6197	0.06			
13	Put	330	0.780	0.30	0.5928	0.11	Heston (1993) $RMSE Parameter Estimates		
14	Put	340	0.803	0.30	0.5311	0.21			
15	Put	350	0.827	0.55	0.5205	0.39	Loss Function		0.1041
16	Put	360	0.851	0.75	0.4838	0.68	Rho (ρ)		-0.3274
17	Put	370	0.874	1.25	0.4669	1.17	Kappa (κ)		1.8946
18	Put	380	0.898	1.91	0.4420	1.95	Theta (θ)		0.5243
19	Put	390	0.922	3.10	0.4267	3.17	Volatility of Variance (σ)		2.0743
20	Put	400	0.945	4.90	0.4120	4.98	Current variance (V₀)		0.1453
21	Put	410	0.969	7.50	0.3974	7.62	Imaginary Part of k (kᵢ)		0.5051
22	Put	420	0.992	11.40	0.3918	11.31	Gamma (γ)		0.0642
23	Call	430	1.016	10.30	0.3783	10.33			
24	Call	440	1.040	6.80	0.3802	6.56			
25	Call	450	1.063	3.90	0.3663	3.99			
26	Call	460	1.087	2.25	0.3653	2.34			
27	Call	470	1.111	1.35	0.3730	1.34			
28	Call	480	1.134	0.70	0.3705	0.76			
29	Call	490	1.158	0.45	0.3857	0.42			
30	Call	500	1.182	0.20	0.3783	0.23			
31	Call	510	1.205	0.15	0.4006	0.13			

FIGURE 9.12 Solution to Exercise 9.2
Source: www.optionmetrics.com

options have a time to maturity of 0.0411 years, which appears in cell D6. The closing price of Google, Inc. on July 6, 2006, was \$423.19. The starting values for the \$RMSE loss function are in cells J5:J11, so in cell J15 we type

$$= \text{RMSEparams}(J5:J11,B10:B31,G5,C10:C31,G4, J4, D6, E10:E31)$$

which produces $\hat{\rho} = -0.3274$, $\hat{\kappa} = 1.8946$, $\hat{\theta} = 0.5243$, $\hat{\sigma} = 2.0743$, $\hat{V}_0 = 0.1453$, $\hat{k}_i = 0.5051$, and $\gamma = 0.0642$. Note that all of the conditions for permissible parameters are satisfied. The value of the loss function is 0.1041, which implies a mean error of roughly 10.4 cents between the market prices and the Heston (1993) prices. The Heston (1993) prices, obtained using the estimated parameter values and the fundamental transform, appear in cells G10:G31. As expected, these are quite close to the market prices.

9.3 The %RMSE loss function (9.11) is created with the perRMSE() function. This VBA function is identical to the RMSE() function of Exercise 9.2, except for the loop, so only part of the function is reproduced here. This function appears in the Excel file Chapter9Exercise3.

```
Function perRMSE()
' More VBA Statements
For i = 1 To n
  If (PC(i) = "Call") Then
    perRMSE = perRMSE + ((realPrice(i) - HCTrans(S, K(i), r,
        q, VO, t, ki, thet, kappa, SigmaV, rho, gam, "Call"))
        / realPrice(i)) ^ 2
  Else
    perRMSE = perRMSE + ((realPrice(i) - HCTrans(S, K(i), r,
        q, VO, t, ki, thet, kappa, SigmaV, rho, gam, "Put"))
        / realPrice(i)) ^ 2
  End If
Next i
  perRMSE = Sqr(perRMSE / n)
End Function
```

The perRMSEparams() function invokes the Nelder-Mead algorithm. It is identical to the RMSEparams() function except that "PERRMS" appears in the argument to the NelderMead() function, so it will not be reproduced here. Figure 9.13 illustrates these functions on the prices of Google, Inc. options. The starting values for the %RMSE loss function are in cells J5:J11, so in cell J15 we type

$$= \text{perRMSEparams}(J5:J11,B10:B31,G5,C10:C31,G4, J4, D6, E10:E31)$$

which produces $\hat{\rho} = -0.3690$, $\hat{\kappa} = 3.4221$, $\hat{\theta} = 0.9728$, $\hat{\sigma} = 3.8493$, $\hat{V}_0 = 0.0889$, $\hat{k}_i = 0.5289$, and $\gamma = 0.0059$. Note that all of the conditions for

		Strike	Moneyne	Closing	B-S Implied	%RMSE		
1	EXERCISE 9.3							
2	Google, Inc. Market and Fitted Heston (1993) Call and Put Prices						Heston (1993) Parameter Starting Values	
3								
4	Current Date	6-Jul-06	Yearly Risk-Free Rate (r)		0.05185		Dividend Yield (δ)	0
5	Expiry Date	21-Jul-06	Spot Price (S)		423.19		Rho (ρ)	-0.3
6	Time to Maturity (T)	0.0411					Kappa (κ)	3
7							Theta (θ)	0.5
8	Option	Strike	Moneyne	Closing	B-S Implied	%RMSE	Volatility of Variance (σ)	0.9
9	Type	Price	(K/S)	Price	Volatility	Prices	Current variance (v)	0.1
10	Put	300	0.709	0.10	0.6842	0.06	Imaginary Part of k (k₁)	0.5
11	Put	310	0.733	0.15	0.6566	0.10	Gamma (γ)	0.1
12	Put	320	0.756	0.20	0.6197	0.16		
13	Put	330	0.780	0.30	0.5928	0.26	**Heston (1993) %RMSE Parameter Estimates**	
14	Put	340	0.803	0.30	0.5311	0.41	**All Options**	
15	Put	350	0.827	0.55	0.5205	0.62	Loss Function	0.1988
16	Put	360	0.851	0.75	0.4838	0.96	Rho (ρ)	-0.3690
17	Put	370	0.874	1.25	0.4669	1.44	Kappa (κ)	3.4221
18	Put	380	0.898	1.91	0.4420	2.15	Theta (θ)	0.9728
19	Put	390	0.922	3.10	0.4267	3.18	Volatility of Variance (σ)	3.8493
20	Put	400	0.945	4.90	0.4120	4.70	Current variance (v)	0.0889
21	Put	410	0.969	7.50	0.3974	6.91	Imaginary Part of k (k₁)	0.5289
22	Put	420	0.992	11.40	0.3918	10.14	Gamma (γ)	0.0059
23	Call	430	1.016	10.30	0.3783	8.93		
24	Call	440	1.040	6.80	0.3802	5.30	**Excluding Options < $0.50**	
25	Call	450	1.063	3.90	0.3663	3.10	Loss Function	0.0563
26	Call	460	1.087	2.25	0.3653	1.84	Rho (ρ)	-0.3438
27	Call	470	1.111	1.35	0.3730	1.10	Kappa (κ)	3.8376
28	Call	480	1.134	0.70	0.3705	0.67	Theta (θ)	1.0079
29	Call	490	1.158	0.45	0.3857	0.42	Volatility of Variance (σ)	2.8235
30	Call	500	1.182	0.20	0.3783	0.26	Current variance (v)	0.0902
31	Call	510	1.205	0.15	0.4006	0.16	Imaginary Part of k (k₁)	0.5290
32							Gamma (γ)	0.0068

FIGURE 9.13 Solution to Exercise 9.3
Source: www.optionmetrics.com

permissible parameters are satisfied. The value of the loss function is 0.1988, which implies a mean error of roughly 19.88 percent between the market prices and the Heston (1993) prices. The Heston (1993) prices, obtained using these estimated parameter values, appear in cells G10:G31.

To obtain the parameter estimates when options with value less than $0.50 are excluded, in cell J24 we type

$$= perRMSEparams(J16:J22,B15:B28,G5,C15:C28,G4, J4, D6, E15:E28)$$

which produces a value of 0.0563 for the loss function, corresponding to a mean error of roughly 5.63 percent between market prices and the generated prices. This is much lower than when all options are used. As noted by Bakshi, Cao, and Chen (1997), excluding cheap options helps to mitigate the impact of price discreteness on option valuation.

9.4 The ivRMSE() function creates the IVMSE loss function (9.12). This function is identical to the RMSE() function, except for the loop, so only part of the function is reproduced here. This function appears in the Excel file Chapter9Exercise4. Note that the ivRMSE() function requires as one of its inputs a vector of implied volatilities, rather than a vector of option prices.

```
Function ivRMSE(startParams, PC, S, K, r, q, t, realIV)
' More VBA Statements
For i = 1 To n
  If (PC(i) = "Call") Then
    curPrice = HCTrans(S, K(i), r, q, VO, t, ki, thet,
                kappa, SigmaV, rho, gam, "Call")
    ivRMSE = ivRMSE + (realIV(i) - BisecBSV("Call", S, K(i),
                r, t, 0.000001, 4, curPrice)) ^ 2
  Else
    curPrice = HCTrans(S, K(i), r, q, VO, t, ki, thet,
                kappa, SigmaV, rho, gam, "Put")
    ivRMSE = ivRMSE + (realIV(i) - BisecBSV("Put", S, K(i),
                r, t, 0.000001, 4, curPrice)) ^ 2
  End If
Next i
  ivRMSE = Sqr(ivRMSE / n)
End Function
```

	A	B	C	D	E	F	G	H	I	J
1	EXERCISE 9.4									
2		Google, Inc. Market and Fitted Heston (1993) Call and Put Prices							Heston (1993) Parameter Starting Values	
3										
4			Current Date	6-Jul-06	Yearly Risk-Free Rate (r)		0.05185		Dividend Yield (δ)	0
5			Expiry Date	21-Jul-06	Spot Price (S)		423.19		Rho (ρ)	-0.3274
6		Time to Maturity (T)		0.0411					Kappa (κ)	1.8946
7									Theta (θ)	0.5243
8		Option	Strike	Moneyness	Closing	B-S Implied	RMSE		Volatility of Variance (σ)	2.0743
9		Type	Price	(K/S)	Price	Volatility	Prices		Current variance (V0)	0.1453
10		Put	300	0.709	0.10	0.6842	0.06		Imaginary Part of k (ki)	0.5051
11		Put	310	0.733	0.15	0.6566	0.09		Gamma (γ)	0.0642
12		Put	320	0.756	0.20	0.6197	0.16			
13		Put	330	0.780	0.30	0.5928	0.26		Heston (1993) IVRMSE Parameter Estimates	
14		Put	340	0.803	0.30	0.5311	0.42			
15		Put	350	0.827	0.55	0.5205	0.66		Loss Function	0.0214
16		Put	360	0.851	0.75	0.4838	1.04		Rho (ρ)	-0.3691
17		Put	370	0.874	1.25	0.4669	1.58		Kappa (κ)	1.9067
18		Put	380	0.898	1.91	0.4420	2.38		Theta (θ)	0.5887
19		Put	390	0.922	3.10	0.4267	3.54		Volatility of Variance (σ)	3.2077
20		Put	400	0.945	4.90	0.4120	5.19		Current variance (V0)	0.1457
21		Put	410	0.969	7.50	0.3974	7.55		Imaginary Part of k (ki)	0.4827
22		Put	420	0.992	11.40	0.3918	10.89		Gamma (γ)	0.0327
23		Call	430	1.016	10.30	0.3783	9.69			
24		Call	440	1.040	6.80	0.3802	5.94			
25		Call	450	1.063	3.90	0.3663	3.57			
26		Call	460	1.087	2.25	0.3653	2.14			
27		Call	470	1.111	1.35	0.3730	1.29			
28		Call	480	1.134	0.70	0.3705	0.78			
29		Call	490	1.158	0.45	0.3857	0.48			
30		Call	500	1.182	0.20	0.3783	0.29			
31		Call	510	1.205	0.15	0.4006	0.18			

FIGURE 9.14 Solution to Exercise 9.4
Source: www.optionmetrics.com

The ivRMSEparams() function finds the minimum value of ivRMSE(), and is identical to the RMSEparams() and perRMSE() functions, except that "IVRMSE" appears in the argument to the NelderMead() function. Convergence of this function is slow because a cross-section of implied volatilities must be calculated at each iteration of the NelderMead() function. Hence, for starting values to the ivRMSE() function we use parameter estimates obtained with the $RMSE loss function in Exercise 9.2. This is illustrated in Figure 9.14.

9.5 The Excel file Chapter9Exercise5 presents the parameter estimates and corresponding option prices obtained under the three methods with the Google, Inc. data. The parameter estimates are copied directly from the Excel files for

	A	B	C	D	E	F	G	H	I	J	K	L
1	EXERCISE 9.5											
2	Implied Volatilities for Google, Inc. Using Market and Fitted Heston (1993) Prices											
3												
4		Current Date		6-Jul-06		Yearly Risk-Free Rate (*r*)		0.05185				
5		Expiry Date		21-Jul-06		Spot Price (S)		423.19				
6		Time to Mat		0.0411		Dividend Yield (δ)		0.00				
7												
8												
9							Heston Fitted Prices and Implied Volatilities					
10							$RMSE		%RMSE		IVRMSE	
11	Option	Strike	Moneyness	Closing	BS-Implied			Implied		Implied		Implied
12	Type	Price	(K/S)	Price	Volatility	Prices	Volatility	Prices	Volatility	Prices	Volatility
13	Put	300	0.709	0.10	0.684	0.01	0.559	0.06	0.648	0.06	0.644
14	Put	310	0.733	0.15	0.657	0.03	0.546	0.10	0.624	0.09	0.621
15	Put	320	0.756	0.20	0.620	0.06	0.534	0.16	0.603	0.16	0.602
16	Put	330	0.780	0.30	0.593	0.11	0.519	0.26	0.579	0.26	0.579
17	Put	340	0.803	0.30	0.531	0.21	0.505	0.41	0.557	0.41	0.558
18	Put	350	0.827	0.55	0.520	0.39	0.490	0.62	0.532	0.64	0.536
19	Put	360	0.851	0.75	0.484	0.68	0.475	0.96	0.509	1.00	0.514
20	Put	370	0.874	1.25	0.467	1.17	0.460	1.44	0.483	1.53	0.490
21	Put	380	0.898	1.91	0.442	1.95	0.445	2.15	0.458	2.31	0.467
22	Put	390	0.922	3.10	0.427	3.17	0.430	3.18	0.431	3.45	0.443
23	Put	400	0.945	4.90	0.412	4.98	0.415	4.70	0.404	5.10	0.420
24	Put	410	0.969	7.50	0.397	7.62	0.401	6.91	0.378	7.48	0.397
25	Put	420	0.992	11.40	0.392	11.31	0.389	10.14	0.354	10.87	0.376
26	Call	430	1.016	10.30	0.378	10.33	0.379	8.93	0.338	9.69	0.360
27	Call	440	1.040	6.80	0.380	6.56	0.373	5.30	0.331	5.93	0.352
28	Call	450	1.063	3.90	0.366	3.99	0.370	3.10	0.334	3.51	0.351
29	Call	460	1.087	2.25	0.365	2.34	0.370	1.84	0.344	2.07	0.356
30	Call	470	1.111	1.35	0.373	1.34	0.372	1.10	0.355	1.22	0.364
31	Call	480	1.134	0.70	0.371	0.76	0.377	0.67	0.367	0.73	0.373
32	Call	490	1.158	0.45	0.386	0.42	0.381	0.42	0.381	0.44	0.384
33	Call	500	1.182	0.20	0.378	0.23	0.387	0.26	0.392	0.26	0.394
34	Call	510	1.205	0.15	0.401	0.13	0.392	0.16	0.403	0.16	0.404

FIGURE 9.15 Solution to Exercise 9.5
Source: www.optionmetrics.com

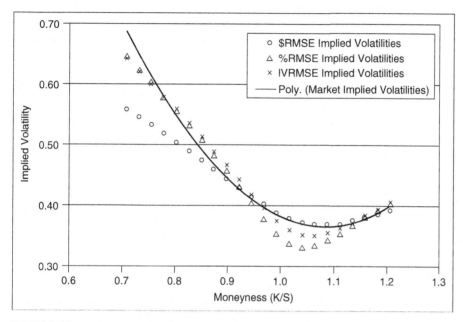

FIGURE 9.16 Solution to Exercise 9.5
Source: www.optionmetrics.com

Exercises 9.2 through 9.4, because the calculation required to obtain these estimates is substantial, especially the IVRMSE estimates. Rather than comparing
the parameter estimates directly, it is preferable to compare the Heston (1993)
prices obtained from the different parameter values, and the implied volatilities
obtained from those prices. These comparisons are included in the left-most part
of the Excel file Chapter9Exercise5, and are illustrated in Figures 9.15 and 9.16.
As expected, the $RMSE estimates produce implied volatilities that are close to
the market implied volatilities for options that are at-the-money or near to the
money, while the %RMSE estimates produce implied volatilities that are close
to market implied volatilities for options that are out-of-the-money. As well,
the IVRMSE estimates produce implied volatilities that are reasonably close to
the market implied volatilities across all moneyness.

CHAPTER 10

Implied Volatility

INTRODUCTION

It was mentioned briefly in Chapter 4 that the Black-Scholes option pricing model suffers from several systematic biases. One way to illustrate these biases is to plot the difference between observed market prices and model prices. One example of such a plot was presented in Figure 5.8, which compared option prices obtained with the Heston (1993) stochastic volatility model, to option prices obtained with the Black-Scholes constant volatility model. This illustration is not perfect. Although it permits to detect absolute differences in call prices, it gives no indication of the relative difference between them. For example, an at-the-money call option with a market price of $5.50 and model price of $5.45 has an absolute difference of $0.05. This corresponds to a relative difference of less than 1 percent, and is not dramatic. On the other hand, a deep out-of-the-money call option on the same stock with a market price of $0.10 and model price of $0.15 also has an absolute difference of $0.05. Although the absolute difference is the same, the relative difference, 50 percent in this case, is quite dramatic. Because of this inconsistency the most frequently used graphical comparison of models is the implied volatility curve.

Implied volatilities are important because they are embedded in option prices, and the prices of options reflect future expectations of market participants. This means that implied volatilities constitute a forward-looking estimate of the volatility of the underlying asset. Chapter 6 presented alternative ways of estimating future volatility, the simple unconditional standard deviation, or the generalized autoregressive conditional heteroskedasticity (GARCH) model. Although these methods are often easy to implement, they constitute a retrospective estimate of asset volatility, since they are based on historical prices. Hence, many authors have advocated the use of implied volatility because it reflects future expectations about volatility, rather than reflecting past realizations.

OBTAINING IMPLIED VOLATILITY

The implied volatility curve is a plot of implied volatilities versus strike price (K), versus spot price (S), or versus moneyness (S/K or K/S). The curve exploits the fact that there exists a one-to-one relationship between volatility and call prices. To illustrate this point, consider the Black-Scholes formula parameters, namely the spot price of the asset S, the strike price K, the risk-free rate r, time to maturity T and stock price volatility σ. Consider two assets with the same spot price, and call options with identical maturity and strike price written on each asset. These calls will have different prices only if the volatility of each asset is different. Hence, if a set of different call prices each with the same spot price, strike price and maturity, differ only with respect to volatility, we should be able to extract volatility from the call prices.

The most popular type of implied volatilities are Black-Scholes implied volatilities. As mentioned in Chapter 4, these are obtained by equating an observed market price with a given strike price and maturity to the Black-Scholes formula with the same strike price and maturity. The value of volatility in the Black-Scholes formula that yields the observed option price is the implied volatility. If σ_{iv} denotes the implied volatility, $C_{obs}(K, T)$ denotes the observed market call price with strike price K and time to maturity T, and $C_{BS}(\sigma, K, T)$ denotes the Black-Scholes price of the call with same strike price and maturity, then σ_{iv} is the value of volatility in the Black-Scholes formula such that

$$C_{obs}(K, T) = C_{BS}(\sigma_{iv}, K, T). \tag{10.1}$$

Since volatility cannot be extracted from the Black-Scholes formula analytically, this must be done numerically, by using a root-finding algorithm. This requires (10.1) to be expressed as the root of the objective function

$$f(\sigma) = C_{BS}(\sigma, K, T) - C_{obs}(K, T), \tag{10.2}$$

so that the objective function takes on the value zero at the value of implied volatility, namely $f(\sigma_{iv}) = 0$.

In Chapter 4 the objective function was defined as the squared difference between market and model prices. A squared objective function, or one that uses the absolute value of the difference, will work for the Newton-Raphson method, but will not work for the bisection method. This is because the bisection method requires that the function has values of opposite sign at the endpoints of each subinterval. Hence, in this chapter objective functions of the form (10.2) are employed.

 In the remainder of this section implied volatilities are obtained by applying the root-finding methods of Chapter 1 to the objective function (10.2). In particular, the Newton-Raphson method, the bisection method, and the Newton-Raphson-bisection method are used. Some of these methods were encountered briefly in Chapter 4, as inputs to the Practitioner Black-Scholes model. In this section these methods are discussed in more detail. All of the VBA functions for implementing these methods are contained in the Excel file Chapter10ImpliedVol.

Newton-Raphson Method

To apply this method the VBA function NewtRaph() introduced in Chapter 1 must be adapted so that the function seeks the root of (10.2). This requires modifying the function declaration statement to include the option parameters S, K, r, and T, an identifier for the option type, PutCall, and an observed price for the option, realC.

```
Function NewtRaph(PutCall, S, K, r, T, x_guess, realC)
Dim EPS As Double
delta_x = 0.000000001: EPS = 0.00001
cur_x = x_guess
  For i = 1 To MAXITER
    fx = realC - bs_price(S, K, r, T, cur_x, PutCall)
    cur_x_delta = cur_x - delta_x
    fx_delta = realC — BS_price(S, K, r, T, cur_x_delta, PutCall)
    dx = (fx - fx_delta) / delta_x
    If (Abs(dx) < EPS) Then
      Exit For
    End If
    cur_x = cur_x - (fx / dx)
  Next i
NewtRaph = cur_x
End Function
```

Note that the objective function (10.2) appears as the statement

```
fx = realC - BS_price(S, K, r, T, cur_x, PutCall)
```

where the Black-Scholes price is obtained using the VBA function BS_price().

```
Function BS_price(S, K, r, T, v, PutCall)
d = (Log(S / K) + T * (r + 0.5 * v ^ 2)) / (v * Sqr(T))
BS_call = S * Gauss(d) — Exp(-r * T) * K * Gauss(d - v * Sqr(T))
If PutCall = "Call" Then
  BS_price = BS_call
Else
  BS_price = BS_call - S + K * Exp(-r * T)
End If
End Function
```

As in Chapter 4 the VBA function Gauss() produces the cumulative distribution function of a standard normal random variable through the Excel function NormS-Dist(), and the VBA function Fz() produces the density function. Both functions are used to conserve space.

The NewtRaph() function returns the implied volatility when the difference between the observed price and the model price is below the tolerance level EPS (set to 1×10^{-5}) or the maximum number of iterations, MAXITER, is reached (set to 500). Recall that the Newton-Raphson algorithm requires that the function's derivative be known explicitly or approximated numerically. The NewtRaph() function above uses the latter approach, by deviating the current volatility by delta_x (set to 1×10^{-9}) and computing the numerical derivative. However, it is known from Chapter 7 that the derivative of the call price with respect to volatility is the vega of the option. Since the observed market price in the objective function (10.2) is a constant, the derivative of (10.2) will simply be vega. By employing vega in the Newton-Raphson function the need to evaluate the derivative numerically can be eliminated, which will make the function more efficient. This is illustrated with the VBA function NewtRaphVega(). The only difference with the NewtRaph() function is that the statement

```
dx = (fx - fx_delta) / delta_x
```

in NewtRaph() is replaced with

```
dx = BSVega(S, K, T, r, cur_x)
```

in the function NewRaphVega(), where BSVega() is the VBA function that produces the option's Black-Scholes vega.

```
Function NewtRaphVega(PutCall, S, K, r, T, x_guess, realC)
Dim EPS As Double
delta_x = 0.000000001
EPS = 0.00001
cur_x = x_guess
  For i = 1 To MAXITER
    fx = BS_price(S, K, r, T, cur_x, PutCall) - realC
    dx = BSVega(S, K, T, r, cur_x)
    If (Abs(dx) < EPS) Then
      Exit For
      End If
    cur_x = cur_x - (fx / dx)
  Next i
NewtRaphVega = cur_x
End Function
Function BSVega(S, K, T, r, v)
d = (Log(S / K) + T * (r + 0.5 * v ^ 2)) / (v * Sqr(T))
  BSVega = S * Fz(d) * Sqr(T)
End Function
```

Bisection Method

Although the Newton-Raphson method is quick to converge to the implied volatility, it requires an initial guess for the volatility. It is well known that this root-finding algorithm is quite sensitive to the location of the initial guess. This implies that the algorithm could deviate drastically from the root. The bisection method, however, is particularly well suited for finding the implied volatility in option prices, when the objective function is (10.2). With the proper function boundaries, the method is always successful at finding the root. In the case of implied volatility, it is easy to find two starting values σ_1 and σ_2 for which the objective function (10.2) takes on values $f(\sigma_1) > 0$ and $f(\sigma_2) < 0$. Since $C_{BS}(\sigma, K, T)$ is an increasing function of volatility, a large value of σ will produce a Black-Scholes price substantially larger than the market price and a positive value for $f(\sigma)$, while the opposite will be true for a very small value of σ. Hence, when using the bisection method to find Black-Scholes implied volatility, we only need to set σ_1 and σ_2 to very large and small values, respectively, such as $\sigma_1 = 4$ (400 percent) and $\sigma_2 = 0.0001$ (0.01 percent), for example. The VBA function BisecBSV() implements the bisection algorithm to find implied volatilities. Again, it requires that the function declaration statement be modified to include option parameters and the observed option prices.

```
Function BisecBSV(PutCall, S, K, r, T, a, b, realC)
TOL = 0.00001
lowCdif = realC - BS_price(S, K, r, T, a, PutCall)
highCdif = realC - BS_price(S, K, r, T, b, PutCall)
test = bs_price(S, K, r, T, a, PutCall)
If (lowCdif * highCdif > 0) Then
  midP = -1
Else
  For cnt = 1 To MAXITER
    midP = (a + b) / 2
    midCdif = realC - BS_price(S, K, r, T, midP, PutCall)
    If (Abs(midCdif) < TOL) Then
      Exit For
    End If
    If (midCdif > 0) Then
      a = midP
    Else
      b = midP
    End If
  Next cnt
End If
BisecBSV = midP
End Function
```

One very important feature of the BisecBSV() function is that it verifies whether or not prices are consistent. When examining options data it is very easy to obtain call prices that are not invertible, which can occur when call price quotes and stock price quotes are not synchronized. If the call price and the stock price quotes are not reported simultaneously and there is a large stock price move, then implied volatility retrieved from the prices will be too low or too high. If the call price is too low, it may be the case that no value of volatility, even zero, will produce a root of (10.2). We can test for such errors by verifying that the implied volatility falls within a certain range defined by the function boundaries. If it does not fall in the range, the observed market price for the option will be classified as an error. This error checking is done by verifying whether the objective function has the same sign for both of the boundary points, using the statement

$$\text{If (lowCdif}^*\text{highCdif} > 0) \text{ Then midP} = -1. \qquad (10.3)$$

If the boundary points have the same sign, the BisecBSV() function returns the value -1 for the implied volatility, signifying an undefined value.

Newton-Raphson-Bisection Method

Although the bisection method always finds the root of the objective function $f(\sigma)$, except when the implied volatility is undefined, it requires more steps than the Newton-Raphson method. The Newton-Raphson method seeks the root at every step of the algorithm, by using the slope of the objective function, while the bisection method cuts the range in half at every step. It is possible to apply both methods simultaneously and achieve faster convergence than by using each method separately, and setting boundary conditions on the objective function, as in (10.3). The VBA function BisNewtVol() modifies the Newton-Raphson function so that at each step, if the current estimate of volatility is outside the current boundaries, a bisection step is performed to ensure convergence.

```
Function BisNewtVol(PutCall, S, K, r, T, a, b, realC)
Dim EPS As Double
EPS = 0.00001
lowCdif = realC - BS_price(S, K, r, T, a, PutCall)
highCdif = realC - BS_price(S, K, r, T, b, PutCall)
midP = 0.5 * (a + b): dxold = (b - a): dx = dxold
midCdif = realC - BS_price(S, K, r, T, midP, PutCall)
midCvega = BSVega(S, K, T, r, midP)
  For i = 1 To MAXITER
    If ((((midP - b) * midCvega - midCdif) * ((midP - a)
       * midCvega - midCdif) > 0) Or
       (Abs(2 * midCdif) > Abs(dxold * midCvega))) Then
      dxold = dx: dx = 0.5 * (b - a): midP = a + dx
    Else
      dxold = dx: dx = midCdif / midCvega
      temp = midP: midP = midP - dx
    End If
  midCdif = realC - BS_price(S, K, r, T, midP, PutCall)
    If (Abs(midCdif) < EPS) Then
      Exit For
    End If
  midCvega = BSVega(S, K, T, r, midP)
    If (midCdif < 0) Then
      b = midP
    Else
      a = midP
    End If
  Next i
BisNewtVol = midP
End Function
```

The BisNewVol() function does not require an initial guess of the volatility, but a range as in the bisection method. The initial guess is defined as the midpoint of the range.

The Excel file Chapter10ImpliedVol contains the four VBA functions described in this chapter. Use of these functions is illustrated in Figure 10.1 on a call option, using $S = K = 100$, $r = 0.05$, and $T = 0.5$ years. In this figure, the market call option price is defined as the Black-Scholes price with volatility $\sigma = 0.35$ in cell C10, and appears in cell C12 as \$11.01. The Black-Scholes formula is used to simulate the market price, so that the true value of volatility is known explicitly. Hence, it is easy to verify the performance of the root-finding algorithms, because these should all produce an implied volatility of $\sigma_{iv} = 0.35$. To implement the Newton-Raphson method, in cell C21 we type

$$= \text{NewtRaph(C11,C6,C7,C8,C9,C14,C12)}$$

which uses $\sigma = 1$ as the initial guess in cell C14, and produces $\sigma_{iv} = 0.35$, as expected. Similarly, using $\sigma_1 = 4$ in cell C18 and $\sigma_2 = 0.00001$ in cell C17 as function boundaries for the bisection method produces the same implied volatility in cell C23. The other methods produce the same implied volatility as well. When calculating implied volatility we can just as easily work with put prices instead of call prices. Indeed, setting "Put" in cell C11 changes the Black-Scholes price of the

	A	B	C	D
3		**Root-Finding Algorithms**		
4				
5		**Option Price Parameters**		
6		Spot Price (S)	100	
7		Strike Price (K)	100	
8		Risk Free Rate (r)	0.05	
9		Time to Maturity (T)	0.5	
10		Actual Volatility (σ)	0.35	
11		Option Type (*Call* or *Put*)	Call	
12		Black-Scholes Call Price	11.01	
13				
14		**Starting Values for σ**		
15		**– Newton-Raphson Method**	1	
16		**– Bisection Method**		
17		Lower Range (σ₂)	0.00001	
18		Upper Range (σ₁)	4	
19				
20		**Implied Volatilities**		
21		Newton-Raphson	0.350000	
22		Newton-Raphson-Vega	0.350000	
23		Bisection Method	0.350000	
24		Newton-Raphson-Bisection	0.350000	

FIGURE 10.1   Implied Volatility Using Root-Finding Algorithms

option to 8.54 in cell C12, but produces exactly the same value for the implied volatility.

Implied Volatilities from Options on Google

This section illustrates the implied volatility curve, using a cross section of calls and puts on Google, Inc. (ticker GOOG), from Yahoo! (finance.yahoo.com). They represent closing prices at July 6, 2006, of calls and puts with expiry date at July 21, 2006. The time to maturity is the difference in days between these two dates, divided by 365, which corresponds to $T = 0.041$ years or roughly two weeks. The closing price of Google on July 6 is \$423.19. The options have a strike price ranging from $K = \$300$ to $K = \$510$. When constructing the implied volatility curve, out-of-the-money and near-the-money options are used since they are more liquid and quotes for these options are readily available.

    The Excel file Chapter10Google contains implied volatility from this set of option prices, obtained with the four methods covered in this section. This is illustrated in Figure 10.2, using the objective function (10.2).

    Closing prices for the puts are in cells C11:C26, with strike prices in cells B11:B26. For the calls these appear in cells C28:C39 and cells B28:B39. The time to maturity is $T = 0.041$ years, the risk-free rate is $r = 0.05185$ and the spot price of the asset is $S = 423.19$. To implement the Newton-Raphson method with a starting value of $\sigma = 1$, in cell F11 we type

$$= \text{NewtRaph("Put",E6,B11,E5,C6,1,C11)}$$

which produces an implied volatility of $\sigma_{iv} = 0.6842$, or 68.42 percent, when the strike price is $K = 300$. Similarly, to implement the bisection method with starting values $\sigma_1 = 4$ and $\sigma_2 = 0.00001$, in cell E11 we type

$$= \text{BisecBSV("Put",E6,B11,E5,C6,0.00001,4,C11)}$$

which produces an identical value, $\sigma_{iv} = 0.6842$. Figure 10.2 indicates that the four methods produce implied volatilities that are identical up to four decimal places. The implied volatilities for calls are obtained analogously expect that the "Put" arguments in the root-finding functions are replaced with "Call".

    To plot the implied volatility curve using values obtained from the bisection method, we use the "Add Trendline" feature in the Chart Wizard of Excel and select a polynomial of order two, which ensures that the curve will be smooth. This implies that we are in fact fitting a quadratic function similar to a simple version

$$\sigma_{iv} = a_0 + a_1 K + a_2 K^2 \tag{10.4}$$

of the deterministic volatility function of Dumas, Fleming, and Whaley (1998), which was introduced in Chapter 4. This fitted curve appears in Figure 10.3 as a solid line, along with the data points $(K/S, \sigma_{iv})$ which appear as crosses.

	A	B	C	D	E	F	G	H
1								
2		**Implied Volatility Using Call and Put Prices on Google**						
3								
4		Date:	6-Jul-06					
5		Exp. Date:	21-Jul-06	Risk-Free Rate (r)	0.05185			
6		Maturity (T)	0.041096	Spot Price (S)	423.19			
7							Implied Volatility	
8		Strike	Market	Moneyness	Bisection	Newton-	Newton-Raphson	Newton-Raphson
9		Price (K)	Price*	K/S	Method	Raphson	Vega	Bisection
10								
11	**PUTS**	300	0.10	0.709	0.6842	0.6842	0.6842	0.6842
12		310	0.15	0.733	0.6566	0.6566	0.6566	0.6566
13		320	0.20	0.756	0.6197	0.6197	0.6197	0.6197
14		330	0.30	0.780	0.5928	0.5928	0.5928	0.5928
15		340	0.30	0.803	0.5311	0.5311	0.5311	0.5311
16		350	0.55	0.827	0.5205	0.5205	0.5205	0.5205
17		360	0.75	0.851	0.4838	0.4838	0.4838	0.4838
18		370	1.25	0.874	0.4669	0.4669	0.4669	0.4669
19		380	1.91	0.898	0.4420	0.4420	0.4420	0.4420
20		390	3.10	0.922	0.4267	0.4267	0.4267	0.4267
21		400	4.90	0.945	0.4120	0.4120	0.4120	0.4120
22		410	7.50	0.969	0.3974	0.3974	0.3974	0.3974
23		420	11.40	0.992	0.3918	0.3918	0.3918	0.3918
24		430	16.30	1.016	0.3815	0.3815	0.3815	0.3815
25		440	22.40	1.040	0.3714	0.3714	0.3714	0.3714
26		450	29.70	1.063	0.3643	0.3643	0.3643	0.3643
27								
28	**CALLS**	400	28.70	0.945	0.4027	0.4027	0.4027	0.4027
29		410	21.70	0.969	0.4019	0.4019	0.4019	0.4019
30		420	15.40	0.992	0.3894	0.3894	0.3894	0.3894
31		430	10.30	1.016	0.3783	0.3783	0.3783	0.3783
32		440	6.80	1.040	0.3802	0.3802	0.3802	0.3802
33		450	3.90	1.063	0.3663	0.3663	0.3663	0.3663
34		460	2.25	1.087	0.3653	0.3653	0.3653	0.3653
35		470	1.35	1.111	0.3730	0.3730	0.3730	0.3730
36		480	0.70	1.134	0.3705	0.3705	0.3705	0.3705
37		490	0.45	1.158	0.3857	0.3857	0.3857	0.3857
38		500	0.20	1.182	0.3783	0.3783	0.3783	0.3783
39		510	0.15	1.205	0.4006	0.4006	0.4006	0.4006
40		* Denotes end-of-day closing prices						

FIGURE 10.2 Implied Volatilities from Google Call Prices
Source: finance.yahoo.com

Note that the curve is slightly negatively sloped and concave. This implies that Google's stock return distribution is negatively skewed and leptokurtic. The degree to which these moments have an effect will be explored deeper in Chapter 12 when higher moments will be introduced.

EXPLAINING SMILES AND SMIRKS

Two of the least tenable assumptions of the Black-Scholes model are that of constant volatility of the underlying asset, and a normal distribution for returns of the underlying asset (equivalently, for a log-normal distribution for prices of the asset). Returns and prices are more skewed, and show greater kurtosis, than the normal

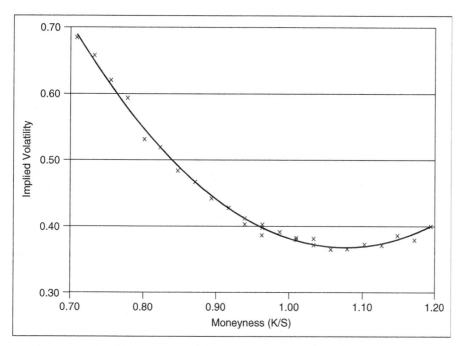

FIGURE 10.3 Implied Volatility Curve for Google Option Prices
Source: finance.yahoo.com

distribution allows. Both of these distributional features are thought to explain smiles and smirks. If returns were normal, then implied volatility would be constant across moneyness and maturity. Smiles can occur, however, because returns show greater kurtosis than stipulated under normality, so that extreme returns are more likely. This implies that deep in-the-money and deep out-of-the-money options are more expensive relative to the Black-Scholes price. Smirks can occur because returns often show negative skewness, which again the normal distribution does not allow. This implies that large negative returns are more likely, leading to implied volatilities for in-the-money calls that are higher than implied volatilities for out-of-the-money calls. Similarly, implied volatilities for out-of-the money puts are higher than implied volatilities for in-the-money puts. When plotted against moneyness, the resulting pattern resembles a smirk.

In general, smiles and smirks are more pronounced for short-term options, and less pronounced for long-term options. This is synonymous with long-term returns being closer to normally distributed than short-term returns. Moneyness and maturity are the two factors thought to most influence the shape of smiles and smirks. Plotting implied volatility as a function of moneyness and maturity produces a three-dimensional graph called an implied volatility surface. Taking a cross section of this surface for a particular value of moneyness produces a pattern that can be described as the term structure of implied volatility, since for a given moneyness it shows how implied volatility depends on the time to maturity of the option. Taking a cross-section for a particular value of maturity yields the implied volatility curve.

In this section we examine how allowing for skewness and kurtosis in option pricing models can generate implied volatility curves that resemble smiles and smirks. Hence, models that incorporate skewness and kurtosis into the price are better suited at capturing the characteristics of the returns distribution.

Fitting the Smile with the Heston (1993) Model

Several explanations have been proposed to explain the smile and smirk patterns in implied volatility curves. Most of these explanations are directed at refuting the Black-Scholes model. It was demonstrated in earlier chapters that different assumptions underlying the return process translate into different option prices. The implied volatility curve is a useful tool for analyzing the fit of different models to return characteristics. Recall that when negative correlation between volatility and return innovations was introduced by setting $\rho = -0.5$ in the Heston (1993) model, options that were in-the-money (out-of-the-money) were priced higher (lower) relative to Black-Scholes prices. This was illustrated in Figure 5.8. As argued in the introduction to this chapter, it is difficult to distinguish relative pricing differences from absolute differences. Using the fact that there is a one-to-one relationship between volatility and call prices, Black-Scholes implied volatilities obtained from option prices simulated with the Heston (1993) model can be plotted. In this section the HCTrans() function of Chapter 5 is used to simulate the prices, using the same data as in Figure 5.8, with $\rho = -0.5$. This curve appears in Figure 10.4, using data contained in the Excel file Chapter10HestonIV.

The sinusoidal curve traced out by the solid line is the difference between the Heston (1993) and Black-Scholes prices. The left vertical axis represents these differences. The dashed line represents the Black-Scholes volatilities implied from the simulated Heston (1993) option prices. The right vertical axis represents implied volatility. The dotted line is the constant Black-Scholes implied volatility $\sigma_{BS} = 0.099561$, or $0.0704 \times \sqrt{2}$, used to compute the Black-Scholes prices. Recall from Chapter 5 that this value is obtained by matching the Black-Scholes volatility to the Heston (1993) volatility over the life of the option. The value is obtained directly from Heston (1993).

The relationship between option prices and implied volatilities is apparent in Figure 10.4. When the implied volatility of the Heston (1993) stochastic volatility model becomes larger than that of the Black-Scholes model, namely at $S = 102$ approximately, the difference between the two prices becomes positive. Recall that changing the ρ parameter in the Heston (1993) model changes the skewness of the underlying return distribution. This is reflected in higher option prices for in-the-money options and lower prices for out-the-money options, relative to Black-Scholes prices, when ρ is negative. Equivalently, the implied volatility curve in Figure 10.4 indicates that a negative value of ρ translates into higher implied volatilities for

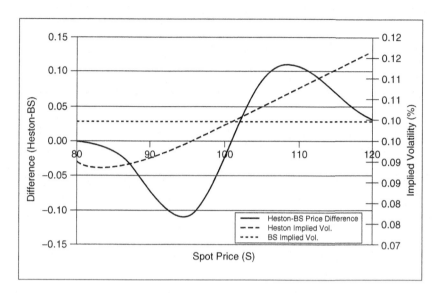

FIGURE 10.4 Effect of Skewness on Heston (1993) Implied Volatility

in-the-money options and lower implied volatilities for out-of-the-money options. This is known as a titling of the implied volatility curve, and produces a curve that resembles a smirk. Bakshi, Kapadia, and Madan (2003), show that the slope of the volatility curve can approximate the degree of skewness in the underlying distribution.

It is also instructive to illustrate the effect of kurtosis on implied volatility. The Excel file Chapter10HestonIV contains the data used to generate the curves in Figure 10.5, using the same parameter values that were used to create Figure 5.10, with $\sigma = 0.2$.

As in the previous figure, the solid line is the difference between the Heston (1993) and Black-Scholes prices, with $\sigma = 0.2$ in the Heston model. The dotted line is the Black-Scholes implied volatility $\sigma_{BS} = 0.100409$, or $0.071 \times \sqrt{2}$, again obtained by matching volatilities, and taken directly from Heston (1993). Finally, the dashed lines are the Heston (1993) implied volatilities, obtained with the bisection method.

Once again the relationship between prices and implied volatilities is evident. When the implied volatility curve of the Heston (1993) model becomes larger than the Black-Scholes model, namely at approximately $S = 93$ and $S = 108$, the pricing difference becomes positive. Recall that changing the volatility of variance parameter (σ) in the Heston (1993) model changes the kurtosis of the underlying return distribution. This reflects the fact that options that are in-the-money and out-of-the-money are more expensive relative to Black-Scholes, and options that are at-the-money are less expensive relative to Black-Scholes. This translates into implied volatilities being lower at-the-money and larger in and out-of-the-money relative to

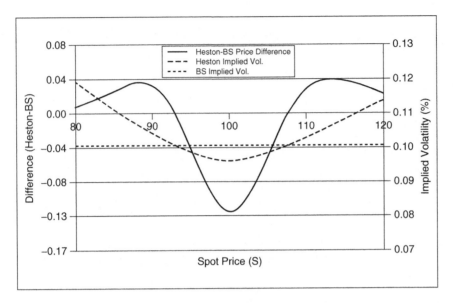

FIGURE 10.5   Effect of Kurtosis on Heston (1993) Implied Volatility

Black-Scholes implied volatilities. Higher kurtosis in the asset spot price distribution can be seen as a concave curvature in the implied volatility curve, which resembles a smile. Note that for options that are deep-in-the-money and deep-out-the-money, the difference between the prices of the two models becomes very small and the solid line in Figures 10.4 and 10.5 each approach zero. This is expected because as the asset price decreases call prices will tend to zero, and as the asset price increases call prices will tend to the value of the stock minus the strike price. However, the implied volatility curve still shows pricing differences because in the deep-in-the-money and deep-out-of-the-money regions, small price differences have larger effects on implied volatilities.

SUMMARY

This chapter presents several algorithms for obtaining implied volatility. The bisection method is particularly well-suited for finding implied volatility, since very large and small starting values of volatility can produce values of the objective function that are opposite in sign. When plotted against moneyness, implied volatilities exhibit a smile or a smirk, which can help identify distributional properties of asset returns. In this chapter it is shown that option prices generated by the Heston (1993) model lead to implied volatilities that show a smirk or smile, depending on the value of model parameters. This model allows for skewness and kurtosis, and is thus able to capture distributional features in asset returns that the Black-Scholes model is unable to capture.

EXERCISES

10.1 The following closing prices on IBM call options were obtained on January 10, 2006, for strike prices of $K = 75, K = 80$, and $K = 85$. The prices are obtained from Yahoo! (finance.yahoo.com), and are the midpoint of the last posted bid and ask prices. The closing price of IBM on January 10, 2006, was $S = 84.07$.

Expiry Date	Closing Call Price		
	$K = 75$	$K = 80$	$K = 85$
January 20, 2006	9.20	4.50	1.20
February 17, 2006	9.50	5.05	1.85
April 21, 2006	10.45	6.40	3.35
July 21, 2006	11.60	7.90	4.90
January 19, 2007	13.95	10.50	7.60

Obtain the implied volatility for the call prices, assuming a yearly risk-free rate of $r = 0.0502$. For each strike price, plot the implied volatility as a function of maturity. This approximates the term structure of implied volatility.

10.2 Use the ordinary least-squares regression function of Chapter 1 to fit the deterministic volatility function (10.4) to the cross-section of Google call prices contained in the Excel file Chapter10Google.

10.3 Since skewness and kurtosis in asset prices can explain smiles and smirks, it is reasonable to expect that implied volatilities obtained from option prices generated by the Edgeworth binomial tree of Rubinstein (1998) covered Chapter 3 will produce such patterns. Replicate Figures 10.4 and 10.5 using call prices generated by the Edgeworth binomial tree with $K = 30, r = 0.05, \sigma = 0.30$, with $n = 100$ steps and S running from \$15 to \$55 in increments of \$2. For the first figure use $\xi = -0.2$ and $\kappa = 4$, and for the second figure use $\xi = 0$ and $\kappa = 5$.

SOLUTIONS TO EXERCISES

This section provides exercises that deal with implied volatility. Solutions are contained in the Excel file Chapter10Exercises.

10.1 No new functions are needed for this exercise. The time to maturity is obtained by dividing the number of days between the expiry date and the current date by 365, which produces the maturities in cells D6:D10 of Figure 10.6. The bisection method with starting values 0.000001 and 4.0 is used to obtain the implied volatilities. For example, in cell I6 we type

$$= BisecBSV("Call", C3,I2,C4,D6,0.000001,4,E6),$$

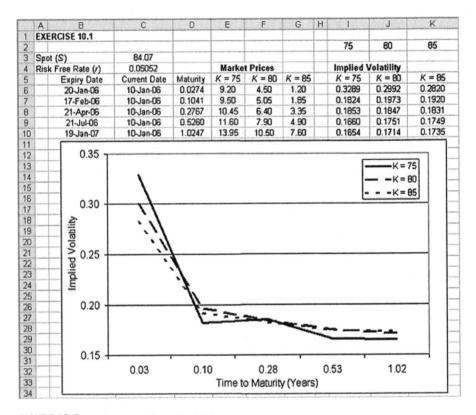

	A	B	C	D	E	F	G	H	I	J	K
1	**EXERCISE 10.1**										
2									75	80	85
3	Spot (S)		84.07								
4	Risk Free Rate (r)		0.05052		**Market Prices**				**Implied Volatility**		
5		Expiry Date	Current Date	Maturity	K = 75	K = 80	K = 85		K = 75	K = 80	K = 85
6		20-Jan-06	10-Jan-06	0.0274	9.20	4.50	1.20		0.3289	0.2992	0.2820
7		17-Feb-06	10-Jan-06	0.1041	9.50	5.05	1.85		0.1824	0.1973	0.1920
8		21-Apr-06	10-Jan-06	0.2767	10.45	6.40	3.35		0.1853	0.1847	0.1831
9		21-Jul-06	10-Jan-06	0.5260	11.60	7.90	4.90		0.1660	0.1751	0.1749
10		19-Jan-07	10-Jan-06	1.0247	13.95	10.50	7.60		0.1654	0.1714	0.1735

FIGURE 10.6 Solution to Exercise 10.1

which produces an implied volatility of 0.3289, or 32.89 percent. The implied volatilities for each strike price are plotted as a function of maturity. The plots clearly indicate a tendency for implied volatility to decrease as maturity increases.

10.2 This problem requires a slight modification of the PBSparams() and PBSvol() functions introduced in Chapter 4, to allow for the simpler specification (10.4) of the deterministic volatility function (DVF).

```
Function PBSparams(impV, K)
Dim RHS() As Double
n = Application.Count(impV)
ReDim RHS(n, 3) As Double
  For cnt = 1 To n
    RHS(cnt, 1) = 1
    RHS(cnt, 2) = K(cnt)
    RHS(cnt, 3) = K(cnt) ^ 2
  Next cnt
  betas = OLSregress(impV, RHS)
  PBSparams = betas
```

```
End Function
Function PBSvol(p, K)
  PBSvol = p(1) + p(2) * K + p(3) * K ^ 2
End Function
```

Use of these functions is illustrated in Figure 10.7.

	A	B	C	D	E	F	G	H
1	EXERCISE 10.2							
2						DVF Parameters		
3		Date:	6-Jul-06			$a_0 =$	2.6490759	
4		Exp. Date:	21-Jul-06	Risk-Free Rate (r)	0.05052	$a_1 =$	-0.0099008	
5		Maturity (T)	0.041096	Spot Price (S)	423.19	$a_2 =$	0.0000108	
6								
7		Strike	Market Call	Moneyness	Bisection	DVF Fitted		
8		Price (K)	Price*	(K/S)	Implied Vol	Volatility		
9		400	28.70	0.945	0.4033	0.40906		
10		410	21.70	0.969	0.4024	0.39714		
11		420	15.40	0.992	0.3897	0.38738		
12		430	10.30	1.016	0.3786	0.37976		
13		440	6.80	1.040	0.3804	0.37430		
14		450	3.90	1.063	0.3665	0.37098		
15		460	2.25	1.087	0.3655	0.36981		
16		470	1.35	1.111	0.3732	0.37080		
17		480	0.70	1.134	0.3707	0.37393		
18		490	0.45	1.158	0.3858	0.37922		
19		500	0.20	1.182	0.3784	0.38666		
20		510	0.15	1.205	0.4007	0.39624		
21		* Denotes end-of-day closing prices						

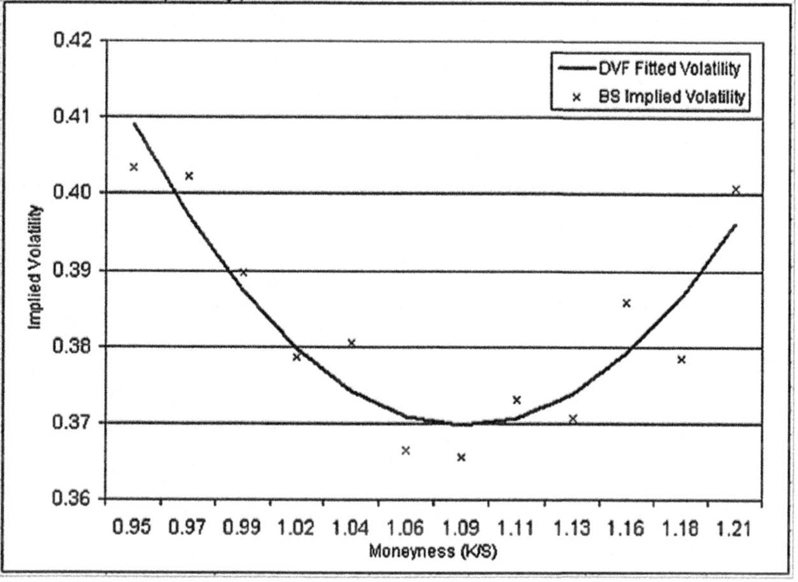

FIGURE 10.7 Solution to Exercise 10.2
Source: finance.yahoo.com

The implied volatilities are in cells E9:E20, and the strike prices in cells B9:B20. Hence, to obtain OLS estimates of the coefficients of (10.4), in cells G3 we type

$$= \text{PBSparams(E9:E20,B9:B20)}$$

and copy to cells G4 and G5, which produces the estimates $\hat{a}_0 = 2.6490, \hat{a}_1 = -0.0099$, and $\hat{a}_2 = 0.0000108$. To obtain the fitted implied volatilities, in cell F9 we type

$$= \text{PBSvol(G3:G5,B9)}$$

which produces the fitted value of $\hat{\sigma}_{iv} = 0.40906$. Copying to cells F10:F20 produces the other values, which are then used to generate the graph. Note that the graph matches that of Figure 10.3 closely. The advantage of the DVF is that an estimate of implied volatility can be obtained at a strike price which is not included in the Google data. For example, the implied volatility of a call with strike price $K = 435$ would be

$$\hat{\sigma}_{iv} = 2.6490 - 0.0099 \times 435 + 0.0000108 \times 435^2 \text{ or } \hat{\sigma}_{iv} \approx 0.3768.$$

10.3 By copying the EWBin() function from Chapter 3, it is straightforward to reproduce the figures. To obtain Edgeworth implied volatilities we use call

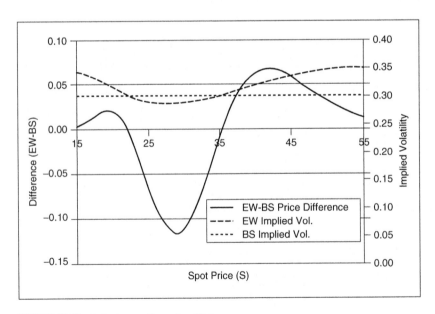

FIGURE 10.8 Solution to Exercise 10.3

prices simulated by the Edgeworth binomial tree as inputs to (10.2). The first figure with $\xi = -0.2$ and $\kappa = 4$ appears as Figure 10.8. The figure bears a striking resemblance to Figure 10.4. Again, note that the price difference becomes positive at $S = 21$ and $S = 37$ approximately, corresponding to where the Edgeworth implied volatilities become larger than the Black-Scholes implied volatilities. The second figure uses $\xi = 0$ and $\kappa = 5$, and is not presented here, but resembles Figure 10.5 closely.

CHAPTER 11

Model-Free Implied Volatility

INTRODUCTION

The models presented in the previous chapters all use the same basic methodology to price options. First, a process for the price of the underlying asset is specified, then parameters for the process are estimated, and finally an option price based on the process is produced. Usually, the parameters of the process are fixed, but sometimes they are dynamic—in Chapters 5 and 6, the asset volatility was treated as a dynamic parameter. In both cases, however, the parameters must be consistent with the distribution of the asset price. In the Black-Scholes formula presented in Chapter 4, for example, the standard deviation of the underlying asset returns is sometimes used as an estimator of the asset volatility.

The methods presented in this chapter use a reverse approach. Rather than specifying a model and estimating model parameters in order for them to fit the asset price distribution, these methods start with a cross-section of option prices and calculate volatility that need not depend on any parametric model. Implied volatilities that are produced non-parametrically are therefore known as model-free implied volatilities.

Chapter 10 discussed the use of Black-Scholes implied volatility as a forecast for future volatility. It was shown that the choice of moneyness is quite important for calculating implied volatilities, since implied volatilities often exhibit a smile. Many researchers in the implied volatility literature use at-the-money implied volatilities only in their forecasting experiments. This alleviates the smile problem, but discards all potential information contained in the rest of the option prices.

THEORETICAL FOUNDATION

Britten-Jones and Neuberger (2000) derive a model-free implied volatility measure that incorporates the whole cross-section of option prices, not only at-the-money prices. Under the assumptions that the underlying asset does not make dividend payments and the risk-free rate is zero, they derive the risk-neutral expected sum of squared returns between two dates (T_1, T_2) as

$$E^Q \left[\int_{T_1}^{T_2} \left(\frac{dS_t}{S_t} \right)^2 \right] = 2 \int_0^\infty \frac{C(T_2, K) - C(T_1, K)}{K^2} \, dK, \qquad (11.1)$$

where $E^Q[]$ refers to expectation under the risk-neutral measure Q, $C(T, K)$ is an observed call price with maturity T and strike price K, and S_t is the asset price at time t. Note that the asset return variance $(dS_t/S_t)^2$, which is also the squared volatility, is a function only of the observed call prices at one point in time. No model for the underlying asset price is required in the derivation of (11.1), hence it is a "model-free" measure of variance. It only requires two cross sections of call prices with varying K, one with time to maturity T_1 and the other with time to maturity T_2.

Since (11.1) is the model-free implied variance, the model-free implied volatility is obtained as its square root. Unfortunately, as pointed out by Britten-Jones and Neuberger (2000), this produces an upward-biased estimator of model-free volatility, so that

$$E^Q \left[\sqrt{\int_{T_1}^{T_2} \left(\frac{dS_t}{S_t} \right)^2} \right] \leqslant \sqrt{2 \int_0^\infty \frac{C(T_2, K) - C(T_1, K)}{K^2} \, dK}. \qquad (11.2)$$

Nevertheless, in this chapter we use the right-hand side of (11.2) as an estimator of model-free implied volatility.

IMPLEMENTATION

Jiang and Tian (2005) show how to implement model-free implied volatility in practice. They explain how the assumptions of no dividends and a zero risk-free rate can be relaxed, which requires several modifications to (11.1). To implement model-free volatility on a stock that pays dividends, the present value of the dividends from the current stock price must be removed. Hence, the current stock price S_t becomes S_t^*, given by

$$S_t^* = S_t - PV[D], \qquad (11.3)$$

where D denotes the total amount of dividends paid and $PV[D]$ their present value at time t. To relax the interest rate assumption a security F_t is created, given by

$$F_t = S_t^* e^{-r(T-t)}, \qquad (11.4)$$

which has zero drift under the risk-neutral measure. It can easily be shown that a call option on F_t with strike price K is equivalent to an option on S_t^* with strike price Ke^{rT}. Incorporating both of these features produces the following modification of (11.1)

$$E^Q\left[\int_{T_1}^{T_2}\left(\frac{dS_t}{S_t}\right)^2\right] = 2\int_0^\infty \frac{C(T_2, Ke^{rT_2}) - C(T_1, Ke^{rT_1})}{K^2} dK, \tag{11.5}$$

which allows for dividends and a nonzero risk-free rate.

To produce a volatility measure that is comparable to implied volatility, the asset return variance between the current date and some later date T must be obtained. This is done by setting $T_1 = 0$ and $T_2 = T$, where T is the maturity to be evaluated. In this case the model-free variance formula simplifies to

$$E^Q\left[\int_0^T\left(\frac{dS_t}{S_t}\right)^2\right] = 2\int_0^\infty \frac{C(T, Ke^{rT}) - \max(S_0 - K, 0)}{K^2} dK. \tag{11.6}$$

Note that only a single cross-section of option prices is needed to compute the model-free variance in (11.6).

There are two problems that arise when computing model-free implied variance with (11.6), discretization of call prices and truncation of the integration domain. The right-hand side of (11.6) specifies an integral over a continuum of strike prices ranging from zero to infinity. Market call prices, however, are available only over a subset of this range, which implies that the integration domain will be truncated. Moreover, these prices are available only at a finite set of values—often in intervals of five dollars—which induces a discretization problem. Jiang and Tian (2005) discuss how to deal with these problems.

Recall from Chapter 2 that integrals can be approximated with numerical integration techniques. The simplest of these techniques is the left-point rule. When applied to (11.6), the left-point rule produces the following approximation

$$2\int_0^\infty \frac{C(T, Ke^{rT}) - \max(S_0 - K, 0)}{K^2} dK$$

$$\approx 2\sum_{K=K_L}^{K_H} \frac{C(T, Ke^{rT}) - \max(S_0 - K, 0)}{K^2} \Delta K \tag{11.7}$$

where

$$\max(S_0 - K, 0) = \text{time-zero value of a call with strike price } K \text{ (with zero time to maturity)}$$
$$K_L = \text{lowest available strike price}$$
$$K_H = \text{highest available strike price}$$
$$\Delta K = \text{difference between adjacent strike prices, typically } \Delta K = \$2.50 \text{ or } \Delta K = \$5.00.$$

In this section the model-free variance given by (11.7) will be implemented, and the biases introduced by truncation and discretization will be dealt with. The Excel file Chapter11SimpleMFV contains the VBA function SimpleMFV() to implement (11.7).

```
Function SimpleMFV(calldata, S, r, T)
n = Application.Count(calldata) / 2
SimpleMFV = 0
delta_K = calldata(2, 1) - calldata(1, 1)
For i = 1 To n
  adjK = calldata(i, 1) * Exp(-r * T)
  SimpleMFV = SimpleMFV + 2 * delta_K * (calldata(i, 2) -
          Application.Max(S - adjK, 0)) / adjK ^ 2
Next i
End Function
```

In this function, calldata() is a matrix of dimension $n \times 2$ for a cross-section of n strike prices and call prices, all with the same maturity. This function uses call options only, although puts could be used, by transforming them into calls using put-call parity. Later in this chapter a method is introduced that uses puts and calls directly.

Use of this function is illustrated in Figure 11.1, using call prices generated with the Heston (1993) model and the same parameters as in the experiment from Chapter 5, namely $S = 100, r = 0, \tau = 0.5, v = 0.04, \rho = -0.5, \kappa = 2, \theta = 0.04, \lambda = 0$, and $\sigma = 0.225$. The strike price varies from $K = 80$ to $K = 120$. Cells containing these parameters have been assigned range names for convenience. In cell F6, for example, we type

$$= \text{Heston(PutCall,kappa,theta, lambda,rho, sigmav, dtm, E6,S, rf,V)}$$

which produces a call price of \$20.04 when the strike price is $K = 80$ in cell E6. To compute the model-free implied variance using the SimpleMFV() function, we select lower and upper values K_L and K_U for the summation in (11.7). In Figure 11.1, 10 pairs of such possible values are used, in columns H and I, respectively (these will be used to illustrate the truncation bias). For example, to compute model-free implied variance over the range $K_L = 84$ to $K_U = 116$, in cell K8 we type

$$= \text{SimpleMFV(E10:F42,S,rf,dtm)},$$

which produces a value of 0.0049. The model-free implied volatility is the square root of this value, and appears in cell L8 as 0.0700. Note that as the integration range (radius) decreases, the approximation error increases. This will be investigated in the next section.

	A	B	C	D	E	F	G	H	I	J	K	L	M
1													
2		Jiang and Tian (2003) Model-Free Implied Volatility							Heston Volatility =		0.0706		
3		Using Heston (1993) Call Prices											
4					Strike	Call			Integration Range				Approx.
5		**Heston Parameters**			Price	Price		K_L	K_U	Radius	MFV	√ MFV	Error
6		Spot Price (S_t)	100		80	20.04		80	120	0.20	0.0050	0.0705	-0.132%
7		Current Variance (v)	0.01		81	19.05		82	118	0.18	0.0049	0.0703	-0.414%
8		Rho (ρ)	-0.5		82	18.06		84	116	0.16	0.0049	0.0700	-0.867%
9		Kappa (κ)	2		83	17.08		86	114	0.14	0.0048	0.0695	-1.585%
10		Theta (θ)	0.01		84	16.10		88	112	0.12	0.0047	0.0687	-2.718%
11		Lambda (λ)	0		85	15.13		90	110	0.10	0.0045	0.0674	-4.519%
12		Volatility of Variance (σ)	0.225		86	14.16		92	108	0.08	0.0043	0.0654	-7.408%
13		Strike Price (K)	100		87	13.20		94	106	0.06	0.0038	0.0620	-12.153%
14		Risk Free Rate (r)	0		88	12.25		96	104	0.04	0.0032	0.0563	-20.194%
15		Time to Maturity ($T - t$)	0.5		89	11.31		98	102	0.02	0.0021	0.0461	-34.672%
16		Type (*Call* or *Put*)	Call		90	10.39							

FIGURE 11.1   Illustration of Model-Free Implied Volatility

Truncation and Discretization Bias

Recall that in the experiment from Chapter 5, call prices from the Heston (1993) stochastic volatility model were compared to call prices from the Black-Scholes model. In order for this to be done properly, the Black-Scholes model volatility was matched to the square root of the variance of the spot return in the Heston (1993) model, over the life of the option. For the parameter values in Figure 11.1, this was given in Heston (1993) as 7.06 percent.

The Excel file Chapter11SimpleMFV is used to illustrate the bias brought on by truncation of the integration domain. Notice that the left-hand side of (11.6) is the variance of the spot return over the life of the option. We can therefore compare the square root of this variance, which appears in column L, to 7.06 percent. In Figure 11.1, the different ranges of integration appear in cells H6:I15. For each range, the radius is defined as the half-width of the strike price range relative to the spot price, namely $\frac{1}{2}(R_U - R_L)/S_t$, and appears in column J. The model-free volatility is computed for each range, and the approximation error is defined as the deviation of the model-free volatility from the Heston (1993) volatility of 7.06 percent. The errors are presented in column N and clearly indicate that the error decreases as the range of integration gets wider. With the most narrow range, $K_L = 98$ and $K_U = 102$, the error is −34.67 percent, and with the widest range, $K_L = 80$ and $K_U = 120$ the error is reduced drastically, to 0.152 percent. Plotting the approximation error versus the radius produces the graph in Figure 11.2, which is also included in the Excel file Chapter11SimpleMFV.

With strike prices of approximately 10 percent (relative to the spot price) in each direction, the approximation error becomes smaller than 5 percent. When the radius is at its largest, however (at 0.2), the integrated variance of is still slight under-estimated, at −0.132 percent. This could be due to the very rudimentary integration algorithm being used. It could also be due to the one-dollar discretization used for the strike price range. Although one dollar is a smaller step than available for most

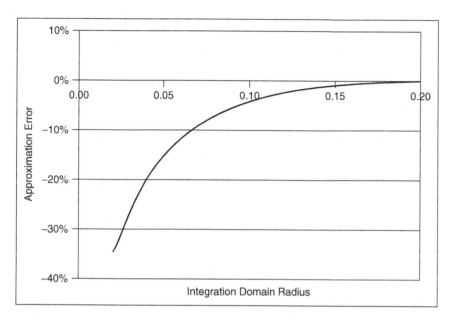

FIGURE 11.2 Approximation Error Due to Truncation

equity options, the range is still not continuous. Both of these sources of error are examined in this section.

We now turn our attention to the bias brought on by discretization of the strike prices. For this experiment call prices are again generated using the Heston (1993) model, using the same parameter values as in the previous experiment. The integration radius at kept at 0.2 in all cases (since the range of integration is always $K_L = 80$ and $K_U = 120$), and the discreteness of the strike prices is allowed to vary from \$0.50 to \$5. The results of this experiment are contained in the Excel file Chapter11DiscreteMFV and illustrated in Figure 11.3.

Clearly, when the smallest strike price step of \$0.50 is used, the approximation error in cell H10 is negligible, but when the large price step of \$10.00 is used, the approximation error is largest, at 15.511 percent in cell H16. Note that when a step of \$1.00 is used, corresponding to the step size in Figure 11.1, the approximation error is −0.132 percent in cell H11, exactly that in cell M6 of Figure 11.1. Figure 11.4 illustrates the portion of the Chapter11DiscreteMFV file that contains the strike and call prices used in the VBA function SimpleMFV().

For a strike step of \$0.50, the strike prices appear in column I and the Heston (1993) call prices for each strike in column J. Only these option prices need to be computed, because the prices in the other columns can be obtained with the VLOOKUP function in Excel. To obtain the call price when the strike step size is 1.00, for example, in cell L6, we type "=VLOOKUP(K6,I6:J86,2)", which yields 20.04. This saves a considerable amount of redundant computing time.

	A	B	C	D	E	F	G	H
1								
2		**Sensitivity of Strike Discreteness on Model-Free Implied Volatility**						
3		**Using Heston (1993) Call Prices**						
4								
5		**Heston Parameters**			Heston Volatility =		0.0706	
6		Spot Price (S_t)	100					
7		Current Variance (v)	0.01					
8		Rho (ρ)	-0.5		Strike			Approx.
9		Kappa (κ)	2		Step	MFV	√ MFV	Error
10		Theta (θ)	0.01		0.50	0.0050	0.0704	-0.287%
11		Lambda (λ)	0		1.00	0.0050	0.0705	-0.132%
12		Volatility of Variance (σ)	0.225		2.00	0.0050	0.0709	0.424%
13		Strike Price (K)	100		2.50	0.0051	0.0712	0.824%
14		Risk Free Rate (r)	0		4.00	0.0052	0.0724	2.497%
15		Time to Maturity ($T - t$)	0.5		5.00	0.0054	0.0734	3.991%
16		Type (*Call* or *Put*)	Call		10.00	0.0067	0.0816	15.511%

FIGURE 11.3   Discretization Bias on Model-Free Implied Volatility

	I	J	K	L	M	N	O	P	Q	R
1										
2	**Heston (1993) Call Prices Using Different Strike Steps**									
3	Step = 0.50		Step = 1.00		Step = 2.00		Step = 2.50		Step = 4.00	
4	Strike	Call	Strike	Call	Strike	Call	Strike	Call	Strike	Call
5	Price	Price	Price	Price	Price	Price	Price	Price	Price	Price
6	80.0	20.04	80.0	20.04	80.00	20.04	80.00	20.04	80.00	20.04
7	80.5	19.54	81.0	19.05	82.00	18.06	82.50	17.57	84.00	16.10
8	81.0	19.05	82.0	18.06	84.00	16.10	85.00	15.13	88.00	12.25
9	81.5	18.56	83.0	17.08	86.00	14.16	87.50	12.73	92.00	8.59
10	82.0	18.06	84.0	16.10	88.00	12.25	90.00	10.39	96.00	5.29
11	82.5	17.57	85.0	15.13	90.00	10.39	92.50	8.15	100.00	2.66
12	83.0	17.08	86.0	14.16	92.00	8.59	95.00	6.07	104.00	1.01
13	83.5	16.59	87.0	13.20	94.00	6.88	97.50	4.21	108.00	0.29
14	84.0	16.10	88.0	12.25	96.00	5.29	100.00	2.66	112.00	0.07
15	84.5	15.61	89.0	11.31	98.00	3.87	102.50	1.50	116.00	0.02
16	85.0	15.13	90.0	10.39	100.00	2.66	105.00	0.76	120.00	0.00
17	85.5	14.64	91.0	9.48	102.00	1.70	107.50	0.35		
18	86.0	14.16	92.0	8.59	104.00	1.01	110.00	0.15		
19	86.5	13.68	93.0	7.72	106.00	0.56	112.50	0.06		
20	87.0	13.20	94.0	6.88	108.00	0.29	115.00	0.03		
21	87.5	12.73	95.0	6.07	110.00	0.15	117.50	0.01		
22	88.0	12.25	96.0	5.29	112.00	0.07	120.00	0.00		
23	88.5	11.78	97.0	4.56	114.00	0.04				
24	89.0	11.31	98.0	3.87	116.00	0.02				

FIGURE 11.4   Strike Price Ranges for Discretization Error Analysis

Turning back to Figure 11.3, the approximation errors can be plotted as a function of the strike price discreteness, to illustrate how fast the error decreases when the strike steps are made smaller. This plot appears in the Excel file Chapter11DiscreteMFV and is illustrated in Figure 11.5.

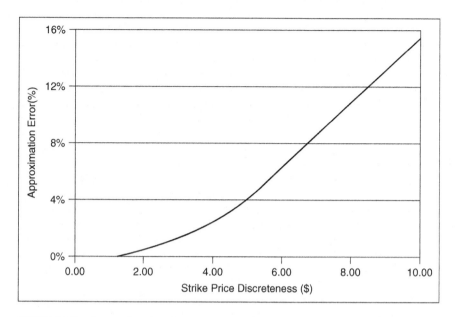

FIGURE 11.5 Approximation Error versus Strike Price Discreteness

Depending on the value of a firm's stock, equity options typically trade with discrete strike prices of $2.50 or $5.00. Figures 11.4 and 11.5 suggest that at these steps, approximation errors of 0.824 percent and 3.99 percent, respectively, can be expected from model-free estimation of implied volatility.

INTERPOLATION-EXTRAPOLATION METHOD

Jiang and Tian (2005) develop a technique to mitigate the truncation and discretization bias induced when model-free volatility is implemented on a range of discrete strike prices with finite range. This method uses puts and calls, and not calls only. It is an interpolation-extrapolation (IE) method implemented in the following steps:

1. Transform all put and call prices into implied volatilities to obtain an implied volatility curve.
2. Extrapolate the implied volatility curve to obtain a desired domain of integration. For strike prices below (above) the available strike price, use the implied volatility of the lowest (highest) available strike price. Using cubic splines, interpolate the points on the entire curve to obtain a desired discretization of strike prices.
3. Obtain call prices for all desired strike prices on the interpolated-extrapolated curve.
4. Compute the model-free implied volatility from these fitted call prices.

Note that step 2 implies that the extrapolated curve is concave within the range of available strike prices, but is a horizontal line for strike prices outside the range.

The Excel file Chapter11MFV contains the VBA function MFV() to implement this technique. To increase the accuracy of the integration, we use trapezoidal integration instead of the left-point rule. This implies that the approximation to (11.6) becomes

$$2 \int_0^\infty \frac{C(T, Ke^{rT}) - \max(S_0 - K, 0)}{K^2} \, dK \approx \sum_{i=1}^{m} [g(T, K_i) + g(T, K_{i-1})] \Delta K \quad (11.8)$$

where $\Delta K = (K_U - K_L)/m$, and m is the number of abscissas. The MFV() function nests two additional VBA functions, IEpoints() and IEcurve(). The first of these functions obtains the implied volatilities in step 1. The first loop in the IEpoints() function calculates the implied volatilities based on put prices. The second loop calculates the implied volatility based on call prices, while adjusting for overlaps in the strikes of calls and puts. This adjustment consists of taking the average of the implied volatilities when a call and put have the same strike price. Finally, the last loop outputs a vector of strike prices along with a vector of implied volatilities.

```
Function IEpoints(S, CallK, CallP, PutK, PutP, r, T)
Dim impVc() As Double, impVp() As Double
Dim nCall As Integer, nPut As Integer, curCnt As Integer
Dim outKIV() As Double, passoutKIV() As Double
nCall = Application.Count(CallK)
nPut = Application.Count(PutK)
ReDim impVc(nCall) As Double, impVp(nPut) As Double
ReDim outKIV(nCall + nPut, 2) As Double
For cntp = 1 To nPut
  pIV = BisecBSV("Put", S, PutK(cntp), r, T, 0.00000001, 5, PutP(cntp))
  outKIV(cntp, 2) = pIV
  outKIV(cntp, 1) = PutK(cntp)
Next cntp
curCnt = nPut
For cntc = 1 To nCall
  cIV = BisecBSV("Call", S, CallK(cntc), r, T, 0.00000001, 5, CallP(cntc))
  addflag = 1
  For cntp = 1 To nPut
    If (CallK(cntc) = outKIV(cntp, 1)) Then
      outKIV(cntp, 2) = (outKIV(cntp, 2) + cIV) / 2
      addflag = 0
      Exit For
    End If
  Next cntp
  If (addflag = 1) Then
    curCnt = curCnt + 1
    outKIV(curCnt, 1) = CallK(cntc)
```

```
      outKIV(curCnt, 2) = cIV
    End If
Next cntc
ReDim passoutKIV(curCnt, 2) As Double
For cnt = 1 To curCnt
  passoutKIV(cnt, 1) = outKIV(cnt, 1)
  passoutKIV(cnt, 2) = outKIV(cnt, 2)
Next cnt
  IEpoints = passoutKIV
End Function
```

The second nested function, IEcurve(), performs the interpolation-extrapolation in step 2, using the NSpline() function described in Chapter 1 for natural cubic spline interpolation. The lower and upper limits of the interpolated-extrapolated implied volatility curve are given by $S/(1 + u)$ and $S(1 + u)$, respectively, with a step size of dK. The implied volatilities for strike prices less than the lowest market strike price are set to the implied volatility of the lowest market strike price. Similarly, the implied volatilities for strike prices greater than the largest market strike price are set to the implied volatility of the largest market strike price. This implies that interpolated volatilities within the range of market strikes are interpolated along the implied volatility curve, but volatilities beyond the range of market strikes are extrapolated as horizontal lines. Finally, the IEcurve() function outputs a matrix of strike prices and implied volatilities.

```
Function IEcurve(passKIV, u, dK, S)
Dim outKIV() As Double
Dim K() As Double, impv() As Double
n = Application.Count(passKIV) / 2
hS = Round(S * (1 + u))
lS = Round(S / (1 + u))
numV = Int((hS - lS) / dK) + 1
ReDim outKIV(numV, 2), K(n) As Double, impv(n) As Double
For cnt = 1 To n
  K(cnt) = passKIV(cnt, 1)
  impv(cnt) = passKIV(cnt, 2)
Next cnt
For cntK = 1 To numV
  cK = lS + (cntK - 1) * dK
  outKIV(cntK, 1) = cK
  If (cK < K(1)) Then
    outKIV(cntK, 2) = impv(1)
  ElseIf (cK > K(n)) Then
    outKIV(cntK, 2) = impv(n)
  Else
    outKIV(cntK, 2) = NSpline(cK, K, impv)
  End If
Next cntK
  IEcurve = outKIV
End Function
```

Lastly, the MFV() function calculates the corresponding call prices for each of the interpolated-extrapolated implied volatilities. The model-free implied volatility in step 4 is obtained using the trapezoidal rule, and appears at the bottom of the function.

```
Function MFV(passCallK, passCallP, passPutK, passPutP, S, r, T)
uniPoints = IEpoints(S, passCallK, passCallP, passPutK, passPutP, r, T)
u = 3
dK = 0.1
outKIV = IEcurve(uniPoints, u, dK, S)
Dim CallK() As Double, CallP() As Double, PutK() As Double, PutP() As
              Double
n = UBound(outKIV)
nCall = 0
nPut = 0
ReDim calldata(n, 2) As Double
For cnt = 1 To n
  curK = outKIV(cnt, 1)
  calldata(cnt, 1) = curK
  calldata(cnt, 2) = bs_price("Call", S, curK *
              Exp(-r * T), r, T, outKIV(cnt, 2))
Next cnt
MFV = 0
delta_K = calldata(2, 1) - calldata(1, 1)
For i = 2 To n
  adjK1 = calldata(i - 1, 1) * Exp(-r * T)
  adjK2 = calldata(i, 1) * Exp(-r * T)
  G1 = 2 * (calldata(i - 1, 2) - Application.Max(S - adjK1, 0))
              / adjK1 ^ 2
  G2 = 2 * (calldata(i, 2) - Application.Max(S - adjK2, 0)) / adjK2 ^ 2
  MFV = MFV + delta_K * 0.5 * (G1 + G2)
Next i
End Function
```

Although the MFV() function seems much more complicated than the SimpleMFV() function described earlier, the extrapolation and interpolation in steps 2 and 3 constitute most of the code, whereas the model-free volatility integration of step 4, which uses the trapezoidal rule, uses very little VBA code.

The Excel file Chapter11MFV illustrates both functions, using call prices generated by the Heston (1993) model with the same parameter values as in the previous figures in this chapter. Only four strike prices are used, $K = 90, 95, 105,$ and $110,$ corresponding to a step size of $5.00. This is illustrated in Figure 11.6.

The approximation error with the SimpleMFV() function appears in cell F18 as -29.41 percent, which is very large. This is not surprising in light of the large step size used for the strike prices. The MFV() function, on the other, hand, produces an error of -0.52 percent in cell F19, which is much smaller. Hence, even with such a small cross-section of call prices, the interpolation-extrapolation technique produces a very good approximation.

It is informative to compare the performance of the SimpleMFV() and MFV() functions, using a plot similar to that in Figure 11.2. The Excel file Chapter11-Compare1 compares the performance of the SimpleMFV() and MFV() functions, using the same integration ranges as in Figure 11.1. This is illustrated in Figure 11.7.

With a radius of roughly 0.16 or greater, both methods produce small approximation errors. When the radius decreases, however, the MFV() function for the improved method produces much smaller errors than the SimpleMFV() function for the simple method. Plotting both errors as a function of the radius produces Figure 11.8, which is also included in the Excel file Chapter11Compare1.

	A	B	C	D	E	F
1						
2		Jiang and Tian (2003) Model-Free Implied Volatility				
3		Correction for Truncation and Discretization Biases				
4						
5		Heston Parameters				
6		Spot Price (S)	100			
7		Current Variance (v)	0.01		Strike	Call
8		Kappa (κ)	2		Price	Price
9		Theta (θ)	0.01		90.00	10.39
10		Lambda (λ)	0		95.00	6.07
11		Rho (ρ)	-0.5		105.00	0.76
12		Volatility of Variance (σ)	0.225		110.00	0.15
13		Risk Free Rate (r)	0			
14		Time to Maturity (T − t)	0.5			
15		Type (Call or Put)	Call			
16					Heston	Approx.
17			MFV	√ MFV	Volatility	Error
18		**Simple Technique**	0.0025	0.0497	0.0704	-29.41%
19		**Exact Technique**	0.0049	0.0700	0.0704	-0.52%

FIGURE 11.6 Bias Correction for Model-Free Implied Volatility

	A	B	C	D	E	F	G	H	I	J	K	L	M	N	O
1															
2		Comparison of Model-Free Implied Volatility							Heston Volatility =		0.0706				
3		Obtained With Two Methods													
4					Strike	Call	Put		Strike Price Range			Simple Method		Improved Method	
5		Heston Parameters			Price	Price	Price		K_L	K_U	Radius	√ MFV	Error	√ MFV	Error
6		Spot Price (S)	100		80	20.04	0.04		80	120	0.20	0.0705	-0.132%	0.0706	-0.040%
7		Current Variance (v)	0.01		81	19.05	0.05		82	118	0.18	0.0703	-0.414%	0.0705	-0.149%
8		Rho (ρ)	-0.5		82	18.06	0.06		84	116	0.16	0.0700	-0.867%	0.0704	-0.318%
9		Kappa (κ)	2		83	17.08	0.08		86	114	0.14	0.0695	-1.585%	0.0702	-0.582%
10		Theta (θ)	0.01		84	16.10	0.10		88	112	0.12	0.0687	-2.718%	0.0699	-0.961%
11		Lambda (λ)	0		85	15.13	0.13		90	110	0.10	0.0674	-4.519%	0.0695	-1.514%
12		Volatility of Variance (σ)	0.225		86	14.16	0.16		92	108	0.08	0.0654	-7.408%	0.0690	-2.255%
13		Risk Free Rate (r)	0		87	13.20	0.20		94	106	0.06	0.0620	-12.153%	0.0684	-3.175%
14		Time to Maturity (T − t)	0.5		88	12.25	0.25		96	104	0.04	0.0563	-20.194%	0.0676	-4.194%
15					89	11.31	0.31		98	102	0.02	0.0461	-34.672%	0.0670	-5.055%

FIGURE 11.7 Comparison of Model-Free Implied Volatility under Two Methods

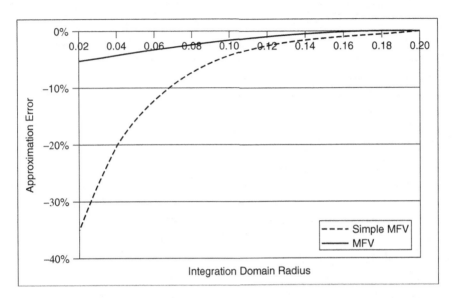

FIGURE 11.8 Approximation Error under Two Methods

Finally, the Excel file Chapter11Compare2 produces a comparison of the effect of discretization on the approximation errors, under both methods. A selected part of the right-most section of this file contains the Heston (1993) call and put prices, and appears in Figure 11.9.

To save computing time, only the Heston (1993) call prices are computed directly. The prices of puts are obtained by put-call parity, using the VBA function PutCallPar(), which includes the option price as one of its function arguments.

```
Function PutCallPar(PutCall, Price, S, K, r, tau)
If PutCall = "Put" Then
  PutCallPar = Price + K * Exp(-r * tau) - S
Else
  PutCallPar = Price - K * Exp(-r * tau) + S
End If
End Function
```

Note also that this sheet uses the Excel function VLOOKUP() to copy call and put prices, which avoids redundant computations. A comparison of the errors introduced by discretization appears in the left-most part of the Excel file Chapter11Compare2, and is illustrated in Figure 11.10.

Both methods produce small errors for strike steps less than $2.00, but for steps greater than $2.00 the MFV() function produces approximations that are vastly superior to those produced by the SimpleMFV() function. This is evident from Figure 11.11, which plots the approximation errors under both methods as a function of the strike price step. This plot is also included in the Excel file Chapter11Compare2.

	J	K	L	M	N	O	P	Q	R	S	T	U
1	Heston (1993) Option Prices											
2												
3		Step = 0.50			Step = 1.00			Step = 2.00			Step = 2.50	
4	Strike	Call	Put	Strike	Call	Put	Strike	Call	Put	Strike	Call	Put
5	Price	Price	Price	Price	Price	Price	Price	Price	Price	Price	Price	Price
6	80.00	20.04	0.04	80.00	20.04	0.04	80.00	20.04	0.04	80.00	20.04	0.04
7	80.50	19.54	0.04	81.00	19.05	0.05	82.00	18.06	0.06	82.50	17.57	0.07
8	81.00	19.05	0.05	82.00	18.06	0.06	84.00	16.10	0.10	85.00	15.13	0.13
9	81.50	18.56	0.06	83.00	17.08	0.08	86.00	14.16	0.16	87.50	12.73	0.23
10	82.00	18.06	0.06	84.00	16.10	0.10	88.00	12.25	0.25	90.00	10.39	0.39
11	82.50	17.57	0.07	85.00	15.13	0.13	90.00	10.39	0.39	92.50	8.15	0.65
12	83.00	17.08	0.08	86.00	14.16	0.16	92.00	8.59	0.59	95.00	6.07	1.07
13	83.50	16.59	0.09	87.00	13.20	0.20	94.00	6.88	0.88	97.50	4.21	1.71
14	84.00	16.10	0.10	88.00	12.25	0.25	96.00	5.29	1.29	100.00	2.66	2.66
15	84.50	15.61	0.11	89.00	11.31	0.31	98.00	3.87	1.87	102.50	1.50	4.00
16	85.00	15.13	0.13	90.00	10.39	0.39	100.00	2.66	2.66	105.00	0.76	5.76
17	85.50	14.64	0.14	91.00	9.48	0.48	102.00	1.70	3.70	107.50	0.35	7.85
18	86.00	14.16	0.16	92.00	8.59	0.59	104.00	1.01	5.01	110.00	0.15	10.15
19	86.50	13.68	0.18	93.00	7.72	0.72	106.00	0.56	6.56	112.50	0.06	12.56
20	87.00	13.20	0.20	94.00	6.88	0.88	108.00	0.29	8.29	115.00	0.03	15.03
21	87.50	12.73	0.23	95.00	6.07	1.07	110.00	0.15	10.15	117.50	0.01	17.51
22	88.00	12.25	0.25	96.00	5.29	1.29	112.00	0.07	12.07	120.00	0.00	20.00
23	88.50	11.78	0.28	97.00	4.56	1.56	114.00	0.04	14.04			
24	89.00	11.31	0.31	98.00	3.87	1.87	116.00	0.02	16.02			
25	89.50	10.85	0.35	99.00	3.24	2.24	118.00	0.01	18.01			
26	90.00	10.39	0.39	100.00	2.66	2.66	120.00	0.00	20.00			

FIGURE 11.9 Strike Price Ranges for Discretization Analysis

	A	B	C	D	E	F	G	H	I
1									
2		**Comparison of Model-Free Implied Volatility**							
3		**Obtained With Two Methods**							
4					Heston Volatility =		0.0706		
5		**Heston Parameters**							
6		Spot Price (S_t)	100		Strike	Simple Method		Improved Method	
7		Current Variance (v)	0.01		Step	√ MFV	Error	√ MFV	Error
8		Rho (ρ)	-0.5		0.50	0.0704	-0.287%	0.0706	-0.040%
9		Kappa (κ)	2		1.00	0.0705	-0.132%	0.0706	-0.040%
10		Theta (θ)	0.01		2.00	0.0709	0.424%	0.0706	-0.040%
11		Lambda (λ)	0		2.50	0.0712	0.824%	0.0706	-0.039%
12		Volatility of Variance (σ)	0.225		4.00	0.0724	2.497%	0.0706	-0.037%
13		Risk Free Rate (r)	0		5.00	0.0734	3.991%	0.0706	-0.039%
14		Time to Maturity ($T - t$)	0.5		10.00	0.0816	15.511%	0.0706	-0.004%

FIGURE 11.10 Comparison of Discretization Bias under Both Methods

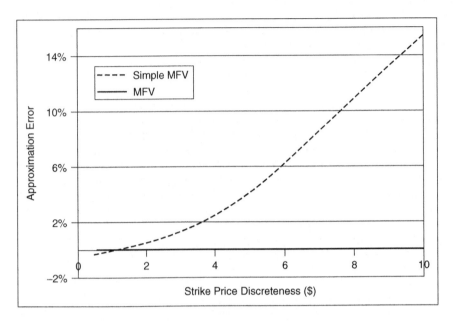

FIGURE 11.11 Plot of Approximation Errors under Both Methods

To summarize, the interpolation-extrapolation method of Jiang and Tian (2005) is able to eliminate almost all of the approximation error induced by discreteness of the strike prices and truncation of the integration domain.

MODEL-FREE IMPLIED FORWARD VOLATILITY

Up to this point, only model-free volatility from the current day going forward has been examined. The forward volatility from $t = T_1$ to $t = T_2$ can be estimated by noting that with (11.6), (11.5) can be written as

$$2 \int_0^\infty \frac{C(T_2, Ke^{rT_2})}{K^2} \, dK - 2 \int_0^\infty \frac{C(T_1, Ke^{rT_1})}{K^2} \, dK$$

$$= 2 \int_0^\infty \frac{C(T_2, Ke^{rT_2}) - \max(S_0 - K, 0)}{K^2} \, dK$$

$$- 2 \int_0^\infty \frac{C(T_1, Ke^{rT_1}) - \max(S_0 - K, 0)}{K^2} \, dK. \qquad (11.9)$$

Hence, the model-free implied forward variance over the time interval (T_1, T_2) can be expressed as the difference of two model-free implied variances, one over $(0, T_1)$

and the other, over $(0, T_2)$. As usual, the model-free implied forward volatility is defined by taking the square root of (11.9).

$$\sqrt{2 \int_0^\infty \frac{C(T_2, K) - \max(S_0 - K, 0)}{K^2} \, dK - 2 \int_0^\infty \frac{C(T_1, K) - \max(S_0 - K, 0)}{K^2} \, dK}.$$

$$(11.10)$$

The Excel file Chapter11Forward contains the VBA function MFV2() to implement model-free implied variance using market prices for calls. This function is identical to the MFV() function described earlier, except that in the first loop, the function verifies whether the market price and strike price produce a positive value for the Black-Scholes implied volatility. If so, the market price and strike price are retained; otherwise, the next pair is used.

```
Function MFV2(incalldata, S, r, T)
For i = 1 To n
  curVol = BisecBSV("Call", S, incalldata(i, 1), r, T,
                    0.00001, 4, incalldata(i, 2))
  If (curVol > 0) Then
    cnt = cnt + 1
    impK(cnt) = incalldata(i, 1)
    impv(cnt) = curVol
  End If
Next i
n = cnt
ReDim Preserve impv(cnt) As Double, impK(cnt) As Double
ReDim calldata(800, 2)
'More VBA Statements
End Function
```

The use of this function is illustrated in Figure 11.12, using market call prices on June 21, 2006 for Morgan Stanley (ticker:MS), with times to maturity July 21, 2006, October 20, 2006, January 19, 2007, and January 18, 2008, with strike prices ranging from $K = 30$ to $K = 80$.

The closing price of Morgan Stanley on June 21, 2006, was \$59.79, in cell B4. To obtain the model-free implied volatility from the first set of call prices and strike prices in cells B10:C18, which have a time to maturity of 0.08 years (roughly one month) shown in cell A13, in cell D10 we type

$$= \text{MFV2(B10:C18,B4,B5,A13)}$$

which produces a model-free implied variance of 0.00379 and a volatility of 0.06155 in cell E10. To obtain the annualized model-free implied volatility, we divide by the square root of the maturity. Hence, in cell F10 we type "=E10/SQRT(A13)", which produces 0.21470. The call price of \$1.50 in cell C15 and strike price of \$60 in cell B15 are used to obtain the at-the-money Black-Scholes implied volatility with the

	A	B	C	D	E	F	G	H	I	J	K	L	M
2	**Model-Free Implied Forward Volatility**												
3				Bisection Method Starting Values									
4	Spot Price (S)	59.79			$\sigma_1 =$	0.0000001							
5	Risk Free Rate (r)	0.05147			$\sigma_2 =$	5							
6	Current Date (T_1)	21-Jun-06											
7					Model-Free Implied Volatility						Model-Free Implied Forward Volatility		
8		Strike	Call	and Black Scholes Implied Volatility							Starting Date T_1		
9	Maturity Date (T_2)	Price	Price	MFV	√ MFV	Annualized			21-Jun-06	21-Jul-06	20-Oct-06	19-Jan-07	18-Jan-08
10	21-Jul-06	35	24.20	0.00379	0.06155	0.21470		21-Jun-06	—	—	—	—	—
11		40	15.50					21-Jul-06	0.06155	—	—	—	—
12	Time ($T_2 - T_1$) / 365	45	11.60				Ending	20-Oct-06	0.12413	0.10779	—	—	—
13	0.08	50	10.00				Date T_2	19-Jan-07	0.16868	0.15705	0.11422	—	—
14		55	5.10	B-S Implied Voaltility		De-Annualized		18-Jan-08	0.27245	0.26541	0.24253	0.21396	—
15		60	1.50	0.21628		0.06201							
16		65	0.15										
17		70	0.05										
18		75	0.05										
19	Maturity Date (T_2)			MFV	√ MFV	Annualized							
20	20-Oct-06	40	20.20	0.01541	0.12413	0.21559							
21		45	12.20										
22	Time ($T_2 - T_1$) / 365	50	10.90										
23	0.33	55	6.40	B-S Implied Voaltility		De-Annualized							
24		60	3.40	0.21862		0.12587							
25		65	1.35										
26		70	0.40										
27		75	0.10										
28		80	0.10										

FIGURE 11.12   Model-Free Implied Forward Volatility

bisection method, whose starting values are in cells F4 and F5. Hence in cell D15 we type

$$= \text{BisecBSV}(\text{``Call''}, \text{B4}, \text{B15}, \text{B5}, \text{A13}, \text{F4}, \text{F5}, \text{C15})$$

which produces an annual implied volatility of 0.21628, comparable to the annualized model-free value of 0.21470 in cell F10. To express this in terms of the time to maturity, it must be "deannualized." Hence in cell F15 we type "=D15*SQRT(A13)", which produces 0.06201, comparable to the model-free value of 0.06155 obtained earlier.

Continuing for the other maturities, a series of model-free and Black-Scholes implied volatilities are obtained, and these can be plotted against time to maturity. This appears in Figure 11.13. Clearly, the implied volatilities match closely, for all maturities.

Finally, model-free implied forward volatilities can be obtained, by using (11.10). For example, the model-free variance for October 20, 2006, is 0.01541 in cell D20, while that for January 19, 2007, is 0.02845 in cell D30. The model-free implied forward volatility from October 20, 2006, to January 19, 2007, is the square root of the difference of these two values. Hence, in cell K13 we type "=SQRT(D30-D20)" which produces a value of 0.11442. The other model-free implied forward volatilities are obtained analogously.

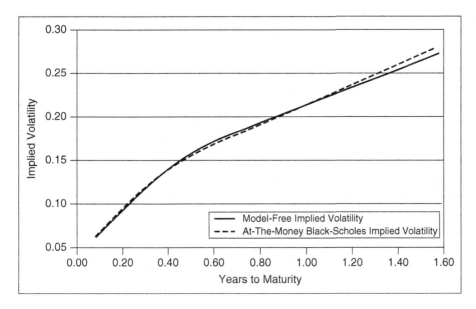

FIGURE 11.13 Black-Scholes and Model-Free Implied Volatility

THE VIX INDEX

The updated Chicago Board Options Exchange® (CBOE) volatility index, the VIX, constitutes one important application of model-free volatility. The VIX was originally defined in terms of Black-Scholes implied volatilities calculated from at-the-money options on the Standard and Poor's (S&P) 100 index. The recent revision of the VIX uses options on the S&P 500 index, on a wide range of moneyness, not only at-the-money. It also uses model-free implied volatility rather than Black-Scholes implied volatility. Figure 11.14 is a plot of the daily closing values of the VIX index, from January 2, 1990, to July 5, 2006. The data are contained in the Excel file Chapter11HistoricalVIX and are downloaded from the CBOE Web site (www.cboe.com). In this section we explain how to calculate the VIX index from a cross section of out-of-the money option prices. This discussion is taken from a white paper produced by the Chicago Board Options Exchange® (CBOE, 2003). Carr and Wu (2006b) explain the derivation of the VIX, and its relation to approximating a 30-day variance swap rate.

To encompass a 30-day calendar period, the VIX index requires option prices from the two nearest-term expiration months. Hence, the first set of options is those with maturities closest to 30 days, from all options with maturities less than 30 days. The second is those with maturities closest to 30 days, from all options with maturities greater than 30 days. The time to maturity T_i $(i = 1, 2)$ of each set

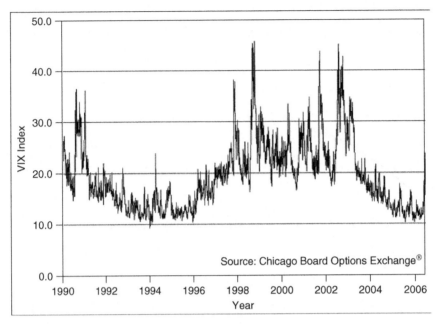

FIGURE 11.14   The CBOE Volatility Index (VIX)
Source: cboe.com

of options is calculated in minutes, from the time of calculation on the current day, and expressed in years:

$$T_i = N_{T_i}/M_Y = (M_C + M_S + M_O)/M_Y \qquad (11.11)$$

where N_{T_i} = number of minutes to expiration of option set i
$\quad\;\; M_C$ = number of minutes from calculation time until midnight of current day
$\quad\;\; M_S$ = number of minutes from midnight until 8:30 AM the next day
$\quad\;\; M_O$ = number of minutes from next day to expiration day

and where $N_{T_i} = M_C + M_S + M_O$. Hence it is always true that $M_S = 8.5 \times 60 = 510$ and $M_Y = 365 \times 24 \times 60 = 525,600$, regardless of the time of calculation on the current day. In the example from CBOE (2003) the time of calculation is 8:30 AM, which corresponds to $M_C = 15.5 \times 60 = 930$, and the options have 16 and 44 days to expiration, so that $M_O = (16 - 2) \times 24 \times 60 = 20,160$ in the first case, and $M_O = (44 - 2) \times 24 \times 60 = 60,480$ in the second case. Hence, the options with 16 and 44 days to expiration have a time to maturity of $N_{T_1} = 21,600$ and $N_{T_2} = 61,920$ minutes, respectively, corresponding to $T_1 = 0.0411$ years and $T_2 = 0.1178$ years.

CBOE (2003) explain how to calculate the VIX with two sets of option prices in three steps. Each set of option prices are sorted by strike price, and each set includes no more than two consecutive deep out-of-the-money options with zero price. For each option, the midpoint between ask and bid quotes is used as the option price.

In the first step, options are selected to be used in the VIX calculation and the forward index level F for each set of options is obtained. The reference strike price K^* is the strike at which the difference in absolute value between the call and put prices is the smallest. The forward index level is calculated using this difference as

$$F = K^* \exp(rT) \times \text{Difference} \qquad (11.12)$$

while the strike price immediately below F is denoted K_0. Out-of-the-money options are selected by retaining only puts with strike price less than K_0, and calls with strike price greater than K_0. The option price at a strike price equal to K_0 is defined as the average of the put and call with that strike price.

In the second step, the model-free implied variance is computed in each set of prices as

$$\sigma^2 = \frac{2}{T} \sum_i \frac{\Delta K_i}{K_i^2} \exp(rT) Q(K_i) - \frac{1}{T} \left(\frac{F}{K_0} - 1 \right)^2 \qquad (11.13)$$

where

$$K_i = \text{strike price for out-of-the money option } i$$
$$\Delta K_i = \text{distance between successive strikes}$$
$$Q(K_i) = \text{mid-point of bid-ask spread for an option with strike } K_i$$

and where the summation i runs over out-of-the-money calls (for $K_i > F$) and out-of-the-money puts (for $K_i < F$). As explained by Carr and Wu (2006b), equation (11.13) is a discretized version of the risk-neutral expected value of the future variance, given by

$$E[\sigma^2] = \frac{2}{T} e^{rT} \int_0^\infty \frac{Q(K)}{K^2} \, dK. \qquad (11.14)$$

The extra term $(F/K_0 - 1)^2$ in (11.13) is an adjustment for using part of the in-the-money calls at K_0.

In the third step, σ_1^2 and σ_2^2 obtained from (11.13) under each set of option prices are interpolated to obtain a variance representing a time to maturity of 30 days. Finally, the square root is taken and multiplied by 100 to produce the VIX 30-day volatility

$$\sigma_{VIX} = 100\% \times \sqrt{\left[T_1\sigma_1^2 \left(\frac{N_{T_2} - N_{30}}{N_{T_2} - N_{T_1}} \right) + T_1\sigma_1^2 \left(\frac{N_{30} - N_{T_1}}{N_{T_2} - N_{T_1}} \right) \right] \times \left(\frac{365}{30} \right)}$$

$$(11.15)$$

where N_{30} = number of minutes in 30 days, or 43,200.

The Excel files Chapter11VIX and Chapter11RealVix each include a set of VBA functions to calculate the VIX volatility in (11.15). The functions Mat(), SmallK(), F(), and K0() calculate the maturity T from (11.11), the reference strike K^*, the forward index level F from (11.12), and K_0. The last three functions require as inputs a vector strike prices (Strike), prices of calls (CallOp) and puts (PutOp), the risk-free rate (r), the number of days until expiration minus two (Ndays), and the time of calculation (CalcTime).

```
Function Mat(Ndays, CalcTime)
  H = Hour(CalcTime)
  M = Minute(CalcTime)
  T = H + M / 60
  Mat = ((24 - T) * 60 + 510 + 60 * 24 * Ndays) / 525600
End Function

Function SmallK(Strike, CallOp, PutOp)
N = Application.Count(Strike)
Dim Diff() As Double, NewDiff() As Double
ReDim Diff(N) As Double, NewDiff(N) As Double
For i = 1 To N
  Diff(i) = Abs(CallOp(i) - PutOp(i))
Next i
SmallK = Diff(1)
For i = 2 To N
  If Diff(i) < Diff(i - 1) Then
    SmallK = Strike(i)
  End If
Next i
End Function

Function F(Strike, CallOp, PutOp, r, Ndays, CalcTime)
N = Application.Count(Strike): T = Mat(Ndays, CalcTime)
K = SmallK(Strike, CallOp, PutOp)
For i = 1 To N
  If Strike(i) = K Then
    F = K + Exp(r * T) * Abs(CallOp(i) - PutOp(i))
  End If
Next i
End Function

Function K0(Strike, CallOp, PutOp, r, Ndays, CalcTime)
N = Application.Count(Strike): T = Mat(Ndays, CalcTime)
Fi = F(Strike, CallOp, PutOp, r, Ndays, CalcTime)
K0 = Strike(1): Diff = Fi - Strike(1)
For i = 2 To N
```

```
      If (Fi - Strike(i) < Diff) And (Fi - Strike(i)) > 0 Then
        KO = Strike(i)
      End If
    Next i
    End Function
```

The VBA function Prices() retains the prices of out-of-sample calls and puts, and calculates the average of the put and call price for the strike equal to K_0.

```
Function Prices(Strike, CallOp, PutOp, r, Ndays, CalcTime)
N = Application.Count(Strike)
Dim P() As Double
ReDim P(N) As Double
K_0 = KO(Strike, CallOp, PutOp, r, Ndays, CalcTime)
For i = 1 To N
  If Strike(i) = K_0 Then
    j = i
  End If
Next i
P(j) = (CallOp(j) + PutOp(j)) / 2
For i = (j + 1) To N
  P(i) = CallOp(i)
Next i
For i = (j - 1) To 1 Step -1
  P(i) = PutOp(i)
Next i
Dim output() As Double
ReDim output(N, 2) As Double
For i = 1 To N
  output(i, 1) = Strike(i)
  output(i, 2) = P(i)
Next i
  Prices = output
End Function
```

The function SubVar() calculates the individual variances σ_1^2 and σ_2^2.

```
Function SubVar(Strike, CallOp, PutOp, r, Ndays, CalcTime)
T = Mat(Ndays, CalcTime)
N = Application.Count(Strike)
Dim K() As Double, P() As Double, Price() As Double, DeltaK() As Double,
            Term() As Double
ReDim K(N) As Double, P(N, 2) As Double, Price(N) As Double, DeltaK(N) As
            Double, Term(N) As Double
K_0 = KO(Strike, CallOp, PutOp, r, Ndays, CalcTime)
Fi = F(Strike, CallOp, PutOp, r, Ndays, CalcTime)
P = Prices(Strike, CallOp, PutOp, r, Ndays, CalcTime)
For i = 1 To N
  K(i) = P(i, 1)
  Price(i) = P(i, 2)
    If i > 1 Then
      DeltaK(i) = K(i) - K(i - 1)
```

```
      End If
   Term(i) = DeltaK(i) / K(i) ^ 2 * Exp(r * T) * Price(i)
Next i
DeltaK(1) = K(2) - K(1)
Term(1) = DeltaK(1) / K(1) ^ 2 * Exp(r * T) * Price(1)
SubVar = 2 / T * Application.Sum(Term)
        - (Fi / K_0 - 1) ^ 2 / T
End Function
```

Finally, the function VIX() calculates the variance in accordance with (11.15).

```
Function VIX(Strike1, CallOp1, PutOp1, Ndays1, Strike2, CallOp2, PutOp2,
             Ndays2, r, CalcTime)
Var1 = SubVar(Strike1, CallOp1, PutOp1, r, Ndays1, CalcTime)
Var2 = SubVar(Strike2, CallOp2, PutOp2, r, Ndays2, CalcTime)
H = Hour(CalcTime): M = Minute(CalcTime): T = H + M / 60
NT1 = (24 - T) * 60 + 510 + Ndays1 * 60 * 24
NT2 = (24 - T) * 60 + 510 + Ndays2 * 60 * 24
T1 = NT1 / 525600: T2 = NT2 / 525600: N30 = 43200
Factor1 = T1 * Var1 * (NT2 - N30) / (NT2 - NT1)
Factor2 = T2 * Var2 * (N30 - NT1) / (NT2 - NT1)
   VIX = Sqr((Factor1 + Factor2) * 365 / 30) * 100
End Function
```

The Excel file Chapter11VIX illustrates these functions using the example in CBOE (2003). This file is illustrated in Figure 11.15. The two nearest-term options range in strike price from $K = 775$ to $K = 1025$. The strike prices and the midpoint of the bid-ask quote for calls and puts are in cells B10:D20 and cells G10:I20. The options have 16 and 44 days to maturity, respectively, which implies 14 and 42 days to expiration after the current day, as indicated in cells C22 and H22. The risk-free rate of 0.01162 is in cell C4 and the time of calculation (8:30 AM) is in cell H4.

Range names have been created for the number of days, the strikes, and the call and put prices. To calculate the value of the VIX with these option prices, in cell E23 we type

$$= \text{VIX(Strike1, CallOp1, PutOp1, Day1, Strike2, CallOp2, PutOp2,}$$
$$\text{Day2, RF, CalcTime)}$$

which produces the value 25.36 percent. This is the only function that needs to appear in the spreadsheet, as the other functions are contained in VIX(). The other functions can be invoked for illustration. For example, in cell C41 we type

$$= \text{SubVar(Strike1,CallOp1,PutOp1,RF,Day1, CalcTime)}$$

which produces $\sigma_1^2 \approx 6.65$ percent.

We now reproduce the closing value of the VIX on January 3, 2005. The Excel file Chapter11RealVIX contains data on options written on the S&P 500 index on January 3, 2005. The options data were obtained from OptionMetrics

	A	B	C	D	E	F	G	H	I	J
1										
2		**Replication of VIX Index Calculation From CBOE (2003)**								
3										
4		Risk Free Rate	0.01162				Calculation Time	8:30		
5										
6			Nearest Term Options					Next Nearest-Term Options		
7										
8		Strike	Call Mid-Quote	Put Mid-Quote	Price		Strike	Call Mid-Quote	Put Mid-Quote	Price
9		Price	Price	Price	Difference		Price	Price	Price	Difference
10		775	125.48	0.11	125.37		775	128.78	2.72	126.06
11		800	100.79	0.41	100.38		800	105.85	4.76	101.09
12		825	76.7	1.30	75.40		825	84.14	8.01	76.13
13		850	45.01	3.60	41.41		850	64.13	12.97	51.16
14		875	34.05	8.64	25.41		875	46.38	20.18	26.20
15		900	18.41	17.98	0.43		900	31.40	30.17	1.23
16		925	8.07	32.63	24.56		925	19.57	43.31	23.74
17		950	2.68	52.23	49.55		950	11.00	59.70	48.70
18		975	0.62	75.16	74.54		975	5.43	79.10	73.67
19		1000	0.09	99.61	99.52		1000	2.28	100.91	98.63
20		1025	0.01	124.52	124.51		1025	0.78	124.38	123.60
21										
22		Days until Exp =	14				Days until Exp =	42		
23				VIX in % =	**25.36**					
24		$T_1 =$	0.04109589				$T_2 =$	0.11780822		
25		$F_1 =$	900.43				$F_2 =$	901.23		
26		$K_0 =$	900				$K_0 =$	900		
27										
28		Strikes	Prices				Strikes	Prices		
29		775	0.11				775	2.72		
30		800	0.41				800	4.76		
31		825	1.30				825	8.01		
32		850	3.60				850	12.97		
33		875	8.64				875	20.18		
34		900	18.20				900	30.79		
35		925	8.07				925	19.57		
36		950	2.68				950	11.00		
37		975	0.62				975	5.43		
38		1000	0.09				1000	2.28		
39		1025	0.01				1025	0.78		
40										
41		$\sigma_1^2 =$	0.066477				$\sigma_2^2 =$	0.063668		

FIGURE 11.15 Replication of VIX Index Calculation Example
Source: cboe.com

(www.optionmetrics.com). The nearest term set options are those with expiry on January 22, and the next nearest are those with expiry on February 19. Options for the nearest term range from $K = 500$ to $K = 1500$, while options for the next nearest term range from $K = 700$ to $K = 1300$. Only part of the sheet is reproduced in Figure 11.16.

Strike prices with the smallest differences are in cells C7 and H7, namely $K_1^* = 1205$ and $K_2^* = 1210$, respectively. These correspond to price differences of 0.105 and 4.5, in cells E56 and J43 (these do not appear in the figure). The time of

	A	B	C	D	E	F	G	H	I	J
1										
2		**VIX Index Calculations Using Options Data on the S&P 500 Index**								
3										
4		Date	3-Jan-05				Date	3-Jan-05	Risk-Free Rate	0.0231
5		Expiry	22-Jan-05				Expiry	19-Feb-05	Calculation Time	15:45
6		$N_{T1} =$	17				$N_{T2} =$	45		
7		$K_1^* =$	1205				$K_2^* =$	1210	VIX =	**14.63**
8		$F_1 =$	1205.15				$F_2 =$	1214.51	Historical =	**14.08**
9		$K_0 =$	1205				$K_0 =$	1210		
10		$T_1 =$	0.0484874				$T_2 =$	0.125200		
11										
12			Nearest Term Options					Next Nearest Term Options		
13		Strike	Call Mid-Quote	Put Mid-Quote	Price		Strike	Call Mid-Quote	Put Mid-Quote	Price
14		Price	Price	Price	Difference		Price	Price	Price	Difference
15		500	704.700	0.050	704.650		700	504.300	0.250	504.050
16		600	604.800	0.050	604.750		725	479.400	0.250	479.150
17		650	554.800	0.050	554.750		750	454.400	0.250	454.150
18		700	504.900	0.050	504.850		775	429.500	0.250	429.250
19		750	455.000	0.050	454.950		800	404.600	0.250	404.350
20		800	405.000	0.050	404.950		825	379.700	0.075	379.625
21		825	380.100	0.050	380.050		850	354.700	0.250	354.450
22		850	356.100	0.050	356.050		875	329.800	0.250	329.550
23		875	330.100	0.025	330.075		900	304.900	0.250	304.650
24		900	305.100	0.050	305.050		925	280.000	0.275	279.725
25		925	280.200	0.050	280.150		950	255.100	0.275	254.825
26		950	255.200	0.075	255.125		975	230.300	0.250	230.050

FIGURE 11.16   Reproduction of the VIX Index
Source: optionmetrics.com

calculation is 3:45 PM, in cell J5. To obtain the value of the VIX index at that time, in cell J7 we type

$$= \text{VIX(Strike1,CallOp1,PutOp1,Ndays1,Strike2,CallOp2,}$$

$$\text{PutOp2,Ndays2,RF,CalcTime)}$$

which produces a value of 14.63 percent. The Excel file Chapter11HistoricalVIX indicates that the historical value of the VIX on January 3, 2005, was 14.08 percent. This small discrepancy can be explained by the fact that the CBOE computes the VIX index using option quotes updated every five minutes. The OptionMetrics database, however, contains the last daily bid-ask quote only, which might not correspond to the data used by CBOE for their final end-of-day calculation.

SUMMARY

The methods of model-free implied volatility covered in this chapter constitute a powerful method to extract implied volatility from option prices. Unlike Black-Scholes implied volatilities, model-free implied volatilities do not rely on any particular model of option prices. Moreover, they utilize the whole cross-section of option prices, rather than at-the-money prices only. In practice, fitting model-free implied volatilities using simple methods is problematic, since the underlying theory specifies options covering a continuum of strike prices along an infinite range. Using options at discrete strike prices and bounded above and below introduces discretization and truncation biases. The method proposed by Jiang and Tian (2005), and described in this chapter, help to mitigate these biases. We show also how model-free forward implied volatility is obtained from model-free forward variances, which themselves are constructed as a difference of model-free variances. Finally, the updated VIX index, produced by the Chicago Board Options Exchange® (www.cboe.com), constitutes an important application of model-free implied volatility. This chapter demonstrates how to construct this index, and illustrates its calculation with an example, using two cross-sections of options on the S&P 500 index, obtained from OptionMetrics (www.optionmetrics.com).

EXERCISES

This section provides exercises that deal with model-free implied volatility. Solutions are contained in the Excel file Chapter11Exercises.

11.1 Use put-call parity to show that Equation (11.6)

$$2 \int_0^\infty \frac{C(T,K) - \max(S_0 - K, 0)}{K^2} \, dK$$

is equivalent to

$$2 \int_0^{S_0} \frac{P(T,K)}{K^2} \, dK + 2 \int_{S_0}^\infty \frac{C(T,K)}{K^2} \, dK. \qquad (11.16)$$

Use a risk-free rate equal to zero. This equation will be encountered in Chapter 13.

11.2 Use simulated Black-Scholes prices to show that the two sets of equations in Exercise 11.1 are equivalent. Use $S_0 = 30, r = 0, T = 1$ year, $\sigma = 0.30$, and a strike price range running from $K = 15$ to $K = 45$ for the integration. Use the TRAPnumint() function for trapezoidal numerical integration introduced in Chapter 2, and the BS_Price() function for Black-Scholes prices introduced in Chapter 4.

SOLUTIONS TO EXERCISES

11.1 The first step is to divide the integral into two parts at $dK = S_0$:

$$2 \int_0^{S_0} \frac{C(T,K) - \max(S_0 - K, 0)}{K^2} \, dK + 2 \int_{S_0}^\infty \frac{C(T,K) - \max(S_0 - K, 0)}{K^2} \, dK.$$

Note that the first integral runs from $dK = 0$ to $dK = S_0$, which implies that $\max(S_0 - K, 0) = S_0 - K$, while the second integral runs from $dK = S_0$ to $dK = \infty$, which implies that $\max(S_0 - K, 0) = 0$. Replacing the max() functions with these equalities in both integrals produces

$$2 \int_0^{S_0} \frac{C(T, K) - S_0 + K}{K^2} \, dK + 2 \int_{S_0}^{\infty} \frac{C(T, K)}{K^2} \, dK.$$

The put-call relation with a zero risk-free rate is $C(T, K) + K = P(T, K) + S_0$. Replacing the denominator of the first integrand with $P(T, K)$ produces the desired result

$$2 \int_0^{S_0} \frac{P(T, K)}{K^2} \, dK + 2 \int_{S_0}^{\infty} \frac{C(T, K)}{K^2} \, dK.$$

11.2 The solution to this exercise is illustrated in Figure 11.17. The Black-Scholes prices of calls and puts are in columns F and G. For example, to obtain the call price when $K = 15$, in cell F6 we type

$$= \text{BS\_Price}(\text{F4, S,E6, rf, T, v})$$

which produces $C(1, 15) = 15.02$. The intrinsic values of the calls, $\max(S_0 - K, 0)$, are in column H, and the weights $1/K^2$ in column I. Values of the first integrand, $(C(T, K) - \max(S_0 - K, 0))/K^2$, are in column J. For example, in cell J6 we type "=(F6-H6)*I6", which produces 0.0001. Applying the trapezoidal rule to the range of values in column I, produces the value of the first integral. Hence in cell C11 we type

$$= 2*\text{TRAPnumint}(\text{E6:E36,J6:J36})$$

which produces $\sigma^2 = 0.0876$. This corresponds to a volatility of $\sigma = 0.30$, exactly that used to generate the Black-Scholes prices. To obtain the value of the two integrals in (11.16), the IF()function in Excel is used to select either calls or puts for the integration. The IF() statement will select $P(T, K)/K^2$ if $K < S_0$ or $C(T, K)/K^2$ if $K > S_0$. For example, in cell K6 we type

$$= \text{IF}(\text{E6} < \text{S,G6*I6,F6*I6})$$

which returns $P(T, K)/K^2 = 0.0001$. In cell K26 we type

$$= \text{IF}(\text{E26} < \text{S,G26*I26,F26*I26})$$

	A	B	C	D	E	F	G	H	I	J	K
1	EXERCISE 11.2										
2											
3	**Simulated Black-Scholes Call and Put Prices**										
4					Strike	Call	Put	Call Intrinsic	Weight	MFV	MFV
5	Underlying Price (S)		30.00		Price (K)	Price (C)	Price (P)	Value	1/K²	All Calls	OTM options
6	Risk-Free Rate (r)		0.00		15	15.02	0.02	15.00	0.0044	0.0001	0.0001
7	Time to Maturity (T)		1.00		16	14.04	0.04	14.00	0.0039	0.0002	0.0002
8	Volatility of the Underlying (σ)		0.30		17	13.08	0.08	13.00	0.0035	0.0003	0.0003
9					18	12.13	0.13	12.00	0.0031	0.0004	0.0004
10	**Variance**				19	11.20	0.20	11.00	0.0028	0.0005	0.0005
11	All Calls		0.087585		20	10.30	0.30	10.00	0.0025	0.0007	0.0007
12	OTM Calls and OTM Puts		0.087585		21	9.43	0.43	9.00	0.0023	0.0010	0.0010
13					22	8.60	0.60	8.00	0.0021	0.0012	0.0012
14	**Volatility**				23	7.81	0.81	7.00	0.0019	0.0015	0.0015
15	All Calls		0.30		24	7.06	1.06	6.00	0.0017	0.0018	0.0018
16	OTM Calls and OTM Puts		0.30		25	6.36	1.36	5.00	0.0016	0.0022	0.0022
17					26	5.71	1.71	4.00	0.0015	0.0025	0.0025
18					27	5.10	2.10	3.00	0.0014	0.0029	0.0029
19					28	4.55	2.55	2.00	0.0013	0.0033	0.0033
20					29	4.04	3.04	1.00	0.0012	0.0036	0.0036
21					30	3.58	3.58	0.00	0.0011	0.0040	0.0040
22					31	3.16	4.16	0.00	0.0010	0.0033	0.0033
23					32	2.78	4.78	0.00	0.0010	0.0027	0.0027
24					33	2.44	5.44	0.00	0.0009	0.0022	0.0022
25					34	2.14	6.14	0.00	0.0009	0.0019	0.0019
26					35	1.87	6.87	0.00	0.0008	0.0015	0.0015
27					36	1.63	7.63	0.00	0.0008	0.0013	0.0013
28					37	1.42	8.42	0.00	0.0007	0.0010	0.0010
29					38	1.24	9.24	0.00	0.0007	0.0009	0.0009
30					39	1.07	10.07	0.00	0.0007	0.0007	0.0007
31					40	0.93	10.93	0.00	0.0006	0.0006	0.0006
32					41	0.80	11.80	0.00	0.0006	0.0005	0.0005
33					42	0.69	12.69	0.00	0.0006	0.0004	0.0004
34					43	0.60	13.60	0.00	0.0005	0.0003	0.0003
35					44	0.52	14.52	0.00	0.0005	0.0003	0.0003
36					45	0.45	15.45	0.00	0.0005	0.0002	0.0002

FIGURE 11.17   Solution to Exercise 11.2

which returns $C(T, K)/K^2 = 0.0015$. Applying the trapezoidal rule to the range of values in column K produces the desired result. Hence, in cell C12 we type

$$= 2*\text{TRAPnumint}(E6:E36,K6:K36)$$

which returns exactly the same value for the variance, $\sigma^2 = 0.0876$.

CHAPTER 12

Model-Free Higher Moments

INTRODUCTION

In the previous chapter, it was shown that volatility can be estimated directly from market option prices, without having to rely on any particular functional form for those prices. The model-free methods covered in this chapter extend this estimation to higher moments of the risk-neutral distribution, namely skewness and kurtosis. Similar to model-free volatility, model-free skewness and kurtosis use a cross-section of options. In this chapter we outline the theoretical foundation for extracting model-free skewness and kurtosis, and present three methods for implementation. The basic method uses a crude numerical integration rule and produces biased estimates. The adapted method corrects for this bias and increases the approximation accuracy. Finally, the advanced method uses an interpolation-extrapolation technique on option prices, and is the most accurate of the three methods. The accuracy of each method is compared using option prices generated from the Gram-Charlier model, for which the skewness and kurtosis are known. This allows each set of estimates to be compared to the true value.

Finally, we note that methods have been proposed to extract the entire risk-neutral distribution from option prices, such as those proposed by Breeden and Litzenberger (1978), Rubinstein (1994), Stutzer (1996), Buchen and Kelly (1996), and Jackwerth and Rubinstein (1996). In this book, however, we concentrate solely on extracting risk-neutral moments.

THEORETICAL FOUNDATION

Bakshi, Kapadia, and Madan (2003) outline a methodology to extract the volatility, skewness, and kurtosis of the risk-neutral return distribution from a set of out-of-the-money calls and puts. Their approach is heavily dependent on a relationship between payoff functions and option prices derived by Carr and Madan (2001).

Define a payoff function $H[S]$ that depends on the terminal stock price S. The price of the payoff can be obtained through risk-neutral valuation as

$$E^q\{H[S]\} = \int_0^\infty H[S]q[S]\,dS \tag{12.1}$$

where $q[S]$ is the risk-neutral pricing density and $E^q\{\}$ is the expectation under q. For example, if $H[S] = e^{-r\tau}(S - K)^+$, then risk-neutral valuation produces the price of a European call option

$$C(t, \tau; K) = \int_0^\infty e^{-r\tau}(S - K)^+ q[S]\,dS, \tag{12.2}$$

where r is the risk-free rate and τ is the time to maturity and where $(x)^+ = \max(0, x)$. The price of a European put is similarly defined as

$$P(t, \tau; K) = \int_0^\infty e^{-r\tau}(K - S)^+ q[S]\,dS. \tag{12.3}$$

Carr and Madan (2001) show that any payoff function $H[S]$ with bounded expectations can be spanned by a continuum of out-of-the-money calls and puts. If the payoff function is twice continuously differentiable, then it can be spanned algebraically as

$$H[S] = H[\bar{S}] + (S - \bar{S})H_S[\bar{S}] + \int_{\bar{S}}^\infty H_{SS}[K](S - K)^+\,dK$$

$$+ \int_0^{\bar{S}} H_{SS}[K](K - S)^+\,dK \tag{12.4}$$

where $H_S = \partial H/\partial S$ and $H_{SS} = \partial^2 H/\partial S^2$ are the first and second partial derivatives of $H[S]$, respectively, and $H[\bar{S}]$ and $H_S[\bar{S}]$ are the value of the payoff function and its derivative evaluated at some value $\bar{S}$. Discounting the payoff expressed in (12.4) by the risk-free rate and taking the risk-neutral expectation produces the arbitrage-free price

$$E^q\{e^{-r\tau}H[S]\} = (H[\bar{S}] - \bar{S}H_S[\bar{S}])e^{-r\tau} + H_S[\bar{S}]S(t)$$

$$+ \int_{\bar{S}}^\infty H_{SS}[K]C(t, \tau; K)\,dK + \int_0^{\bar{S}} H_{SS}[K]P(t, \tau; K)\,dK. \tag{12.5}$$

This equation indicates that any payoff can be replicated by three positions in market-traded assets:

1. A position of $H[\bar{S}] - \bar{S}H_S[\bar{S}]$ in a zero-coupon bond
2. A position of $H_S[\bar{S}]$ in the stock
3. A position that is a linear combination of out-of-the-money calls and puts, with weights $H_{SS}[K]$

Bakshi, Kapadia, and Madan (2003) apply this result to the pricing of higher moments. They first define the τ-period return as $R_{t,\tau} = \ln[S_{t+\tau}/S_t]$, and then define three contracts based on $R_{t,\tau}$. The volatility contract has the payoff $H[S] = R_{t,\tau}^2$, the cubic contract has the payoff $H[S] = R_{t,\tau}^3$, and the quartic contract has the payoff $H[S] = R_{t,\tau}^4$. The prices of these contracts are obtained by discounted risk-neutral expectation, and are denoted $V(t,\tau) \equiv E^q\{e^{-r\tau}R_{t,\tau}^2\}$, $W(t,\tau) \equiv E^q\{e^{-r\tau}R_{t,\tau}^3\}$, and $X(t,\tau) \equiv E^q\{e^{-r\tau}R_{t,\tau}^4\}$, respectively. Baskhi, Kapadia, and Madan (2003) show that by applying (12.5) and evaluating the arbitrage-free price at $\bar{S} = S_t$, the three defined contracts have the following form:

$$V(t,\tau) = \int_{S_t}^{\infty} \frac{2(1 - \ln[K/S_t])}{K^2} C(t,\tau;K)\,dK$$

$$+ \int_0^{S_t} \frac{2(1 + \ln[S_t/K])}{K^2} P(t,\tau;K)\,dK, \tag{12.6}$$

$$W(t,\tau) = \int_{S_t}^{\infty} \frac{6\ln[K/S_t] - 3(\ln[K/S_t])^2}{K^2} C(t,\tau;K)\,dK$$

$$- \int_0^{S_t} \frac{6\ln[S_t/K] + 3(\ln[S_t/K])^2}{K^2} P(t,\tau;K)\,dK, \tag{12.7}$$

$$X(t,\tau) = \int_{S_t}^{\infty} \frac{12(\ln[K/S_t])^2 - 4(\ln[K/S_t])^3}{K^2} C(t,\tau;K)\,dK$$

$$- \int_0^{S_t} \frac{12(\ln[S_t/K])^2 + 4(\ln[S_t/K])^3}{K^2} P(t,\tau;K)\,dK. \tag{12.8}$$

Moreover, each price can be constructed using a portfolio of options indexed by their strikes. In the appendix to Bakshi, Kapadia, and Madan (2003), it is shown how these prices are used in the spanning equation (12.4) and the pricing equation (12.5) to produce the risk-neutral variance

$$VAR(t,\tau) \equiv E^q\{(R_{t,\tau} - E^q[R_{t,\tau}])^2\}$$

$$= e^{r\tau} V(t,\tau) - \mu(t,\tau)^2, \tag{12.9}$$

the risk-neutral skewness

$$SKEW(t,\tau) \equiv \frac{E^q\{(R_{t,\tau} - E^q[R_{t,\tau}])^3\}}{E^q\{(R_{t,\tau} - E^q[R_{t,\tau}])^2\}^{3/2}}$$

$$= \frac{e^{r\tau} W(t,\tau) - 3e^{r\tau}\mu(t,\tau)V(t,\tau) + 2\mu(t,\tau)^3}{[e^{r\tau} V(t,\tau) - \mu(t,\tau)^2]^{3/2}}, \tag{12.10}$$

and the risk-neutral kurtosis

$$
\begin{aligned}
KURT(t, \tau) &\equiv \frac{E^q\{(R_{t,\tau} - E^q[R_{t,\tau}])^4\}}{E^q\{(R_{t,\tau} - E^q[R_{t,\tau}])^2\}^2} \\
&= \frac{e^{r\tau}X(t,\tau) - 4e^{r\tau}\mu(t,\tau)W(t,\tau) + 6e^{r\tau}\mu(t,\tau)^2 V(t,\tau) - 3\mu(t,\tau)^4}{[e^{r\tau}V(t,\tau) - \mu(t,\tau)^2]^2},
\end{aligned}
\tag{12.11}
$$

where

$$
\begin{aligned}
\mu(t,\tau) &\equiv E^q \ln\left[\frac{S_{t+\tau}}{S_t}\right] \\
&= e^{r\tau} - 1 - \frac{e^{r\tau}}{2}V(t,\tau) - \frac{e^{r\tau}}{6}W(t,\tau) - \frac{e^{r\tau}}{24}X(t,\tau).
\end{aligned}
\tag{12.12}
$$

These expressions can be derived by computing the derivatives of the payoff functions $H[S]$ of each contract with respect to the terminal stock price S and applying equation (12.5). The first partial derivatives $H_S[S] = \partial H/\partial S$ are

$$
H_S[S] = \begin{cases}
\dfrac{2[\ln(S_{t+\tau}/S_t)]}{S_{t+\tau}} & \text{volatility contract} \\[2mm]
\dfrac{3[\ln(S_{t+\tau}/S_t)]^2}{S_{t+\tau}} & \text{cubic contract} \\[2mm]
\dfrac{4[\ln(S_{t+\tau}/S_t)]^3}{S_{t+\tau}} & \text{quartic contract,}
\end{cases}
\tag{12.13}
$$

and the second partial derivatives $H_{SS}[S] = \partial^2 H/\partial S^2$ are

$$
H_{SS}[S] = \begin{cases}
\dfrac{2(1 - \ln(S_{t+\tau}/S_t))}{S_{t+\tau}^2} & \text{volatility contract} \\[2mm]
\dfrac{6\ln(S_{t+\tau}/S_t) - 3[\ln(S_{t+\tau}/S_t)]^2}{S_{t+\tau}^2} & \text{cubic contract} \\[2mm]
\dfrac{12[\ln(S_{t+\tau}/S_t)]^2 - 4[\ln(S_{t+\tau}/S_t)]^3}{S_{t+\tau}^2} & \text{quartic contract.}
\end{cases}
\tag{12.14}
$$

Each of these functions is evaluated at the current stock price S_t. Recall that the pricing equation (12.5) requires a position of $H[\bar{S}] - \bar{S}H_S[\bar{S}]$ in a zero coupon bond, and a position of $H_S[\bar{S}]$ in the stock. Each of these positions is zero when evaluated at S_t. This implies that only the linear combination of calls and puts is needed to obtain the arbitrage-free price.

IMPLEMENTATION

In this section, model-free higher moments are implemented using three methods. The basic method is the simplest because it uses the left-point rule for approximating the required integrals. The adapted method is more accurate because it regroups two integrals into a single integral, which avoids the possibility of the middle interval of strikes being excluded from the integration. Finally, the advanced method uses extrapolation and interpolation of prices and is the most accurate of the three methods under consideration.

Basic Implementation

With the prices $V(t,\tau)$, $W(t,\tau)$, and $X(t,\tau)$, it is straightforward to obtain the variance, skewness, and kurtosis in (12.9) through (12.11). Evaluating the moments requires an approximation to the integrals in (12.6), (12.7), and (12.8). Bakshi, Kapadia, and Madan (2003) approximate the integrals using summation equations, which is equivalent to the left-point rule. As in their paper, we use the cubic contract (12.7) for illustration. The long position in out-of-the-money calls can be estimated by

$$\sum_j w[S_t + j\Delta K]C(t,\tau; S_t + j\Delta K)\Delta K. \tag{12.15}$$

In this expression, the summation runs from $j = 1$ to $j = (\overline{K} - S_t)/\Delta K$, where $\overline{K}$ denotes the largest available call strike price. The long position in out-of-money puts can be estimated by

$$\sum_j w[j\Delta K]P(t,\tau; j\Delta K)\Delta K, \tag{12.16}$$

where the summation runs from $j = 1$ to $j = (S_t - \Delta K)/\Delta K$. In both (12.15) and (12.16), $w[K]$ is defined as

$$w[K] \equiv \frac{6\ln[K/S_t] - 3(\ln[K/S_t])^2}{K^2}. \tag{12.17}$$

The volatility and quartic contracts are constructed similarly, by modifying the function in (12.17). While this approach is easy to implement, it uses the left-point rule, which is the most rudimentary numerical integration technique. Dennis and Mayhew (2002) use the trapezoidal rule instead, which produces far more accurate approximations and is only slightly more complicated to implement. The Excel files for this chapter contain VBA functions that use the trapezoidal rule to approximate the prices in (12.6), (12.7), and (12.8) and the model-free variance, skewness, and kurtosis in (12.9), (12.10), and (12.11). The functions BV(), BW(), and BX() compute $V(t,\tau)$, $W(t,\tau)$, and $X(t,\tau)$ under the basic implementation, using the TRAPnumint()

function for trapezoidal integration in two instances, once for the calls, and once for the puts. These functions require as inputs a set of prices and strikes for calls and puts, the current stock price, the risk-free rate, and the time to maturity.

```
Function BV(CallK, CallP, PutK, PutP, S, r, tau)
Dim call_int() As Double, call_intV() As Double
Dim put_int() As Double, put_intV() As Double
callcnt = Application.Count(CallK)
putcnt = Application.Count(PutK)
ReDim call_int(callcnt) As Double, call_intV(callcnt) As Double
ReDim put_int(putcnt) As Double, put_intV(putcnt) As Double
For cloop = 1 To callcnt
  K = CallK(cloop)
  C = CallP(cloop)
  call_int(cloop) = K
  call_intV(cloop) = ((2 * (1 - Application.Ln(K / S))) / (K ^ 2)) * C
Next cloop
  BV = TRAPnumint(call_int, call_intV)
For ploop = 1 To putcnt
  K = PutK(ploop)
  P = PutP(ploop)
  put_int(ploop) = K
  put_intV(ploop) = ((2 * (1 + Application.Ln(S / K))) / (K ^ 2)) * P
Next ploop
  BV = BV + TRAPnumint(put_int, put_intV)
End Function

Function BW(CallK, CallP, PutK, PutP, S, r, tau)
Dim call_int() As Double, call_intW() As Double
Dim put_int() As Double, put_intW() As Double
callcnt = Application.Count(CallK)
putcnt = Application.Count(PutK)
ReDim call_int(callcnt) As Double, call_intW(callcnt) As Double
ReDim put_int(putcnt) As Double, put_intW(putcnt) As Double
For cloop = 1 To callcnt
  K = CallK(cloop)
  C = CallP(cloop)
  call_int(cloop) = K
  call_intW(cloop) = ((6 * Application.Ln(K / S)
       - 3 * (Application.Ln(K / S) ^ 2)) / (K ^ 2)) * C
Next cloop
  BW = TRAPnumint(call_int, call_intW)
For ploop = 1 To putcnt
  K = PutK(ploop)
  P = PutP(ploop)
  put_int(ploop) = K
put_intW(ploop) = -((6 * Application.Ln(S / K)
       + 3 * (Application.Ln(S / K) ^ 2)) / (K ^ 2)) * P
Next ploop
  BW = BW + TRAPnumint(put_int, put_intW)
End Function
```

```
Function BX(CallK, CallP, PutK, PutP, S, r, tau)
Dim call_int() As Double, call_intX() As Double
Dim put_int() As Double, put_intX() As Double
callcnt = Application.Count(CallK)
putcnt = Application.Count(PutK)
ReDim call_int(callcnt) As Double, call_intX(callcnt) As Double
ReDim put_int(putcnt) As Double, put_intX(putcnt) As Double
For cloop = 1 To callcnt
  K = CallK(cloop)
  C = CallP(cloop)
  call_int(cloop) = K
  call_intX(cloop) = ((12 * (Application.Ln(K / S) ^ 2)
        - 4 * (Application.Ln(K / S) ^ 3)) / (K ^ 2)) * C
Next cloop
  BX = TRAPnumint(call_int, call_intX)
For ploop = 1 To putcnt
  K = PutK(ploop)
  P = PutP(ploop)
  put_int(ploop) = K
put_intX(ploop) = ((12 * (Application.Ln(S / K) ^ 2)
        + 4 * (Application.Ln(S / K) ^ 3)) / (K ^ 2)) * P
Next ploop
  BX = BX + TRAPnumint(put_int, put_intX)
End Function
```

Once these three prices are obtained it is easy to write functions for the variance, skewness and kurtosis, in accordance with equations (12.9), (12.10), and (12.11). This is achieved with the VBA functions BMFVar(), BMFSkew(), and BMFKurt(), respectively.

```
Function BMFVar(CallK, CallP, PutK, PutP, S, r, tau)
Dim V As Double, W As Double, X As Double
V = BV(CallK, CallP, PutK, PutP, S, r, tau)
W = BW(CallK, CallP, PutK, PutP, S, r, tau)
X = BX(CallK, CallP, PutK, PutP, S, r, tau)
er = Exp(r * tau)
mu = er - 1 - (er / 2) * V - (er / 6) * W - (er / 24) * X
BMFVar = (er * V - mu ^ 2)
End Function

Function BMFSkew(CallK, CallP, PutK, PutP, S, r, tau)
Dim V As Double, W As Double, X As Double
V = BV(CallK, CallP, PutK, PutP, S, r, tau)
W = BW(CallK, CallP, PutK, PutP, S, r, tau)
X = BX(CallK, CallP, PutK, PutP, S, r, tau)
er = Exp(r * tau)
mu = er - 1 - (er / 2) * V - (er / 6) * W - (er / 24) * X
BMFSkew = (er * W - 3 * mu * er * V + 2 * (mu ^ 3))
        / ((er * V - mu ^ 2) ^ (3 / 2))
End Function
```

```
Function BMFKurt(CallK, CallP, PutK, PutP, S, r, tau)
Dim V As Double, W As Double, X As Double
V = BV(CallK, CallP, PutK, PutP, S, r, tau)
W = BW(CallK, CallP, PutK, PutP, S, r, tau)
X = BX(CallK, CallP, PutK, PutP, S, r, tau)
er = Exp(r * tau)
mu = er - 1 - (er / 2) * V - (er / 6) * W - (er / 24) * X
BMFKurt = (er * X - 4 * mu * er * W + 6 * er * (mu ^ 2)
        * V - 3 * (mu ^ 4)) / ((er * V - mu ^ 2) ^ 2)
End Function
```

Later in this chapter these functions will be demonstrated using option prices generated under different models.

Adapted Implementation

Using two separate integrals—one for puts and the other for calls—can lead to problems when estimating the prices of the volatility, cubic, and quartic contracts $V(t, \tau)$, $W(t, \tau)$, and $X(t, \tau)$. This is best explained with a hypothetical example. Suppose that the current stock price is $S_t = 102$. As mentioned in earlier chapters, market options will not be available on a continuum of strike prices, but rather on standardized strike prices, usually in increments of $2.50 or $5.00. A stock price with current price $S_t = 102$ will typically have market options available over a strike price range of $K = 75$ to $K = 130$ in increments of $5.00. This implies that the integrals for the three contracts, which run over a combined integration domain of $[0, \infty)$, will be approximated in two parts, the first from $K = 75$ to 100 using out-of-the-money puts, and the second from $K = 105$ to 130 using out-of-the-money calls. With this approach, since the current underlying price does not fall on a particular strike price, the middle interval of strikes $(100,105)$ is not included in either of the integrals.

 This problem can be avoided by employing one integral to estimate the contract prices, instead of two integrals. This is the adapted implementation. The integrals are combined into a single integral, and the integrand is adjusted according to whether the strike price is below or above the spot price. In the hypothetical example, the integral runs from $K = 75$ to 130, without excluding the middle interval. The area under the middle interval is obtained by joining the value of the integrand at each endpoint of the middle interval with a line segment, and evaluating the area under the line segment. The Excel files for this chapter contain the VBA functions AV(), AW(), and AX() for approximating the prices of the volatility, cubic, and quartic contracts, respectively, under the adapted implementation.

```
Function AV(CallK, CallP, PutK, PutP, S, r, tau)
Dim all_int() As Double, all_intV() As Double
callcnt = Application.Count(CallK)
putcnt = Application.Count(PutK)
ReDim all_int(callcnt + putcnt) As Double, all_intV(callcnt + putcnt) As
        Double
```

```vba
For ploop = 1 To putcnt
  K = PutK(ploop)
  P = PutP(ploop)
  all_int(ploop) = K
  all_intV(ploop) = ((2 * (1 + Application.Ln(S / K))) / (K ^ 2)) * P
Next ploop
For cloop = 1 To callcnt
  K = CallK(cloop)
  C = CallP(cloop)
  all_int(putcnt + cloop) = K
  all_intV(putcnt + cloop) = ((2 * (1 - Application.Ln(K / S)))
                / (K ^ 2)) * C
Next cloop
  AV = TRAPnumint(all_int, all_intV)
End Function

Function AW(CallK, CallP, PutK, PutP, S, r, tau)
Dim all_int() As Double, all_intW() As Double
callcnt = Application.Count(CallK)
putcnt = Application.Count(PutK)
ReDim all_int(callcnt + putcnt) As Double, all_intW(callcnt + putcnt) As
                Double
For ploop = 1 To putcnt
  K = PutK(ploop)
  P = PutP(ploop)
  all_int(ploop) = K
  all_intW(ploop) = -((6 * Application.Ln(S / K)
        + 3 * (Application.Ln(S / K) ^ 2)) / (K ^ 2)) * P
Next ploop
For cloop = 1 To callcnt
  K = CallK(cloop)
  C = CallP(cloop)
  all_int(putcnt + cloop) = K
  all_intW(putcnt + cloop) = ((6 * Application.Ln(K / S)
        - 3 * (Application.Ln(K / S) ^ 2)) / (K ^ 2)) * C
Next cloop
  AW = TRAPnumint(all_int, all_intW)
End Function
Function AX(CallK, CallP, PutK, PutP, S, r, tau)
Dim all_int() As Double, all_intX() As Double
callcnt = Application.Count(CallK)
putcnt = Application.Count(PutK)
ReDim all_int(callcnt + putcnt) As Double, all_intX(callcnt + putcnt) As
                Double
For ploop = 1 To putcnt
  K = PutK(ploop)
  P = PutP(ploop)
  all_int(ploop) = K
  all_intX(ploop) = ((12 * (Application.Ln(S / K) ^ 2)
        + 4 * (Application.Ln(S / K) ^ 3)) / (K ^ 2)) * P
Next ploop
For cloop = 1 To callcnt
  K = CallK(cloop)
```

```
      C = CallP(cloop)
      all_int(putcnt + cloop) = K
      all_intX(putcnt + cloop) = ((12 * (Application.Ln(K / S)
          ^ 2) - 4 * (Application.Ln(K / S) ^ 3)) / (K ^ 2)) * C
   Next cloop
      AX = TRAPnumint(all_int, all_intX)
   End Function
```

The AMFVar(), AMFSkew(), and AMFKurt() functions are the same as their BMFVar(), BMFSkew(), and BMFKurt() counterparts and are not presented here. The only difference is that they invoke the AV(), AW(), and AX() functions above.

Advanced Implementation

The accuracy of the integral approximation can be further increased by applying the smoothing techniques developed by Jiang and Tian (2005) and presented in Chapter 11. The cubic spline interpolation and extrapolation technique of the implied volatility curve is implemented, and these implied volatilities are converted back into the appropriate call and put prices depending if the strike price is below or above the current underlying spot price. Once a large, finely spaced cross-section of out-of-the-money calls and puts is obtained, the adapted implementation is used to calculate model-free variance, kurtosis, and skewness.

The VBA function MFVar() is used to implement this method on model-free variance. The function nests the VBA functions IEpoints() and IEcurve() presented in Chapter 11, so these two functions are not presented here.

```
Function MFVar(passCallK, passCallP, passPutK, passPutP, S, r, T)
uniPoints = IEpoints(S, passCallK, passCallP, passPutK, passPutP, r, T)
u = 3
dK = 0.1
outKIV = IEcurve(uniPoints, u, dK, S)
Dim CallK() As Double, CallP() As Double, PutK() As Double, PutP() As
                  Double
n = UBound(outKIV)
nCall = 0
nPut = 0
For cnt = 1 To n
  curK = outKIV(cnt, 1)
    If (curK < S) Then
      nPut = nPut + 1
    Else
      nCall = nCall + 1
    End If
Next cnt
ReDim CallK(nCall) As Double, CallP(nCall) As Double
ReDim PutK(nPut) As Double, PutP(nPut) As Double
nCall = 0
nPut = 0
```

```
For cnt = 1 To n
  curK = outKIV(cnt, 1)
    If (curK < S) Then
      nPut = nPut + 1
      PutK(nPut) = curK
      PutP(nPut) = bs_price("Put", S, curK, r, T, outKIV(cnt, 2))
    Else
      nCall = nCall + 1
      CallK(nCall) = curK
      CallP(nCall) = bs_price("Call", S, curK, r, T, outKIV(cnt, 2))
    End If
Next cnt
  MFVar = AMFVar(CallK, CallP, PutK, PutP, S, r, T)
End Function
```

The last part of this function invokes the AMFVar() function for implementing the risk-neutral variance defined in (12.9).

```
Function AMFVar(CallK, CallP, PutK, PutP, S, r, tau)
Dim V As Double, W As Double, x As Double
V = AV(CallK, CallP, PutK, PutP, S, r, tau)
W = AW(CallK, CallP, PutK, PutP, S, r, tau)
x = AX(CallK, CallP, PutK, PutP, S, r, tau)
er = Exp(r * tau)
mu = er - 1 - (er / 2) * V - (er / 6) * W - (er / 24) * x
AMFVar = (er * V - mu ^ 2)
End Function
```

The functions MFSkew() and MFKurt() are similar to the MFVar() function, except that the functions AMFSkew() and AMFKurt(), respectively, are invoked at the end of the functions. These last two functions, in turn, are identical to the AMF-Var() function, except that the last statements employ the expressions in (12.10) and (12.11), respectively.

Comparison of the Three Methods

In this section, the accuracy of the three methods—basic, adapted, and advanced—is compared using out-of-the-money put and call prices generated through different pricing models for which the variance, skewness, and kurtosis are known. The simplest is the Black-Scholes model. A comparison of the three methods using Black-Scholes prices is in the Excel file Chapter12BKM-BS. This file is illustrated in Figure 12.1, using a spot price of $S = 102$, a yearly volatility $\sigma = 0.20$, a risk-free rate $r = 0.05$, and time to maturity $T = 0.25$ years. The skewness and kurtosis for this model are that of the normal distribution, namely $\gamma_1 = 0$ and $\gamma_2 = 3$, respectively. Strike prices range from $K = 75$ to 130, in increments of \$5.

Parameter values for the Black-Scholes model are in cells C6:C11, and the out-of-the-money option puts and calls are generated in cells E6:E11 and G6:G11 using the Black-Scholes pricing functions developed in Chapter 4. The true values of the T-period variance, skewness and kurtosis are in cells C15, C16, and C17,

	A	B	C	D	E	F	G
1							
2		**Model Free Risk-Neutral Variance, Skewness, and Kurtosis**					
3							
4		**Black-Scholes Parameters**		**OTM Black-Scholes Option Prices**			
5				Strike	Put	Strike	Call
6		Underlying Price (S)	102.00	75.00	0.00	105.00	3.31
7		Risk-Free Rate (r)	0.05	80.00	0.02	110.00	1.69
8		Time to Maturity (T)	0.25	85.00	0.09	115.00	0.78
9		Volatility (σ)	0.20	90.00	0.37	120.00	0.32
10		Skewness (γ_1)	0.00	95.00	1.10	125.00	0.12
11		Kurtosis (γ_2)	3.00	100.00	2.59	130.00	0.04
12							
13		**Model-Free Moments**	**True**	**Estimated Values**			
14			**Values**	**Basic**	**Adapted**	**Advanced**	
15		T-Period Variance (σ_T^2)	0.0100	0.0068	0.0097	0.0100	
16		T-Period Skewness (γ_{1T})	0.0000	-0.0474	-0.0116	-0.0001	
17		T-Period Kurtosis (γ_{2T})	3.0000	5.9995	3.1061	2.9925	
18							
19				**Approximation Error**			
20				**Basic**	**Adapted**	**Advanced**	
21				0.0032	0.0003	0.0000	
22				0.0474	0.0116	0.0001	
23				2.9995	0.1061	0.0075	

FIGURE 12.1 Model-Free Moments with Black-Scholes Prices.

respectively. To obtain the T-period variance σ_T^2, we scale the yearly variance by the time to maturity, so that $\sigma_T^2 = \sigma^2 T$. In cell C15 we type "=C9^2*C8", which produces $\sigma_T^2 = 0.20^2 \times 0.25$ or $\sigma_T^2 = 0.01$. Since the skewness and kurtosis of the normal distribution are always zero and three, we have $\gamma_{1T} = 0$ and $\gamma_{2T} = 3$. The model-free estimates generated by the basic, adapted, and advanced methods are in cells D15:D17, E15:E17, and F15:F17. For example, to obtain model-free variance under the basic method, in cell D15 we type

$$= \text{BMFVar}(F6:F11,G6:G11,D6:D11,E6:E11,C6,C7,C8)$$

which produces a value of $\hat{\sigma}^2 = 0.0068$. The other values are obtained similarly.

The absolute approximation errors of the variance and the kurtosis, estimated under each method, appear at the bottom of the sheet and are given by $|\theta - \hat{\theta}|$, where θ and $\hat{\theta}$ are the true and estimated values of the moment. The basic method does very poorly, and not only does the adapted method have faster execution time, but it is much more accurate. The advanced method with a large integration radius $u = 3$ and fine strike price interval $dK = 0.1$ is extremely accurate. To illustrate why there is such an improvement over the three methods we can plot the integrands for the prices of the volatility contract $V(t, \tau)$, the cubic contract $W(t, \tau)$, and quartic contract $W(t, \tau)$. The Excel file Chapter12PlotVar contains the data to plot the integrand for the volatility contract as a function of strike price. This is illustrated in Figure 12.2, using puts from $K = 80$ to 100 and calls from $K = 105$ to 130, when $S = 102$. To generate the figure, the functions for the volatility contract were modified to return integrand values rather than the integral itself.

Under the basic method, the integrand is made up of two parts, one that includes the points from $K = 80$ to 100 inclusive, and the other that includes points $K = 105$ to 130 inclusive, so that $V(t, \tau)$ is estimated as the area under the two curves made up of solid line segments in Figure 12.2. The adapted method adds the area under the dashed line, which spans the strike interval (100,105), and is therefore more accurate. Finally, the advanced method generates the solid peaked curve using the Jiang and Tian (2005) cubic spline interpolation and extrapolation technique. The integrand is extrapolated beyond $K = 80$ and $K = 130$ imposed by the data, and the method estimates $V(t, \tau)$ as the area under the solid smoothed line.

The Excel file Chapter12PlotSkew contains the integrand values for the cubic contract $W(t, \tau)$. A plot of these integrand values as a function of the strike price appears in Figure 12.3. Again, the basic method corresponds to the area under the two curves joined by solid line segments, the adapted method adds the area under the dashed line, and the advanced method corresponds to the area under the smooth

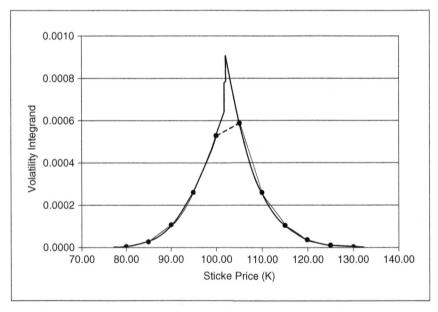

FIGURE 12.2 Integrand Plot for the Volatility Contract
Source: finance.yahoo.com

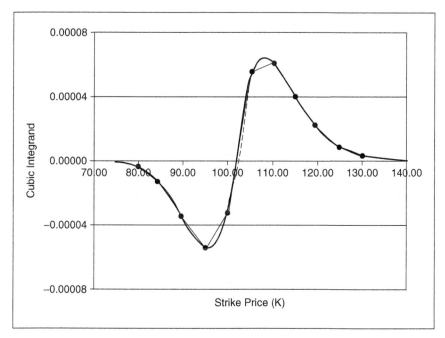

FIGURE 12.3 Integrand Plot for the Cubic Contract
Source: finance.yahoo.com

curve. In this particular example, omitting the area under the dashed line does not lead to a dramatic bias.

The Excel file Chapter12Kurt contains integrand values for the quartic contract $X(t, \tau)$, which are plotted in Figure 12.4. The interpretation of the plots is identical to that in Figures 12.2 and 12.3.

It is evident from Figure 12.2, which plots the integrand for $V(t, \tau)$, that not including the center of the integration domain leads to a downward biased estimate of the variance contract. It is much harder to quantify the effects on skewness and kurtosis since they are functions of $V(t, \tau)$, $W(t, \tau)$, and $X(t, \tau)$. These effects are better investigated by implementing the methods on model-generated option prices whose higher moments are known explicitly. This is done in the following section.

VERIFYING IMPLIED MOMENTS

Since both the skewness and kurtosis in the Gram-Charlier model are known parameters that are used as inputs to the option prices, we can use prices generated by this model to verify the accuracy of the three methods used to extract model-free implied moments from those generated prices. As explained in Chapter 4, the Gram-Charlier option pricing model is an extension of the Black-Scholes model.

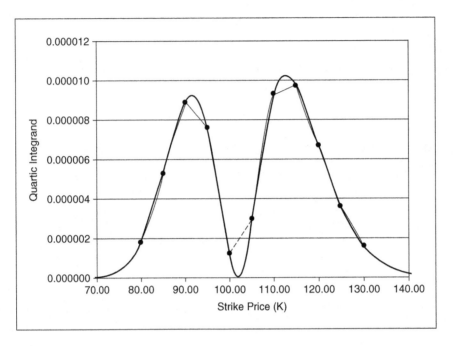

FIGURE 12.4 Integrand Plot for the Quartic Contract

The distribution of the stock price follows a Gram-Charlier expansion of the normal distribution, which allows for skewness and excess kurtosis.

Earlier in this chapter, Black-Scholes option prices were generated, and it was demonstrated that the advanced estimation technique was the most accurate of the three methods. There are two problems with the Black-Scholes model, skewness and excess kurtosis both equal to zero, and constant volatility. Since constant volatility corresponds to a flat implied volatility curve, the advanced estimation method has an unfair advantage because the method extrapolates linearly along the curve.

The Excel file Chapter12BKM-GC contains estimates of model-free moments using out-of-the-money call and put prices generated with the Gram-Charlier model. Strike prices range from $K = 75$ to 130 in intervals of \$5, and the one-period skewness and kurtosis are set to $\gamma_1 = -0.6$ and $\gamma_2 = 2$, respectively, where the periods are months. This file is illustrated in Figure 12.5 using a spot price of $S = 102$, a yearly volatility of $\sigma = 0.20$, corresponding to a one-period volatility of $0.20/\sqrt{12} \approx 0.0577$, a yearly risk-free rate of $r = 0.05$, and a time to maturity of three months.

As in Figure 12.1, care must be taken to obtain the T-period moments from the one-period moments. Since $\sigma_T^2 = \sigma^2 T$, in cell C21 we type "=C14^2*C12", which produces $\sigma_T^2 = 0.0577^2 \times 3$, or $\sigma_T^2 = 0.01$. For skewness, since $\gamma_{1T} = \gamma_1/\sqrt{T}$, in cell C22 we type "=C15/SQRT(C12)" which produces $\gamma_{1T} = -0.6/\sqrt{3} \approx -0.3464$.

	A	B	C	D	E	F	G
1							
2		**Model Free Risk-Neutral Variance, Skewness, and Kurtosis**					
3							
4		**Gram-Charlier Parameters**		**OTM Gram-Charlier Option Prices**			
5		**Period = Monthly**					
6				Strike	Put	Strike	Call
7		Underlying Price (S)	102.00	75.00	0.01	105.00	3.13
8		Risk Free Rate Per Year (r×12)	0.05	80.00	0.05	110.00	1.49
9		Risk Free Rate Per Period (r)	0.0042	85.00	0.18	115.00	0.63
10		Foreign Rate or Dividend Yield Per Year (q×12)	0	90.00	0.50	120.00	0.25
11		Foreign Rate or Div Yield Per Period (q)	0	95.00	1.18	125.00	0.10
12		Periods Until Maturity (T)	3	100.00	2.53	130.00	0.04
13		Volatility Per Year (σ×√12)	0.2000				
14		One-Period Volatility (σ)	0.0577				
15		One-Period Skewness (γ_1)	-0.6000				
16		One-Period Kurtosis (γ_2)	2.0000				
17							
18							
19		**Model-Free Moments**	**True**	**Estimated Values**			
20			**Values**	**Basic**	**Adapted**	**Advanced**	
21		T-Period Variance (σ_T^2)	0.01000	0.0069	0.0097	0.0100	
22		T-Period Skewness (γ_{1T})	-0.3464	-0.6244	-0.3674	-0.3510	
23		T-Period Kurtosis (γ_{2T})	3.6667	7.0742	3.7319	3.6351	
24							
25				**Approximation Error (%)**			
26				**Basic**	**Adapted**	**Advanced**	
27				-30.61%	-3.37%	0.09%	
28				80.26%	6.05%	1.33%	
29				92.93%	1.78%	-0.86%	

FIGURE 12.5   Model-Free Moments with Gram-Charlier Prices

Finally, recall that the Gram-Charlier model uses excess kurtosis, and that the T-period excess kurtosis is $\gamma_{2T} = \gamma_2/T$. To convert this to raw kurtosis, we must add three to the fraction. Hence, in cell C23 we type "=C16/C12+3" which produces $\gamma_{1T} = 2/3 + 3$ or $\gamma_{1T} \approx 3.6667$

The results of the approximations in Figure 12.5 lead to the same conclusion as those in Figure 12.1. Approximation errors for the estimated moments are defined as $(\theta - \hat{\theta})/\theta \times 100\%$. Clearly, using typical market strike price ranges and intervals, there is a large improvement in precision when moving from the basic method to the adapted method, and from the adapted method to the advanced method. This last method produces the smallest approximation error for all three moments.

GRAM-CHARLIER IMPLIED MOMENTS

The Gram-Charlier model can also be used to extract implied moments from option prices. Using the techniques presented in Chapter 9, the parameters of the

Gram-Charlier model can be estimated using a cross-section of option prices. Since the parameters of the Gram-Charlier model define the moments, the estimated parameters are implied by the options. This is illustrated with the option prices written on Google, Inc. first used in Chapter 10, and using the three loss functions of Chapter 9 to estimate the parameters. Recall from Chapter 9 that the dollar root mean squared error loss function $RMSE assigns more weight to near-to-the-money options and at-the-money options, the relative root mean squared error loss function %RMSE assigns more weight to out-of-the-money options, and the implied volatility root mean square error loss function IVRMSE assigns almost equal weight to all options. The weighting is not exactly equal, because in the presence of high kurtosis deep-out-of-the-money options will have higher implied volatilities.

The Excel file Chapter12GoogleIV contains implied moments calculated from option prices generated by the Gram-Charlier model. The market option prices are

	M	N	O	P	Q
1					
2		**Gram-Charlier Option Pricing Model Starting Parameters**			
3		**Period = Monthly**			
4					
5		Risk Free Rate Per Year ($r \times 12$)	0.05		
6		Risk Free Rate Per Period (r)	0.004		
7		Foreign Rate or Dividend Yield Per Year ($q \times 12$)	0		
8		Foreign Rate or Div Yield Per Period (q)	0		
9		Periods Until Maturity (T)	0.4932		
10		Volatility Per Year ($\sigma \times \sqrt{12}$)	0.3707		
11		One-Period Volatility (σ)	0.1070		
12		One-Period Skewness (γ_1)	-0.3300		
13		One-Period Kurtosis (γ_2)	0.7000		
14					
15			**Loss Function Estimates**		
16		**One-Period Moments**	**$RMSE**	**%RMSE**	**IVRMSE**
17		Loss Function	0.1052	0.4526	0.0727
18		Volatility	0.1167	0.1215	0.1336
19		Skewness	-0.3306	-0.4556	-0.6038
20		Kurtosis	0.4646	0.6174	0.8418
21					
22		**Time to Maturity Moments**			
23		Volatility	0.0819	0.0854	0.0938
24		Skewness	-0.4708	-0.6487	-0.8599
25		Kurtosis	3.9422	4.2520	4.7070
26					
27		**Model-Free Moments for Time to Maturity**			
28		Variance	0.0070		
29		Volatility	0.0836		
30		Skewness	-0.8257		
31		Kurtosis	6.4539		

FIGURE 12.6 Parameter Estimates for Gram-Charlier Model
Source: finance.yahoo.com

obtained from Yahoo! (finance.yahoo.com). The part of the spreadsheet presented in Figure 12.6 shows estimates of volatility, skewness, and kurtosis obtained by using the three loss functions, and by using model-free estimation. It uses the functions RMSEparams(), perRMSEparams(), and ivRMSEparams() developed in Chapter 9.

One-period moment estimates using the $RMSE, %RMSE, and IVRMSE loss functions appear in cells O18:O20, P18:P20, and Q18:Q20, respectively. These are obtained using market prices of calls and puts. They are contained in the right part of the Chapter12GoogleIV Excel file and are illustrated in Figure 12.6. The value of the loss function appears immediately above each set of estimates. For example, to obtain the $RMSE moment estimates, in cell O17 we type

$$= \text{RMSEparams(O11:O13,B12:B36,H6,C12:C36,H5,O8,O9,E12:E36)}$$

and copy down to the next three cells, which produces estimates of monthly volatility, skewness, and kurtosis of $\hat{\sigma} = 0.1167$, $\hat{\gamma}_1 = -0.3306$, and $\hat{\gamma}_2 = 0.4646$, respectively. The value of the $RMSE loss function is 0.1052. To obtain values corresponding to the time to maturity (0.4932 months or roughly two weeks), we scale each estimate by the appropriate factor. For example, in cell O23, we type "=O18*SQRT(O9)", which produces a value of $\hat{\sigma} = 0.1167 \times \sqrt{0.4932}$, or approximately 0.0819 for the two-week volatility. Monthly and time-to-maturity estimates using the other loss functions are obtained similarly. The model-free estimates of the moments are in cells O28:O31, using the advanced method described earlier. For example, in cell O30 we type

$$= \text{MFSkew(C27:C36,E27:E36,C12:C26,E12:E26,H6,H4,D6)}$$

which produces a model-free time-to-maturity skewness of $\gamma_1 = -0.8257$, comparable to the IVRMSE estimate of $\gamma_1 = -0.8599$ in cell Q24.

Note that the implied volatility loss function is the closest to the model-free approach for skewness and kurtosis, but overestimates the volatility compared to the dollar and relative root mean squared error loss functions. Another interesting way of examining the model fit to the implied moments is by examining the implied volatility curves induced by each of the parameters, and comparing these curves to the actual implied volatility curve. The Excel file Chapter12GoogleIV contains these implied volatilities. This is illustrated in Figure 12.7.

The market prices of the calls and puts on Google, Inc., are in column E. To obtain the Black-Scholes implied volatilities from these market prices, we use the bisection method with starting values $\sigma_1 = 0.000001$ and $\sigma_2 = 4$. For example, in cell F12 we type

$$= \text{BisecBSV(B12,H6,C12,H4,D6,0.000001,4,E12)}$$

which produces an implied volatility of $\sigma_{iv}^{BS} = 0.7500$. The Gram-Charlier prices using parameters obtained with the $RMSE, %RSME, and IVRMSE loss functions,

	A	B	C	D	E	F	G	H	I	J	K	L
1												
2		**Implied Volatilities for Google, Inc. Using Market and Gram-Charlier Prices**										
3												
4		Current Date	6-Jul-06		Yearly Risk-Free Rate (r)		0.05185					
5		Expiry Date	21-Jul-06		Monthly Risk-Free Rate		0.00432					
6		Time to Mat	0.0411		Spot Price (S)		423.19					
7												
8							**Gram-Charlier Implied Volatilities**					
9					Market	B-S	$RMSE		%RMSE		IVRMSE	
10		Option	Strike	Moneynes	Closing	Implied	G-C	Implied	G-C	Implied	G-C	Implied
11		Type	Price	(K/S)	Price	Volatility	Price	Volatility	Price	Volatility	Price	Volatility
12		Put	280	0.662	0.05	0.7500	0.0000	0.4678	0.0001	0.4971	0.0014	0.5649
13		Put	290	0.685	0.10	0.7447	0.0003	0.4734	0.0009	0.5042	0.0059	0.5743
14		Put	300	0.709	0.10	0.6842	0.0016	0.4790	0.0040	0.5115	0.0209	0.5838
15		Put	310	0.733	0.15	0.6566	0.0068	0.4843	0.0155	0.5185	0.0618	0.5926
16		Put	320	0.756	0.20	0.6197	0.0239	0.4886	0.0489	0.5245	0.1559	0.5998
17		Put	330	0.780	0.30	0.5928	0.0701	0.4912	0.1295	0.5285	0.3399	0.6040
18		Put	340	0.803	0.30	0.5311	0.1737	0.4910	0.2932	0.5292	0.6499	0.6035
19		Put	350	0.827	0.55	0.5205	0.3721	0.4869	0.5783	0.5252	1.1082	0.5963
20		Put	360	0.851	0.75	0.4838	0.7068	0.4781	1.0162	0.5151	1.7185	0.5813
21		Put	370	0.874	1.25	0.4669	1.2258	0.4648	1.6352	0.4988	2.4833	0.5586
22		Put	380	0.898	1.91	0.4420	2.0034	0.4480	2.4874	0.4777	3.4421	0.5303
23		Put	390	0.922	3.10	0.4267	3.1715	0.4301	3.6876	0.4545	4.7100	0.4999
24		Put	400	0.945	4.90	0.4120	4.9367	0.4134	5.4362	0.4324	6.4897	0.4713
25		Put	410	0.969	7.50	0.3974	7.5575	0.3993	7.9965	0.4135	9.0396	0.4470
26		Put	420	0.992	11.40	0.3918	11.2790	0.3883	11.6266	0.3986	12.6087	0.4276
27		Call	430	1.016	10.30	0.3783	10.3599	0.3801	10.6034	0.3873	11.4701	0.4128
28		Call	440	1.040	6.80	0.3802	6.6226	0.3745	6.7679	0.3792	7.4758	0.4018
29		Call	450	1.063	3.90	0.3663	4.0227	0.3711	4.0904	0.3737	4.6211	0.3938
30		Call	460	1.087	2.25	0.3653	2.3384	0.3698	2.3559	0.3707	2.7210	0.3886
31		Call	470	1.111	1.35	0.3730	1.3183	0.3708	1.3124	0.3704	1.5458	0.3863
32		Call	480	1.134	0.70	0.3705	0.7354	0.3743	0.7259	0.3733	0.8707	0.3877
33		Call	490	1.158	0.45	0.3857	0.4156	0.3804	0.4130	0.3800	0.5083	0.3941
34		Call	500	1.182	0.20	0.3783	0.2423	0.3890	0.2493	0.3907	0.3226	0.4064
35		Call	510	1.205	0.15	0.4006	0.1463	0.3993	0.1607	0.4043	0.2265	0.4239
36		Call	520	1.229	0.15	0.4365	0.0904	0.4101	0.1082	0.4190	0.1709	0.4440

FIGURE 12.7 Gram-Charlier Implied Volatilities
Source: finance.yahoo.com

are in columns G, I, and K, respectively. The corresponding implied volatilities are obtained using the bisection method also, and are in columns H, J, and L.

Figure 12.8 contains a plot of the market implied volatility curve and the Gram-Charlier implied volatility curve. As in Chapter 10, a quadratic curve has been fitted to the market Black-Scholes implied volatility curve, and this curve appears in the figure as a solid quadratic curve.

SUMMARY

While the model-free estimators of volatility dealt with in the previous chapter have important applications, such as the construction of the VIX index, it is useful

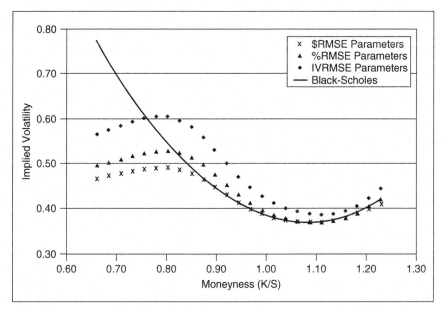

FIGURE 12.8   Implied Volatility Curves
Source: finance.yahoo.com

to have model-free estimators of higher moments such as skewness and kurtosis. The methodology introduced by Bakshi, Kapadia, and Madan (2003), which is based on an expression for the payoff function derived by Carr and Madan (2001), forms the theoretical basis of this chapter. The basic implementation calls for the evaluation of two separate integrals using a simple numerical integration technique. When the spot asset price does not correspond to any available option strike price, however, this approach produces biased estimates of variance, skewness and kurtosis, since the middle interval of strikes will not be included in any of the integrals. The adapted implementation circumvents this problem by combining the two integrals into a single integral. The area under the middle interval is obtained by joining the value of the integrand at each middle interval endpoint with a line segment. The advanced implementation is based on the cubic spline interpolation and extrapolation technique of Jiang and Tian (2005) introduced in Chapter 11. In this chapter it is shown that moving from the basic to the adapted implementation and from the adapted to the advanced implementation, produces estimates of model-free variance, kurtosis, and skewness that are increasing in accuracy. Since the Gram-Charlier model produces option prices based on known variance, skewness, and kurtosis, the accuracy of the methods covered in this chapter can be evaluated by using Gram-Charlier prices to extract model-free estimates of these moments, and comparing the estimates to the known values. The results confirm that the advanced implementation produces the most accurate estimates of model-free moments.

Finally, the Gram-Charlier model can be used to obtain implied higher moments from option prices. This is done by estimating the parameters of the model—which are also the higher moments—with the methods described in Chapter 9.

EXERCISES

This section provides exercices that deal with model-free higher moments. Solutions are contained in the Excel file Chapter12Exercises.

12.1 Repeat the analysis in Figure 12.5, using the same spot price and interest rate, same time to maturity, same strikes for calls and puts, but using the Edgeworth binomial tree to generate option prices. For the Edgeworth parameters, use $\xi = -0.4$ and $\kappa = 4.5$, with $n = 250$ time steps. Compare the approximation error of each model-free implementation method.

12.2 Generate option prices with the Practitioner Black-Scholes (PBS) model of Chapter 4, using the following deterministic volatility function (DVF):

$$\sigma_{iv} = a_0 + a_1(K/S - 1) + a_2(K/S - 1)^2.$$

Implement three PBS models, using three different sets of values for (a_0, a_1, a_2). For the first set of values use $(0.2, 0, 0)$, which corresponds to a constant yearly volatility of 20 percent. For the second set use $(0.2, -0.2, 0)$, which corresponds to a negatively sloped implied volatility curve, and for the third set use $(0.19, -0.035, 1)$, which corresponds to a concave implied volatility curve. For each set of parameter values, generate put prices with strikes ranging from $K = 75$ to $K = 100$, and call prices with strikes ranging from $K = 105$ to $K = 130$, with a strike price interval of 5 for each set of options. Use a spot price of $S = 100$, a risk-free rate of $r = 0.05$, and a time to maturity of $T = 0.25$ years. For each set of generated prices, compute the model-free annualized volatility, skewness, and kurtosis using the VBA functions introduced in this chapter.

SOLUTIONS TO EXERCISES

12.1 The solution to this exercise is illustrated in Figure 12.9. The model-free variance calculates the variance over a period corresponding to the time to maturity. Since the yearly volatility used as input to the Edgeworth prices is $\sigma = 0.20$, the time to maturity variance is $\sigma^2 = (0.2)^2 \times 0.25 = 0.01$. This value appears in cell C17 in Figure 12.9, and the option prices in cells E8:E13 and G8:G13. The EWBin() function is taken from Chapter 3. To obtain the put price when $K = 95$, for example, in cell E12 we type

= EWBin(S,D12,Rf,V,T,N,Skew,Kurt,"Put","Euro")

A	B	C	D	E	F	G
1	EXERCISE 12.1					
2						
3	**Model Free Risk-Neutral Variance, Skewness, and Kurtosis**					
4						
5	**Edgeworth Parameters**			**OTM Edgeworth Option Prices**		
6						
7	Underlying Price (S)	102.00	Strike	Put	Strike	Call
8	Risk Free Rate (r)	0.05	75.00	0.02	105.00	2.99
9	Volatility (σ)	0.2000	80.00	0.08	110.00	1.40
10	Time to Maturity (T)	0.25	85.00	0.24	115.00	0.63
11	Numer of Steps (n)	250	90.00	0.55	120.00	0.30
12	Skewness (ξ)	-0.4	95.00	1.16	125.00	0.16
13	Kurtosis (κ)	4.5	100.00	2.42	130.00	0.09
14						
15	**Model-Free Moments**	True		Estimated Values		
16		Values	Basic	Adapted	Advanced	
17	Variance (σ²)	0.010	0.0070	0.0096	0.0100	
18	Skewness (ξ)	-0.400	-0.7416	-0.4501	-0.4126	
19	Kurtosis (κ)	4.500	8.0943	4.3849	4.4012	
20						
21				Approximation Error (%)		
22			Basic	Adapted	Advanced	
23			-29.78%	-3.75%	0.05%	
24			85.40%	12.52%	3.15%	
25			79.87%	-2.56%	-2.20%	

FIGURE 12.9 Solution to Exercise 12.1

which produces a price of \$1.16. To implement the model-free moment estimators, we proceed exactly as in Figure 12.5, except that the time to maturity need not be divided by 12, since it is already expressed in years. For example, to obtain the model-free kurtosis under the adapted method, in cell E19 we type

= AMFKurt(F8:F13,G8:G13,D8:D13,E8:E13,C7,C8,C10)

which produces $\hat{\kappa} = 4.3849$. The approximation errors at the bottom of the sheet indicate that, again, the advanced implementation method produces the most accurate estimates.

12.2 The solution to this exercise is illustrated in Figure 12.10. The DVFs with the three different sets of parameters appear in columns H, J, and L. For each given strike price, the DVFs are used as input volatilities to the Black-Scholes model. For example, under DFV 2 the parameter values are $(a_0, a_1, a_2) = (0.2, -0.2, 0)$ in cells C19:C21. To obtain the value of DVF 2 when $K/S - 1 = -0.15$ in cell G11 (corresponding to $K = 85$), in cell J11 we type

= C19+C20*G11+C21*G11∧2

	A	B	C	D	E	F	G	H	I	J	K	L	M
1	EXERCISE 12.2												
2													
3		Estimated Model-Free Moments Using 3 Different Deterministic Volatility Functions (DVF)											
4													
5		Black-Scholes Parameters				Simulated Option Prices Using Three Different DVFs							
6													
7		Underlying Price (S)	100.00		Option	Strike	Moneyness	DVF	Option	DVF	Option	DVF	Option
8		Risk-Free Rate (r)	0.05		Type	Price	Minus 1	1	Price	2	Price	3	Price
9		Time to Maturity (T)	0.25		Put	75	-0.25	0.20	0.00	0.25	0.03	0.26	0.04
10		Skewness (γ₁)	0.00		Put	80	-0.20	0.20	0.03	0.24	0.10	0.24	0.09
11		Kurtosis (γ₂)	3.00		Put	85	-0.15	0.20	0.15	0.23	0.29	0.22	0.23
12					Put	90	-0.10	0.20	0.55	0.22	0.75	0.20	0.59
13			DVF 1		Put	95	-0.05	0.20	1.53	0.21	1.69	0.19	1.44
14		a₀ =	0.200		Put	100	0.00	0.20	3.37	0.20	3.37	0.19	3.18
15		a₁ =	0.000		Call	105	0.05	0.20	2.48	0.19	2.29	0.19	2.30
16		a₂ =	0.000		Call	110	0.10	0.20	1.19	0.18	0.91	0.20	1.14
17					Call	115	0.15	0.20	0.51	0.17	0.27	0.21	0.58
18			DVF 2		Call	120	0.20	0.20	0.20	0.16	0.05	0.22	0.34
19		a₀ =	0.200		Call	125	0.25	0.20	0.07	0.15	0.01	0.24	0.23
20		a₁ =	-0.200		Call	130	0.30	0.20	0.02	0.14	0.00	0.27	0.19
21		a₂ =	0.000										
22							Estimated Model-Free Moments						
23			DVF 3				PBS 1	PBS 2	PBS 3				
24		a₀ =	0.190		Annualized Var (σₜ²)		0.2001	0.2025	0.2025				
25		a₁ =	-0.035		Skewness (γ₁ₜ)		-0.0001	-0.5963	0.0081				
26		a₂ =	1.000		Kurtosis (γ₂ₜ)		2.9923	3.5057	5.0859				

FIGURE 12.10   Solution to Exercise 12.2

which produces $\hat{\sigma}_{iv} = 0.23$. Using this value for volatility produces a Black-Scholes price of \$0.29, or 29 cents, for the put. To compute the model-free variance, skewness, and kurtosis, we use the out-of-the-money calls and puts generated by the three PBS models. The model-free variance must be scaled by the time to maturity before taking the square root to produce the annualized model-free volatility. For example, to obtain the annualized model-free volatility under the first PBS model, in cell G24 we type

$$= \text{SQRT(MFVar(F15:F20, I15:I20, F9:F14, I9:I14, C7, C8, C9)/C9)}$$

which produces $\sigma = 0.2001$, close to the true value of 0.20. To produce the model-free skewness, in cell G25 we type

$$= \text{MFSkew(F15:F20, I15:I20, F9:F14, I9:I14, C7, C8, C9)}$$

which produces $\gamma_{1T} = -0.0001$, close to the true value of zero. Finally, to produce the model-free kurtosis, in cell G26 we type

$$= \text{MFKurt(F15:F20, I15:I20, F9:F14, I9:I14, C7, C8, C9)}$$

which produces $\gamma_{2T} = 2.9923$, again close to the true value of 3. The model-free higher moments for the other PBS models are obtained analogously.

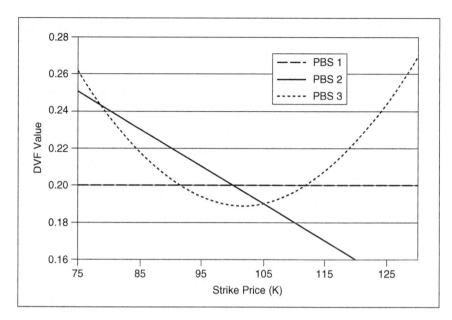

FIGURE 12.11 Solution to Exercise 12.2

Note that all three PBS models have the same annualized model-free volatility. Their higher moments, however, are not the same. It is instructive to plot the DVF function for each of the three PBS models, to see how the model-free implied moments are consistent with the shape of each DVF. This plot appears in Figure 12.11. Recall that return distributions with negative skewness exhibit negatively sloped implied volatility curves. The results in Figure 12.10 indicate that PBS model 2 has a model-free skewness of -0.5963. This is reflected in the shape of its DVF, represented by the solid line in Figure 12.11. Recall also that returns that have a higher kurtosis than the normal distribution exhibit concave-shaped implied volatility curves. Figure 12.10 indicates that PBS model 3 has a model-free kurtosis of 5.0859. Again, the shape of its DVF, represented by the dotted line in Figure 12.11, is consistent with this high value of kurtosis. Finally, PBS model 1 has no skewness or kurtosis, consistent with normally distributed returns, so that its DVF is a straight flat line, represented by the dashed line in Figure 12.11.

CHAPTER 13

Volatility Returns

INTRODUCTION

In this chapter, volatility investments are introduced. There are many reasons for investing in volatility. In light of the negative correlation between volatility and returns, investors may want to hedge their portfolios against rising market volatility. Equity investors often speculate on the direction of a stock. It is easy for them to do this, simply by holding a long or short position in the stock. Similar bets can be placed on volatility. An investor who believes that volatility is low, for example, can speculate on future rising volatility by holding a portfolio that earns a profit when volatility increases. This chapter examines three different trading strategies that investors can employ to speculate on volatility: straddles, delta-hedged options, and volatility swaps.

The first volatility investment is a long position in a straddle, also known as a bottom straddle. This investment can be used to speculate on volatility being higher than expected. It is constructed by holding a put and call with the same strike price and expiration. The payoff of this combination is V-shaped, so a profit is realized if the stock price moves up or down by a substantial amount. The position can be reversed to bet against volatility, by taking a short position in a straddle. This is known as a top straddle and is constructed by shorting a put and a call with the same strike price and expiration.

The second type of volatility investment is the delta-hedged option. Stock options are not pure volatility investments, because they are exposed to both the direction of the stock price and the stock price volatility. The exposure to the stock price can be eliminated by delta-hedging the option, so that the only remaining exposure is volatility risk. This is not a perfect strategy, however, because the delta is often calculated using the Black-Scholes formula. As seen in previous chapters, many of the assumptions underlying the Black-Scholes model are rarely met. Volatility cannot be perfectly estimated, stocks are not priced continuously, and investors cannot ignore transaction costs.

The third type of volatility investment is the volatility swap. A volatility swap is a forward contract whereby the holder agrees to swap the realized volatility of the underlying for a predetermined volatility rate. In this chapter it is shown how such contracts can be created synthetically, and it is proved under simplifying assumptions that this type of investment is a pure investment in volatility.

STRADDLE RETURNS

This section analyzes straddles, the first type of volatility investment we consider. As mentioned in the introduction to this chapter, straddles allow investors to speculate on the future volatility of a stock price. Straddles are constructed using plain-vanilla European calls and puts, each with the same strike price, usually at-the-money. Simple straddles consist of a single call and put. Zero-beta straddles are more sophisticated, and are designed to have zero market risk. In this section we also show how straddles can be rebalanced periodically, and we present a simple model for valuation of straddle options.

Simple Straddles

The simplest type of straddle is a simple straddle, which consists of an equal weighing of one call and one put. This is illustrated with the following example. On January 3, 2006, the closing price of IBM was $82.06. To construct the simple straddle contract, a call and a put nearest to this closing price are selected. A call expiring January 20, 2006 (maturity of 17 days), with a strike price of $K = 80$ was valued at $2.95, and a put with the same expiration and strike price was valued at $0.85. The cost of the straddle is the sum of the call and put price, and its payoff is the sum of the payoffs at expiration of holding long one call and one put. In the absence of transaction costs, the profit is the sum of the payoffs minus the cost of constructing the straddle (Call Payoff + Put Payoff − Cost).

The Excel file Chapter13SimpStraddle illustrates the profit generated by the simple straddle, for various values of the spot price at expiration of the put and call. The straddle return is the ratio of the profit to the cost. This is illustrated in Figure 13.1.

The total cost of the straddle is $2.95 + 0.85 = 3.80$ in column F. The call and put payoffs are in column G and H, respectively, the total profit is in column I, and the straddle return in column J. No VBA functions are required to calculate these simple returns, only simple Excel functions.

The current spot price is $82.06, so the call and put are not exactly at-the-money. The call is slightly in-the-money and the put is slightly out-of-the-money. The straddle contract costs $3.80 to construct, and both the call and put have a strike price of $80. If the stock price were $S = 76.80$ at expiration of the call and put, the payoff of the call would be zero and that of the put would be 3.80. This would exactly offset the cost of the straddle, so the straddle return would be zero. If the stock price were $S = 83.80$, the payoff of the call would be 3.80 and that of the put would be zero, which would again result in a return of zero. Hence, the break-even point of the strategy occurs at these two prices. Note that the contract

	A	B	C	D	E	F	G	H	I	J
1										
2		**Simple Straddle Returns**								
3		**Using Put and Call on IBM on January 3, 2006**								
4					Spot Price	Straddle	Call	Put	Total	Simple
5					time T	Cost ($)	Payoff ($)	Payoff ($)	Profit ($)	Straddle Returns
6		Underlying Price (S)	82.06		70	3.80	0.00	10.00	6.20	163.16%
7		Risk Free Rate (r)	0.05		72	3.80	0.00	8.00	4.20	110.53%
8		Days to Maturity (DTM)	17		74	3.80	0.00	6.00	2.20	57.89%
9		Call Price (K=80 and DTM=17)	2.95		76	3.80	0.00	4.00	0.20	5.26%
10		Put Price (K=80 and DTM=17)	0.85		78	3.80	0.00	2.00	-1.80	-47.37%
11		Strike Price (K)	80		80	3.80	0.00	0.00	-3.80	-100.00%
12					82	3.80	2.00	0.00	-1.80	-47.37%
13					84	3.80	4.00	0.00	0.20	5.26%
14					86	3.80	6.00	0.00	2.20	57.89%
15					88	3.80	8.00	0.00	4.20	110.53%
16					90	3.80	10.00	0.00	6.20	163.16%
17										
18		**Break Even Points**			76.20	3.80	0.00	3.80	0.00	0.00%
19					83.80	3.80	3.80	0.00	0.00	0.00%

FIGURE 13.1 Simple Straddle Returns

loses the most, a return of -100 percent, when the terminal stock price is $S = 80$. This strategy will tend to make money when the stock price is more volatile than expected, since it constitutes a bet on the size of the price movement, rather than a bet on a movement in any particular direction. In other words, the returns are symmetric about $S = 80$, so that the straddle makes the same amount of money regardless of which direction the stock price moves.

Zero-Beta Straddles

Although a simple straddle represents a bet on increasing volatility, it does not guarantee that the beta of the straddle, or its market exposure, is zero. It is important for the straddle to have a zero market exposure, since in that case the straddle returns do not depend on the market, only on volatility. Rather than construct straddles by using calls and puts in equal proportions, Coval and Shumway (2001) propose to use calls and puts in proportion to their market beta. This results in a straddle contract that has a zero beta with the market, but that is still sensitive to volatility. These are called zero-beta or zero-delta straddles.

According to portfolio theory, the capital asset pricing model (CAPM) beta of a portfolio can be obtained as a weighted average of the CAPM betas of its components. The zero-beta straddle is a portfolio with two components, a proportion θ of calls (in terms of dollar value), and a proportion $1 - \theta$ of puts. Since the beta of this portfolio must be zero, this implies

$$\beta_{STR} = \theta\beta_C + (1 - \theta)\beta_P = 0 \tag{13.1}$$

where β_{STR}, β_C and β_P are the market betas for the straddle, call, and put, respectively. Black and Scholes (1973) use the CAPM in an alternative derivation of their option pricing formula. They find the beta of a call option to be

$$\beta_C = \frac{S}{C}\Phi\left[\frac{\ln(S/K) + (r - q + \sigma^2/2)T}{\sigma\sqrt{T}}\right]\beta_S = \frac{S}{C}\Delta_C\beta_S \tag{13.2}$$

where $\Phi[]$ = the standard normal cumulative distribution function
β_S = the market beta of the underlying asset
q = the dividend yield of the asset
C = the call price
S = the spot price
Δ_C = the delta of the call option.

Using put-call parity and the relation in Equation (13.2), the market beta of the call can be written

$$\beta_C = \frac{P}{C}\beta_P + \frac{S}{C}\beta_S. \tag{13.3}$$

Using these two last equations the market beta of the put can be written

$$\beta_P = \left(\frac{S}{C}\Delta_C\beta_S - \frac{S}{C}\beta_S\right)\frac{C}{P} = \frac{S}{P}(\Delta_C - 1)\beta_S = \frac{S}{P}\Delta_P\beta_S. \tag{13.4}$$

Substituting the call and put beta equations into the straddle beta equation, and solving for the proportion of calls produces

$$\theta = \frac{\Delta_P}{\Delta_P - \frac{P}{C}\Delta_C}. \tag{13.5}$$

The proportion of puts is therefore

$$(1 - \theta) = \frac{\Delta_C}{\Delta_C - \frac{C}{P}\Delta_P}. \tag{13.6}$$

Coval and Shumway (2001) define θ as the proportion of calls used in the straddle, expressed in dollars. To obtain the proportion in terms of number of contracts, suppose that the straddle is constructed with a single call option, and that the cost of a call option is \$C. Suppose also that in order for $\beta_{STR} = 0$ to hold, an amount \$X must be invested in puts. This implies that

$$C\beta_C + X\beta_P = 0 \tag{13.7}$$

Substituting for $\beta_P = S\Delta_P\beta_S/P$ and $\beta_C = S\Delta_C\beta_S/C$, where P is the price of a put, produces

$$1 \times \Delta_C + Y \times \Delta_P = 0. \tag{13.8}$$

Solving this last equation yields the number of puts required when one call is used to construct the zero-beta straddle

$$Y = -\frac{\Delta_C}{\Delta_P}, \tag{13.9}$$

where $Y = X/P$ is the number of puts. It is evident from (13.8) that a straddle constructed with one call option and Y put options has a beta of zero, and equivalently, a delta of zero.

Implementing the zero-beta straddle in VBA is relatively straightforward. The VBA function BSDelta() from Chapter 7 is used to compute Δ_C. Recall that the parameters needed to compute the Black-Scholes delta of an option are the same as those to compute the price. These are the underlying spot price S, the strike price K, the risk-free rate r, the time to maturity T and the volatility σ. The main difficulty in the implementation is specifying which volatility to use for calculating the delta. Using Black-Scholes implied volatility assumes the Black-Scholes model is correct. This volatility, however, would vary depending on the strike price and the type of option used to obtain the implied volatility. Using the unconditional variance of returns assumes that volatility is constant. One possible way to allow for time-varying volatility is to use a rolling window of returns, and compute the variance in each window. Unfortunately, the resulting variance would be sensitive to the choice of window size, which is arbitrary. Moreover, returns across windows would not be independent. One effective approach to estimating daily time-varying volatility is to use the GARCH(1,1) model covered in Chapter 6. This approach was used by Bakshi and Kapadia (2003) for delta-hedged gains, which will be covered in the next section.

 Estimation of GARCH(1,1) parameters, therefore, constitutes the first step in constructing a zero-beta straddle. This construction is illustrated using returns on IBM over the January 4, 2005, to February 1, 2006, period and options written on IBM on January 3, 2006, obtained from Yahoo! (finance.yahoo.com). The results are in the Excel file Chapter13ZBStraddle, which appears in Figure 13.2. Note that only returns for the days close to January 3, 2006, are included, since the aim of this sheet is not to illustrate GARCH estimation.

The GARCH(1,1) parameters were estimated using the VBA function GARCH-params() presented in Chapter 6, and pasted directly into the spreadsheet as $\hat{\omega} = 0.000031, \hat{\alpha} = 0.350389, \hat{\beta} = 0.481114$ for illustration only. The daily GARCH variance for the day of the options, January 3, 2006, is $\sigma_t^2 = 0.000073$ in cell H20. This variance is used to compute the annualized volatility, using the YearVol() presented in Chapter 6 and reproduced here for convenience.

```
Function YearVol(T, alpha, beta, omega, V0)
  Var = omega / (1 - alpha - beta)
  a = -Log(alpha + beta)
  YearVol = Sqr(252 * (Var + (1 - Exp(-a * T)) / a / T * (V0 - Var)))
End Function
```

	C	Spot Price time T	Straddle Cost ($)	Call Payoff ($)	Put Payoff ($)	Total Profit ($)	Zero-Beta Straddle Returns
Zero-Beta Straddle Returns							
Using Put and Call on IBM on January 3, 2006							
Underlying Price (S)	82.06	70	1.00	0.00	5.50	4.50	450.26%
Risk Free Rate (r)	0.05	72	1.00	0.00	4.40	3.40	340.21%
Days to Maturity (DTM)	17	74	1.00	0.00	3.30	2.30	230.16%
Call (K=80 and DTM=17)	2.95	76	1.00	0.00	2.20	1.20	120.10%
Put (K=80 and DTM=17)	0.85	78	1.00	0.00	1.10	0.10	10.05%
Strike Price (K)	80	80	1.00	0.00	0.00	-1.00	-100.00%
Yearly Volatility	0.193889	82	1.00	0.36	0.00	-0.64	-63.91%
Long Call Weight (θ)	0.532278	84	1.00	0.72	0.00	-0.28	-27.83%
Long Put Weight ($1-\theta$)	0.467722	86	1.00	1.08	0.00	0.08	8.26%
		88	1.00	1.44	0.00	0.44	44.35%
		90	1.00	1.80	0.00	0.80	80.43%

	C	Date	Return R_t	Return² R_t^2	Variance σ_t^2
Numbers of Calls and Puts					
Number of Calls θ / C	0.180433		Return	Return²	Variance
Number of Puts ($1-\theta$) / P	0.550262	Date	R_t	R_t^2	σ_t^2
Black-Scholes Call Delta Δ_C	0.753066	3-Jan-06	-0.001715	0.000003	0.000073
Black-Scholes Put Delta Δ_P	-0.246934	30-Dec-05	-0.002445	0.000006	0.000084
Number of Puts $Y = -\Delta_C / \Delta_P$	3.049672	29-Dec-05	-0.007663	0.000059	0.000068
		28-Dec-05	0.000606	0.000000	0.000077
		27-Dec-05	-0.005923	0.000035	0.000070
GARCH(1,1) Parameters		23-Dec-05	0.003139	0.000010	0.000075
Omega (ω)	0.000031	22-Dec-05	0.001210	0.000001	0.000091
Alpha (α)	0.350389	21-Dec-05	0.007655	0.000059	0.000082
Beta (β)	0.481114	20-Dec-05	-0.003410	0.000012	0.000097

FIGURE 13.2 Zero-Beta Straddle Returns
Source: finance.yahoo.com

The days to maturity is in cell C8, so in cell C12 we type

$$= \text{YearVol}(C8, \text{alpha}, \text{beta}, \text{omega}, H20)$$

which produces an annualized volatility of 0.1939. The function ZBStraddleWeight() computes the weight θ in accordance with (13.5).

```
Function ZBStraddleWeight(S, K, T, r, v, C, P)
  CallDelta = BSdelta(S, K, T, r, v, "Call")
  PutDelta = CallDelta - 1
  ZBStraddleWeight = PutDelta / (PutDelta - (P / C) * CallDelta)
End Function
```

To invoke this function, in cell C13 we type

$$= \text{ZBStraddleWeight}(C6,C11,C8/365,C7,C12,C9,C10)$$

which produces $\theta = 0.532278$. Note that since T is expressed in days, the third input to the function must be $T/365$. The put weight is $1 - \theta = 0.467722$ in cell C14.

To obtain the number of required calls and puts, θ/C and $(1-\theta)/P$, in cells C18 and C19 we type "=C13/C9" and "=C14/C10" which produces 0.180433 and 0.550262, respectively. When there is a single call, the number of puts is given by (13.9) and appears in cell C22 as 3.049672, using the Black-Scholes deltas in cells C20 and C21. It is easy to verify that the relative magnitude of each amount is same, namely that

$$\frac{1}{3.049672} = \frac{0.180433}{0.550262}.$$

The zero-beta straddle can now be constructed, using these weights. The cost of the straddle is $(\theta/C) \times C + ((1-\theta)/P) \times P = 1$. For example, in cell F6 we type "=C18*C9+C19*C10", which produces a cost of \$1 to construct the straddle. The payoffs from the options, the profit, and the returns are calculated exactly as in the simple straddle.

It is informative to compare the straddle returns from the simple straddle and the zero-beta straddle graphically. The simple straddle returns are included in the right part of the Excel file Chapter13ZBStraddle for reference. These returns are plotted along with those of the zero-beta straddle returns in Figure 13.3.

The returns from the two straddles are similar, except that the zero-beta straddle is tilted to the right. The closing price of IBM stock was \$81.36 on January 20, 2006, so a profit of −64.21 percent was realized for the simple straddle and a profit of −75.46 percent was realized for the zero-beta straddle. Clearly the price movement

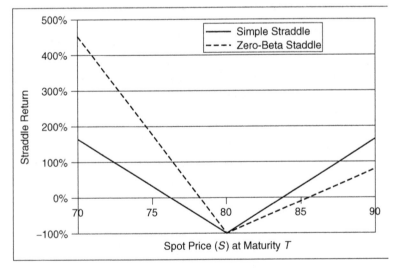

FIGURE 13.3 Simple and Zero-Beta Straddle Returns
Source: finance.yahoo.com

of IBM over the time to maturity of 17 days was not large enough for either straddle to make a profit.

Straddle Rebalancing

The analyses of the previous section were performed under the assumption that the straddle is held until expiration of the calls and puts with which it is constructed. It is possible, however, to rebalance the straddle every day, by selling the straddle and buying a new zero-beta straddle. With the VBA function ZBStraddleWeight() described in the previous section, implementing such a rebalancing strategy is easy. This entails buying a zero-beta straddle constructed with options closest to the money every day, and then selling it the next day to buy a new zero-beta closest to the money straddle. Recall from Chapter 7 that an option's sensitivity to volatility, or its vega, is largest when the option is at-the-money. Thus, by buying a straddle and holding it until maturity, the investor is not receiving constant volatility exposure. Deep-in-the-money and deep-out-of-money options have a vega of close to zero, so if there is a large stock price move after the straddle is entered into the investor might not have as much volatility exposure as desired. This can be remedied by rebalancing the position.

 This rebalancing strategy is illustrated using options on IBM with expiry on January 20, 2006, over the one-week period of January 3, 2006, to January 10, 2006, obtained from Yahoo! (finance.yahoo.com). Each day, calls and puts are selected that are closest to the money. The next day, the calls and puts are sold at the current market price, and the daily payoff from the straddle is calculated. A daily interest charge is deducted from the straddle to produce the net profit. The next-day calls and puts are used to construct the straddle for the following day, again by selecting the closest-to-the-money options, which maximizes volatility exposure. This example is contained in the Excel file Chapter13Rebalance, and illustrated in Figure 13.4. It is convenient to write a VBA function that produces the number of calls θ/C and number of puts $(1 - \theta)/P$ directly. The function NumOption() does this by nesting the ZBStraddleWeight() function.

```
Function NumOption(S, K, T, r, V, C, P, PutCall As String)
Theta = ZBStraddleWeight(S, K, T, r, V, C, P)
  If PutCall = "Call" Then
    NumOption = Theta / C
  ElseIf PutCall = "Put" Then
    NumOption = (1 - Theta) / P
  End If
End Function
```

The top part of the figure contains option data on the IBM stock. All options expire on January 20, 2006. The bottom part represents the profits and losses from daily rebalancing of the straddle. The bottom part of the sheet also contains GARCH parameters and volatilities that do not appear in the figure, but that are needed to compute the volatilities in cells H8:H13. Note that these volatilities each

	A	B	C	D	E	F	G	H	I	J	K	L	M
1													
2		**Daily Rebalanced Zero-Beta Straddle Returns**											
3		**Using Puts and Calls on IBM on January 3, 2006**											
4													
5					**IBM Options Data**								
6								Closing	DTM		Daily Prices		Next Day Prices	
7		Expiry Date	20-Jan-06		Day	DTM	Price	Volatility	Strike	Call	Put	Call	Put
8		Risk-Free Rate	0.05		3-Jan-06	17	82.06	0.1939	80	2.95	0.85	2.90	0.80
9					4-Jan-06	16	81.95	0.1767	80	2.90	0.80	3.30	0.65
10					5-Jan-06	15	82.50	0.1744	80	3.30	0.65	5.40	0.25
11					6-Jan-06	14	84.95	0.1718	80	5.40	0.25	4.10	0.35
12					9-Jan-06	11	83.73	0.1622	85	1.10	2.15	1.20	2.00
13					10-Jan-06	10	84.07	0.1581	85	1.20	2.00	0.95	3.40
14													
15		**Zero-Beta Straddle Profits**			**Daily Rebalancing Profits**								
16													
17						Number of	Number of	Daily	Next-Day	Interest	Total		
18		Dollar Gain ($)	0.35		Date	Calls	Puts	Cost	Profit	Payment	Profit		
19		As a % of Spot Price	0.43%		3-Jan-06	0.1804	0.5503	1.00	-0.0365	0.0002	-0.0367		
20		As a % of Straddle Price	35.40%		4-Jan-06	0.1808	0.5947	1.00	-0.0169	0.0002	-0.0171		
21					5-Jan-06	0.1556	0.7487	1.00	0.0272	0.0002	0.0270		
22					6-Jan-06	0.0766	2.3460	1.00	0.1351	0.0002	0.1349		
23					9-Jan-06	0.4733	0.2230	1.00	0.0139	0.0002	0.0137		
24					10-Jan-06	0.4289	0.2427	1.00	0.2325	0.0002	0.2323		
25													
26								Total	0.35520	0.0012	0.3540		
27													

FIGURE 13.4   Zero-Beta Straddle Rebalancing
Source: finance.yahoo.com

correspond to the maturities specified in cells F8:F13. On the first day, January 3, 2006, the closing price is $S = 82.06$, the nearest strike price is $K = 80$, and the call and put selected to construct the straddle for that day have a price of 2.95 and 0.85 in cells J8 and K8, respectively. The 17-day annualized volatility is obtained using the YearVol() function and the daily GARCH variance value of $\sigma_t^2 = 0.0000732$ appears in cell H43. Hence, in cell H8 we type

$$= \text{YearVol}(\text{F8, alpha, beta, omega, H43})$$

which produces $\sigma(17)^2 = 0.1939$. The strike price for that day is in cell I8, the days to maturity is in cell F8, and the risk-free rate is in cell C8, so to obtain the number of calls needed to construct the straddle, in cell F19 we type

$$= \text{NumOption}(\text{G8,I8,F8/365,C8,H8,J8,K8, ''Call''})$$

which produces $\theta/C = 0.1804$. Similarly, in cell G19 we type

$$= \text{NumOption}(\text{G8,I8,F8/365,C8,H8,J8,K8,''Put''})$$

which produces $(1 - \theta)/P = 0.5503$. These are of course the same numbers that appear in Figure 13.2. Note that, as before, the time to maturity is expressed in days and must be divided by 365 in the function argument. The cost of the straddle is obtained by typing "=F26*J8+G26*K8" in cell H19, which produces a cost of $1, as expected.

The closing price on January 4 is $S = 81.95$, so the next day the closest-to-the-money options again have a strike price of $K = 80$. The price of these options is now 2.90 and 0.80 for the call and put, respectively. Hence, the payoff of the straddle on January 4 is a function of the current option prices and the prior day's weights, namely $0.1804 \times 2.90 + 0.5503 \times 0.80$, or roughly 96 cents. To obtain the profit (payoff minus cost) in cell I19 we type

$$= (F19*L8+G19*M8)-H19$$

which produces a value of -0.0365. When the interest payment of 0.0002 is deducted, the total profit from the straddle is -0.0367 in cell K19.

Continuing in this way produces a series of daily profits from the daily straddle rebalancing strategy, which are aggregated over the life of the strategy. There are three ways of expressing the aggregated profit: the dollar profit, the profit as a percentage of the spot price, and the dollar as a percentage of the initial straddle price. The dollar profit is simply the sum of the daily profits, obtained in cell C18 by typing "=SUM(K19:K24)" and equal to 0.35. In cell C19 we type "=C18/G8", which produces 0.43 percent, the profit as a percentage of the spot price on January 3. Finally, in cell C20 we type "=C18/H19", which produces 35.40 percent, the profit as a percentage of the straddle price.

There are variations of straddles, called strips, straps, and strangles. A strip is a straddle with more puts than calls, and a strap is a straddle with more calls than puts. Zero-beta straddles are not pure straddle positions, and are therefore considered strips and straps, depending on the relationship between the put and call betas. A strangle is a straddle where the put has a lower strike price than the call. Its payoff is no longer a V-shaped pattern because the payoff has a flat area in the middle before the put or the call become in-the-money. A strangle is a cheaper version of a straddle, because both options are purchased out-of-the-money. This strategy requires larger price movements to be profitable.

Options on Straddles

Instead of purchasing call and put options to form a straddle, investors can purchase a straddle option (STO), which is a call option on a simple straddle. Brenner, Ou, and Zhang (2006) propose a valuation model for such an option. At maturity, time T_1, the holder of the STO has the option to buy an at-the-money bottom simple straddle with exercise price K_{STO}. If exercised, the holder receives a call and a put, each with maturity T_2 $(T_2 > T_1)$, with strike price equal to the forward price of the underlying asset at time T_1. The valuation model of Brenner, Ou, and Zhang (2006) allows for stochastic volatility, by allowing the stock price and the volatility to each follow a diffusion process. In this chapter, however, we treat the simplest case, corresponding to the Black-Scholes assumptions. Under these assumptions the stock volatility is σ_1 in the interval $(0, T_1)$ but can switch to σ_2 in the interval (T_1, T_2). In this simplest case the price of the straddle option at time t $(0 \leqslant t < T_1)$ is given by

$$STO_t = \alpha S_t \Phi(d) - K_{STO} e^{-r(T_1-t)} \Phi(d - \sigma_1 \sqrt{T_2 - T_1}) \qquad (13.10)$$

where
$$\alpha = 2[2\Phi(d_1) - 1]$$
$$d_1 = \tfrac{1}{2}\sigma_2 \sqrt{T_2 - T_1}$$
$$d = \frac{\ln(\alpha S_t / K_{STO}) + (r + \tfrac{1}{2}\sigma_1^2)(T_1 - t)}{\sigma_1 \sqrt{T_1 - t}}$$
$$S_t = \text{stock price at time } t.$$

The Excel file Chapter13STO contains the VBA function STO() for implementing the price of a straddle option under Black-Scholes, in accordance with (13.10). As before, the function N() obtains values of the standard normal cumulative distribution function, and is used to conserve space.

```
Function N(d)
  N = Application.NormSDist(d)
End Function

Function STO(K, S, r, V1, V2, T1, T2, T)
  d1 = V2 * Sqr(T2 - T1) / 2
  alpha = 2 * (2 * N(d1) - 1)
  d = (Log(alpha * S / K) + (r + V1 ^ 2 / 2) * (T1 - T))
    / V1 / Sqr(T1 - T)
  STO = alpha * S * N(d) - K * Exp(-r * (T1 - T))
    * N(d - V1 * Sqr(T1 - T))
End Function
```

This function is illustrated in Figure 13.5, using the same data used by Brenner, Ou, and Zhang (2006).

To obtain the price of a straddle option, in cell C14 we type

$$= STO(K, S, rf, Var1, Var2, Time1, Time2, Time0)$$

which produces a price of $STO_0 = 9.324$ at $t = 0$. Straddle prices for various values of the strike price K_{STO} appear in cells F5:F24. These are slightly different than those in Brenner, Ou, and Zhang (2006), since in our illustration a nonzero risk-free rate is used.

It is also possible to obtain the price of a straddle option by simulation. This is done by first generating stock prices over the interval $(0, T_1)$, assuming the stock price follows the Black-Scholes diffusion $dS = rSdt + \sigma_1 S \sqrt{dt}\varepsilon$, where $\varepsilon \sim N(0, 1)$. Next, for each terminal stock price S_{T_1}, the price of a call and put option each with strike price $S_{T_1} e^{r(T_2-T_1)}$ and time to maturity $T_2 - T_1$ is obtained. The sum of these two prices is the cost of the straddle. The payoff of the straddle option is $\max(\text{Cost} - K_{STO}, 0)$, and this is discounted back to time zero. Finally, the simulated

	A	B	C	D	E	F
1						
2		**Brenner, Ou, and Zhang (2006) Straddle Option**				
3		**Under Black-Scholes**			Strike Price	STO
4					K_{STO}	Price
5		Asset Price $S(t)$	100		1	10.299
6		Strike Price K_{STO}	2		2	9.324
7		STO Maturity Date T_1	0.5		3	8.348
8		Straddle Maturity Date T_2	1		4	7.373
9		Time 1 Volatility (σ_1)	0.2		5	6.398
10		Time 2 Volatility (σ_2)	0.2		6	5.423
11		Time of Contract (t)	0		7	4.447
12		Risk Free Rate (r)	0.05		8	3.474
13					9	2.518
14		**Straddle Option Price at t**	9.324		10	1.639
15					11	0.931
16		**Simulated Straddle Option Price**	9.317		12	0.455
17					13	0.192
18					14	0.071
19					15	0.023
20					16	0.007
21					17	0.002
22					18	0.000
23					19	0.000
24					20	0.000
25						

FIGURE 13.5 Straddle Option Prices

straddle option price is obtained by taking the average of these discounted payoffs over each simulated terminal stock price.

 The Excel file Chapter13STO contains the function Sim(), which can be used to perform this simulation. The function uses 10 time steps to simulate each stock price path, and performs 5,000 simulations.

```
Function Sim(S, KSTO, r, T1, T2, v)
Maturity = T2 - T1
Increments = 10
Nsims = 5000
Dim Straddle() As Double
ReDim Straddle(Nsims) As Double
Stock = S
For j = 1 To Nsims
  Stock = S
  For i = 2 To Increments
    dt = Maturity / Increments
    dz = Application.NormSInv(Rnd)
    dS = r * Stock * dt + v * Stock * dz * Sqr(dt)
```

```
      Stock = Stock + dS
   Next I
   fStock = Stock * Exp(r * (T2 - T1))
   CallOp = bs_price(Stock, fStock, r, Maturity, v, "Call")
   PutOp = bs_price(Stock, fStock, r, Maturity, v, "Put")
   Cost = CallOp + PutOp
   Straddle(j) = Exp(-r * T1) * Application.Max(Cost - KSTO, 0)
Next j
   Sim = Application.Average(Straddle)
End Function
```

The simulated straddle option price appears in Figure 13.5 also. To invoke this function with the given parameter values, in cell C16 we type

$$=\text{Sim(S, K,rf, Time1, Time2, Var2)}$$

which produces a time-zero price of $STO_0 = 9.317$, close to the true value of 9.324.

DELTA-HEDGED GAINS

The second type of volatility investment analyzed in this chapter is delta-hedged options. This strategy consists of a long position in a call option, dynamically hedged by a short position in the stock so that the net return of the strategy is the risk-free rate. The profits made in excess of the risk-free rate are the delta-hedged gains. Similar to the zero-beta straddle, this strategy dynamically delta-hedges the underlying asset, so the investor is exposed to volatility risk only.

Bakshi and Kapadia (2003) show that under stochastic volatility, and when volatility risk is not priced, delta-hedged gains are equal to zero on average. This strategy consists of a portfolio that requires continuous rebalancing. In practice, the portfolio is rebalanced at discrete time steps $t_0, t_1, \ldots, t_T$, where $t_0 = 0$ and $t_T = T$. This discretization induces a bias, but fortunately this bias is small. The profit of the portfolio at time T is

$$\pi = \max(S_T - K, 0) - C_0 - \sum_{n=1}^{T} \Delta_{t_{n-1}}(S_{t_n} - S_{t_{n-1}}) - \sum_{n=1}^{T} r_{n-1}(C_0 - \Delta_{t_{n-1}} S_{t_{n-1}})$$

$$(13.11)$$

where S_T = stock price at expiration
       K = strike price
       C_0 = time-zero cost of a call option with strike K
       Δ_{t_n} = delta of the call at time t_n
       S_{t_n} = value of the stock at time t_n
       r_n = risk-free rate at time t_n.

Equation (13.11) consists of four distinct terms. The first term, $\max(S_T - K, 0)$, is the value of the call at expiration (time T). The second term, C_0, is the cost of call at the time the portfolio is created (at $t = 0$). The third term, $\sum \Delta_{t_{n-1}}(S_{t_n} - S_{t_{n-1}})$, is the cost of the delta hedge, namely the amount of money lost or gained through stock price movements. Finally, the fourth term, $\sum r_{n-1}(C_0 - \Delta_{t_{n-1}}S_{t_{n-1}})$, is the cost of creating the strategy, assuming that capital can be borrowed and lent each day at the risk-free rate. Money needs to be borrowed to buy the call, but money can be lent after shorting the stock in an amount equivalent to delta.

This strategy is easily implemented in Excel with the VBA function BSDelta(), the GARCH estimated volatility path, and the function YearVol() for the volatility term structure. No new VBA functions are required. As mentioned previously, calculating delta-hedged gains is a two-step process. First, the volatility path must be estimated, which can be done using a GARCH(1,1) model. Second, the profit of the dynamically rebalanced portfolio must be calculated. There are three different ways of expressing the profits, as dollar delta-hedged gains (π), delta-hedged gains as a percentage of the stock price (π/S_0) or delta-hedged gains as percentage of the call price (π/C_0).

Delta-hedged gains are illustrated using a closest-to-the-money IBM call option on January 3, 2006, obtained from Yahoo! (finance.yahoo.com). This is contained in the Excel file Chapter13DHGains, and presented in Figure 13.6. In this example, the portfolio is rebalanced daily, over a period of 17 days.

The GARCH parameters in cells C25:C27 were estimated by maximum likelihood, using the GARCHparams() function introduced in Chapter 6. The daily GARCH(1,1) variances in cells H27:H38 were generated using these parameter values. The volatilities in cells H6:H17 are each for the maturity time horizon in cells F6:F17, and are created with the YearVol() function. The deltas Δ_{t_n} are in cells I6:I17 and are created with the BSDelta() function. For example, to create the delta for January 11, in cell I12 we type

$$= \text{BSDelta}(\text{G12,C8,F12/365,C6,H12,”Call”})$$

which produces $\Delta_{t_n} = 0.944$. Note that, as before, the time to maturity must be expressed in years, so this function requires "F12/365" as the third argument. The hedging profits $\Delta_{t_{n-1}}(S_{t_n} - S_{t_{n-1}})$ are in cells J7:J18. Hence, to calculate the profit at January 11, in cell J12 we type "=I11*(G12-G11)", which produces a profit of 0.09, or 9 cents. The interest payments $r_{n-1}(C_0 - \Delta_{t_{n-1}}S_{t_{n-1}})$ are in cells K7:K17, so to calculate the interest payment on the same day, in cell K12 we type

$$= (\text{C6/252})*(\text{C5-I11*G11})$$

which produces a payment of -0.01, or a loss of one cent. Finally, to compute the profit of the portfolio, the hedge profits and interest payments are aggregated in cells G22 and H22, respectively. These are subtracted from the call payoff $\max(S_T - K)$ in cell E22 and from C_0 in cell F22 to produce the profit $\pi = -0.20$, or a loss of 20 cents, in cell I22.

	B	C	D	E	F	G	H	I	J	K
2	**Delta-Hedged Gains**									
3	**Using a Call on IBM on January 3, 2006**									
4						Closing Price	DTM	Call	Hedging	Interest
5	Call Price ($)	2.95		Date	DTM	S_t	Volatility	Delta	Profits	Payments
6	Risk Free Rate (r)	0.05		3-Jan-06	17	82.06	0.194	0.753		
7	Date of Maturity	20-Jan-06		4-Jan-06	16	81.95	0.191	0.750	-0.08	-0.01
8	Strike Price (K)	80		5-Jan-06	15	82.50	0.189	0.809	0.41	-0.01
9				6-Jan-06	14	84.95	0.191	0.953	1.98	-0.01
10				9-Jan-06	11	83.73	0.257	0.860	-1.16	-0.02
11				10-Jan-06	10	84.07	0.239	0.905	0.29	-0.01
12				11-Jan-06	9	84.17	0.211	0.944	0.09	-0.01
13				12-Jan-06	8	83.57	0.192	0.944	-0.57	-0.02
14				13-Jan-06	7	83.17	0.187	0.940	-0.38	-0.02
15				17-Jan-06	3	83.00	0.167	0.993	-0.16	-0.01
16				18-Jan-06	2	83.80	0.153	1.000	0.79	-0.02
17				19-Jan-06	1	83.09	0.164	1.000	-0.71	-0.02
18				20-Jan-06	0	81.36			-1.73	-0.02
19	**Delta-Hedged Gain**									
20	Dollar Gain ($)	-0.20		Terminal	Call Cost	Hedging	Interest	Profit π		
21	As a % of Spot Price S_0	-0.24%		Payoff ($)	C_0 ($)	Profits ($)	Payments ($)	($)		
22	As a % of Call Price C_0	-6.81%		1.36	2.95	-1.22	-0.17	-0.20		
23										
24	**GARCH(1,1) Parameters**									
25	Omega (ω)	3.07E-05			Return	Return^2	Variance			
26	Alpha (α)	0.350389		Date	R_t	R_t^2	σ_t^2			
27	Beta (β)	0.481114		19-Jan-06	-0.00856	0.00007	0.00010			
28				18-Jan-06	0.00965	0.00009	0.00007			
29				17-Jan-06	-0.00206	0.00000	0.00009			
30				13-Jan-06	-0.00483	0.00002	0.00010			
31				12-Jan-06	-0.00720	0.00005	0.00011			
32				11-Jan-06	0.00120	0.00000	0.00017			
33				10-Jan-06	0.00408	0.00002	0.00028			
34				9-Jan-06	-0.01444	0.00021	0.00037			
35				6-Jan-06	0.02920	0.00085	0.00008			
36				5-Jan-06	0.00673	0.00005	0.00006			
37				4-Jan-06	-0.00135	0.00000	0.00007			
38				3-Jan-06	-0.00172	0.00000	0.00007			

FIGURE 13.6 Delta-Hedged Gains
Source: finance.yahoo.com

VOLATILITY EXPOSURE

Delta-hedged gains use a single call option in the portfolio, so the volatility exposure of the delta-hedged portfolio is simply the vega of the option. Recall from Chapter 4 that the Black-Scholes vega is $V = S\phi(d)\sqrt{T}$. Plotting vega against the asset price S produces the graph in Figure 13.7, which appears in the Excel file Chapter13Vega.

Clearly, while the delta-hedged option portfolio is able to hedge away variations in the asset price, the vega of the portfolio is not constant. When the asset price is less than $S = 80$ or greater than $S = 120$ approximately, the portfolio is insensitive to changes in volatility because its vega is nearly zero.

Demeterfi et al. (1999) show how to construct a portfolio whose vega is insensitive to the asset price, namely, a portfolio with constant vega across all values of

	A	B	C	D	E	F	G	H
1								
2		**Delta-Hedge Gain**			**Vega Variation With Change in Asset Spot Price**			
3		**Black-Scholes Setting**						
4					Spot Price	Vega		
5		Strike Price (K)	100		70.00	0.000		
6		Years to Maturity (T)	0.0833		72.50	0.000		
7		Interest Rate (r)	0.05		75.00	0.000		
8		Volatility (v)	0.2		77.50	0.001		
9					80.00	0.008		

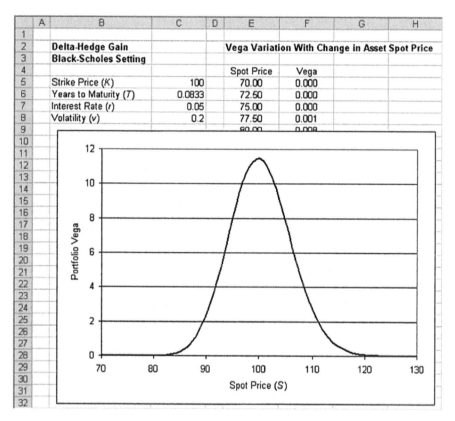

FIGURE 13.7 Delta-Hedged Gains Volatility Sensitivity

S. This portfolio is given by

$$\Pi(S, S_*, \sigma\sqrt{\tau}) = \sum_{K>S_*} \frac{1}{K^2} C(K) + \sum_{K<S_*} \frac{1}{K^2} P(K), \qquad (13.12)$$

where $C(K)$ and $P(K)$ are the values of out-of-the money calls and puts, respectively, each with maturity τ and volatility σ, when the spot price is S. As explained in the next section, S_* is a strike price that defines the boundary between liquid calls and puts. Equation (13.12) can be obtained using the Carr and Madan (2001) payoff function (12.4), using the payoff $H[S_T] = \ln(S_T/S_*)$, which produces $H_S[S_T] = 1/S_T$ and $H_{SS}[S_T] = -1/S_T^2$. Substituting these values into (12.4) with $\bar{S} = S_*$ and noting that $H[S_*] = 0$, produces

$$-\ln\left[\frac{S_T}{S_*}\right] + \left(\frac{S_T - S_*}{S_*}\right) = \int_{S_*}^{\infty} \frac{1}{K^2}(S_T - K)^+ \, dK + \int_{0}^{S_*} \frac{1}{K^2}(K - S_T)^+ \, dK. \quad (13.13)$$

This equation is identical to that for model-free variance (11.6) from Chapter 11, by substituting the in-the-money calls with out-of-the-money puts using put-call parity. As explained by Demeterfi et al. (1999), the left-hand side of (13.13) represents the time-T payoff of a short position of a log contract with reference price S_* (Neuberger 1994), plus the payoff of a long position on $1/S_*$ forward contracts on the asset, with delivery price S_*. The right-hand side is the time-T payoff from a long position of $1/K^2$ in call options over a continuum of strikes ranging over (S_*, ∞), and a long position of $1/K^2$ in put options over a continuum of strikes ranging over $(0, S_*)$. The time-t value of the portfolio is therefore the time-t value of the right-hand side, namely

$$\int_{S_*}^{\infty} \frac{1}{K^2} C(K)\, dK + \int_0^{S_*} \frac{1}{K^2} P(K)\, dK, \qquad (13.14)$$

where $C(K)$ and $P(K)$ are the time-t values of out-of-the-money calls and puts, respectively, each with maturity $\tau = T - t$. Equation (13.12) approximates (13.14) when calls and puts are available at a discrete set of strike prices.

It is useful to compare the vega obtained from a portfolio that weighs all options equally, to one that weighs options by $1/K^2$, namely that given by (13.12). The Excel file Chapter13Vega3 performs this comparison using three options, with strikes $K = 90, K = 100$, and $K = 110$. This is illustrated in Figure 13.8.

The quantities $1/K_i^2$ are contained in cells C10, C13, and C16, and their sum $\Psi = \sum_{i=1}^{3} 1/K_i^2$ in cell C18. The normalized weights are therefore $(1/K_i^2)/\Psi$ for $i = 1, 2, 3$. The BSVega() function from Chapter 4 is used to compute the option vegas. For example, to obtain the vega for the option with $K = 100$ when $S = 80$, in cell G10 we type

$$= \text{BSVega(E10,C12,C5,C6,C7)}$$

which produces $V = 0.008$. To obtain the equally-weighted vega when $S = 80$, based on the option vegas in cells F10, G10, and H10, in cell I10 we type

$$= (1/3)\text{*F10}+(1/3)\text{*G10}+(1/3)\text{*H10}$$

which produces $V_{EW} = 0.471$. To obtain the vega weighted inversely to the squared strike price, in cell J10 we type

$$= (\text{C10/C18})\text{*F10}+(\text{C13/C18})\text{*G10}+(\text{C16/C18})\text{*H10}$$

which produces $V_{KW} = 0.570$. The plots of the equally weighted and inverse squared strike price weighted vegas are represented by solid and dashed lines, respectively. Even with three options, the vega of the $1/K^2$ weighted portfolio is flatter than that of the equally weighted portfolio.

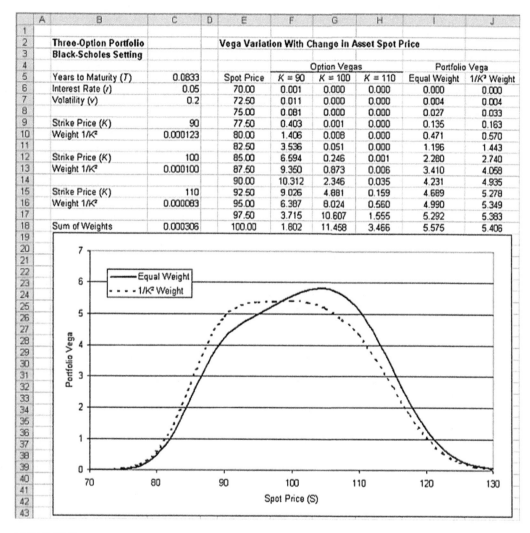

A	B	C	D	E	F	G	H	I	J
	Three-Option Portfolio			**Vega Variation With Change In Asset Spot Price**					
	Black-Scholes Setting								
						Option Vegas		Portfolio Vega	
	Years to Maturity (*T*)	0.0833		Spot Price	*K* = 90	*K* = 100	*K* = 110	Equal Weight	1/*K²* Weight
	Interest Rate (*r*)	0.05		70.00	0.001	0.000	0.000	0.000	0.000
	Volatility (*v*)	0.2		72.50	0.011	0.000	0.000	0.004	0.004
				75.00	0.081	0.000	0.000	0.027	0.033
	Strike Price (*K*)	90		77.50	0.403	0.001	0.000	0.135	0.163
	Weight 1/*K²*	0.000123		80.00	1.406	0.008	0.000	0.471	0.570
				82.50	3.536	0.051	0.000	1.196	1.443
	Strike Price (*K*)	100		85.00	6.594	0.246	0.001	2.280	2.740
	Weight 1/*K²*	0.000100		87.50	9.360	0.873	0.006	3.410	4.058
				90.00	10.312	2.346	0.035	4.231	4.935
	Strike Price (*K*)	110		92.50	9.026	4.881	0.159	4.689	5.278
	Weight 1/*K²*	0.000083		95.00	6.387	8.024	0.560	4.990	5.349
				97.50	3.715	10.607	1.555	5.292	5.383
	Sum of Weights	0.000306		100.00	1.802	11.458	3.466	5.575	5.406

FIGURE 13.8 Three-Option Portfolio Vega

This comparison can easily be repeated with more than three options. The Excel file Chapter13Vega13 contains vegas of the equally and $1/K^2$ weighted portfolios, using thirteen options. The leftmost part of this file is illustrated in Figure 13.9.

The 13 strike prices range from $K = 70$ to $K = 130$, in increments of \$5, and are contained in row 4. The inverse squared strikes appear in row 5, and the normalized weights $(1/K_i^2)/\Psi$ $(i = 1, \ldots, 13)$ in row 6. As in the previous figure, the vega of the equally weighted portfolio is plotted with a solid line, and that of the $1/K^2$ weighted portfolio, with a dashed line. With 13 options, the advantage of weights inversely proportional to the squared strike price is remarkably noticeable. The vega of the

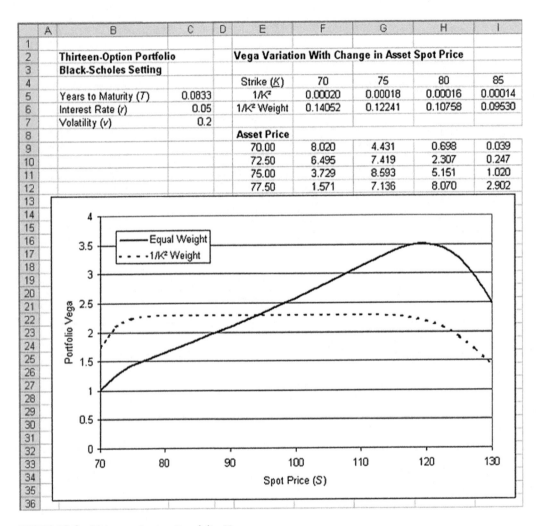

	A	B	C	D	E	F	G	H	I
1									
2		**Thirteen-Option Portfolio**			**Vega Variation With Change in Asset Spot Price**				
3		**Black-Scholes Setting**							
4					Strike (*K*)	70	75	80	85
5		Years to Maturity (*T*)	0.0833		1/*K*²	0.00020	0.00018	0.00016	0.00014
6		Interest Rate (*r*)	0.05		1/*K*² Weight	0.14052	0.12241	0.10758	0.09530
7		Volatility (*v*)	0.2						
8					**Asset Price**				
9					70.00	8.020	4.431	0.698	0.039
10					72.50	6.495	7.419	2.307	0.247
11					75.00	3.729	8.593	5.151	1.020
12					77.50	1.571	7.136	8.070	2.902

FIGURE 13.9 Thirteen-Option Portfolio Vega

portfolio is flat across all spot prices from approximately $S = 75$ to $S = 115$. The vega of the equally weighted portfolio, though flatter than when three options are used, is not nearly as insensitive to the asset price.

VARIANCE SWAPS

A variance swap is a forward contract on future variance, entered into at time t, and with expiry at time T. This contract resembles a call option. Its payoff at time T is $N(\sigma_{t,T}^2 - K_{var})$, where $\sigma_{t,T}^2$ is the annualized realized variance over $(t, t + T)$, calculated at T, K_{var} is delivery value for the variance, specified at inception of the contract, and N is the notional amount of the swap. Similarly, a volatility swap is a forward contract on future volatility. The payoff at time T of a volatility swap is $N(\sigma_{t,T} - K_{vol})$, where $\sigma_{t,T}$ is the annualized realized volatility over $(t, t + T)$ and K_{vol} is the delivery value. To obtain the price of a variance swap, an estimator of K_{var} must be produced. This estimator is based on model-free variance. See Carr and Wu (2004) for a theoretical treatment.

Swap Rate Adjustment

Demeterfi et al. (1999) show how to price a variance swap when implied volatilities show a volatility skew. In their setting, the liquidity of option contracts is not uniform across moneyness levels. Instead of dividing options into out-of-the-money calls and puts about a moneyness of $K/S = 1$, they modify the moneyness boundary so that a sufficient amount of both calls and puts can be obtained. This approach exploits the fact that out-of-the money options are usually more liquid and readily available for purchase. The value of the variance swap when the forward contract is entered into, at time zero, is $E[e^{-rT}(\sigma_T^2 - K_{var})]$, where K_{var} is the strike, r is the risk-free rate, σ_T^2 is the realized variance over $(0, T)$ and T is the time to maturity. If the stock price evolves in accordance with the diffusion

$$\frac{dS_t}{S_t} = r\,dt + \sigma\,dZ_t, \tag{13.15}$$

where $Z_t = \sqrt{dt}\varepsilon_t$ and $\varepsilon_t \sim N(0, 1)$, then K_{var} can be specified as the risk-neutral expected variance over $(0, T)$

$$K_{var} = \frac{1}{T}E\left[\int_0^T \sigma_t^2\,dt\right]. \tag{13.16}$$

Using Itô's Lemma, the process driving $d\log S_t$ is identical to that in (13.15), except that the drift is replaced by $r - \sigma^2/2$. This leads to a difference between them equal to

$$\frac{dS_t}{S_t} - d\log S_t = \frac{1}{2}\sigma^2\,dt. \tag{13.17}$$

Multiplying (13.17) by $2/T$, integrating over $(0, T)$, and taking the risk-neutral expected value produces the following expression for the strike in (13.16)

$$K_{var} = \frac{2}{T}E\left[\int_0^T \frac{dS_t}{S_t} - \log\frac{S_T}{S_0}\right]. \tag{13.18}$$

The idea is to obtain K_{var} using plain-vanilla calls and puts. Under the process (13.17), the first expectation in (13.18) is rT, while the second corresponds to the payoff at time T of a log contract (Neuberger, 1999). Since no such contract is traded, its payoff must be replicated. Demeterfi et al. (1999) show how this can be achieved by using a combination of a forward contract on the stock, and out-of-the-money (OTM) calls and puts along with (13.13). An adjustment must be made in order to have a sufficient amount of each type of OTM option, so a boundary parameter S_* is introduced. This parameter specifies the boundary between calls and puts, so that the liquidity of each type of option is roughly the same. Hence, the strike is written as

$$K_{\text{var}} = \frac{2}{T}\left[rT - \left(\frac{S_0}{S_*}e^{rT} - 1\right) - \log\frac{S_*}{S_0} + e^{rT}\int_0^{S_*}\frac{P(K)\,dK}{K^2} + e^{rT}\int_{S_*}^{\infty}\frac{C(K)\,dK}{K^2}\right],$$

$$(13.19)$$

where $P(K)$ and $C(K)$ are the time zero values of puts and calls with strike K. Equation (13.19) for K_{var} requires a continuum of puts, with strike prices over $(0, S_*)$, and a continuum of calls, with strike prices over (S_*, ∞).

Demeterfi et al. (1999) suggest the following approximation to (13.19) when strikes are available at discrete time intervals

$$K_{\text{var}} = \frac{2}{T}\left[rT - \left(\frac{S_0}{S_*}e^{rT} - 1\right) - \log\frac{S_*}{S_0}\right] + e^{rT}\Pi_{CP}.$$

$$(13.20)$$

In this expression, Π_{CP} is the time zero value of the portfolio of options with payoff at time T given by

$$f(S_T) = \frac{2}{T}\left(\frac{S_T - S_*}{S_*} - \log\frac{S_T}{S_*}\right).$$

$$(13.21)$$

To approximate the payoff $f(S_T)$ with a piecewise linear function, a series of call options with strike prices $K_0 < K_{1c} < K_{2c} < \cdots$, and a series of put options with strike prices $K_0 > K_{1p} > K_{2p} > \cdots$ are needed, where $K_0 = S_*$. The numbers of calls and puts to use at each strike are given by

$$w_c(K_{n,c}) = \frac{f(K_{n+1,c}) - f(K_{n,c})}{K_{n+1,c} - K_{n,c}} - \sum_{i=0}^{n-1} w_c(K_{i,c})$$

$$(13.22)$$

$$w_p(K_{n,p}) = \frac{f(K_{n+1,p}) - f(K_{n,p})}{K_{n,p} - K_{n+1,p}} - \sum_{i=0}^{n-1} w_p(K_{i,p})$$

$$(13.23)$$

respectively. With these weights, the value of the portfolio in (13.20) is

$$\Pi_{CP} = \sum_n w_p(K_{n,p})P(S, K_{n,p}) + \sum_n w_c(K_{n,c})C(S, K_{n,c}).$$

$$(13.24)$$

Substituting Π_{CP}, r, T, the current stock price S_0 and the boundary point S_* into (13.20) produces the approximation to K_{var}.

The Excel file Chapter13KSwap contains the VBA function Kvar() for implementing this swap. It requires as inputs the spot price S, the boundary S_*, the risk-free rate r and the time to maturity T, as well as four columns of numbers corresponding to implied volatilities and strike prices for puts and calls. The weights for the calls and puts are stored in the arrays CallW() and PutW(), respectively, while the total cost of the portfolio, Π_{CP}, is stored in the variable BigPi. The function uses Black-Scholes prices for the puts and calls in (13.24).

```
Function Kvar(Spot, Sb, r, T, PutV, PutK, CallV, CallK)
'Call Options
n = Application.Count(CallV)
For i = 1 To n - 1
  Temp(i) = (f(CallK(i + 1), Sb, T) - f(CallK(i), Sb, T))
        / (CallK(i + 1) - CallK(i))
  Value(i) = BS_price(Spot, CallK(i), r, T, CallV(i), "Call")
Next i
CallW(1) = Temp(1)
For i = 2 To n - 1
  CallW(i) = Temp(i) - Temp(i - 1)
Next i
For i = 1 To n - 1
  CallC(i) = Value(i) * CallW(i)
Next i
Pi1 = Application.Sum(CallC)
' PutOptions
' Flip the Vectors for Convenience
n = Application.Count(PutV)
For i = 1 To n
  K(i) = PutK(n - i + 1)
  V(i) = PutV(n - i + 1)
Next i
For i = 1 To n - 1
  Temp2(i) = (f(K(i + 1), Sb, T) - f(K(i), Sb, T)) / (K(i) - K(i + 1))
  Value2(i) = bs_price(Spot, K(i), r, T, V(i), "Put")
Next i
PutW(1) = Temp2(1)
For i = 2 To n - 1
  PutW(i) = Temp2(i) - Temp2(i - 1)
Next i
For i = 1 To n - 1
  PutC(i) = Value2(i) * PutW(i)
Next i
Pi2 = Application.Sum(PutC)
BigPi = Pi1 + Pi2
Kvar = 2 / T * (r * T - (Spot / Sb * Exp(r * T) - 1)
    - Log(Sb / Spot)) + Exp(r * T) * BigPi
End Function
```

	A	B	C	D	E	F	G	H	I	J
1										
2		**Demeterfi, Derman, Kamal, and Zou (1999)**								
3		**Approximation to Variance Swap**								
4						Strike	Implied	Black-Scholes		Price
5		Boundary Price (S⁎)	100			Price	Volatility	Option Price	Weight*	Contribution
6		Spot Price (S₀)	100		Puts	45	0.31			
7		Risk Free Rate (r)	0.05			50	0.30	0.000003	160.81	0.00042
8		Time to Maturity (T)	0.25			55	0.29	0.000029	132.78	0.00391
9						60	0.28	0.000237	111.50	0.02646
10		K_{var} =	0.041868			65	0.27	0.001461	94.96	0.13870
11		$\sqrt{K_{var}}$ =	0.204616			70	0.26	0.007177	81.84	0.58735
12						75	0.25	0.029089	71.27	2.07316
13						80	0.24	0.099623	62.62	6.23866
14						85	0.23	0.293344	55.46	16.26869
15						90	0.22	0.751960	49.46	37.19127
16						95	0.21	1.693229	44.38	75.15031
17						100	0.20	3.372770	20.69	69.79175
18										
19					Calls	100	0.20	4.614990	19.36	89.33409
20						105	0.19	2.288609	36.32	83.12771
21						110	0.18	0.907295	33.09	30.02426
22						115	0.17	0.267001	30.27	8.08329
23						120	0.16	0.052854	27.80	1.46943
24						125	0.15	0.006156	25.62	0.15772
25						130	0.14	0.000350	23.69	0.00830
26						135	0.13	0.000007	21.96	0.00016
27						140	0.12			
28		* The weights have been multiplied by 10,000						Total Portfolio Cost (π_{CP}) =		419.6756

FIGURE 13.10 Variance Swap

The VBA function Kvar() uses the BS_price() function defined in Chapter 4 for the Black-Scholes price of puts and calls, and the following function for the terminal payoff function $f(S_T)$ defined in (13.21)

```
Function f(S, Sb, T)
  f = 2 / T * ((S - Sb) / Sb - Log(S / Sb))
End Function
```

Figure 13.10 illustrates this function, using the same input values as those in Exhibit 5 of Demeterfi et al. (1999). The strikes for the puts range from 50 to 100, and those for the calls from 100 to 135, in increments of 5. The implied volatility is $\sigma = 0.20$ at $S_* = 100$ and rises (decreases) by 0.01 for every \$5 decrease (increase) in the strike price.

The put with strike 45 and the call with strike 140 are used as extra points to initialize the weights. The option prices in column H are obtained using the VBA function BS_price(). In cell C10 we type

$$= \text{Kvar}(S, Sb, rf, T, G6:G17, F6:F17, G19:G27, F19:F27),$$

while in cell C11 we type "=SQRT(C10)", which produces $K_{\text{var}} \approx (0.20462)^2$.

The functions CallWeight() and PutWeight() are extracted from the VBA function Kvar(), and produce the weights in column I. Note that these functions multiply the weights by 10,000 to make them comparable to the weights in Exhibit 5 of Demeterfi et al. (1999). This has the effect of expressing K_{var} in terms of percentage points instead of decimals.

To value a volatility swap with delivery K_{vol}, Demeterfi et al. (1999) suggest the approximation

$$\sigma_{t,T} - K_{\text{vol}} \approx \frac{1}{2K_{\text{vol}}}(\sigma_{t,T}^2 - K_{\text{vol}}^2). \tag{13.25}$$

Hence, a volatility contract with notional amount $N = 1$ and delivery K_{vol} corresponds to a variance contract with notional amount $N = 1/(2K_{\text{vol}})$ and delivery K_{vol}^2. This assumes that the delivery of the volatility contract is the square root of the delivery of the variance contract, $K_{\text{vol}} = \sqrt{K_{\text{var}}}$. As shown by Demeterfi et al. (1999), the approximation (13.25) works best when the future realized volatility is close to K_{vol}.

SUMMARY

In this chapter various tools for investing in volatility are introduced. Simple straddles are the easiest way to speculate on volatility. They are constructed with a single call and put with the same expiry and strike price. Alternatively, one can opt for an option on this type of straddle, rather than the straddle itself. Zero-beta straddles have the advantage of zero exposure to market risk. It is also possible to build a dynamic straddle, by rebalancing daily the puts and calls that make up the straddle. This maintains the highest exposure to volatility, and allows for the calculation of daily profits. Delta-hedged options are hedged against movements in the underlying stock price. They attempt to isolate exposure to volatility. Since a delta-hedged option is constructed with a single call option, however, the vega of the option varies with stock price movements. A portfolio whose vega is insensitive to stock price movements can be constructed by using out-of-the-money calls and puts, weighted by the inverse of their squared strike prices. The cost of variance in a variance swap is constructed in this manner. The holder of a variance swap receives realized variance for a delivery value at expiration of the swap.

EXERCISES

This section provides exercises that deal with volatility returns. Solutions are contained in the Excel file Chapter13Exercises.

13.1 Demeterfi et al. (1999) explain that the mismatch between the variance and volatility swap in the approximation (13.25) is the convexity bias given by $(\sigma_{t,T} - K_{vol})^2/(2K_{vol})$. Plot this bias as a function of $\sigma_{t,T}$, with $K_{vol} = 0.30$ and with $\sigma_{t,T}$ ranging from 0.15 to 0.40. On the same graph, plot the values of the left-hand side and right-hand side of (13.25).

13.2 Create an at-the-money simple straddle and a zero-beta straddle on January 3, 2006, using a call and put option for Intel Corporation that each expire on January 20, 2006. Download daily closing prices for Intel, adjusted for dividends and stock splits, from January 3, 2005, to January 3, 2006, to calculate daily returns and to estimate the yearly unconditional volatility based on those returns. Use this volatility measure in the calculation of call and put betas. Use a call and a put each with strike price $K = 25$ and prices $C = 0.95$ and $P = 0.35$, and a risk-free rate of $r = 0.05$. Select the weights of each straddle so that the cost of constructing each straddle is $1. Graph the profit of the simple straddle and the zero-beta straddle as a function of the terminal stock price from $S_T = 20$ to $S_T = 30$. The closing price of Intel on January 20, 2006, was $S_T = 21.76$. Calculate the actual straddle returns and indicate them on the profit diagrams.

13.3 Use closing prices on Intel Corporation from January 3, 2006, to January 20, 2006, to dynamically delta-hedge a call, using a call option with a strike price of $K = 25$. Use a 252-day rolling window unconditional volatility estimator as input to the Black-Scholes delta, and a risk-free rate of $r = 0.05$.

13.4 The Excel file IntelOptions on the CD-ROM contains the following option prices for Intel Corporation on January 3, 2006. All options expire on January 20, 2006, corresponding to a time to maturity of 17 days. These are listed in Table 13.1. The unadjusted closing price of Intel on January 3, 2006, was 25.57. Using these option prices and the MFV() function for model-free implied volatility of Chapter 11, show that the annualized realized volatility of

TABLE 13.1 Option Prices for Intel on January 3, 2006

Strike Price	Call Price	Put Price
22.50	3.10	0.05
25.00	0.95	0.35
27.50	0.10	1.95
30.00	0.05	4.70

Intel Corp. over the 17-day period was higher than the annualized model-free implied volatility. Use the puts with strikes 22.50, 25, and 27.50, and the calls with strikes 25, 27.50, and 30, and use a risk-free rate of $r = 0.05$. This confirms that the straddles of Exercise 13.2 and the delta-hedged portfolio of Exercise 13.3 would have earned a profit.

SOLUTIONS TO EXERCISES

13.1 No new VBA functions are required for this exercise. The left-hand side of (13.25) produces a straight line, while the right-hand side, a convex curve. The convexity bias is a parabola that takes on positive values only. This exercise, which reproduces Exhibit 14 of Demeterfi et al. (1999), shows that using the right-hand side of (13.25) as an approximation to a volatility swap works best when the realized volatility is close to the strike volatility K_{vol}.

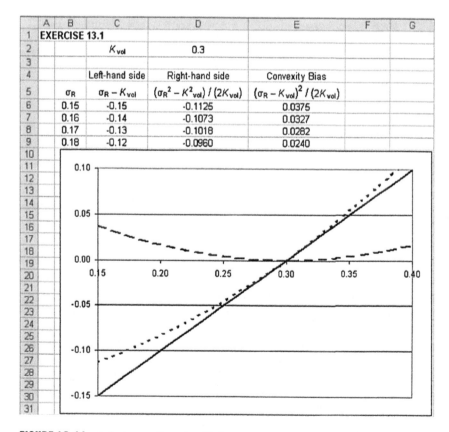

	A	B	C	D	E	F	G
1	EXERCISE 13.1						
2			K_{vol}	0.3			
3							
4			Left-hand side	Right-hand side	Convexity Bias		
5		σ_R	$\sigma_R - K_{vol}$	$(\sigma_R^2 - K^2_{vol}) / (2K_{vol})$	$(\sigma_R - K_{vol})^2 / (2K_{vol})$		
6		0.15	-0.15	-0.1125	0.0375		
7		0.16	-0.14	-0.1073	0.0327		
8		0.17	-0.13	-0.1018	0.0282		
9		0.18	-0.12	-0.0960	0.0240		

FIGURE 13.11   Solution to Exercise 13.1

EXERCISE 13.2

Straddle Returns Using At-The-Money Put and Call
on Intel Corporation for January 3, 2006

			Straddle Weight	
			Simple	Zero-Beta
Risk-Free Rate	0.05			
Current Date	03-Jan-06	Number of Calls	0.769	0.54227
Expiry Date	20-Jan-06	Number of Puts	0.769	1.38526
Time to Maturity (T)	0.0466	Straddle Cost	1	1
Underlying Price (time = 0)	25.57			
Terminal Price (time = T)	21.76			
Strike Price (K)	25			
Call Price ($)	0.95			
Put Price ($)	0.35			
Current Annual Volatility	0.2071			

Spot Price	Simple Straddle			Zero-Beta Straddle		
	Call Payoff	Put Payoff	Return	Call Payoff	Put Payoff	Return
20.00	0.00	3.85	284.6%	0.00	6.93	592.6%
20.50	0.00	3.46	246.2%	0.00	6.23	523.4%
21.00	0.00	3.08	207.7%	0.00	5.54	454.1%
21.50	0.00	2.69	169.2%	0.00	4.85	384.8%
22.00	0.00	2.31	130.8%	0.00	4.16	315.6%
22.50	0.00	1.92	92.3%	0.00	3.46	246.3%
23.00	0.00	1.54	53.8%	0.00	2.77	177.1%
23.50	0.00	1.15	15.4%	0.00	2.08	107.8%
24.00	0.00	0.77	-23.1%	0.00	1.39	38.5%
24.50	0.00	0.38	-61.5%	0.00	0.69	-30.7%
25.00	0.00	0.00	-100.0%	0.00	0.00	-100.0%
25.50	0.38	0.00	-61.5%	0.27	0.00	-72.9%
26.00	0.77	0.00	-23.1%	0.54	0.00	-45.8%
26.50	1.15	0.00	15.4%	0.81	0.00	-18.7%
27.00	1.54	0.00	53.8%	1.08	0.00	8.5%
27.50	1.92	0.00	92.3%	1.36	0.00	35.6%
28.00	2.31	0.00	130.8%	1.63	0.00	62.7%
28.50	2.69	0.00	169.2%	1.90	0.00	89.8%
29.00	3.08	0.00	207.7%	2.17	0.00	116.9%
29.50	3.46	0.00	246.2%	2.44	0.00	144.0%
30.00	3.85	0.00	284.6%	2.71	0.00	171.1%
21.76	0.00	2.49	149.2%	0.00	4.49	348.8%

Date	Adjusted Close	Return
3-Jan-06	25.18	0.0245
30-Dec-05	24.57	-0.0045
29-Dec-05	24.68	-0.0149
28-Dec-05	25.05	-0.0008
27-Dec-05	25.07	-0.0197
23-Dec-05	25.57	0.0000
22-Dec-05	25.57	0.0035
21-Dec-05	25.48	0.0028
20-Dec-05	25.41	0.0012
19-Dec-05	25.38	-0.0230
16-Dec-05	25.97	-0.0077
15-Dec-05	26.17	-0.0019
14-Dec-05	26.22	-0.0034
13-Dec-05	26.31	0.0038
12-Dec-05	26.21	0.0204
9-Dec-05	25.68	0.0149
8-Dec-05	25.30	-0.0176

FIGURE 13.12   Solution to Exercise 13.2

13.2 The solution appears in Figure 13.12. The returns for 2005 for Intel Corporation are in cells D19:D270, so to calculate the unconditional annual volatility, in cell D15 of Figure 13.12 we type

$$= SQRT(252*VAR(D19:D270))$$

which produces the value $\sigma = 0.2071$. The cost of constructing the straddles with the call (with price $C = 0.95$) and the put (with price $P = 0.35$) must be $1. This implies that the number of calls and puts are each $1/(0.95 + 0.35)$ or 0.769 for the simple straddle. These appear in cells G7:G8. The number of calls for the zero-beta straddle is obtained from the ZBStraddleWeight() function. This function must be scaled by the option prices in cell D13 and D14, to make the cost of constructing the zero-beta straddle equal to $1. To obtain the number of calls, in cell H7 we type

$$= ZBStraddleWeight(S,K,T,rf,D15,D13,D14) / D13$$

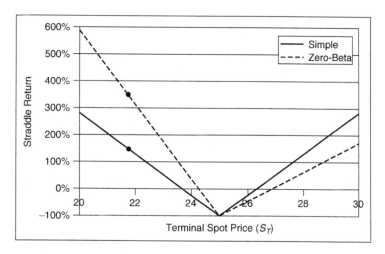

FIGURE 13.13   Solution to Exercise 13.2

which produces 0.54227. To obtain the number of puts, in cell H8 we type

$$= (1\text{-}ZBStraddleWeight(S,K,T,rf,D15,D13,D14))/D14$$

which produces 1.38526. Finally, the payoffs of the calls and puts are obtained using the Excel function MAX() with the strike price of $K = 20$ and the spot prices in column F.

Plotting the returns as a function of the terminal spot price produces the graph in Figure 13.13. The closing price of Intel on January 20, 2006, was $S_T = 21.76$. Cells I35 and L35 of Figure 13.12 indicate that the payoff of the simple and zero-beta straddle for that value of S_T are 149.2 and 348.8 percent, respectively. These payoffs are represented by the black circles in Figure 13.13.

13.3 The solution appears in Figure 13.14. Since 252-day rolling windows are used to obtain volatility estimates, returns from January 5, 2005, to January 20, 2006, are needed. These are in cells E27:E290, and are obtained from the adjusted closing prices for Intel Corporation in cells D27:D291. The closing prices for Intel are in cells G7:G19. Note that these do not match the adjusted closing prices exactly. To calculate returns, closing prices adjusted for dividends must be used, since dividends are part of returns. To obtain the annualized volatility on January 4, 2006, using the adjusted closing prices, in cell F38 we type

$$= SQRT(252*VAR(E38:E289))$$

which uses returns from January 5, 2005, to January 4, 2006, to produce $\sigma = 0.2064$. To obtain the call delta for January 4, 2006, corresponding to a

	A	B	C	D	E	F	G	H	I	J	K
1	EXERCISE 13.3										
2											
3		**Delta-Hedged Gains Using a Call Option**									
4		**on Intel Corporation on January 3, 2006**									
5							Closing Price	DTM	Call	Hedging	Interest
6		Call Price ($)	0.95			Date	DTM	S_t	Volatility	Delta	Profits	Payments
7		Risk Free Rate (r)	0.05			3-Jan-06	17	25.57	0.2071	0.719		
8		Date of Maturity	20-Jan-06			4-Jan-06	16	25.91	0.2064	0.816	0.2443	-0.00346
9		Strike Price (K)	25			5-Jan-06	15	26.27	0.2065	0.895	0.2937	-0.00401
10						6-Jan-06	14	26.31	0.2061	0.909	0.0358	-0.00448
11						9-Jan-06	11	26.47	0.2065	0.951	0.1454	-0.00456
12						10-Jan-06	10	26.12	0.2059	0.910	-0.3328	-0.00481
13						11-Jan-06	9	26.14	0.2044	0.926	0.0182	-0.00453
14						12-Jan-06	8	25.97	0.2039	0.905	-0.1574	-0.00461
15						13-Jan-06	7	25.79	0.2040	0.875	-0.1630	-0.00448
16						17-Jan-06	3	25.52	0.2378	0.838	-0.2362	-0.00429
17						18-Jan-06	2	22.60	0.2375	0.000	-2.4459	-0.00405
18						19-Jan-06	1	22.40	0.2393	0.000	0.0000	0.00019
19						20-Jan-06	0	21.76			0.0000	0.00019
20		Delta-Hedged Gain									
21		Dollar Gain ($)	1.78			Terminal	Call Cost	Hedging	Interest	Profit π	Number of	Total Profit π
22		As a % of Cost	177.96%			Payoff ($)	C_0 ($)	Profits ($)	Payments ($)	per Call ($)	Calls	($)
23						0.00	0.95	-2.60	-0.04	1.69	1.053	1.78
24												
25				Adjusted			Annualized					
26			Date	Close	Return	Volatility						
27			20-Jan-06	21.42	-0.0290	0.2393						
28			19-Jan-06	22.05	-0.0090	0.2375						
29			18-Jan-06	22.25	-0.1217	0.2378						
30			17-Jan-06	25.13	-0.0103	0.2040						
31			13-Jan-06	25.39	-0.0071	0.2039						
32			12-Jan-06	25.57	-0.0066	0.2044						
33			11-Jan-06	25.74	0.0008	0.2059						
34			10-Jan-06	25.72	-0.0131	0.2065						
35			9-Jan-06	26.06	0.0062	0.2061						
36			6-Jan-06	25.90	0.0015	0.2065						
37			5-Jan-06	25.86	0.0136	0.2065						
38			4-Jan-06	25.51	0.0130	0.2064						
39			3-Jan-06	25.18	0.0245	0.2071						

FIGURE 13.14   Solution to Exercise 13.3

maturity of $T = 16$ days in cell F8, a spot price for Intel of $S = 25.91$ in G8, a risk-free rate of $r = 0.05$ in cell C7, a strike price of $K = 25$ in cell C9, and a volatility of $\sigma = 0.2064$ in H8 copied directly from cell F38, in cell I8 we type

$$= \text{BSDelta}(\text{G8,C9,F8/365,C7,H8,"Call"})$$

which produces $\Delta_C = 0.816$. Note that the third argument is "F8/365" since the time to maturity in the BSDelta() function must be expressed in years. The cost of the delta hedge is obtained by entering "=I7*(G8-G7)" in cell J8, which produces $\Delta_{t_{n-1}}(S_{t_n} - S_{t_{n-1}}) = 0.2443$. The cost of creating the strategy is obtained by entering "=(C7/252)*(C6-I7*G7)" in cell K8, which produces $r_{n-1}(C_0 - \Delta_{t_{n-1}}S_{t_{n-1}}) = -0.00346$. Aggregating these last quantities produces -2.60 in cell G23 and -0.04 in cell H23. The profit per call is obtained

	A	B	C	D	E	F	G
1	**EXERCISE 13.4**						
2							
3		Unadjusted Closing Price (S)	25.57		Strike	Call	Put
4		Current Date	3-Jan-06		Price	Price	Price
5		Date of Maturity	20-Jan-06		22.50	3.10	0.05
6		Time to Maturity (T − t)	0.0466		25.00	0.95	0.35
7		Risk Free Rate (r)	0.05		27.50	0.10	1.95
8					30.00	0.05	4.70
9							
10		**Model-Free**				Adjusted	
11		Period Variance	0.0109		Date	Close	Return
12		Annualized Variance	0.2342		20-Jan-06	21.42	-0.0290
13		Annualized Volatility	0.4839		19-Jan-06	22.05	-0.0090
14					18-Jan-06	22.25	-0.1217
15		**Realized**			17-Jan-06	25.13	-0.0103
16		Daily Variance	0.0013		13-Jan-06	25.39	-0.0071
17		Annualized Variance	0.3288		12-Jan-06	25.57	-0.0066
18		Annualized Volatility	0.5735		11-Jan-06	25.74	0.0008
19					10-Jan-06	25.72	-0.0131
20					9-Jan-06	26.06	0.0062
21					6-Jan-06	25.90	0.0015
22					5-Jan-06	25.86	0.0136
23					4-Jan-06	25.51	0.0130
24					3-Jan-06	25.18	0.0245
25					30-Dec-05	24.57	-0.0045
26					29-Dec-05	24.68	-0.0149
27					28-Dec-05	25.05	-0.0008

FIGURE 13.15   Solution to Exercise 13.4

from (13.11) as \$1.69 in cell I23. Finally, to compare the delta-hedge gain to the straddles in Exercise 13.2, the profit when \$1 is invested at the outset (corresponding to 1.053 calls) is 1.78 or 178 percent in cell C22. Referring back to Figure 13.13, this profit lies in between that obtained from the simple straddle and the zero-beta straddle.

13.4 This exercise is illustrated in Figure 13.15. To obtain the daily variance using returns over the 17-day period, in cell C16 we type "=VAR(G12:G24)" which produces 0.0013. Scaling the square root of this number by $\sqrt{252}$ produces the annualized realized volatility, which appears in cell C18 as $\sigma_R = 0.5735$. To obtain the model-free variance for the same period, in cell C11 we type

$$= \text{MFV(E6:E8,F6:F8,E5:E7,G5:G7,C3,C7,C6)}$$

which produces the 17-day model-free variance of 0.0109. To annualize this variance, we divide by the time to maturity in cell C6, so in cell C12 we type "=C11*(1/C6)". The model-free annualized volatility is the square root of this number, $\sigma_{MF} = 0.4839$, which is indeed smaller than the realized volatility.

A VBA Primer

In this appendix we provide a very brief description of how VBA functions are written with the VBA editor. The VBA editor is accessed under the Tools menu in Excel, by selecting Macro, and then Visual Basic Editor, or simply by pressing ALT and F11. The first step to writing VBA code is to insert a VBA module by selecting Module from the Insert menu. A VBA function always begins with the declaration statement Function and always ends with the statement End Function. The Function statement includes all parameters that are passed to the function.

```
Function SumNum(a,b)
  SumNum = a + b
End Function
```

To use the function in Excel, the function name is typed into any cell, preceded by an equal sign (=). Hence, in any cell we type "=SumNum(5,4)", which produces 9. If the numbers are in, say, cells A1 and A2, then we type "=SumNum(A1,A2)".

Using built-in functions in Excel requires that the function name be preceded by Application. Hence, the built-in Sum function in Excel could be used, so that the function would be

```
Function SumNum2(a)
  SumNum = Application.Sum(a)
End Function
```

If the numbers that need to be summed are in cells A1:A5, then in any cell we type "=SumNum(A1:A5)".

$$= SumNum2(A1:A5)$$

It is sometimes useful to create VBA functions to apply built-in functions, to save space. The following function returns the standard normal cumulative distribution function:

```
Function Gauss(X)
  Gauss = Application.NormSDist(X)
End Function
```

If there are many such Excel functions to invoke within the VBA function, we could use the With Application statement and precede each function with a period.

```
Function Gauss(X)
  With Application
    Gauss = .NormSDist(X)
  End With
End Function
```

Parameters can also be text strings, in which case the parameter name must be followed by "As String" in the function declaration. This is used often in the option pricing formulas, to incorporate the call and put price into a single function, as is the case with the BlackScholes() function.

```
Function BlackScholes(S, K, r, T, v, PutCall As String)
  d = (Log(S / K) + T * (r + 0.5 * v ^ 2)) / (v * Sqr(T))
  bs_call = S * Gauss(d) - Exp(-r * T) * K
            * Gauss(d - v * Sqr(T))
  If PutCall = "Call" Then
    BlackScholes = bs_call
  ElseIf PutCall = "Put" Then
    BlackScholes = bs_call - S + K * Exp(-r * T)
  End If
End Function
```

Instead of the If-ElseIf-EndIf statements, we could use the Select statement, which is better than nesting If statements when there are many cases to choose from

```
Select Case PutCall
  Case "Call"
    BlackScholes = bs_call
  Case "Put"
    BlackScholes = bs_call - S + K * Exp(-r * T)
End Select
```

Iterative processing in VBA is done analogously to other programming languages. The For loop, for example, processes a loop a given number of times.

```
Function Repeat(n)
  For i = 1 To n
    MsgBox "Iteration Number is " & i
  Next i
End Function
```

The iteration can also be run backwards from $i = n$ to $i = 1$. This is accomplished with the Step statement, which specifies a step size of -1 in this example:

```
Function Repeat2(n)
  For i = n To 1 Step -1
    MsgBox "Iteration Number is " & i
  Next i
End Function
```

In both functions, the statements "Next i" could both be changed to "Next". When there are multiple loops nested within one another, however, including the looping variable with the Next statement makes the code easier to read.

The Do-While loop executes a loop until a certain condition is met. The BisMet() function of Chapter 1, for example, finds the root of a function using a Do-While loop. The Do-While loop continues the bisection algorithm until a tolerance of EPS is met.

```
Function BisMet(fname As String, a, b)
  EPS = 0.000001
  If (Run(fname, a) < Run(fname, b)) Then
    tmp = b
    b = a
    a = tmp
  End If
  Do While (Run(fname, a) - Run(fname, b) > EPS)
    midPt = (b + a) / 2
      If Run(fname, midPt) < 0 Then
        b = midPt
      Else
        a = midPt
      End If
  Loop
BisMet = (b + a) / 2
End Function
```

Sometimes the VBA function needs to return an array of numbers rather than just a single value. In this case, it is convenient to define an array within VBA and assign the function value to the array name once the array is filled with the values to output. In this example, terminal values from the CRR binomial tree of Chapter 3 are transferred to the array Out(). The dimensions of an array are set by the Dim statement, and can later be redimensioned using the ReDim statement. When using the ReDim statement, the values contained in the array can be preserved using the Preserve option. The Option Base 1 statement sets the first element of the array to be indexed as 1 instead of as 0. The latter value is the default value, but in our opinion it is more intuitive to index array elements starting with 1.

```
Option Base 1
Function CRRTree(Spot, T, sigma, n)
dt = T / n
u = Exp(sigma * (dt ^ 0.5))
d = 1 / u
p = (Exp(r * dt) - d) / (u - d)
Dim S() As Double, Out() As Double
ReDim S(n + 1, n + 1) As Double
ReDim Out(n + 1) As Double
For i = 1 To n + 1
  For j = i To n + 1
    S(i, j) = Spot * u ^ (j - i) * d ^ (i - 1)
    If j = n + 1 Then Out(i) = S(i, j)
```

	A	B	C	D	E	F	G	H
1								
2		**Terminal Values for CRR Binomial Tree**						
3					*S(i,n+1)*			
4		Spot Price (S)	100		160.70			
5		Time to Maturity (T)	0.5		132.92			
6		Volatility (σ)	0.3		109.95			
7		Number of Steps (n)	5		90.95			
8					75.23			
9					62.23			
10								
11		**All Values for CRR Tree**						
12					*S(i,j)*			
13			100.00	109.95	120.89	132.92	146.15	160.70
14				90.95	100.00	109.95	120.89	132.92
15					82.72	90.95	100.00	109.95
16						75.23	82.72	90.95
17							68.42	75.23
18								62.23

FIGURE A.1 The CRR Binomial Tree

```
    Next j
    Next i
    CRRTree = Application.Transpose(Out)
    End Function
```

The Out() array produces a row vector, so the array must be transposed if the terminal prices are to be outputted as a column vector. To output the $n + 1$ terminal values, we must use the combination of the keys SHIFT, CTRL, and ENTER. This is illustrated with the Excel file Appendix and Figure A.1 below, using a spot price of $S = 100$, a time to maturity of $T = 0.5$ years, an annual volatility of $\sigma = 0.30$, and $n = 5$ steps.

In cell E4, we type

$$= \text{CRRTree}(C4,C5,C6,C7)$$

and press ENTER, which produces the terminal price $S(1, n + 1) = 160.70$. Next, since $n + 1 = 6$ cells are needed for the output, we highlight cells E4:E9, press F2 (EDIT), and then CTRL-SHIFT-ENTER simultaneously. To output the entire tree values, it is convenient to Dim the Out() array as Variant, so that blank values can be outputted to cells where there is no price (the lower diagonal of the array), rather than zeros. The output is achieved in the second loop.

```
Function CRRTree2(Spot, T, sigma, n)
dt = T / n
u = Exp(sigma * (dt ^ 0.5))
```

```
d = 1 / u
p = (Exp(r * dt) - d) / (u - d)
Dim S() As Double, Out() As Variant
ReDim S(n + 1, n + 1) As Double
ReDim Out(n + 1, n + 1) As Variant
For i = 1 To n + 1
  For j = i To n + 1
    S(i, j) = Spot * u ^ (j - i) * d ^ (i - 1)
  Next j
Next i
For i = 1 To n + 1
  For j = 1 To n + 1
    If j >= i Then
      Out(i, j) = S(i, j)
    Else
      Out(i, j) = " "
    End If
  Next j
Next i
CRRTree2 = Out
End Function
```

Referring to Figure A.1, to output the entire CRR binomial tree in cell C13 we type

$$= \text{CRRTree2(C4,C5,C6,C7)}$$

and press ENTER, which produces $S(1, 1) = 100$. Since a six-by-six array is needed for the output, we highlight cells C13:H18, press F2, and press CTRL-SHIFT-ENTER simultaneously. If a tree with more steps is required, we change the value of $n + 1$ in cell C7, and we select a larger number of cells to highlight.

References

Ait-Sahalia, Y. 2002. "Maximum Likelihood Estimation of Discretely Sampled Diffusions: A Closed-Form Approximation Approach." *Econometrica*, Vol. 70, No. 1, pp. 223–262.

Ait-Sahalia, Y., and R. Kimmel. 2007. "Maximum Likelihood Estimation of Stochastic Volatility Models." *Journal of Financial Economics*, forthcoming.

Babbs, S. 2000. "Binomial Valuation of Lookback Options." *Journal of Economic Dynamics and Control*, Vol. 24, No. 11–12, pp. 1499–1525.

Backus D., S. Foresi, and L. Wu. 2004. "Accounting for Biases in Black-Scholes." Working Paper, Stern School of Business, New York University.

Bakshi, G., C. Cao, and Z. Chen. 1997. "Empirical Performance of Alternative Option Pricing Models." *Journal of Finance*, Vol. 52, No. 5, pp. 2003–2049.

Bakshi, G., and N. Kapadia. 2003. "Delta-Hedged Gains and the Negative Market Volatility Risk Premium." *Review of Financial Studies*, Vol. 16, No. 2, pp. 527–566.

Bakshi, G., N. Kapadia, and D. Madan. 2003. "Stock Return Characteristics, Skew Laws, and the Differential Pricing of Individual Equity Options." *Review of Financial Studies*, Vol. 16, No. 1, pp. 101–143.

Bakshi, G., and D. Madan. 2000. "Spanning and Derivative-Security Valuation." *Journal of Financial Economics*, Vol. 55, pp. 205–238.

Black, F., and M. Scholes. 1973. "The Pricing of Options and Corporate Liabilities." *Journal of Political Economy*, Vol. 81, No. 3, pp. 637–654.

Bollerslev, T., R. Chou, and K. Kroner. 1992. "ARCH Modeling in Finance: A Review of the Theory and Empirical Evidence." *Journal of Econometrics*, Vol. 52, pp. 5–59.

Boyle, P. P. 1986. "Option Valuation Using a Three-Jump Process." *International Options Journal*, Vol. 3, pp. 7–12.

Boyle, P. P., and S. H. Lau. 1994. "Bumping Up against the Barrier with the Binomial Method." *Journal of Derivatives*, Summer, pp. 6–14.

Breeden, D. T. 1979. "An Intertemporal Asset Pricing Model with Stochastic Consumption and Investment Opportunities." *Journal of Financial Economics*, Vol. 7, pp. 265–296.

Breeden, D. T., and R. H. Litzenberger. 1978. "Prices of State-Contingent Claims Implicit in Option Prices." *Journal of Business*, Vol. 51, No. 4, pp. 621–651.

Brenner, M., E. Y. Ou, and J. E. Zhang. 2006. "Hedging Volatility Risk." *Journal of Banking and Finance*, Vol. 30, No. 3, pp. 811–821.

Britten-Jones, M., and A. Neuberger. 2000. "Option Prices, Implied Price Processes, and Stochastic Volatility." *Journal of Finance*, Vol. 55, No. 2, pp. 839–866.

Broadie, M., P. Glasserman, and S. G. Kou. 1999. "A Continuity Correction for Discrete Barrier Options." *Mathematical Finance*, Vol. 7, No. 4, pp. 325–348.

Broadie, M., P. Glasserman, and S. G. Kou. 1997. "Connecting Discrete and Continuous Path-Dependent Options." *Finance and Stochastics*, Vol. 3, pp. 55–82.

Broadie, M., and K. Özgür. 2005. "Exact Simulation of Stochastic Volatility and Other Affine Jump Diffusion Processes." Working Paper, Columbia University.

Buchen, P., and M. Kelly. 1996. "The Maximum Entropy Distribution of an Asset Inferred from Option Prices." *Journal of Financial and Quantitative Analysis*, Vol. 31, No. 1, pp. 143–159.

Burden, R. L., and J. D. Faires. 2001. *Numerical Analysis*, 7th ed. Pacific Grove, Calif.: Brooks/Cole.

Carr, P., and D. Madan. 2001. "Optimal Positioning in Derivative Securities." *Quantitative Finance*, Vol. 1, No. 1, pp. 19–37.

Carr, P., and L. Wu. 2006a. "Stochastic Skew for Currency Options." Working Paper, New York University and Baruch College.

Carr, P., and L. Wu. 2006b. "A Tale of Two Indices." *Journal of Derivatives*, Vol. 13, No. 3, pp. 13–29.

Carr, P., and L. Wu. 2004. "Variance Risk Premia." Working Paper, New York University and Baruch College.

Chernov, M., and E. Ghysels. 2000. "Estimation of Stochastic Volatility Models for the Purpose of Option Pricing." In: Abu-Mostafa, Y. S., B. LeBaron, A. W. Lo, and A. S. Weigend (eds.), *Computational Finance—Proceedings of the Sixth Annual International Conference*, MIT Press, pp. 567–582.

Cheuk, T. H., and T. C. F. Vorst. 1997. "Currency Lookback Options and Observation Frequency: A Binomial Approach." *Journal of International Money and Finance*, Vol. 16, No. 2, pp. 173–187.

Chicago Board Options Exchange. 2003. "VIX: CBOE Volatility Index." White Paper, www.cboe.com.

Choi, S., and M. Jameson. 2003. "Lookback Option Valuation: A Simplified Approach." *Journal of Derivatives*, Winter, pp. 53–64.

Chriss, N. 1997. *Black-Scholes and Beyond: Option Pricing Models*. Chicago: Irwin Professional Publishing.

Christoffersen, P., and K. Jacobs. 2004a. "The Importance of the Loss Function in Option Pricing." *Journal of Financial Economics*, Vol. 72, No. 2, pp. 291–318.

Christoffersen, P., and K. Jacobs. 2004b. "Which GARCH Model for Option Valuation?" *Management Science*, Vol. 50, No. 9, pp. 1204–1221.

Christoffersen, P., K. Jacobs, and K. Mimouni. 2006. "An Empirical Comparison of Affine and Non-Affine Models for Equity Index Options." Working Paper, McGill University.

Coval, J. D., and T. Shumway. 2001. "Expected Option Returns." *Journal of Finance*, Vol. 56, No. 3, pp. 983–1009.

Cox, J. C., J. E. Ingersoll, and S. A. Ross. 1985. "A Theory of the Term Structure of Interest Rates." *Econometrica*, Vol. 53, pp. 385–408.

Cox, J., S. Ross, and M. Rubinstein. 1979. "Option Pricing: A Simplified Approach." *Journal of Financial Economics*, Vol. 7, pp. 229–264.

Dai, M., Y. K. Kwok, and L. Wu. 2004. "Optimal Shouting Policies of Options with Strike Reset Right." *Mathematical Finance*, Vol. 14, No. 3, pp. 383–401.

Davidson, R., and J. G. MacKinnon. 1993. *Estimation and Inference in Econometrics*. New York: Oxford University Press.

Dennis, P., and S. Mayhew. 2002. "Risk-Neutral Skewness: Evidence from Stock Options." *Journal of Financial and Quantitative Analysis*, Vol. 37, No. 3, pp. 471–493.

Demeterfi, K., E. Derman, M. Kamal, and J. Zou. 1999. "A Guide to Volatility and Variance Swaps." *Journal of Derivatives*, Vol. 6, No. 4, pp. 9–32.

Derman, E., and I. Kani. 1994. "The Volatility Smile and Its Implied Tree." *Risk*, 7-2, pp. 139–145, pp. 32–39. Also available at www.ederman.com.

Derman, E., I. Kani, and N. Chriss. 1996. "Implied Trinomial Trees of the Volatility Smile." *Journal of Derivatives*, Vol. 4, No. 3, pp. 7–22. Also available at www.ederman.com.

Derman, E., I. Kani, D. Ergener, and I. Bardhan. 1995. "Enhanced Numerical Methods for Options with Barrier." *Financial Analysts Journal*, November–December, pp. 65–74. Also available at www.ederman.com.

Duan, J.-C. 1995. "The GARCH Option Pricing Model." *Mathematical Finance*, Vol. 5, No. 1, pp. 13–32.

Duan, J.-C., G. Gauthier, C. Sasseville, and J.-G. Simonato. 2003. "Approximating American Option Prices in the GARCH Framework." *Journal of Futures Markets*, Vol. 23, No. 10, pp. 915–929.

Dumas, B., J. Fleming, and R. E. Whaley. 1998. "Implied Volatility Functions: Empirical Tests." *Journal of Finance*, Vol. 53, No. 6, pp. 2059–2106.

Eraker, B. 2001. "MCMC Analysis of Diffusion Models with Application to Finance." *Journal of Business and Economic Statistics*, Vol. 19, No. 2, pp. 177–191.

Eraker, B., M. Johannes, and N. Polson. 2003. "The Impact of Jumps in Volatility and Returns." *Journal of Finance*, Vol. 58, No. 3, pp. 1269–1300.

Figlewski, S., and B. Gao. 1999. "The Adaptive Mesh Model: A New Approach to Efficient Option Pricing." *Journal of Financial Economics*, Vol. 53, pp. 313–351.

Haug, E. G. 2001. "Closed Form Valuation of American Barrier Options." *International Journal of Theoretical and Applied Finance*, Vol. 4, No. 2, pp. 355–359.

Haug, E. G. 1998. *The Complete Guide to Option Pricing Formulas*. New York: McGraw-Hill.

Hentschel, L. 1995. "All in the Family: Nesting Symmetric and Asymmetric GARCH Models." *Journal of Financial Economics*, Vol. 39, No. 1, pp. 71–104.

Heston, S. L. 1993. "A Closed-Form Solution for Options with Stochastic Volatility with Applications to Bond and Currency Options." *Review of Financial Studies*, Vol. 6, No. 2, pp. 327–343.

Heston, S. L., and S. Nandi. 2000. "A Closed-Form GARCH Option Valuation Model." *Review of Financial Studies*, Vol. 31, No. 3, pp. 585–625.

Huang, C., and R. H. Litzenberger. 1988. *Foundations for Financial Economics*. Upper Saddle River, N.J.: Prentice Hall.

Hull, J. C. 2006. *Options, Futures, and Other Derivatives*, 6th ed. Upper Saddle River, N.J.: Prentice Hall.

Hull, J. C., and A. White. 1993. "Efficient Procedures for Valuing European and American Path-Dependent Options." *Journal of Derivatives*, Vol. 1, No. 1, pp. 21–31.

Hull, J. C., and A. White. 1987. "The Pricing of Options on Assets with Stochastic Volatilities." *Journal of Finance*, Vol. 42, No. 2, pp. 281–300.

Jackwerth, J. C., and M. Rubinstein. 1996. "Recovering Probability Distributions from Option Prices." *Journal of Finance*, Vol. 51, No. 5, pp. 1611–1631.

Jacquier, E., N. G. Polson, and P. E. Rossi. 2004. "Bayesian Analysis of Stochastic Volatility Models with Fat Tails and Correlated Errors." *Journal of Econometrics*, Vol. 122, No. 1, pp. 185–212.

Jiang, G. J., and Y. S. Tian. 2005. "The Model-Free Implied Volatility and Its Information Content." *Review of Financial Studies*, Vol. 18, No. 4, pp. 1305–1342.

Johannes, M., N. Polson, and J. Stroud. 2006. "Optimal Filtering of Jump-Diffusions: Extracting Latent States from Asset Prices." Working Paper, Columbia University and University of Chicago.

Kamrad, B., and P. Ritchken. 1991. "Multinomial Approximating Models for Options with k State Variables." *Management Science*, Vol. 37, No. 12, pp. 1640–1652.

Kendall, M., and A. Stuart. 1977. *The Advanced Theory of Statistics, Volume One*, 4th ed. New York: Macmillan.

Krantz, S. G. 1999. *Handbook of Complex Variables*. Boston: Birkhäuser.

Kwok, Y. K., and M. Dai. 2004. "Knock-In American Options." *Journal of Futures Markets*, Vol. 24, No. 2, pp. 179–192.

Lagarias, J. C., J. A. Reeds, M. H. Wright, and P. E. Wright. 1999. "Convergence Properties of the Nelder-Mead Simplex Method in Low Dimensions." *SIAM Journal of Optimization*, Vol. 9, No. 1, pp. 112–147.

Leisen, D. P. J., and M. Reimer. 1996. "Binomial Models for Option Valuation—Examining and Improving Convergence." *Applied Mathematical Finance*, Vol. 3, No. 4, pp. 319–346.

Lewis, A. L. 2000. *Option Valuation Under Stochastic Volatility, With Mathematica*^{TM} *Code.* Newport Beach, Calif.: Finance Press.

Neter, J., M. H. Kutner, C. J. Nachtsheim, and W. Wasserman. 1996. *Applied Linear Statistical Models*, 4th ed. New York: McGraw-Hill.

Neuberger, A. 1994. "The Log Contract." *Journal of Portfolio Management*, Vol. 20, No. 2, pp. 74–80.

Pelsser, A., and T. Vorst. 1994. "The Binomial Model and the Greeks." *Journal of Derivatives*, Spring, pp. 45–49.

Press, W. H., B. P. Flannery, S. A. Teukolsky, and W. T. Vetterling. 2002. *Numerical Recipes in C: The Art of Scientific Computing*, 2nd ed. New York: Cambridge University Press.

Rubinstein, M. 1994. "Implied Binomial Trees." *Journal of Finance*, Vol. 49, No.3, pp. 771–818.

Rubinstein, M. 1998. "Edgeworth Binomial Trees." *Journal of Derivatives*, Spring, pp. 20–27.

Stutzer, M. 1996. "A Simple Nonparametric Approach to Derivative Security Valuation." *Journal of Finance*, Vol. 51, No. 5, pp 1633–1652.

Taleb, N. N. 1997. *Dynamic Hedging: Managing Vanilla and Exotic Options*. New York: John Wiley & Sons.

Tian, Y. 1999. "A Flexible Binomial Option Pricing Model." *Journal of Futures Markets*, Vol. 19, No. 7, pp. 817–843.

About the CD-ROM

INTRODUCTION

This appendix provides information on the contents of the CD that accompanies this book. For the latest updated information, please refer to the ReadMe file located at the root of the CD.

SYSTEM REQUIREMENTS

- A PC with a processor running at 120 Mhz or faster
- At least 32 MB of total RAM installed on your computer; for best performance, we recommend at least 64 MB
- Microsoft Excel version 2002 for Windows 2000 Service Pack 4 or later.
- A CD-ROM drive.

Note: The files that appear on this CD-ROM are designed to run under Microsoft Excel. Other spreadsheet programs are capable of reading Microsoft Excel files. However, users should be aware that the VBA functions running within the files may not work when using a program other than Microsoft Excel, or versions of Excel earlier than version 2002.

USING THE CD WITH WINDOWS

To install the items from the CD to your hard drive, follow these steps:

1. Insert the CD into your computer's CD-ROM drive.
   Note: The interface won't launch if you have autorun disabled. In that case, click Start-->Run. In the dialog box that appears, type **D:\start.exe**. (Replace D with the proper letter if your CD drive uses a different letter. If you don't know the letter, see how your CD drive is listed under My Computer.) Click OK.
2. The CD-ROM interface will appear. The interface provides a simple point-and-click way to explore the contents of the CD.

WHAT'S ON THE CD

This CD-ROM contains Excel files for implementing all of the option pricing and volatility models covered in this book. Each Excel file contains one or more VBA functions that are described in the book chapters. Some of the files contain graphs of the file content, but these may be located in a separate worksheet in the file. Other files contain option data downloaded from Yahoo! (**finance.yahoo.com**) and OptionMetrics (**www.optionmetrics.com**).

The following sections provide a summary of the software and other materials found on the CD.

Content

Each chapter of the book includes its own set of Excel files, which are contained in sub-directories named according to the chapter in which the file is described. These are arranged in the sub-directories Chapter 1 through Chapter 13. The Excel file for the Appendix is in the sub-directory Appendix, and the Excel files that contain option prices on IBM Inc. and Intel Corporation are in the sub-directory named Yahoo.

All of the option pricing and volatility models covered in this book are implemented using VBA. The contents of each Excel file appear as a figure in the book, so this is exactly what users will see when they open the files. Users can use the Excel files as template, and substitute their own data into the spreadsheet to generate their own option prices and volatility calculations.

The VBA functions can be accessed from the VBA Editor in Excel. The VBA functions are not password protected, so it is possible for them to be modified by the user. Please note, however, that doing so may introduce errors and produce results that are inaccurate. It is recommended that users familiarize themselves with VBA before attempting to change any of the VBA functions contained on the CD-ROM.

While using the files requires no programming experience or knowledge of VBA, some knowledge of Excel is recommended. The Appendix provides a brief introduction to VBA, for those readers with no prior programming experience.

Most of the graphs in the book are produced using the VBA functions contained on the CD-ROM. These graphs are contained in the Excel files also. Please note that the graphs are linked to the data contained in the files, so changing data values will alter the appearance of the graphs.

Applications

The following applications are on the CD:

Excel Viewer   Excel Viewer is a freeware viewer that allows you to view, but not edit, most Microsoft Excel spreadsheets. Certain features of Microsoft Excel documents may not work as expected from within Excel Viewer.

Shareware programs are fully functional, trial versions of copyrighted programs. If you like particular programs, register with their authors for a nominal fee and receive licenses, enhanced versions, and technical support.

Freeware programs are copyrighted games, applications, and utilities that are free for personal use. Unlike shareware, these programs do not require a fee or provide technical support.

GNU software is governed by its own license, which is included inside the folder of the GNU product. See the GNU license for more details.

Trial, demo, or evaluation versions are usually limited either by time or functionality (such as being unable to save projects). Some trial versions are very sensitive to system date changes. If you alter your computer's date, the programs will "time out" and no longer be functional.

TROUBLESHOOTING

If you have difficulty installing or using any of the materials on the companion CD, try the following solutions:

- **Turn off any antivirus software that you may have running.** Installers sometimes mimic virus activity and can make your computer incorrectly believe that it is being infected by a virus. (Be sure to turn the antivirus software back on later.)
- **Close all running programs.** The more programs you're running, the less memory is available to other programs. Installers also typically update files and programs; if you keep other programs running, installation may not work properly.
- **Reference the ReadMe:** Refer to the ReadMe file located at the root of the CD-ROM for the latest product information (if any) at the time of publication.

CUSTOMER CARE

If you have trouble with the CD-ROM, please call the Wiley Product Technical Support phone number at (800) 762-2974. Outside the United States, call 1(317) 572-3994. You can also contact Wiley Product Technical Support at **http://support.wiley.com**. John Wiley & Sons will provide technical support only for installation and other general quality control items. For technical support on the applications themselves, consult the program's vendor or author.

To place additional orders or to request information about other Wiley products, please call (877) 762-2974.

About the Authors

Fabrice Douglas Rouah is a senior quantitative analyst at a large financial institution and is based in Boston, MA. He obtained both his PhD in finance and his MSc in statistics from McGill University, and his BSc in applied mathematics from Concordia University. Fabrice is a former faculty lecturer and consulting statistician in the Department of Mathematics and Statistics at McGill University. His research interests are in hedge funds, risk management, and equity option pricing. He is coauthor and coeditor of four books on hedge funds. This is his third book with John Wiley & Sons.

Gregory Vainberg is a corporate risk specialist with a large multinational consulting firm, and is based in Montreal, Quebec. He obtained both his PhD in finance and his BEng in computer engineering from McGill University. Prior to obtaining his PhD, he was lead developer for Summit Tech, a Montreal-based consultancy, where he developed software applications in VBA, C++, and PHP for companies such as Bombardier, CAE, and Ericsson. His research interests are equity option pricing, stochastic volatility, volatility swaps, and empirical finance. He is the creator of the top finance and math VBA site www.vbnumericalmethods.com.

Page numbers followed by an *f* indicate figures.
Page numbers followed by a *t* indicate tables.

For more information about the CD-ROM see the **About the CD-ROM** section on page 413.

CPSIA information can be obtained
at www.ICGtesting.com
Printed in the USA
BVOW11s1222270417
482425BV00006B/18/P